CROWN COURT INDEX 2007

AUSTRALIA
Law Book Co
Sydney

CANADA and USA
Carswell
Toronto

NEW ZEALAND
Brookers
Wellington

SINGAPORE and MALAYSIA
Sweet & Maxwell Asia
Singapore and Kuala Lumpur

INDEX OF TITLES

CROWN COURT INDEX

TWENTY-SEVENTH EDITION

By

His Honour IAN McLEAN
Formerly a Circuit Judge

and

His Honour Judge SAM KATKHUDA

LONDON
SWEET & MAXWELL
2007

Published in 2007 by Sweet & Maxwell Limited
100 Avenue Road
London NW3 3PF
Typeset by Servis Filmsetting Ltd, Manchester
Printed and bound in Great Britain by
William Clowes Ltd, Beccles, Suffolk

First published 1964
Twentieth edition 2000
Twenty-First edition 2001
Twenty-Second edition 2002
Twenty-Third edition 2003
Twenty-Fourth edition 2004
Twenty-Fifth edition 2005
Twenty-Sixth Edition 2006
Twenty-Seventh Edition 2007

No natural forests were destroyed to make this product;
only farmed timber was used and replanted

A CIP catalogue record for this book is available from the
British Library

ISBN 10 184703005X
ISBN 13 9781847030054

PREFACE

THIS EDITION has seen a good deal of re-writing and revision, both for the purposes of revising the text in the light of new authorities but also for the purpose of streamlining the text. Increase in size has been a problem for some years. It is still a problem. The authors have always seen this work as a concise practicable *aide memoire* for the practitioner, enabling him to find a short answer to a practical problem without recourse to textbook. Keeping it to a manageable size has proved increasingly difficult as the criminal justice system is overwhelmed by *minutiae*, most, if not all, of which need to be dealt with if such a work as this is to be of any real value. The authors have sought to further reduce the size this year but still ask for consideration in respect of its length.

Fortunately the profession has not been so overburdened with new legislation this year, although the amendments to CPR 2005 are significant, and the authors have taken the opportunity to tidy up some of those sections which were acquiring "barnacles". ABSOLUTE AND CONDITIONAL DISCHARGE, ANTI-SOCIAL BEHAVIOUR ORDERS, BREACH, AMENDMENT AND REVOCATION, have all benefitted from this treatment. In CASE MANAGEMENT the law and procedure in relation to statutory preparatory hearings and interlocutory appeals from them has been rewritten. COMMUNITY SENTENCES has been streamlined to avoid repeated mention of specific community orders in other sections such as DEFERMENT OF SENTENCE, and IMPRISONMENT, where such orders are directly relevant to custody plus orders and suspended sentence orders. In CONFISCATION a section has been added on the seizure and forfeiture of cash. In IMPRISONMENT there has been wide revision of the section on custody plus orders and suspended sentence orders. Both RECOMMENDATION FOR DEPORTATION and SEX OFFENDERS ORDERS have been rewritten in the light of the new authorities.

As far as important new material is concerned a section on the new approach to procedural defects has been added to CASE MANAGEMENT in the light of the decisions in *Soneji* and *Sekhon*. CDS FUNDING has been revised in the light of provision for financial eligibility and contribution orders. A section on victim impact statements and the victim representation scheme being piloted has been added in the light of the Protocol issued by the President of the Queen's Bench Division. The practice in relation to dangerous offenders in IMPRISONMENT has had to be rewritten in the light of the Court of Appeals guidance in *R. v Lang*.

The authors have decided to remove the section on EVIDENCE (CJA 2003) which was only intended as an overview of the subject for the convenience of readers. The case law on that subject is now quite substantial, and evidence was never a subject designed for inclusion in a work of this kind. HUMAN RIGHTS as a separate section has been removed. It was, again, only an introduction to the topic; the relevant provisions are dealt with throughout the other sections. The section on SCOTTISH & WELSH DEVOLUTION MATTERS has attracted little practical attention and has been removed.

The authors record with regret the death at Southampton General Hospital on November 26, 2005, of Peter Morrish, whose brain-child and pride this work was. He was closely involved with 26 editions of "Morrish & McLean" as it is still colloquially known. The 26th arrived at his home a few days before his death. The present authors trust that they will be able to maintain his high standards.

The law is stated as of October 12, 2006.

TABLE OF ABBREVIATIONS

The following abbreviations appear in the text and refer to the respective enactments shown:

ECHR	European Convention on Human Rights
CLA 1826	Criminal Law Act 1826
OAPA 1861	Offences Against the Person Act 1861
CPA 1865	Criminal Procedure Act 1865
BBEA 1879	Bankers' Books Evidence Act 1879
ESA 1883	Explosive Substances Act 1883
POA 1907	Probation of Offenders Act 1907
AJ(MP)A 1933	Administration of Justice (Miscellaneous Provisions) Act 1933
CYPA 1933	Children and Young Persons Act 1933
ABOOA 1956	Magistrates' Courts (Appeals from Binding Over Orders) Act 1956
SOA 1956	Sexual Offences Act 1956
MHA 1959	Mental Health Act 1959
AJA 1960	Administration of Justice Act 1960
CYPA 1963	Children and Young Persons Act 1963
CP(I)A 1964	Criminal Procedure (Insanity) Act 1964
LA 1964	Licensing Act 1964
CP(AW)A 1965	Criminal Procedure (Attendance of Witnesses) Act 1965
M(ADP)A 1965	Murder (Abolition of Death Penalty) Act 1965
CJA 1967	Criminal Justice Act 1967
CLA 1967	Criminal Law 1967
CAA 1968	Criminal Appeal Act 1968
FA 1968	Firearms Act 1968
JPA 1968	Justices of the Peace Act 1968
TA 1968	Theft Act 1968
CYPA 1969	Children and Young Persons Act 1969
AJA 1970	Administration of Justice Act 1970
CA 1971	Courts Act 1971
CDA 1971	Criminal Damage Act 1971
IA 1971	Immigration Act 1971
MDA 1971	Misuse of Drugs Act 1971
CJA 1972	Criminal Justice Act 1972
JA 1974	Juries Act 1974
ROA 1974	Rehabilitation of Offenders Act 1974
BA 1976	Bail Act 1976
CLA 1977	Criminal Law Act 1977

TABLE OF ABBREVIATIONS

IA 1978	Interpretation Act 1978
TA 1978	Theft Act 1978
CEMA 1989	Customs and Excise Management Act 1979
LP(E)A 1980	Licensed Premises (Exclusion of Certain Persons) Act 1980
MCA 1980	Magistrates' Courts Act 1980
CAA 1981	Criminal Attempts Act 1981
CCA 1981	Contempt of Court Act 1981
SCA 1981	Supreme Court Act 1981
CJA 1982	Criminal Justice Act 1982
MH(A)A 1982	Mental Health (Amendment) Act 1982
MHA 1983	Mental Health Act 1983
PACE 1984	Police and Criminal Evidence Act 1984
RTRA 1984	Road Traffic Regulation Act 1984
POA 1985	Prosecution of Offences Act 1985
CDDA 1986	Company Directors Disqualification Act 1986
DTOA 1986	Drug Trafficking Offences Act 1986
GA 1986	Gaming (Amendment) Act 1986
POrA 1986	Public Order Act 1986
CJA 1987	Criminal Justice Act 1987
CJA 1988	Criminal Justice Act 1988
LA 1988	Licensing Act 1988
RTA 1988	Road Traffic Act 1988
RTOA 1988	Road Traffic Offenders Act 1988
CA 1989	Children Act 1989
FSA 1989	Football Spectators Act 1989
CJ(IC)A 1990	Criminal Justice (International Co-operation) Act 1990
CLSA 1990	Courts and Legal Services Act 1990
CJA 1991	Criminal Justice Act 1991
CP(IUP)A 1991	Criminal Procedure (Insanity and Unfitness to Plead) Act 1991
RTA 1991	Road Traffic Act 1991
AVTA 1992	Aggravated Vehicle Taking Act 1992
B(A)A 1993	Bail (Amendment) Act 1993
CJA 1993	Criminal Justice Act 1993
PCP(S)A 1993	Prisoners and Criminal Proceedings (Scotland) Act 1993
CJPOA 1994	Criminal Justice and Public Order Act 1994
DTA 1994	Drug Trafficking Act 1994
CAA 1995	Criminal Appeals 1995
CEA 1995	Civil Evidence Act 1995
PCA 1995	Proceeds of Crime Act 1995
CPIA 1996	Criminal Procedure and Investigations Act 1996
CSA 1997	Crime (Sentences) Act 1997
F(A)A 1997	Firearms (Amendment) Act 1997
JPA 1997	Justices of the Peace Act 1997

TABLE OF ABBREVIATIONS

PHA 1997	Protection from Harassment Act 1997
SOA 1997	Sex Offenders Act 1997
CDA 1998	Crime and Disorder Act 1998
HRA 1998	Human Rights Act 1998
AJA 1999	Access to Justice Act 1999
FOD 1999	Football (Offences and Disorder) Act 1999
IAA 1999	Immigration and Asylum Act 1999
YJCEA 1999	Youth Justice and Criminal Evidence Act 1999
CJCSA 2000	Criminal Justice and Court Services Act 2000
FDA 2000	Football Disorder Act 2000
IA 2000	Insolvency Act 2000
PCC(S)A 2000	Powers of Criminal Courts (Sentencing) Act 2000
RIPA 2000	Regulation of Investigatory Powers Act 2000
Terr A 2000	Terrorism Act 2000
CJPA 2001	Criminal Justice and Police Act 2001
PCA 2002	Proceeds of Crime Act 2002
PRA 2002	Police Reform Act 2002
ASBA 2003	Anti-Social Behaviour Order Act 2003
CA 2003	Courts Act 2003
C(IC)A 2003	Crime (International Co-operation) Act 2003
CJA 2003	Criminal Justice Act 2003
CJCSA 2003	Criminal Justice and Courts Services Act 2003
EA 2003	Extradition Act 2003
SOA 2003	Sexual Offences Act 2003
DVA 2004	Domestic Violence, Crime and Victims Act 2004
CRCA 2005	Commissioners for Revenue and Customs Act 2005
SOCA 2005	Serious Organised Crime and Police Act 2005
CDSA 2006	Criminal Defence Service Act 2006
RHA 2006	Racial and Religious Hatred Act 2006

Subordinate legislation

R.	Criminal Procedure Rules 2005
MC(F)R 1981	Magistrates' Courts (Forms) Rules 1981
GR 1986	Costs in Criminal Cases (General) Regulations 1986
GR(A)R 1991	Costs in Criminal Cases (General) (Amendment) Regulations 1991
DTLR 1997	Criminal Procedure and Investigations Act 1996 (Defence Disclosure Time Limits) Rules 1997
CPR 1998	Civil Procedure Rules 1998
CVHCCR 2001	Criminal Defence Service (Choice in Very High Cost Cases) Regulations 2001
GR 2001	Criminal Defence Service (General) Regulations 2001
RDCOR 2001	Criminal Defence Service (Recovery of Defence Costs) Regulations 2001

ROAR 2001	Criminal Defence Service (Representation Order: Appeals) Regulations 2001
DTTO 2002	Drugs Testing and Treatment Order 2002
CACCRRR 2003	Criminal Appeal (Confiscation, Restraint and Receivership) Rules 2003
PCAO 2003	Proceeds of Crime Act 2002 (Appeals under Part 2) Order 2003
CPR 2005	Criminal Procedure Rules 2005

Miscellaneous

ARA	Assets Recovery Agency
CACD	Court of Appeal (Criminal Division)
CCP 2004	Code for Crown Prosecutors 2004
CPS	Crown Prosecution Service
DARA	Defence Aviation Repair Agency
DRC	Director of Revenue and Customs
DSFO	Director of the Serious Fraud Office
EPE	electronic presentation of evidence
HO 1990	Home Office publication *Sentence of the Court* (1990)
ISO	individual support order
JSB	Judicial Studies Board
LSC	Legal Services Commission
PCMH	plea and case management hearing
PD	Practice Direction
PD 2004	Practice Direction (Criminal; Consolidated) 2004
PDC 2004	Practice Direction (Costs) 2004
RCPO	Revenue and Customs Prosecution Office
RSHO	risk of sexual harm order
RT	road traffic
SFO	Serious Fraud Office
SGC 1	Sentencing Guidelines Council, 'Reduction in sentence for a guilty plea'
SGC 2	Sentencing Guidelines Council, 'Overarching principles – seriousness'
SGC 3	Sentencing Guidelines Council, 'New sentences CJA 2003'
SOCA	Serious Organised Crime Agency
SOPO	Sexual Offences Prevention Order

TABLE OF CASES

TABLE OF CASES

TABLE OF CASES

TABLE OF STATUTES

TABLE OF STATUTES

Table of Statutes

Table of Statutes

Table of Statutes

Table of Statutes

Table of Statutes

Table of Statutes

Table of Statutes

TABLE OF STATUTORY INSTRUMENTS

TABLE OF STATUTORY INSTRUMENTS

TABLE OF STATUTORY INSTRUMENTS

1 ABSCONDING ACCUSED

General

1–001 An accused has, in general, a right to be present at his trial and to be legally represented. He may waive those rights, separately or together:

(1) wholly if, knowing when and where his trial is to take place, he deliberately and voluntarily absents himself, or withdraws his instructions from those representing him; or
(2) partly if, being present and represented at the outset, during the course of the trial he behaves in such a way as to obstruct the proper course of the proceedings and/or withdraws his instructions from those representing him.

In such cases, the trial judge has a discretion as to whether a trial should take place or continue in the absence of the accused and/or his legal representative. Nor is there anything in the European jurisprudence which suggests that such a procedure offends against the European Convention (*R. v Jones* [2002] Cr.App.R. 9, also PD 2004, I.13.17–19).

The discretion needs to be exercised with great care, and only in a rare case in favour of the trial taking place or continuing, particularly if the accused is unrepresented; fairness to the defence is of prime importance, but fairness to the prosecution needs also to be taken into account. (*R. v Jones* (above); *R. v O'Hare* [2006] Crim.L.R. 950). The judge must have regard to all the circumstances of the case (see 1–002–1–004, below).

As to making a confiscation order in relation to an absconding accused, see 24 CONFISCATION ORDERS.

A clear additional safeguard to the fairness of the trial is the presence of an advocate on behalf of the accused, who can ensure that all points which can be put forward in the absence of the accused's evidence are clearly before the jury (*R. v O'Hare*, above).

The nature and circumstances of the accused's behaviour

1–002 The judge needs to consider:

(1) the nature and circumstances of the accused's behaviour in absenting himself from the trial, or disrupting it, as the

case may be, and in particular, whether his behaviour was deliberate, voluntary and such as plainly waived his right to appear;

(2) whether an adjournment might result in the accused being apprehended, or attending voluntarily and/or not disrupting the proceedings; and

(3) the likely length of such an adjournment.

The needs of the defence case

1–003 The judge needs to consider also:

(1) whether the accused, though absent, is, or wishes to be, legally represented at the trial or has, by his conduct, waived his right to representation;

(2) whether the legal representatives of an absent accused are able to receive instructions from him during the trial and the extent to which they are able to present his defence;

(3) the extent of the disadvantage to the accused in not being able to give his account of events, having regard to the nature of the evidence against him, and

(4) the risk of the jury reaching an improper conclusion about the absence of the accused.

The public interest

1–004 The judge also needs to consider:

(1) the general public interest and the particular interests of the victims and witnesses that a trial should take place within a reasonable time of the events to which it relates;

(2) the effect of delay on the memories of witnesses; and

(3) where there is more than one accused, and not all have absconded, the undesirability of separate trials and the prospects of a fair trial for those who are present.

The seriousness of the offence though a relevant factor or is not an overriding consideration (*R. v O'Hare* above).

Considerations of fairness

1–005 Where the judge decides that the trial should take place or continue in the absence of an unrepresented accused, he must ensure that the trial is as fair as circumstances permit. In particular, he must take reasonable steps, both during the giving of evidence and in the summing-up, to expose any weaknesses in the prosecution case and to make such points on behalf of the accused as the evidence permits. He ought to warn the jury, in a trial with a jury, that absence is not an admission of guilt, and adds nothing to the case for the Crown.

Accused refusing to come to court

1–006 An accused in custody refusing to come to court, even when he is in the course of giving evidence, should not be compelled by the use or threat of force. The trial may be continued in his absence and/or he may be dealt with for contempt (see 25 CONTEMPT OF COURT) (*R. v Boyle* 92 Cr.App.R. 202).

Judge's direction

1–007 As to the direction required where the accused absconds and the trial proceeds in his absence, see *R. v Gough* [2002] 2 Cr.App.R. 8.

2 ABSOLUTE AND CONDITIONAL DISCHARGE

General

2–001 A discharge, whether absolute, or conditional may be appropriate: PCC(S)A 2000, s.12(1); CJA 2003, s.304, Sch.32, Pt I. para.93

(1) generally, for any age of offender, provided the offence is not one for which the sentence is fixed by law, or falls to be imposed under PCC(S)A 2000, ss.109, 110(2), 111(2) (required custodial sentences for certain repeat offences), FA 1968, s.51A(2) (minimum sentences for certain firearms offences, CJA 2003, ss.225, 226 (dangerous offenders), or ss.227, 228 (extended sentences), and
(2) specifically, where the nature of the offence and the character of the offender make the infliction of punishment inexpedient.

A discharge is not a "community order" in terms of CJA 2003, s.177.

Absolute and Conditional Discharge

Absolute discharge

2–002 An absolute discharge is appropriate where the judge considers no action is required beyond the mere finding of guilt, reflecting:

(1) the triviality of the offence (*R. v King* [1977] Crim.L.R. 627);
(2) the circumstances in which it came to be prosecuted (*Smedleys Ltd v Breed* [1974] A.C. 839); or
(3) factors relating to the offender (*R. v O'Toole* (1971) 55 Cr.App.R. 206).

It is not an order likely to be made frequently in the Crown Court.

Conditional discharge

2–003 The effect of an order is to discharge an offender subject to a *single condition* that he commit no offence during the period specified in the order (the "operational period"), which may not exceed three years. PCC(S)A 2000, s.12(3)

An order may not be made:

CDA 1998, ss.1(11), 65, 66(4); SOA 2003, s.13(3); CJA 2003, s.304, Sch.32, para.93(b)

(1) where a person has been warned by a constable under CDA, s.65 and is convicted of an offence within two years of that warning, save in exceptional circumstances which the judge must spell out in open court;
(2) on the breach of a sexual offences prevention order (see 56 SEX OFFENDER ORDERS)
(3) on the breach of an anti-social behaviour order (see 9 ANTI-SOCIAL BEHAVIOUR ORDERS AND ISOs).

The judge has a general duty under CJA 2003, s.174 (see 29 DEALING WITH AN OFFENDER): and should explain that:

(a) in view of the nature of the offence and any mitigating factors (including a plea of guilty) he does not propose to *punish* the offender;
(b) instead he proposes to discharge the offender conditionally for x months or years on condition that he commit no further offence during the period;
(c) if he stays out of trouble for that period he will not be punished for the instant offence, but if he does commit another offence he may be brought back and sentenced in a different way, which might include a custodial sentence as well as being dealt with for the fresh offence.

Improper combinations

2–004 The judge may not, except where permitted by statute, combine with a discharge *on the same count of the indictment* (*cf. R. v Bainbridge* (1979) 1 Cr.App.R.(S.) 216) any additional order with a "punitive element", such as: a custodial or a community sentence (*R. v Savage* (1983) 5 Cr. App. R.(S.) 216), or a fine (*R. v McClelland* (1951) 35 Cr.App.R. 22; *R. v Sanck* (1990) 12 Cr.App.R.(S.) 262).

Ancillary orders

2–005 On making an order for discharge, the judge may: PCC(S)A 2000, s.12(6)(7)

(1) in the case of a conditional discharge, if he thinks it expedient for the purpose of the offender's reformation, allow any person who consents to do so, to give **security for the offender's good behaviour**;
(2) when discharging an offender absolutely or conditionally in respect of an offence, make an order for **costs** against him, or make a **compensation order** under PCC(S)A

2000, s.130, a **deprivation order** under *ibid.* s.143 or a **restitution order** under *ibid.* s.148; and

(3) make a recommendation for **deportation** (IA 1971, s.6(3); PCC(S)A 2000, s.14(1)).

(4) make an anti-social behaviour order, see 9 ANTI-SOCIAL BEHAVIOUR ORDERS AND ISOs.

In an appropriate case, the judge must:

(a) give his reasons for not making a compensation order where personal injury, loss or damage is involved;

(b) discharge any duty under RTOA 1988, s.46(1) to **disqualify** a road traffic offender, or to order the **endorsement** of his licence.

Effect of discharge

2–006 A conviction of an offence for which an absolute or conditional discharge is made is deemed not to be a conviction for any purpose other than the purposes of the proceedings in which the order was made, or of any subsequent proceedings taken against the offender under *ibid.* s.13 for a breach (see e.g. *R. v Longworth* [2006] 1 W.L.R. 313, HL, where the imposition of a conditional discharge was held not to activate the notification procedures of SOA 1997), though: PCC(S)A 2000, s.14

(1) where the offender was aged 18 or over at the time of his conviction of the offence in question, and is subsequently sentenced under s.13, this provision ceases to apply;

(2) the "deeming" provision does not affect:

  (a) any right of the offender to rely on his conviction in bar of any subsequent proceedings for the same offence;

  (b) the restoration of any property in consequence of his conviction; or

  (c) the operation in relation to him, of any enactment or instrument in force on July 1, 1974, which is expressed to extend to persons dealt with under POA 1907, s.1(1) as well as to convicted persons, and

(3) in any event, the conviction is to be disregarded for the purposes of an enactment or instrument which imposes any disqualification or disability on convicted persons, or authorises or requires the imposition of such and

(4) the deeming provisions have effect subject to CAA 1968, s.50(1A) and MCA 1980, s.108(1A), and do not prevent an appeal against conviction, or otherwise.

Conviction of further offence

2–007 An offender convicted in any part of Great Britain of an offence committed during the "operational period" of a conditional discharge, and who is dealt with in respect of that further offence, is liable to be dealt with for the offence for which he was made the subject of the order. PCC(S)A 2000, s.13

Where the original order was made by:

(1) the Crown Court, and the subsequent conviction is in a magistrates' court, that court may commit him to the Crown Court, a judge of which, if satisfied of the breach, may deal with him for the offence for which the order was made in any way in which he could deal with him if he had just been convicted before him of that offence;

(2) the Crown Court, as is the subsequent conviction, a judge may deal with the offender as if he had just been convicted before him of the original offence; and

(3) a magistrates' court, and the subsequent conviction is in the Crown Court, or the offender is dealt with in the Crown Court after committal under (1) above:

(a) the judge's powers are limited to dealing with the offender in a manner in which the lower court could have dealt with him had he just been convicted before it, unless

(b) the original order was made when the offender was under 18, in respect of an offence triable only on indictment in the case of an adult, in which case the judge's powers in dealing with the original offence extend to a fine not exceeding £5,000, or the lower court's powers in relation to an offence punishable with imprisonment for a term not exceeding six months (see 20 COMMITTALS FOR SENTENCE).

The relevant date for considering the appropriate sentencing option on the commission of a further offence is the date of subsequent sentence (*R. v Keelan* (1975) 61 Cr.App.R. 212).

Orders made on appeal

2–008 Where an order for conditional discharge has been made on appeal, for the purposes of s.13 above, it is deemed: PCC(S)A 2000, s.15(1)

(1) if it was made on an appeal brought from a magistrates' court, to have been made by that magistrates' court; and

(2) if it was made on an appeal brought from the Crown Court or from CACD, to have been made by the Crown Court.

Procedure on the breach

2–009 In dealing with the alleged commission of a further offence during the operational period of a conditional discharge, the accused must be asked in terms whether;

(1) on the date specified he was convicted of the offence and made the subject of a conditional discharge;
(2) he admits that his subsequent conviction was within the operational period of that order; and
(3) he realises that he is liable to be dealt with for the original offence.

Should he dispute (1) or (2) above, the issue falls to be determined by the judge, not by the verdict of a jury. PCC(S)A 2003, s.15(3)

While there is no statutory obligation to deal with an offender for breach of the order, failure to do so, save for good reason, renders the making of the original order pointless.

Generally there should be a sentence which is more than nominal, though there is nothing to prevent the judge dealing with the breach by a fresh conditional discharge where the circumstances are exceptional and such a course is justified.

Termination of the order

2–010 If a person conditionally discharged under s.12, is sentenced for the offence in respect of which the order was made, the order ceases to have effect though a compensation order made when the original order was made remains in force (*R. v Evans* [1963] 1 Q.B. 979). PCC(S)A 2000, s.12(5)

3 ABUSE OF PROCESS

The underlying principle

3–001 It is well established that the Crown Court, like any other court, has jurisdiction to prevent abuse of its process, the discretionary power to stay an indictment (or part of an indictment—*R. v Munro* (1993) 97 Cr.App.R. 183) being conferred to ensure that there is a fair trial according to law, involving as it does fairness both to the accused and to the prosecutor. The right to a fair trial is guaranteed by ECHR, Art.6.

"Abuse of process" has been defined as "something so unfair and wrong that the court should not allow a prosecutor to proceed with what is, in all other respects, a regular proceeding" (*R. v Hui Chi-Ming* [1992] 1 A.C. 34, PC). This may be because the judge concludes that the accused cannot receive a fair trial, or that it would be unfair for the accused to be tried (*R. v Beckford* [1996] Cr.App.R.(S.) 94 at 101).

Where abuse may arise

3–002 The cases show that there may be abuse of process where:

(1) the prosecution has manipulated or misused the process of the court so as to deprive an accused of a protection afforded by the law, or to take advantage of a technicality (*R. v Liverpool MC Ex p. Slade* [1998] 1 All E.R. 60);

(2) the proceedings before the court have only been made possible by acts which offend the court's conscience as being contrary to the rule of law, or would otherwise bring the administration of justice into disrepute (e.g. *R. v Horseferry Rd MC Ex p. Bennett* [1994] 1 A.C. 42);

(3) illegal conduct by the police or the prosecutor is so grave as to threaten or undermine the rule of law itself (*R. v Grant, The Times*, May 12, 2005);

(4) on a balance of probabilities, the accused has been, or will be, prejudiced in the preparation or conduct of his defence by delay on the part of the prosecution which is unjustifiable, being not due, for example, to:

  (a) the complexity of the enquiry and the preparation of the prosecution case;

  (b) the action of the accused or one or more co-accused

Abuse of Process

(c) genuine difficulties of service (*R. v Derby CC Ex p. Brooks* (1985) 80 Cr.App.R. 164); or

(5) a prosecuting authority ignores or fails to comply with its own declared prosecuting criteria (*R. v Adaway* 168 J.P. 645).

Potential prejudice to the accused: a "fair trial"

3–003 An application to stay is, in effect, a plea in bar of trial and should not succeed where there are other methods of achieving a fair hearing of the case (*DPP v. Hussain* (1994) 158 J.P.N. 570, DC).

The crux of the matter is whether, in all the circumstances, the situation created by any apparent abuse is such as to make any trial unfair (see, e.g. *Tan v Cameron* [1993] 2 All E.R. 493, PC, *Att-Gen of Hong Kong v Cheung Wai-bun* [1993] 2 All E.R. 510, PC).

It is well established that where there is no fault on the part of the police or the prosecutor, it will be very rare for a stay to be justified. Even where the judge finds that there has been an abuse of process in the conduct of the proceedings, whatever the category of abuse, in general, he:

(1) must consider as a "further and separate" question, whether there is potential prejudice to the accused;
(2) has a discretion, even where he finds abuse of process, to allow the trial to proceed, where he finds no potential prejudice to the accused (*R. v Gloucester CC Ex p. Jackman* [1993] 12 C.L. 118); unless

the unlawful acts by the police or the prosecutor are so great an affront to the intergrity of the justice system and therefore to the rule of law, that the associated prosecution should not be countenanced by the courts, whether or not prejudice is caused to the accused (*R. v Grant*, *The Times*, May 12, 2005).

A stay should not be granted in the absence of prejudice to the accused so serious that no fair trial could be held. When assessing "serious prejudice" the judge needs to bear in mind, however, his control over the admission of evidence and the important fact that the trial process itself will ensure that all factual issues arising will be properly before the jury (*R. v S (Stephen Paul) The Times*, March 26, 2006, CACD).

Thus:

(a) it is important to distinguish between the sort of case in which the issues at the trial will depend upon the recollection of witnesses about some event, and a case which turns largely upon documents (*R. v Buzalek & Schiffer* [1991] Crim.L.R. 116);

(b) the complexities of the case and the difficulties of investigation are a factor to be considered; there may be cases where the case is so complex that, despite the diligent efforts of the Crown, the delay is such that a fair trial is impossible (*cf. R. v Telford JJ. Ex p. Badham* [1991] 2 Q.B. 78; *H v L* [1998] 1 W.L.R. 854).

Special situations: (1) propriety of investigative methods

3–004 Action by the investigating body, luring persons into committing acts forbidden by law and then seeking to prosecute them for doing so, amounts to an abuse of the process of the court, and a judge has an inherent power and duty to prevent it. The boundary between acceptable and unacceptable behaviour, will depend in each case on its own facts, but a useful guide to identifying the limits of the type of conduct which is acceptable, is to consider whether, in the particular circumstances, the investigators did no more than present the accused with an unexceptional opportunity to commit a crime.

Thus:

(1) if the conduct of the investigators preceding the commission of the offence was no more than might have been expected from others in the circumstances, they are not to be regarded as having instigated or incited the crime, for

(2) if they did no more than others might be expected to do, they were not creating crime artificially, but

the investigatory technique of providing an opportunity to commit crime should not be applied in a random fashion or be used for wholesale virtue-testing without good reason.

The greater the degree of intrusiveness, the closer will be the need for the judge to scrutinise the reason for using it.

While:

(a) the investigators must act in good faith, and having reasonable suspicion is one way in which such good faith might be established;

(b) reasonable suspicion of a particular individual will not always be necessary; and

(c) in deciding what is acceptable, the judge must have regard to the accused's circumstances, including his vulnerability (*R. v Loosely; Att-Gen's Reference (No.3 of 2000)* [2001] 1 W.L.R. 2060).

The prosecution must disclose fully the role of any prosecution witness as a participating informant (*R. v Patel* [2002] Crim. L.R. 304. See also *R. v Early and Others* [2003] 1 Cr.App.R. 19.

Special situations: (2) missing exhibits

3–005 The absence of an exhibit does not, of itself, give rise to abuse of process (*R. v Beckford* [1995] Crim.L.R. 712). A distinction needs to be drawn between the *deliberate destruction* of evidence (*R. v Birmingham* [1992] Crim.L.R. 117), and the *loss* of an exhibit (*R. v McNamara & McNamara* [1998] Crim.L.R. 278; *R. v Medwa* [2000] Crim.L.R. 415; *R. v T* [2000] Crim.L.R. 832; *R. v Feltham MC Ex p. Ebraham* [2001] All E.R. 831; see also *R. v Feltham Magistrate's Court, Mouat v DPP* [2001] 1 All E.R. 831, DC, *R. v Boyd* [2004] R.T.R. 7).

The judge should:

(1) consider the nature of the investigator/prosecutor's duty to obtain and/or retain, the evidence; if there was none before the defence first sought its retention, no question of a trial being unfair on that ground arises (see *R. v Parker* [2003] Archbold News 1);

(2) bear in mind, if the evidence was not obtained and/or retained in breach of the obligations set out in the Code of Practice [CPIA 1996, ss.23, 25] or under the Attorney-General's Revised Guidelines issued in April 2005, that the ultimate objective is to ensure that there be a fair trial according to law and while this involves fairness both to the prosecutor and to the defence;

   (a) the trial process is equipped to deal with the examination of complaints, and there will be few cases in which the judge will be able to conclude that a trial would be unfair;

   (b) it is commonplace in criminal trials for the defence to rely on gaps in the Crown case, and if, in such a case, there is sufficient credible evidence which, if believed, would justify a safe conviction, then the trial may proceed, leaving the defence to seek to persuade the jury, if there is one, or the judge, not to convict owing to the unavailability, through no fault of their own, of the evidence in question;

(3) stay the proceedings, if the conduct of the Crown has been such that it would be unfair to put the accused on trial. The most useful test is to ask whether there has been bad faith, or at least some serious fault on the part of the

investigating body or of the Crown (see *R. v ARA* [2001] 4 All E.R. 559, *R. v Feltham MC Ex p. Ebrahim*, above and see PD 2004, I.V.36 at 3.10 below.

See, as to missing video recordings, *DPP v S* 67 JCL 87; and as to gaps in video evidence, *R. v Brooks* (2004) 148 S.J. 1031.

Special situations: (3) delay

3–006 Delay is relevant to the right to the fair trial guaranteed by ECHR, Art.6; it is normally taken to run from the date of charge or summons *Att-Gen's Reference (No.2 of 2001)* [2004] 2 W.L.R. 1).

Where delay in the proceedings is put forward as amounting to abuse, the judge must consider the reasons for the delay and the potential unfairness, if any, to the accused.

In considering the question of whether there is potential prejudice to the accused, relevant factors will be:

(1) the *length* of the delay;
(2) any *reasons* given by the prosecutor for that delay; and
(3) any *efforts* made by the accused to assert his rights.

The longer the delay the more likely it will be that the prosecution is at fault, and that the delay has caused prejudice to the accused; the less the prosecution has to offer by way of explanation, the more easily can prejudice be inferred.

Delay in reporting by the young victim of a sexual assault due to reticence is not uncommon, and is wholly understandable (*R. v L.P.B.* (1990) 91 Cr.App.R. 359).

A permanent stay on the ground of delay should be the exception rather than the rule. The discretion whether or not to grant a stay as an abuse of process because of delay is an exercise in judicial assessment dependent on judgment rather than on any conclusion as to fact based on evidence. The correct approach for a judge to whom an application for such a stay is made is to bear in mind the following principles:

(a) even where delay was unjustifiable, a permanent stay should be the exception rather than the rule:
(b) where there was no fault on the part of the complainant or the prosecution, it should be very rare for a stay to be granted;
(c) no stay should be granted in the absence of serious prejudice to the defence so that no fair trial can be held;
(d) when assessing possible serious prejudice, he should bear in mind his power to regulate the admissibility of evidence and that the trial process itself should ensure that

all relevant factual issues arising from delay will be placed before the jury for their consideration in accordance with appropriate directions from him; and

(e) if, having considered all those factors, his assessment is that a fair trial is possible, he should not grant a stay.

(*R. v S (Crime: Delay in prosecution) The Times*, March 29, 2006) considering *Att-Gen's Reference (No. 1 of 1990)* [1992] Q.B. 630, 644, which was followed in *Att-Gen's Reference (No. 2 of 2001)* [2001] 1 W.L.R. 1869, *R. v Hooper* (unreported [2003] EWCA Crim. 2427 para.7), *R. v B* [2003] 2 Cr.App.R. 197, paras 15 to 18) and *R. v Smolinksi* [2004] 2 Cr.App.R. 661 para.7.

As to delay in enforcement proceedings under e.g. PCA 2002, see *R. (Lloyd) v Bow St MC* [2004] Crim.L.R. 136; also *R. v Smolindhi* [2004] Archbold News 1; *R. v B* [2005] 2 Cr.App.R. 13.

Special situations: (4) undertaking not to prosecute

3–007 There may be abuse of process where an unequivocal promise has been made to an accused that he will not be prosecuted. A prosecution undertaking ought to be relied on, and it is not right to allow a prosecution to proceed unless the prosecutor can show affirmatively that the original decision was exclusively evidentially based and was clearly wrong (*DPP v Taylor* [2004] 7 Archbold News).

Where the offender admits an offence and, with his agreement, is formally cautioned by the police under CDA 1998 on their assurance that he will not be brought before a criminal court in connection with the matter, it is an abuse of the court's process to permit the victim subsequently to bring a private prosecution in respect of that offence (*Jones v Whalley The Times*, July 31, 2006, HL).

In general, the circumstances of the case need to be exceptional (see e.g. *R. v Croydon JJ. Ex p. Dean* [1994] 98 Cr.App.R.76; *R. v Horseferry Rd MC Ex p. Bennett, above; R. v Slesinger* [1995] Crim.L.R. 137; *R. v Latif* [1996] 1 W.L.R. 104; *R. v Mullen* [1999] Crim.L.R. 561), *R. v Townsend and Others* [1997] 2 Cr. App. R.540 makes it plain that breach of a promise not to prosecute does not necessarily give rise to abuse (*cf R. v Bloomfield* [1997] 1 Cr. App. R. 235 where an assurance had been given to the judge that no evidence would be offered).

Where the prosecutor has elected not to proceed against a co-accused, although such proceedings were possible, such a decision does not amount to abuse of process (*R. v Forsyth*

[1997] 2 Cr.App.R. 299). See also *Environment Agency v Stanford* [1999] Env.L.R. 286.

There is a convention that if the prosecutor fails to secure a conviction on two occasions he will not seek a further retrial (*Henworth v UK The Times* November 22, 2004, EctHR). *Cf. R. v Henworth* [2001] 2 Cr.App.R. 4; *DPP v Edgar* (2002) 164 J.P. 471).

Special situations: (5) adverse publicity

3–008 As to a stay owing to the publicity surrounding a case, see *R. v Stone* [2001] Crim.L.R. 405, and the Scots cases of *Montgomery v HMA, Coulter v HMA* [2001] 2 W.L.R. 779.

Procedure on application

3–009 The following procedure applies (PD 2004, IV.36.1) where an accused proposes to make an application to stay an indictment on the grounds of abuse of process:

(1) written notice of application must be given to the prosecuting authority and to any co-accused not later than 14 days before the date fixed or warned for trial ("the relevant date");

 (a) specifying the name of the case, and the indictment number;
 (b) stating the fixed date or the warned date for trial, as appropriate;
 (c) specifying the nature of the application;
 (d) setting out in numbered sub-paragraphs the grounds upon which the application is to be made; and
 (e) being copied to the Chief Listing Officer at the court centre where the case is to be heard.

 Any co-accused who wishes to make a like application must give a like notice not less than 7 days before the relevant date, setting out any additional grounds relied upon (PD 2004, IV.36.2);

(2) the following automatic directions apply (PD 2004, IV.36.3). The advocate for the:

 (a) applicant(s) must, not later than 5 clear working days before the date fixed or warned for trial ("the relevant date") lodge with the court and serve on all other parties, a skeleton argument in support of the application and, if reference is to be made to any document not in the existing trial documents, a paginated and indexed bundle of such documents must be provided with the skeleton argument.

(b) prosecution must lodge with the court and serve on all other parties a responsive skeleton argument at least two clear working days before the relevant date together with a supplementary bundle if appropriate.

All skeleton arguments must specify any propositions of law to be advanced (together with the authorities relied on in support with page references to passages relied on), and where appropriate include a chronology of events and a list of the *dramatis personae* (PD 2004, IV.36.4).

In all instances where reference is made to a document, the reference in the trial documents or supplementary bundle must be given.

Time limits; plea and case management hearing

3–010 The above time limits are minimum time limits; in appropriate cases the court may (PD 2004, IV.36.5) order longer lead times.

In all cases where defence advocates are, at the time of the PCMH considering the possibility of an abuse of process application, this must be raised with the judge dealing with the matter, who will order a different timetable if appropriate, and may wish, in any event, to give additional directions about the conduct of the application.

Spelling it out

3–011 In giving judgment on an application, a few sentences showing the judge's command of the law on the topic will usually suffice, followed by a summary of the reasons for granting or rejecting the application (*R. v Manchester CC Ex p. Brockenbrow*, *The Times*, October 31, 1991, DC; *R. v Feltham Magistrates' Court, Mouat v DPP* [2001] 1 All E.R. 831, DC).

4 ACCESS TO TRIAL JUDGE

General principle

4–001 Meetings between advocates and the trial judge in the latter's private room may be necessary for the purposes of discussing the progress of the case, or for other reasons, but should be kept to a minimum since:

(1) the more relaxed atmosphere of the private room may tend to blur the formal outlines of the trial;
(2) there is room for misunderstanding as to how far any confidence is to extend; there is a risk that counsel and solicitors for the other parties may hear something said to the judge which they would rather not hear, putting them into a state of conflict between their duties to their clients, and their obligation to maintain the confidentiality of the private room;
(3) the accused has to learn what the judge said at second-hand and may afterwards complain that he was not given an accurate account;
(4) the accused does not hear what counsel says and cannot, therefore, intervene to correct a misstatement or an excess of authority.

Types of case

4–002 Such meetings are unnecessary where:

(1) the accused seeks an indication of sentence on a plea of guilty; a formal procedure is now provided (within the framework of *R. v Goodyear* [2005] EWCA Crim 888) for that matter to be raised in open court, in his presence, with both sides represented, and a full record being kept, (see 41 INDICATION OF SENTENCE);
(2) it is sought to inform the judge of assistance given, or to be given by the accused to the authorities; a form of proceedings is now prescribed under SOCA 2005, (see 29 DEALING WITH AN OFFENDER);

There may still be cases, where, for instance, it is sought to inform the judge of a matter which for compassionate reasons it is not thought proper to communicate to the accused (e.g. the diagnosis of a terminal illness) where it may be proper to see the judge privately, but generally such matters may be communicated in writing.

5 ACCUSED NOT GIVING EVIDENCE

Accused's right to give or not to give evidence

5–001 At the conclusion of the evidence for the prosecution, in a trial on indictment with a jury, CJPOA 1994, s.35(2), (as amended by CJA 2003, s.331, Sch.36, Pt 4, para.62) requires the judge to satisfy himself that the accused is aware that the stage has been reached at which evidence can be given for the defence and that, PD 2004, IV.44.1

(1) if he wishes, he may give evidence; and,
(2) if he chooses not to give evidence, or having been sworn, without good cause refuses to answer any questions, it will be permissible for the jury to draw such inferences as appear proper from his failure to give evidence or his refusal, without good cause, to answer any question.

Accused legally represented

5–002 Where the accused's legal representative informs the judge in the presence of the jury, if there is one, that the accused: PD 2004, IV.44.2, 3, 4

(1) *will give evidence*, the case proceeds in the normal way;
(2) *does not intend to give evidence* (or the judge is not informed that he does), the judge must address the advocate as follows:

> *"Have you advised your client that the stage has now been reached at which he may give evidence and, if he chooses not to do so or, having been sworn, without good cause refuses to answer any question, the jury may draw such inferences as appear proper from his failure to do so?"*

If the representative replies that the accused has been so advised, the case will proceed in the normal way; if the judge is informed that the accused has not been so advised, then he will direct the representative to advise his client of the consequences set out in IV.44.3 and should adjourn briefly for this purpose before proceeding.

Accused not legally represented

5–003 If the accused is not represented, the judge must, at the conclusion of the evidence for the prosecution and in the presence of the jury, if there is one, say to the accused: PD 2004, IV.44.5

> *"You have heard the evidence against you. Now is the time for you to make your defence. You may give evidence on oath,*

> *and be cross-examined like any other witness. If you do not give evidence or, having been sworn, without good cause refuse to answer any question, the jury may draw such inferences as appear proper. That means they may hold it against you. You may call any witness whom you have arranged to attend court. Afterwards you may also, if you wish, address the jury by arguing your case from the dock. But you cannot at that stage give evidence. Do you now intend to give evidence?"*

Directions to jury

5–004 There will be cases where the judge will consider it necessary to discuss with the advocates in the absence of a jury, the form of his direction. In the ordinary case the recommended direction to a jury is as follows:

> *"The accused has not given evidence. That is his right. But, as he has been told, the law is that you may draw such inferences as appear proper from his failure to do so. Failure to give evidence on its own cannot prove guilt but depending on the circumstances, you may hold his failure against him when deciding whether he is guilty."*

In a case where there is such evidence the judge may add:

> *"There is evidence before you on the basis of which the counsel for the defence invites you not to hold it against the accused that he has not given evidence before you namely . . . If you think that because of this evidence you should not hold it against him that he has not given evidence, do not do so. But if the evidence he relies on presents no adequate explanation for his absence from the witness box then you may hold his failure to give evidence against him. You do not have to do so.*
>
> *What proper inferences can you draw from his decision not to give evidence before you? If you conclude that there is a case for him to answer you may think that he would have gone into the witness box to give you an explanation for or an answer to the case against him. If the only sensible explanation for his decision not to give evidence is that he has no answer to the case against him, or none that could have stood up to cross-examination, then it would be open to you to hold against him his failure to give evidence. It is for you to decide whether it is fair to do so."*

As to the position where the accused absconds and the trial proceeds in his absence, see *R. v Gough* [2002] 2 Cr.App.R.8.

Basic essentials

5–005 *R. v Cowan* (1996) 1 Cr.App.R. 1, CACD highlighted certain essentials in relation to a trial with a jury.

The judge:

(1) must tell the jury that the burden of proof remains upon the prosecution throughout, and define the required standard;

(2) must make clear to the jury that the accused is entitled to remain silent; it is his right and his choice;
(3) must tell the jury that an inference from failure to give evidence cannot, on its own, prove guilt (it is expressly stated in CJPOA 1994, s.38(3)); therefore, they must be satisfied that the prosecution have established a case to answer before drawing any inferences from silence (see *R. v Alford's Transport and Others* (1997) 2 Cr.App.R. 326; *R. v Birchall*, *The Times*, February 10, 1998).
(4) may tell them that if, despite any evidence relied upon to explain his silence, or in the absence of any such evidence, they conclude that silence can only sensibly be attributed to the accused's having no answer, or none that would stand up to cross-examination, they may draw an adverse inference.

5–006 It is not possible to anticipate all the circumstances in which a judge might think it right to direct or advise a jury against drawing an adverse inference. Adopting the reasoning of a Northern Ireland case (*R. v McLernon* [1992] N.I. 168) the court said in *R. v Cowan* that:

> *"the [jury] has then a complete discretion as to whether inferences should be drawn or not. In these circumstances it is a matter for the [jury] in any criminal case (1) to decide whether to draw inferences or not; and (2) if it decides to draw inferences what their nature, extent and degree of adversity, if any, may be. It would be improper and indeed quite unwise for any court to set out the bounds of either steps (1) or (2). Their application will depend on factors peculiar to the individual case."*

CACD accepted in *R. v Cowan*: that:

(a) apart from the mandatory exceptions in s.35(1), it will be open to a jury to decline to draw an adverse inference from silence at his trial and for a judge to direct or advise them against drawing such inference if the circumstances of the case justify such a course;
(b) there would, however, need either to be some evidential basis for doing so or some exceptional factors in the case, making that a fair course to take;
(c) the inferences permitted by the section are only such "as appear proper"; the use of that phrase was no doubt intended to leave a broad discretion to the trial judge to decide in all the circumstances whether any proper inference is capable of being drawn by the jury. If not, he should tell them so; otherwise it is for the jury to decide whether, in fact, an inference should properly be drawn.

ACCUSED NOT GIVING EVIDENCE

The possession of a previous criminal record upon which he could be cross-examined (if he has attacked prosecution witnesses) is no good reason for directing a jury that they should not hold his silence against him. (See *R. v Becouarn* [2005] 1 W.L.R. 2589).

Counsel is not entitled to give evidence dressed up as a submission; it cannot be proper for him to give to the jury reasons for his client's silence at trial in the absence of evidence to support such reasons.

Medical reasons

5–007 Where it is contended under s.35(1)(b) that the accused's physical or mental condition makes it undesirable for him to give evidence, that issue must be properly raised (see *R. v Friend* [1997] 2 Cr.App.R. 231; *R. v A* [1997] Crim.L.R. 883) and must be decided by the judge (s.35(1)(b)). If the judge decides in favour of the accused the jury must be directed not to draw any adverse inference. It is a matter for the judge whether he hears evidence on the *voir dire* (*R. v Chadwick* [1998] 7 Archbold News 3, CA).

6 AGE OF OFFENDER

A. The relevant date

Under or over 18

6–001 Some of the principal sentences and ancillary orders which may be made by a judge of the Crown Court depend on the age of the offender. The form of sentence generally depends on whether the offender is under 18 or is 18 years or over. PCC(S)A 2000, s.164(1)

Where the offender's age is in doubt or in dispute, the judge should adjourn and obtain proper evidence of age before sentence.

Age of Offender

Particular orders

6–002 For the purposes of the following orders (there are certain exceptions see below) the relevant age is the age of the offender *on the day of conviction* (*R. v Danga* (1992) 13 Cr.App.R.(S.) 408) *R. v Robson* [2006] Crim.L.R. 935:

(1) liability to a custodial sentence,
(2) community orders,
(3) community rehabilitation orders,
(4) community punishment orders,
(5) community punishment and rehabilitation orders,
(6) curfew orders,
(7) drug abstinence orders,
(8) drug treatment and testing orders,
(9) exclusion orders,
(10) supervision orders, and
(11) attendance orders.

For the purposes of the following orders the age of the offender is deemed to be, after considering any available evidence on the day of conviction, *what it appears to the judge to be* (again there are exceptions, as to which see below):

(a) imprisonment,
(b) detention in a young offender institution,
(c) detention under PCC(S)A 2000, s.91; and
(d) a detention and training order.

AGE OF OFFENDER

Exceptions

6–003 There are a number of exceptions to the basic rules stated in 6–002:

(1) an offender committed to the Crown Court for sentence under PCC(S)A 2000, ss.3, 4 or 6 must be sentenced on the basis of *his age on the day he appears before the Crown Court*;

(2) an *offender* subject to:
  (a) a community rehabilitation order,
  (b) a community punishment order,
  (c) a community punishment and rehabilitation order,
  (d) a curfew order,
  (e) a drug abstinence order, or
  (f) a drug treatment and testing order, or

who appears before the Crown Court for sentence, *while the community order is in force*, must be sentenced on the basis of his age when he appears before the Crown Court *if the judge revokes the community order* and passes a further sentence for the offence;

(3) an offender who is found to be *in breach* of:
  (a) a community rehabilitation order,
  (b) a community punishment order,
  (c) a community punishment and rehabilitation order,
  (d) a curfew order,
  (e) a drug abstinence order,
  (f) a drug treatment and testing order, or
  (g) an exclusion order

and in whose case *the order is revoked* must be sentenced on the basis of *his age when he appears before the court which revokes the order*;

(4) an offender who is *subject to a community order under CJA 2003 and* in whose case the community *order is revoked* following a breach or subsequent conviction must be sentenced on the basis of his *age when the original order was made;*

(5) an offender subject to a conditional discharge convicted of a further offence during the operational period of the order where the conditional discharge is *revoked*, any sentence imposed for the original offence must be based on the offender's *age when he is so sentenced* (*R. v Keelan* (1975) 61 Cr. App. R. 212).

(6) an offender convicted *at any age* of a murder *committed when he was under 18* must be sentenced to be detained during HM Pleasure;

(7) the power to make an RT disqualification order depends on the offender's age *when he committed the offence*.

B. Sentences relevant by age

The starting point

6–004 The starting point is the sentence which the offender would have been likely to receive if he had been sentenced on the date of the commission of the offence (see *R. v M* [2003] 2 Cr.App.R.(S.) 26, *R. v Jones* [2003] Crim.L.R. 639).

1. Orders & sentences available for all ages

Absolute and Conditional discharge

6–005 Applies to a person of any age, convicted of any offence not being an offence for which the sentence is fixed by law or falls to be imposed under PCC(S)A 2000 ss.109 where that section still applies, 110(2), 111(2) (required custodial sentences for certain repeat offences), FA 1968, s.51A(2), CJA 2003, ss.225, 226, 227 or 228, but a conditional discharge must not be made in respect of:

(1) an offender aged under 18 who:

  (a) is convicted of an offence under CDA 1998, s.2(1) of offending against an anti-social behaviour order; or

  (b) within two years of the offence for which he is being sentenced, has been the subject of a constable's warning under CDA 1998, s.61, unless he is of the opinion that there are exceptional circumstances relating to the offence or to the offender which justify his doing so; or

(2) the breach of a sexual offences prevention order (CJA 2003, s.304, Sch.32, para.93(b).

Fines

6–006 In the case of an offender aged under 18 the judge may, and if he is under 16 must order any sum to be paid by the parent or guardian of the offender in the circumstances set out at 19–024 *et seq*. As to local authorities see 19–026, below; the level of fines, etc. which may be imposed on a juvenile are those of general application, as to which see 36 FINES AND ENFORCEMENT.

Deferred sentence
6–007 See 30 DEFERRING SENTENCE.

2. Sentences on conviction for offenders aged 18 and over

(a) Custodial sentences

Imprisonment for less than 12 months
6–008 Sentences of imprisonment for less than 12 months (for offenders aged 21 and over) will be replaced by custody plus orders under CJA 2003, s.181 (when that section comes into force), see 40–020 to 40–024, below.

Detention in young offender institution (ages 18, 19 & 20) for less than 12 months
6–009 Sentences of detention in a young offender institution for less than 12 months (for offenders aged 18, 19 and 20) will be replaced by custody plus orders under CJA 2003, s.181 (when that section comes into force), but note the prohibition on sentencing persons under 21 years old to imprisonment contained in PCC(S)A 2000, s.89(1). No doubt the provision contained CJCSA 2000, s.61 will be brought into force at the same time as CJA 2003, s.181 substituting "18 years" for "21 years" in s.89(1).

Custody plus order: imprisonment for less than 12 months under CJA 2003
6–010 See 40–020 to 40–024, below.

Intermittent custody order (for persons aged 21 or more)
6–011 This sentence is available only for offenders aged 21 and over on the date of conviction; see 24–026 to 40–033, below.

Suspended sentence order (for persons aged 21 or more)
6–012 This sentence is available for offenders aged 21 and over on the date of conviction; CJA 2003, s.189(1) – for offenders aged at least 18 but under 21. See suspended sentence of detention in a young offender institution at 40–080 to 40–092, below. For offences committed before April 4, 2005 see 40–071 to 40–079, below.

Suspended sentence of detention in YOI (ages 18, 19 & 20)

6–013 Detention in a young offender institution may be suspended in respect of offenders aged at least 18 but under 21 on the date of conviction (in respect of offences committed on and after April 4, 2005) (CJA 2003, s.189(1); Criminal Justice Act 2003 (Sentencing) (Transitory Provisions) Order 2005 (SI 2005/643), art.3(2).

Imprisonment (ages 21 and over) for 12 months or more

6–014 See 40–001 and 40–016, below.

Detention in a YOI (ages 18, 19 & 20) for 12 months or more

6–015 See 31–005 to 31–007, below.

Required minimum sentences under PCC(S)A 2000, ss.109–111

6–016 PCC(S)A 2000, ss.109 where still appropriate, 110 (third offence of Class A drug trafficking) 111 (third offence of domestic burglary).

Required minimum sentence FA 1968, s.51A

6–017 FA 1968, s.51A was inserted by CJA 2003, s.287 with effect from January, 22, 2004. PCC(S)A 2000, s.89(1) prohibits the imprisonment of persons under 21 years of age. An odd position now obtains because the Home Secretary has not made transitory and consequential provisions in relation to those aged 18, 19 and 20. Thus, an offender aged 21 and over convicted of one of the qualifying offences under FA 1968, s.5 (as amended) is liable to a required minimum sentence of *five years imprisonment*; an offender aged 16 years and under is liable to a minimum term of *three years detention* under PCC(S)A 2000, s.91 (see *R. v Rehman & Wood* [2005] *The Times*, September 27, 2005).

In view of PCC(S) 2000, s.89(1) offenders aged 18, 19 and 20 are not liable to a minimum required sentence, though this anomaly could be remedied by the bringing into force of CJCSA 2000, s.61 which substitutes "18 years" for "21 years" in s.89(1) or by a further transitional provision being made in compliance with the powers conferred of the Home Secretary under CJA 2003, s.333 (see *R. v Campbell* [2006] EWCA Crim 726; [2006] Crim.L.R. 654).

AGE OF OFFENDER

Until CJCA 2000, s.61 is implemented offenders who fall under this provision must be sentenced in the ordinary way by imposing an appropriate discretionary sentence of detention in a YOI.

Extended sentence of imprisonment (ages 21 and over), CJA 2003, s.227

6–018 Available for offenders aged 21 and over for offences committed on and *after April 4, 2005* which are "specified violent or sexual offences", see CJA 2003, s.224 and Sch.15. As to extended sentences for offenders aged 21 and over on the date of conviction in relation to offences committed *after September 30, 1998 and before April 4, 2005* see PCC(S)A 2000, s.85 and 40–041, 40–042, below.

Extended sentence of detention in a YOI (ages 18, 19 & 20), CJA 2003, s.227

6–019 See 31–027 and 31–028, below.

Imprisonment (21 and over) for public protection, CJA 2003, s.225

6–020 See 40–043–24–049, below.

Detention in a YOI (ages 18, 19 and 20) for public protection, CJA 2003, s.225

6–021 Relates to "dangerous offenders" for which CJA 2003, ss.224, 225: (a) The offence must be a violent or sexual offence as specified in APPENDIX A and either punishable with a life sentence but not sufficiently serious (by itself or with any other associated offence/s to justify such a sentence) or by a determinate sentence of 10 years and over; and (b) there must be a significant risk to the public of serious harm being caused by the offender committing further such offences.

Imprisonment for life (21 and over), CJA 2003, s.225

6–022 See 29–014, below.

Custody for life (ages 18, 19 and 20) CJA 2003, s.225

6–023 Available for offenders aged 18, 19 or 20 where (a) the offence he is convicted of is a violent or sexual offence as specified in APPENDIX A (b) such offence is punishable with a life sentence and (c) it is sufficiently serious (either by itself or with any associated offence(s) to justify a life sentence; in addition, there must be a significant risk to the public of serious harm being caused by the offender committing further such offence(s).

(b) Non-custodial sentences

Community order

6–024 A community order may be made only where the offender is 18 years old or over at the time of conviction. Although CJA 2003, s.177(1) refers to offenders aged 16 and 17 these provisions do not come into force until April 4, 2007 (CJA 2003 (Commencement No. 8 and Transitional and Savings Provisions) Order 2005, SI 2005/950, art.2(2). A community order may include any of the requirements set out below 6–025 to 6–036.

Unpaid work requirement

6–025 Not less than 40 hours and not more than 300 hours (CJA 2005, s.199(2), (5)). The prescribed period is 12 months (s.200(2)). May be accompanied by an electronic monitoring requirement.

Activity requirement

6–026 The total number of days must not exceed 60 days (CJA 2003, s.201(5)). Where this requirement forms part of a community sentence, the maximum period is three years (s.177(5). There is no minimum prescribed period other than the number of days specified in the order.

Where the requirement forms part of a suspended sentence order, the period must end not less than six months or more than two years from the date of the order (s.189(3)).

Where it is a requirement forming part of a condition of licence under a custody plus order or intermittent custody order, the period must not exceed that of the licence period.

May be accompanied by an electronic monitoring requirement unless arrangements are not available or a third party whose cooperation is needed does not consent (ss.177(4), 182(4), 185(2), 190(4), 215(2) and 218(4), (6) and (7).

Programme requirement

6–027 'Accredited Programme' is defined in s.202(2), (3). CJA 2003 does not prescribe a minimum and maximum number of days.

Where this requirement forms part of a community order, the maximum period is three years (s.177(5)). No minimum period is prescribed save for the actual number of days specified in the order.

Where the requirement forms part of a suspended sentence order, the period must not end less than six months or more than two years from the date of the order (s.189(3)).

Where the requirement forms part of a condition of licence under a custody plus order or an intermittent custody order, the period of the requirement must not exceed that of the licence period.

Electronic monitoring may accompany a programme requirement unless arrangements are not available or a third party whose cooperation is needed does not consent (ss.177(4), 182(4), 185(2), 190(4), 215(2) and 218(4), (6) and (7).

Prohibited activity requirement

6–028 There is no prescribed number of days, either minimum or maximum. Where the requirement forms part of a community order, the maximum period is three months (s.177(5)). Where it forms part of a suspended sentence order, the period of the requirement must not end less than six months or more than two years from the date of the order (s.189(3)). Where it is a condition of a licence under a custody plus order or an intermittent custody order, the period must not exceed the licence period.

May be accompanied by an electronic monitoring requirement unless arrangements are not available or a third party whose cooperation is needed does not consent (ss.177(4), 182(4), 185(2), 190(4), 215(2) and 218(4), (6) and (7).

Curfew requirement

6–029 The curfew on any one day may not be less than two hours and not more than 12 hours; however it may specify different places and different periods for different days (s.204(2)).

Where an order forms part of a community order or a sus pended sentence order, the maximum period is six months (there is no minimum period) (s.204(3)). Where it forms part of a custody plus order, the maximum period is six months from the beginning of the licence (s.204(4)). Where it forms part of an intermittent custody order, the maximum is 182 days (s.204(5)).

Electronic monitoring *must* accompany a curfew requirement unless arrangements are not available or a third party whose cooperation is needed does not consent, or the judge considers that such an order inappropriate (ss.177(3), 182(3), 185(2), 190(3), 215(2) and 218(2), (5) and (8)).

Exclusion requirement

6–030 Exclusion may be from a single specified place or places or from a specified area or areas and will continue to run throughout the specified period (s.205(3)).

Where an exclusion requirement is part of a community order, the maximum period is two years (s.205(2)). Where it is part of a suspended sentence order, the minimum period is six months or more and the maximum period is two years from the date of the order (s.189(3)). Where it is a condition of a licence under a custody plus order or an intermittent custody order, the period must not exceed the licence period.

An electronic monitoring requirement *must* accompany an exclusion requirement unless arrangements are not available or a third party whose cooperation is needed does not consent, or the judge considers such a requirement as inappropriate: ss.177(3), 182(3), 185(2), 190(3), 215(2) and 218(4), (5) and (8).

Residence requirement

6–031 This requirement is available as part of a community order (s.177(1)) or a suspended sentence order (ss.189(1)(7), 190(1)). If it forms part of a community order it may be made up to three years in length (s.177(5)). If it forms part of a suspended sentence order the period must end not less than six months and not more than two years from the date of the order (s.189(3)).

Electronic monitoring may accompany a programme requirement unless arrangements are not available or a third party whose cooperation is needed does not consent (ss.177(4), 182(4), 185(2), 190(4), 215(2) and 218(4), (6) and (7)).

Before imposing this requirement take notice of the provisions of CJA 2003, ss.206(2), 217(1).

Mental health treatment requirement

6–032 This requirement is available as part of a community order (s.177(1)) or a suspended sentence order (ss.189(1)(7), 190(1)). There must be evidence (written or oral) from a medical practitioner (s.207(5)) and the medical practitioner must be approved under MHA 1983, s.12 (CJA 2003, s.207(3)(a)).

Where the requirement forms part of a community order the period of the requirement must not exceed three years (s.177(5)); where it is part of a suspended sentence order, the period must end not less than six months and no more than two years from the date of the order (s.189(3)). Note that different periods of treatment may be specified by the medical practitioner and the psychologist (ss.207(1), 207(2)(c)).

Electronic monitoring may accompany a programme requirement unless arrangements are not are not available or a third party whose cooperation is needed does not consent (ss.177(4), 182(4), 185(2), 190(4), 215(2) and 218(4), (6) and (7)).

Where the offender does not agree to the making of this requirement, a custodial sentence may be passed (s.152(3)(a)).

Drug rehabilitation requirement

6–033 This requirement is available as part of a community order (s.177(1)) or a suspended sentence order (ss.189(1) and (7) and 190(1)).

Where it forms part of a community order the period of the DRR must not be less than six months (s.209(3)) but not more than three years (s.177(5)). Where it forms part of a suspended sentence order the period must not end less than six months and not more than two years from the date of the order (ss.189(3) and 209(3)). Where the treatment and testing period is more than 12 months, reviews are mandatory at intervals of not less than one month (s.210(1)(a)), otherwise reviews are optional (s.210(1)).

Electronic monitoring may accompany a programme requirement unless arrangements are not available or a third party whose cooperation is needed does not consent (ss.177(4), 182(4), 185(2), 190(4), 215(2) and 218(4), (6) and (7)).

Where the offender does not agree to the making of this requirement, a custodial sentence may be passed (s.152(3)(a)).

Alcohol treatment requirement

6–034 This requirement is available as part of a community order (s.177(1)) or a suspended sentence order (ss.189(1)(7), 190(1)). Where it forms part of a community order, the period of alcohol treatment must be not less than six months (s.210(4)) and not more than three years (s.177(5)). Where it forms part of a suspended sentence order, the period must end not less than six months and not more than two years from the date of the order (ss.189(3), 210(4)).

Electronic monitoring may accompany a programme requirement unless arrangements are not available or a third party whose cooperation is needed does not consent (ss.177(4), 182(4), 185(2), 190(4), 215(2) and 218(4), (6) and (7)).

Where the offender does not agree to the making of this requirement, a custodial sentence may be passed (s.152(3)(a)).

Supervision requirement

6–035 This requirement is available as part of a community order (s.177(1)) or a suspended sentence order (ss.189(1)(7), 190(1)) or as a condition of the licence under a custody plus order (when it comes into force); or as a condition of the licence under an intermittent custody order (ss.181(3)(4), 182(1), 183(1)(2) and 196(2)).

Where this requirement forms part of a community order, the period is that for which the order remains in force (maximum is three years) (ss.213(3)(a), 177(5)). Where it forms part of a suspended sentence order, the period of supervision must be not less than six months and not more than two years from the date of the order (ss.213(3)(d), 189(3)). Where it is a condition of a licence under either a custody plus order or an intermittent custody order, the period is equal to the licence period(s) (ss.213(3)(b)(c), 181(3)(b), 183(3)).

An electronic monitoring requirement may accompany a supervision requirement unless arrangements are not available or a third party whose cooperation would be needed does not consent (ss.177(4), 190(4), 215(2), 218(4)(6)(7)).

Attendance centre requirement

6–036 This requirement is available as part of a community order (s.177(1)), a suspended sentence order (ss.189(1)(7), 190(1)) or as part of the conditions of a licence under custody plus order or an intermittent custody order (ss.181(3)(4), 182(1), 183(1)(2) and 196(2)). The number of hours must be not less than 12 and not more than 36 (s.214(2)).

An electronic monitoring requirement may accompany an attendance centre requirement unless arrangements are not available or a third party whose cooperation is needed does not consent (ss.177(4), 190(4), 215(2), 218(4)(6)(7)).

Electronic monitoring requirement

6–037 This requirement:

(1) must accompany a curfew requirement or an exclusion requirement unless arrangements are not available; or a third party whose cooperation would be needed does not consent; or the judge considers such a requirement to be inappropriate (ss.177(3), 182(3), 185(2), 190(3), 215(2), 218(4), (5) and (8)).

(2) *may* form part of a community order (s.177(3)(4) or of a suspended sentence order (ss.189(1)(7), 190(1)); or of the conditions of a licence under a custody plus order or an intermittent custody order (ss.181(3)(4), 182(1), 183(1)(2) and 196(2)).

An electronic monitoring requirement may not be imposed on its own; its purpose is to ensure the offender's compliance with such other requirement/s as has/have been imposed (s.215(1)).

Unless arrangements are not available or a third party whose cooperation would be required does not consent, an electronic

Age of Offender

monitoring requirement may accompany the following requirements:

(1) Unpaid work requirement
(2) Activity requirement
(3) Programme requirement
(4) Prohibited activity requirement
(5) Residence requirement
(6) Mental health treatment requirement
(7) Drug rehabilitation requirement
(8) Alcohol treatment requirement
(9) Supervision requirement
(10) Attendance centre requirement

3. Sentences on conviction for offenders aged under 18

(a) Custodial sentences

Detention and training order (ages 12–17)

6–038 The length of a detention and training order must be for one of the following periods:4/6/8/10/12/18 or 24 months.

Where the defendant was aged *12, 13 or 14* when convicted an order may not be imposed unless the judge considers him to be a *persistent offender* (stating his reasons).

Detention s.91 (PCC(S)A 2000) for less than 12 months

6–039 Applies to an offender:

(1) under 18 convicted of certain specified offences only, namely an offence:

   (a) punishable in the case of an offender aged 21 or over with 14 years imprisonment, not being an offence for which the sentence is fixed by law; or
   (b) under SOA 2003, s.3 (sexual assault); or
   (c) under SOA 2003, s.13 (child sex offences committed by children or young persons); or
   (d) under SOA 2003, s.25 (sexual activity with a child family member);
   (e) under SOA 2003, s.26 (inciting a child family member to engage activity);

(2) aged at least 14 but under 18 is convicted of certain specified offences, namely;

(a) causing death by dangerous driving under RTA 1988, s.1; or
(b) causing death by careless driving while under the influence of drink or drugs;

the sentence may not exceed the maximum term of imprisonment to which a person aged 21 or over would be liable.

Detention s.91 (PCC(S)A 2000) for 12 months or more

6–040 See above 6–039.

Required minium sentence, FA 1968, s.51A (offenders under 18)

6–041 See above 6–017.

Extended sentence of detention; CJA 2003, s.228

6–042 The court is required to pass an extended sentence of detention under s.228 in respect of an offender who is aged under 18 on the date of conviction if:

(1) he committed a violent or a sexual offence specified in APPENDIX A; and
(2) there is a significant risk to the public of serious harm being caused by the offender committing further such specified offence/s; and
(3) one of the following three circumstances applies:

(a) the offence of which he was convicted carries a life sentence, but is not sufficiently serious to justify a life sentence, and an extended sentence, rather than a sentence for public protection, is sufficient to protect the public from serious harm from him; or
(b) the offence of which he was convicted carries 10 years or more, and an extended sentence, rather than a sentence for public protection, is sufficient to protect the public from serious harm from him; or
(c) the offence of which he was convicted carries a determinate sentence of less than 10 years, and an extended sentence would be adequate rather than a sentence which would otherwise be imposed.

As to assessment of significant risk to the public of serious harm see *R. v Lang* [2006] Crim.L.R. 174 (death or serious personal injury).

See also 31–027, below.

Detention for public protection, CJA 2003, s.226

6–042A The judge is required to pass a sentence of detention for public protection on an offender who is aged under 18 on the date of conviction if:

(1) the offence of which he was convicted is a violent or sexual offence specified in APPENDIX A; and

- (a) the offence carries a life sentence, but is not sufficiently serious to justify a life sentence, or
- (b) the offence is punishable by a determinate sentence of 10 years or more; and

(2) there is a significant risk to the public of serious harm being caused by the offender committing further such specified offence(s); and

(3) an extended sentence under s.228 would not be adequate to protect the public from serious harm from him.

Detention for life, CJA 2003, s.226

6–043 The judge is required to pass a sentence of detention for life on an offender aged under 18 on the date of conviction if:

(1) The offence of which he was convicted is:

- (a) a violent or sexual offence specified in APPENDIX A; and
- (b) carries a life sentence; and
- (c) sufficiently serious to justify a life sentence; and

(2) there is a significant risk to the public of serious harm being caused by the offender committing further such specified offence(s).

(b) Non-custodial sentences

6–044 When passing sentence on an offender under 18 the judge may make one or more of the following *youth community orders:*

A curfew order (for persons aged 10–17)
An exclusion order (for persons aged 10–17)
An attendance centre order (for persons aged 10–17)
A supervision order (for persons aged 10–17)
An action plan order (for persons aged 10–17)
A community rehabilitation order (for persons aged 16 or 17)
A community punishment order (for persons aged 16 or 17)
A community punishment and rehabilitation order (for persons aged 16 or 17)
A drug treatment and testing order (for persons aged 16 or 17)

Curfew order (Ages 10–17)

6–045 PCC(S)A 2000, ss.37 to 40.

The maximum period is three months (s.37(3)(a), (4)); the order may specify different days, different places and different periods; on any one day the curfew must not be less than two hours and not more than 12 hours.

Exclusion order (ages 10–17)

6–046 PCC(S)A 2000, ss.40A to 40C.

The maximum period is three months (s.40A(1); usually the exclusion will be from a specific place or area, however, the order may specify different places or areas for different periods or for different days.

Attendance centre order (ages 10–17)

6–047 PCC(S)A 2000, ss.60 to 62.

The total aggregate of hours must be 12 but if the offender is under 14 and the judge considers 12 hours are excessive he may order a shorter period. If he considers 12 hours to be inadequate, then he may increase the maximum number of hours up to 24.

Supervision order (ages 10–17)

6–048 PCC(S)A 2000, ss.63 to 68.

The maximum period is three years (s.63(7)); to assist the "supervisor" of the order the judge may impose requirements as set out in Sch.6 (as amended by CJA 2003, s.304, Sch.32, para.127), see 21–071, below.

Action plan order (ages 10–17)

6–049 PCC(S)A 2000, ss.69 to 72; see 21–081 to 21–085, below.

Section 69(1)(a) provides that the action plan order be for three months. For requirements that may be imposed with this order see 21–083, below.

A community rehabilitation order (ages 16 or 17)

6–050 PCC(S)A 2000, ss.41 to 45; see 21–004, below. Not less than six months and not more than three years (s.41(1)).

A community punishment order (ages 16 or 17)

6–051 PCC(S)A 2000, ss.46 to 50; see 21–005 and 21–006, below.

Not less than 40 hours and not more than 240 hours to be performed, in general, within 12 months.

A community punishment and rehabilitation order (ages 16 or 17)

6–052 PCC(S)A 2000, s.51; see 21–007, below.

The period of the order must not be less than 12 months and no more than three years (s.51(1)(b)). Additional requirements under the rehabilitation element may be imposed. The number of hours of work must not be less than 40 and not more than 100 (s.51(1)(b)).

A drug treatment and testing order (ages 16 or 17)

6–053 PCC(S)A 2000, ss.52 to 58. The order is now available only for offenders aged 16 or 17.

It must last for at least six months but no more than three years (s.52(1)(a)). There will be reviews (which the offender must attend) to monitor his progress under the order. The intervals between reviews must be of not less than one month (s.54(6)(a)).

7 ALLOCATION AND DEPLOYMENT OF CASES

Case sent for trial; date of trial

7–001 The trial of a person whose case is sent to the Crown Court for trial must:

SCA 1981, s.77; CJPOA 1994, Sch.4, para.52; CJA 2003, s.332, Sch.37, Pt 4

(1) not begin until the expiration of 14 days beginning with the date it was sent for trial, except with the consent of the person charged; and
(2) unless the Crown Court has otherwise ordered, begin not later than the expiration of eight weeks beginning with that date.

A trial is taken to "begin" to this purpose, when the accused is arraigned.

The time limits were said in *Ex p. Scott* (1988) 85 Cr.App.R. 382 to be "directory only", but see the decisions of the House of Lords in *R. v Soneji* [2005] 3 W.L.R. 303 and the decisions of CACD in *R. v Sekhon and Others* [2003] 1 W.L.R. 1655 and *R. v Ashton* [2006] *The Times*, April 18, referred to at para.16–014 below.

CJPOA1994, Sch.4, para.52(5) requires the judge to have regard to the desirability of avoiding prejudice to the welfare of any witness which may be occasioned by unnecessary delay.

Allocation of business

7–002 The cases, or classes of cases, in the Crown Court suitable for allocation respectively to a judge of the High Court and to a Circuit Judge or a Recorder, and all other matters relating to the distribution of Crown Court business, are determined in accordance with directions given by or on behalf of the Lord Chief Justice.

SCA 1981, s.75(1)(2)

The same applies to the cases or classes of cases suitable for allocation to a court comprising magistrates. The directions at present in force are those given in PD 2004, III.21 *et seq.,* as amended (see *The Times*, June 7, 2005), set out below, and taking effect from June 6, 2005.

Classification

7–003 For the purposes of trial in the Crown Court, offences are to be classified as follows

Class 1: (a) Misprision of treason and treason felony; (b) murder; (c) genocide; (d) torture, hostage-taking and offences under the War Crimes Act 1991; (e) an offence under the Official Secrets Acts; (f) manslaughter; (g) infanticide; (h) child destruction; (i) abortion (OAPA 1861, s.58); (j) sedition; (k) an offence under s.1 of the Geneva Conventions Act 1957; (l) mutiny; (m) piracy; (n) soliciting, incitement, attempt or conspiracy to commit any of the above offences.

Class 2: (a) rape; (b) sexual intercourse with a girl under 13; (c) incest with a girl under 13; (d) assault by penetration; (e) causing a person to engage in sexual activity; (f) rape of a child under 13; (g) assault of a child under 13 by penetration; (h) causing or inciting a child to engage in sexual activity, where penetration is involved; (i) sexual activity with a person with a mental disorder; (j) inducement to procure sexual activity with a mentally disordered person, where penetration is involved; (k) paying for sexual services of a child where child is under 13 and penetration is involved; (l) committing an offence with intent to commit a sexual offence, where the offence is kidnapping or false imprisonment; (m) soliciting, incitement, attempt or conspiracy to commit any of the above offences.

Class 3: All other offences not listed in classes 1 or 2.

7–004 Cases committed, transferred or sent for trial

A magistrates' court upon either committing a person for trial under MCA 1980, s.6 or sending a person for trial under CDA 1998, s.51, must:

(a) if the offence, or any of the offences, is included in Class 1, specify the most convenient location of the Crown Court where a High Court Judge, or where a Circuit Judge duly authorised by the Lord Chief Justice to try Class 1 cases regularly sits;

(b) if the offence, or any of the offences, is included in Class 2, specify the most convenient location of the Crown Court where a judge duly authorised to try Class 2 cases, regularly sits; these courts on each Circuit will be identified by the Presiding Judges with the concurrence of the Lord Chief Justice, on each circuit.

(c) if an offence is in Class 3, specify the most convenient location of the Crown Court.

Where a case is transferred under CJA 1987, s.4 or CJA 1991, s.53, the authority must, in specifying the proposed place of trial in the notice of transfer, comply with the above provisions. PD 2004, III.21.2

In selecting the most convenient location of the Crown Court, the magistrates must have regard to the considerations referred to in MCA 1980, s.7 and CDA 1998, s.51(10), and to the location or locations of the Crown Court designated by a Presiding Judge as the location to which cases should normally be committed, from their petty sessions area. PD 2004, III.21.3

Where on one occasion a person is committed in respect of a number of offences, all the committals must be to the same location of the Crown Court and that location must be the one where a High Court Judge regularly sits if such a location is appropriate for any of the offences. PD 2004, III.21.4

Committals following breach

7–005 Where, in the Crown Court, a community order or an order for conditional discharge has been made, or a suspended sentence has been passed, and the offender is subsequently found or alleged to be in breach before a magistrates' court which decides to commit the offender to the Crown Court, he must be committed in accordance with paras III.21.6, III.21.7 or III.21.8 below. Thus: PD 2004, III.21.5

(1) he must be committed to the location of the Crown Court where the order was made or the suspended sentence was passed, unless it is inconvenient, impracticable or inappropriate to do so in all the circumstances; PD 2004, III.21.6
(2) if, for whatever reason, he is not so committed and the order was made by a High Court Judge he must be committed to the most convenient location of the Crown Court where a High Court Judge regularly sits; PD 2004, III.21.7
(3) in all other cases he must be committed to the most convenient location of the Crown Court; PD 2004, III.21.8

In selecting the most convenient location of the Crown Court, the magistrates must have regard to the locations of the Crown Court designated by a Presiding Judge as the locations to which cases should normally be committed from their court. PD 2004, III.21.9

Serious or complex fraud cases

7–006 Where notice of transfer is served under CJA 1987, s.4 the proposed place of trial to be specified in the notice must be one of the Crown Court centres designated by the Senior Presiding Judge. PD 2004, III.21.10

Child witness cases

7–007 Where a notice of transfer is served under CJA 1991, s.53 (child witness cases), the proposed place of trial to be specified in accordance with CJA 1991, Sch.6, para.1(1) must be a Crown Court centre which is equipped with live television link facilities. PD 2004, III.21.11

Transfer of cases from one circuit to another

7–008 An application that a case be transferred from one circuit to another should not be granted unless the judge is satisfied that: PD 2004, IV.31.1

(1) the approval of the Presiding Judges and the Regional Director for each Region/Circuit has been obtained; or
(2) the case may be transferred under general arrangements approved by the Presiding Judges and Regional Directors.

Transfer of proceedings between locations of the Crown Court

7–009 Without prejudice to the provisions of SCA 1981, s.76 (committal for trial; alteration of place of trial), directions may be given for the transfer from one location of the Crown Court to another of: PD 2004, IV.32.1–3

(a) appeals; and
(b) proceedings on committal for sentence, or to be dealt with.

Such directions may be given in a particular case by an officer of the Crown Court, or generally, in relation to a class or classes of case, by the Presiding Judge or a judge acting on his behalf.

If dissatisfied with such directions given by an officer of the Crown Court, any party to the proceedings may apply to a judge of the Crown Court who may hear the application in chambers.

Alteration of venue

7–010 Without prejudice to the above provisions, directions, or further directions, altering the place of any trial on indictment, whether by varying the decision of the magistrates' court under MCA 1980, s.7, (or CDA 1998, s.51 – *R. v Croydon CC Ex p. Britton* 164 J.P. 729) or by substituting some other place for the place specified in a notice of transfer or varying a previous decision of the Crown Court, may be given by or on behalf of the Crown Court by a Crown Court officer. Where a preparatory hearing has been ordered under CJA 1987, s.7, such SCA 1981, ss.8(1), 76(1)(2); CJA 1987, s.15, Sch.2; CJPOA 1994, s.168(1), Sch.9, para.17; CJA 2003, s.331, Sch.32, para.47

directions may be given at any time before the jury is sworn (or would be sworn but for the making of an order under CJA 2003, Pt 7 (trial without jury).

If dissatisfied with the place of trial as:

(1) fixed by the magistrates' court;
(2) specified in a transfer notice under CJA 1987, s.4 or CJA 1991, s.53; or
(3) fixed by the Crown Court,

a party may apply to the Crown Court for a direction, or a further direction, varying the place of trial, and the Crown Court must take the matter into consideration, and may comply with or refuse the application, or give a direction not in compliance with the application, as it thinks fit.

Allocation of business within the Crown Court

General

7–011 Cases in: PD 2004, IV.33.1

Class 1 may be tried only by:

(1) a High Court Judge; or
(2) a Circuit Judge, a Deputy High Court Judge or a Deputy Circuit Judge provided that:
   (a) in all cases save attempted murder such judge is authorised by the Lord Chief Justice to to try murder cases, or in the case of attempted murder, to try murder or attempted murder; and
   (b) the Presiding Judge has released the case for trial by such a judge.

Class 2 may be tried by: PD 2004, IV.33.2

(1) a High Court Judge;
(2) a Circuit Judge, a Deputy High Court Judge or Deputy Circuit Judge or a Recorder, provided that in all cases such judge is authorised to try Class 2 cases by the Lord Chief Justice and the case has been assigned to the judge by order under the direction of either the Presiding Judge or Resident Judge in accordance with guidance given by the Presiding Judges.

Class 3 may be tried by a High Court Judge or, in accordance with guidance given by the Presiding Judges, by a Circuit Judge, Deputy Circuit Judge or a Recorder. A Class 3 case must not be PD 2004, IV.33.3

listed before a High Court Judge except with the consent of a Presiding Judge.

Appeals from decisions of magistrates:

7–012 Appeals from decisions of magistrates must be heard by: PD 2004, IV.33.45

(1) a Resident Judge; or
(2) a Circuit Judge who regularly sits at that Crown Court centre, nominated by the Resident Judge; or
(3) an experienced Recorder or Deputy Circuit Judge specifically approved by or under the direction of the Presiding Judges for the purpose; or
(4) where no Circuit Judge or Recorder satisfying the requirements above is available and it is not practicable to obtain the approval of the Presiding Judges, by a Circuit Judge, Recorder or Deputy Circuit Judge selected by the Resident Judge to hear a specific case or cases listed on a specific day.

Plea and management hearings

7–013 With the exception of courts operating the management and directions scheme referred to in para.41.1, the following arrangements for **pre-trial proceedings** apply: PD 2002, para.33.6

(1) to applications or matters arising before trial (including those relating to bail) should be listed where possible before the judge by whom the case is expected to be tried. Where a case is to be tried by a High Court Judge who is not available the application or matter should be listed before any other High Court Judge then sitting at the Crown Court centre at which the matter has arisen; before a Presiding Judge; before the Resident Judge for the centre, or with the consent of the Presiding Judge, before a Circuit Judge nominated for the purpose.
(2) in other cases, if the Circuit Judge or Recorder who is expected to try the case is not available, the matter must be referred to the Resident Judge or, if he is not available, to any judge or Recorder then sitting at the centre.

Committals following breach

7–014 Committals following breach (such as a matter in which a community order has been made or a suspended sentence passed) should, where possible, be listed before the judge who originally dealt with the matter or, if not, before a judge of the same or higher level. PD 2004, IV.33.5.

Application for removal of a driving disqualification

7–015 Application should be made to the location of the Crown Court where the order of disqualification was made. PD 2004, IV.33.6.

Absence of Resident Judge

7–016 A Resident Judge must appoint a deputy to exercise his functions when he is absent from his centre (PD 2004, IV.33.7).

Presiding Judges' guidance

7–017 For the just, speedy and economical disposal of the business of a circuit, the Senior Presiding Judge, or the Presiding Judges with his approval, (PD 2004, IV.33.8) may issue guidance to Resident Judges in relation to the allocation and management of the work at their court.

With the approval of the Senior Presiding Judge, general directions may be given by the Presiding Judges of the South Eastern Circuit concerning the distribution and allocation of business of all classes (all cases or classes of cases) at the Central Criminal Court (PD 2004, IV.33.9).

Guidance for Resident Judges

General responsibilities

7–018 A Resident Judge has the general responsibility, subject to the guidance of the Presiding Judges, within his court centre for the allocation of criminal judicial work, to ensure the just and efficient despatch of the business of the court or group of courts. This includes the overseeing of the deployment of allocated judges at the court or group, including the distribution of work between all the judges allocated to that court.

Under PD 2004, IV.33.7 (see 7–017 above) the Senior Presiding Judge and the Presiding Judge issued guidance (dated May 26, 2005 and taking effect on June 6, 2005) in relation to cases which must be referred to:

(1) a Presiding Judge for release; and
(2) the Resident Judge before being assigned to a Judge or Recorder to hear.

It is applicable to all Crown Courts, but its application at certain Crown Courts may be modified by the Presiding Judges, with the approval of the Senior Presiding Judge, through the provision of further specific guidance applicable to such Crown Courts as are identified in the further guidance. Note that:

(a) cases which do not come within (1) or (2) are not specifically covered by this Guidance, but are subject to the directions given to the Listing Officer by the Resident Judge at each centre;

(b) this Guidance does not seek to prescribe the way in which the Resident Judge gives directions as to listing policy to the listing officer; its purpose is to ensure that there is appropriate judicial control over the listing of cases specified in this Guidance;

(c) in view of the changes effected to this Guidance in respect of Class 2 cases, it is essential that a Resident Judge nominates a judge to act on his behalf and discharge his responsibilities when he is away.

Cases to be referred to a Presiding Judge

7–019 The following cases must be referred to a Presiding Judge:

(1) all Class I cases (see 7–003 above);

(2) all cases expected to last four weeks or more. If there are serious fraud cases (as defined by the Lord Chief Justice in 1998) that are estimated to last less than this, they must also be referred;

(3) all cases involving rape or other sexual offences which are of especial sensitivity or likely to attract publicity such as those involving well known persons or circumstances of particular difficulty or notoriety or serial cases. Paragraph 7 020 sets out the cases which must bc referred to the Resident Judge and para.7–021 sets out the procedure for assignment by the Resident Judge or Judge who is to try such cases without reference to the Presiding Judge;

(4) terrorist and firearms cases;

(5) cases involving explosives, terrorism or the actual discharge of firearms in the course of another crime; also the more serious cases of possession of firearms, especially where possession is in the context of robbery or other serious crime.

The form is attached as Annex A to the Guidance. Of particular importance when a release request is made are a case summary, which can be very brief in a standard sort of case, a clear recommendation by the Resident Judge about the judges available to try the case, and any brief comments or reasons he/she thinks helpful.

Cases to be referred to the Resident Judge

7–020 The following cases must be referred by listing officers to the Resident Judge:

(1) all cases under (1)–(5) above which are required to be referred to a Presiding Judge must in the first instance be referred to the Resident Judge;
(2) all sexual offences (not merely those in Class 2, see 7–003 above); he may deal with them, in accordance with 7–021 without reference to the Presiding Judge, save in the circumstances specified in 7–019 at (3);
(3) all cases involving firearms or imitation firearms;
(4) cases involving causing death by dangerous or careless driving;
(5) arson;
(6) kidnapping and false imprisonment;
(7) cases where any accused is under 18;
(8) any case which appears to raise particularly complex, sensitive or serious issues.

Administrative arrangements

7–021 It is the Resident Judge's duty to arrange with the Listing Officer a satisfactory means of ensuring that all cases listed at their court are listed before judges or recorders of suitable seniority and experience, subject to the following:

(1) if a case is referred to the Presiding Judge, and the Presiding Judge does not assign the judge who is to try the case, the assignment of the judge must be made by the Resident Judge; the time at which the assignment is made is at his discretion;
(2) in all rape cases and other sexual offences falling within Class 2 (see 7–003 above), the judge who is to try the case must be assigned by or under the direction of the Resident Judge, the time at which the assignment is made being at his discretion. The judge assigned must have been authorised to try Class 2 cases. It is a condition of the authorisation that it does not take effect until the judge has attended the relevant JSB course; the Resident Judge should check in the case of newly authorised judges that they have attended the course;
(3) the following offences, save in exceptional circumstances specifically authorised by the Resident Judge, should also be tried by a judge authorised to try Class 2 cases who is assigned to try the case by the Resident Judge; **all serious sexual offences** including:

- cases of buggery with a person under 16;
- all cases of serious cases of indecent assault and indecency, especially those involving children or vulnerable complainants whether under the 2003 Act or otherwise;
- unlawful sexual intercourse with young girls; indictable-only offences under the 2003 Act — see ss.9 and 25;
- cases involving breach of trust — see ss.38–41;
- any other cases which are potentially sensitive;

(4) all cases specified in 7–020(3)–(8) must be assigned for trial to a judge by or under direction of the Resident Judge; the time at which the assignment is made being a matter for his discretion.

8 ALTERATION OF SENTENCE

Introduction

8–001 Ordinarily, a sentence imposed, or other order, made by the Crown Court when dealing with an offender, takes effect from the beginning of the day on which it is imposed, unless the judge otherwise directs (PCC(S)A 2000, ss.154, 155; CJA 2003, s.34, Sch.32, para.121), but:

(1) as a court of record, the Crown Court has an inherent jurisdiction to rectify mistakes in its record (*R. v Saville* [1981] Q.B. 12); and, more importantly;
(2) a sentence or order may be varied or rescinded under the provisions of PCC(S)A 2000, s.155(1), (2), (3), see below; and
(3) a "discounted" sentence passed upon an offender in view of an undertaking to assist the authorities, may be subsequently reviewed (under SOCA 2005, s.74) where it is shown that such assistance is not forthcoming;
(4) special rules apply in relation to adjusting a sentence in subsequent proceedings under PCA 2002, see 24 CONFISCATION ORDERS.

1. Variation of sentence; PCC(S)A 2000, ss.154, 155

General

8–002 A sentence or other order may be varied or rescinded:

(1) within, and only within (*R. v Menocal* [1980] A.C. 598; *R. v Hart* (1983) 5 Cr.App.R.(S.) 25; *R. v Stillwell* (1992) 94 Cr.App.R. 65), the period of 28 days beginning with the day on which the sentence was imposed or other order was made;
(2) within, and only within, any specified time limit imposed by any other statutory provision (unless it is of a formal nature);
(3) where two or more persons are jointly tried on indictment, not later than the expiration of whichever is the shorter or the following periods, i.e.:

    (a) 28 days beginning with the conclusion of the joint trial; or

(b) 56 days beginning with the day on which the sentence or other order was imposed or made;
(c) bearing in mind that a joint trial is concluded for these purposes on the latest of the dates on which any of the accused is acquitted or sentenced or a special verdict is returned;

(4) in open court (*R. v Dowling* (1989) 88 Cr.App.R. 88) in the presence of the offender (*R. v Hussein* [1999] Crim.L.R. 1004) and after his representatives have had an opportunity to make submissions on the alteration, unless he has waived the right, either expressly or by implication—as by absconding (*R. v May* (1981) 3 Cr.App.R. 165; *R. v Cleere* (1983) 5 Cr.App.R. (S.) 465; *R. v McLean* (1988) 10 Cr.App.R.(S.) 18) and
(5) by the court constituted as it was when sentence was passed or the other order was made or, where the Crown Court comprised one or more justices, a court so constituted save for the omission of any one or more of those justices.

The sentence or order as varied takes effect from the beginning of the day on which it was originally imposed or made, unless the court otherwise directs.

"Order", "sentence" defined

8–003 "Order" does not include a contribution order under AJA 1999, s.17(2) (CDS funding); it was held under the previous law to include a confiscation order under DTA 1994 (*R. v Miller* (1991) 92 Cr.App.R. 191), and thus probably, a confiscation order under PCA 2002.

A "sentence" includes a recommendation for deportation, also a forfeiture order made in consequence of a conviction (*R. v Menocal* [1980] A.C. 598).

"Variation" defined

8–004 The word "varied" is an ordinary English word and bears its dictionary meaning (*R. v Sodhi* (1978) 66 Cr.App.R. 260). The provisions empower the judge, in an appropriate case, to:

(1) correct minor errors made in sentencing;
(2) change the nature of the sentence where necessary (e.g. *R. v Grice* (1978) 66 Cr.App.R. 167 (imprisonment varied to hospital order);
(3) reduce the sentence imposed if, after further reflection, it appears too severe; and

(4) increase the sentence originally passed, but only in exceptional cases (*R. v Newsome* (1970) 54 Cr.App.R. 485 (under previous legislation); *cf. R. v Grice*, (above)) where, e.g.:

   (a) additional material is put before the judge (*R. v Reilly* [1982] Q.B. 1208); or
   (b) it is clear that the original sentence was passed on an incorrect factual basis (*R. v Hart* (1983) 5 Cr.App.R. (S.) 25; *R. v McLean* (1988) 10 Cr.App.R.(S.) 18; *R. v Hadley* (1995) 16 Cr.App.R.(S.) 358), *cf. R. v Woop* [2002] 2 Cr.App.R.(S.) 65).

As to the problems caused by "rescinding" rather than varying a sentence, see *R. v Smith* [1995] Crim. L.R. 662, and *R. v Dunham* [1996] 1 Cr.App.R.(S.) 438. Where the judge, in imposing consecutive sentences for two offences, has properly had regard to the totality principle but in imposing one of the sentences has exceeded the maximum, he may vary the sentence under s.47(2), so as to reduce the unlawful sentence and increase the other, provided the total is not increased: *R. v Lees* [1999] 1 Cr.App.R.(S.) 194. *Cf. R. v Evans* 13 Cr.App.R.(S.) 377.

Ancillary orders

8–005 Where the judge is contemplating making an ancillary order, such as a compensation order or a confiscation order, which requires consideration of further evidence as to the amount, etc., he ought to state that he is postponing that question at the time he passes the substantive sentence. He cannot otherwise make, for example, a compensation order after the expiration of the 28 day period: see *R. v Dorrian* [2001] 1 Cr.App.R.(S.) 135.

2. Review of discounted sentence under SOCA 2005

General

8–006 Where a judge of the Crown Court has passed a sentence on a person in respect of an offence, and that person receives: SOCA 2005, s.74(1) (1)–(3), 13

(1) a discounted sentence in consequence of his having offered in pursuance of a written agreement to give assistance to the prosecutor or investigator of an offence and knowingly fails to any extent to give assistance in accordance with the agreement; or

(2) a discounted sentence in consequence of his having offered in pursuance of a written agreement to give assistance to the prosecutor or investigator of an offence and, having given the assistance in accordance with the agreement, in pursuance of another written agreement gives or agrees to give further assistance; or

(3) a sentence which is not discounted, and in pursuance of a written agreement he subsequently gives or offers to give assistance to the prosecutor or investigator of an offence,

a specified prosecutor (i.e. the DPP, the DRCP, the DSFO, the DPP for Northern Ireland, or a prosecutor designated for the purposes of this section by one of those), may at any time refer the case back to the court by which the sentence was passed, if that person is still serving his sentence, and the specified prosecutor thinks it is in the interests of justice to do so.

A person does not fall within SOCA 2005, s.74(2) if he was convicted of an offence for which the sentence is fixed by law, and he did not plead guilty to the offence for which he was sentenced.

The hearing

8–007 A case referred as above must, if possible, be heard by the judge who passed the sentence to which the referral relates. SOCA 2005, s.74(4)–(7)

Where that judge is satisfied that the person concerned under (1) above knowingly failed to give the assistance, he may substitute for the sentence to which the referral relates such greater sentence (not exceeding that which the original judge would have passed but for the agreement to give assistance) as he thinks appropriate.

In a case of a person who falls within (2) or (3) above, the judge may take into account the extent and nature of the assistance given or offered; and substitute for the sentence to which the referral relates such lesser sentence as he thinks appropriate (s.74(6)).

Any part of the sentence to which the referral relates which the person has already served must be taken into account in determining when a greater or lesser sentence imposed by s.71(5) or (6) has been served. CJA 2003, s.174(1)(a) or s.270 as the case may be applies to a sentence substituted under SOCA 2005, s.74(5) above unless the court thinks that it is not in the public interest to disclose that the person falls within s.74(2)(a)).

The public may be excluded in relation to proceedings under SOCA 2005, s.74(3). SOCA 2005, s.75

Appeal

8–008 A person in respect of whom a reference is made under s.74(3), and the specified prosecutor are each given the right, subject to the leave of CACD, to appeal to that court against the decision of the judge of the Crown Court, CAA 1968, s.33(3) (limitation on appeal from CACD) does not prevent a further appeal to the House of Lords/Supreme Court). SOCA 2005, s.74 (8)(9)

Procedure on such an appeal is governed by SOCA 2005 (Appeals under Section 74) Order 2006 (SI 2006/2135) Pts 2 and 3.

Where CACD allow an appeal under s.74(8) they:

(1) may, in a case where the judge substituted a sentence under s. 74(5) or (6), vary that substituted sentence; and

(2) may, in a case where the judge did not substitute a sentence, vary the sentence to which the referral under s.74(3) Act relates; but

(3) must not exercise their powers under (1) and (2) so that the sentence imposed on the offender exceeds the sentence that the judge would have passed but for the agreement to give assistance; and

(4) if the offender falls within s.74(2)(c) of the Act and the judge did not substitute a sentence under s.74(6), must not so exercise their powers under (1) and (2) so that the offender is dealt with more severely than he was originally dealt with for the offence, the sentence for which the referral under s.74(3) of the Act relates.

The Criminal Procedure (Amendment No. 2) Rules 2006 (SI 2006/2636) assimilates the procedure for such an appeal to appeals under CAA 1968. See 18 CHALLENGING THE CROWN COURT.

3. Reduction and amendment of sentence on subsequent proceedings under PCA 2002

8–009 Where a judge varies a confiscation order under PCA 2002, ss.21, 22, 23, 29, 32 or 33, the effect of the variation is to vary the maximum period applicable in relation to the order under PCC(S)A 2000, s.139(4) and: PCA 2002, s.39

(1) the result is that that maximum period is less than the term of imprisonment or detention fixed in respect of the order under PCC(S)A 2000, s.139(2), the judge must fix a reduced term of imprisonment or detention in respect of the confiscation order under s.139(2) in place of the term previously fixed; or

(2) if (1) is not the case, the judge may amend the term of imprisonment or detention fixed in respect of the confiscation order under PCC(S)A 2000, s.139(2).

See generally 24 CONFISCATION ORDERS.

9 ANTI-SOCIAL BEHAVIOUR ORDERS AND ISOs

General

9–001 An anti-social behaviour order for a specified period of not less than two years may be made whether on application or otherwise, where;

(1) an offender is convicted of an offence committed after December 2, 2002; and
(2) the judge considers that:

(a) the offender has acted, at any time since the above date, in an anti-social manner, that is to say in a manner that caused, or was likely to cause harassment, alarm or distress to one or more persons not of the same household as himself; and CDA 1998, s.1C; SI 2002/2750
(b) that such an order is necessary to protect persons in any place (in England and Wales) from an offence as described above, or from further anti-social acts by him.

The order is preventative in nature. It is designed for the protection of others and is not a penalty for an offence. The approach should be to sentence for the offence, and then to consider whether an order should be made, albeit at the same hearing where that is appropriate.

An order may cover a multitude of matters but will commonly include harassment, noise nuisance, writing graffiti and verbal abuse.

Necessity is the test

9–002 The test for the making of an order is one of necessity, in that each separate order prohibiting the doing of a specified thing has to be necessary to protect persons from further anti-social acts by the offender. The test requires judgment and evaluation; it does not require proof beyond a reasonable doubt that the order is necessary (*R. v Wadmore and Another* [2006] Crim.L.R. 857. The order must be tailor-made for the individual offender, not designed on a word processor for use in every case (*R. (Lonergan) v Lewes CC*, *The Times*, April 25, 2005; *R. v Boness and Others*, *The Times*, October 24, 2005).

The judge is not required to consider what sentence he would have imposed (whether by way of curfew or otherwise), if he had been sentencing the same person for one or more of the same acts which justified the making of the order (*R. (McCann) v Manchester CC* [2003] 1 A.C. 787 HL).

The order must be substantially, not just formally, prohibitory; a curfew order which imposes a restraint upon leaving or travelling between specified premises between particular times meets that test (*R. (Lonergan) v Lewes CC*, above).

The judge must also consider making an ISO, see below.

Procedure

9–003 An order cannot stand alone; it is an ancillary order which may be attached to any sentence imposed for an offence as described above, or to a conditional discharge. It may be initiated by the judge of his own motion, or on application. A warrant may be issued where the offender fails to appear on an adjourned hearing.

There is no specified procedure where an order is made on application. The proceedings are civil in nature and hearsay evidence is admissible *(R. v Wadmore and Another,* above). Where:

(1) an application is made for an order, the judge should require the prosecutor to identify the particular facts that constitute the anti-social behaviour, and if the offender accepts those facts they should be reduced into writing in the same way as the basis of a plea of guilty (see 34–008 below); if not accepted the facts must be proved to the criminal standard before being acted upon *(R. v Wadmore and Another*, above);

(2) the judge acts of his own motion, he should state the basis on which he is minded to make the order, and the material on which he proposes to rely, so that the offender may make meaningful submissions as to why an order should not be made, or made in the form provisionally proposed (*C (etc.) v Sunderland YC, etc.* [2004] 1 Cr.App.R.(S.) 75).

The whole of the procedure should take place in the presence of the accused; also

(a) the terms of any order must be precise and capable of being understood by the accused, to whom they must be explained;

(b) the findings of fact giving rise to the making of the order must be recorded;

(c) the exact terms of the order must be pronounced in open court, and explained to the offender, and the written order must accurately reflect the order as pronounced.

(*R. v Parkin* [2004] Crim.L.R. 490; *R. v Shane Tony P* [2004] EWCA Crim 287).

Form of order

9–004 The form of order is set out in PD 2004, Annex D. The duration of the order ought to be for a determinate period: *R. v Vittles* [2005] 1 Cr.App.R.(S.) 7 (where five years was substituted for an indeterminate period; see also *R. v Werner* [2004] EWCA Crim 2931]). R 50.4

It is a cardinal principle of the sentencing procedure that the judge seek carefully to match the prohibitions in the order with the type of behaviour it was necessary to prohibit for the purposes in the Act (*CPS v T, The Times*, April 13, 2006). Thus a term of the order purporting to ban the offender from "committing any criminal offence" is too wide and is unenforceable (*W v DPP, The Times*, June 20, 2005, as is a term "not to act in an anti-social manner in the City of Manchester" (*CPS v T*, below).

As to forms of prohibition, see Thomas L.J.'s *ASBO Guidance for the Judiciary*, published by HM Court Service on their website.

Where an order prohibits conduct which is also a distinct criminal offence care should be exercised in deciding whether to make an order, if made

(a) it must be justified with reference to CDA 1998, s.1C(2)(a)(b);

(b) it should not be made simply for the purpose of increasing the sentence available on a breach beyond the maximum provided for that other offence; but

(c) if the maximum is prescribed by statute, there is no rule that the sentence in respect of the breach should be limited to the statutory maximum for that offence (*R. v Lamb, The Times*, December 1, 2005, following *R. v Braxton* [2005] 1 Cr.App.R.(S.) 167 rather than *R. v Morrison* [2006] Crim.L.R. 69; *H. Stevens v Lovegrove* [2006] Crim.L.R. 569).

As to variation and discharge, see 14 BREACH, AMENDMENT AND REVOCATION. Appeal lies under CDA 1998, s.4.

Suspended order

9–005 An order ordinarily takes effect on the day it is made, but the judge may provide that any requirements of the order as he may specify be suspended until the offender is released from any period of custody during which he is detained.

Where a custodial offence of more than a few months is passed, the offender being liable to be released on licence, and subject to recall, the need for a suspended order taking effect on release, is limited, though there may be cases where, e.g. geographical restraints might conveniently supplement the licence conditions (*R. v Parkin*, above).

Breach of order

9–006 An offender in breach of the order commits an offence (maximum five years on indicttment). CACD upheld a term of 18 months in *R. v Thomas* [2005] 1 Cr.App.R.(S.) 35, and three and a half years in *R. v Braxton* [2005] 1 Cr.App.R.(S.) 35. As to the position where a condition is included in an interim order but not replicated in the final order see *Parker v DPP*, *The Times*, June 20, 2005). CDA 1998, s.10C; SOCA 2005, s.130(2)

In proceedings for an offence under s.1(10) a copy of the original order, certified as such by the proper officer of the court which made it, is admissible as evidence of its having been made and of its contents to the same extent that oral evidence of those things is admissible in those proceedings.

Individual support orders (ISOs)

9–007 Where the judge makes an anti-social behaviour order in respect of a person under 18 he must consider whether the individual support conditions are made out. CDA 1998, s.1AA; CJA 2003, s.322

These are that:

(1) an individual support order (ISO) would be desirable in the interests of preventing any repetition of the kind of behaviour which led to the making of the anti-social behaviour order;
(2) the offender is not already subject to an ISO; and
(3) the judge has been notified that arrangements for implementing such orders are available in the area in which it appears to it that the offender resides or will reside.

If the judge is satisfied that these conditions are fulfilled, he must make an order requiring the offender to comply:

(a) for a period not exceeding six months, with such requirements as are specified in the order; and

(b) with any directions given by the responsible officer with a view to the implementation of the requirements under (a).

If he is not satisfied that these conditions are fulfilled, he must state in open court that he is not so satisfied and why.

Preconditions to making of ISO

9–008 Before making an order, the judge must obtain a report from a social worker of a local authority social services department or a member of a youth offending team, and consider any information which he considers necessary in order to determine whether the individual support conditions are fulfilled, or to determine what requirements should be imposed by the order if made. CDA 1998, s.1AA(9); CJA 2003, s.322

"Responsible officer" in relation to an ISO means a social worker of a local authority social services department, a person nominated by a person appointed as Chief Education Officer under the Education Act 1996, s.532, or a member of a youth offending team.

The requirements of the order

9–009 The requirements that may be specified are any that the judge considers desirable in the interests of preventing any repetition of the kind of behaviour which led to the making of the anti-social behaviour order. CDA 1998, s.1AA(5)–(8); CJA 2003, s.322

The requirements included in, and the directions given under such an order by the responsible officer, may require the offender to do all or any of the following things:

(1) to participate in activities specified in the requirements (or directions) at a specified time or times;
(2) to present himself to a specified person or persons at a place or places and at a time or times so specified;
(3) to comply with any specified arrangements for his education,

provided the requirements (or directions) do not require the offender to attend (whether at the same place or at different places) on more than two days in any week; and "week" here means a period of seven days beginning with a Sunday. The requirements must, as far as practicable, be such as to avoid any conflict with the offender's religious beliefs, and any interference with the times, if any, at which he normally works or attends school or any other educational establishment.

Spelling it out

9–010 Before making an order, the judge must explain to the offender in ordinary language: CDA 1998, s.1B(1)(3); CJA 322

(1) the effect of the order and of the requirements proposed to be included in it;
(2) the consequences which may follow if he fails to comply with any of those requirements; and
(3) that the judge has power (under s.1B(6)) to review the order on the application either of the offender or of the responsible officer.

The consequences of failing without reasonable excuse to comply with any requirement included in the order, are that the offender is guilty of an offence and liable on summary conviction to a fine, not exceeding, if he is aged 14 or over at the date of his conviction, of £1,000 or if he is aged under 14, £250. (As to payment by parent or guardian, see 19 CHILDREN AND YOUNG PERSONS.)

Variation etc. of ISO

9–011 Both the offender and the responsible officer may apply to the court which made the order for a variation or discharge, and if the order is varied, the court varying it may, by further order vary or discharge it. CDA 1998, s.1B(5)-(7) 2003, CJA 2.322

If the anti-social behaviour order, as a result of which the ISO was made, ceases to have effect, the ISO, if it has not previously ceased to have effect, ceases to have effect at the same time. (CDA 1998, s.1B(5)(6)(7); CJA 2003, s.322.) Appeal lies under CDA 1998, s.4 as amended by CJA 2003, s.323(2).

Variation etc. of ASBO

9–012 An offender subject to an anti-social behaviour order made in the Crown Court may apply to the court that made it for it to be varied or discharged, but not before the end of the period of two years beginning with the date on which the order took effect. CDA 1998, s.1C(6)(8)

10 APPEALS

10–001 The Crown Court exercises all appellate and other jurisdiction conferred on it by order under the provisions of the SCA 1981, or exercisable by it immediately before the commencement of that Act (SCA 1981, s.45(1)). CA 1971, s.8, Sch.1 vested in the Crown Court all jurisdiction formerly conferred on courts of quarter session, or any committee of the same. Rights of appeal to the Crown Court are governed by MCA 1980, ss.108–110 and the Criminal Procedure Rules 2005, r.63.

Rights of appeal: (1) general

10–002 A general right of appeal to the Crown Court is given to a person convicted in a magistrates' court where he pleaded: MCA 1980, s.108(1); PCC(S)A 2000, s.165, Sch.9, para.71

(1) guilty, against his sentence;
(2) not guilty, against his conviction and sentence.

Subject to the rare exceptional case (see 10–020 below), a plea of guilty in the magistrates' court is a bar to an appeal against conviction to the Crown Court (*R. v Birmingham CC Ex p. Sharma* [1988] Crim. L.R. 741).

"Sentence" includes any "order made on conviction" by a magistrates' court except an order: MCA 1980, s.108(3); CJA 1982, Sch.16

(a) for the payment of costs (*R. v Tottenham JJ. Ex p. Joshi* (1982) 75 Cr.App.R. 72);
(b) under the Protection of Animals Act 1911, s.2 (which enables a court to order the destruction of an animal); or
(c) made in pursuance of an enactment under which the court has no discretion as to the making of the order or its terms;

and also includes a declaration of relevance under FSA 1989.

Note that (c) above does not prevent an appeal against a surcharge imposed under CJA 2003, s.161A (MCA 1980, s.108(3)(d); DVA 2004, s.58(1), Sch.10, para.10).

An invalid sentence does not nullify the conviction on which it is based, which remains a "conviction" entitling the Crown Court to entertain an appeal (*R. v Birmingham JJ. Ex p. Wyatt* (1975) 61 Cr.App.R. 306).

Rights of appeal: (2) "orders made on conviction"

10–003 An "order made on conviction" is an order made as a consequence of the conviction for the particular offence of which the appellant was convicted. In consequence the following do not qualify:

(1) an order which does not depend upon the fact of conviction (*R. v Hayden* (1975) 60 Cr.App.R. 304 — a legal aid contribution order);
(2) an order sending a case to the Crown Court for trial (see (*R. v London Sessions Appeals Committee Ex p. Beaumont* [1951] 1 K.B. 557); or
(3) an order committing an accused to the Crown Court for sentence under PCC(S)A 2000, s.3.

By statute the following may be appealed:

(a) a recommendation for deportation (which is treated as a "sentence" (IA 1971, s.6(5)(a));
(b) a guardianship or hospital order (MHA 1983, s.70);
(c) an RT disqualification under RTOA 1988, s.34 or s.35.

Rights of appeal: (3) other specific cases

10–004 Appeal also lies to the Crown Court from a magistrates' court by:

(1) an offender sentenced for an offence in respect of which a conditional discharge was previously made; MCA 1980, s.108(2)
(2) an offender sentenced for breach of the requirements of a community order; CJA 2003, s.179, Sch.8, para.21(4)
(3) a juvenile sentenced in respect of the breach of an attendance centre order, or the rules of the centre; PCC(S)A 2000, s.61, Sch.5, paras 2(6), 4(4)
(4) a juvenile against an order made under PCC(S)A 2000 Sch.3 paras 2(2), 5(1) or 6(3) on the breach of a supervision order; PCC(S)A 2000, s.65, Sch.7, para.11
(5) a person ordered, under JPA 1968 or otherwise to enter into a recognisance, with or without sureties, to keep the peace; ABOOA 1956, s.1
(6) a person, or the parent or guardian of a juvenile, on the making of a hospital or guardianship order without proceeding to conviction; MHA 1983, s.45(1)
(7) a parent or guardian ordered to pay a fine, compensation or costs in respect of a juvenile; PCC(S)A 2000, s.137(7)
(8) a parent or guardian ordered to enter into recognisances to ensure payment of outstanding sums owed by a juvenile offender; PCC(S)A 2000, s.150(8)

(9) a parent or guardian ordered to enter into recognisances to take proper care and exercise proper control of a relevant minor; PCC(S)A 2000, s.150(8)

(10) against the extension or further extension of a custody time limit, or the giving of a direction by the court under POA 1985, s.6A; POA 1985, s.22(8); CDA 1998, s.43(6)

(11) a person aggrieved by the making of an order under FSA 1989, s.22(7); FOD 1999, s.7

(12) against an order making or dispensing with, or refusing to dispense with reporting restrictions in the case of juveniles; YJCEA 1999, s.44(11)

(13) a party to any proceedings in which the forfeiture of cash is made by a magistrates' court under CJ(IC)A 1990, s.26; CJ(IC)A 1990, s.24A; CJA 1993, s.25

(14) against the making of an anti-social behaviour order, or an individual support order (ISO); CDA 1998, s.4(1), (2); CJA 2003, s.323(2)

(15) by a parent or guardian against the making of a parenting order; CDA 1998, s.10(1)

(16) by an offender against any order made on the breach of an action-plan order or a reparation order, except one that could have been made in his absence by virtue of PCC(S) A 2000, Sch.8 para.6(9), and against the dismissal of an application to revoke an order; PCC(S)A 2000, ss.72, 75, Sch.8, para.7

(17) by a juvenile offender dealt with for an offence on the revocation of a referral order made under PCC(S)A 2000, ss.16–32; PCC(S)A 2000, s.32

(18) a person against whom a forfeiture order has been made under Terr A 2000, s.23(5); Terr A 2000, s.29

(19) a person in whose case a notification order under SOA 2003, s.97, or an interim order under s.100 has been made; SOA 2003, s.101

(20) a person against whom a sexual offences prevention order (SOPO) under SOA 2003, s.104, has been made or an interim order under s.109; SOA 2003, s.110

(21) a person against whom a foreign travel order under SOA 2003, s.114 or an order making or refusing an order under s.118; SOA 2003, s.119

(22) a person against whom a risk of sexual harm order (RSHO) under SOA 2003, s.123, or an interim order under s.126 has been made; SOA 2003, s.127

(23) by the Security Industry Authority or the individual against the grant or refusal of a licence under the Private Security Industry Act 2001; Private Security Industry Act 2001, s.11(4)

(24) by a person against whom a third party costs order is made in the magistrates' court (POA 1985, s.19B); SI 2004/2408, reg.7

(25) against the making of an anti-social behaviour order in the magistrates' court; CDA 1998, s.4(1)

(26) against the making of a parental compensation order; CDA 1998, s.13D; SOCA 2005, s.134, Sch.11
(27) against a financial reporting order.
(28) against seizure or forfeiture of cash, see 24 CONFISCATION ORDERS, at 24–065 below. SOCA 2005, ss.76 *et seq*

As to appeals against refusal to excuse, etc. from jury service, see 43 JURY MANAGEMENT.

Rights of appeal: (4) contempt of court

10–005 The effect of MCA 1980, s.108, combined with the CCA 1981, s.12(5), seems to give a right of appeal to a person sentenced in a magistrates' court for contempt, against the sentence imposed but not against the finding (*R. v Havant JJ. Ex p. Palmer* (1985) 149 J.P. 609).

Rights of appeal: (5) the unsuccessful prosecutor

10–006 An unsuccessful prosecutor:

(1) has no right of appeal to the Crown Court against the dismissal of an information or an acquittal in the magistrates' court, unless conferred by statute, e.g. Commissioners for Revenue & Excise under CEMA 1979, s.147(2).
(2) has, by statute, a right of appeal to the Crown Court:
    (a) against the refusal to extend, or further extend, the overall custody time limits, or a refusal to give a direction under POA 1985, s.22, and see 28 CUSTODY TIME LIMITS); and POA 1985, s.22(8); CDA 1998, s.43(7)
    (b) against the grant of bail, where B(A)A 1993 applies (see 11 BAIL). B(A)A 1993, s.1

Reference by Criminal Cases Review Commission

10–007 The Commission may refer a case before the magistrates' court to the Crown Court for consideration. Such a reference is treated for all purposes as an appeal under MCA 1980, s.108(1), whether or not the appellant pleaded guilty, though on a reference the Crown Court may not award any punishment more severe than that awarded by the court below. CAA 1995, s.11

The reference of a sentence is treated for all purposes as an appeal under MCA 1980, s.108(1) against the sentence, and against any other sentence imposed on, or in subsequent proceedings relating to, the conviction or any related conviction, i.e. a conviction of the same person by the same court on the same day, but again, the Crown Court may not award a punishment more severe than that awarded by the court below.

Procedure: (1) notice

10–008 The requirements of giving notice of appeal to the Crown Court are: R.63.2(1)–(4)

(1) notice in writing served on a court officer for the magistrates' court and any other party to the appeal;
(2) stating the grounds of the appeal;
(3) within 21 days after the day on which the decision appealed against was given, which means that:
   (a) if the trial was adjourned after conviction, the day on which the appellant was sentenced or otherwise dealt with; and
   (b) if sentence was deferred under PCC(S)A, 2000, s.1(1), the day on which the magistrates' court deferred sentence.

Appeal by a person aggrieved by forfeiture of cash under PCA 2002, s.295 must be made within 30 days beginning with the date on which the order was made. PCA 2002, s.299

The procedure in relation to appeals concerning custody time limits is dealt with under 28 CUSTODY TIME LIMITS; that relating to binding over orders under 13 BIND OVER.

Procedure: (2) extension of time

10–009 An extension beyond the 21 days, whether before or after the period has expired, requires: R.63.2(5)–(7)

(1) an application in writing to be sent to the Crown Court officer;
(2) specifying the grounds of the application.

If a judge of the Crown Court extends the time, the Crown Court officer will give notice to the appellant and any other party to the appeal.

The applicant has no right to an oral hearing, though in a rare case the judge may, in his discretion, grant one (*R. v Croydon CC Ex p. Smith* (1983) 77 Cr.App.R. 277). The judge need give no reasons for his decision; he may grant an extension in respect of sentence only, if that is appropriate.

If the judge grants an extension, notice will be given to the applicant and to the magistrates' court. It is for the appellant to give notice to any other party.

Procedure: (3) bail

10–010 Bail may be granted to a person giving notice of appeal by either the magistrates' court or the Crown Court. The statutory presumption in favour of bail before conviction has no SCA 1981, s.81(1)(b); PCC(S)A 2000,

application. The Crown Court may find it expedient, following the practice of CACD, to expedite the hearing instead of granting bail. The Crown Court may also grant bail to a person whose conviction or sentence is referred to it by the Criminal Cases Review Commission. Any time during which such a person is released on bail does not count towards sentence. s.165, Sch.9, para.87; CAA 1995, s.13(7)

Procedure: (4) suspension of RT disqualification

10–011 If a person convicted of an offence and disqualified from holding or obtaining a driving licence appeals to the Crown Court, either: RTOA 1988, ss.39(1), 40(1), (2), (6)

(1) the magistrates' court; or
(2) the Crown Court,

may suspend the disqualification pending the appeal, on such terms as the court thinks fit.

Procedure: (5) interim hospital order

10–012 The fact that an appeal to the Crown Court is pending does not affect the power of the magistrates' court which has made an interim hospital order to: SCA 1981, s.48(7); MH(A)A1982, Sch.3; MHA 1983, Sch.4

(1) renew or terminate the order; or
(2) deal with the accused on its termination.

Entry of appeal; notice of hearing

10–013 On receiving notice of appeal, the Crown Court officer will: R.63, 4

(1) enter the appeal; and
(2) give notice of the time and place of the hearing to,
    (a) the appellant;
    (b) any other parties to the appeal; and
    (c) the magistrates' court officer.

If an appeal is adjourned and no date is fixed for its resumption, the appropriate officer of the Crown Court will notify the appellant and any other party, in the same manner (*R. v London QS Appeals Committee Ex p. Rossi* [1956] 1 Q.B. 682).

Non-appearance

10–014 Where neither party appears, either personally or by advocate, an appeal may be struck out. If the appellant fails to appear one of several courses may be adopted:

(1) if neither appellant nor his advocate appears, and notice of hearing is proved, the appeal should be dismissed

(*R. v Spokes Ex p. Buckley* (1912) 76 J.P. 354; *R. v Croydon CC Ex p. Clair* [1986] 2 All E.R. 716); it should not be treated as impliedly abandoned (*R. (Hayes) v Chelmsford CC* 167 J.P. 65);

(2) if notice of appeal has been given, has not been withdrawn and no application to abandon is made, the appeal may be heard in the appellant's absence (*R. v Guildford CC Ex p. Brewer* (1988) 87 Cr.App.R. 265);

(3) if an advocate appears on his behalf, the appeal may go on (*R. v Croydon CC Ex p. Clair (*1986) 83 Cr.App.R. 202).

Nothing prevents the court from setting aside its own order, and hearing the appeal, if this is an appropriate course (*R. v London QS Appeals Ex p. Rossi* [1956] 1 Q.B. 682); if the respondent does not appear, either personally or by advocate, and service of notice, etc. is proved, any conviction or sentence appealed may be quashed (*R. v Croydon CC Ex p. Clair* (above)), but before taking such a step, the judge ought to consider the position of any victim, who may be deprived of compensation (*R. (CPS) v Portsmouth CC* [2004] Crim.L.R. 224).

The judge should certainly not take it upon himself to conduct the respondent's case where an advocate fails to appear: *R. v Wood Green CC Ex p. Taylor* [1995] Crim.L.R. 879.

The magistrates as respondents

10–015 The prosecutor in the case below invariably takes upon himself the conduct of the respondent's case on the appeal.

The magistrates have an absolute right to appear, instruct counsel and call evidence in support of their decision. They seldom do, but:

(1) they may need to where the "other party" has no interest in defending the appeal;

(2) if they do, they appear as amicus curiae, and should not enter into disputes, or make themselves a party to the appeal; in which case,

(3) no costs may be awarded against them.

(*R. v Kent JJ. Ex p. MPC* [1936] 1 K.B. 547; *R. v Preston CC Ex p. Pamplin* [1981] Crim.L.R. 338).

Abandonment before hearing; costs; bail

10–016 Without prejudice to the power of the Crown Court to give leave for an appeal to be abandoned, an appellant may abandon his appeal by giving notice in writing not later than the third day (excluding Saturdays, Sundays and Bank Holidays) before the date fixed for hearing the appeal to: R.78.1(4)

(1) the magistrates' court officer;
(2) the Crown Court officer; and
(3) any other party to the appeal; and

thus avoiding any order for costs which might otherwise be made against him (R.63.5). No order for costs may be made by the Crown Court on the abandonment of an appeal from a magistrates' court by giving notice under R.63.5 (*ibid* R.78.1(3)).

On the abandonment of an appeal otherwise than under R.63.5 the Crown Court may make an order for costs on dismissing an appeal where the appellant has failed to proceed with the appeal.

If the Crown Court allows an appellant to abandon an appeal, there is no power to increase sentence (*R. v Gloucester CC Ex p. Betteridge* (1997) 161 J.P. 721).

Such notice, deliberately given, is final; it cannot be afterwards withdrawn. It may be treated as a nullity only if the Crown Court finds, after investigation, that it was given under a mistake or as a result of fraudulent inducement, so that there has been no real abandonment. There is no other jurisdiction to relist the appeal (*R. v Essex Q.S. Ex p. Larkin* [1961] 3 All E.R. 930; *R. v Knightsbridge CC Ex p. C.E.C.* [1986] Crim.L.R. 324).

Failure to appear when bailed to do so is not to be treated as an implied abandonment; provided service of the notice of hearing is proved the case may be treated as one of non-appearance (see 10–14 above).

Where notice of abandonment is given by the appellant, any recognisance conditioned for his appearance at the hearing has effect as if conditioned for his appearance before the magistrates' court from whose decision the appeal was brought, at a time and place to be notified to him by the officer of that court. R.63.6

The hearing: (1) composition of the court

10–017 The court hearing an appeal must consist of: SCA 1981, ss.8, 73, 74(1); CA 2003, s.6; R.63.7.8

(1) a judge of the High Court, a Circuit Judge, a Recorder or, once CA 2003, s.66 comes into force, a District Judge (Magistrates' Courts), sitting with not less than two nor more than four lay magistrates;
(2) on an appeal from a youth court, a judge sitting with two lay magistrates, each of whom subject to (3) below and to any directions given under SCA 1981, s.74(4), is a member of a youth panel, and including both a man and a woman; though
(3) where it appears to the judge that the court cannot be so constituted without unreasonable delay, one lay

magistrate, or one who is a member of a youth panel, as the case may be.

Nothing prevents the court from continuing at any stage, where one or more of the magistrates initially comprising the court has withdrawn or is absent.

A lay magistrate is disqualified from sitting on the hearing of an appeal in a matter on which he ajudicated (R.63.9) but not merely because the proceedings are not at a place within the local justice area to which he is assigned, or because the proceedings are not related to that area in any other way.

Objection to the constitution of the court needs to be taken not later than the time the proceedings are entered upon, or when the irregularity begins.

SCA 1981, s.74(6); SCA 1981, s.8(2); CA 2003, s.109(9), Sch.8, para.259

Special provisions apply to appeals under the Licensing Act 1964, the Betting, Gaming and Lotteries Act 1963, and the Gaming Act 1968.

The hearing: (2) status of the lay magistrates

10–018 Where a judge, Recorder or District Judge (Magistrates' Courts) sits with lay magistrates, he presides, and:

(1) the decision of the court may be by a majority; and
(2) if the members are equally divided, the judge, District Judge or Recorder has a second and casting vote;
(3) interlocutory decisions are taken by the court as a whole, though on questions of law the lay magistrates are likely to defer to the judge's views (*R. v Orpin* (1974) 59 Cr.App.R. 231).
(4) where the exercise of discretion arises, as where the admissibility of a confession is in issue (*R. v Orpin*, above), or otherwise, the discretion falls to be exercised by the whole court, but where, as a matter of law, the discretion can only be exercised in one way, the lay magistrates are bound by the judge's decision (*Cook v DPP* [2001] Crim.L.R. 321).

The hearing: (3) abandonment, lapse

10–019 An appellant who has not taken advantage of R.63.5 (abandonment before hearing) may still apply to the court on the day of the hearing to abandon his appeal, but such an application differs from the procedure under R.63.5, in that:

(1) the court has a discretion whether to permit him to do so or not; and
(2) he has no immunity from costs.

Only in the most exceptional circumstances would the court:

(a) refuse the application if it is made before the hearing of the appeal has begun;
(b) grant the application, once the hearing has begun.

(*R. v Manchester CC Ex p. Welby* (1981) 73 Cr.App.R. 248; *R. v Knightsbridge CC Ex p. C.E.C.* [1986] Crim.L.R. 324.)

The appellant cannot bring his appeal to an end merely by failing to appear or to instruct counsel, so obliging the court to dismiss it (*R. v Guildford CC Ex p. Brewer* (1988) 87 Cr.App.R. 265).

The proceedings will ordinarily lapse on the death of the appellant; not on the death of the informant (*R. v Jefferies* [1969] 1 Q.B. 120).

The hearing: (4) equivocal plea

10–020 An appellant may contend that he has a right of appeal against conviction because his plea of guilty in the magistrates' court was an equivocal one. To be "equivocal" the appellant must have added to his plea a qualification which, if substantiated, might show that he was not guilty of the offence (*Foster (Haulage) Ltd v Roberts* (1978) 67 Cr.App.R. 305). It is an issue that the Crown Court must determine as a preliminary point (*R. v Durham Q.S. Ex p. Virgo* [1952] 1 All E.R. 466).

The procedure to be followed is this (*R. v Marylebone JJ. Ex p. Westminster City Council* [1971] 1 All E.R. 1025; *R. v Rochdale JJ. Ex p. Allwork* (1981) 73 Cr.App.R. 319):

(1) evidence must be heard from or on behalf of the appellant as to the basis of the plea;
(2) if that evidence casts no doubt on the validity of the plea, or falls short of establishing "equivocality", the issue is resolved and the court proceeds to hear any appeal against sentence;
(3) if the evidence for the appellant does disclose *prima facie* that the plea in the magistrates' court was equivocal, help should be sought from the court below as to what happened at the hearing;
(4) the magistrate, chairman or clerk should be called upon to swear an affidavit as to what happened, and only after considering that evidence should the court determine the issue (and see *R. v Coventry CC Ex p. Manson* (1978) 67 Cr.App.R. 315);
(5) in appropriate circumstances, the case may be remitted to the magistrates for a fresh hearing. SCA 1981, s.48(2)(b)

Provided the Crown Court has made a proper enquiry before determining the issue, the remittal for a fresh hearing must be complied with by the court below (*R. v Plymouth JJ. Ex p. Hart* (1986) 83 Cr.App.R. 81). If a dispute arises as to whether there was a proper enquiry, the issue can only be resolved by the High Court on judicial review.

In exceptional circumstances an appellant may be permitted to appeal against conviction, even though his plea of guilty was unequivocal, where his plea was entered under duress (*R. v Huntingdon CC Ex p. Jordan* [1981] Q.B. 857).

The fact that an unequivocal plea was entered below does not prevent an appellant putting forward a plea of *autrefois convict* or *autrefois acquit* at the hearing of the appeal (*Cooper v New Forest DC* [1992] Crim.L.R. 877).

The hearing: (5) procedure

10–021 An appeal to the Crown Court is by way of rehearing; the customary practice and procedure with respect to appeals to Quarter Sessions is continued by SCA 1981. In an appeal against:

(1) *conviction*,

- (a) the party seeking an order or conviction proves his case again;
- (b) there is no obligation on the prosecution to put its case in the same way as in the court below (*Hingley-Smith v DPP* [1998] 1 Arch. News 2, DC);
- (c) evidence is heard afresh;
- (d) the Crown Court does not "review" the decision of the lower court; it takes the place of the magistrates, forming its own view and substituting its opinion for that of the court below, in regard to conviction and/or sentence (*Drover v Rugman* [1950] 2 All E.R. 575; *Sagnata Ltd v Norwich Corpn* [1971] 2 All E.R. 1441; *R. v Swindon CC Ex p. Murray* (1998) 162 J.P. 36; *Hingley-Smith v DPP*, above); and
- (e) it may find the case proved on a different basis from that found in the lower court (*Hingley-Smith v DPP, above*);

(2) *sentence*,

- (a) there is a rehearing from conviction onwards;
- (b) the Crown Court is not limited to considering whether the sentence imposed by the lower court was within its jurisdiction. The court goes through the sentencing process afresh, including, where appropriate, the

inspection of driving licences, etc. (*Dyson v Ellison* (1974) 60 Cr.App.R. 191; *R. v Knutsford CC Ex p. Jones* (1985) 7 Cr.App.R. (S.) 448), and the examination of any suggested "special reasons" for not disqualifying (*DPP v O'Connor* (1992) 95 Cr.App.R. 135);

(3) *binding over order*,

- (a) there is a rehearing; and
- (b) unless the appellant is prepared to admit the evidence which was before the magistrates, the facts must be proved by sworn evidence (*Shaw v Hamilton* (1982) 75 Cr.App.R. 288);
- (c) the issue is whether or not the court below was justified in making the order, *not* whether the appellant is likely to repeat the conduct (*Hughes v Holley* (1988) 86 Cr.App.R. 130);

(4) *refusal of a firearms certificate*, (see 10–032 below).

- (a) there is a rehearing;
- (b) the views of the police being only one of the factors to be taken into consideration (*Cliff v MPC* (1973) 117 S.J. 855).

Special considerations govern appeals against local government decisions, see, e.g. *Stepney B.C. v Joffe* [1949] 1 All E.R. 256; *Northern Ireland Trailers Ltd v Preston Corp* [1972] 1 All E.R. 260.

The Crown Court is empowered to determine an appeal on a factual basis which differs from that adopted by the magistrates' court (see *Hingley-Smith v DPP* [1998] Archbold News 2). Any such question is determined in precisely the same way as on a plea to an indictment. The court is not bound by any finding of fact made in the magistrates' court which might limit its power of sentence.

If the Crown Court decides not to accept the express view of the court below, it should explain that to the appellant: *Bussey v DPP* [1999] 1 Cr.App.R.(S.) 125.

The hearing: (6) powers

10–022 In the course of an appeal, the court may:

(1) correct any error or mistake in the order or judgment incorporating the decision which is the subject of the appeal; but
(2) *not* purport to amend the substance of the information on which the appellant was tried below (*Meek v Powell* [1952] 1 All E.R. 347; *Garfield v Maddocks* (1973) 57

Cr.App.R. 372; *Fairgrieve v Newman* (1986) 82 Cr.App.R. 60; *R. v Swansea CC Ex p. Stacey* [1990] RTR 183; *R. v Norwich CC Ex p. Russell* [1993] Crim. L.R. 518);

(3) hear the appeal on the basis of the unamended information and may exercise the same jurisdiction as the court below, e.g. in the use of MCA 1980, s.123 (*R. v Swansea CC Ex p. Stacey* [1990] R.T.R. 183).

Powers: (1) general

10–023 On the termination of the hearing of an appeal, the court may, in relation to the: SCA 1981, s.48(2), (3); CJA 1988, s.156

(1) *decision*,
  (a) confirm, reverse or vary any part of the decision appealed against, including a determination not to impose a separate penalty; or
  (b) remit the matter with its opinion thereon to the authority whose decision is appealed against; or
  (c) make such order in the matter as it thinks just, and by such order exercise any power which that authority might have exercised, subject to any enactment which expressly restricts or limits its powers.

(2) *sentence*, whether the appeal was against conviction or sentence, SCA 1981, s.48(4); CAA 1995, s.11(6)
  (a) award any punishment, whether more or less severe than that awarded by the magistrates whose decision is appealed, provided it is a punishment which those magistrates might have awarded at the time the appellant was sentenced by them (*R. v Portsmouth CC Ex p. Ballard* (1990) 154 J.P. 109) provided that the power to increase sentence may not be exercised where the appeal is referred to the court by the Criminal Cases Review Commission;
  (b) if the appeal is against one of several convictions on the same occasion, vary the sentences imposed for all the offences (*Dutta v Westcott* (1987) 84 Cr.App.R. 103).

The Crown Court should not increase sentence without giving a clear warning of its intention (see, e.g. *R. (Tottman) v DPP* [2004] EWHC 258 (Admin)).

"Sentence" includes any order made by a court when dealing with an offender, including a hospital order, and a recommendation for deportation. SCA 1981, s.48(6); MHA 1983, Sch.4

Powers: (2) interim hospital order

10–024 If, on the termination of an appeal, the Crown Court: SCA 1981, s.48(7); MH(A)A 1982, Sch.3; MHA 1983, Sch.4

(1) quashes an interim hospital order made by the magistrates, but does not pass any sentence or make any other order, it may direct the appellant to be kept in custody or released on bail pending his being dealt with by the magistrates;

(2) makes an interim hospital order, the court below:
   (a) has the power to renew or terminate the order, and to deal with the accused on its termination;
   (b) is to be treated for the purposes of absconding offenders (MHA 1983, s.31(8)) as the court which made the order.

Powers: (3) recommendation for deportation

10–025 Where the appellant appeals against a recommendation for deportation made by the magistrates, or the conviction in respect of which it is made, the court may direct his release in accordance with the Act, without setting aside the recommendation. (See also *R. v Ofori* (1994) 99 Cr.App.R. 219.) IA 1971, Sch.3; CJA 1982, s.64, Sch.10

Powers: (4) forfeiture of cash under PCA 2002, s.298

10–026 An appeal by a party to proceedings in which a cash forfeiture order is made under PCA 2002, s.298, is by way of rehearing. The Crown Court may make any order it thinks appropriate, and if it upholds the appeal may order the release of the cash. PCA 2002, s.299

Powers: (5) anti-social behaviour, sex offenders, parenting orders

10–027 Where the appellant appeals against the making of an anti-social behaviour order, parenting order or sex offender order, the Crown Court may: CDA 1998, s.4(1), (2), (3)

   (a) make such orders as may be necessary to give effect to its determination of the appeal; and
   (b) make such incidental or consequential orders as appear to it to be just.

Any order, other than one directing a rehearing by a magistrates' court, is treated as an order of the court from which the appeal was brought, not of the Crown Court.

Powers: (6) reparation and action plan orders

10–028 An offender may appeal to the Crown Court: PCC(S)A 2000, ss.72, 75, Sch.8, para.7

(1) against an order of a magistrates' or youth court dismissing an application to discharge a reparation or action plan order or varying it;
(2) where a magistrates' or youth court, being satisfied the offender has failed to comply with any requirement included in such an order:
   (a) has fined the offender or made an attendance centre order or a curfew order in respect of him; or
   (b) has discharged such an order *and* dealt with him in some other way for the offence in respect of which the order was made.

Powers: (7) costs; taxation

10–029 Where an appellant's:

(1) conviction is set aside, or a less severe punishment is awarded, the court may make a "defence costs order" in his favour; POA 1985, ss.16(3), 18(1); R.78.2
(2) appeal against conviction or sentence is dismissed, it may make any order for costs to be paid by the appellant.

Where an indictable offence is concerned, the court may order the payment of costs out of central funds to a prosecutor other than a public authority ((6) and see generally 26 COSTS AND TAXATION). POA 1985, ss.17(1)(a), (2)

A successful appellant should have his costs under POA 1985, s.16 unless there are positive reasons for not making an order; the reasons for refusal (*Cunningham v Exeter CC* 167 J.P. 93) or for not awarding the amount claimed (*R. Galandauer v Sharesbrook CC, The Times* August 15, 2006, QBD) should be stated.

As to third party costs, see 26 COSTS AND TAXATION.

Where under R.78 a judge of the Crown Court makes an order for the costs of any proceedings to be paid by a party and does not fix a sum, the amount of the costs to be paid will be ascertained as soon as practicable by the Crown Court officer ("the taxing authority"), who will allow such costs reasonably incurred in or about the prosecution and conviction or the defence, as the case may be (R.78.3). Any party dissatisfied with that order may apply to the taxing authority to review his decision, by giving notice to the taxing authority and to any other party to the taxation within 14 days of the taxation, specifying the items in respect of which the application is made and the grounds of objection. A party to whom notice is thus given may within 14 days of the service of the notice deliver to the taxing authority answers in writing to the objections specified in that notice to the taxing authority and, if he does, will send copies to the applicant for the review and to any other party to the taxation. The taxing authority must reconsider his taxation in the light of the objections and answers, if any, of the parties and of any oral representations made by or on their behalf and notify them of the result of his review (R.78.4).

10–030 A party dissatisfied with the result of this may, within 14 days of receiving notification of it:

(1) request the taxing authority to supply him with reasons in writing for his decision; and
(2) within 14 days of the receipt of such reasons apply to the Chief Taxing Master for a further review giving notice of the application to the taxing authority and to any other party to the taxation, to whom he shall also give a copy of the reasons given by the taxing authority.

The application must state whether the applicant wishes to appear or be represented, or whether he will accept a decision given in his absence and must be accompanied by a copy of the notice given under R.78.4, of any answer which may have been given under R.78.4(3) and of the reasons given by the taxing authority for his decision, together with the bill of costs and full supporting documents. Any other party receiving notice of an application must also inform the Chief Taxing Master whether he wishes to appear or be represented at a further review, or whether he will accept a decision given in his absence.

The further review will be conducted by a Taxing Master, who will inform the applicant or any other party who has given notice of his intention to appear or be represented, of the date on which the further review will take place. Before reaching his decision the Taxing Master may consult the judge who made the order for costs and the taxing authority and, unless the Taxing Master otherwise directs, no further evidence will be received on the hearing; and no ground of objection will be valid which was not raised on the review under R.78.4.

In making his review, the Taxing Master may alter the assessment of the taxing authority in respect of any sum allowed, whether by increase or decrease, and he will communicate the result of the further review to the parties and to the taxing authority (R.78.5). The Taxing Master may make such order as he thinks just in respect of the costs of the hearing of the further review (R.78.7).

A party dissatisfied with the result of this further review may, within 14 days of receiving notification of the result appeal by originating summons to a judge of the Queen's Bench Division of the High Court if, but only if, the Taxing Master certifies that the question to be decided involves a point of principle of general importance. On the hearing of the appeal the judge may reverse, affirm or amend the decision appealed against or make such other order as he thinks appropriate (R.78.6). The judge may make such order as he thinks just in respect of the costs of the hearing of the appeal (R.78.7).

Any of the time set out by the rules (Rr.78.4, 78.5, 78.6) may be extended by the taxing authority, Taxing Master or judge of the High Court on such terms as he thinks just (R.78.7).

Powers: (8) search

10–031 On the determination of an appeal, if money is payable by the appellant by virtue of:

PCC(S)A 2000, s.142; DVA 2004, s.58(1), Sch.10, para.53

(1) an order of the Crown Court; or
(2) a conviction or order of the court below;

the appellant may, if he is before the court, be searched and any money found on him applied to payment.

Powers: (9) reasons for decision

10–032 The judge presiding in the Crown Court is obliged to give reasons for the decision of the court, at least sufficient to demonstrate that the court has identified the main issues in the case and how it has resolved them (*R. v Harrow CC Ex p. Dave* [1994] 1 W.L.R. 98, DC) and so that an appellant can know the reasons for the decision as soon as is reasonably possible, see the nature of the criminality found and consider whether to appeal (*R. v ILCC Ex p. Lambeth LBC* [2000] Crim.L.R. 303). Failure to do so may vitiate the decision, unless the reasons are obvious, the case is simple or the subject matter of the appeal unimportant: *R. v Kingston CC Ex p. Bell* 164 J.P. 633. Reasons should be given contemporaneously with the decision (*R. v Snaresbrook CC Ex p. Input Management Ltd* (1999) 163 J.P. 533; *R. v ILCC Ex p. Lambeth LBC* [2000] Crim.L.R. 303).

Appeals under the Firearms Act 1968

10–033 An appeal against a decision of a chief officer of police under FA 1968, ss.28A, 29, 30A, 30B, 30C, 34, 36, 37 or 38 lies to the Crown Court. It is determined on the merits and not by way of review.

FA 1968, s.44; F(A)A 1997, s.41; FA 1968, Sch.5, Pt II

APPEALS

The procedure for initiating the appeal is similar to that for other appeals to the Crown Court, thus:

(1) notice of appeal must be given within 21 days after the date on which the appellant received notice of the decision of the chief officer of police by which he is aggrieved;
(2) the notice must be given both to the designated officer of the magistrates'court and to the chief officer, and must state the general grounds of his appeal;
(3) the Crown Court officer will give notice of the date and place of the hearing both to the appellant and to the chief officer, who is entitled to appear and be heard on the appeal;
(4) the appellant may abandon his appeal at any time, not less than two clear days before the date fixed for the hearing by giving notice in writing to the magistrates' court and to the chief officer.

On the hearing of the appeal, the Crown Court may either dismss the appeal or give the chief officer such directions as it thinks fit as respects the certificate or the register which is the subject of the appeal.

11 BAIL

11–001 A judge of the Crown Court may grant bail to persons:

(A) appearing or brought before the Crown Court; or
(B) still before the magistrates' court.

As to the requirements of bail where the custody time limits expire, see 28 CUSTODY TIME LIMITS; as to persons subject to investigation under CJA 2003, Pt 10, see 53 RETRIAL.

Quick guide

A. Bail in the Crown Court (below)
B. Crown Courts' control over bail in magistrates' court (11–003, below)
C. Procedure in the Crown Court (11–009, below)
D. General principles
   1. Whether bail is appropriate (11–013, below)
   2. Consideration governing grant (11–017, below)
   3. Unconditional or subject to conditions (11–025, below)
   4. Sureties/Security (11–027, below)
   5. Other requirements (11–031, below)
   6. Record, variation, breach (11–036, below)
   7. Absconding (11–040, below)
   8. Estreatment; forfeiture of security (11–046, below)

A. Grant of bail in the Crown Court

11–002 A judge of the Crown Court may, subject to CJPOA 1994, s.25 (see 11–014, below), grant bail to any person:

SCA 1981, s.81(1); CJA 1982, ss.29, 60; CJPOA 1994, s.25; CDA 1998, s.119; Sch.8, para.37; CJA 2003, s.41, Sch.3, para.54(5)

(1) who has been sent in custody to the Crown Court for trial under CDA 1998, s.51 or s.51A;
(2) who is in custody pursuant to a sentence imposed by a magistrates' court and who has appealed to the Crown Court against his conviction or sentence;
(3) who is in the custody of the Crown Court pending the disposal of his case by that court;
(4) who, after the decision of his case by the Crown Court, has applied to the court for a case to be stated for the opinion of the High Court on that decision or is seeking a quashing order in respect of that decision;

(5) to whom the Crown Court has granted a certificate under CAA 1968 ss.1(2) or 11(1A), or SCA 1981, s.81(1B) that a case is fit for appeal (see 18 CHALLENGING THE CROWN COURT).

Where an accused is sent for trial to the Crown Court, the magistrates' bail ceases when the accused surrenders to the Crown Court, whether for arraignment or otherwise, and the judge, if releasing him again on bail, must consider the appropriateness of any conditions afresh, including the position of any surety (*R. v Kent CC Ex p. Jodka* (1997) 161 J.P. 638).

As to grant of bail during the trial, see 11–023 below.

It should always be made to clear to an accused granted bail that if he fails to attend his trial, the consequences may be that it will proceed in his absence and without legal representation (*R. v O'Hare* [2006] EWCA Crim 471).

B. Crown Court's control over bail in the magistrates' court

11–003 The Crown Court has jurisdiction to entertain an appeal by the person concerned where a magistrates' court:

BA 1976, s.5(6A); CJA 1982, s.60(3); PCC(S)A 2000, s.165, Sch.9, para.53; CJA 2003, s.16(1), (2)

(1) adjourns a case under:
   (a) MCA 1980, s.10;
   (b) MCA 1980, s.17C (intention as to plea);
   (c) MCA 1980, s.18 (initial procedure on information against an adult for an offence triable either way);
   (d) MCA 1980, s.24C (intention to plead by child or young person);
   (e) CDA 1998, s.52(5) (cases sent for trial s.51); or
   (f) PCC(S)A 2000, s.11 (remand for medical examination); and
(2) that court:
   (a) refuses to grant bail;
   (b) refuses to entertain an application by the accused for a rehearing; or
   (c) grants bail subject to the specified conditions set out below.

Certificate of full argument

11–004 A magistrates' court, remanding a person in custody in any of the above situations, must issue a certificate in the prescribed form (MC(F)R 1981, Form 151A), stating that it

BA 1976, s.5(6A); CJA 1982, s.60(3);

has heard full argument on the application before refusing it, thus entitling the person refused bail to apply to the Crown Court.

PCC(S)A 2000, s.165, Sch.9, para.53; CJA 2003, s.13

Appeal by accused where bail granted with conditions

11–005 CJA 2003, s.16 provides a new avenue for an accused to appeal to the Crown Court against conditions attached to the grant of bail by the magistrates' court; it implements s.17 which abolishes the right of appeal to the High Court where jurisdiction is duplicated in the Crown Court. Where a magistrates' court grants bail to a person on adjourning the proceedings in one of the above situations, the person concerned may appeal to the Crown Court against any such condition of bail, being a requirement:

CJA 2003, ss.16(3)–(6)

(1) that he resides away from a particular place or area;
(2) that he resides at a particular place other than a bail hostel;
(3) for the provision of a surety or sureties or the giving of a security;
(4) that he remains indoors between certain hours; or
(5) imposed under BA 1976, s.3(6ZAA) (requirements with respect to electronic monitoring); or
(6) that he make no contact with another person,

Provided that such appeal may not be brought unless:

(a) the application to the magistrates' court under BA 1976, s.3(8)(a) was made and determined before the appeal was brought; or
(b) the application to the magistrates' court under under BA 1976, s.3(8)(b) (application by constable or prosecutor), or under BA 1976, s.5B(1) (application by prosecutor), was made and determined before the appeal was brought.

The judge, under this provision, may vary the conditions of bail, but where he determines such an appeal the person concerned may not bring a further appeal under the section in respect of the conditions of bail, unless an application or a further application to the magistrates' court under BA 1976, s.3(8)(a) is made and determined after the appeal.

CJA 2003, ss.16(7), (8)

Bail

Appeal by prosecutor

11–006 Where a magistrates' court grants bail to a person who is charged with, or convicted of, an offence punishable by imprisonment, the prosecution, in a case conducted:

B(A)A 1993, s.1(1), (2), (10)(a); CJA 2003, s.18(1), (2)

(1) by or on behalf of the DPP; or

(2) by or on behalf of a prescribed person (see below),

may appeal to a judge of the Crown Court against the granting of bail, provided that such an appeal lies only where:

(a) in relation to offences punishable with less than a term of five years or more, the case was committed, transferred or sent, or a voluntary bill was preferred, after **April 4, 2005** (SI 2005/950);
(b) the prosecution made representations that bail should not be granted; and
(c) such representations were made before it was granted.

For those persons prescribed under (2) above, see SI 1994/1438, as amended by SI 2001/1149, and SI 2005/1129, i.e. the DSFO, the Secretary of State for Trade and Industry, the Secretary of State for Social Services, the Director of Revenue and Customs Prosecutions for the Commissioners of Customs and Excise, and the Commissioners of Inland Revenue, and a universal service provider under the Postal Services Act 2000.

As far as procedure is concerned: B(A)A 1993, s.1(4), (5), (7), (8), (10)(b); rr.19.16(1)–(9)

(a) oral notice of appeal must be given to the magistrates' court and to the person concerned at the conclusion of the proceedings in which such bail was granted, and before the release of the person concerned;
(b) the magistrates will remand the person concerned in custody (or in local authority accommodation in the case of a juvenile) until the appeal is determined or otherwise disposed of;
(c) oral notice must be followed by written notice within two hours of the conclusion of the proceedings, otherwise the appeal will be deemed to have been disposed of;
(d) if, having given oral notice of appeal, the prosecution fails to serve written notice within the appropriate period, the person concerned will be released.

Where written notice of appeal is served on the magistrates' court, the Crown Court officer will, as soon as is practicable, be provided with a copy, the notes of argument made under the Rules, and a note of the date or dates when the person concerned is next due to appear in the magistrates' court. R.19.6(10)

Crown Court procedure: R.19.17

11–007 The written notice of appeal required by B(A)A 1993, s.1(5):

(1) is in the form set out in PD 2004, Annex D; and
(2) must be served on the magistrates' court officer; and the person concerned (within the meaning of B(A)A 1993, s.1).

The Crown Court officer will enter the appeal and give notice of the time and place of the hearing to the prosecution, the person concerned or his legal representative and the magistrates' court officer.

The person concerned is not entitled to be present at the hearing of the appeal unless he is acting in person or, in any other case of an exceptional nature, a judge of the Crown Court is of the opinion that the interests of justice require him to be present and gives him leave to be so.

Where a person concerned has not been able to instruct a solicitor to represent him at the appeal:

(1) he may give notice to the Crown Court requesting that the Official Solicitor represent him at the appeal; and
(2) the court may, if it thinks fit, assign the Official Solicitor to act for the person concerned accordingly.

At any time after the service of written notice of appeal, the prosecution may abandon the appeal by giving notice in writing in the form set out in PD 2004, Annex D and served on the person concerned or his legal representative, the magistrates' court officer and the Crown Court officer.

The appeal hearing must begin within 48 hours, excluding weekends and public holidays (construed as "two working days", see *R. v Middlesex Guildhall Crown Court Ex p. Okoli* [2001] 1 Cr.App.R. 1; see also *R. (Jeffrey) v Warwick CC* [2003] Crim.L.R. 190).

Under B(A)A 1993, s.1, the proceedings are expressly stated to be a rehearing, the judge having power to remand in custody or to release on bail on such conditions as he thinks fit.

If the judge upholds the prosecutor's appeal, he must fix a date on which the accused is to appear before the magistrates in accordance with the magistrates' powers under MCA 1980, ss.128, 128A and 129 (as amended by CJA 2003, ss.41, 304, 337, Sch.3, para.51(7), Sch.37, Pt 4) otherwise the accused will be unlawfully detained once the eight days of the remand have expired (*Re Szakal* [2001] 1 Cr.App.R. 248).

Administrative provisions; record

11–008 Any record required by BA 1976, s.5 (together with any note of reasons required by s.5(4) to be included) is made by way of an entry in the file relating to the case in question and the record will include the following particulars, namely;

(1) the effect of the decision;
(2) a statement of any condition imposed in respect of bail, indicating whether it is to be complied with before or after release on bail; and
(3) where bail is withheld, a statement of the relevant exception to the right to bail (as provided in Sch.1 to the 1976 Act) on which the decision is based.

The Crown Court officer will, as soon as practicable after the hearing of the appeal, give notice of the decision and of the matters required by the preceding paragraph to be recorded to the person concerned or his legal representative, the prosecution, the police, the magistrates' officer and the governor of the prison or person responsible for the establishment where the person concerned is being held. R.19.17(8)

In addition to the methods of service permitted by R.4.3 (service of documents Crown Court proceedings), the notices required by R.19.17(3), (5), (7) and (9) may be sent by way of facsimile transmission and the notice required by R.19.17(3) may be given by telephone.

CJA 2003, s.17 abolishes the inherent power of the High Court to entertain any applications in relation to bail where a judge has determined such an application under:

(1) BA 1976, s.3(8); or
(2) SCA 1981, s.81(1)(a), (b), (c) or (g),

though this does not affect that court's jurisdiction to grant bail in other matters (such as case stated), or in *habeas corpus* applications. The High Court, however, retains the jurisdiction to entertain an application for judicial review of a refusal of bail, a determination being based on the *Wednesbury* principles "robustly applied", at any time before the start of his trial at the Crown Court (*R. (Shergill) v Harrow CC* [2005] EWHC 648 (Admin)).

A reference to an "application in relation to bail" includes an application for:

(i) bail to be granted;
(ii) bail to be withheld;
(iii) the conditions of bail to be varied.

A reference to the withholding of bail includes a reference to the revocation of bail. CJA 2003, ss.17(7), (8)

C. Procedure in the Crown Court

Applications to the Crown Court before trial

11–009 Where an application in relation to bail is made to the Crown Court otherwise than during the hearing of proceedings, notice in writing of the intention to make such application must be given (in the form set out in PD 2004, Annex D), at least 24 hours before the application is made: R.19.18(1)(2)(4)

(1) to the prosecutor; and
(2) if the prosecution is being carried on by the CPS, to the appropriate Crown Prosecutor; or
(3) if the application is to be made by the prosecutor or a constable under BA 1976, s.3(8), to the person to whom bail was granted,

and the applicant must give a copy of the notice to the Crown Court officer.

A person making an application relating to bail must inform the court of any earlier application to the High Court, or to the Crown Court relating to bail in the course of the same proceedings (R.19.18(10)).

On receiving the notice, the prosecutor, or the appropriate Crown Prosecutor or, as the case may be the person to whom bail was granted, must: R.19.18(3)

(a) notify the Crown Court officer, and the applicant, that he wishes to be represented at the hearing of the application or that he does not oppose it; or
(b) give to the Crown Court officer, for the consideration of the court, a written statement of his reasons for opposing the application, sending a copy, at the same time, to the applicant.

Special provisions apply in the case of bail granted on the expiry of a custody time limit under POA 1985, s.22 (see 28 CUSTODY TIME LIMITS).

Assignment of Official Solicitor

11–010 It is unlikely that the need will arise, in the Crown Court at any rate, preceding the trial, for the Official Solicitor to be assigned to an applicant, since any representation order granted in the magistrates' court will cover such an application. R.19.18(6), (7)

Where, however, the necessity arises (as where the representation order has been revoked), a person in custody, or on bail, who desires to make an application in relation to bail and who has been unable to instruct a solicitor to apply on his behalf, may give notice in writing to the Crown Court of his desire to make an application requesting that the Official Solicitor act for him, and the court may, if it thinks fit:

(1) assign the Official Solicitor to act for him and, if it does so,
(2) dispense with the requirements of giving notice in advance of the application, and
(3) deal with the application in a summary manner.

Hearing applications

11–011 An application for bail is normally heard in chambers, and where possible will be listed before the judge by whom the case is expected to be tried, or before the Resident Judge.

PD 2002, para.33.6 provided that where a case:

(1) is to be tried by a High Court Judge who is not available, the application should be listed before any other High Court Judge then sitting at the Crown Court centre at which the application has arisen, before a Presiding Judge, before the Resident Judge for the centre, or, with the consent of a Presiding Judge, before a Circuit Judge nominated for the purpose;
(2) does not fall within (1) and the Circuit Judge or Recorder who is expected to try the case is not available, the matter must be referred to the Resident Judge, or, if he is not available, to any judge or Recorder then sitting at the centre.

This direction does not seem to be repeated in PD 2004.

Except where an application is made by the prosecutor or a constable under BA 1976, s.3(8), an applicant is not entitled to be present on the hearing of the application unless the judge gives leave (R.19.18(5)).

Note that:

(a) Under B(A)A 1993, s.1(9) the proceedings are expressly stated to be a rehearing, the judge having power to remand in custody or to release on bail on such conditions as he thinks fit. B(A)A 1993, s.1(9)
(b) If the judge upholds the prosecutor's appeal, he must fix a date on which the accused is to appear before the magistrates in accordance with the magistrates' powers under MCA 1980, ss.128, 128A and 129. SCA 1981, s.81(IB)

Reconsideration; subsequent applications

11–012 If a judge decides not to grant bail to an applicant, it is his duty to consider at each subsequent hearing, while a person to whom the presumption under BA 1976, s.4 (see BA 1976, Sch.1, Pt IIA; CJA 1988, s.154

below) applies and remains in custody, whether he ought to be granted bail:

(1) at the first hearing after that at which the judge decided not to grant bail, the applicant may support an application for bail with any argument as to fact or law which he desires, whether or not he has advanced that argument previously;
(2) at subsequent hearings the judge need not hear arguments as to fact or law which he has heard previously.

The jurisdiction to grant bail is that of the court, not the individual judges of the court; thus applications are not to be made, simultaneously or immediately consecutively, to more than one judge of the court (*R. v Reading CC Ex p. Malik* (1981) 72 Cr.App.R. 146).

A decision based on BA 1976, Sch.1, para.5 (not practicable to have sufficient information) is not a decision for these purposes (*R. v Calder JJ. Ex p. Kennedy* (1992) 156 J.P. 716).

Where the judge, in reconsidering bail, refuses to withhold bail after hearing representations from the prosecution in favour of withholding bail, he must give reasons for refusing to withhold bail, and include a note of those reasons in the record of his decision, providing a copy to the prosecution if requested.

BA 1976, s.5B(8A); CJPA 2001, s.129(3)

D. General Principles

1. Whether bail appropriate

Bail

Right to bail before conviction

11–013 The seriousness of the offence is not to be treated as a conclusive reason for withholding bail to an unconvicted suspect. Decisions as to whether an unconvicted suspect should be released on bail subject to conditions pending trial raise questions of importance both to the individual and to the community at large. The individual has an interest in remaining at liberty, until he is convicted of a crime serious enough to justify depriving him of it; the community has a countervailing interest in ensuring that the course of justice is not thwarted by the flight of the suspect, or perverted by his interference with witnesses or evidence, and that he does not commit further offences pending trial (*Hurnam v State of Mauritius* [2005] UKPC 49, *per* Lord Bingham of Cornhill).

BAIL

Under the general provisions of BA 1976, but subject to CJPOA 1994, s.25 (restrictions on bail in certain serious offences, see below) a person who:

BA 1976, s.4, Sch.1, Pt1; CJA 1991, Sch.11, para.21; CJPOA 1994, s.25, Sch.10, para.32; PCC(S)A 2000, s.166, Sch.9, para.54; CJA 2003, s.332, Sch.37, Pt 4

(1) appears or is brought before the Crown Court in the course of, or in connection with, proceedings for an offence; or
(2) applies to the Crown Court for bail in connection with the proceedings; or
(3) has been convicted of an offence and whose case is adjourned for reports before sentence, has a right to bail unless one of the exceptions under BA 1976, Sch.1 is made out, and the judge exercises his discretion to refuse bail.

As to :

(a) bail during the trial, see 11–023 below;
(b) POA 1985 and the Regulations made thereunder see 28 CUSTODY TIME LIMITS.

Restrictions on bail; previous conviction for certain serious offences

11–014 This provision applies to the following offences:

CJPOA 1994, s.25; CDA 1998, s.56; PCC(S)A 2000, s.165, Sch.9, para.160; CJPA 2001, s.129(4); SOA 2003, s.139, Sch.6, para.32; CJA 2003, s.304, Sch.32, Pt 1, para.67

(1) murder;
(2) attempted murder;
(3) manslaughter;
(4) rape under the law of Scotland or Northern Ireland;
(5) an offence under SOA 1956, s.1 (rape);
(6) an offence under SOA 2003, s.1 (rape);
(7) an offence under SOA 2003, s.2 (assault by penetration);
(8) an offence under SOA 2003, s.4 (causing a person to engage in sexual activity without consent) where the activity involved penetration within s.4(4)(a)–(d);
(9) an offence under SOA 2003, s.5 (rape of a child under 13);
(10) an offence under SOA 2003, s.6 (assault of a child under 13 by penetration);
(11) an offence under SOA 2003, s.8 (causing or inciting a child under 13 to engage in sexual activity) where an activity involved penetration within s.8(3)(a)–(d) was caused;
(12) an offence under SOA 2003, s.30 (sexual activity with a person with a mental disorder impeding choice) where the touching involved penetration within s.30(3)(a)–(d);
(13) an offence under SOA 2003, s.31 (causing or inciting a person with a mental disorder impeding choice to engage in sexual activity) where an activity involving penetration within s.31(3)(a)–(d) was caused; and
(14) an attempt to commit an offence within any of the para. (d) to (m) above.

A person charged with, or convicted of, any of the above offences, who:

(a) has been previously convicted in any part of the UK of such an offence; or
(b) in the case of a previous conviction for manslaughter or culpable homicide, was then a child or young person and was sentenced to long term detention,

may be granted bail in those proceedings only if the judge is satisfied that there are exceptional circumstances which justify it.

Section 25 should be construed as a guide to the proper operation of BA 1976. Additionally it operates to dis-apply the ordinary requirements of the Custody Time Limits Regulations 1987 that bail be granted automatically to an accused where the custody time limit has expired. If a person to whom s.25 applies, if granted bail, is likely to fail to surrender, to offend on bail or to interfere with witnesses or otherwise obstruct the course of justice, bail should not be granted. If, however, taking all the circumstances into consideration the accused does not create such an unacceptable risk, he is an exception to the norm and should be granted bail (*R. (O) v Harrow CC* [2003] 1 W.L.R. 2756). The section does not breach ECHR, Art.5 (*R. (O) v Harrow CC*, *The Times*, August 11, 2006, HL).

Drug users

11–015 CJA 2003, ss.19, 20 is designed to meet the problem of drug users who, once released on bail, reoffend by committing acquisitive offences to fund their habit.

BA 1976, Sch.1, Pt 1, paras 6A, 6B, 6C; CJA 2003, ss.19, 20

Where arrangements are in force in the court's area, there will be a presumption against bail in the case of a person aged 18 or over, charged with an imprisonable offence; unless the judge is satisfied that there is no significant risk of his committing another offence while on bail, where:

(1) he tests positive for a specified (CJCSA 2000, Pt 3) Class A drug; and
(2) he does not consent to:
    (a) undergo an assessment as to his dependency or propensity to use drugs; or
    (b) following assessment, any relevant follow up action recommended.

A sample (taken under PACE 1984, s.63B in connection with the offence, or under CJA 2003, s.161 after conviction and before sentence) must have revealed the presence in the accused's body of a specified Class A drug, and either:

(i) the offence must be one under MDA 1971, s.5(2) or 5(3), and relate to a specified Class A drug; or
(ii) the judge must be satisfied that there are substantial grounds for believing that misuse by the accused of a specified Class A drug caused or contributed to the offence; or, even if it did not, the offence was motivated wholly or partly by his intended misuse of such a drug; and

if an assessment or a follow-up is proposed and agreed to, it must be a condition of bail that it be undertaken. See HO Circular 22/2004.

Restrictions on bail; extradition cases

11–016 Where the Home Secretary has given an undertaking in connection with a person's extradition to the United Kingdom which includes terms that that person be kept in custody until the conclusion of any proceedings against him for an offence, a judge may grant bail only if he considers that there are exceptional circumstances which justify it. EA 2003, s.154

2. Considerations governing grant

Grant or variation

11–017 In taking the decision whether to grant, withhold or vary bail in the case of a person accused or convicted (before the coming into force of para.2A of the Schedule) of an imprisonable offence, the judge is bound to have regard to such of the following considerations as appear to be relevant, that is to say: BA 1976, s.4(1), Sch.1, Pt I; CJPOA 1994, Sch.10, para.32; CDA 1998, s.119, Sch.8, para.38; PCC(S)A 2000, s.165, Sch.9, para.54

(1) the nature and seriousness of the offence (or default) and the probable method of dealing with the accused for it;
(2) the character, antecedents, associations and community ties of the accused;
(3) the accused's record as respects the fulfilment of his obligations under previous grants of bail in criminal proceedings; and
(4) except in the case of an accused whose case is adjourned for inquiries or a report, the strength of the evidence of his having committed the offence (or having defaulted), as well as to any others which appear to be relevant.

In making the decision, the considerations to which the judge must have regard, include, so far as is relevant, any misuse of controlled drugs by the accused (BA 1976, s.4(9); CJCSA 2000, s.58).

11–018 It is common sense that:

(a) the presumption of innocence which is clearly a factor, is one which does not exclude competing factors which may be more formidable in the circumstances of the case;
(b) previous convictions per se should not be regarded as an automatic reason for refusing bail, but if there is a significance in the record and the nature of the charges to be preferred, protection of the public needs to be considered;
(c) the allegation at the time of the alleged commission of the offence that the accused was in a position of trust to behave as a good citizen and not breach the law is an important factor. This may arise where, e.g. he is on bail in respect of another offence, subject to a community sentence, on licence or parole; or subject to a deferred sentence (or a suspended sentence one might add) when, unless there are cogent reasons for deciding otherwise, bail ought to be refused;
(d) vague or unspecified arguments that the police are still, after the case has been sent to the Crown Court for trial, making enquiries are hardly a good ground for refusing bail, but it is otherwise where the prosecutor can prove that it is in the interests of the public administration of justice that the accused be detained while those enquiries are made.

Refusing bail; imprisonable offence: Sch.1, Pt I

11–019 The judge may refuse to grant bail to an accused (subject to expiry of the custody time limits) where, in the case of an imprisonable offence:

BA 1976, Sch.1, Pt. I; CJA 1991, Sch.11, para.2; CJPOA 1994, s.26; PCC(S)A 2000, s.165, Sch.9 para.54; CJCSA 2000, s.58; CJA 2003, ss.13(3), (4)

(1) there exist substantial grounds for the belief (see *R. v Slough JJ. Ex p. Duncan* (1982) 75 Cr.App.R. 384, *cf. R. v Mansfield JJ. Ex p. Sharkey* [1985] Q.B. 613) that if released on bail, whether with sureties or not, he will:
    (a) fail to surrender;
    (b) commit an offence while on bail; or
    (c) interfere with witnesses or otherwise obstruct the course of justice, whether in relation to himself or any other person;
(2) it appears he was on bail in criminal proceedings on the date of the offence, unless he is satisfied that there is no significant risk of his committing an offence while on bail, whether subject to conditions or not;
(3) he is satisfied that the accused should be kept in custody for his own protection (or welfare in the case of a juvenile);

Bail

(4) the accused is already in custody in pursuance of the sentence of a court or of any authority acting under the Services Acts; or
(5) he is satisfied that it has not been practicable to obtain sufficient information for the purpose of taking the decisions in (1)–(3) above for want of time since the institution of proceedings against him.

In deciding whether he is satisfied that there are substantial grounds for believing that the accused, if released on bail, whether subject to conditions or not, would commit an offence while on bail, **the judge must give particular weight to the fact that he was on bail in criminal proceedings on the date of the offence**.

Non-imprisonable offences

11–020 Part II of BA 1976, Sch.1 makes different, less stringent, provisions where the accused faces, or is convicted of, a non-imprisonable offence, applicable only where; BA 1976, Sch.1, Pt II, paras 2–5; CJA 2003, s.13(4)

(1) it appears that, having been previously granted bail in criminal proceedings he has failed to surrender to custody in accordance with his obligations under the grant of bail; and
(2) the judge believes, in view of that failure, that the accused, if released on bail (whether subject to conditions or not) would fail to surrender to custody.

In such a case, bail need not be granted if the judge is satisfied that:

(a) he should be kept in custody for his own protection or, if he is a child or young person, for his own welfare;
(b) he is in custody in pursuance of the sentence of a court or of any authority acting under any of the Services Acts; or
(c) if:
 (i) having been released on bail in or in connection with the proceedings for the offence, he has been arrested in pursuance of BA 1976, s.7; and
 (ii) the judge is satisfied that there are substantial grounds for believing that if released on bail, (whether subject to conditions or not), he would fail to surrender to custody, commit an offence on bail or interfere with witnesses or otherwise obstruct the course of justice (whether in relation to himself or any other person).

There is nothing to prevent conditions being imposed in such a case (*R. v Bournemouth MC Ex p. Cross etc.* [1989] Crim. L.R. 207).

Adults defaulting on bail

11–021 Where the accused is aged 18 or over, and it appears that: BA 1976, Sch.1, Pt I, paras 2A(1), 6(1), (2), (3); CJA 2003, ss.14, 15

(1) he was on bail in criminal proceedings on the date of the offence, or
(2) having been released on bail in or in connection with the proceedings for the offence, he failed to surrender to custody,

he may not be granted bail (once CJA 2003, ss.14, 15 come into force) unless the judge is satisfied that there is no significant risk of his committing an offence while on bail (whether subject to conditions or not), or failing to surrender to custody.

Where it appears that the accused had reasonable cause for his failure to surrender to custody, (2) above does not apply unless it also appears that he failed to surrender to custody at the appointed place as soon as reasonably practicable after the appointed time.

In the case of an accused under 18, **the judge must give particular weight to the fact that he has failed to surrender to bail in assessing the risk of future offending**.

Exercise of discretion

11–022 Before the discretion to refuse bail arises:

(1) the judge must be satisfied that one of the five conditions in 11–019 obtains. With regard to (1) above, it is the existence of substantial grounds for the belief, not the belief itself, which is the crucial factor (*R. v Slough JJ. Ex p. Duncan* [1982] 75 Cr.App.R. 384);
(2) in deciding whether substantial grounds exist, the judge must act compatibly with ECHR, Art.5(3) which limits pre-trial custody; he must take into account *all* relevant considerations, including those relating to the character of the person involved, his morals, his home, his occupation, his assets, his family ties and all kinds of links with his community and country (*Letellier v France* (1992) 14 E.H.H.R. 83);
(3) there should be evidence to support objections to bail, but it seems that the strict rules of evidence need not apply. Evidence upon which the prosecution intend to rely in

opposing bail should be disclosed (*Lamy v Belgium* (1989) 11 E.H.R.R. 529).

Bail during the trial

11–023 Once a trial has begun, the further grant of bail, subject to BA 1976, (especially s.4), whether during the short adjournment or overnight, is in the discretion of the trial judge. It may be a proper exercise of this discretion to refuse bail during the short adjournment if the accused cannot otherwise be segregated from witnesses and jurors. PD 2004 III.25.1–5

In particular:

(1) an accused who was on bail while on remand should not be refused overnight bail during the trial unless in the opinion of the judge there are positive reasons to justify this refusal. Such reasons are likely to be:
   (a) that a point has been reached where there is a real danger that the accused will abscond, either because the case is going badly for him, or for any other reason;
   (b) that there is a real danger that he may interfere with witnesses or jurors;
(2) there is no universal rule of practice that bail shall not be renewed when the summing-up has begun; each case must be decided in the light of its own circumstances and having regard to the judge's assessment from time to time of the risks involved;
(3) once the jury has returned a verdict a further renewal of bail should be decided in the light of the gravity of the offence and the likely sentence to be passed in all the circumstances of the case.

It may be a proper exercise of that discretion to insist on the accused surrendering earlier and being released later than the times during which other persons are present, particularly in courts where no proper segregated refreshment facilities for jurors and witnesses are available. *Burgess v S of S* [2001] 1 W.L.R. 93.

Bail on remand for inquiries or reports

11–024 Where an offender's case is adjourned for inquiries or reports, and the offence, or one of the offences, of which he is convicted in the proceedings is punishable with imprisonment, he need not be granted bail if it appears that it would be impracticable to complete the inquiries or make the report without keeping him in custody (e.g. the obvious case of the offender BA 1976, s.4(1), Sch.1, Pt I

who has a history of not attending upon an officer of a local probation board).

Prior to the passing of CJA 1991 it could be said that:

(1) where an offender had never been to prison before; or
(2) where the judge, in order to impose a custodial sentence, had to be satisfied, after considering reports, that a custodial sentence was the only proper disposal,

very good reasons were required to justify refusing bail pending reports being obtained (BA 1976, Sch.1, Pt II). Whether that principle can be maintained now that reports are mandatory even in the case of an offender who must inevitably receive a custodial sentence for what is a grave, though an either-way, offence, is doubtful.

3. Unconditional or subject to conditions

Imposing conditions

11–025 Bail in criminal proceedings is either unconditional or subject to conditions. No condition is to be imposed unless it appears necessary to do so for the purpose of:

BA 1976, ss.1(6), 4(5), Sch.1, Pt I; CJA 1988, s.131(2); CJA 1991, Sch.1; PCC(S)A 2000, s.165, Sch.9 para.54; CJA 2003, s.13(1)

(1) preventing a person's failure to surrender, his commission of offences while on bail, or interference with witnesses or obstruction of the course of justice; or
(2) the accused's own protection, or, if he is a child or young person, for his own welfare or in his own interests;
(3) in an appropriate case, of his making himself available for the purpose of enabling enquiries or a report to be made, to assist the court in dealing with him for the offence and, in this case, only where it is necessary.

Surety, security and requirements

11–026 In general (BA 1976, s.3(3)) no security for his surrender is to be taken from an accused, nor is he required to provide a surety, nor is any other requirement to be imposed upon him as a condition of bail. Nevertheless, under the section, an accused may be required:

BA 1976, ss.3(3)(4), (5), (6); CDA1998, s.54(1); CJA 2003, s.13(1)

(1) before release on bail, to provide a surety or sureties or to give security, which may be given by himself or on his behalf, before being released, for his surrender (though neither of these provisions applies in the case of a person granted bail on the expiry of a time limit under POA 1985, s.22); and

(2) before release on bail, or later, to comply with such requirements as appear to be necessary to secure that he surrenders to custody, commits no offence while on bail, does not interfere with witnesses or obstruct justice, for his own protection, or, if he is a child or young person, for his own welfare or in his own interests, or makes himself available for the purpose of enquiries or a report being made, or before the time appointed for him to surrender to custody, he attends an interview with an authorised advocate or authorised litigator, as defined by CLSA 1990, s.119(1).

The former precondition to requiring security, namely that the accused would not be likely to remain in the United Kingdom for his trial, was removed by CDA 1998, s.54(1). As to the nature of the security envisaged by the Act, see *R. (Stevens) v Truro MC* [2002] 1 W.L.R. 144.

As to drug users, see 11–034, below; as to murder cases, see 11–032, 11–033, below. As to procedure, see 11–029, below.

4. Sureties/security

General

11–027 In considering the suitability of a surety required under BA 1976, s.3(4), the judge needs to have regard, among other things, to the surety's: BA 1976, s.8(1)(2)

(1) financial resources;
(2) character and previous convictions, if any; and
(3) proximity, whether in point of kinship, place of residence or otherwise, to the person for whom he is a surety.

In considering "financial resources":

(a) it is the resources of the surety, rather than of the principal, that are relevant;
(b) in relation to the wife of the principal, it is important to consider whether she has sufficient means to discharge her liability out of her separate property, and no account should be taken of any joint property or of the matrimonial home (*R. v Southampton JJ. Ex p. Green* [1975] 2 All E.R. 1073).

There will be cases where only a token investigation into the resources of a surety will suffice; in other cases it will be sensible to insist on examining bank accounts, building society books and other documents. "Jewellery" will seldom fetch the value suggested, nor is there likely to be an opportunity to sell a house or other immovable property.

A surety is not to be equated with a guarantor; he is not discharged from his recognisance by operation of law where the judge changes other conditions of bail (*R. v Bow Street MC Ex p. Hall* (1986) 136 N.L.J. 1111).

Parent or guardian

11–028 Where the parent or guardian of a child or young person consents to be a surety for him, that person may be required to secure that the juvenile comply with any requirement of bail imposed upon him (under BA 1976, s.3(6) or (6A)), save that: BA 1976, s.3(7)

(1) no requirement is to be imposed on that person where it appears that the juvenile will attain the age of 17 before the time appointed for him to surrender to custody;
(2) the parent or guardian is not to be required to secure compliance with a requirement to which he does not agree; and
(3) the parent or guardian must not, in respect of the requirements to which he does agree, be bound in a sum greater than £50.

Procedure

11–029 Where the Crown Court grants bail in criminal proceedings, the recognisance of any surety may be taken forthwith, after enquiry into his suitability, or subsequently.

Where the court is unable to release the accused because no surety, or no suitable surety, is available, the judge must fix the amount of the surety, which may be taken subsequently, in accordance with BA 1976, ss.3(4), (5) and (6). BA 1976, s.8(3)

In such circumstances the recognisance of the surety may be entered into before: BA 1976, s.8(3), (4); r.19.22

(1) an officer of the Crown Court; or
(2) the governor or keeper of any prison or other place of detention in which the person granted bail is held;
(3) those other persons specified in BA 1976, s.8(4), i.e. a magistrate, the designated officer of a magistrates' court, a police officer who is either of or above the rank of inspector, or in charge of a police station, or, where bail is granted by the Crown Court, the Crown Court officer.

In a case where the proposed surety resides in Scotland the judge may, if satisfied of the suitability of the proposed surety, BA 1976, s.8(3), (6)

Bail

direct that arrangements be made for the surety to be entered into there, before a constable having charge at any police office or station there.

A person proposing to enter into a recognisance must, unless the court otherwise directs, give notice to the prosecutor at least 24 hours before he enters into it (R.19.22(3)).

Where a surety seeks to enter into a recognisance before a person such as one of those specified in BA 1976, s.8(4), and that person declines to take it because he is not satisfied of the surety's suitability, the proposed surety may apply either to: BA 1976, s.8(5)

(a) the court which fixed the amount in which the surety was to be bound; or
(b) a magistrates' court for the local justice area in which he resides, for the court to take his recognisance, and that court must do so if satisfied of his suitability.

Where a recognisance is entered into before a court other than that which fixed the amount of the recognisance, the same consequences follow as if it had been entered into before the original court. BA 1976, s.8(7)

"Bail as before"

11–030 A judge granting "bail as before" needs to be careful with the procedure. Bail granted on a previous occasion ceases on the surrender of the accused, or offender.

Where the judge:

(1) contemplates granting bail on the same conditions as it was granted previously, and
(2) a surety was required on that occasion,

then unless he proposes to remove the requirement of a surety, he must consider the surety's position (*R. v Maidstone CC Ex p. Jodka* (1997) 161 J.P. 638) and see *R. v Dimond* [2000] 1 Cr.App.R. 21.

5. Other requirements of bail

No closed list

11–031 There can be no closed list of requirements which may be imposed, but common requirements are those as to residence, including sleeping every night at a named address, reporting periodically at a named police station between specified hours on specified days, observing a curfew between specified hours, residing in a specified hostel, surrender of passport and restrictions on entering or leaving certain defined areas.

Special conditions apply to bail pending appeal to the CACD (see 18 CHALLENGING THE CROWN COURT).

A requirement may be added:

(1) that before the time appointed for surrender to custody, the accused attend an interview with an advocate or authorised litigator as defined by CLSA 1990, s.119(1); BA1976, s.3(6)(e); CDA 1998, s.54(2); SI 1998/2327

(2) where bail is granted pending reports, that the offender "attend on an officer of a local probation board or a medical practitioner — as directed".

(3) where one of the conditions imposed is residence in a bail or probation hostel, that he comply with the rules of the hostel; BA 1976, s.3(6A); CJA 1988, s.131

(4) subject to s.3AA (see 11–035) in the case of a child or young person, that he be required to be subject to electronic monitoring requirements, that is requirements imposed for the purpose of securing the electronic monitoring of his compliance with any other requirement imposed on him as a requirement of bail. BA 1976, ss.3(6ZAA), (6ZAB)

(5) "not to drive", but before imposing it the judge ought to consider whether it may have possibly unjust results (*R. v Kwame* (1975) 60 Cr.App.R. 64); there is power to impose an interim disqualification under RTA 1991, on remanding an accused.

11–032 Where the judge imposes a requirement to be complied with before a person's release on bail, he may give directions as to the manner in which, and the person or persons before whom, the requirement is to be complied with. R. 19.22(2), (3)

Murder cases

11–033 In the case of a person accused of murder, the judge, when granting bail must, unless he considers that satisfactory reports on his mental condition have already been obtained, impose as a condition of bail, a requirement that: BA 1976, s.3(6A), (6B); MH(A)A1982, s.34(1), (2); MHA 1983, s.4

(1) the accused is examined by two medical practitioners for the purpose of enabling reports to be prepared; and

(2) he attend such institution or place as the judge directs, and comply with such other directions as may be given to him for the purpose by either of those medical practitioners.

Of those medical practitioners, at least one must be a practitioner approved for the purposes of MHA 1983, s.12. Failure to impose such a requirement renders the grant of bail a nullity (*R. v CCC Ex p. Porter* [1992] Crim.L.R. 121).

Drug users

11–034 Where the court has been notified that arrangements for conducting a relevant assessment, or, as the case may be, providing relevant follow-up, have been made for the local justice area in which it appears that the person referred to in subs. (6D) would reside if granted bail; and the notice has not been withdrawn, then, in relation to a person to whom BA 1976, Sch.1, para.6B(1)(a) and (b) apply, and who: BA 1976, ss. 3(6C), (6D), (6E); CJA 2003, S.19(2)

(1) after analysis, has been offered a relevant assessment or, if a relevant assessment has been carried out, has had relevant follow-up proposed to him; and
(2) has agreed to undergo the relevant assessment or, as the case may be, to participate in the relevant follow-up,

the judge, if he grants bail, must impose as a condition of bail that that person both undergo the relevant assessment and participate in any relevant follow-up proposed to him or, if a relevant assessment has been carried out, that he participate in the relevant follow-up.

In this provision:

(a) "relevant assessment" means an assessment conducted by a suitably qualified person of whether that person is dependent upon or has a propensity to misuse any specified Class A drugs;
(b) "relevant follow-up" means, in a case where the person who conducted the relevant assessment believes that person to have such a dependency or propensity, such further assessment, and such assistance or treatment in connection with the dependency or propensity, as the person who conducted the relevant assessment (or conducts any later assessment) considers to be appropriate in his case,

and in para. (a) above "Class A drug" and "misuse" have the same meaning as in MDA 1971, and "specified" (in relation to a Class A drug) has the same meaning as in CJCSA 2000, Pt 3, as to both of which, see 11–015, above.

Electronic monitoring requirement; children and young persons

11–035 A judge may not impose electronic monitoring requirements on a child or young person unless each of the following conditions is satisfied; namely that: BA 1976, s.3AA; CJPA 2001, s.131

(1) he has attained the age of 12 years;

(2) he is charged with, or has been convicted of:
  (a) a violent or sexual offence; or
  (b) an offence punishable in the case of an adult with imprisonment for 14 years or more; or
  (c) one or more imprisonable offences which, together with any other imprisonable offences of which he has been convicted in any proceedings, amount, or would amount, if he were convicted of the offences with which he is charged, to a recent history of repeatedly committing imprisonable offences while remanded on bail or to local authority accommodation;

(3) the court has been notified by the Home Secretary that such arrangements exist for children and young persons and the necessary provisions can be made.

The requirement must include a provision making a person responsible for the monitoring.

6. Record; variation; breach

Reasons and record; notification of recognisance, etc.

11–036 A judge: BA 1976, s.5(3)–(5)

(1) granting or withholding bail, or
(2) varying conditions,

in relation to a person to whom the right to bail before conviction applies, must, with a view to enabling that person to consider applying to another court, give his reasons, though he need not do so, where that person is represented by a solicitor or counsel, unless asked to do so.

His reasons will be entered on the court file and a copy of the note will be given to the person in relation to whom the decision was taken, unless his representative does not ask for it. BA 1976, s.5(1)

Where a recognisance is entered into, or a requirement is complied with, before any person, that recognisance, or a statement of the requirement, must be transmitted forthwith to the Crown Court officer, a copy being sent at the same time to the governor or keeper of any prison or place of detention in which the person named is detained, unless, of course, the recognisance was entered into, or the requirement was complied with, before that person. R.19.22(4)

Variation of conditions

11–037 On an application by, or on behalf of, the person to whom bail was granted, or by the prosecutor or a constable, a judge of the Crown Court may, if that court has granted bail, BA 1976, s.5(1); CLA 1977, Sch.1

or a magistrates' court has committed a person to it for trial or to be sentenced or otherwise to be dealt with, or has sent a person for trial under CDA 1998, s.51 (see *R. v Lincoln MC Ex p. Mawer* (1996) 160 J.P. 219), vary any conditions of bail or impose conditions in respect of bail granted unconditionally.

Breach of condition

11–038 A person arrested under BA 1976, s.7(2) as being likely to abscond or to breach his conditions, or as having breached a condition of his bail (even where that bail was granted by the Crown Court) must be brought before a justice of the peace for the local justice area in which he is arrested (and not before the Crown Court) (BA 1976, s.7(4), (5), (6); CLA 1977, Sch.2). A recorder of the Crown Court is not a justice for this purpose (*Re Marshall* [1994] Crim.L.R. 915).

BA 1976, s.7(4)–(6); CLA 1977, Sch.2

That justice may remand him, or commit him to custody, or grant him bail on the same or different conditions. He has no power to send him to the Crown Court to be dealt with for the breach. See *Re Teeside MC Ex p. Elliott*, *The Times*, February 20, 2000.

Unlike failure to surrender which is a contempt of court and may be dealt with as such, breach of a bail condition is not, and should be dealt with under BA 1976 (*R. v Ashley* [2004]Crim. L.R. 297).

"Withdrawal" of surety

11–039 There is no right for a surety, believing that his principal is about to abscond or has already absconded, to "withdraw" his recognisance, unless the principal is before the court. He is entitled to make an application in writing at a police station, stating that the accused is unlikely to surrender, which empowers an officer to arrest the accused without warrant (*R. v Wood Green CC Ex p. Howe* [1992] 3 All E.R. 366).

7. Absconding

Effect of bail in criminal proceedings

11–040 A person granted "bail in criminal proceedings" under the Act has a duty to surrender to custody, that is to surrender himself into the custody of the court at the time and place for the time being appointed for him to do so.

BA 1976, ss.2(2), 3(1), (2), 6(1); PCC(S)A 2000, s.165, Sch.9, para.51

"Court" includes an official of the court where the accused has followed the procedure he is directed to follow (*DPP v Richards* [1988] Q.B. 701).

No recognisance for his surrender is taken from him but where:

(1) he fails without reasonable cause to surrender, or
(2) having reasonable cause for such failure he has failed to surrender, and then fails to surrender to custody at the appointed place as soon after the appointed time as is reasonably practicable, he commits an offence (see 11–041 *et seq*).

"Bail in criminal proceedings" means bail grantable: BA 1976, s.1(1)

(a) in or in connection with proceedings for an offence, to a person accused of the offence; or
(b) in connection with an offence to a person under arrest for the offence, or for whose arrest for the offence a warrant endorsed for bail is being issued.

In proceedings other than "criminal proceedings", the traditional system of principal and surety obtains.

An adult not admitted to bail is remanded in custody. As to the remand of juveniles see 19 CHILDREN AND YOUNG PERSONS.

Absconding on bail: (1) a criminal offence

11–041 A person released on bail in criminal proceedings who: BA 1976, ss.6(1), (2), (5), (7); CJA 2003, s.41, Sch.3, para.48(4)

(1) fails without reasonable excuse to surrender to custody; or
(2) having reasonable cause for such failure, then fails to surrender at the appointed place as soon after the appointed time as is reasonably practicable,

commits an offence, which in the Crown Court is punishable as if it were a criminal contempt of court and the offender is liable to imprisonment for up to 12 months or to a fine or both. (See also *R. v Reader* (1987) 84 Cr.App.R. 294.)

Note that:

(a) a person surrenders to custody when he complies with the procedure of the court at which he is due to appear, directing him to report to a particular office or particular official;
(b) it is not sufficient for him simply to attend the courthouse; he must report and comply with the procedure; and thereafter,
(c) though not physically restrained, he is in the custody of the court and should be instructed not to leave the building without consent (*DPP v Richards* (1989) 88 Cr.App.R. 97).

Where an accused is arraigned he surrenders to custody if he has not done so at an earlier stage (*R. v CCC Ex p. Guney* [1996] 2 Cr.App.R. 352).

The fact that such an offence is to be treated as if it were a criminal contempt does not alter the fact that it is an offence, and therefore:

(i) a person convicted of absconding in the magistrates' court and committed under BA 1976, s.6(6) to the Crown Court for sentence is liable to the same penalties;
(ii) an offender must be dealt with in respect of a suspended sentence on the ordinary principles; and
(iii) as in the case of any other offence, the *de minimis* principle may be applied.

An accused who commits an offence contrary to BA 1976, s.6(1), (2) commits an offence that stands apart from the proceedings in respect of which bail was granted. The seriousness of the offence can be reflected by an appropriate penalty being imposed for the Bail Act offence.

The fact that the accused is acquitted of the substantive offence for which he is being tried or dealt with does not preclude the court, in a proper case, from imposing an immediate custodial sentence for the offence of absconding (*R. v Kohli* (1983) 5 Cr.App.R.(S.) 175); nor does the fact that a fine is imposed on the substantive offence prevent a custodial sentence being imposed on the bail offence (*R. v Uddin* (1992) 13 Cr.App.R.(S.) 114).

Absconding on bail: (2) general

11–042 Breach of bail in the magistrates' court is not indictable and can be tried in the Crown Court only where the magistrates commit the offender for sentence under BA 1976, s.6(6) (see 20 COMMITTALS FOR SENTENCE).

The failure of an accused to comply with the terms of his bail by not surrendering can undermine the administration of justice; it can disrupt proceedings. The resulting delays impact on victims, witnesses and other court users and also waste costs. Failure to surrender affects not only the case with which the accused is concerned, but also the courts' ability to administer justice more generally by damaging the confidence of victims, witnesses and the public in the effectiveness of the court system and the judiciary. It is, therefore most important that accused persons who are granted bail appreciate the significance of the obligation to surrender to custody in accordance with the terms of their bail and that courts take appropriate action if they fail to do so. PD 2004, I.13.4–5

There are at least three courses of action for the judge to consider:

(1) imposing a penalty for the failure to surrender;
(2) revoking bail or imposing more stringent bail conditions; and
(3) conducting the trial in the absence of the accused (see 1 ABSCONDING ACCUSED).

Absconding on bail: (3) approach

11–043 The judge should deal with the absconding offence as soon as is practicable, taking into account:

(1) when the proceedings in respect of which bail was granted are expected to conclude;
(2) the seriousness of the offence for which the accused is already being prosecuted;
(3) the type of penalty that might be imposed for the breach of bail and the original offence; as well as
(4) any other relevant circumstances.

If:

(a) there is no good reason for postponing dealing with the breach until after the trial, the breach should be dealt with as soon as practicable;
(b) the disposal of the breach of bail is postponed, then it is still necessary to consider imposing a separate penalty at the trial; and the sentence for the breach of bail should usually be:
   (i) custodial; and
   (ii) consecutive to any other custodial sentence and in addition,

bail should usually be revoked in the meantime.

In the case of offences which cannot, or are unlikely to, result in a custodial sentence, trial in the absence of the accused may be a pragmatic sensible response to the situation (see 1 ABSCONDING ACCUSED). This is not a penalty for the Bail Act offence; a penalty may also be imposed for the Bail Act offence.

Absconding on bail: (4) initiation and conduct of proceedings

11–044 Where a person granted bail by a court subsequently fails to surrender to custody, he should normally, on arrest, be brought as soon as appropriate before the court at which the proceedings in respect of which bail was granted are to be PD 2004, I.13.8

heard. (The six month time limit does not apply where bail was granted by the court.) Should he commit another offence outside the jurisdiction of the bail court, the Bail Act offence should, where practicable, be dealt with by the new court at the same time as the new offence. If impracticable, the accused may, if this is appropriate, be released formally on bail by the new court so that the warrant may be executed for his attendance before the first court in respect of the substantive and the Bail Act offences.

It is appropriate that the court should initiate the proceedings its own motion. The judge will be invited to do so by the prosecutor, if he considers proceedings are appropriate.
Note that:

(1) proceedings under BA 1976, s.6 may be conducted either as a summary offence or as a criminal contempt of court;
(2) where the court is invited to take proceedings by the prosecutor, the prosecutor will conduct the proceedings and, if the matter is contested, call the evidence;
(3) where the court initiates proceedings without such an invitation the same role can be played by the prosecutor at the request of the court, where this is practicable;
(4) the burden of proof is on the accused to prove that he had reasonable cause for his failure to surrender to custody (BA 1976, s.6(3)).

If the court decides to proceed, the Bail Act offence should be concluded as soon as practicable.

11–045 Still relevant from para.56(1) of the previous *Practice Direction* are that:

(1) it is neither necessary nor desirable that a formal charge or indictment should be laid in order to commence proceedings in the Crown Court;
(2) the nature of the offence, which is tantamount to a defiance of a court order, makes it more appropriate that the judge initiate proceedings of his own motion, following an express invitation by the Crown;
(3) the Crown ought to invite the judge to deal with the matter only where, having considered all the circumstances, proceedings are considered appropriate;
(4) counsel for the Crown should conduct the proceedings and, where the issue is contested, call the evidence.

Absconding is a criminal charge which must be proved following the correct procedure (*R. v Davies* (1986) 8 Cr.App.

R.(S.) 97; *R. v Woods* (1989) 11 Cr.App.R.(S.) 551; *R. v O'Boyle* (above)).

The judge must:

(a) give the accused the opportunity to explain himself;
(b) invite submissions from counsel appearing for him; and
(c) make a finding of guilt or otherwise as the case may be.

A document purporting to be a copy of the prescribed record which relates to the time and place appointed for the accused to surrender to custody, and duly certified to be a true copy, is evidence of the time and place appointed for that person to surrender. BA 1976, s.6(8)

8. Estreatment forfeiture of recognisances, security

Estreatment of recognisance

11–046 Where a recognisance has been entered into in respect of a person granted bail to appear before the Crown Court, and it appears to the judge that a default has been made in performing the conditions of that recognisance where: R.19.23, 24

(1) that recognisance was conditioned for the appearance of the accused at the Crown Court, and the accused fails to appear in accordance with the condition, the judge *must* declare the recognisance to be estreated;
(2) the default is other than by failing to appear at the crown court in accordance with such condition, the judge *may* order the recognisance to be estreated.

In either case, before the recognisance is actually estreated or forfeited, a notice under R.19.23(2) or a summons under R.19.24(2) must be given to the person by whom the recognisance was entered into, to enable him to show cause why it should not be estreated.

At the time specified in the summons, the judge may proceed in the absence of the person by whom the recognisance was entered into, if satisfied that the summons has been served.

Breach of these provisions may result in any order of estreatment being quashed (*R. v CCC Ex p. Naraghi & Binji* (1980) 2 Cr.App.R.(S.) 104).

11–047 The authorities were considered in *R. v Uxbridge Justices Ex p. Heward-Mills* [1983] 1 All E.R. 530 and the more important principles derived from them were stated to be as follows:

Bail

(1) when an accused for whose attendance a person has stood surety fails to appear, the full recognisance should be forfeited unless it appears fair and just that a lesser sum should be forfeited or none at all;
(2) the burden of satisfying the judge that the full sum should not be forfeited rests on the surety and is a heavy one; it is for him to lay before the court the evidence of want of culpability and of means on which he relies;
(3) where a surety is unrepresented the judge should assist him by explaining the principles in ordinary language, and giving him an opportunity to call evidence and advance argument in relation to them;
(4) a lack of culpability on the surety's part, or even a commendable diligence, is not of itself a reason for reducing or setting aside the obligation into which he has freely entered, but the judge has a broad discretion as to whether and to what extent it would be fair to remit some or all of the recognisance (*R. v Maidstone CC Ex p. Lever* [1995] 2 All E.R. 35). The basis of forfeiture is not culpability; it is non-attendance.

What is reasonable in any given case depends on the circumstances of that case (*R. v York Crown Court Ex p. Coleman* (1988) 86 Cr.App.R. 151). The judge may, and should, look at the conduct of the surety to see whether there are mitigating circumstances (*R. v ILCC Ex p. Springall* (1987) 85 Cr.App.R. 214; *R. v Reading CC Ex p. Bello* [1992] 3 All E.R. 353, CA; *R. v Wood Green CC Ex p. Howe* (1991) 93 Cr.App.R. 213).

Where a wife's recognisance is estreated, it should come out of her own property and not out of her husband's, nor out of their joint property or the matrimonial home (*R. v Southampton JJ. Ex p. Green* [1975] 2 All E.R. 1073).

Enforcement of estreated recognisances

11–048 When the judge forfeits a person's recognisance, he:

(1) *must* make an order fixing a term of imprisonment which he is to undergo if, any sum which he is liable to pay is not duly paid or recovered; in which case PCC(S)A 2000, s.139(2)
  (a) the maximum default term is that set out in the table applicable to fines (see 36 FINES AND ENFORCEMENT); and
  (b) the restrictions as to immediate imprisonment or detention apply as they do in the case of a fine (see 36 FINES AND ENFORCEMENT);

(2) *may* make an order; PCC(S)A 2000, ss.139(1), 142

(a) in the case of a person before the court, that he be searched, and any money found on him be applied, unless otherwise directed, to the payment of the recognisance;

(b) allowing time for payment of the amount due under the recognisance;

(c) directing payment of the amount by instalments of such amounts and on such dates as may be specified in the order;

(d) discharging the recognisance or reducing the amount thereunder.

Forfeiture of security (s.3(5))

11–049 Where an accused has given security before his release on bail (under BA 1976, s.3(5)), and the judge is satisfied that he has failed to surrender to custody, then, unless it appears that he had reasonable cause for failure, the judge may order the forfeiture of the security, or such amount less than the full value that it thinks fit. The Crown Court officer will give notice of the decision to the person before whom security was given. BA 1976, s.5(7), (8); R.19.21(5)

Such order, unless previously revoked, takes effect at the end of 21 days beginning with the day on which it is made. If the security consists of money it is accounted for and paid in the same way as a fine imposed by the Crown Court, if it does not, it is enforced by such magistrates' court as is specified in the order. BA 1976, s.5(8A), (9); CLA 1977, Sch.12)

If the judge is satisfied on an application made by or on behalf of the person who gave security, that he did after all have reasonable cause for his failure to surrender, he may: BA 1976, s.5(8B), (8C), (9A)

(1) remit the forfeiture; or

(2) declare that the forfeiture extend to such an amount less than the full value as it sees fit to order.

An order for remission may be made before or after the original order has taken effect but an application is not to be entertained unless the judge is satisfied that the prosecution were given reasonable notice of the applicant's intention to make it. Where an order for remission is made after the order for forfeiture had taken effect, any balance due to the person concerned will be repaid.

Where security is provided to the accused by a third person, that person has no right to demand its return where the accused fails to appear (*R. (Stevens) v Truro MC* [2002] 1 W.L.R. 144).

12 BENCH AND WITNESS WARRANT

12–001 A bench warrant may be issued at the Crown Court for the arrest of a person:

(1) released on bail in criminal proceedings, and thus under a duty to surrender to the custody of the court, who: BA 1976, s.7(1), (2); SCA 1981, s.81(4)
   (a) fails to surrender at the appointed time and place; or
   (b) having surrendered, absents himself at any time and before the court is ready to begin or resume the hearing of the proceedings

   unless he is absent in accordance with leave given by or on behalf of the court; or

(2) where an indictment has been signed but the person charged has not been sent for trial, where a summons is inappropriate. SCA 1981, s.80(2); CJA 2003, s.41, Sch.3, para.54(5)

A warrant may, in an appropriate case, be backed for bail.

Contempt by witness

12–002 A person who, without just excuse, disobeys a witness order or witness summons requiring him to attend before the Crown Court is guilty of contempt and may be punished summarily as if his contempt had been in the face of the court (see 25 CONTEMPT OF COURT). The maximum term of imprisonment is three months. For sentencing principles, see *R. v Montgomery* [1995] 2 Cr.App.R. 23. CP(AW)A 1965, s.3

Witness summons

12–003 In criminal proceedings a judge may issue a summons: CP(AW)A 1965, ss.2(1), (2), (3); CPIA 1996, s.66

(1) on application, under the Rules, where he is satisfied that:
   (a) a person is likely to be able to give evidence likely to be material evidence or to produce any document or thing likely to be material evidence, for the purpose of any criminal proceedings before the Crown Court; and
   (b) it is in the interests of justice to issue a summons to secure the attendance of that person to give evidence or to produce the document or thing; or CP(AW)A 1965, s.2D; CPIA 1996, s.66; SOCA 2005, s.151(1)

(2) of his own motion,

in which circumstances a summons will be issued directing the person concerned to attend at a specified time and place and to give the evidence or produce the document, or produce it for inspection. Under (1) a summons may be refused if any requirement relating to the application is not fulfilled.

The procedure is set out in R.28.3.

Where a person has been sent for trial for any offence to which the proceedings relate, an application must be made as soon as practicable after service on that person of the documents (in pursuance of the Regulations made under CDA 1998, Sch.3, para.1) relevant to that offence. CP(AW)A 1965, ss.2(4), (5), (6); CPIA 1996, s.66; CJA 2003, ss.41, 332, Sch.3, para.42, Sch.37, Pt 4

No further need for summons

12–004 Where a document or thing is produced in pursuance of a summons, or the applicant no longer needs the requirement, and he applies, in accordance with R.28.4 to the Crown Court for a direction, the court may direct that the summons be of no further effect. CP(AW)A 1965, S.2B; CPIA 1996, s.66

Setting aside summons

12–005 A person to whom a summons is directed may apply to the Crown Court, and if: R.28.5, 28.6

(1) in the case of a summons issued on application by a party, he satisfies the judge that he was not served with notice of the application to issue the summons and that he was neither present nor represented at the hearing of the application; and CP(AW)A 1965, ss.2C, 2E; CPIA 1996, s.66
(2) whether the summons was issued on application or by the judge of his own motion, he satisfies the judge that he cannot give any evidence likely to be material evidence, or as the case may be, produce any document or thing likely to be material evidence,

the court may direct that the summons shall be of no effect.

The general principles are that material required to be produced on a summons;

(a) must be *prima facie* admissible (*R. v Cheltenham JJ. Ex p. SoS for Trade and Industry* [1977] 1 All E.R. 460, see also *R. v Derby MC Ex p. B* [1996] 1 Cr.App.R. 385, *R. v H(L)* [1997] 1 Cr.App.R. 176); and
(b) must be material, i.e. relevant to an issue in the case (*R. v Reading JJ. Ex p. Berkshire CC* [1996] 1 Cr.App.R. 239);
(c) must *not* be subject to public interest immunity (*R. v Cheltenham JJ.* (above); *R. v K* (*Trevor Douglas*) (1993) 97 Cr.App.R. 342).

It is immaterial for these purposes whether the Rule requires such a person to be served with notice of the application or CP(AW)A 1965, s.2C(2); CPIA 1996, s.66

enable such a person to be present or represented at the hearing of the application to issue the summons.

The court may refuse to make such a direction if any requirement relating to it under the Rules is not fulfilled. CP(AW)A 1965, ss.2C(4), 2E(2); CPIA 1996, s.66

Costs

12–006 Where a summons is issued on application by a party and the court later makes a direction under s.2C that it shall be of no effect, the person on whose application the summons was issued may be ordered to pay the whole or any part of the costs of the application under this section, to be taxed by the Crown Court officer. CP(AWA) 1965, s.2C(8), (9); CPIA 1996, s.66

The issue of a purely speculative summons may well amount to an "improper, unreasonable or negligent act" capable of being the subject of a wasted costs order (*R. v Cheltenham JJ.* (above), also *Re Ronald A Prior & Co (Solicitors)* [1996] 1 Cr.App.R. 248).

Witness warrant

12–007 A warrant may be issued for the arrest of a witness who:

(1) is required by virtue of a witness order or a witness summons to give evidence; or CP(AW)A 1965, s.4(2)
(2) fails to attend in compliance with a summons or order,

provided the Crown proves that notice has been given (*R. v Abdulaziz* [1989] Crim.L.R. 717).

The judge may:

(a) cause notice to be served on the witness requiring him to attend forthwith or at a specified time; or
(b) if he is satisfied there are reasonable grounds for believing that there is no just excuse for the witness's failure to attend, or he has already failed to comply with a notice under (a), he may issue a warrant.

Culpable forgetfulness is not a "reasonable excuse" (*R. v Lennock* (1993) 97 Cr.App.R. 228).

A witness brought before the court in pursuance of the warrant may be remanded in custody or on bail, with or without sureties, until such time as the court appoints for receiving his evidence or otherwise dealing with him. CP(AW)A 1965, s.4(3)

Service outside the UK

12–008 A summons or order requiring a person to attend before the court for the purpose of giving evidence in criminal proceedings may be issued or made notwithstanding that the CJ(IC)A 1990, s.2

person in question is outside the UK, and may be served outside the UK in accordance with arrangements made by the Secretary of State.

Such service does not impose any obligation under the law of England and Wales to comply with it, so that failure to do so does not constitute contempt of court, nor is it a ground for issuing a warrant, unless that person is subsequently served in the UK.

Where a witness summons is issued or a witness order is made by the Crown Court in such circumstances, it is sent to the Secretary of State with a view to its being served in accordance with arrangements made by him. R.32

Warrant of arrest

12–009 A judge of the Crown Court, if satisfied on oath that a witness in respect of whom a witness summons or order is in force is unlikely to comply with it, may issue a warrant for his arrest provided that in the case of a witness subject to a witness summons, he is satisfied that the witness is likely to be able to give material evidence or produce a document or thing likely to be material evidence in the proceedings. CP(AW)A 1965, s.4(1); CPIA 1996, s.66(8)

"Unlikely to attend" may include a situation where the witness is willing but because of factors outside his control he is unable to attend (*R. v Sokolovics* [1981] Crim.L.R. 788).

13 BIND OVER

General

13–001 The court's jurisdiction over:

(1) an *offender* may be exercised at common law or under statute, principally the JPA 1968;
(2) *any other person*, is exercisable only under statute, again, principally the JPA 1968.

Since there are technical distinctions applicable to the form of each order, it is important in making an order to specify which jurisdiction is being exercised (thus avoiding the difficulties arising in *R. v Finch* (1962) 47 Cr.App.R. 58 and *R. v Ayu* (1959) 43 Cr.App.R. 31).

As to binding over the parents or guardians of juveniles, see 13–010 below.

An offender must consent to the making of an order, and that consent is not vitiated by the fact that a custodial sentence is the only realistic alternative (*R. v Williams* [1982] 1 W.L.R. 1398). The court cannot force him to enter into recognisances, or treat him as bound where he declines to be. The remedy, where a person over the age of 18 refuses to be bound, is to commit him to prison (see 40 IMPRISONMENT) until he agrees (*Veater v Glennon* (1981) 72 Cr.App.R. 331).

The court is powerless in respect of persons under 18 (*Veater v Glennon* (above); *Howley v Oxford* (1985) 81 Cr.App.R. 246; *Surrey Chief Constable v Ridley* [1985] Crim.L.R. 725); unless they consent (*Conlan v Oxford* (1983) 5 Cr.App.R.(S.) 237).

A. Common law bind over; respited judgment

13–002 Where judgment is pending, an appeal is pending, or in any other case where the circumstances make it expedient in the interests of justice, an offender may be required: SCA 1981, s.79(2),(b)

(1) to enter into recognisances, with or without sureties, in a specific amount or amounts;
(2) to come up for judgment within a reasonable, specified period, if called upon to do so; and
(3) meanwhile to keep the peace and/or be of good behaviour and the order needs to be carefully couched in these very terms.

BIND OVER

The Act has not been amended to reflect the decision in *Hashman & Harrup v UK* [2000] Crim.L.R. 185, that binding over "to be of good behaviour" offends ECHR, Art.10(1).

Distinctive features

13–003 A common law bind over differs from one under JPA 1968 in that:

(1) conditions other than the general one to keep the peace may be imposed (*R. v Randall* (1986) 8 Cr.App.R.(S.) 433); FA 1968, s.52(1) envisages a condition, in a proper case, that the offender should not possess, use or carry a firearm;
(2) a common law bind over ranks as a penalty, not as an ancillary order, and cannot therefore be combined with any other penalty such as fine or imprisonment (*R. v Ayu* (1959) 43 Cr.App.R. 31);
(3) an offender called upon to come up for judgment is liable to be sentenced for the original offence, not merely to estreatment of recognisances;
(4) a common law bind over ranks as a conviction, and even where no sentence is subsequently passed for the offence, appeal lies to the Court of Appeal (*R. v Abrahams* (1952) 36 Cr.App.R. 147; *R. v Williams* (1982) 75 Cr.App.R. 378).

But see, in relation to ECHR, *Hashmaur and Hardop v UK* [2000] Crim.L.R. 185.

Condition to leave jurisdiction

13–004 It may be a condition of a common law bind over (but not of an order under JPA 1968), provided the offender consents, that he leave the jurisdiction and not return for a specified period. The CACD has said that the power should be used very sparingly. Thus, in the following cases, the conditions listed below were imposed:

(1) *R. v Ayu* (above) "to return to Nigeria forthwith and not to return to Great Britain during the period of the recognisance";
(2) *R. v Flaherty* [1958] Crim.L.R. 556 "to return to Ireland and not land again in this country for at least three years";
(3) *R. v Hodges* (1967) 51 Cr.App.R. 361 to attend a Carmelite organisation in the Republic of Ireland, which was prepared to accept the offender, and "not to return to England for ten years".

Only in exceptional circumstances should it be used to return an offender to a country of which he is not a citizen, and in which he does not habitually reside (*R. v Williams* (1982) 75 Cr.App.R. 378).

Appearing for judgment

13–005 An offender may be called upon to come up for judgment for something less than the commission of a further offence (*R. v McGarry* (1945) 30 Cr.App.R. 187). When he appears:

(1) the facts of any breach must be proved as if they were allegations of an offence;
(2) he must be given an opportunity to give evidence or call witnesses;
(3) if the matter of complaint is his failure to leave the country, the judge should enquire into whether that failure was a deliberate one (*R. v Philbert* [1973] Crim. L.R. 129);
(4) he may be dealt with for the original offence; the judge is not limited to estreating any recognisances.

B. Justices of the Peace Act 1968, s.1

13–006 A bind over under the Act is not dependent on conviction and, in a proper case, an acquitted accused may be bound over (*R. v Inner London Crown Court Ex p. Benjamin* (1987) 85 Cr.App.R. 267), as where no evidence is offered. Jurisdiction extends beyond the offender, to any person who, or whose case, is before the court, requiring that person: JPA 1968, s.1

(1) to enter into recognisances, with or without sureties, in a specific sum;
(2) to keep the peace, for a specified period, usually but not necessarily, 12 months; or
(3) to go to prison if he does not comply.

For the distinctions between such a bind over and one at common law, see 13–001, above. See also *Hashmaur and Hardop v UK* (above).

"Persons before the court"

13–007 A "person before the court":

(1) includes a witness who gives evidence, whether for the Crown or for the accused (*Sheldon v Bromfield* [1964] 2 All E.R. 131);

(2) does not include a person who is not a party and is not called as a witness (*R. v Swindon CC Ex p. Singh* (1984) 79 Cr.App.R. 137; *R. v Kingston CC Ex p. Guarino* [1986] Crim.L.R. 325; *R. v Lincoln CC Ex p. Jones*, *The Times*, June 16, 1989).

Procedure under the Act

13–008 If the court is minded to bind over a person under the Act, the authorities show that:

(1) there must be material, though it need not be sworn evidence, before the court, justifying the conclusion that, unless such a step is taken, there is the risk of a breach of the peace;
(2) a witness or complainant who is to be bound over should be given the opportunity of being heard, though this is not strictly necessary in the case of the accused;
(3) an acquitted accused or an accused in respect of whom it is proposed to leave counts on the file ought, as a matter of courtesy, to be warned of the court's intention and it is of particular importance in such a case that the court is *sure* that the accused is a potential threat to others and is a man of violence, not merely that it believes that he *may* pose a threat (*R. v Middlesex CC Ex p. Khan* (1997) 161 J.P. 240; *R. v Lincoln CC Ex p. Jude* [1997] 3 All E.R. 737);
(4) a person causing a disturbance in court need not receive a warning, nor need he be given an opportunity to make representations; but
(5) unless the amount of the proposed recognisance is trifling, the court must enquire into the means of the person to be bound over, and give him or his advocate an opportunity to make representations (*R. v CCC Ex p. Boulding* (1984) 79 Cr.App.R. 100; *R. v Atkinson* (1988) 10 Cr.App.R.(S.) 470; *R. v Nottingham CC Ex p. Brace* (1990) 154 J.P.N. 63; *R. v Lincoln CC Ex p. Jude* (above));
(6) there is no power to insert specific conditions in a bind over under the Act (*R. v Randall* (1986) 8 Cr.App.R.(S.) 433).

Enforcement of orders; estreatment

13–009 A breach of a recognisance needs to be proved under the criminal burden of proof (*R. v Marlow JJ. Ex p. O'Sullivan* (1983) 5 Cr.App.R.(S.) 279). It can be enforced only by estreatment (see 11 BAIL), and committal to prison can follow only in default of payment.

The court, before taking steps to estreat the recognisance, must make such enquiries as are required before estreating the recognisance of a surety for bail (*R. v Marlow JJ. Ex p. O'Sullivan* [1984] Q.B. 381).

C. Parents and guardians of juvenile offenders

13–010 Where a person under 18 is convicted of an offence, the judge: PCC(S)A 2000, ss.150(1), (2)

(1) *may*; and
(2) where the offender is under 16 when sentenced, *must*, if satisfied having regard to the circumstances of the case that it would be desirable in the interest of preventing the commission by him of further offences,

with the consent of that person, order the parent or guardian to enter into a recognisance to take proper care of him and exercise proper control over him, and

(a) if the parent or guardian refuses consent and the judge considers that refusal unreasonable, order that person to pay a fine not exceeding £1,000; and
(b) where the judge has passed a community sentence on the offender he may include in the recognisance a provision that the parent or guardian ensure that the offender complies with the requirements of the sentence.

Where he does not exercise his duty under (2) above, the judge must state in open court that he is not satisfied as mentioned in that paragraph, and why.

Amount and period of recognisances

13–011 In fixing the amount of a recognisance under these provisions, the court must take into account, among other things, the means of the parent or guardian so far as they appear or are known to him, and an order shall not require him to enter into a recognisance: PCC(S)A 2000, ss.150(3), (7)

(1) for an amount exceeding £1,000; or
(2) for a period exceeding three years or where the young person will attain the age of 18 in a shorter period, for a period exceeding that shorter period.

BIND OVER

A parent or guardian may appeal to the CACD against the making of such an order, as if he had been convicted on indictment and the order were a sentence passed on his conviction. The court may vary or revoke an order made by it if, on the application of the parent or guardian, it appears, having regard to any change in circumstances since the order was made, to be in the interests of justice to do so. PCC(S)A 2000, ss.150(9), (10)

14 BREACH, AMENDMENT AND REVOCATION

14–001 A judge of the Crown Court may be required to deal with the breach of sentencing orders made by the Crown Court, or, in certain circumstances, as on appeal, by the magistrates' courts. As far as amendment and revocation of community orders and requirements is concerned, the judge will need, in making any order to direct expressly that amendment, etc. be left to the apropriate magistrates' court; if he does not, amendments, etc. will be referred to the Crown Court.

There is no uniform code for dealing with these matters, and it is necessary to consider separately:

A Deferred sentence, under PCC(S)A 2000, ss.1B-1D (14–002 to 14–006)
B Community orders, under CA 2003, Sch.8 (14–007)
C Youth community orders:
D 1. Curfew and exclusion orders, under PCC(S)A 2000, Sch.3, (14–027)
  2. Attendance centre orders, under PCC(S)A 2003, Sch.5 (14–035)
  3. Supervision orders, under PCC(S)A 2003, Sch.7, (14–037)
  4. Action plan orders, under (14–039)
E "Custody plus" orders and "intermittent custody orders," under CJA 2003, Sch.10 (14–041)
F Suspended sentence orders, under CJA 2003, Sch.12 (14–048)
G Sexual offences prevention order under SOA 2002, s.104 (14–064)
H Anti-social behaviour order under CDA 1998, s.1C (14–065)

A. Deferred sentence; CJA 2003, Sch.23

Breach of undertaking(s)

14–002 A court which has deferred passing sentence on an offender under PCC(S)A 2000, s.1 may, whether the offence for which sentence was deferred was committed before or after

PCC(S)A 2005, s.1B; CJA 2003, s.278, Sch.23, para.1

April 4, 2005, deal with him before the end of the period of deferment where:

(1) sentence was deferred ;
(2) the offender undertook to comply with one or more requirements imposed under s.1(3)(b) in connection with the deferment; and
(3) a person appointed to act as a supervisor in relation to the offender has reported to the court that the offender has failed to comply with one or more of those requirements; and
(4) he appears or is brought before the Crown Court, and the judge is satisfied that he has failed to comply with one or more requirements imposed in connection with the deferment.

To bring him before the court, the Crown Court may issue:

(a) a summons requiring the offender to appear before the court at a time and place specified in the summons; or
(b) a warrant to arrest him and bring him before the court at a time and place specified in the warrant.

Conviction of further offence

14–003 A court which has deferred passing sentence on an offender may deal with him before the end of the period of deferment if during that period he is convicted in Great Britain, whether before or after April 4, 2005, of any offence. PCC(S)A 2005, s.1C: CJA 2003, s.278, Sch.23, para.1

Where a court has, under PCC(S)A 2000, s.1 deferred passing sentence on an offender in respect of one or more offences and:

(1) during the period of deferment the offender is convicted in England or Wales of any offence ("the later offence"), then,
(2) whether or not the offender is sentenced for the later offence during the period of deferment), the court which passes sentence on him for the later offence may also, if this has not already been done,
(3) deal with him for the offence or offences for which passing of sentence has been deferred, except that:

   (a) this power must not be exercised by a magistrates' court if the court which deferred passing sentence was the Crown Court; and
   (b) a judge of the Crown Court, in exercising that power in a case in which the court which deferred passing

sentence was a magistrates' court, must not pass any sentence which could not have been passed by a magistrates' court in exercising that power.

Where a court which has deferred passing sentence on an offender proposes to deal with him under these provisions before the end of the period of deferment, it may issue a summons requiring him to appear at a time and place specified, or a warrant to arrest him and bring him before the court at a time and place specified.

Powers on due date

14–004 Where the passing of sentence on an offender has been deferred, the power of the judge under that section to deal with the offender at the end of the period of deferment and any power in relation to the breach of an undertaking under s.1B(1) or a further conviction under s.1C(1) or of any other court which deals with him under s.1C(3); PCC(S)A 2000, s.1D: CJA 2003, s.278, Sch.23, para.1

(1) is a power to deal with him, in respect of the offence for which passing of sentence has been deferred, in any way in which the original court could have dealt with him if it had not deferred passing sentence; and
(2) where;
    (a) the passing of sentence on an offender in respect of one or more offences has been deferred under s.1; and
    (b) a magistrates' court deals with him in respect of the offence or any of the offences by committing him to the Crown Court under PCC(S)A 2000, s.3 the power of the Crown Court to deal with him includes the same power to defer passing sentence on him as if he had just been convicted of the offence or offences on indictment before the court.

It should be noted that under the former legislation:

(i) it was not necessary that the offender be dealt with exactly on the date originally specified; there was nothing to prevent the court adjourning or postponing the hearing of the matter, provided there is no further deferment (*R. v Ingle* (1974) 59 Cr.App.R. 306); but
(ii) if sentence was deferred to a date after the expiry of the six-month period, the court was deprived of its jurisdiction (*R. v W London*

Stipendiary Magistrate, Ex p. Watts, The Times, May 30, 1987);

(iii) it was desirable that the judge who passed sentence should be the same as the judge who deferred sentence in the first place, but if that was not possible the second judge should be fully apprised of the first judge's views (*R. v Gurney* [1974] Crim.L.R. 472);

(iv) the advocate who represented the offender on the earlier occasion should, if possible, appear for him on the date when sentence is to be passed (*R. v Ryan* [1976] Crim.L.R. 508).

14–005 The purpose of deferment must be ascertained, and the judge needs to determine if the offender has substantially conformed or attempted to conform with the proper expectations of the judge who deferred. If he has, then he may legitimately expect that an immediate custodial sentence will not be imposed. If he has not, the judge should be careful to state with precision in what respects he has failed (*R. v George* (1984) 79 Cr.App.R. 26). He should not be influenced by proceedings which are pending but incomplete (*R. v Aquilina* (1989) 11 Cr.App.R.(S.) 431).

Nature of sentence on deferred date

14–006 On the day on which the sentence originally deferred is dealt with, the judge is bound to approach the matter on a fair consideration of the offender's progress, if any, during the period of deferment. Thus:

(1) it is wrong to imprison the offender if he has fulfilled that which was required of him (*R. v Gilby* (1975) 61 Cr.App.R. 112; *R. v Head* (1976) 63 Cr.App.R. 157; *R. v Smith* (1979) 1 Cr.App.R. (S.) 339); and

(2) if the report made to the court is not unfavourable, a substantial custodial sentence is probably not appropriate.

B. Community orders

CJA 2003, Sch.8 deals with the breach, revocation and amendment of community orders made under CJA 2003 on or after April 4, 2005. In respect of offenders aged 18 or over, the provisions do not apply to persons aged 16 or 17. Persons not coming with the above provisions fall to be dealt with under PCC(S)A.

1. Breach of requirement

Process

14–007 If a community order made by the Crown Court does not include a direction that failure to comply with the requirements is to be dealt with by a magistrates' court, then if, at any time, it appears to a judge of the Crown Court that the offender has failed to comply with any of the requirements of the order, a summons may be issued, or if the information is on oath, a warrant, to bring him before the court. If he does not appear on a summons, a warrant may be issued.

CJA 2003, s.179, Sch.8, para.8

Powers of Crown Court

14–008 Where the offender appears or is brought before the Crown Court and it is proved to the judge's satisfaction that he has failed without reasonable excuse to comply with any of the requirements of the order, the judge may deal with him in respect of that failure in any one of the following ways, taking into account the extent to which the offender has complied with any of the requirements, namely:

CJA 2003, s.179, Sch.8, para.10(1)–(5)

(1) by amending the terms of the order so as to impose more onerous requirements which he could impose if he were then making the order;
(2) by dealing with the offender for the offence in respect of which the order, was made in any way in which he could deal with him if he had just been convicted before the Crown Court of the offence; and revoking the order if it is still in force;
(3) in the case of an offender who has willfully and persistently failed to comply, by imposing a custodial sentence, and, if the order was made in respect of an offence punishable with imprisonment, a sentence of imprisonment may be passed notwithstanding the restrictions imposed on community sentences by CJA 2003, s.152(2) (see 29 DEALING WITH AN OFFENDER).
(4) where;

(a) the offence in respect of which the order was made was not an offence punishable by imprisonment, but
(b) the offender is aged 18 or over, and
(c) the offender has willfully and persistently failed to comply with the requirements of the order, by dealing with him, in respect of that offence by imposing a

sentence of imprisonment for a term not exceeding 51 weeks, notwithstanding anything in CJA 2003, s.152(2) (see above), and revoking the order if it still in force.

In dealing with an offender under (1) above, the judge may extend the duration of particular requirements (subject to any limit in respect of individual requirements imposed by CJA 2003, Pt 12, Ch. 4) but may not extend the period beyond the maximum of three years specified under *ibid*, s.177(5).

Any question whether the offender has failed to comply with the requirements of the order is to be determined by the judge and not by the verdict of a jury; the ordinary rules as to the presentation of the prosecution case apply (*R. v Gainsborough JJ. Ex p. Green* (1983) 78 Cr.App.R. 9). CJA 2003, s.179, Sch.8, para.10(6)

Approach to breach

14–009 SGC 2, 2.1.46 makes it clear that the primary objective should be to ensure that the requirements of the (original) sentence are completed. If a custodial sentence is imposed for the breach, without adequate consideration being given to alternatives, the judge is in danger of imposing a sentence that is not commensurate with the seriousness of the original offence and is solely a punishment for breach. This may undermine the purposes identified, originally, as being important.

The judge must:

(1) take account of the extent to which the offender has complied with the requirements of the order;
(2) the reasons for the breach; and
(3) the point at which the breach has occurred.

Where a breach takes place towards the end of the operational period and the judge is satisfied that the offender's appearance before the court is likely to be sufficient in itself to ensure future compliance, then since it is not open to the judge to make 'no order', he may sentence in a way that enables the original order to be completed properly, for example, by a differently constructed community sentence that aims to secure compliance with the purposes of the original sentence.

If the judge decides to increase the onerousness of an order, he ought to:

(a) give careful consideration (with advice from the Probation Service), to the offender's ability to comply; and

(b) consider the impact on the offender's ability to comply and the possibility of precipitating a custodial sentence for further breach.

For that reason, and particularly where the breach occurs towards the end of the sentence, he may consider that:

(i) extending the supervision or operational periods will be more sensible; or
(ii) in other cases he might choose to add punitive or rehabilitative requirements instead.

In making these changes he must be mindful of the legislative restrictions on the overall length of community sentences and on the supervision and operational periods allowed for each type of requirement.

Where an offender has wilfully and persistently failed to comply with an order made in respect of an offence that is not itself punishable by imprisonment, the judge may impose a maximum sentence of 51 weeks custody (see 14–008).

A custodial sentence should be the last resort, where all reasonable efforts to ensure that an offender completes a community sentence have failed.

In dealing with an offender for breach of a requirement, as opposed to dealing with him in respect of a new offence, non-compliance is not to be taken as an aggravation of the original offence; he must be sentenced on the facts upon which the original order was made (*R.v Clarke* [1997] 2 Cr.App.R.(S.) 163).

If an RT disqualification was imposed at the time the relevant order was made, there is no power to impose a further disqualification when the order is revoked and the offender is re-sentenced (*R. v Coy* (1992) 13 Cr.App.R.(S.) 619);

Treatment cases

14–010 An offender who is required by any of the following requirements of a community order: CJA 2003, s.179, Sch.8, para.11

(1) "a mental health treatment requirement";
(2) "a drug rehabilitation requirement", or
(3) "an alcohol treatment requirement",

to submit to treatment for his mental condition, or his dependency on, or propensity to misuse, drugs or alcohol, is not to be treated for these purposes as having failed to comply with that requirement on the ground only that he had refused to undergo any surgical, electrical or other treatment if, in the judge's opinion, his refusal was reasonable having regard to all the circumstances.

The judge may not, under these provisions amend a mental health treatment requirement, a drug rehabilitation requirement or an alcohol treatment requirement unless the offender expresses his willingness to comply with the requirement as amended.

2. Revocation with or without re-sentencing

14–011 Where there is in force a community order made by the Crown Court: CJA 2003, s.179, Sch.8, para.14

(1) which does not include a direction that any failure to comply with the order be dealt with by a magistrates' court, and
(2) the offender or the responsible officer applies to the Crown Court for the order to be revoked or for the offender to be dealt with in some other way for the offence in respect of which the order was made,

then, if it appears to the judge to be in the interests of justice to do so, having regard to circumstances which have arisen since the order was made, he may;

(a) revoke the order, or
(b) both revoke the order, and deal with the offender for the offence in respect of which the order was made, in any way in which the court could deal with him if he had just been convicted of that offence by or before the court which made the order.

The circumstances in which an order may be revoked include the offender's making good progress or his responding satisfactorily to supervision or treatment, as the case requires.

In dealing with an offender under this provision the judge must take into account the extent to which the offender has complied with the requirements of the order.

Where the judge proposes to exercise its powers under this paragraph otherwise than on the application of the offender, he must be summoned to appear before the court and, if he does not appear in answer to the summons, a warrant may be issued for his arrest.

Illness or disability

14–012 Where revocation is on the ground that the offender is unable to comply by reason of illness or disability, the imposition of a custodial sentence depends on the circumstances, thus, under the previous legislation it was held that:

(1) in general it should not be imposed (*R. v Fielding* (1993) 14 Cr.App.R.(S.) 494), particularly
(2) where the offender made it clear from the outset that there might be difficulties (*R. v Johnson* [2000] Cr.App.R.(S.) 405); but
(3) it may well be appropriate where the offender failed to disclose any difficulties at the time (*R. v Hannoni* [1998] 2 Cr.App.R.(S.) 202).

If the application is based on grounds which amount, in effect, to an alleged breach of the order, the judge should satisfy himself as to the grounds for revocation by hearing evidence, as if on a breach (*R. v Jackson* [1984] Crim.L.R. 573).

3. Amendment of order

14–013 The appropriate magistrates' court has wide powers of amendment of community orders, even those made by the Crown Court, and the Crown Court order will generally include a direction that failure to comply with any requirements is to be dealt with by the magistrates' court. This will, however, not always be the case. CJA 2003, s.179, Sch.8, para.25

Where no such direction has been included, and the judge proposes to exercise his powers of amendment, save for an order cancelling a requirement, or reducing the period of any requirement, or subsituting a new local justice area or a new place for the one specified in the order, and otherwise than on the offender's application:

(1) the offender must be summoned to appear, and
(2) if he does not appear in answer to the summons, a warrant may be issued.

Change of residence

14–014 In relation to an order made by the Crown Court which does not include a direction that failure to comply with any of the requirements of the order be dealt with by the magistrates' court, the judge, if he is satisfied that the offender proposes to change, or has changed, his residence from the local justice area concerned to another such area, may, and on the application of the responsible officer *must*, amend the order by substituting the other area for the area specified in the order, but where the order contains requirements which, in his opinion, cannot be complied with unless the offender continues to reside CJA 2003, s.179, Sch.8, paras 16(1)–(5), 24(1) in the local justice area concerned unless, in accordance with para.17 (below), he either:

(1) cancels those requirements, or
(2) substitutes for those requirements other requirements which can be complied with if the offender ceases to reside in that area.

He has the same powers in relation to a drug rehabilitation requirement which is subject to review made by the Crown Court.

He may not amend under this paragraph a community order imposing a programme requirement unless it appears that the accredited programme specified in the requirement is available in the other local justice area.

No order under this provision may be made while an appeal against the order is pending.

4. Amendment of requirements

14–015 In relation to an order made by the Crown Court which does not include a direction that any failure to comply with any of the requirements of the order be dealt with by the magistrates' court, the judge may, on the application of the offender or the responsible officer, amend an order CJA 2003, s.179, Sch.8, para.24(1), (2)

(1) by cancelling any of the requirements of the order, or
(2) by replacing any of those requirements with a requirement of the same kind, which the judge could include if he were then making the order,

provided that he may *not* amend under this paragraph a mental health treatment, a drug rehabilitation or an alcohol treatment requirement unless the offender consents to the requirement as amended.

He has the same powers in respect of a drug rehabilitation requirement (see 14–017) which is subject to review, imposed by the Crown Court.

No application may be made while an appeal against the community order is pending except in a case where it relates to a "mental health", "drug rehabilitation" or "alcohol treatment requirement", and the offender consents to comply with the requirement as amended.

If the offender fails to consent to the proposed amended requirement, the judge may;

(a) revoke the community order, and
(b) deal with him for the offence in respect of which the order was made, in any way in which he could deal with him if

he had just been convicted in the Crown Court of the offence, but

in dealing with the offender he must take into account the extent to which the offender has complied with the requirements of the order.

He may impose a custodial sentence (where the order was made in respect of an offence punishable with such a sentence) notwithstanding the restrictions imposed by CJA 2003, s.152(2) (see 29 DEALING WITH AN OFFENDER).

Amendment of treatment requirements

14–016 Where the medical practitioner or other person by whom, or under whose direction, an offender is, in pursuance of: CJA 2003, s.179, Sch.8, para.18

(1) "a mental health treatment requirement",
(2) "a drug rehabilitation requirement", or
(3) "an alcohol treatment requirement",

being treated for his mental condition or his dependency on or propensity to misuse drugs or alcohol:

(a) is of the opinion;

 (i) that the treatment of the offender should be continued beyond the period specified in that behalf in the order,
 (ii) that the offender needs different treatment,
 (iii) that the offender is not susceptible to treatment, or
 (iv) that the offender does not require further treatment, or

(b) is for any reason unwilling to continue to treat or direct the treatment of the offender,

he must make a report in writing to that effect to the responsible officer and that officer must apply to the appropriate court for the variation or cancellation of the requirement.

Review of drug rehabilitation requirement

14–017 Where the responsible officer is of the opinion that a community order imposing a drug rehabilitation requirement which is subject to review should be so amended as to provide for each subsequent periodic review (required by CJA 2003, s.191) to be made without a hearing instead of at a review hearing, or vice versa, he must apply under para.17 to the court responsible for the order for the variation of the order. CJA 2003, s.179, Sch.8, para.19

Extension of unpaid work requirement

14–018 Where, in relation to any community order made by the Crown Court which does not include a direction that any failure to comply with any of the requirements of the order be dealt with by the magistrates' court, an unpaid work requirement is in force, and, on the application of the offender or the responsible officer it appears to the judge that it would be in the interests of justice to do so, having regard to circumstances which have arisen since the order was made, he may extend the period beyond the 12 months specified in CJA 2003, s.200(2). CJA 2003, s.179, Sch.8, paras 20, 24(1)

C. Powers following subsequent conviction

Process

14–019 Where a judge of the Crown Court proposes to exercise the above powers otherwise than on the offender's application: CJA 2003, s.179, Sch.8, para.25

(1) the offender must be summoned to appear, and
(2) if he does not appear in answer to the summons, a warrant may be issued for his arrest.

Revocation and fresh sentence

14–020 Where an offender in respect of whom a community order is in force is: CJA 2003, s.179, Sch.8, para.23

(1) convicted of an offence in the Crown Court, or
(2) brought or appears before the Crown Court having been committed by a magistrates' court for sentence, and

it appears to the judge that it would be in the interests of justice to exercise his powers under this provision, having regard to circumstances which have arisen since the community order was made, he may:

(a) revoke the order, or
(b) both:

(i) revoke the order, and
(ii) deal with the offender for the offence in respect of which the order was made, in any way in which the court which made the order could deal with him if he had just been convicted of that offence by or before the court which made the order,

taking into account under (b)(ii) the extent to which the offender has complied with the requirements of the community order.

Sentence on the breach

14–021 The fact that an offence committed during the currency of a relevant order is different in character from that or those for which the community order was passed, does not prevent the court revoking the order and dealing with the offender by imposing, for instance, a custodial sentence (*R. v Fleming* (1989) 11 Cr.App.R.(S.) 137).

There is no binding principle that it can never be right to impose a consecutive term for an offence committed before offences for which a community sentence was passed; it depends in each case on what the interests of justice require (*R. v Newton* [1999] 2 Cr.App.R.(S.) 172).

In an appropriate case, the sentence passed on a breach may be a substantial one (*R. v Barresi* [1981] Crim.L.R. 268) though some discount ought to be given for:

(1) any hours worked under an unpaid work requirement (*R. v Baines* (1983) 5 Cr.App.R.(S.) 264; *R. v Whittingham* (1986) 8 Cr.App.R.(S.) 116; *R. v Williams* (1986) 8 Cr.App.R.(S.) 230); and
(2) any time spent in custody for the offence before the community order was made (*R. v McDonald* (1988) 10 Cr.App.R.(S.) 458; *R. v Gyorgy* (1989) 11 Cr.App.R.(S.) 1; *R. v Needham* (1989) 11 Cr.App.R.(S.) 506; *R. v Mcintyre* (1985) 7 Cr.App.R.(S.) 196; *R. v Mackenzie* (1988) 10 Cr.App.R.(S.) 299; *R. v Wiltshire* (1992) 13 Cr.App.R.(S.) 642).

The fact that a community sentence was originally imposed does not mean that the offence was not one qualifying for a custodial sentence. If the commission of a further offence destroys any mitigation there may have been, a custodial sentence may be appropriate. An offender cannot tie the hands of the court by seeking to complete, e.g. the specified hours of unpaid work, once breach proceedings have begun (*R. v Tebbutt* (1989) 10 Cr.App.R.(S.) 88).

There is no obligation to take into account time spent in custody before the order was made (*R. v Broomfield* [2004] Crim.L.R. 672).

Offence committed prior to order

14–022 Where a person is sentenced in the Crown Court for an offence committed before a current community sentence was imposed, it is uncertain whether the Crown Court should revoke the earlier community sentence and re-sentence for the earlier offence (*R. v Neville* [1993]14 Cr.App.R.(S.) 765; *R. v Cawley*

(1993) 15 Cr.App.R.(S.) 209; *R. v Kenny* [1996] 1 Cr.App. R.(S.) 397; *R. v Saphier & and Pearsal* [1997] 1 Cr.App.R.(S.) 235; *R. v Day* [1997] 2 Cr.App.R.(S.) 328; *R. v Newton* [1993] 2 Cr.App.R.(S.) 172; *R. v Reid* [1998] 2 Cr.App.R.(S.) 40; *R. v Brighton* [1999] 2 Cr.App.R.(S.) 196).

Magistrates' courts orders

14–023 Different divisions of CACD have had difficulty in interpreting the provisions of the former legislation (CJA 1991, Sch.2, para.8(2)(b)), in relation to the sentencing powers of the Crown Court where a judge revokes a community order made by a magistrates' court:

(1) in *R. v Mackness & Wilson* (1994) 16 Cr.App.R.(S.) 549 and in *R. v Doyle* [1996] 1 Cr.App.R.(S.) 239 it was held that the judge's powers on indictment applied;
(2) in *R. v Kosser & Armstrong* (1994) 16 Cr.App.R.(S.) 737 and in *R. v Hewitt* [1996] 2 Cr.App.R.(S.) 14 it was held that the judge was restricted to magistrates' sentencing powers;
(3) in *R. v Ogden* [1996] 2 Cr.App.R.(S.) 387, CACD followed (2).

1. Administrative Provisions

14–024 On the making of an order revoking or amending a community order, the Crown Court officer must CJA 2003, s.179, Sch.8, para.27

(1) provide copies of the revoking or amending order to the offender and the responsible officer
(2) in the case of an amending order which substitutes a new local justice area, provide a copy of the amending order to:
    (a) the local probation board acting for that area, and
    (b) the magistrates' court acting for that area, and
(3) in the case of an amending order which imposes or amends a requirement specified in the first column of CJA 2003, Sch.14, provide a copy of so much of the amending order as relates to that requirement to the person specified in relation to it in the second column of that Schedule.
(4) where under sub-para.(1)(b) the proper officer of the court provides a copy of an amending order to a magistrates'

court acting for a different area, he must also provide to that court such documents and information relating to the case as he considers likely to be of assistance to a court acting for that area in the exercise of its functions in relation to the order.

D. Youth Community Orders

General

14–025 While orders of this nature are generally more appropriately made by the youth court and such offenders may be remitted to such a court for sentence under the duty imposed by PCC(S)A 2000, s.8 (see 19 CHILDREN AND YOUNG PERSONS), this provision will often be inappropriate, and the orders are dealt with below.

PCC(S)A 2000, s.33; CJA 2003, s.304, Sch.32, Para.95; SI 2005/950

A youth community order means any of the following;

(1) a curfew order;
(2) an exclusion order;
(3) an attendance centre order;
(4) a supervision order; and
(5) an action plan order;
(6) a community rehabilitation order;
(7) a community punishment order;
(8) a community punishment and rehabilitation order;
(9) a drug treatment and testing order (ages 16 or 17);

A "community sentence" means a sentence which includes a community order under CJA 2003, s.60 or one or more youth community orders.

Electronic monitoring

14–026 Where the judge is informed that monitoring arrangements are available, and that provision can be made under those arrangements, a community order may include requirements for securing the electronic monitoring of the offender's compliance with the order. However, where there is a person other than the offender without whose cooperation the order will not be practicable, the order must not be made without that person's consent. Further, a requirement must *not* be included where one is already included, and the order must make an appropriate person responsible for monitoring the requirement.

PCC(S)A 2000, s.36B; CJCSA 2000, s.52; CJA 2003, s.304, Sch.32, para.96

1. Curfew and exclusion orders

(1) breach of requirement

Issue of summons or warrant

14–027 If at any time while an order is in force in respect of an offender it appears on information to a magistrate acting for the local justice area concerned that the offender has failed to comply with any of the requirements of the order, he may issue a summons requiring the offender to appear or if the information is in writing and on oath, issue a warrant for his arrest. If the relevant order was made by the Crown Court and included a direction that any failure to comply with any of the requirements of the order be dealt with by the Crown Court, the summons will direct appearance before the Crown Court. PCC(S)A 2000, Sch.3; CJA 2003, s.304, Sch.32, para.12

Where:

(1) the summons requires an offender to appear before the Crown Court and the offender does not appear in answer to it, the Crown Court may issue a further summons requiring the offender to appear at the place and time specified in it;
(2) the original summons or a further summons issued by the Crown Court requires the offender to appear before the Crown Court and he does not appear, a warrant may be issued for his arrest.

Powers of Crown Court

14–028 Where the offender is brought or appears before the Crown Court and it is proved to the judge's satisfaction that he has failed without reasonable excuse to comply with any of the requirements of the relevant order, the judge may deal with him in respect of the failure in one of the following ways (and must deal with him in one of those ways if the relevant order is in force): PCC(S)A 2000, SCh.3, para.5; CJA 2003, s.304, Sch.32, Pt I, para.125

(1) by making a curfew order in respect of him (subject to Sch.3, para.7 below);
(2) by making an attendance centre order in respect of him (subject to para.8 below); or
(3) by dealing with him for the offence in respect of which the order was made in any way in which he could have been dealt with for that offence by the court which made the order if the order had not been made.

Where the judge deals with the offender under (3) he must revoke the relevant order if it is still in force.

In dealing with the offender the judge:

(a) *must* take into account the extent to which the offender has complied with the requirements of the relevant order; and

(b) *may*, in the case of an offender who has wilfully and persistently failed to comply with those requirements, impose a custodial sentence (where the relevant order was made in respect of an offence punishable with such a sentence) notwithstanding the restrictions imposed by CJA 2003, s.152(2) (see 29 DEALING WITH AN OFFENDER).

Any question whether the offender has failed to comply with the requirements of the relevant order are to be determined by the judge not by the verdict of a jury.

Exclusions from paragraphs 4 and 5

14–029 Without prejudice to any power to revoke the order (Sch.3, paras 10 and 11 below), an offender convicted of a further offence while a relevant order is in force in respect of him must not on that account, be dealt with under para.4 or 5 of Sch.3 (above) in respect of a failure to comply with any requirement of the order. PCC(S)A 2000, Sch.3, para.6; CJA 2003, s.304, Sch.32, Pt I, para.125

Curfew orders; attendance centre order

14–030 Where the judge has power to deal with an offender under these provisions for failure to comply with any of the requirements of a relevant order, he may make a curfew order under PCC(S)A 2000, s.37 modified by Sch.3, para.7. PCC(S)A 2000, Sch.3, paras 7, 8; CJA 2003, Sch.32, Pt I, para.125

He may also make an attendance centre order under PCC(S)A 2000, s.60(1), again subject to certain modifications (stated in Sch.3, para.8).

Continuance of order

14–031 The exercise of the powers in paras 4(2)(a) and 5(2)(a) above is without prejudice to the continuance of the relevant order.

(2) Revocation of order

Revocation of order on conviction, etc.

14–032 Where: PCC(S)A 2000, Sch.3, para.11; CJA 2003, s.304, Sch.32, Pt I, para.125

(1) a relevant order made by the Crown Court is in force in respect of an offender and he or the responsible officer applies to the Crown Court for the order to be revoked or for the offender to be dealt with in some other way for the offence in respect of which the order was made; or

(2) an offender in respect of whom a relevant order is in force is convicted of an offence before the Crown Court or, having been committed by a magistrates' court to the Crown Court for sentence, is brought or appears before the Crown Court,

then, if it appears to the judge to be in the interests of justice to do so, having regard to circumstances which have arisen since the order was made, he may;

(a) revoke the order; or
(b) both revoke the order and deal with the offender for the offence in respect of which the order was made, in any way in which he could have been dealt with for that offence by the court which made the order if the order had not been made,

taking into account under (b) the extent to which the offender has complied with the requirements of the relevant order.

Revocation following custodial sentence by magistrates' court

14–033 Where:

(1) an offender in respect of whom a relevant order is in force is convicted of an offence by a magistrates' court unconnected with the order, and; PCC(S)A 2000, Sch.3, paras 12, 13; CJA 2003, s.304, Sch.32, Pt I, para.125
(2) being an order made by the Crown Court, the magistrates commit the offender in custody or release him on bail until he can be brought or appear before the Crown Court,

and it appears to the judge to be in the interests of justice to do so, having regard to circumstances which have arisen since the relevant order was made, he may revoke the order.

(3) Amendment of order

14–034 The amendment of such orders is a function of the relevant magistrates' court (PCC(S)A 2000, Sch.3, paras 15–19 as substituted by CJA 2003, s.304, Sch.32, Pt 1, para.125).

2. Attendance centre orders

Variation and discharge; dealing with the offender

14–035 Variation and discharge of attendance centre orders is dealt with under PCC(S)A 2000, Sch.5 as amended by CJA

2003, ss.203, 304, Sch.32, para.126.

Applications to vary an order are made to a magistrates' court acting for the local justice area in which the centre is situated. An order may be discharged by application either to the court which made it, or to a magistrates' court acting for the local justice area in which the centre is situated, on behalf of the offender or of the officer in charge of the centre, unless the original order was made by the Crown Court which reserved to itself the power of discharge.

The power to discharge an order includes the power to deal with the offender for the offence for which the order was made, in any manner in which he could have been dealt with for that offence by the court which made the order, if the order had not been made.

The Crown Court officer will send or deliver a copy of the order to the offender and to the officer in charge of the centre.

Breach of the order: PCC(S)A 2000, Sch.5

14–036 If it is proved to the satisfaction of the Crown Court that an offender has:

(1) failed to attend under the order; or
(2) committed a breach of the rules of the centre which cannot be adequately dealt with under those rules;

the offender may be dealt with in any manner in which the Crown Court could have dealt with him if it had not made the order.

In the case of an offender who has wilfully and persistently failed to comply with the requirements, the Court may impose a custodial sentence, notwithstanding the restrictions imposed by CJA 2003, s.152(2) (see 29 DEALING WITH AN OFFENDER).

Where a judge deals with an offender under the above provision he must revoke the attendance centre order.

Questions as to whether the offender is in breach of the order are for the judge, not a jury, to determine.

3. Supervision orders

General

14–037 If, while a supervision order made by the Crown Court is in force in respect of an offender it is proved to the satisfaction of the magistrates' court that the offender has failed to comply with any requirement included in the order, it may commit him to the Crown Court in custody or on bail, PCC(S)A 2000, Sch.7, paras 1, 2

certifying the particulars of the offender's failure, and such other particulars of the case as may be.

Where the offender is brought before the Crown Court and the judge is satisfied that he has failed to comply with the requirement in question, he may deal with him for the offence in respect of which the supervision order was made, in any way in which he could have dealt with him for that offence if the order had not been made, taking into account the extent to which he has complied with the requirements of the order. He must revoke the supervision order if it is still in force.

A curfew order or an attendance centre order may be made on a breach, subject to the modifications made by paras 3 and 4 above.

Amendment and revocation

14–038 Amendment and revocation of supervision orders is a matter for the appropriate magistrates' court (paras 5–8).

4. Action plan orders

General

14–039 Similar provisions apply to the breach, etc. of action plan orders under PCC(S)A 2000, Sch.8 as amended by CJA 2003, s.304, Sch.32, Pt 1, para.129, as apply to supervision orders under Sch.7.

If, while a supervision order made by the Crown Court is in force in respect of an offender it is proved to the satisfaction of the magistrates' court that the offender has failed to comply with any requirement included in the order, it may commit him to the Crown Court in custody or on bail, certifying the particulars of the offender's failure, and such other particulars of the case as may be. PCC(S)A 2000, Sch.8, Para 1, 2.

Where the offender is brought before the Crown Court and the judge is satisfied that he has failed to comply with the requirement in question, he may deal with him for the offence in respect of which the supervision order was made, in any way in which he could have dealt with him for that offence if the order had not been made, taking into account the extent to which he has complied with the requirements of the order. He must revoke the supervision order if it is still in force.

A curfew order or an attendance centre order may be made on a breach, subject to the modifications made by PCC(S)A 2000, Sch.8, paras 2(3) and 2(4). (*Ibid.* Sch.8, para.2(5).)

Amendment and revocation

14–040 Amendment and revocation of supervision orders is a matter for the magistrates' court (paras 5–7).

E. "Custody plus" orders and "intermittent custody orders"

General

14–041 The "appropriate court" for dealing with the revocation and amendment of these orders (see 40 IMPRISONMENT) is the Crown Court where a judge of that court made the order, and in any other case, a magistrates' court acting for the local justice area for time being specified in the order. CJA 2003, s.187, Sch.10, Paras 1, 2

Where an order was made on appeal to CACD, it is to be taken to have been made by the Crown Court.

Revocation or removal

14–042 Where at any time while a "custody plus order" or an "intermittent custody order" is in force, it appears to a judge of the Crown Court, being the appropriate court (see above), on the application of the offender or the responsible officer that, having regard to circumstances which have arisen since the order was made, it would be in the interests of justice to do so, he may: CJA 2003, s.187, Sch.10, para.3

(1) in the case of a "custody plus order", revoke the order, and
(2) in the case of an "intermittent custody order", amend the order so that it contains only a provision specifying periods for the purposes of s.183(1)(b)(i), during which the offender is to be released.

Revocation of a custody plus order does not affect the sentence of imprisonment to which the order relates, except in relation to the conditions of the licence.

Change of residence

14–043 Where, at any time during the term of imprisonment to which a "custody plus order" or an "intermittent custody order" relates, a judge of the Crown Court, being the appropriate court (see above), is satisfied that the offender proposes to change, or has changed, his residence during the licence period from that local justice area to another such area, he may, and on the application of the responsible officer must, amend the order by substituting the other local justice area for the area specified in the order, unless: CJA 2003, s.187, Sch.10, para.4

(1) the order contains requirements which, in his opinion, cannot be complied with unless the offender resides in the petty sessions area concerned unless, in accordance with para.5, he either;

(a) cancels those requirements, or
(b) substitutes for those requirements other requirements which can be complied with if the offender does not reside in that area; or

(2) the order imposes a programme requirement, unless the accredited programme specified is available in the other local justice area.

Amendment of requirements

14–044 At any time during the term of imprisonment to which an order relates, a judge of the Crown Court, being the appropriate court (see above) may, on the application of the offender or the responsible officer, by order amend any requirement of a "custody plus order" or an "intermittent custody order": CJA 2003, s.187, Sch.10, para.5

(1) by cancelling the requirement, or
(2) by replacing it with a requirement of the same kind (i.e. falling within the same paragraph of s.182(1)) imposing different obligations, which he could include if he were then making the order.

Alteration of pattern of temporary release

14–045 At any time during the term of imprisonment to which an "intermittent custody order" relates, a judge of the Crown Court, being the appropriate court, see above, may, on the application of the offender or the responsible officer, amend the order so as to: CJA 2003, s.187, Sch.10, para.6

(1) specify different periods for the purposes of s.183(1)(b)(i); or
(2) provide that he is to remain in prison until the number of days served by him in prison is equal to the number of custodial days

provided he has received from the Secretary of State that suitable prison accommodation is available for the offender during the periods which, under the order as amended, will be custodial periods.

Supplementary

14–046 Note that;

(1) none of the above applications may be made while an appeal against the sentence of which the custody plus or intermittent custody order forms part is pending. CJA 2003, s.187, Sch.10, paras 7, 8, 9

(2) subject to sub-para.(2), where a court proposes to exercise its powers under para.5 or 6, otherwise than on the application of the offender, the court:

  (a) must summon him to appear before the court, and
  (b) if he does not appear in answer to the summons, may issue a warrant for his arrest.

(3) on the making of an order revoking or amending a custody plus order or amending an intermittent custody order, the Crown Court officer must:

  (a) provide copies of the revoking or amending order to the offender and the responsible officer,
  (b) in the case of an amending order which substitutes a new local justice area, provide a copy of the amending order to the local probation board acting for that area, and the magistrates' court acting for that area,
  (c) in the case of an order which cancels or amends a requirement specified in the first column of Sch.14, the court provide a copy of so much of the amending order as relates to that requirement to the person specified in relation to that requirement in the second column of that Schedule.

Where the proper officer of the court provides a copy of an amending order to a magistrates' court acting for a different area, the officer must also provide to that court such documents and information relating to the case as it considers likely to be of assistance to a court acting for that area in the exercise of its functions in relation to the order.

Transfer of order to Scotland and Northern Ireland

14–047 The transfer of "custody plus orders" and "intermittent custody orders" to Scotland and Northern Ireland is governed by the provisions of CJA 2003, s.188 and Sch.11.

F. Suspended sentence order
(The provisions apply to sentences suspended by the Crown Court in respect of offences committed on or after April 4, 2005)

1. Procedure

Issue of summons or warrant by Crown Court

14–048 If at any time while a suspended sentence order made by the Crown Court (save one where a direction was included that failure to comply with the community requirements of it be dealt with by a magistrates' court) is in force in respect of an offender it appears on information that the offender has failed to comply with any of the community requirements of the order, the Crown Court may; CJA 2003, s.193, Sch.12, para.7(2)

(1) issue a summons requiring the offender to appear at the place and time specified in it, or
(2) if the information is in writing and on oath, issue a warrant for his arrest.

Where the summons requires the offender to appear before the Crown Court and the offender does not appear in answer to it, a judge may issue a warrant for his arrest.

Powers on breach of community requirement or conviction of further offence

14–049 Where

(1) it is proved to the judge's satisfaction that the offender has failed without reasonable excuse to comply with any of the community requirements of the suspended sentence order, or CJA 2003, s.193, Sch.12, para.8
(2) the offender is convicted of an offence committed during the operational period of a suspended sentence (other than one which has already taken effect) and either:
   (a) he is so convicted by or before a court having power under para.11 to deal with him in respect of the suspended sentence, or
   (b) he subsequently appears or is brought before such a court,

the judge must consider his case and deal with him in one of the following ways, that is to say he may:

(i) order that the suspended sentence is to take effect with its original term and custodial period unaltered,

(ii) order that the sentence is to take effect with either or both of the following modification, that is to say:

- the substitution for the original operational term of a lesser term complying with CJA 2003, s.181(2) (see 40 IMPRISONMENT); and
- the substitution for the original custodial period of a lesser custodial period complying with s.181(5) and (6);

(iii) amend the order by doing any one or more of the following:

- imposing more onerous community requirements which he would have had power to include if he were then making the order,
- subject to s.189(3) and (4) (i.e. not less than six months, nor more than two years) extending the supervision period, or
- subject to s.189(3) above, extending the operational period.

The judge *must* make an order under (1) or (2) unless he is of the opinion that it would be unjust to do so in view of all the circumstances, including those stated below in (i) and (ii) and where it is of that opinion the court must state its reasons.

The matters referred to in the preceding paragraph are;

(i) the extent to which the offender has complied with the community requirements of the suspended sentence order, and

(ii) in a case falling within sub-para.(2) above, the facts of the subsequent offence.

Where the judge deals with an offender in respect of a suspended sentence, the appropriate officer of the court must notify the appropriate officer of the court which passed the sentence of the method adopted.

The appropriate officer will notify the appropriate officer of the court which passed the sentence of the method adopted.

Approach to breach

14–050 The judge has several options, including extending the operational period of the sentence:

(1) the presumption (which also applies where breach is by virtue of the commission of a further offence) is that the

suspended prison sentence will be activated (either with its original custodial term or a lesser term), unless the judge takes the view that this would, in all the circumstances, be unjust; in reaching that decision, he may take into account both the extent to which the offender has complied with the requirements and the fact of any new offence;

(2) if he considers that the sentence needs to be activated, he may activate it in full or with a reduced term; again, the extent to which the requirements have been complied with will be relevant;

(3) if, instead of activating the suspended term, he amends the order, he must either:

   (a) make the requirements more onerous; or
   (b) extend the supervision or operational periods (provided these remain within the limits defined by s.189(3) and (4) of the Act).

(SGC 2, 3.2.15–17).

The judge must state his reasons for not activating the suspended sentence, which might include the extent to which the offender has complied with requirements, or the facts of the subsequent offence.

14–051 The guidelines make four further points (SGC 2, 3.2.18–21):

(1) if the offender near the end of the operational period, has complied with the requirements imposed, but commits another offence, it may be more appropriate to amend the order rather than activate the sentence;

(2) if the new offence is of a less serious nature than the offence for which the suspended sentence was passed, it may justify activating the sentence with a reduced term, or amending the terms of the order;

(3) it is expected that the activated suspended term will be consecutive to any sentence imposed for the new offence;

(4) if the new offence is non-imprisonable, the judge ought to consider whether it is appropriate to activate the suspended sentence at all.

Where the judge decides to amend the original rather than activate the custodial sentence, he should give serious consideration to extending the supervision or operational periods, within the statutory limits, rather than making the requirements more onerous (SGC 2, 3.2.21).

Further provisions as to order that suspended sentence is to take effect

14–052 When making an order under para.8(2)(a) or (b) above, that a sentence is to take effect (with or without any variation of the original term and custodial period), the judge: CJA 2003, s.193. Sch.12, para.9

(1) must also make a "custody plus order", and
(2) may order that the sentence is to take effect immediately or that the term of that sentence is to commence on the expiry of another term of imprisonment passed on the offender by him or by another court,

subject, in the case of (2) to CJA 2003, s.265 (restriction on consecutive sentences for released prisoners, for which see 40 IMPRISONMENT).

In proceedings for dealing with an offender in respect of a suspended sentence which take place before the Crown Court, any question whether the offender has been convicted of an offence committed during the operational period of the suspended sentence is to be determined by the judge and not by the verdict of a jury.

For the purpose of any enactment conferring rights of appeal in criminal cases, an order made under para.8(2)(a) or (b) is to be treated as a "sentence" passed on the offender by that court for the offence for which the suspended sentence was passed.

Restrictions where treatment required

14–053 An offender who is required by any of the following community requirements of a suspended sentence order: CJA 2003, s.193, Sch.12, para.10

(1) a mental health treatment requirement,
(2) a drug rehabilitation requirement, or
(3) an alcohol treatment requirement,

to submit to treatment for his mental condition, or his dependency on or propensity to misuse drugs or alcohol, is not to be treated for the purposes of para.8(1)(a) as having failed to comply with that requirement on the ground only that he had refused to undergo any surgical, electrical or other treatment if, in the opinion of the court, his refusal was reasonable having regard to all the circumstances.

A judge may not, under para.8(2)(c)(i) amend the requirements (1)–(3) above unless the offender consents to the amended requirement.

Court by which suspended sentence may be dealt with under para.8(1)(b)

14–054 An offender may be dealt with under para.8(1)(b) in respect of a suspended sentence by the Crown Court or, where the sentence was passed by a magistrates' court, by any magistrates' court before which he appears or is brought. CJA 2003, s.193, Sch.12, para.11

Where an offender is convicted by a magistrates' court of any offence and the court is satisfied that the offence was committed during the operational period of a suspended sentence passed by the Crown Court:

(1) the court may, if it thinks fit, commit to the Crown Court, and
(2) if it does not, must give written notice of the conviction to the Crown Court officer.

For the purposes of this paragraph and of para.11, a suspended sentence passed on an offender on appeal is to be treated as having been passed by the court by which he was originally sentenced.

Conviction of further offence; judge not dealing with suspended sentence

14–055 If it appears to the judge where the Crown Court has jurisdiction in accordance with sub-para.(2), (above), or to a magistrate having jurisdiction in accordance with that subparagraph that: CCJA 2003, s.193, Sch.12, para.12

(1) an offender has been convicted in the United Kingdom of an offence committed during the operational period of a suspended sentence, and
(2) that he has not been dealt with in respect of the suspended sentence,

that court or magistrate may, subject to the following provisions of this paragraph, issue a summons requiring the offender to appear at the place and time specified in it, or a warrant for his arrest.

Jurisdiction for the purposes of sub-para.(1) may be exercised:

(a) if the suspended sentence was passed by the Crown Court, by a judge of that court;
(b) if it was passed by a magistrates' court, by a magistrate acting for the area for which that court acted.

Where:

(i) an offender is convicted in Scotland or Northern Ireland of an offence, and

(ii) the judge is informed that the offence was committed during the operational period of a suspended sentence passed in England or Wales,

that court must give written notice of the conviction to the appropriate officer of the court by which the suspended sentence was passed.

Amendment of suspended sentence order

Cancellation of community requirements

14–056 Where at any time while a suspended sentence order is in force, it appears to the Crown Court that: CJA 2003, s.193, Sch.12, para.13

(1) in the case of an order which is subject to review, the Crown Court is responsible for the order, or
(2) the order was made by the Crown Court,

then, on the application of the offender or the responsible officer that, having regard to the circumstancess which have arisen since the order was made, it would be in the interests of justice to do so, a judge may cancel the community requirements of the suspended sentence order.

The circumstances in which he may exercise this power in these circumstances include the offender's making good progress or his responding satisfactorily to supervision.

No application may be made by the offender while an appeal against the suspended sentence is pending.

Change of residence

14–057 Where, at any time while a suspended sentence is in force, the Crown Court, as the appropriate court, (see 14–014, above), is satisfied that the offender proposes to change, or has changed, his residence from the local justice area concerned to another, a judge may, and on the application of the responsible officer must, amend the suspended sentence order by substituting the other local justice area for the area specified in the order, unless: CJA 2003, s.193, Sch.12, para.14

(1) the suspended sentence order contains requirements which, in his opinion, cannot be complied with unless the offender resides in the local justice area concerned unless, in accordance with para.15 below, he either cancels those requirements, or substitutes for them other requirements which can be complied with if the offender does not reside in that area; or

Breach, Amendment and Revocation

(2) where the order imposes a programme requirement, unless it appears to him that the accredited programme specified in the requirement is available in the other local justice area.

Amendment of community requirements

14–058 At any time during the supervision period, a judge of the Crown Court, as the appropriate court (see 14–015, above) may, on the application of the offender or the responsible officer, by order amend any community requirement of a suspended sentence order, by cancelling it, or by replacing it with a requirement of the same kind, which he could include if he were then making the order, but: CJA 2003, s.193, Sch.12, para.15

(1) he may not under this paragraph amend a mental health treatment requirement, a drug rehabilitation requirement or an alcohol treatment requirement unless the offender consents to the amended requirement; and
(2) if the offender fails to consent to comply any of the proposed amended requirements, specified in (1) above, the judge may:
   (a) revoke the suspended order and the suspended sentence to which it relates, and
   (b) deal with him, for the offence in respect of which the suspended sentence was imposed, in any way in which it could deal with him if he had just been convicted by or before the court of the offence.

In dealing with the offender under (b), the judge must take into account the extent to which the offender has complied with the requirements of the order.

Note that:

(i) a requirement is of the same kind as another if they fall within the same paragraph of CJA 2003, s.190(1), (setting out the requirements which may be imposed (see 40 IMPRISONMENT);
(ii) an electronic monitoring requirement is a requirement of the same kind as any requirement falling within s.190(1) to which it relates.

Amendment of treatment requirements on practitioner's report

14–059 Where the medical practitioner or other person by whom, or under whose direction, an offender is, in pursuance of CJA 2003, s.193, Sch.12, para.16

any requirement, being treated for his mental condition or his dependency on or propensity to misuse drugs or alcohol:

(1) is of opinion that:

  (a) the treatment of the offender should be continued beyond the period specified in that behalf in the order,
  (b) the offender needs different treatment,
  (c) the offender is not susceptible to treatment, or
  (d) the offender does not require further treatment, or

(2) is for any reason unwilling to continue to treat or direct the treatment of the offender, he must make a report in writing to that effect to the responsible officer and that officer must apply under Sch.12 para.15 above, to the appropriate court for the variation or cancellation of the requirement.

Review of drug rehabilitation requirement

14–060 Where the responsible officer is of the opinion that a suspended sentence order imposing a drug rehabilitation requirement which is subject to review should be amended as to provide or each periodic review (required by CJA 2003, s.191) to be made without a hearing instead of at a review hearing, or vice versa, he must apply under Sch.12 para.18 below to the court responsible for the order for a variation of the order. CJA 2003, s.193, Sch.12, para.17

Appeal pending

14–061 No application may be made under Sch.8 paras 12, 14 or 17, and no order may be made under *ibid* para.13, while an appeal against the suspended sentence is pending. CJA 2003, s.193, Sch.12, para.19(1)

Process

14–062 Where a judge of the Crown Court proposes to exercise his powers under para.14, otherwise than on the application of the offender, and apart from an order cancelling a community requirement, the offender must be summoned to appear, and if he does not appear in answer to the summons, a warrant may be issued for his arrest. CJA 2003, s.193, Sch.12, para.20

Administrative matters

14–063 On the making of an order amending a suspended sentence order, the Crown Court officer must provide: CJA 2003, s.193, Sch.12, para.22

(1) copies of the amending order to the offender and the responsible officer,

(2) in the case of an amending order which substitutes a new local justice area, a copy of the amending order to:

(a) the local probation board acting for that area, and
(b) the magistrates' court acting for that area, and

in the case of an amending order which imposes or amends a requirement specified in the first column of Sch.14, provide a copy of so much of the amending order as relates to that requirement to the person specified in relation to that requirement in the second column of that Schedule.

Where under (l)(b) above, the proper officer provides a copy of an amending order to a magistrates' court acting for a different area, he must also provide to that court such documents and information relating to the case as he considers likely to be of assistance to a court acting for that area in the exercise of its functions in relation to the order.

G. Sexual offences prevention order under SOA 2003, s.104

14–064 In relation to a sexual offences prevention order (see 56 SEX OFFENDER ORDERS) made by the Crown Court or CACD the offender, the chief officer of police for the area in which he resides, or a chief officer of police who believes that the offender is in, or is intending to come to his police area, may apply to the Crown Court for an order varying, renewing or discharging the order. SOA 2003, s.108(1)–(3), (7) (8)

Subject to subss (5) and (6), on application, the judge, after hearing the applicant and (if they wish to be heard), the other persons mentioned above, may make any order, varying, renewing or discharging the order, that he considers appropriate. SOA 2003, s.108(4)(5)

An order may be renewed, or varied, by imposing additional prohibitions on the accused, only if it is necessary to do so for the purpose of protecting the public, or any particular members of the public, from serious sexual harm from him, and any renewed or varied order may contain only such prohibitions as are necessary for this purpose. SOA 2003, s.108(5)

The judge must not discharge an order before the end of five years beginning with the day on which it was made, without the consent of the accused and: SOA 2003, s.108(6)

(a) where the application is made by a chief officer of police, that chief officer, or
(b) in any other case, the chief officer of police for the area in which the accused resides.

H. Anti-social behaviour order

14–065 An offender subject to an anti-social behaviour order made in the Crown Court may apply to the court which made it for it to be varied or discharged, but not before the end of the period of two years beginning with the date on which the order took effect. CDA 1998, s.1C(6),(8)

15 CASES COMMITTED, TRANSFERRED, SENT, FOR TRIAL

A. Present (pre-CJA 2003) position

General

15–001 Until CJA 2003, Sch.3 comes into force in the autumn of 2007, cases are moved from the magistrates' courts to the Crown Court for trial in four ways, namely in the case of:

(1) offences triable either way, by committal proceedings under MCA 1980, s.6;
(2) certain offences involving children, by notice of transfer under CJA 1991, s.53, Sch.3;
(3) serious fraud cases, by notice of transfer under CJA 1987, s.4;
(4) indictable-only offences, under the provisions of CDA 1998, ss.51 *et seq.*

A judge of the Crown Court may be required to deal with applications for dismissal in cases arising under (2)–(4) above.

As to the effect of CJA 2003, Sch.3, see 15–034–15–049, below.

(1) Committal for trial; summary offences (s.41)

15–002 Where a magistrates' court commits a person to the Crown Court for trial for an offence triable either way, or a number of such offences, it may also commit to the Crown Court for trial proceedings against that person for any summary offence with which he is also charged, and which:

CJA 1988, s.41(1)(3); DVA 2004, Sch.10, para.28

(1) is punishable with imprisonment or carries obligatory or discretionary RT disqualification; and
(2) arises out of circumstances that appear to be the same as, or connected with, those giving rise to the either-way offence(s);

whether or not evidence relating to the summary offence(s) appears on the papers. (In the magistrates' court the information charging the summary offence(s) will be treated as if it had been adjourned under MCA 1980, s.10 *sine die*.

Committal for trial cannot be challenged in the Crown Court, but *certiorari* will lie in an appropriate case (see *R. v Miall* [1992] Q.B. 836).

Notice under section 41

15–003 The magistrates' court will give notice both to the accused and to the Crown Court stating which of the either-way offences appears to arise out of circumstances which are the same as, or connected with, those giving rise to the summary offence(s). CJA 1988, s.41(2)

Crown Court procedure

15–004 Liability to be dealt with for a s.41 offence does not arise unless the accused is convicted of the either-way offence. If he is not convicted, or the Crown offers no evidence on the either-way offence, he cannot be required to answer the summary offence(s). CJA 1988, s.41(2)

A s.41 offence is not put to the accused unless he is convicted on the indictment of the either-way offence.

If he is convicted:

(1) the judge considers whether the preconditions for committal of the summary offence(s) are made out;
(2) if the judge is satisfied as to (1), the substance of the summary offence(s) is put to the accused and he is called upon to plead;
(3) if the accused pleads guilty to the summary offence(s) he may be dealt with in any manner in which the magistrates could have dealt with him for the offence(s) (see *R. v Avbunudje* [1999] 2 Cr.App.R.(S.) 189);
(4) if the accused does not plead guilty to the summary offence(s), any powers of the Crown Court to deal with the accused in respect of the summary offence(s) cease; and
(5) if the Crown indicates that it does not wish to submit evidence on a summary offence the judge will dismiss it.

The magistrates' court will be informed of the outcome of the proceedings (CJA 1988, s.41(10)).

(2) Notice of transfer procedure

Effect of notice

15–005 The effect of a notice of transfer, whether given under CJA 1991, s.53 or under CJA 1987, s.4 is to: CJA 1987, s.5(6), (7); CJA

(1) deprive the magistrates' court of its jurisdiction to conduct a preliminary enquiry into the facts of the case; 1988, s.144(1), (3); CJA 1991, Sch.5, paras 2(5), (6), (7)

(2) restrict the powers of the magistrates' court in dealing with applications for bail, public funding, enlargement of recognisances and the making of witness orders; and

(3) impose on the Crown Court the management of the case.

The notice will specify the proposed place of trial and the charge(s) to which it relates.

Remand, necessity for appearance

15–006 Matters of remand and bail are dealt with in the magistrates' court, but where a notice is given after the person to whom it relates has been remanded on bail to appear before a magistrates' court on an appointed day:

(1) the requirement that he appear ceases on the giving of the notice, unless the notice states that it shall continue;

(2) if the requirement ceases, it is his duty to appear before the Crown Court at the place specified in the notice as the proposed place of trial, or at any place substituted for it by a direction under SCA 1981, s.76 (see 7 ALLOCATION AND DEPLOYMENT OF CASES);

(3) if the notice states that the requirement is to continue, then where the person to whom the notice relates appears before the magistrates' court, that court may grant bail, and enlarge the recognisances of any surety, so that the surety is bound to secure the appearance of the person charged before the Crown Court.

An application for dismissal of the charge or charges is made to a judge of the Crown Court (see 15–019, 15–012, 15–017, below).

(a) Certain cases involving children

General

15–007 If a person has been charged with an offence to which CJA 1988, s.32(2) applies (sexual offences and offences involving violence or cruelty), and the DPP is of opinion that: CJA 1991, s.53(1)–(4), Sch.3, para.1

(1) the evidence of the offence would be sufficient for proceedings against a person charged to be transferred for trial;

(2) a child who is alleged:

 (a) to be the person against whom the offence was committed; or

(b) to have witnessed the commission of the offence, will be called as a witness at the trial; and

(3) for the purpose of avoiding any prejudice to the welfare of the child the case should be taken over and proceeded with without delay by the Crown Court;

notice of transfer certifying that opinion, and specifying the charge or charges to which it relates, and any other requisite information, may be served by or on behalf of the DPP on the magistrates' court in whose jurisdiction the offence has been charged.

This must happen not later than the time at which the DPP would be required to serve a notice of the prosecution's case under MCA 1980, s.5, and the functions of the magistrates' court cease except for the making of ancillary orders. The decision is not subject to appeal.

Definition of "child"

15–008 For the purposes of s.53, "child" means, in the case of an offence falling within: CJA 1991, s.53(6)(7)

(1) CJA 1988, s.32(2)(a) or (b), under 14 years of age, or if he was under that age when a video recording (under s.32A(2) of that Act) was made in respect of him, under 15;
(2) CJA 1988, s.32(2)(c), under 17, or if under that age when the recording was made, under 18.

References to such offences include offences of attempting or conspiring to commit them, or aiding, abetting, etc. their commission.

In *R. v T & K* [2001] 1 Cr.App.R. 446, CACD stated that notices of transfer should not be given in the case of an accused under 18 unless the DPP concluded that the justices would be likely to commit on account of the seriousness of the charge (MCA 1980, s.24(1)) and that a statement to that effect should be included in the notice.

Application for dismissal

15–009 Where notice of transfer has been given, any person to whom it relates, may, at any time before he is arraigned (and whether or not an indictment has been preferred against him), apply, orally or in writing, to the Crown Court sitting at the place specified by the notice of transfer as the proposed place CJA 1991, Sch.6, paras 5(1)–(6)

of trial, for the charge, or any of the charges in the case, to be dismissed.

The judge must dismiss a charge, and accordingly quash a count relating to it in any indictment preferred against the applicant, if it appears to him that the evidence against the applicant would not be sufficient for a jury properly to convict him.

Dismissal of a charge against the applicant has the same effect as a refusal by examining justices to commit, save that *no* further proceedings may be brought on the dismissed charge except by means of the preferment of a voluntary bill of indictment.

Note that:

(1) an oral application for dismissal may not be made unless the applicant has given written notice of his intention to do so to the Crown Court at the place specified by the notice of transfer as the proposed place of trial; and
(2) oral evidence may be given on an application only with the leave of the judge or by his order, and the judge will give leave only if it appears to him, having regard to any matters stated in the application, that the interests of justice require him to do so. If he does give leave or make an order permitting or requiring a person to give oral evidence, and that person does not do so, the judge may disregard any document indicating the evidence that he might have given.

As to procedure, R.13, at 15–026 *et seq.*, below.

Reporting restrictions

15–010 Reporting restrictions similar to those imposed in the case of committal proceedings in magistrates' courts are imposed in relation to applications for dismissal of charges under s.5(3). CJA 1991, Sch.6, para.5(1)–(3)

It is unlawful to publish a report of proceedings which contains matter other than that permitted by para.6 unless on the order of the judge dealing with the case.

The matters permitted by para.6(8) are:

(1) the identity of the court and the name of the judge;
(2) the names, ages, home addresses and occupations of the accused and witnesses;
(3) the offence(s), or a summary of them, with which the accused is or are charged;
(4) the names of counsel and solicitors engaged in the proceedings;

(5) where the proceedings are adjourned, the date and place to which they are adjourned;
(6) any arrangements as to bail; and
(7) whether a representation order was granted to the accused.

Objection may be taken to the judge making an order "lifting" the restrictions. Where, in the case of two or more accused, one of them objects, the judge will make the order only if satisfied after hearing the representations of the accused, and in the light of international law and practice which has drawn attention to the need to protect the welfare and privacy of juveniles involved in criminal cases, that it is in the interests of justice to do so.

The power should be exercised with great care, caution and circumspection (*McKerry v Teesdale & Wear Valley JJ.* 164 J.P. 355, DC), and only where there is good reason for making an order, and in deciding whether there is good reason, the judge must give considerable weight to the offender's age (*R. v CCC Ex p. S* (1999) 163 J.P. 776).

(b) Serious fraud cases

Giving of notice

15–011 A notice of transfer may be given to a magistrates' court, other than in a case to which CDA 1998, s.48 applies, where: CJA 1987, s.4; CJPOA 1994, Sch.4, para.54, Sch.9, para.29; CDA 1998, s.119, Sch.8, para.65

(1) a person has been charged with an indictable offence;
(2) in the opinion of a "designated authority" or one of its officers the evidence of the offence would be sufficient for the person charged to be committed to the Crown Court; and
(3) it reveals a case of such seriousness or complexity, that it is appropriate that the management of the case be taken over by the Crown Court without delay.

A "designated authority" includes the DPP, the Director of the Serious Fraud Squad, the Director of Revenue and Customs Prosecutions and the Secretary of State. The decision to give notice of transfer is not subject to appeal, or liable to be questioned in any court (CJA 1987, s.4(3)).

The notice must be given not later than the time at which the authority would be required to serve a notice of the prosecution case under MCA 1980, s.5, and that court's functions then cease CJA 1987, s.4(1)(c); CJPOA 1994, Sch.4, para.64

in relation to the case except as provided by CJA 1987, ss.5(3), 5(7A) and (8), and by AJA 1999 (public funding).

The notice will specify:

(a) the proposed place of trial; and
(b) the charge(s) to which it relates.

CJA 1987, s.5(1)(2); CPIA 1996, s.45(1)–(3)

As to the places of trial for such offences, see 7 ALLOCATION AND DEPLOYMENT OF BUSINESS.

Dismissal of transferred charge(s)

15–012 Where notice of transfer has been given, any person to whom it relates, at any time before he is arraigned (and whether or not an indictment has been preferred against him), may apply, orally or in writing, to the Crown Court sitting at the place specified by the notice of transfer as the proposed place of trial, for the charge, or any of the charges in the case, to be dismissed. CJA 1987, s.6; CJA 1988, s.144(5)

The judge may dismiss a charge, and quash a count relating to it in any indictment preferred against the applicant, if it appears to him that the evidence against the applicant would not be sufficient for a jury properly to convict him.

As to procedure, see R.13, at 15–026 *et seq.*, below.

Dismissal of the charge(s) against the applicant has the same effect as a refusal by examining justices to commit, save that no further proceedings may be brought on a dismissed charge except by means of the preferment of a voluntary bill of indictment. CJA 1987, s.6; CJA 1988, s.144

Oral application

15–013 An oral application for dismissal may not be made unless the applicant has given written notice in the prescribed form to the Crown Court at the place specified by the notice of transfer as the proposed place of trial. CJA 1987, s.6(2); CJA 1988, s.144(5)

As to procedure, see R.13, at 15–026 *et seq.*, below.

Oral evidence

15–014 Oral evidence may be given on an application for dismissal only with the leave of the judge or by his order, and he will give leave or make an order only if it appears to him having regard to any matters stated in the application for leave, that the interests of justice require him to do so. CJA 1987, s.6(3), (4); CJA 1988, s.144(5)

If he does give leave, or make an order, permitting or requiring a person to give oral evidence and that person does not do so, the judge may disregard any document indicating the evidence that he might have given.

(3) Sending for trial CDA 1998, s.51

General

15–015 Where: CDA 1998, s.51(1)–(6), (12)

(1) a person aged 18 or over, appears or is brought before a magistrate's court, charged with an offence triable only on indictment, the court must send him immediately to the Crown Court for trial for:

(a) that offence; and
(b) any either-way or summary offence with which he is charged, and which appears to be related to the indictable-only offence, and in the case of a summary offence, is punishable with imprisonment or involves obligatory or discretionary RT disqualification;

(2) such a person, who has been sent for trial, is subsequently brought before a magistrates' court charged with an either-way or summary offence which fulfills those conditions, he may be sent forthwith to the Crown Court;
(3) another person aged 18 or over appears or is brought before the magistrates' court on the same occasion, charged jointly with him with an either-way offence, and that offence appears to be related to the indictable-only offence, that person may be sent to the Crown Court with him;
(4) the magistrates send a person aged 18 or over to the Crown Court in either of the above circumstances, they may send with him, any child or young person brought before them on the same occasion, charged jointly with the adult in the indictable-only offence and on any summary or either-way offence which fulfils the requisite conditions.

An either-way offence is "related to" an indictable-only offence if the charge for the either-way offence could be joined in the same indictment as the indictable-only offence. A summary offence is "related to" an indictable-only offence if it arises out of circumstances which are connected with those giving rise to the indictable-only offence.

As to where a Newton Hearing was held in the Magistrates' Court, see *R. v Warley MC Ex p. DPP* [1998] 2 Cr.App.R. 307.

Listing of first Crown Court appearance

15–016 A Crown Court officer to whom notice has been given under CDA 1998, s.51(7) will list the first appearance in the R.12.2

Crown Court of the person to whom the notice relates in accordance with any directions given by the magistrates' court.

Application for dismissal

15–017 A person sent for trial in such circumstances, on any charge or charges may, at any time: CDA 1998, s.52(6), Sch.3, para.2(1)(2)(3)

(1) after he has been served with copies of the documents containing the evidence on which the charge or charges are based; and
(2) before he is arraigned (and whether or not the indictment has been preferred against him),

apply orally, or in writing, to the Crown Court sitting at the place specified in the notice served upon him (under s.48(5)) for the charge, or any of the charges in the case to be dismissed.

No oral application may be made unless the applicant has given written notice to the court of his intention to make the application.

Note that:

(a) oral evidence may be given on the application only with the leave of the judge, or by his order. He will give leave, or make an order, only if it appears to him, having regard to any matters stated in the application for leave, that the interests of justice require him to do so. If he does give leave, or makes an order requiring a person to give evidence, and that person does not do so, the judge may disregard any document indicating the evidence he might have given; CDA 1998, s.52(6), Sch.3, para.2(4)(5)
(b) notice in writing of intention to apply orally or any written application must be served no later than 14 days after service of the documents containing the prosecution case and must also be served on the prosecution and any joint defendant. Application to extend this time limit may be made before or after it has expired in writing to the court, specifying the grounds. A copy must be sent to the prosecutor and any joint defendant. Any written application to dismiss must be accompanied by a copy of any statement or other document, and identify any article on which the applicant relies. A copy must be given to the prosecution and any joint defendant;
(c) any notice of application to dismiss must specify the charge or charges to which it relates and state whether the leave of the judge is sought to adduce oral evidence on the application, indicating what witnesses it is

proposed to call at the hearing. The prosecution may, within seven days of service by the defence of the appropriate notice, make similar applications to call oral evidence, or to have an oral hearing where a written application has been made.

The judge must dismiss a charge (and accordingly quash any count relating to it in any indictment preferred against the applicant), which is the subject of the application, if it appears to him that the evidence against the applicant would not be sufficient for a jury properly to convict him. CDA 1998, s.52(6), Sch.3, para.2(2)(6)

As to applications based on alleged defects in the s.51(7) notice, see *Bentham v Wandsworth Prisoner Governor* [2006] Crim.L.R. 855.

If the charge, or any of the charges, is dismissed, no further proceedings may be brought on it except by means of the preferment of a voluntary bill, and unless the applicant is in custody otherwise than on the dismissed charge, he must be discharged.

Reporting restrictions

15–018 Reporting restrictions similar to those imposed on committal proceedings are imposed in such a case. CDA 1998, s.52(6), Sch.3, para.3

Dealing with summary offences

15–019 Where the magistrates' court has sent a person for trial under s.42 for offences which include a summary offence, the procedure at the Crown Court is as follows: CDA 1998, s.52(6), Sch.3, para.6

(1) if that person is convicted on indictment, the judge will consider whether the summary offence is "related" (see above) to the offence or offences triable only on indictment;
(2) if he finds that it is, the substance of the offence will be put to the accused and he will be asked to plead it;
(3) if the accused pleads guilty, he will be convicted, the judge's powers of sentencing being limited to those of the magistrates' court;
(4) if the accused does not plead guilty, the Crown Court ceases to have powers in the matter, unless the prosecution inform the judge that they do not wish to offer any evidence on the charge, when he may dismiss it.

Summary offences under CJA 1988, s.40

15–020 If the summary offence is one to which s.40 applies, the Crown Court may exercise in relation to it, the powers conferred by that section, but where the accused is tried on indictment for such an offence, the functions of the court under this paragraph cease. CDA 1998, s.52(6), Sch.3, para.6(8)

No indictable only offence remaining

15–021 Where a person has been sent for trial in this manner, but has not been arraigned, and is charged on an indictment which, as a result of amendment, or a successful application to dismiss or for any other reason, no longer includes any offence triable on indictment-only, the court will proceed as follows: CDA 1998, s.52(6), Sch.3, paras 7, 8, 9

(1) each count of the indictment charging an offence triable either-way, will be read to the accused;
(2) he will be informed in ordinary language, that in relation to each of those offences he may indicate whether, if it were to proceed to trial, he would plead guilty or not guilty, and that if he pleads guilty he will be treated as if he had pleaded guilty on arraignment;
(3) he will then be asked whether, if the offence in question were to proceed to trial, he would plead guilty or not guilty;
(4) if he indicates that he would plead guilty, the court will proceed as if had been arraigned on the count in question and had pleaded guilty;
(5) if he indicates that he would plead not guilty, or fails to indicate how he would plead, the judge will consider whether the offence is more suitable for summary trial or for trial on indictment.

Where, in the exceptional case, the judge considers that because of his disorderly conduct before the court, it is not practicable for the proceedings to be conducted in the presence of the accused, and he considers that the proceedings should be conducted in his absence:

(a) provided that the accused is legally represented;
(b) the judge will cause each count of the indictment charging an either-way offence to be read to the representative; and
(c) that representative will be asked whether, if the offence were to proceed to trial the accused would plead guilty or not guilty;
(d) depending on the representative's reply, the ordinary procedure (outlined above) will apply.

Whether more suitable for trial summarily or on indictment

15–022 In considering the question whether an offence is more suitable for summary trial or for trial on indictment, the judge must: CDA 1998, s.52(6), Sch.3, para.9

(1) first afford the prosecutor, and then the accused, an opportunity to make representations as to which mode of trial would be more suitable; and
(2) in considering the question, have regard to:
    (a) any representations so made;
    (b) the nature of the case, and whether the circumstances make it one of a serious character;
    (c) whether the punishment which a magistrates' court would have power to impose for it would be adequate;
    (d) any other circumstances which appear to the judge to make it more suitable for the case to be dealt with in one way rather than the other.

Special provisions apply (see Sch.3, para.14) in the case of "schedule offences".

15–023 Where:

(1) the judge considers that such an offence is more suitable for summary trial, he will: CDA 1998, s.52(6), Sch.3, para.11
    (a) explain to the accused in ordinary language that it appears to him more suitable that he be tried summarily for the offence, and that he can either consent to be so tried, or if he wishes, be tried by a jury; and
    (b) explain that if he is tried summarily and convicted, he may still be committed for sentence to the Crown Court (under MCA 1980, s.38) if the lower court is of such opinion as is mentioned in s.38(2); and
    (c) ask the accused whether he wishes to be tried summarily or by a jury;
    (d) remit him for trial to a magistrates' court acting for the place from which he was sent for trial, if the accused indicates that he wishes to be tried summarily if the accused does not give such an indication, the Crown will retain its functions and proceed accordingly,
(2) the judge considers that the offence is more suitable for trial on indictment he will tell the accused that he has so decided and the Crown Court will retain its functions and proceed accordingly.

Powers of Law Officers

15–024 Where the prosecution is being carried on by the Attorney General, the Solicitor-General or the DPP, and he applies for an offence which may be tried on indictment to be so tried, the Crown Court will retain its functions in any event and CDA 1998, s.52(6), Sch.3, para.12

paras 5(4)–(8), 6(2)(b)–(d), 6(3) and (7)–(9) will not apply. The power of the DPP under this provision is not to be exercised except with the consent of the Attorney General.

Power to proceed in absence of accused

15–025 The judge may deal with any of the procedures under paras 7–11 in the absence of the accused, provided he is legally represented by a representative who signifies to the court the accused's consent to such a course, and the judge is satisfied that there is good reason for proceeding in the accused's absence. In such a case, any explanations and questions to, and any consents to be given by, the accused will be given to and answered by the legal representative. CDA 1998, s.52(6), Sch.3, para.15

B. Application for dismissal; present (pre-CJA 2003) procedure

General

15–026 CPR 2005, R.13 governs the procedure in all cases where: R.13.1

(1) notice of transfer has been given under CJA 1987 or CJA 1991; or
(2) a person has been sent for trial under CDA 1998;

and the person concerned proposes to apply orally under:

(a) CJA 1987, s.6(1);
(b) CJA 1991, Sch.6, para.5(1); or
(c) CDA 1998, Sch.3, para.2(1),

for any charge in the case to be dismissed.

Note that:

(i) "notice of transfer" means a notice referred to in CJA 1987, s.4(1) or CJA 1991, s.53(1); and
(ii) "the prosecution" means the authority by or on behalf of whom notice of transfer was given under the Acts or the authority by or on behalf of whom documents were served under CDA 1998, Sch.3, para.1.

Requirement of notice

15–027 Such person must give notice of his intention in writing to the Crown Court officer at the place specified by the notice of transfer under the 1987 or 1991 Acts or the notice given under s.51(7) of the 1998 Act as the proposed place of trial. Notice of intention to make an application under the 1987 R.13.2.(1)

or 1991 Acts must be in the forms prescribed in PD 2004, Annex D.

Notice of intention to make an application must be given in the case of an application to dismiss charges:

(1) transferred under the 1987 Act, not later than 28 days after the day on which notice of transfer was given;
(2) transferred under the 1991 Act, not later than 14 days after the day on which notice of transfer was given; and
(3) sent under the 1998 Act, not later than 14 days after the day on which the documents were served under para.1 of Sch.3 to that Act;

and a copy of the notice must be given at the same time to the prosecution and to any person to whom the notice of transfer relates or with whom the applicant for dismissal is jointly charged. R.13.2(2)

Extension of time

15–028 The time for giving notice may be extended, before it expires, by the Crown Court, on an application in writing, specifying the grounds for it, and sent to the Crown Court officer, a copy being given at the same time to the prosecution and to any other person to whom the notice of transfer relates or with whom the applicant for dismissal is jointly charged. R.12.2(3), (4)

Notice will be given by the Crown Court to all parties, in the form prescribed in PD 2004, Annex D as appropriate, of the judge's decision as to an extension of time. R.13.2(5)

Notice of intention to make an oral application for dismissal under any of the Acts mentioned above must be accompanied by a copy of any material on which the applicant relies, and the notice must: R.13.2(6)

(1) specify the charge or charges to which it relates; and
(2) state whether leave is sought to adduce oral evidence on the application, indicating the witnesses it is proposed to call; and
(3) in the case of a transfer under CJA 1991 (certain offences involving children) confirm in relation to each witness that he is not a child to whom Sch.6, para.5(5) of the Act applies.

The Crown Court officer will give notice in the same form, as appropriate of the judge's decision as to oral evidence being given, and indicating what witnesses are to be called, if applicable, and the appropriate officer will list the application for hearing. R.13.2(7), (8)

Written application

15–029 An application may be made for dismissal under R.13.3(1)–(3)

(1) CJA 1987, s.6(1);
(2) CJA 1991, Sch.6, para.5(1); or
(3) CDA 1998, Sch.3, para.2(1),

may be made without an oral hearing. It must be made in writing in the form at PD 2004, Annex D and sent to the Crown Court officer, accompanied by a copy of any statement or other document, and identifying any article, on which the applicant relies. A copy of the application, and of any accompanying documents must be given, at the same time, to the prosecution and to any other person to whom the notice of transfer relates, or with whom the applicant is jointly charged.

Such application must be made not later than: R.13.3(4)

(1) 28 days after the day on which notice of transfer was given under (1) above;
(2) 14 days after the day on which notice of transfer was given under (2) above; or
(3) 14 days after the day on which documents required by CDA 1998, Sch.3 were served

unless the time for making the application is extended, either before or after it expires, by the Crown Court, in which case Rr.13.2(4) and (5) (see 15–028, above) apply as if references to giving notice of intention to make an oral application were references to making a written one.

Prosecution reply

15–030 The prosecution may apply to the Crown Court under CJA 1987, s.6(3), CJA 1991, Sch.6, para.5(4), or CDA 1998, Sch.3, para.2(4): R.13.4(1), (2)

(1) not later than seven days from the date of service of notice of intention to apply orally for the dismissal of any charge contained in a notice of transfer or based on documents served under CDA 1998, Sch.3, para.1, the prosecution for leave to adduce oral evidence at the hearing of the application, indicating what witnesses it proposes to call; and
(2) not later than seven days from the date of receiving a copy of an application for dismissal under R.13.3, for an oral hearing of the application.

Such applications must be served on the Crown Court officer in writing in the form prescribed in PD 2004, Annex D and, in the case of (2) above must state whether the leave of the judge is sought to adduce oral evidence and, if so, must indicate what witnesses it is proposed to call.

Where, having received the material specified (in R.13.2 or, as the case may be, R.13.3), the prosecution proposes to adduce in reply, any written comments or any further evidence, they must serve on the Crown Court officer: R. 13.4(5)

(a) any such comments, copies of the statements or other documents outlining the evidence of any proposed witnesses;
(b) copies of any further documents; and
(c) in the case of an application to dismiss charges transferred under the 1991 Act, copies of any video recordings which it is proposed to tender in evidence,

not later than 14 days from the date of receiving the material, and must, at the same time serve copies on the applicant for dismissal and any other person to whom the notice of transfer relates or with whom the applicant is jointly charged. In the case of a defendant acting in person, copies of video recordings need not be served but must be made available for viewing by him.

Leave to adduce oral evidence

15–031 Where leave is sought to adduce oral evidence under CJA 1991, Sch.6, para.5(4), the application should confirm in relation to each such witness that he is not a child to whom CJA 1991, sch.6, para.5(5) applies. In proceedings under the 1987 or 1991 Acts, such an application must be in the form set out in PD 2004, Annex D. Rr.13.4(1)–(3)

Notice of the judge's determination, indicating what witnesses, if any, are to be called will be served in writing by the Crown Court officer on: R.13.4(4)

(1) the prosecution;
(2) the applicant for dismissal; and
(3) any other party to whom the notice of transfer relates or with whom the applicant for dismissal is jointly charged. In proceedings under the 1987 or 1991 Acts,

in the form set out at PD 2004, Annex D.

Extension of time

15–032 The time for: R.13.4(6), (7)

(1) making an application under (1) or (2) above; or
(2) serving any material on the Crown Court officer (under 15–047, below)

may be extended, either before or after it expires, by the Crown Court, on application. Such application must be made in writing and must be served on the Crown Court officer, a copy being served at the same time on the applicant for dismissal and on any other person to whom the notice of transfer relates or with whom the applicant for dismissal is jointly charged. In proceedings under the 1987 or 1991 Acts an application must be in the form set out in PD2004, Annex D.

Determination of applications; supplementary

15–033 Note that:

(1) a judge may grant leave for a witness to give oral evidence on an application for dismissal notwithstanding that notice of intention to call the witness has not been given in accordance with the Rules (R.13.5(1)); and
(2) where an application for dismissal is determined otherwise than at an oral hearing, the Crown Court officer will, as soon as practicable, send to all the parties to the case written notice of the outcome of the application. In proceedings under the 1987 and 1991 Acts the notice will be in the form prescribed in PD 2004, Annex D.

C. Scheme introduced by CJA 2003, Pt 6, Sch.3

General

15–034 CJA 2003, Pt 6 with Sch.3, **not yet in force**, will make wide-ranging alterations to the manner in which cases are moved from the magistrates' court to the Crown Court for trial.

It lays down:

(1) the procedure to be followed by magistrates' courts in determining whether cases triable either way should be tried summarily or on indictment; and
(2) the procedure for sending to the Crown Court such cases as need to go there.

The effects are that:

(a) committal proceedings under MCA 1980, s.6 are abolished, and the magistrates' court ceases to have the role of "examining magistrates";
(b) the notice of transfer procedure in relation to both
    (i) certain cases involving children, and
    (ii) serious fraud cases,

will be assimilated into the proceedings for "sending" cases for trial under CDA 1998, ss.51 *et seq.*;

(c) the procedure for sending indictable-only offences for trial under CDA 1998, s.51 will be extended to offences triable either-way, in a manner replicating the former "notice of transfer" procedure in the cases of serious fraud, and child witness cases, and will be the only avenue for moving cases from the magistrates' courts to the Crown Court; and

(d) scutiny of the evidence will be by a judge of the Crown Court, who will have the power of dismissal (see 15–014, below).

Adults and corporations sent for trial

15–035 Adults (i.e. accused aged 18 and over) and corporations may be sent for trial under CDA 1998, s.51(1), (2) as amended in respect of:

CDA 1998, s.51(2), (11); CJA 2003, Sch.3, para.18

(1) indictable only offences other than those in respect of which notice has been given under CDA 1998, s.51B or s.51C inserted by CJA 2003, Sch.3, para.18 (see 15–036 and 15–037, below);

(2) either-way offences where the magistrates' court is required under MCA 1980, ss.20(9)(b), 21, 23(4)(b) or (5) or 25(2D) to proceed in accordance with (1); or

(3) cases in which notice is given under s.51B or s.51C in respect of the offence under s.51(1), (2) as amended by CJA 2003, Sch.3, para.18).

The offences for which such a person is sent to the Crown Court may include:

(a) any either-way offence appearing to be related to (1) above; and

(b) any summary offence appearing to be related to the offence in (1) above (and punishable with imprisonment or a discretionary RT disqualification).

A child or young person charged jointly with the adult with an indictable offence for which the adult is sent for trial, or an indictable offence which appears to the court to be related to that offence, may also, subject to MCA 1980, ss.24A and 24B, which provide for certain cases involving children and young persons to be tried summarily where considered necessary in the interests of justice be sent with the adult for trial for the indictable offence, and the same rules as to either-way and summary offences apply.

CDA 1998, s.51(7), (8), (9); CJA 2003, s.41, Sch.3, para.18

Children and young persons

15–036 Children and young persons (i.e. those aged under 18) may be sent to the Crown Court under CDA 1998, s.51A, as inserted by CJA 2003, Sch.3, para.18, subject to MCA 1980, ss.24A and 24B, which provide for certain offences involving children or young persons to be tried summarily, where:

CDA 1998, s.51A(1), (2), (3); CJA 2003, s.41, Sch.3, para.18

(1) the offence is one of homicide;
(2) each of the requirements of FA 1968, s.51A (minimum sentences in respect of certain firearms offences) would be satisfied with respect to the offence and the person charged with it if he were convicted of the offence;
(3) the offence is one of those grave offences mentioned in PCC(S)A 2000, s.91(1) or (2) (other than one mentioned in (5) below) in relation to which the court considers that if he is found guilty of the offence it ought to be possible to sentence him under s.91(3);
(4) notice is given to the court under s.51B or s.51C below in respect of the offence; or
(5) the offence is a specified offence (within the meaning of CJA 2003, s.224) (see APPENDIX, Section 2) and it appears to the court that if he is found guilty of the offence the criteria for the imposition of a sentence under s.226(3) or s.228(2) (dangerous offenders) would be met.

There is a strong presumption against sending young offenders to the Crown Court unless it is clearly required and the case is so serious that a sentence above two years is required.

When such a situation arises;

(1) the general policy of the legislation is that offenders under 18 and particularly those under 15 should, wherever possible be tried by the youth court;
(2) it is a further purpose of the legislation that generally speaking first time offenders aged 12–14 and offenders under 12 should not be detained in custody and in deciding on jurisdiction the court should have regard to the fact that the exceptional power to detain for grave offences should not be used to water down the general principle; those under 15 who rarely attract a period of detention, and even more rarely those under 12, should not be detained in custody;
(3) in each case the magistrates' court should ask itself whether there was a real prospect, having regard to the accused's age, that he might require a sentence of, or in excess of, two years or alternately whether, although the

sentence might be less then two years there was some unusual feature which entitled the magistrates' court to decline jurisdiction

(*R. (on the application of H, A & O) v Southampton YC* [2005] Crim.L.R. 395).

An adult charged jointly with a juvenile with an indictable offence for which the juvenile is sent for trial, or an indictable offence which appears to the court to be related to that offence, may also be sent with the adult for trial for the indictable offence (CJA 1998, s.51A(6), (7); CJA 2003, Sch.3, para.18) and the same rules as to either-way and summary offences apply. CDA 1998, s.51A(4); CJA 2003, s.41, Sch.3, para.18

Serious or complex fraud cases

15–037 Serious or complex fraud cases involving an indictable offence may be sent to the Crown Court where the designated authority (see below) is of the opinion that the evidence of the offence charged: CDA 1998, s.51B(1), (2), (5), (6); CJA 2003, s.41, Sch.3, para.18

(1) is sufficient for the person charged to be put on trial for the offence; and
(2) reveals a case of fraud of such seriousness or complexity that it is appropriate that the management of the case should without delay be taken over by the Crown Court,

and notice is given to the magistrates' court at which the person charged appears, or before which he is brought, before any summary trial begins, the effect of which is that the functions of the magistrates' court in relation to the case will cease except:

(a) for the purposes of selecting the place of trial (s.51D);
(b) in relation to defence public funding, as provided by AJA 1999, Sch.3, para.2; and
(c) in connection with remanding the person charged (whether in custody or on bail).

A "designated authority" includes the DPP, the Director of the Serious Fraud Squad, the Director of Revenue and Customs Prosecutions and the Secretary of State. The decision to give notice of transfer is not subject to appeal, or liable to be questioned in any court.

Certain cases involving children

15–038 A case may be sent to the Crown Court under CDA 1998, s.51C, where notice is given by the DPP to a magistrates' CDA 1998, s.51C(7); CJA court at which a person charged appears or is brought, and before any summary trial begins, in respect of an offence: 2003, s.41, Sch.3, para.18

(1) which involves an assault on, or injury or a threat of injury to, a person;
(2) under CYPA 1933, s.1 (cruelty to persons under 16);
(3) under SOA 1956, the Protection of Children Act 1978, or SOA 2003; or
(4) of kidnapping or false imprisonment, or an offence under the Child Abduction Act 1984; s.1 or s.2;
(5) which consists of attempting or conspiring to commit, or of aiding, abetting, counselling, procuring or inciting the commission of such an offence, and where he is of the opinion (to be certified in the notice) that:
    (a) the evidence of the offence charged is sufficient for the person charged to be put on trial for the offence;
    (b) a child would be called as a witness at the trial; and
    (c) for the purpose of avoiding any prejudice to the welfare of the child, the case should be taken over and proceeded with without delay by the Crown Court.

The provisions of s.51B(4), (5) and (6) above, in relation to serious or complex frauds then apply.

"Child" here means:

(i) a person who is under the age of 17; or
(ii) any person of whom a video recording was made when he was under the age of 17 with a view to its admission as his evidence in chief in the trial of a person charged with the offence which is the subject of the notice under this section.

Content of notices; place of trial

15–039 The magistrates' court will specify in a notice: CDA 1998, s.51D; CJA 2003, s.41, Sch.3, para.18

(1) the offence or offences for which a person is sent for trial under s.51 or s.51A; and
(2) the place at which he is to be tried (which, if a notice has been given under s.51B, must be the place specified in that notice),

and a copy of the notice will be served on the accused and given to the Crown Court sitting at that place.

In a case where a person is sent for trial under s.51(1) or s.51A(2) for more than one offence and the court includes any further offence in the notice, the court will specify in the notice the offence to which the further offence appears to the court to be related.

In selecting the place of trial, the magistrates must have regard to:

(a) the convenience of the defence, the prosecution and the witnesses;
(b) the desirability of expediting the trial; and
(c) any direction given by or on behalf of the Lord Chief Justice under SCA 1981, s.75(1).

Listing of first Crown Court appearance

15–040 A Crown Court officer to whom notice has been given under CDA 1998, s.51(7), must list the first Crown Court appearance of the person to whom notice relates in accordance with any directions given by the magistrates' court. No set period is now prescribed. R.12.2

Dismissal; no case to answer

15–041 A person sent for trial on any charge or charges may, at any time: CDA 1998, s.52(6), Sch.3, para.2(1), (2), (3); CJA 2003, ss.41, 331, Sch.3, paras 20, 36, Pt 4, para.73

(1) after he has been served with copies of the documents containing the evidence on which the charge or charges are based; and
(2) before he is arraigned (and whether or not the indictment has been preferred against him),

apply orally, or in writing, to the Crown Court sitting at the place specified in the notice served upon him (under s.51D(1)) for the charge, or any of the charges in the case, to be dismissed.

The judge is required to take into account the whole of the evidence against the accused, and to decide whether:

(a) there is any evidence to go to a jury, where there is one; and
(b) that evidence is sufficient for a jury to convict.

The question for decision is the sufficiency of the evidence.

The criteria to be applied on consideration of an application are those ordinarily applied to a submission of "no case to answer" (*R. v X* [1989] Crim.L.R. 726).

Where the evidence is largely documentary, the judge must assess the inferences which the prosecutor proposes to ask the jury to draw from the documents and decide whether it appears to him that such inferences might properly be drawn (*R. (IRC) v Kingston CC* [2001] 4 All E.R. 721).

Reporting restrictions

15–042 Reporting restrictions similar to those previously imposed on committal proceedings (see 15–010, above) are imposed in such a case. CDA 1998, s.52(6), Sch.3, para.3

Result of dismissal or amendment

15–043 The result of the above proceedings before the judge may be that:

(1) the indictment no longer contains any indictable only offence; or
(2) any remaining offences triable either-way may not be, in the judge's opinion, suitable for trial on indictment;
(3) there are summary offences remaining to be dealt with.

No indictable only offence remaining

15–044 Where a person has been sent for trial under s.51 or s.51A, but has not been arraigned, and is charged on an indictment which, as a result of amendment, or a successful application to dismiss, or for any other reason, no longer includes any "main offence", as defined below, the procedure is as follows: CDA 1998, s.52(6), Sch.3, para.7(9); CJA 2003, s.41, Sch.3, para.20(7)

(1) each remaining count of the indictment charging an offence triable either way, is read to the accused;
(2) he is informed that in relation to each of those offences he may indicate whether, if the court were to proceed to trial, he would plead guilty or not guilty, and that if he pleads guilty he will be treated as if he had pleaded guilty on arraignment;
(3) he is then asked whether, if the offence in question were to proceed to trial, he would plead guilty or not guilty;
(4) if he indicates that he would plead guilty, the judge proceeds as if he had been arraigned on the count in question and had pleaded guilty;
(5) if he indicates that he would plead not guilty, or fails to indicate how he would plead, the judge will decide whether the offence is more suitable for summary trial or for trial on indictment.

Where, in the exceptional case, the judge considers that because of his disorderly conduct before the court, it is not practicable for the proceedings to be conducted in his presence, and he considers that the proceedings should be conducted in his absence, then provided that the accused is legally represented:

(a) the judge will cause each count of the indictment charging an either-way offence to be read to the representative;
(b) that representative will be asked whether, if the offence were to proceed to trial, the accused would plead guilty or not guilty; and
(c) depending on the representative's answer, the ordinary procedure (outlined above) will apply (CDA 1998, s.52(6), Sch.3, paras 7, 8, 9; CJA 2003, s.41, Sch.3, para.20(7)).

A "main offence" for the purposes of the above provisions is:

(i) an offence for which the person has been sent to the Crown Court for trial under s.51(1); or
(ii) an offence:

- for which the person has been sent to the Crown Court for trial under s.51(5) or s.51A(6) ("the applicable sub section"); and
- in respect of which the conditions for sending him to the Crown Court for trial under the applicable subsection (as set out in s.51(5) (a) to (c) or s.51A(6)(a) and (b)), continue to be satisfied.

Modifications are made to the procedure by Sch.3, para.8 where, in view of the accused's disorderly behaviour, the court proceeds in his absence.

Summary trial or trial on indictment

15–045 Before deciding the question whether an offence is more suitable for summary trial or for trial on indictment, the judge must give: CDA 1998, s.52(6), Sch.3, para.9; CJA 2003, s.41, Sch.3, para.20(9)

(1) the prosecutor an opportunity to inform the court of the accused's previous convictions in Great Britain (if any); and
(2) the accused an opportunity to make representations as to whether summary trial or trial on indictment would be more suitable.

In deciding the question, he must consider:

(a) whether the sentence which a magistrates court would have power to impose for the offence would be adequate; and
(b) any representations made by the prosecution or the accused,

and must have regard to any allocation guidelines, or revised allocation guidelines, issued under CJA 2003, s.170 (see 7 ALLOCATION AND DEPLOYMENT OF BUSINESS).

Where:

(i) the accused is charged on the same occasion with two or more offences; and
(ii) it appears to the judge that they constitute or form part of a series of two or more offences of the same or a similar character,

para.(a) above has effect as if references to the sentence which a magistrates' court would have power to impose for the offence were a reference to the maximum aggregate sentence which a magistrates' court would have power to impose for all of the offences taken together.

Special provisions apply (see Sch.3, para.14) in the case of "schedule offences" (i.e. those offences of criminal damage and aggravated vehicle taking set out in MCA 1980, Sch.2).

Offence more suitable for summary trial

15–046 Where the judge decides that such an offence is more suitable for summary trial: CDA 1998, s.52(6), Sch.3, para.10; CJA 2003, s.41, Sch.3, para.20(10)

(1) he will explain to the accused that:
   (a) it appears to him more suitable for the accused to be tried summarily for the offence;
   (b) he can either consent to be so tried or, if he wishes, be tried on indictment; and
   (c) in the case of a "specified offence" (within the meaning of CJA 2003, s.224) (see APPENDIX A, Section 2), that if he is tried summarily and is convicted by the magistrates' court, he may be committed for sentence to the Crown Court under PCC(S)A 2000, s.3A if the committing court is of such opinion as is mentioned in subs.(2) of that section (see 20 COMMITTALS FOR SENTENCE).
(2) he will then ask the accused whether he wishes to be tried summarily or on indictment;
(3) if the accused indicates that he wishes to be tried summarily, the judge will remit him for trial to a magistrates' court acting for the place from which he was sent for trial;
(4) if the accused does not give such an indication, the Crown Court will retain its functions and proceed accordingly.

Offence more suitable for trial on indictment

15–047 Where the judge considers that the offence is more suitable for trial on indictment: CDA 1998, s.52(6), Sch.3, para.11; CJA 2003, s.41, Sch.3, para.20(11)

(1) he will tell the accused that he has so decided; and
(2) the Crown Court will retain its functions and proceed accordingly.

Children and young persons

15–048 Where a child or young person has been: CDA 1998, s.52(6), Sch.3, para.13; CJA 2003, s.35, Sch.3, para.17

(1) sent for trial under s.51 or s.51A but has not been arraigned; and
(2) is charged on indictment which (following amendment, or for any other reason) includes no "main offence",

instead of following paras 7 to 12 of the Schedule, the judge must remit the child or young person for trial to a magistrates' court acting for the place where he was sent to the Crown Court for trial.

A "main offence" for the purposes of this provision is:

(a) an offence for which the child or young person has been sent to the Crown Court for trial under s.51A(2); or
(b) an offence—
  (i) for which the child or young person has been sent to the Crown Court for trial under s.51(7); and
  (ii) in respect of which the conditions for sending him to the Crown Court for trial under that subsection (as set out in paras (a) and (b) of that subsection) continue to be satisfied.

Dealing with summary offences

15–049 Where the magistrates' court has sent a person for trial under s.51 or s.51A for offences which include a summary offence, the procedure at the Crown Court is as follows, if: CDA 1998, s.52(6), Sch.3, para.6; CJA 2003, s.41, Sch.3, para.20(6)

(1) that person is convicted on indictment, the judge will consider whether the summary offence is "related" (see 15–015) to the indictable offence for which he was sent for trial, or, as the case may be, any of the indictable offences for which he was so sent; and
(2) he finds that it is, the substance of the offence will be put to the accused and he will be asked to plead to it;
(3) the accused pleads guilty, he will be convicted, the judge's powers of sentencing being limited to those of the magistrates' court;

(4) the accused does not plead guilty, the Crown Court ceases to have powers in the matter unless the prosecution inform the judge that they do not wish to offer any evidence on the charge, in which case he may dismiss it.

Power to proceed in absence of accused

15–050 The judge may deal with any of the procedures under paras 7–11 of Sch.3 in the absence of the accused, provided he is legally represented by a representative who signifies to the court the accused's consent to such a course, and the judge is satisfied that there is good reason for proceeding in the accused's absence. In such a case, any explanations and questions to, and any consents to be given by the accused, will be given to and answered by the legal representative.

CDA 1998, s.52(6), Sch.3, para.8

16 CASE MANAGEMENT

Introduction

16–001 The following may be classed as aspects of case management:

(1) plea and case management hearings (16–015 *et seq.*);
(2) preparatory hearings in serious fraud and other matters (16–026 *et seq.*);
(3) statutory pre-trial hearings under CPIA 1996, Pt IV (16–027).

Disclosure of unused material, though a part of case management, is a subject of increasing importance and is dealt with at 32 DISCLOSURE OF UNUSED MATERIAL.

The Criminal Procedure Rules 2005 (CPR 2005), **applying in general, on or after April 4, 2005** state the overriding objective of the Rules and the duties of the parties in relation to criminal proceedings. These are set out below.

PD 2004 also added a further paragraph to Pt V and an Annex D, which set out forms to be used under Rule 3.11(1) of the new Criminal Procedure Rules. Almost all are identical to those in use before that date, and accordingly a form in use before that date which corresponds with one set out in Annex D may still be used in connection with the rule to which it applied. The table at the beginning of Annex D lists the forms set out in that annex and shows the Rule in connection with which each form applies; describes each form in the case of a form in use before the Criminal Procedure Rules came into force; and shows the legislation by which the form is prescribed and by what number, if any, it is known.

As to the control and management of heavy fraud and other complex criminal cases, see 16–049 *et seq.*, below.

As to terrorism cases, see 16–062 *et seq.*, below.

A. CPR 2005 Objective and duties

General

16–002 The overriding objective of CPR 2005 is stated to be that criminal cases be dealt with justly, which includes: R.1.1

(1) acquitting the innocent and convicting the guilty;
(2) dealing with the prosecution and the defence fairly;

(3) recognising the rights of an accused, particularly those under ECHR, Art. 6;
(4) respecting the interests of witnesses, victims and jurors and keeping them informed of the progress of the case;
(5) dealing with a case efficiently and expeditiously;
(6) ensuring that appropriate information is available to the court when bail and sentence are considered; and
(7) dealing with the case in ways that take into account:

(a) the gravity of the offence alleged,
(b) the complexity of what is in issue,
(c) the severity of the consequences for the accused and others affected, and
(d) the needs of other cases.

The duty of the participants in a criminal case

16–003 The Rules impose duties and burdens on all the participants in a criminal trial, including the judge, and the preparation and conduct of criminal trials is dependent on and subject to the Rules (*R. v K and Others*, *The Times*, May 12, 2006 CA). Each participant, in the conduct of a criminal case (and that includes anyone involved in any way with the case), is under a duty to: R.1.2

(1) prepare and conduct the case in accordance with the overriding objective;
(2) comply with the Rules, practice directions and directions made by the court; and
(3) at once inform the court and all parties of any significant failure (whether or not that participant is responsible for that failure) to take any procedural step required by the Rules, any practice direction or any direction of the court. A failure is significant if it might hinder the court in furthering the overriding objective.

Application by the court

16–004 The court has a duty to further the overriding objective, in particular when: R.1.3

(1) exercising any power given to it by legislation (including the Rules);
(2) applying any practice direction; or
(3) interpreting any rule or practice direction.

Case management; the court's duty

16–005 The court has a duty to further the overriding objective by actively managing the case. Active case management includes: R.3.2(2)

(1) the early identification of the real issues;
(2) the early identification of the needs of witnesses;
(3) achieving certainty as to what must be done, by whom, and when, in particular by the early setting of a timetable for the progress of the case;
(4) monitoring the progress of the case and compliance with directions;
(5) ensuring that evidence, whether disputed or not, is presented in the shortest and clearest way;
(6) discouraging delay, dealing with as many aspects of the case as possible on the same occasion, and avoiding unnecessary hearings;
(7) encouraging the participants to co-operate in the progression of the case; and
(8) making use of technology.

The court must actively manage the case by giving any direction appropriate to the needs of that case as early as possible.

Case management; the duty of the parties

16–006 Each party is under a duty actively to assist the court in fulfilling its duty under R.3.2 above without or if necessary with a direction; and to apply for a direction if needed to further the overriding objective. R.3.3

Case progression officers and their duties

16–007 At the beginning of the case each party must unless the court otherwise directs, nominate an individual responsible for progressing that case; and tell other parties and the court who he is and how to contact him. The court will, in fulfilling its duty under R.3.2, where appropriate, nominate a court officer responsible for progressing the case; and make sure the parties know who he is and how to contact him. R.3.4

A person so nominated is called a case progression officer whose duty is to: R.3.4.(3)(4)

(1) monitor compliance with directions;
(2) make sure that the court is kept informed of events that may affect the progress of that case;
(3) make sure that he can be contacted promptly about the case during ordinary business hours;
(4) act promptly and reasonably in response to communications about the case; and
(5) if he will be unavailable, appoint a substitute to fulfil his duties and inform the other case progression officers.

CASE MANAGEMENT

The court's case management powers

16–008 In fulfilling its duty under R.3.2, the court may give any direction and take any step actively to manage a case unless that direction or step would be inconsistent with legislation, including the Rules. In particular, it may: R.3.5

(1) nominate a judge to manage the case;
(2) give a direction on its own initiative or on application by a party;
(3) ask or allow a party to propose a direction;
(4) for the purpose of giving directions, receive applications and representations by letter, by telephone or by any other means of electronic communication, and conduct a hearing by such means;
(5) give a direction without a hearing;
(6) fix, postpone, bring forward, extend or cancel a hearing;
(7) shorten or extend (even after it has expired) a time limit fixed by a direction;
(8) require that issues in the case should be determined separately, and decide in what order they will be determined; and
(9) specify the consequences of failing to comply with a direction.

The above powers enable the judge with preliminary matters exclusively by reference to written submissions limited to a length specified by him if he thinks it right to do so. He is not bound to allow oral submissions, but if he does so he is entitled to put a time limit on them. The necessary public element of any hearing will be suffieiciently achieved if the accused and representatives of the media in court are supplied with copies of written submissions if they wish to see them. No particular method of approach is prescribed, as case management decisions are case specific (*R. v K and Others*, above).

A magistrates' court may give a direction that will apply in the Crown Court if the case is to continue there, and conversely, the Crown Court may give a direction that will apply in a magistrates' court if the case is to continue there. R.3.5.(3)(4)

Application to vary a direction

16–009 A power to give a direction under these provisions includes a power to vary or revoke that direction. R.3.5(5)

A party may apply to vary a direction (R.3.6(1)) if:

(1) the court gave it without a hearing;
(2) the court gave it at a hearing in his absence; or
(3) circumstances have changed.

The party who applies to vary a direction must apply as soon as practicable after he becomes aware of the grounds for doing so; and give as much notice to the other parties as the nature and urgency of his application permits. R.3.6

Agreement to vary a time limit fixed by a direction

16–010 The parties may agree to vary a time limit fixed by a direction, but only if: R.3.7

(1) the variation will not:

(a) affect the date of any hearing that has been fixed; or
(b) significantly affect the progress of the case in any other way;

(2) the court has not prohibited variation by agreement; and
(3) the court's case progression officer is promptly informed.

The court's case progression officer must refer the agreement to the court if he doubts the conditions in (l)(a) and (b) are satisfied.

Case preparation and progression

16–011 At every hearing:

(1) if a case cannot be concluded there and then, the court must give directions so that it can be concluded at the next hearing or as soon as possible after that. R.3.8(1)
(2) the court must, where relevant: R.3.8(2)

(a) if the accused is absent, decide whether to proceed nonetheless;
(b) take the accused's plea (unless already done) or if no plea can be taken find out whether the accused is likely to plead guilty or not guilty;
(c) set, follow or revise a timetable for the progress of the case, which may include a timetable for any hearing including the trial or the appeal;
(d) in giving directions, ensure continuity in relation to the court and to the parties' representatives where that is appropriate and practicable; and
(e) where a direction has not been complied with, find out why, identify who was responsible, and take appropriate action.

The case management forms set out in the Practice Direction must be used, and where there is no form then no specific formality is required. The court must make available to the parties a record of any directions given. R.3.11

Readiness for trial or appeal

16–012 In relation to a party's preparation for trial or appeal, (and in this rule and r.3.10 trial includes any hearing at which evidence will be introduced) each party must, in fulfilling his duty under r.3.3 above: R.3.9

(1) comply with directions given by the court;
(2) take every reasonable step to make sure his witnesses will attend when they are needed;
(3) make appropriate arrangements to present any written or other material; and
(4) promptly inform the court and the other parties of anything that may—
  (a) affect the date or duration of the trial or appeal, or
  (b) significantly affect the progress of the case in any other way.

The court may require a party to give a certificate of readiness.

Conduct of trial or an appeal

16–013 In order to manage the trial or appeal, the court may require a party to identify: R.3.10

(1) which witnesses he intends to give oral evidence;
(2) the order in which he intends those witnesses to give their evidence;
(3) whether he requires an order compelling the attendance of a witness;
(4) what arrangements, if any, he proposes to facilitate the giving of evidence by a witness;
(5) what arrangements, if any, he proposes to facilitate the participation of any other person, including the accused;
(6) what written evidence he intends to introduce;
(7) what other material, if any, he intends to make available to the court in the presentation of the case;
(8) whether he intends to raise any point of law that could affect the conduct of the trial or appeal; and
(9) what timetable he proposes and expects to follow.

The prevailing approach to procedural defects

16–014 A number of points may be made based on the far-reaching decisions of the House of Lords in *R. v Soneji* [2005] 3 W.L.R. 303 and the decisions of CACD in *R. v Sekhon and Others* [2003] 1 W.L.R. 1655 and *R. v Ashton* [2006] EWCA Crim 794:

(1) The purpose of rules of procedure is not usually to give or take away a court's jurisdiction, rather procedural

requirements provide a convenient and just machinery enabling the court to exercise its jurisdiction.

They:

(a) may be, but usually are not, conditions that have to be fulfilled to give the court jurisdiction;

(b) more usually do no more than:

 (i) enable the court if they are not complied with to make orders to require something to be done if it has not been done in accordance with the statutory provisions; or

 (ii) in the same circumstances to dismiss the proceeding.

Moreover, "substantive provisions" giving the court its jurisdiction are not to be automatically defeated in the ordinary way by non-compliance with procedural requirements unless this is necessary to achieve the statutory purpose;

(2) the rigid mandatory and directory distinction, and its many artificial refinements, has outlived its usefulness; a better test for determining the issue of validity is to ask whether it was a purpose of the legislation that an act done in breach of the provision should be invalid.

(3) the prevailing approach is to avoid determining cases on technicalities (when they do not result in real prejudice and injustice) but instead to ensure that they are decided fairly on their merits. This approach is reflected in CPR 2005 and, in particular, the overriding objective;

(4) in the absence of a clear indication that Parliament intended jurisdiction automatically to be removed following procedural failure, the judge's decision should be based on a wide assessment of the interests of justice, with particular focus on whether there is a real possibility that the prosecution or the accused may suffer prejudice. If that risk is present, the judge should then decide whether it is just to permit the proceedings to continue;

(5) a procedural failure should result in a lack of jurisdiction only if this is necessary to ensure that the criminal justice system serves the interests of justice and thus the public, or where there is at least a real possibility of the accused suffering prejudice as a consequence of that procedural failure.

Accordingly, where a judge is confronted with procedural failure in the progress of an accused's case through the courts (as opposed to the markedly different situation where a court acts without jurisdiction), he should first ask himself whether the intention of the legislature was that any act done following that procedural failure should be invalid.

If the answer to that question is "no", then he should go on to consider the interests of justice generally, and most particularly whether there is a real possibility that either the prosecution or the defence may suffer prejudice on account of the procedural failure; if there is such a risk, he must decide whether it is just to allow the proceedings to continue;

It is otherwise where a court acts without jurisdiction, as for instance where a magistrates' court purports to try an accused on a charge of homicide, in those circumstances the proceedings will usually be invalid.

As to the rectification of defects by assuming the powers of a District Judge (Magistrates' Courts) under CA 2003, s.66 see 42 JURISDICTION at 42–002, below.

B. Case Management Hearings

1. Plea and Case Management Hearings (PCMH)

General

16–015 An amendment to PD 2004, dated March 22, 2005, replaces the existing para.IV.41 **taking effect from April 4, 2005**, when CPR 2005 came into force. It applies to the sending, committal or transfer of cases by magistrates' courts to the Crown Court for trial where that event took place on or after that date, and to the subsequent management of those cases in the Crown Court. The existing para.41 of Pt IV continues to apply to cases sent, committed or transferred for trial before that date.

Active case management at plea and case management hearings are intended to reduce the number of ineffective and disrupted trials.

A magistrates' court committing, transferring or sending a case for trial to the Crown Court:

(1) must order a plea and case management hearing at the Crown Court in every case; and
(2) may, where it considers it necessary, order a pre-trial hearing.

The date of such hearing will be fixed by arrangement with the Crown Court.

For cases

(a) committed to the Crown Court for trial under MCA 1980, s.6 the case progression form to be used in the magistrates' court is set out in Annex E with guidance notes. A plea and case management should be ordered by the magistrates court in every case, to be held within about seven weeks after committal; PD 2004, IV.45.1.6

(b) transferred to the Crown Court for trial under CJA 1987, s.14(1) or under CJA 1991, s.53(1) the directions contained in the case progression form used in cases for committal for trial applies as if the case had been committed on the date of the notice of transfer. A plea and case management hearing should be listed by the Crown Court to be held **within about seven weeks after transfer**. PD 2004, IV.41.7

Where both hearings are ordered, both dates should be fixed at the same time.

Management of cases to be heard in the Crown Court

16–016 Part IV.41 supplements the rules in Pt 3 of the Criminal Procedure Rules as they apply to the management of cases to be heard in the Crown Court. Note that: PD 2004, IV.41.1.2

(1) where time limits or other directions in PD 2004 appear inconsistent with this section, the directions in this section take precedence;

(2) the case details form set out in Annex E should be completed by the Crown Court case progression officer in all cases to be tried on indictment.

As to the control and management of heavy fraud and other complex criminal cases, see 16–046 *et seq.*, below.

Necessity for preliminary hearing

16–017 A preliminary hearing is not required in every case sent for trial under CDA 1998, s.51 (see R.12.2, which alters the Crown Court rule from which it is derived). PD 2004, IV.41.3–5

A preliminary hearing should be ordered by the magistrates' court (or by the Crown Court), subject to any directions by the Resident Judge only where (according to the guidance notes):

(1) there are case management issues which call for such a hearing;

(2) the case is likely to last for more than four weeks;

(3) it is desirable to set an early trial date;
(4) the accused is a child or young person;
(5) there is likely to be a guilty plea and the accused could be sentenced at the preliminary hearing; or
(6) it seems that it is a case suitable for a preparatory hearing in the Crown Court (see below).

The preliminary hearing form to be used in the Crown Court is set out in Annex E with guidance notes.

The form provides a detailed timetable to enable the plea and case management hearing to be effective. Whether or not a magistrates' court order a preliminary hearing it should order a preliminary hearing to be held within about 14 weeks after sending for trial where a defendant is in custody and within about 17 weeks after sending for trial where a defendant is on bail.

Plea and case management hearing

16–018 The effectiveness of a plea and case management hearing in a contested case depends in large measure upon preparation by all concerned and upon the presence of the trial advocate or an advocate who is able to make decisions and give the court the assistance which the trial advocate could be expected to give. PD 2004, IV.41,8,9

Special provisions apply in the case of heavy fraud and other complex criminal cases, see 16–049 *et seq.*, below. Resident judges in setting the listing policy, should ensure that listing officers fix cases as far as possible to enable the trial advocate to conduct the plea and case management hearing and the trial.

In Class 1 and Class 2 cases, and in all cases involving a serious sexual offence against a child, the plea and case management hearing must be conducted:

(1) by a High Court judge, by a Circuit Judge or by a Recorder to whom the case had been assigned in accordance with para.33 of Pt IV (allocation of business within the Crown Court) (see 7 ALLOCATION AND DEPLOYMENT OF BUSINESS); or
(2) by a judge authorised by the Presiding Judges to conduct such hearings.

In the event of a guilty plea in such a case before an authorised judge, the case must be adjourned for sentencing by a High Court Judge or by a Circuit Judge or Recorder to whom the case had been assigned.

Pilot schemes; other courts

16–019 In:

(1) pilot courts (the Central Criminal Court, Preston Crown Court and Nottingham Crown Court) the plea and case management hearing form as set out in Annex B to this work is to be used in accordance with the guidance notes; PD 2004, IV.41,10

(2) other courts, the Resident Judge should exercise discretion as to the manner in which the form used taking account of the views of the local criminal justice agencies and of practitioners. PD 2004, IV.41.11

In the event of the Resident Judge deciding to use the forms in a manner that was not agreed to by either the local criminal justice agencies or the practitioners, the resident judge should consult the Presiding Judges of his circuit before doing so.

The form

16–020 The form on which the hearing takes place (see APPENDIX B) is self-explanatory. Copies are provided at the court. Notes for Guidance are attached to it.

The parties must complete only one copy of the form and make it available to the judge at or before the hearing (if there are more than five defendants, a further form should be filled in only so far as necessary). The answers to the questions in bold must be filled in before the hearing. The proposed italicised orders should be filled in before the hearing, if possible. The "Not applicable" box should be ticked if no part of the section is relevant. Local practice will determine how the form should be completed and by whom and whether electronically or not. The directions must be easily understood by, and made available to, the case progression officers. Time limits should normally be expressed by reference to a particular date rather than by the number of days allowed, to make the task of the case progression officers easier.

The court may make rulings (see 16–045, below) which have binding effect (subject to being discharged or varied) under CPIA 1996, s.40 as to:

"(a) any question as to the admissibility of evidence;
(b) any other question of law relating to the case concerned."

The extent to which courts exercise the power to make these rulings at this hearing is a matter for the judge after considering representations.

Except where otherwise required, a direction to "serve" material means serve on the other parties and file with the Crown Court.

Where a direction requires a party to respond to a proposal (e.g. a proposed edited interview) the party responding will be expected to suggest a counter-proposal.

Further pre-trial hearings after the plea and case management hearing

16–021 Additional pre-trial hearings should be held only if needed for some compelling reason. Where necessary the power to give, vary or revoke a direction without a hearing should be used. PD 2004, IV.41.13

Paragraph 5 of the plea and case management hearing form enables the court to require the parties' case progression officers to inform the Crown Court case progression officer that the case is ready for trial, that it will proceed as a trial on the date fixed and will take no more or less time than that previously ordered.

Abuse of process

16–022 Where the defence are considering making an abuse of process application, the matter should be raised at the plea and case management hearing (see 3 ABUSE OF PROCESS).

Children and young persons

16–023 Where a young person is indicted jointly with an adult accused, the judge should, at the plea and case management hearing: PD 2004, IV.39.4, 5

(1) consider whether the young accused should be tried on his own, and should ordinarily so order unless of opinion that a joint trial would be in the interests of justice and would not be unduly prejudicial to his welfare; if he is to be tried jointly with an adult, the ordinary procedures will apply subject to such modifications, if any, as the judge may see fit to order;

(2) consider and so far as practicable give directions on the matters covered by PD 2004, IV.39, 9–15.

Custody time limits; fixing a date

16–024 Where difficulties may arise in relation to custody time limits, the matter should, ideally, be raised at the plea and case management hearing, so that a date can be fixed for the trial. If it is not possible to agree a date, the matter should be re-listed (see 28 CUSTODY TIME LIMITS).

It should always be made to clear to an accused on bail that if he fails to attend his trial, the consequences may be that it will proceed in his absence and without legal representation (*R. v O'Hare* [2006] EWCA Crim 471).

General note

16–025 Experience from the operation of the former PDHs discloses a number of points:

(1) the directions judge needs to have a very firm control of the proceedings, and having studied the papers, needs to be very aware of the issues involved and the nature of the evidence to be adduced by the Crown;
(2) since two of the objects of the procedure are to concentrate the minds of both sides on the issues involved and the requirements as to witnesses, at a very early stage, to avoid the situation where witnesses at the trial are sent away as superfluous, the attention of counsel must be concentrated on all the issues relevant to the hearing;
(3) if any relevant matter is unresolved, the case should not be released until it has been or, if that is not practicable, an adjourned hearing should be fixed; and
(4) only in the most exceptional circumstances should there be no arraignment—one of the principal purposes of the hearing is to establish the plea; this is done by arraignment, not by vague indications of pleas that will eventually be entered at the trial.

As to the control and management of heavy fraud and other complex criminal cases, see 16–049 *et seq.*, below.

2. Preparatory hearings

(1) General

General

16–026 A statutory preparatory hearing *may* be ordered, either on application by the prosecutor or an accused or of the judge's own motion in two distinct types of case namely in:

CJA 1987, s.7(1); CJPOA 1994, Sch.9, para.39; CPIA 1996, Sch.3, para.3; CJA 2003, ss.45(4), 310(1), 331, Sch.36, paras 52, 53/CPIA 1996, ss.28, 29; CJA 2003, 310(1), 331, Sch.36, Pt 4, para.66; Terrorism Act 2006, s.16

(1) **serious and complex fraud cases**, under CJA 1987, ss.7–10 where, before the time when the jury are sworn it appears to a judge of the Crown Court, that the evidence on the indictment reveals a case of fraud of such seriousness or complexity that substantial benefits are likely to accrue from a preparatory hearing, for the purpose of; and
(2) **cases other than serious fraud**, under CPIA 1996, where, in relation to an offence:

(a) an accused is committed for trial, or sent for trial under CDA 1998, s.51 for the offence concerned; or
(b) proceedings for trial on the charge concerned are transferred to the Crown Court (or when CJA 2003, Sch.3 comes into force the subject of a notice under CDA 1998, s.51C); or
(c) a voluntary bill of indictment is preferred,

a case of such complexity, or of such seriousness, is revealed, or a case whose trial is likely to be of such a length that substantial benefits are likely to accrue from a preparatory hearing at the time the jury are sworn.

The reference to the time the jury was sworn is to be read, in the case of a trial without a jury, as a reference to the time when, if the trial were conducted with a jury, the jury would be sworn (CJA 1987, s.7(2B)/CPIA 1996, s.29(5), CJA 2003, s.304, Sch.36, Pt 4, para.66).

In a case in which it appears to a judge of the Crown Court that evidence on an indictment reveals a case of fraud of such seriousness or complexity as is mentioned CJA 1987, s.1 (above): CPIA 1996, s.29(3); Terrorism Act 2006, s.16

(i) the judge may make an order for a preparatory hearing under CPIA 1996, s.29 only if he is required to do so by s.29(1B) or (1C) (below);
(ii) before making an order in pursuance of either of those subsections, he must determine whether to make an order for a preparatory hearing under that section; and
(iii) he is not required by either of those subsections to make an order for a preparatory hearing under s.29 if he determines that an order should be made for a preparatory hearing under that section;

and, in a case in which an order is made for a preparatory hearing under that section, requirements imposed by those subsections apply only if that order ceases to have effect.

Terrorist cases; mandatory hearing

16–026A An order for a preparatory hearing *must* be made in every case which is a case: CPIA 1996, s.29(1B)(1C); Terrorism Act 2006, s.16

(1) in which at least one of the offences charged in the indictment against at least one of the persons charged is a **terrorist offence** (as defined in s.29(6)); or
(2) at least one of the persons charged by the indictment against at least one of the persons charged is an offence carrying a maximum of **10 years** imprisonment (see

s.29(7)) and it appears that evidence on the indictment reveals that conduct in respect of which that offence is charged has a **terrorist connection**, i.e. it is or takes place in the course of an act of terrorism (see Terrorism Act 2001, s.1) or is for the purposes of terrorism.

Statutory purposes

16–027 The purposes of such hearing are laid down by statute: CJA 1987, s.7(1)); CJPOA 1994, Sch.9, para.39; CJA 2003, ss.310(2), 331, Sch.36, Pt 4, paras 52, 53/CPIA 1996, ss.28,29; CJA 2003, ss.310(1), 331, Sch.36, Pt 4, para.66

(1) identifying the issues which are likely to be material to the verdict of the jury (under CJA 2003), and the determinations and findings which are likely to be required during the trial;
(2) assisting the comprehension of any such those issues;
(3) expediting the proceedings before the jury, or determining an application to which CJA 2003, s.45 (application for trial without jury) once that provision is in force, applies;
(4) assisting the judge's management of the trial; or
(5) considering questions as to the severance or joinder of charges.

"Expediting the proceedings" includes dealing with issues of evidence, and those questions which typically arise under PACE 1984, s.78 (*R. v Claydon* [2004] 1 W.L.R. 1575).

The judge who is to conduct the hearing should be, save in the most exceptional cases, the judge who is to conduct the trial (*R. v Southwark CC Ex p. Commrs of C & E, etc.* [1993] 1 W.L.R. 764).

A preparatory hearing:

(a) needs to be distinguished from an informal pre-trial review (*Re Gunawardena* (1990) 91 Cr.App.R. 55); it is to be used for the purposes specified in the statute, and for no others (*ibid.*);
(b) is concerned with matters which will facilitate the trial not with applications to prevent it taking place (*R. v Hedworth* [1997] 1 Cr.App.R. 421).

The judge's ruling relating, e.g. as to whether the indictment is to be construed as involving a wide-ranging conspiracy or only a narrower cell conspiracy, is a ruling as to the construction of the indictment, within the words of CJA 1987, s.7(1)(a) as identifying issues which are likely to be material to the verdict of a jury, furthermore such a purpose was pro-active case management to ensure that the jury were not over-burdened (*R. v G, S and N* [2002] Crim.L.R. 59).

As to consideration of evidence and issues under PACE 1984, s.78, see *R. v Claydon*, above.

16–028 A preparatory hearing may be held only where the statutory provisions set out in 16–027 above are fulfilled (not e.g. merely to allow points of law to be decided and then tested by interlocutory appeal: *R. v Pennine Acute Hospital NHS Trust etc* (2003) 147 S.J. 1426). In relation to (2) in 16–026 there must be a case of such complexity, a case of such seriousness, or a case whose trial is likely to be of such a length that a hearing would be beneficial, where, e.g.:

(1) the process of proper disclosure can be conducted;
(2) the marshalling of evidence can be prepared with direct reference to the live issues in the case;
(3) issues as to the proper interpretation of the relevant legislation, and as to directions to be given to the jury may be resolved,

but it is important for the judge to bear in mind that his power to make rulings on questions of law is confined to questions of law "relating to the case" (*R. v Shayler* [2002] 2 W.L.R. 754, HL).

The hearing

16–029 If a preparatory hearing is ordered:

(1) for purposes connected with the hearing the trial starts with that hearing (*R. v H (Evidence; Admissibility)* 2005, *The Times*, August 22, 2005), and arraignment takes place at the start of the hearing, if it has not taken place already; CJA 1987, s.8; CPIA 1996, s.31
(2) the judge needs, therefore, to bear in mind the effect on the custody time limits of the decision to hold such a hearing (*Re Kanaris* [2003] 1 W.L.R. 443, HL);
(3) in most cases, the decision to hold a hearing should be in respect of all accused joined in the same indictment (*Re Kanaris* above);
(4) any matter dealt with before the jury is sworn is to be treated as forming part of the preparatory hearing, provided that the purpose of dealing with it at that stage was one of the objects set out in the statute (*R. v Jennings* (1994) 98 Cr.App.R. 308).

Rulings and orders made

16–030 At the hearing, the judge may determine: CJA 1987, s.9; CJA 1988, Sch.16; CJA 1993, s.6(8); CPIA 1996, s.72, Sch.3,

(1) any question arising under CJA 1993, s.6 (relevance of external law to certain charges of conspiracy, attempt and incitement);

(2) any question as to the admissibility of evidence; and
(3) any other questions of law relating to the case.

para.3, s.74(1), (4); CJA 2003, s.310(2), 331, Sch.36, paras 18, 52, 54; CPIA 1996, s.31(1)(2)(3)(11)

but note that:

(a) he may not give a ruling which is tantamount to an order granting a stay or quashing the indictment (*R. v Hoogstraten, The Times*, December 24, 2003);
(b) any ruling has effect throughout the trial unless it appears to him, on application, that the interests of justice require him to vary or discharge it;
(c) he must be prepared to vary his rulings where required (*R. v Shayler* [2002] 2 W.L.R. 754, HL).

He may adjourn the hearing from time to time.

In relation to cases under CPIA 1996, there will be cases where the judge decides that orders under s.30(4)–(7) should be made before the hearing. In such a case he may make an order either before or at the hearing, and the above provisions apply accordingly (*ibid.,* s.32).

An order or ruling made by the judge has effect during the trial unless it appears to the judge, on an application made to him during the trial, that the interests of justice require him to discharge it.

CJA 1987, s.9(10); CPIA 1996, Sch.2

Disclosure by prosecutor

16–031 The judge may order the prosecutor:

CJA 1987, s.9(4) as amended above)/CPIA 1996 s.31(4), (5); CJA 2003, s.331, Sch.36, Pt 4, para.67

(1) to supply the court and each accused with a written "case statement", of the following, namely:
    (a) the principal facts of the prosecution case;
    (b) the witnesses who will speak to those facts;
    (c) any exhibits relevant to those facts;
    (d) any propositions of law on which the prosecutor intends to rely; and
    (e) the consequences in relation to any of the counts in the indictment which appear to him to flow from the matters stated in (a)–(d).
(2) to prepare his evidence and other explanatory material in such form as appears likely to aid the comprehension of a jury and to supply it in that form to the court and to each accused;
(3) give the court and each accused notice of documents, the truth of the contents of which ought, in the prosecutor's view, to be admitted, and of any other matters which ought to be agreed; and

(4) to make any amendments to any case statement supplied that appear to the judge to be appropriate, having regard to any objections made by any accused.

The judge may specify the time within which any requirement is to be complied with.

Disclosure by accused

16–032 Where the judge has ordered the prosecution to supply a case statement and the prosecutor has complied, the judge may order each accused to: CJA 1987, s.9(5)

(1) give to the court and the prosecutor, a statement in writing setting out in general terms the nature of his defence and indicating the principal matters on which he takes issue with the prosecution;
(2) give the court and the prosecutor notice of any objections that he has to the case statement;
(3) inform the court and the prosecution of any point of law (including points as to the admissibility of evidence) which he wishes to take, and any authority on which he intends to rely for that purpose; and
(4) give the court and the prosecution notice stating the extent to which he agrees with the prosecutor as to the documents and other matters to which it relates, and the reasons for any disagreement.

Paragraphs (1) and (4) above will be rendered otiose once the enhanced disclosure provisions of CJA 2003 come into force.

If he considers the reasons inadequate, the judge will inform the party concerned and has the power to require further or better reasons.

Where the judge decides that any order which could be made at the hearing should be made *before* the hearing, he may act accordingly. CJA 1987, s.9A; CPIA 1996, Sch.3, para.4

An order may specify the time within which any requirement contained in it is to be complied with. Orders under s.9(5) should be clear, comprising short questions identifying matters upon which the Crown require the defendant's agreement. In the case of several defendants, each defendant's case should be the subject of individual orders (*Case Statements made under CJA 1987, s.9* (1993) 97 Cr.App.R. 417). CJA 1987, s.9(9)

Certain consequences may flow from failure to comply with such orders (see 16–034 below), and the judge will need to warn each accused of them. In making an order he must warn the accused of the possible consequences of not CJA 1987, s.9(7); CPIA 1996, Sch.3, para.3; CPIA 1996, s.31(6), complying with it; if it appears to him that the reasons given in pursuance of s.2(b) are inadequate, he will inform the person giving them, and may require him to give further or better reasons. (7), (9); CJA 2003, s.331, Sch.36, Pt 4, s.66

Case statements of no evidential value

16–033 It has been said (*R. v Mayhew* unreported, November 18, 1991) that neither the prosecutor's case statement nor the defence statement has any evidential value, nor do they limit the respective parties in the evidence they may call. The object of ordering a case statement is to:

(1) inform the other side of the case that is intended to be put forward;
(2) facilitate preparation for trial, and to avoid surprise; and
(3) to enable comment to be made under s.10 where there is a significant departure from the statement.

The judge should not permit a case statement to be put before the jury as a matter of course, as if it were particulars of the indictment.

Later stages of the trial; departure from case at trial

16–034 A party may depart from the case he disclosed in pursuance of a requirement under s.9 or s.31 respectively but where: CJA 1987, s.10; CPIA 1996, Sch.3, para.5; CJA 2003, s.331, Sch.36, Pt 4, para.55/CPIA 1996, s.34; CJA 2003, s.331, Sch.36, Pt 4, para.68

(1) he does so; or
(2) fails to comply with the requirement to disclose,

The judge, or with his leave, any other party, may make such comment as appears appropriate, and the jury, or in the case of a trial without a jury, the judge will be able to draw such inferences as appear proper, though no part of the case statement or any other information relating to the accused may be disclosed after the jury have been sworn without the consent of the accused concerned.

The judge, in doing anything under this provision, or in deciding whether to do anything under it, may have regard to such matters as the extent of any departure or failure and whether it is justified.

(2) Procedure

CPR 2005, as amended by SI 2006/353, lays down a common procedure in a single part (Pt 15) in relation to preparatory hearings under both CJA 1987and CPIA 1996.

Application for preparatory hearing;

16–035 A party who wants the court to order a preparatory hearing under CJA 1987, s.7(2) or under CPIA 1996, s.29(4) must: R.15.1

(a) apply in the form set out in PD 2004, Annex D;
(b) include a short explanation of the reasons for applying; and
(c) serve the application on the court officer and all other parties.

A prosecutor who wants the court to order that:

(i) the trial will be conducted without a jury under CJA 2003, ss.43 or 44; or
(ii) the trial of some of the counts included in the indictment will be conducted without a jury under DVA 2004, s.17,

must apply under this rule for a preparatory hearing, whether or not the accused has applied for one.

Time for applying

16–036 A party who applies under r.15.1 must do so not more than 28 days after: R.15.2

(a) the committal of the accused;
(b) the consent to the preferment of a bill of indictment in relation to the case;
(c) the service of a notice of transfer; or
(d) where a person is sent for trial, the service of copies of the documents containing the evidence on which the charge or charges are based.

A prosecutor who applies under r.15.1 because he wants the court to order a trial without a jury under CJA 2003, s.44 (jury tampering) must do so as soon as reasonably practicable where the reasons do not arise until after that time limit has expired.

The court may extend the time limit, even after it has expired, A form of application is set out in PD 2004, Annex D specifying the grounds of the application which must be served on the Crown Court officer, a copy of the application being served at the same time on any other party.

Representations concerning an application

16–037 A party who wants to make written representations concerning an application made under r.15.1 must: R.15.3

(a) do so within 7 days of receiving a copy of that application; and
(b) serve those representations on the court officer and all other parties.

An accused who wants to oppose an application for an order that the trial will be conducted without a jury under CJA 2003, ss.43 or 44 must serve written representations under this rule, including a short explanation of the reasons for opposing that application.

Determination of application

16–038 Where an application has been made under R.15.1(2) the court must hold a preparatory hearing. R.15.4

Other applications made under r.15.1 should normally be determined without a hearing.

The court officer must serve on the parties in the case, in the form set out in PD 2004, Annex D:

(a) notice of the determination of an application made under r.15.1; and
(b) an order for a preparatory hearing made by the court of its own initiative, including one that the court is required to make.

Orders for disclosure by prosecution or defence

16–039 Any disclosure order under CJA 1987, s.9, or CPIA 1996, s.31 must identify any documents that are required to be prepared and served by the prosecutor under that order. R.15.5

A disclosure order under either of those sections does not require an accused to disclose who will give evidence, except to the extent that disclosure is required by:

(a) s.6A(2) of the 1996 Act (disclosure of alibi); or
(b) CPR 2005, Pt 24 (disclosure of expert evidence).

The court officer must serve notice of the order, in the relevant form set out in PD 2004, Annex D, on the parties.

Service of documents, etc

16–040 The service of notices or other documents is covered by R.15.6 as amended by SI2006/353.

(3) Reporting restrictions

16–041 Reporting restrictions similar to those imposed in the case of committal proceedings in magistrates' courts are imposed in relation to applications for dismissal of charges under CJA 1987, s.6 and to preparatory hearings under both the 1987 and the 1996 Acts.

CJA 1987, s.11; CJA 1988, Sch.15; CPIA 1996, ss.37, 38, Sch.3, para.6; CJA 2003,

It is unlawful to publish a report of proceedings which contains matter other than that permitted by the Acts unless on the order of the judge dealing with the matter, until the conclusion of the trial of the accused or the last of the accused to be tried. s.311(1), (2), s.332, Sch.37, Pt 4/CPIA 1996, s.37; AJA 1999, s.24, Sch.4, para.49; CJA 2003, s.311(5)(6)

The matters permitted are:

(1) the identity of the court, and the name of the judge;
(2) the names, ages, home addresses and occupations of the accused;
(3) any relevant business information (as defined in CJA 1987, s.11(9));
(4) the offence(s) or a summary of them, with which the accused are charged;
(5) the names of counsel and solicitors engaged in the proceedings;
(6) where the proceedings are adjourned, the date and place to which they are adjourned;
(7) any arrangements as to bail; and
(8) whether legal representation was granted to the accused.

Objection may be taken to the judge making an order "lifting" the restrictions. Where, in the case of two or more accused, one of them objects, the judge will make the order only if satisfied, after hearing the representations of the accused, that it is in the interests of justice to do so.

C. Interlocutory appeals

Right of appeal

16–042 Appeal lies, but only with leave from that court, to the CACD, from: CJA 1987, s.9(11), (12)

(1) any order or ruling of a judge;
(2) made within the ambit of a preparatory hearing as defined in CJA 1987, s.7(1), or as the case may be, CPIA 1996, s.31(3); and
(3) involving a question of law within CJA 1987, s.9(3)(b) or (c), (See 18 CHALLENGING THE CROWN COURT.)

As to defence costs, see POA 1985, s.16(4A); CJA 2003, s.257.

An application to quash the indictment is not within the scope of s.7(1), since such a hearing is concerned with matters which will *facilitate* the trial of the charges, not applications to *prevent* the trial from taking place (*R. v Hedworth* [1997] 1 Cr.App.R. 421). A ruling as to the scope of the indictment does fall within s.7(1) as identifying issues which are likely to be material to the verdict of the jury: *R. v G and Others*, *The Times*, March 30, 2001.

The judge may continue the preparatory hearing notwithstanding that leave has been granted to appeal, but the preparatory hearing is not to be concluded until the appeal has been determined or abandoned. (see *R. v Y* [2001] Crim.L.R. 389). CJA 1987, s.9(13), (14); CJA 2003, s.331, Sch.36, Pt 4, para.54

CACD may confirm, vary or reverse the judge's decision.

D. Preliminary hearings; pre-trial rulings

Definitions

16–043 A pre-trial hearing is one which relates to a trial on indictment and takes place: CPIA 1996, s.39; CDA 1998, s.119, Sch.8; CJA 2003, s.331, Sch.36, paras 57, 71

(1) after the accused has been sent for trial for the offence; or
(2) after a voluntary bill of indictment has been preferred; and
(3) before the start of the trial.

The "start" of a trial on indictment (s.39(3)) occurs at the time when a jury is sworn or, if the court accepts a plea of guilty *at* the time when a jury is sworn when that plea is accepted (subject to s.30, and to CJA 1987 in relation to preparatory hearings).

The reference to the time the jury was sworn is to be read, in the case of a trial without a jury, is a reference to the time when, if the trial were conducted with a jury, the jury would be sworn. CDA 1998, s.57 permits the use of TV links at such a hearing where such facilities exist, and the accused is in custody. CPIA 1996, s.39; CJA 2003, s.41, Sch.3, para.66, s.331, Sch.36, Pt 4, para.71

Effect of pre-trial ruling

16–044 At such a hearing, the judge may, either on application by a party or of his own motion, make a ruling:

(1) as to the admissibility of evidence; or
(2) on any question of law in the case.

That ruling has (subject to CPIA 1996, s.40(4)) immediate effect from the time it is made until the case against the accused is disposed of by acquittal or conviction or by the prosecutor deciding not to proceed (*ibid.* s.40).

It is desirable, where the judge is asked to decide whether the facts support a charge, for the facts on which the ruling is sought to be recorded (*R. v Marshall and Others* [1998] 2 Cr.App.R. 282).

Under s.40(4) a judge, whether or not the judge who made the ruling, may, either on application or of his own motion, discharge, vary, or further vary it, if it appears to him to be in the interests of justice so to do, where there has been a change of circumstances since the ruling or the last application was made.

Reporting restrictions

16–045 Reporting restrictions apply to proceedings and rulings under the section but the judge can lift the restrictions in certain circumstances.

A ruling made under s.40(1) is not binding for the purposes of a re-trial where the first jury disagreed. A judge may discharge or vary any ruling of his own motion if it appears to be in the interests of justice to do so. CPIA 1996, ss.41.42

E. Protocol for the control and management of heavy fraud and other complex criminal cases

[2005] 2 All E.R. 429

1. Introduction

General

16–046 This protocol supplements CPR 2005, and summarises good practice which experience has shown may assist in bringing about some reduction in the length of trials of fraud and other crimes that result in complex trials. Flexibility of application of this protocol according to the needs of each case is essential; it is designed to inform but not to prescribe.

This protocol:

(1) is primarily directed towards cases which are likely to last eight weeks or longer; but
(2) should also be followed in all cases estimated to last more than four weeks;
(3) applies to trials by jury, but many of the principles will be applicable if trials without a jury are permitted under CJA 2003, s.43.

The best handling technique for a long case is continuous management by an experienced judge nominated for the purpose.

2. The investigation

Prosecution and defence teams

16–047 While instructed, it is for the lead advocate for the prosecution to take all necessary decisions in the presentation and general conduct of the prosecution case in court. The prosecution lead advocate will be treated by the court as having that responsibility. However, in relation to policy decisions, the lead advocate for the prosecution must not give an indication or undertaking which binds the prosecution without first discussing the issue with the director of the prosecuting authority or other senior officer.

"Policy" decisions should be understood as referring to non-evidential decisions on: the acceptance of pleas of guilty to lesser counts or groups of counts or *available* alternatives; offering no evidence on particular counts; consideration of a re-trial; whether to lodge an appeal; certification of a point of law; and the withdrawal of the prosecution as a whole (for further information see the "Farquharson Guidelines" on the role and responsibilities of the prosecution advocate).

In each case, the lead advocate for the defence will be treated by the court as having responsibility to the court for the presentation and general conduct of the defence case.

In each case, a case progression officer must be assigned by the court, prosecution and defence from the time of the first hearing when directions are given until the conclusion of the trial.

In each case where there are multiple defendants, the Legal Services Commission (LSC) will need to consider carefully the extent and level of representation necessary.

Length of case; initial consideration

16–048 If the prosecutor in charge of the case from the prosecuting authority or the lead advocate for the prosecution consider that the case as formulated is likely to last more than eight weeks, the case should be referred in accordance with arrangements made by the prosecuting authority to a more senior prosecutor. The senior prosecutor will consider whether it is desirable for the case to be prosecuted in that way or whether some steps might be taken to reduce its likely length, whilst at the same time ensuring that the public interest is served.

Any case likely to last six months or more must be referred to the director of the prosecuting authority so that similar considerations can take place.

Special arrangements will be put in place for the early notification by the Crown Prosecution Service (CPS) and other prosecuting authorities, to the LSC and to a single designated officer of the court in each region (circuit) of any case which the CPS or other prosecuting authority consider likely to last over eight weeks.

The court will allocate such cases and other complex cases likely to last four weeks or more to a specific venue suitable for the trial in question, taking into account the convenience to witnesses, the parties, the availability of time at that location, and all other relevant considerations.

3. Designation of trial judge

16–049 In any complex case which is expected to last more than four weeks, the trial judge will be assigned under the direction of the Presiding Judges at the earliest possible moment. Thereafter the assigned judge should manage that case "from cradle to grave"; it is essential that the same judge manages the case from the time of his assignment and that arrangements are made for him to be able to do so. It is recognised that in certain court centres with a large turnover of heavy cases (e.g. Southwark) this objective is more difficult to achieve. But in those court centres there are teams of specialist judges, who are more readily able to handle cases which the assigned judge cannot continue with because of unexpected events; even at such courts, there must be no exception to the principle that one judge must handle all the pre-trial hearings until the case is assigned to another judge.

4. Case management

Obectives

16–050 The number, length and organisation of case management hearings will depend critically on the circumstances and complexity of the individual case. However, thorough, well-prepared and extended case management hearings will save court time and costs overall.

Effective case management of heavy fraud and other complex criminal cases requires the judge to have a much more detailed grasp of the case than may be necessary for many other plea and case management hearings.

Fixing the trial date

16–051 Although it is important that the trial date should be fixed as early as possible, this may not always be the right course. There are two principal alternatives. The trial date should:

(1) be fixed at the first opportunity, i.e. at the first (and usually short) directions hearing, from then on:
   (a) everyone must work to that date;

(b) all orders and pre-trial steps will be timetabled to fit in with that date; and

(c) all advocates and the judge should take note of this date, in the expectation that the trial will proceed on the date determined; or

(2) not be fixed until the issues have been explored at a full case management hearing, after the advocates on both sides have done some serious work on the case. Only then can the length of the trial be estimated.

Which procedure is apposite must depend on the circumstances of each case, but the earlier it is possible to fix a trial date, by reference to a proper estimate and a timetable set by reference to the trial date, the better.

It is generally to be expected that once a trial is fixed on the basis of the estimate provided, that it will be *increased* if, and only if, the party seeking to extend the *time* justifies why the original estimate is no longer appropriate.

The first hearing for the giving of initial directions

16–052 At the first opportunity the assigned judge should hold a short hearing to give initial directions. The directions on this occasion might well include that:

(1) there should be a full case management hearing on, or commencing on, a specified future date by which time the parties will be properly prepared for a meaningful hearing and the defence will have full instructions;

(2) the prosecution should provide an outline written statement of the prosecution case at least one week in advance of that case management hearing, outlining in simple terms:

(a) the key facts on which it relies;

(b) the key evidence by which the prosecution seeks to prove the facts. The statement must be sufficient to permit the judge to understand the case and for the defence to appreciate the basic elements of its case against each defendant. The prosecution may be invited to highlight the key points of the case orally at the case management hearing by way of a short mini-opening. The outline statement should not be considered binding, but it will serve the essential purpose in telling the judge, and everyone else, what the case is really about and identifying the key issues.

(3) a core reading list and core bundle for the case management hearing should be delivered at least one week in advance;
(4) preliminary directions about disclosure.

The first case management hearing

16–053 At the first case management hearing the prosecution advocate should be given the opportunity to highlight any points from the prosecution outline statement of case (which will have been delivered at least a week in advance), and each defence advocate should be asked to outline the defence.

If the defence advocate is not in a position to say what is in issue and what is not in issue, then the case management hearing can be adjourned for a short and limited time and to a fixed date to enable the advocate to take instructions; such an adjournment should only be necessary in exceptional circumstances, as the defence advocate should be properly instructed by the time of the first case management hearing and in any event is under an obligation to take sufficient instructions to fulfill the obligations contained in CJA 2003, ss.33–39.

There should then be a real dialogue between the judge and all advocates for the purpose of identifying

(1) the focus of the prosecution case;
(2) the common ground; and
(3) the real issues in the case (see CPR 2005, r.3.2).

The judge will try to generate a spirit of co-operation between the court and the advocates on all sides. It may be noted that:

(a) the expeditious conduct of the trial and a focussing on the real issues must be in the interests of all parties;
(b) it cannot be in the interests of any defendant for his good points to become lost in a welter of uncontroversial or irrelevant evidence;
(c) in many fraud cases the primary facts are not seriously disputed; the real issue is what each defendant knew and whether that defendant was dishonest. Once the judge has identified what is in dispute and what is not in dispute, he can then discuss with the advocate how the trial should be structured, what can be dealt with by admissions or agreed facts, what uncontroversial matters should be proved by concise oral evidence, what timetabling can be required under CPR 2005, r.3.10, and other directions.

It is important that proper defence case statements be provided as required by CPR 2005; judges will use the powers contained in CPIA 1996, ss.28–34 (and the corresponding provisions of CJA 1987, ss.33 *et seq.*) and CPR 2005 to ensure that realistic defence case statements are provided.

This objective may also be achieved by requiring the prosecution to serve draft admissions by a specified date and by requiring the defence to respond within a specified number of weeks.

Further case management hearings; length of trial

16–054 The date of the next case management hearing should be fixed at the conclusion of the hearing so that there is no delay in having to fix the date through listing offices, clerks and others. If one is looking at a trial which threatens to run for months, pre-trial case management on an intensive scale is essential.

Even intensive case management on the above lines may still be insufficient to reduce the trial to a manageable length:

(1) generally a trial of three months should be the target, but there will be cases where a duration of six months or, in exceptional circumstances, even longer may be inevitable;

(2) if the trial is not estimated to be within a manageable length, it will be necessary for the judge to consider what steps should be taken to reduce the length of the trial, whilst still ensuring that the prosecution has the opportunity of placing the full criminality before the court.

To assist the judge in this task:

(a) the lead advocate for the prosecution should be asked to explain why the prosecution have rejected a shorter way of proceeding; they may also be asked to divide the case into sections of evidence and explain the scope of each section and the need for each section;

(b) the lead advocates for the prosecution and for the defence should be prepared to put forward in writing, if requested, ways in which a case estimated to last more than three months can be shortened, including possible severance of counts or defendants, exclusions of sections of the case or of evidence or areas of the case where admissions can be made.

The judge may consider pruning the indictment by omitting certain charges and/or by omitting certain defendants.

CASE MANAGEMENT

The judge's powers

16–055 The judge must not usurp the function of the prosecution when pruning the indictment, and he must bear in mind that he will, at the outset, know less about the case than the advocates. The aim is to achieve fairness to all parties. Nevertheless, the judge does have two methods of pruning available for use in appropriate circumstances:

(1) persuading the prosecution that it is not worthwhile pursuing certain charges and/or certain defendants;
(2) severing the indictment.

Severance for reasons of case management alone is perfectly proper, although judges should have regard to any representations made by the prosecution that severance would weaken their case. However, before using what may be seen as a blunt instrument, the judge should insist on seeing full defence statements of all affected defendants. Severance may be unfair to the prosecution if, for example, there is a cut-throat defence in prospect. For example, the defence of the principal defendant may be that the defendant relied on the advice of his accountant or solicitor that what was happening was acceptable. The defence of the professional may be that he gave no such advice. Against that background, it might be unfair to the prosecution to order separate trials of the two defendants.

CPR 2005 require the court to take a more active part in case management. Nevertheless these salutary provisions do not have to be used on every occasion. Where the advocates have done their job properly, by narrowing the issues, pruning the evidence and so forth, it may be quite inappropriate for the judge to "weigh in" and *start* cutting out more evidence or more charges of his own volition. It behoves the judge to make a careful assessment of the degree of judicial intervention which is warranted in each case.

In respect of:

(1) **expert evidence**, early identification of the subject matter of expert evidence to be adduced by the prosecution and the defence should be made as early as possible, preferably at the directions hearing. Following the exchange of expert evidence, any areas of disagreement should be identified and a direction should generally be made requiring the experts to meet and prepare, after discussion, a joint statement identifying points of agreement and contention and areas where the prosecution is put to proof on matters of which a positive case to the contrary

is not advanced by the defence. After the statement has been prepared it should be served on the court, the prosecution and the defence. In some cases, it might be appropriate to provide that to the jury.

(2) **surveillance evidence,** where a prosecution is based upon many months' observation or surveillance evidence and it appears that it is capable of effective presentation based on a shorter period, the advocate should be required to justify the evidence of such observations before it is permitted to be adduced, either substantially or in its entirety. Schedules should be provided to cover as much of the evidence as possible and admissions sought.

Disclosure

16–056 In fraud cases the volume of documentation obtained by the prosecution is liable to be immense. The problems of disclosure are intractable and have the potential to disrupt the entire trial process.

(1) The prosecution lawyer (and the prosecution advocate if different) brought in at the outset, each have a continuing responsibility to discharge the prosecution's duty of disclosure, either personally or by delegation, in accordance with the Attorney General's Guidelines on Disclosure.

(2) The prosecution should only disclose those documents which are relevant (i.e. likely to assist the defence or undermine the prosecution — see CPIA 1996, s.3(1) and the provisions of CJA 2003.

(3) It is almost always undesirable to give the "warehouse key" to the defence for two reasons: (a) this amounts to an abrogation of the responsibility of the prosecution; and (b) the defence solicitors may spend a disproportionate amount of time and incur disproportionate costs trawling through a morass of documents.

The judge should therefore try and ensure that disclosure is limited to what is likely to assist the defence or undermine the prosecution.

(4) At the outset the judge should set a timetable for dealing with disclosure issues. In particular, he should fix a date by which all defence applications for specific disclosure must be made.

(5) At the outset (and before the cut-off date for specific disclosure applications) the judge should ask the defence to

indicate what documents they are interested in and from what source. A general list is not an acceptable response to this request. The judge should insist upon a list which is specific, manageable and realistic. The judge may also require justification of any request.

(6) In non-fraud cases, the same considerations apply, but some may be different:

(a) it is not possible to approach many non-fraud cases on the basis that the defendant knows what is there or what they are looking for; but on the other hand this should not be turned into an excuse for a "fishing expedition"; the judge should insist on knowing the issue to which a request for disclosure applies;

(b) if the bona fides of the investigation is called into question, the judge will be concerned to see that there has been independent and effective appraisal of the documents contained in the disclosure schedule and that its contents are adequate. In appropriate cases where this issue has arisen and there are grounds which show there is a real issue, consideration should be given to receiving evidence on oath from the senior investigating officer at an early case management hearing.

Abuse of process

16–057 Applications to stay or dismiss for abuse of process have become a normal feature of heavy and complex cases. Such applications may be based upon delay and the health of defendants. See *R. v Howell and Harris* [2003] EWCA Crim 486. It should be noted that abuse of process is not there to discipline the prosecution or the police. Where the issue arises:

(1) the arguments on both sides must be reduced to writing;
(2) oral evidence is seldom relevant;
(3) the judge should direct full written submissions (rather than "skeleton arguments") on any abuse application in accordance with a timetable set by him; these should identify any element of prejudice the defendant is alleged to have suffered.

And see above, 3–010.

5. The trial

Case management at the trial

16–058 The Protocol recognises that a heavy fraud or other complex trial has the potential to lose direction and focus:

(1) the jury may lose track of the evidence, thereby prejudicing both prosecution and defence;
(2) the burden on the defendants, the judge and indeed all involved will become intolerable; and
(3) scarce public resources will be wasted.

It is necessary for the judge to exercise firm control over the conduct of the trial at all stages. His role in a heavy fraud or other complex criminal trial is different from his role in a "conventional" criminal trial. So far as possible, he should be freed from other duties and burdens, so that he can give the high degree of commitment which a heavy fraud trial requires. The protocol suggests that:

(a) by the outset of the trial at the latest (and in most cases very much earlier) the judge be provided with a schedule, showing the sequence of prosecution (and in an appropriate case defence) witnesses and the dates upon which they are expected to be called;
(b) this schedule should be kept under review by the trial judge and by the parties. If a case is running behind or ahead of schedule, each witness affected must be advised by the party who is calling that witness at the earliest opportunity;
(c) if an excessive amount of time is allowed for any witness, the judge can ask why; he may probe with the advocates whether the time envisaged for the evidence-in-chief or cross-examination (as the case may be) of a particular witness is really necessary;
(d) there should be periodic case management sessions, during which the judge engages the advocates upon a stock-taking exercise: asking, amongst other questions, "where are we going?" and "what is the relevance of the next three witnesses?" This will be a valuable means of keeping the case on track. CPR 2005, r.3.10 will again assist the judge;
(e) "case management notes" from the judge to the advocates, setting out the judge's tentative view on where the trial may be going off track, which areas of future evidence are relevant and which may have become irrelevant (e.g. because of concessions, admissions in cross-examination and so forth, together with written responses may, if

cautiously used, provide a valuable focus for debate during the periodic case management reviews held during the course of the trial;

(f) setting rigid time limits in advance for cross-examination is rarely appropriate, but the judge can and should indicate when cross-examination is irrelevant, unnecessary or time wasting. The judge may limit the time for further cross-examination of a particular witness;

(g) electronic presentation of evidence (EPE) has the potential to save huge amounts of time in fraud and other complex criminal trials and should be used more widely; there should still be a core bundle of those documents to which frequent reference will be made during the trial;

(h) greater use of other modern forms of graphical presentations should be made wherever possible;

(i) the judge should consider extensive editing of self-serving interviews, even when the defence want the jury to hear them in their entirety; such interviews are not evidence of the truth of their contents but merely of the defendant's reaction to the allegation.

Problems have arisen when the LSC have declined to allow advocates or solicitors to do certain work; on occasions the matter has been raised with the judge managing or trying the case. The LSC has provided guidance to judges on how they can obtain information from the LSC as to the reasons for their decisions; further information in relation to this can be obtained from Nigel Field, Head of the Complex Crime Unit, Legal Services Commission, 29–37 Red Lion Street, London, WC1R 4PP.

F. TERRORISM CASES

Introduction

16–059 A protocol issued by the President of the QBD on January 16, 2006 provides for the management of those "terrorism cases" as defined in para.1 which are indictable only and sent to the Crown Court under CDA 1998, s.51 or in cases involving serious fraud, are transferred to the Crown Court under CJA 1987, s.4.

All such cases, wherever they originate in England and Wales, are to be managed in a "terrorism cases list" by the Presiding Judges of the SE Circuit and such other High Court judges nominated by the President of the QBD. They will be heard, unless the President otherwise directs, by a High Court judge nominated by him. Judges hearing such cases will be supported by the London and SE Regional Co-ordinator's Office.

Duties of magistrates' court

16–060 The magistrates' court, both in s.51 cases and in transfers under s.4, to facilitate the preliminary hearing at the Crown Court, require:

(1) the prosecutor, three days prior to the preliminary hearing in the terrorism cases list, to serve on each accused and the Regional Listing Co-ordinator:

(a) a preliminary summary of the case;
(b) the names of those who are to represent the prosecution, if known;
(c) an estimate of the length of the trial;
(d) a suggested provisional timetable which should generally include:

(i) the general nature of further enquiries being made by the prosecution;
(ii) the time needed for the completion of such enquiries;
(iii) the time required by the prosecution to review the case;
(iv) a timetable for the phased service of the evidence;
(v) the time for the provision by the Attorney-General for his consent if necessary;
(vi) the time for service of the detailed defence case statement;
(vii) the date for the case management hearing;
(viii) the estimated trial date

(e) A preliminary statement of the possible disclosure issues setting out the nature and scale of the problem including the amount of unused material, the manner in which the prosecution seeks to deal with these matters and a suggested timetable for discharging their statutory duty; and
(f) any information relating to bail and custody time limits

(2) each accused, one day prior to the preliminary hearing in the terrorist cases list, to serve in writing on the Regional Listing Co-ordinator and the prosecution:

(a) the proposed representation;
(b) observations on the timetable; and
(c) an indication of plea and the general nature of the defence.

When a terrorism case is sent or transferred to the Crown Court it will go into the terrorism list and be managed by the nominated judge.

Preliminary hearing at the Crown Court

16–061 At the preliminary hearing at the Crown Court, the judge will determine whether the case is one to remain in the terrorism list, and if so will give directions setting the provisional timetable. The Legal Services Commission must attend by an authorised officer to assist the judge.

Unless a judge otherwise directs all Crown Court hearings prior to the trial will be conducted by video link for all accused in custody.

17 CDS FUNDING

17–001 LAA 1988 (and the LA (Gen) Regs made under it) was repealed by AJA 1999, amended by CDSA 2006, which establishes a Legal Service Commission having functions in relation to the Community Legal Service and the Criminal Defence Service (CDS) which it sets up. The Commission is under a duty (AJA 1999, s.12(2)) to establish, maintain and develop the Criminal Defence Service (CDS) for the purpose of securing that individuals involved in criminal investigations or criminal proceedings have access to such advice, assistance and representation as the interests of justice require. See also The Criminal Defence Service (General) (No.2) Regulations 2001 (SI 2001/1437), and The Criminal Defence Service (General) (No.2) Regulations 2003 (SI 2003/644). The Criminal Defence (General) (No.2) (Amendment) Regulations 2006 (SI 2006/2491).

Under the existing structure it is the courts which are responsible for granting the right to have funding. CDSA 2006 (SI 2006/2491) enables the Lord Chancellor to confer power to grant such rights on the Legal Services Commission instead of on the court; it provides further for rights to representation being granted only where a person satisfies financial eligibility criteria and for the making of contribution orders where financial eligibility criteria are satisfied.

The Criminal Defence Service (Financial Liability) Regulations 2006 (SI 2006/2492) set out the criteria relating to financial eligibilty which must be satisfied before persons involved in criminal proceedings in a magistrates' court may receive publicly funded representation.

The Criminal Defence Service (Funding) Order 2001 (SI 2001/855), as amended by the Criminal Defence Service (Funding) (Amendment No. 3) Order 2001 (SI 2001/341) and see 17–036 below, makes provison for the funding and remuneration of services provided as part of the CDS.

"Criminal proceedings" defined

General

17–002 "Criminal proceedings" are proceedings: AJA 1999, s.12(1)

(a) before any court for dealing with an individual accused of an offence;

- before any court for dealing with an individual convicted of an offence (including proceedings in respect of a sentence or order);
- for dealing with an individual under the Extradition Act 2003;
- for binding an individual over to keep the peace or to be of good behaviour under MCA 1980, s.115 and for dealing with an individual who fails to comply with an order under that section;
- on an appeal brought by an individual under CAA 1968, s.44A (deceased appellants);
- for contempt committed, or alleged to have been committed, by an individual in the face of the court;
- concerning an individual before any such court or body as may be prescribed (other than the above).

Prescribed proceedings—s.12(2)(g)

17–003 The following have been prescribed as "criminal proceedings" for the purposes of the AJA 1999, s.12(2)(g): GR 2001, reg.2(2)–(4); SI 2004/1196; SI 2006/2491

(a) civil proceedings in a magistrates' court arising from failure to pay a sum due or to obey an order of that court where such failure carries the risk of imprisonment;
(b) proceedings under CDA 1998, ss.1, 2 and 4 relating to anti-social behaviour orders or sex offender orders;
(c) proceedings under the CDA 1998, s.8(I)(b) relating to parenting orders made where an anti-social behaviour order or a sex offender order is made in respect of a child;
(d) proceedings under the CDA 1998, s.8(1)(c) relating to parenting orders made on conviction of a child;
(e) proceedings under CDA 1998, s.9(5) to discharge or vary a parenting order as mentioned in (c) and (d) above;
(f) proceedings under CDA 1998, s.10 to appeal against a parenting order made as mentioned in (c) or (d) above;
(g) proceedings under FSA 1989, as amended, ss.14B, 14D, 14G, 14H, 21B and 21D (banning orders and references to a court); and
(h) proceedings under the Financial Services and Marketing Act 2000, s.137 to appeal against a decision of the Financial Services and Markets Tribunal; and
(i) proceedings under ASBA 2003, ss.2, 5 and 6 relating to the making or extension of a closure order, and appeals against such an order.

Incidental proceedings

17–004 Proceedings in the Crown Court: GR 2001, reg.3(3)

(1) following committal for sentence by a magistrates' court
(2) to quash an acquittal under the CPIA 1996; or
(3) for confiscation and forfeiture in connection with criminal proceedings under CPR 1998, Sch.1 under RSC, Ord.115,

are to be regarded as incidental to the criminal proceedings from which they arise.

Applications for judicial review or *habeas corpus* relating to any criminal investigations or proceedings are not to be regarded as incidental to such criminal investigations or proceedings.

Availability of representation

17–005 A right to representation for the purposes of any kind of criminal proceedings may be granted to an individual such as is mentioned in relation to that kind of proceedings in s.12(2) of the Act (see above). Proceedings may also be granted to an individual to enable him to resist an appeal to the Crown Court otherwise than in an official capacity. AJA 1999, S.14(1), Sch.3, para.1

General power to grant representation

17–006 Whether or not an application has been made for a representation order, the court or a judge of the court may at any stage of the proceedings, in the circumstances provided for under GR 2001, grant such an order. GR 2001, reg.7

Representation orders for a Q.C. alone or more than one advocate

17–007 Such applications made to the Crown Court must be placed before the resident judge of that Crown Court (or in his absence, a judge nominated for that purpose by a Presiding Judge of the circuit) who must determine the application, save that, where the application relates to a case which is to be heard before a named High Court Judge or a named Circuit Judge, he should refer the application to the named judge for determination. CDS(G)(No.2) Regs 2001

This does not apply where an application is made:

- in the course of a trial, or
- of a preliminary hearing;
- pre-trial review, or (d) plea and directions hearing by the judge presiding at that trial or hearing.

In the event of any doubt as to the proper application of this direction, reference should be made by the judge concerned to PD 2004, IV.38.1

a presiding judge of the circuit, who must give such directions as he thinks fit.

Grant and withdrawal of right by court

17–008 A court before which any criminal proceedings take place, or are to take place, may grant a right to representation in the interests of justice: AJA 1999, s.14, Sch.3, para.2; CDSA 2006, s.1; GR 2001, reg.3(4)

(1) in respect of those proceedings;
(2) for the purpose of any related bail proceedings;
(3) for the purpose of any preliminary or incidental proceedings; and
(4) for the purpose of criminal proceedings before another court,

except in relation to proceedings in respect of which the Commission has power to grant a right to representation under *ibid* para.2A, unless regulations otherwise provide or in such other circumstances as may be prescribed.

Applications for judicial review or *habeas corpus* relating to any criminal investigations or proceedings are not to be regarded as incidental to such criminal investigations or proceedings.

A right to representation in respect of proceedings may be withdrawn by any court before which proceedings take place, unless the Commission has power to do, and a court must consider whether to withdraw a right to representation in such circimstances as may be prescribed. See also 17–021, below.

Contempt cases

17–009 In any proceedings for contempt committed, or alleged to have been committed by an individual in the face of the court, a judge may order that the person concerned be granted representation for the purposes of the proceedings, if it appears desirable in the interests of justice. AJA 1999, s.12(2)f)

Financial eligibility; contribution orders

17–009A Once CDSA 2006 comes into force, the power to grant a right to representation may only be exercised in relation to an individual whose financial resources appear to the prescribed authority to be such that under regulations, he is eligible to be granted such a right. A right to representation may be withdrawn if it appears to the prescribed authority in relation to the person concerned that: AJA 1999, S.14, Sch.3, paras 3B; 17A; CDSA 2006, ss.2, 3

(1) his financial resources are not such that, under regulations, he is eligible to be granted that right; or

(2) he has failed, in relation to that right, to comply with regulations about the furnishing of information

Regulations may be made under the Act as amended, providing that in prescribed circumstances, a person granted a right to representation may be ordered to pay the cost of his representation or to make a contribition in respect of that amount of such amount as is fixed by or determined under the regulations.

Statutory criteria

17–010 Any question as to whether a right to representation should be granted must be determined according to the interests of justice. In deciding what the interests of justice are in relation to any individual, the following factors, now statutory, but identical with those obtained in the light of the authorities decided on the previous legislation (but which may be added to or varied by the Lord Chancellor), are to be taken into account. They are whether: AJA 1999, s.14, Sch.3, para.5

(1) the individual would, if any matter arising in the proceedings is decided against him, be likely to lose his liberty or livelihood or suffer serious damage to his reputation;
(2) the determination of any matter arising in the proceedings may involve consideration of a substantial question of law;
(3) the individual may be unable to understand the proceedings or to state his case;
(4) the proceedings may involve tracing, interviewing or expert cross-examination of witnesses (not the cross-examination of expert witnesses (*R. v Liverpool City Magistrates Ex p. McGhee*, below) on his behalf; and
(5) it is in the interests of another person that the applicant be represented.

In considering whether an applicant is likely to lose his liberty, it is not the fact that the offence carries a custodial penalty that is important, but whether on the facts alleged by the Crown, a custodial sentence might be imposed (*R. v Highgate JJ. Ex p. Lewis* [1977] Crim.L.R. 611). A community punishment order is not to be regarded as depriving the applicant of his liberty (*R. v Liverpool City Magistrates Ex p. McGhee* [1993] Crim.L.R. 609).

As to the cross-examination of police witnesses, see *R. v Scunthorpe JJ. Ex p. S* (*The Times*, March 5, 1998).

A right to representation must always be granted in such circumstances as may be prescribed.

Advice prior to grant of representation order

17–011 Advice given prior to the grant of an order in the Crown Court is deemed to have been given under the order where: GR 2001, reg.4A; SI 2004/1196

(1) the interests of justice required that the advice be provided as a matter of urgency;
(2) there was no undue delay in making the application for a representation order; and
(3) the advice was given by the representative subsequently assigned to the order.

Applying for representation: (1) general

17–012 "Representation" here, means representation for the purposes of proceedings and includes the assistance which is usually given by a representative in the steps preliminary or incidental to any proceedings and, subject to any time limits which may be prescribed, advice and assistance as to any appeal. AJA 1999, s.26

Other than where reg.6(3) applies (see below), an application for a representation order in respect of proceedings in the Crown Court may be made, where an application for such an order in respect of the proceedings in a magistrates' court has not been made or has been refused: GR 2001, regs 6, 7, 9; SI 2006/2491

(1) orally or in writing to the Crown Court,
(2) in writing to the Crown Court officer
(3) in writing to the magistrates' court at the conclusion of any proceedings in the magistrates' court;
(4) in writing to the magistrates' court to send a case for trial under CDA 1998, s.51 *et seq*;
(5) where a magistrates' court has been given a notice of transfer under CJA 1987, s.4 (serious fraud cases) in writing to the designated officer of the magistrates' court;
(6) in the case of an appeal to the Crown Court from a magistrates' court, to the designated officer of that court;
(7) where the applicant was committed for trial in the Crown Court under MCA 1980, s.6(2), to the designated officer of the magistrates' court ordering the committal; or
(8) in the case of a retrial ordered under CJA 1968, s.7 orally or in writing to the court ordering the retrial,

and the appropriate officer of the relevant court, or the relevant court, may grant or refuse the application. Where an application is made orally to the court, the court may refer it to the officer for determination.

An application for the grant of representation in respect of the proceedings in the Crown Court which are mentioned in s.12(2)(a)–(f) (above, 17–002) of the Act and in reg.3(2)(h) (above, 17–003) must be made to the Commission. GR 2001 reg.6(3)

The appropriate officer of each court keeps a record of every application to that court for a representation order, and of its outcome.

Where an application is refused, the appropriate officer will provide to the applicant written reasons for the refusal and details of the appeal process.

Applying for representation: (2) voluntary bill procedure

17–013 In the case of an application for a representation order in respect of representation in the High Court against the preferment of a voluntary bill of indictment, it may be made: GR 2001, reg.9(2)

(1) in writing to the Crown Court officer; or
(2) orally to the judge considering the preferment of the bill,

and where it is granted it applies to any proceedings in which the applicant is indicted.

Applying to the Commission: reg.3(2) cases

17–014 Any application for the grant of a representation order in respect of those criminal proceedings set out in the GR 2001, reg.3(2) for the purposes of AJA 1999, s.12(2)(g) (i.e. those listed at 17–003, above) must be made to the Commission, and may only be granted by the Commission, or a person acting on behalf of the Commission where such function has been delegated in accordance with AJA 1999, s.3(4). Where such an application is refused, the applicant will be provided by the Commission with written reasons for the refusal and details of the appeal process. GR 2001, reg.5(2)

Selecting a representative

17–015 An individual who has been granted a representation order may select any representative or representatives willing to act for him. Where he does so, the Commission (under AJA 1999, s.14(1)) will fund such representation, provided the representative selected is: AJA 1999, s.15;GR 2001, regs 9, 11

(1) employed by the Commission to provide such representation; or

(2) authorised to provide such representation under a crime franchise contract with the Commission, which commences on or after April 2, 2001 and specifies the rate of remuneration for such representation.

Representation in magistrates' courts and subsequent proceedings

17–016 In relation to any criminal proceedings in a magistrates' court, any proceedings in the Crown Court coming within reg.3(2) (above) and any proceedings preliminary or incidental thereto (but not proceedings for contempt in the face of the court), representation is restricted to a representative: GR 2001, regs 9, 10

(1) employed by the Commission to provide such representation; or
(2) authorised to provide such representation under a crime franchise contract with the Commission which commences on or after April 2, 2001, and specifies the rate of remuneration for such representation.

An order may include representation by an advocate in a magistrates' court only in the case of an indictable offence, including one triable either way, or proceedings under the Extradition Act 1989, s.9, or Sch.1, para.6.

An "advocate" in this context is a barrister or a solicitor who has obtained a higher advocacy qualification in accordance with regulations and the rules of the Law Society.

Where, however, the court is of opinion that circumstances make the proceedings unusually grave or difficult, it may grant representation by both a solicitor and an advocate, if it considers it would be desirable.

Representation in the Crown Court

17–017 Representation under a representation order in respect of any proceedings in the Crown Court (other than those mentioned in reg.3(2)), the Court of Appeal or the House of Lords is exercisable only in relation to those representatives who are: GR 2001, reg.13

(1) employed by the Commission to provide such representation;
(2) authorised to provide such representation under a crime franchise contract with the Commission; or
(3) involved in a "very high cost" serious fraud case, where representation is limited to a current member of the Serious Fraud Panel.

Note that:

(a) a "very high cost" case is one where the trial is likely to last for 25 days or more, or specific costs are likely to amount to £150,000 or more; and
(b) the "Serious Fraud Panel" is a panel of solicitors appointed under arrangements made by the Commission to deal with such cases.

Such a case is one in which the offence charged is primarily or substantially founded on allegations of fraud or other serious financial impropriety, or involves complex financial transactions. The regulation does not apply to any proceedings referred to in AJA 1999, s.12(2)(f) (proceedings for contempt in the face of the court).

Representation in very high cost cases

17–018 A "very high cost case" is a case with regard to which: CVHCCR 2001, reg.2; SI 2004/598

(1) if the case proceeds to trial, the trial would be likely to last for 25 days or more; or
(2) the defence costs with regard to any one accused or group of accused rerpresented by the same firm of solicitors are likely to amount to £150,000 or greater (including the solicitors' fees and disursements, counsel's fees and VAT).

Any question of whether the case fulfils either of these criteria being a question to be determined by the Commission.

A "very high cost fraud case" means a very high cost case as defined above, with regard to which the offence with which the accused is charged is primarily or substantially founded on allegations of fraud or other serious financial impropriety, or involves complex financial transactions.

Where a representation order has been granted in relation to a very high cost case and the Commission proposes to enter into an individual contract for the provision of funded services in relation to that case, and either: CVHCCR 2001, reg.3(1), (2); SI 2004/598

(a) it serves notice that it does not propose to enter into such a contract with any, or all, of the current representatives; and
(b) any or all of those representatives serves notice that they do not propose to enter into such a contract, or
(c) the current solicitor representatives are not members of the Serious Fraud Panel established by the Commission, and the case is a very high cost fraud case,

then the Commission is no longer required to fund representation by the relevant current representative. The person in whose favour the representation order was made may select a different representative, chosen in accordance with GR 2001, and the representation order may be amended accordingly.

Amendment and revocation

17–019 Where a representation order has been granted by a relevant court or in the relevant circumstances by the Commission, it may be amended or withdrawn, whether by the relevant court or by the Commission. If legal representatives withdraw during the trial, fresh solicitors and counsel must be assigned unless the order is revoked (*R. v Harris* [1985] Crim.L.R. 244; *R. v Chambers* [1989] Crim.L.R. 367; *R. v Dimech* [1991] Crim.L.R. 846). CR 2001, reg.3(1)(2)

In some circumstances, the judge may have to conduct an enquiry as to why an accused has dispensed with his legal representatives (*R. v Seale* [1997] Crim.L.R. 899).

Renewal of application

17–020 An applicant whose application for a representation order has been refused by the Crown Court is entitled to renew his application either orally or in writing to the same court, or in writing to the Crown Court officer of that court. ROAR 2001, regs 4, 6

Where an application is renewed:

(1) to the officer, he may either grant it or refer it to a judge; or
(2) to the court, the court may grant it, refuse it or refer it to the officer, in which case the latter may grant it or refer it to a judge.

A judge of the court to whom to an application is referred may grant or refuse the application, giving reasons for that refusal, and where the application is in writing, reasons must be given in writing.

A person whose application for a grant of a representation order has been refused by the Commission is also entitled to renew it, in writing to the Funding Review Committee, which may grant or refuse it, giving reasons in writing for any refusal.

Withdrawal of representation

17–021 Where any charge or proceedings against the assisted person are varied, the court before which the proceedings are heard, or, in respect of any proceedings mentioned in reg.3(2)(a)–(g), the Commission, must: GR 2001, reg.17; SI 2006/2491

(1) consider whether to interests of justice continue to require that he be represented in respect of the varied charge or proceedings; and

(2) withdraw the representation if the interests of justice do not so require.

The court before which the proceedings are heard, or, in respect of any proceedings mentioned in reg.3(2)(a)–(g), the Commission, must consider whether to withdraw the representation order in any of the following circumstances:

(a) where the assisted person declines to accept a representation order in the terms which are offered;
(b) otherwise at the request of the assisted person; or
(c) where the representative named on the representation order declines to continue to represent the assisted person.

Where representation is withdrawn, the appropriate officer or the Commission, as appropriate, will provide written notification to the assisted person and to the solicitor (or, where there was no solicitor assigned, to the advocate), who must inform any assigned advocate (or, where notification is given to the advocate, any other assigned advocate).

If there is a subsequent application by the assisted person for a representation order in respect of the same proceedings, he must declare the previous withdrawal of representation and the reason for it. Where it was withdrawn in the circumstances set out in (1) or (2) or (a) or (b) above, and a representation order is subsequently granted, the court or the Commission, as appropriate, must select the same representative unless it considers that there are good reasons why a different representative should be selected.

Where a representation order has been withdrawn, appeal lies against such withdrawal on one occasion only, to the body which withdrew the order. Regulations 4 to 6 (above) apply to such appeals. An appeal in writing must be in such form as is from time to time specified. ROAR 2001, reg.7

Magistrates' assignment of Queen's Counsel in Crown Court

17–022 A magistrates' court has power to grant a representation order for Queen's Counsel only in the following circumstances: GR 2001, reg.12(14)

- for Queen's Counsel alone on a committal, transfer or sending for trial for murder; or
- for Queen's Counsel with one junior counsel, upon receiving a notice of transfer under CJA 1987, s.4, where the prosecution is brought by the Serious Fraud Office.

Assignment of two or more counsel

17–023 GR 2001, reg.12(2)(a)(b) and (c) sets out the terms on which representation may be provided for the services of Queen's Counsel, or of more than one advocate. These terms may be varied by reg.12(3) to (9) inclusive.

A representation order may provide for the services of Queen's Counsel or of more than one advocate in any of the following terms:

- Queen's Counsel alone;
- where two advocates are required:
- Queen's Counsel with junior counsel;
- Queen's Counsel with noting junior counsel;
- two junior counsel; or
- junior counsel with noting junior counsel;
- where three advocates are required:
- in any of the terms provided for in (b) above, plus an extra junior counsel; or
- in any terms provided for in (b) above, plus a noting junior.

An order under the terms of:

(1) reg.12(2)(a) above, may be made if and only if:

(a) in the court's opinion the case for the assisted person involves substantial, novel Or complex issues of law or fact which could not be adequately presented except by Queen's Counsel; and GR 2001, reg. 12(3)(a)–(x)

(b) either:

- Queen's Counsel or Senior Treasury counsel has been instructed on behalf of the prosecution; or
- the case for the assisted person is exceptional compared with the generality of cases involving similar offences.

(2) para.2(b)(iii) or (iv) above, may be made if and only if GR 2001, reg.12(4)(a)(b)

(a) in the court's opinion the case for the assisted person involves substantial, novel or complex issues of law or fact which could not be adequately presented by a single advocate; and

(b) either:

- two or more advocates have been instructed on behalf of the prosecution;
- the case for the assisted person is exceptional compared with the generality of cases involving similar offences;

- the number of prosecution witnesses exceeds 80; or
- the number of pages of prosecution evidence, including the witness statements, documentary and pictorial exhibits, and records of interview with the assisted person and other accused, forming part of the committal documents or included in any notice of additional evidence, exceeds 1000.

(3) para.2(b)(i) or (ii) above, may be made if and only if — GR 2001, reg.12(5)(a)(b)

(a) the court is of opinion that the case for the assisted person involves substantial novel or complex issues of law or fact which could not be adequately presented except by Queen's Counsel assisted by junior counsel; and

(b) either:

(i) the case for the assisted person is exceptional compared with the generality of cases involving similar offences; or

(ii) Queen's Counsel or senior Treasury counsel has been instructed on behalf of the prosecution and one of the conditions in reg.4(b)(i)(iii) or (iv) (see above) is satisfied.

The "equality of arms" principle embodied in the European Convention, Art.6 is not breached by the refusal to allow representation by Queen's Counsel where the Crown is so represented (*Att.-Gen.'s Reference (No. 82 of 2000)* [2002] 2 Cr.App.R. 342).

(4) para.(2)(c) above, may be made if and only if — GR 2001, reg.12(6)(a)–(c):

(a) the proceedings arise from a prosecution brought by the Serious Fraud Office;

(b) the court making the order considers that three advocates are required; and

(c) in the case of proceedings in the Crown Court, the conditions in reg.12(4) and (5) (see above) are satisfied.

The fact that a Queen's Counsel has been, or is proposed to be, assigned under this regulation is not by itself a reason for making an order in any of the terms provided for by reg.12 (2)(b) or (c). — GR 2001, reg.12(7)

Restrictions on grant

17–024 No order must be made or amended in the terms of paragraph: GR 2001, reg.12(10)

- 2(b), where two advocates are required, unless the court making the order is of the opinion that the assisted person could not be adequately represented under para.2(a), namely by Queen's Counsel alone;
- 2(b)(i) (Queen's Counsel with junior counsel), unless the court making the order is of the opinion that the assisted person could not be adequately represented under an order in the terms of para.2(b)(ii),(iii) or (iv) (Queen's Counsel with a noting junior, or two junior counsel or junior counsel with a noting counsel);
- 2(b)(ii) (Queen's Counsel with a noting junior), unless the court making the order is of the opinion that the assisted person could not be adequately represented under an order in the terms of para.2(b)(iii) or (iv) (two junior counsel or junior counsel with a noting junior);
- 2(b)(iii) (two junior counsel), unless the court making the order is of the opinion that the assisted person could not be adequately represented under an order in the terms of para.2(b)(iv) (junior counsel with a noting junior);
- (2)(c)(i), unless the court making the order is of the opinion that the assisted person could not be adequately represented under an order in the terms under para.(2)(c)(ii).

Every application for a representation order in any of the terms provided for by reg.12(2), (above) or for an amendment under reg.12(15), must be in writing specifying:

(a) the terms of the order sought and the grounds of the application; and
(b) which of the conditions in paras (3), (4), (5), (6) and (9) is relied upon in support of the order sought, and on what grounds it is contended that each condition is fulfilled.

Before making a representation order or amending an order under para.(15) the court may require from any advocate already assigned to the applicant written advice on the question of what representation is needed in the proceedings. The court making a decision whether to make an order under para.(2) or amending an order under para.(15) must make annotations to the written application, stating whether each of the conditions relied upon in support of the order made or sought is fulfilled. GR 2001, reg.12(11),(12)

Apart from the grant of Queen's Counsel by the magistrates' court, the decision make, or to amend, a representation order for CDS(G)(No.2) Regs, reg.14(3)

Queen's Counsel, or more than one advocate, may only be made:

(i) in the course of the trial;
(ii) at a preliminary hearing;
(iii) at a pre-trial review; or
(iv) at a pleas and directions hearing,

by the judge presiding at that trial or hearing; otherwise, where the proceedings are in the Crown Court, by a High Court judge, the resident judge of the Crown Court or (in the absence of the resident judge) a judge nominated for the purpose by the presiding judge of the circuit.

Amendment of representation order

17–025 A representation order may be amended to provide representation in any of the forms allowed under the provisions of para.(2) (above) or to provide for representation by one junior counsel only. GR 2001, reg.12(15)(16)

Where a representation order is made for the assisted person to be represented by:

(1) Queen's Counsel with a junior;
(2) Queen's Counsel with a noting junior;
(3) two junior counsel; or
(4) junior counsel with a noting junior,

under GR 2001, reg. 12(2)(b), and where three advocates are required under para.(2)(c), it is the duty of:

(a) each representative:
   (i) to keep under review the need for more than one advocate to be present in court or otherwise providing services; and
   (ii) to consider whether the representation order should be amended under para.(15) (above);
(b) Queen's Counsel, where the services of Queen's Counsel are provided, to keep under review the question whether he could act alone.

If they are of opinion that the representation order should be amended as provided for under the regulations, it is their duty to notify that opinion in writing to the other representatives for the assisted person and to the court, and the court must, after considering the opinion and any representations made by any other representatives for the assisted person, determine whether and in what manner the order should be amended. GR 2001, reg.12(17)

Representation by advocate alone

17–026 The court may grant a representation order for representation by an advocate alone: GR 2001, reg.15

(1) in any proceedings for contempt or alleged contempt in the face of the court under AJA 1999, s.12(2)(f);
(2) in respect of an appeal to CACD; or
(3) in cases of urgency where it appears to the court that there is no time to instruct a solicitor:
  (a) in respect of an appeal to the Crown Court; or
  (b) in proceedings in which a person is committed to or appears before the Crown Court for trial or sentence, or appears or is brought before that court to be dealt with.

Change of representatives

17–027 The court may grant or refuse an application for a change of representative. The application may be made to the court before which proceedings are heard to select a representative in place of a representative previously selected. The application must state the grounds on which it is made. GR 2001, reg.16

The court may grant the application where:

- the representative considers himself under a duty to withdraw from the case in accordance with his professional rules of conduct and, in such a case, the representative must provide details of the nature of such duty;
- there is a breakdown in the relationship between the assisted person and the representative such that effective representation can no longer be provided and, in such a case, the representative must provide details of the nature of the breakdown;
- through circumstances beyond his control, the representative is no longer able to represent the assisted person; or
- some other substantial compelling reason exists.

Selection by two or more accused

17–028 Where a person who granted a right of representation is one of two or more accused whose cases are to be tried together, that person must select the same representstive as a co-accused unless unless there is likely to be a conflict of interest. GR 2001, reg.16A; SI 2004/1196

Authorisation of expenditure

17–029 Where it appears necessary for the proper conduct of proceedings in the Crown Court for costs to be incurred under a representation order by taking any of the following steps: GR 2001, reg.19

(1) obtaining the written report of one or more experts;
(2) employing any other person to provide a written report or opinion (otherwise than as an expert);
(3) obtaining any transcripts or recordings; or
(4) doing anything which is unusual in its nature or requires unusually large expenditure, the solicitor may apply to the Costs Committee for prior authority to do so.

Travelling and accomodation expenses

17–030 A representative assigned to an assisted person in the Crown Court may apply to the court for prior authority for the incurring of travelling and accommodation expenses in order to attend at the trial or other main hearing in those proceedings. GR 2001, reg.20

Transfer of documents

17–031 Where a defendant is committed or sent for trial by a lower court to a higher court, or appeals or applies for leave to appeal from a lower court to a higher court, the appropriate officer of the lower court must send to the appropriate officer of the higher court: GR 2001, reg.18

(1) a copy of any representation order previously made in respect of the same proceedings; and
(2) a copy of any application for a representation order which has been refused.

Notification of very high costs cases

17–032 Any solicitor who has conduct of a funded very high cost case must notify the Commission as soon as practicable. If he fails to do so without good reason, and as a result there is a loss to public funds, the court or Commission, as appropriate, may refuse payment of his costs up to the extent of such loss. However, such payment must not be refused without the solicitor being given a reasonable opportunity to show why it should not be refused. GR 2001, reg.23

Duty to report abuse

17–033 Where a representative for an applicant or assisted person knows or suspects that person: GR 2001, reg.24

(1) has intentionally failed to comply with any provision of regulations made under the AJA 1999 concerning the information to be provided by him; or
(2) in furnishing such information, has knowingly made a false statement or false representation,

the representative must immediately report the circumstances to the Commission.This duty is notwithstanding the relationship between or rights of a representative and client or any privilege arising out of such a relationship.

Funding

17–034 The Criminal Defence Service (Funding) Order 2001 (SI 2001/855), as amended by the Criminal Defence Service (Funding) (Amendment No. 3) Order 2001 (SI 2001/3341), which came into force on October 29, 2001, makes provison for the funding and remuneration of services provided as part of the Criminal Defence Service.

These amendments apply in respect of proceedings in which a representation order is made on or after that date: art.3(1). In all other proceedings the principal order has effect as if the third amendment order had not been made: art.3(2).

Recovery of defence costs orders: judge's duty

17–035 A judge of the Crown Court before which criminal proceedings were heard, may make a "recovery of defence costs order" against a funded defendant requiring him to pay some or all of the costs of any representation so funded for him, unless he: RDCOR 2001, regs 6, 10, 12

- was committed for sentence to the Crown Court;
- is appealing against sentence to the Crown Court; or
- has been acquitted, other than in exceptional circumstances.

The order may be made up to a maximum amount of the full cost of representation incurred in any court under the representation order, and may provide for payment to be made forthwith, or in specified instalments.

The judge:

(1) must before making a recovery of defence costs order at the conclusion of the relevant proceedings, consider whether it is reasonable to make such an order in all the circumstances of the case, including any other financial order or penalty; RDCOR 2001, reg.11

(2) may, when making an order request: RDCOR 2001, regs 6, 10, 12

(a) information as to the funded defendant's financial resources which must be provided;

(b) the funded defendant's solicitor to give an estimate of the total costs which are likely to be incurred, or

(c) he may adjourn the making of an order, and order that any further information which is required should be provided.

Where financial information is required under the regulations and such information is not provided, a recovery of defence costs order must, other than in exceptional circumstances, be made for the full cost of the representation incurred under the representation order. RDCOR 2001, reg.13

Any payment under a recovery defence costs order is made to the the Commission in accordance with the order, and in the event of non-payment is enforceable as a civil debt between parties. Where the defendant has paid the amount ordered, the balance will be repaid to him. RDCOR 2001, regs 16, 17

The solicitor for the funded person must inform the Commission if it subsequently transpires that the costs incurred were lower than the amount ordered to be paid (RDCOR 2001, reg.14). See also 26 COSTS AND TAXATION.

Funding of a representation order

17–036 Where a representation order has been made, or is being considered, the court or the appropriate officer may refer the financial resources of the funded defendant to the Commission for a report, and the Commission may investigate the financial resources of the funded defendant and may subsequently require him to provide further information or evidence, and details of any change in his financial circumstances. RDCOR 2001, regs 7–9, 15

For the purposes of calculating the financial resources of the funded defendant, other than in exceptional circumstances, the following assets are not taken into account:

(1) the first £3,000 of capital available to him;
(2) the first £100,000 of equity in his principal residence; and
(3) his income, where the court or the Commission are satisfied that his gross annual income does not exceed £24,500 in respect of orders made on or after April 8, 2002, but excluding the above, in calculating the financial resources of a funded defendant:

    (a) the amount of the value of every source of income and every resource of a capital nature available to him may be taken into account; and
    (b) the financial resources of the defendant's partner are to be treated as the financial resources of the funded defendant.

The "funded defendant's partner" means a person with whom the funded defendant lives as a couple, and includes a person with whom the funded defendant is not currently living, but from whom he is not living separate and apart.

CDS FUNDING

Without prejudice to reg.9(1)(a), (above), where it appears to the judge, the appropriate officer or the Commission that: RDCOR 2001, reg.8

(i) the funded defendant has directly or indirectly transferred any resources to another person;
(ii) another person is, or has been, maintaining him in any proceedings; or
(iii) any resources of another person are, or have been, made available to him,

they (as the case may be) may assess or estimate the value of the resources of that other person, and may treat all or any of such resources as those of the funded defendant.

"Person" includes a company, partnership, body of trustees and any body of persons whether corporate or not corporate.

18 CHALLENGING THE CROWN COURT

General

18–001 Prior to the coming into force of CJA 2003, Pt 9 decisions and orders of the Crown Court might be challenged in three principal ways:

(1) by the offender, after conviction, etc. on indictment, by appeal to the CACD;
(2) in relation to appeals to the Crown Court from the magistrates' courts, by the offender or the prosecution, by way of case stated to the High Court; and
(3) by an offender committed from the magistrates' court for sentence or to be dealt with, in some cases to CACD, and in others to the High Court.

The offender or the prosecution might appeal from rulings made at preparatory hearings, whether in relation to serious fraud cases under CJA 1988, s.9, or in relation to other cases, and in relation to publicity or access under CPIA 1996, ss.35, 36.

An application for review, both of legal points and of over-lenient sentences, lay at the instance of the Attorney-General, see 18–057 below.

As to appeals from reviewed sentences under SOCA 2005, s.74(8), see 8 ALTERATION OF SENTENCE.

CJA 2003, Pt 9, ss.57 *et seq.*, confers:

(a) an interlocutory right of appeal on the prosecution, in relation to criminal proceedings in which the committal for trial, transfer to the Crown Court or the preferment of a voluntary bill; occurred before the April 4, 2005, against a ruling ("terminatory ruling") by the trial judge which has the effect of terminating a trial on indictment, whether the ruling is made at a preparatory hearing or during the trial itself, at any time up to the start of the summing-up;
(b) a right of appeal, relating to evidentiary rulings, or a series of rulings made in the trial of certain "qualifying offences" listed in CJA 2003, Sch.4 (see APPENDIX A, Pt 1), (not yet in force); under that provision the prosecution right of appeal is restricted to rulings which significantly weaken their case, and may only be exercised up to the opening of the defence case;
(c) rights of appeal from:
   (i) the refusal by a judge of an application to which CJA

2003, s.45 (application in relation to trial without a jury), or

(ii) the order of a judge under CJA 2003, s.43 or s.44, made on the determination of such an application, and CJA 2003, s.47

(iii) an order under CJA 2003, s.46(3) ordering the continuation of a trial without a jury.

18–002 Quick guide to the new position:

A. Appeals to CACD (see below)
  (1) By the accused/offender (see below)
  (2) Interlocutory appeals (18–028, below)
  (3) By the Crown against rulings (18–037, below)

B. Reference by A–G (18–057, below)

C. Case stated (18–064, below)

D. Judicial review (18–070, below)

E. Tainted acquittals (18–076, below)

F. High Court varying sentence (18–084, below)

G. Criminal Cases Review Commission (18–085, below)

H. Appeals to CACD under PCA 2002, (18–087, below).

I. Appeal to CACD by a specified prosecutor in respect of sentence substituted by Crown Court under SOCA 2005, s.74 (see 18–097 below).

A. Appeals to the Court of Appeal (Criminal Division)

1. By the accused/offender

(1) General

18–003 All the usual consequences following from a conviction, etc. on indictment, are susceptible to appeal to CACD:

(1) by a person convicted on indictment, against his conviction and/or sentence (not being a sentence fixed by law);

(2) by a person convicted in the magistrates' court and sentenced on committal to the Crown Court in certain limited circumstances (*R. v Gatehouse* [2001] 2 Cr.App.R.(S.) 94);

CAA 1968, ss.1, 10; CAA 1995, s.1; CDA 1998, s.119, Sch.8, paras 12–14; PCC(S)A 2000, s.165, Sch.9, para.28;

(3) by a person in whose case a verdict of not guilty by reason of insanity has been returned — against that verdict.

CAA 1968, s.12; CJA 2003, ss.41, 319, Sch.3, para.44

(4) where there has been a determination under CP(I)A 1964, s.4 of the question of a person's fitness to be tried and the jury has returned findings that he is under disability and that he did the act or made the omission charged against him;

CAA 1968, s.15; CP(IUP)A

(5) by a person who was arraigned on or after March 31, 2005, in whose case the Crown Court makes a hospital order or an interim hospital order by virtue of CP(I)A 1964, s.5 or s.5A or makes a supervision order under *ibid.* s.5.

(6) where, upon conviction at the Crown Court, judgment is respited and the offender is bound over to come up for judgment when called upon, against any sentence subsequently imposed (*R. v Smith* (1925) 89 J.P. 79).

1991, Sch.3, para.2; CAA 1995, s.1(5)

CAA 1968, s.16A; DVA 2005, s.25

As to interlocutory appeals, see 18–028, below.

CACD has jurisdiction under AJA 1960, s.13, to entertain an appeal against a refusal of bail made in the course of contempt proceedings in the Crown Court (*R. v Serumaga* [2005] EWCA Crim 370). See also CJA 2003 (Mandatory Life Sentences: Appeal in Transitional Cases) Order 2005, SI 2005/2798.

Pleas of guilty

18–004 CACD is entitled to allow an appeal against conviction *only* where the conviction is unsafe, not, as was previously the case, where it was unsatisfactory, or there had been a material irregularity (see *R. v Chalkley & Jeffries* [1998] 2 All E.R. 155, accused pleading guilty following judge's ruling). Where the accused pleads guilty *before* being put in charge of the jury, CACD has no power to substitute a conviction for another offence (*R. v Horsman* [1997] 3 All E.R. 385).

Need for leave to appeal

18–005 An appeal to the CACD lies only:

(1) with the leave of CACD, or
(2) if the judge of the court of trial grants a certificate that the case is fit for appeal.

CAA 1968, ss.1(2), 12, 15; CAA 1995, s.1; CA 1968, ss.9, 10, 11(1A); CJA 1982, s.29(2)(A); PCC(S)A 2000, s.165, Sch.9, para.28; CAA 1968, s.16A(2); DVA 2005, s.25

Absconding, etc. appellants

18–006 As to appeals by absconding appellants, see *R. v Charles, R. v Tucker* [2001] 2 Cr.App.R. 15; as to appellants who escape from custody before the hearing of their appeal, see *R. v Gooch* [1998] 2 Cr.App.R. 130, also *R. v Flower* (1966) 50 Cr.App.R. 22, and *R. v Panayi and Another* [1989] 1 W.L.R. 187.

As to appellants failing to answer their bail, see *R. v Whiting* (1987) 85 Cr.App.R. 78, and *R. v Carter* (1994) 98 Cr.App.R. 106.

Appeals in cases of deceased appellant

18–007 In the case of a person since deceased:

(1) any appeal under CAA 1968, ss.1, 9, 12, or 15, or under s.33, which might have been begun by him had he remained alive may be begun by a person approved by CACD (see, e.g. *R. v Whelan* [1997] Crim.L.R. 659); and CAA 1968, s.44A; CAA 1995, s.7

(2) where such an appeal was begun by him while he was alive or is begun in relation to his case by virtue of (1) or by a reference by the Criminal Cases Review Commission, any further step which might have been taken by him in connection with the appeal if he were alive, may be taken by a person so approved.

Approval for these purposes may only be given to a widow or widower of the deceased, or to certain personal representatives, or to a person appearing to the court, or a single judge, by reason of a family or similar relationship with the deceased, to have a substantial financial or other interest in the determination of the appeal. CAA 1968, s.44A(3)(6); CAA 1995, s.7

Except where the case is referred by the Criminal Cases Review Commission (see e.g. *R. v Bentley* [2001] 1 Cr.App.R. 21; *R. v Hanratty*, *The Times*, May 16, 2002) an application for approval must be made within a year beginning with the date of the death. CAA 1968, s.44A(4); CAA 1995, s.7

Meaning of "sentence"

18–008 "Sentence", in terms of CAA 1968, means any order made by a court when dealing with an offender including, in particular: CAA 1968, s.50; CJA 1982, s.66(1); CJA 1991, s.100, Sch.11, para.4; CJA 1993, Sch.5, para.1; DTA 1994, Sch.1, para.2; CSA 1997, s.55, Sch.4, para.6(1); AJA 1999, s.24, Sch.4, para.3; PCC(S)A 2000, s.165(1), Sch.9, para.30; FDA 2000, s.1(3), Sch.5; PCA 2002, s.456, Sch.11, para.4(1)(3)

(a) a hospital order under MHA 1983, Pt III with or without a restriction order;
(b) an interim hospital order under that Part;
(e) a hospital direction and a limitation direction under MHA 1983, Pt III;
(f) a confiscation order under PCA 2002, Pt 2;
(g) an order which varies a confiscation order made under PCA 2002, Pt 2, if the varying order is made under PCA 2002, ss.21, 22 or 29 (but not otherwise);
(h) a recommendation for deportation;
(i) a confiscation order under DTA 1994, other than one made in the High Court;
(j) a confiscation order under CJA 1988, Pt VI (proceeds of major crime);

(h) an order varying a confiscation order of a kind included in (g) or (h) above;
(i) an order made by the Crown Court varying a confiscation order made by the High Court by virtue of DTA 1994, s.19;
(j) a declaration of relevance under FSA 1989.

A mandatory life sentence imposed on conviction for murder under M(ADP)A 1965, s.1(1) is a sentence fixed by law, and therefore excluded from appeal under CAA 1968, s.9(1), except in so far as a question of compatibility with the ECHR arises: *R. v Lichniak, R. v Pyrah, The Times*, May 16, 2001, or the minimum term imposed (*R. v Sullivan and Others, The Times*, July 14, 2004 CACD).

A sentence for contempt of court imposed upon an appellant, whether in respect of his conduct at the trial or for absconding from bail, is treated as a sentence for the purposes of appeal. Where the judge has deferred passing sentence on an offender, the CACD will treat such an order as being a "sentence" within s.50. (*Att.-Gen's Reference (No. 22 of 1992*) (1994) 97 Cr.App.R. 275, *R. v J* [1999] 1 W.L.R. 479).

Single appeal

18–009 Generally the Act provides for a single appeal in respect of each case, but this does not preclude an appeal against a confiscation order under DTA 1994 made subsequent to sentence (*R. v Neal* [1999] 2 Cr.App.R.(S.) 352).

Generally, it will be inappropriate to seek to appeal against conviction until the Crown Court proceedings have been completed, which includes the passing of sentence. It is clear, however, that the word "conviction" in the Act may properly encompass the verdict of the jury, and there may be cases where the Court of Appeal will entertain an appeal short of that stage (*R. v Drew* (1985) 81 Cr.App.R. 190). An offender who has pleaded guilty at the Crown Court may appeal to the CACD against "conviction" before the imposition of any sentence (*R. v Dasour* [1998] 4 Arch. News 1). As to appeal against conviction after a plea of guilty following the trial judge's direction, see *R. v Chalkley, R. v Jefferies* [1998] 2 All E.R. 155.

Criminal Cases Review Commission

18–010 Convictions and sentences in the Crown Court may be referred to CACD by the Criminal Cases Review Commission. See CAA 1995, Pt II, and Criminal Cases Review (Insanity) Act 1999.

(2) Procedure

Notice of appeal and application for extension of time

18–011 Notice of appeal or of an application for leave to appeal under CAA 1968, Pt I (or notice of appeal under AJA 1960, s.13 — appeal in cases of contempt of court, as required by *ibid.* s.18A) against an order or decision of the Crown Court is given by completing the form set out in PD 2004, Annex D (pp. 171–177) and serving it on the Crown Court officer. The notice must be accompanied by the grounds of the appeal or application, including notice of: R.68.3(1)–(4): SI 2006/353

(1) any application to be made to the court for a declaration of incompatibility under HRS 1998, s.4; or
(2) any issue for the court to decide which may lead to the court making such a declaration.

Where the grounds of appeal or application include notice in accordance with (2) above, a copy of the notice must be served on the prosecutor by the appellant.

An appellant who is appealing or applying for leave to appeal against conviction must specify in the form, any exhibit produced at the trial which he wishes to be kept in custody for the purposes of his appeal. R.68.3(9)

If the appellant has been convicted of more than one offence, the notice of appeal or of an application for leave must specify the convictions or sentences against which the appellant is appealing or applying for leave to appeal. R.68.3(5)

Where an appellant does not require leave to appeal, a notice of application for leave to appeal must be treated as a notice of appeal; and where an appellant requires leave to appeal but serves only a notice of appeal, the notice of appeal will be treated as an application for leave to appeal. R.68.3(12)

The grounds of an appeal or application may, with the consent of the court, be varied or amplified within such time as the court may allow. R.68.3(6)

Notice must be served within within 28 days: CAA 1968, s.18

(a) from the date of the conviction appealed against; or
(b) in the case of an application for leave to appeal against sentence, from the date on which sentence was passed; or
(c) in the case of an order made, or treated as made, on conviction, from the date of the making of the order.

In the case of an appeal in relation to a trial conducted without a jury under the provisions of CJA 2003, Pt 7, the date of conviction is the date of the judgment delivered by the Court under s.48(5)(a). CJA 2003, s.48(5)(b)

The time limits must be strictly adhered to: *R. v Long* [1998] 2 Cr.App.R. 326.

Notice of application to extend the the time within which notice of appeal or of an application for leave to appeal may be given under: R.63.3(7)(8); SI 2006/353

(1) Pt I of CAA 1968; or
(2) Art.3 of the CJA 2003 (Mandatory Life Sentences: Appeals in Transitional Cases) Order 2005,

Must be given by completing the form set out in PD 2004, Annex D, and serving it on the Registrar.

Notice of application for leave to appeal under CJA 2003, Sch.22, para.14 (mandatory life sentences), is given by completing the form set out in PD 2004, Annex D and serving it on the Registrar. The notice must specify the grounds of the application.

Any forms to which this Rule relates must be signed by, or on behalf of, the appellant. If a form is not signed by the appellant and the appellant is in custody, the Registrar will, as soon as practicable after receiving the form from the Crown Court, send a copy of it to the appellant. R.68.3(10)(11)

Appeal following reference by Criminal Cases Review Commission

18–012 The Registrar will serve on the appellant written notice of receipt of a reference, and the appellant must then give notice of appeal under R.68.3 (above) by serving it on the Registrar within: R.68.4

(1) 28 days of the date of the notice served under para.(2), in the case of an appeal against sentence; or
(2) 56 days of the date of that notice, in the case of an appeal against conviction, verdict of not guilty by reason of insanity, finding that the appellant was under a disability, or finding that the appellant did the act or made the omission charged.

CACD may extend the time for giving notice of appeal, either before or after it expires.

The grounds of appeal accompanying a notice of appeal must include, where a ground of appeal is said;

(a) to relate to a reason given by the Commission for making the reference, an explanation of how it is related; and
(b) not to be so related, notice of application for leave to appeal on that ground.

If a notice of appeal is not received within the time specified in (1) and (2) above, or within such longer period as the court allows, the reasons given by the Commission for making the reference will stand as the grounds of appeal.

On receiving a notice of appeal the Registrar will serve a copy on the prosecutor and on any other party to the appeal.

Grounds of appeal

18–013 Counsel should not settle grounds of appeal or support them with written advice unless they consider that they are properly arguable. Such grounds must be carefully drafted and properly particularised. Should leave be granted to amend the grounds it is most unlikely that further grounds will be considered. PD 2004, II.15.1

In the case of a mandatory minimum sentence depending on one or more previous convictions under CSA 1997, Pt I, if a relevant previous conviction is set aside by the CACD, thus invalidating the mandatory sentence, notice of appeal against the latter may be given at any time within 28 days from the date on which the previous conviction was set aside.

(1) If a positive advice on appeal is given then, it should always be incorporated into the same document as the grounds of appeal, thus generating a single document rather than two that often appear at the moment. This enables an assessment of the strength of an appeal to be made more easily.

(2) An adverse advice should never be lodged with the Registrar so that if there is a new, personal appeal, there will be nothing adverse in the file and the application can be considered entirely on its merits.

Loss of time

18–014 Both CACD and the single judge have a discretionary power to direct that part of the time during which the applicant is in custody after putting in his notice of application for leave to appeal should not count towards sentence. This power must be borne in mind when contemplating an appeal. Where an application devoid of merit has been refused by the single judge and a direction for loss of time has been made, the full court, on renewal of the application, may direct that additional time shall be lost if it, once again, thinks it right to exercise its discretion in all the circumstances of the case. Although the power has been very sparingly used in recent years, *R. v Kulumba, The Times*, May 17, 2005 indicates that CACD is prepared to use it in the case of unmeritorious appeals and renewed applications. PD 2004, II.16.1

Skeleton arguments

18–015 In all appeals against conviction a skeleton argument from counsel for the appellant is to be lodged with the Registrar and served on the prosecuting authority within 14 days of receipt by counsel of the notification of the grant of leave to appeal, or such longer period as the Registrar or the court may direct. The skeleton argument may refer to an advice, which should be annexed, with an indication of which parts are relied on, and should include any additional arguments to be advanced. PD 2004, II.17

The advocate for the prosecuting authority should lodge with the Registrar, and with counsel for the appellant, his skeleton argument within 14 days of the receipt of the appellant's skeleton arguments, or such longer (or in exceptional cases shorter) period as the court or Registrar may direct.

Skeleton arguments should:

(1) include short headnotes where reliance is placed on unreported cases;
(2) include Criminal Appeal Office correct numbers at the beginning, and the relevant counsel's name at the end;
(3) include a numbered list of the points which counsel intends to argue, grouped under each ground of appeal, stated in no more than one or two sentences;
(4) be as succinct as possible, the object being to identify each point, not to argue it or elaborate on it;
(5) include after each listed point a full reference to the material to which counsel will refer in support of it, that is the relevant passages in the transcripts, authorities etc;
(6) contain anything the advocate would expect the court to take down during the hearing, such as propositions of law, chronologies, etc; if more convenient these can be annexed to the skeleton rather than included in it. Chronologies should, if possible, be agreed with the opposing advocate before the hearing;
(7) state the point of law and cite the principal authority or authorities in support with reference to the passages where the principle is enunciated.

As to listing, see *Practice Direction (Criminal Procedure; Appeals Listing)* [2004] 1 W.L.R. 1285.

Criminal Appeal Office summaries

18–016 Summaries of cases are prepared by the Criminal Appeal Office to assist the court. They are objective, do not contain any advice about how the court should deal with the case or provide any view about its merits. PD 2004, II.18

A summary consists of two parts. Part 1 generally contains:

(1) particulars of the proceedings in the Crown Court, including representation and details of any co-accused;
(2) particulars of the proceedings in the CACD;
(3) the facts of the case, as drawn from the transcripts, counsel's advice, witness statements and/or the exhibits;
(4) the submissions and rulings, summing up and sentencing remarks.

If counsel does not want any factual material in his advice taken into account this should be stated in the advice. The contents of the summary are a matter for the professional judgment of the writer, but counsel wishing to suggest any significant alteration to Part 1 should write to the Registrar.

If the Registrar does not agree, the summary and the letter will be put before the court for decision. The court will not generally be willing to hear oral argument about the content of the summary. Part 1 of the summary may be shown to counsel's professional or lay clients (but to no one else) if they believe it would help to check facts or formulate arguments. Normally, permission will not be given in cases involving children or sexual offences, or where the Crown Court has made an order restricting reporting. Part 1 will also be supplied to appellants who seek to represent themselves before the full court or who renew to the full court their applications for leave to appeal against conviction or sentence, unless a High Court judge or the Registrar gives a direction to the contrary in any particular case involving material of an explicitly salacious or sadistic nature.

Part II, which is supplied to the court alone, contains:

(a) a summary of the grounds of appeal; and
(b) in appeals against sentence (and applications for such leave), summaries of the antecedent histories of the parties and of any relevant pre-sentence, medical or other reports.

All of the source material is provided to the court and advocates are able to draw attention to anything in it which may be of particular relevance.

Subsequent procedure

18–017 Subsequent procedure is within the jurisdiction of CACD, (see rr.68.6, 9–30), as amended by SI 2006/353 supervised by the single judge and the Registrar. The only matters which come within the purview of the Crown Court are the granting of a certificate by a judge in a proper case, the grant of PD 2004, II.1.1

bail in the rare case in which it is appropriate, and the transmission of the trial papers.

In the case of appeals against sentence the relevant prosecuting authority will be notified by the Registrar in the event that:

(a) leave to appeal is granted;
(b) an application for leave is referred to the Full Court for determination; or
(c) he becomes aware that counsel for the applicant will be appearing at a renewed application for leave.

(3) Fitness for appeal; trial judge's certificate

General

18–018 A certificate may be given, in a proper case: CAA 1968, ss.1(2),12,15(2); SCA 1981, ss.81(c), 81(1B); CJA 1982, s.29

(1) that a case is fit for appeal against conviction, etc., on a question of fact, or one of mixed law and fact — by the trial judge;
(2) that a case is fit for appeal against sentence under s.9 — by the trial judge;
(3) that a case is fit for appeal against sentence under s.10 — by the judge who passed the sentence;
(4) as a pre-condition to granting bail, that a case is fit for appeal on a ground involving a question of law alone — by the trial judge.

Where the judge has taken the view, in the course of the trial, that he has of necessity ruled on the interpretation of primary or subordinate legislation in a manner which is not compatible with any provision of the ECHR, it is anticipated that he will give a certificate in order to give the CACD the opportunity to make a declaration of incompatibility which the Crown Court has no power to make.

An exceptional course

18–019 Only in rare cases, where there is a particular and cogent ground of appeal against sentence should application be made to the trial judge for his certificate. It should be granted only where the clarity and cogency of the ground warrants it, otherwise it is probably better to leave the matter to the Court of Appeal or to the single judge, who are in a better position to judge whether leave should be granted (*Practice Direction* (1984) 78 Cr.App.R. 40).

In particular, the trial judge should not give his certificate merely in the light of mitigation to which he has, in his opinion, already given due weight (*R. v Killeen* [1985] Crim.L.R. 331).

Procedure

18–020 If, at the conclusion of the trial, an issue is clarified which might warrant the granting of a certificate, then:

(1) if the trial judge, acting on his own initiative considers the point to be one which ought to be investigated by CACD, it will be convenient if:
   (a) he drafts the question which he considers ought to be investigated; and
   (b) he reads the draft to counsel so that they have an opportunity of agreeing the formulation of the question before it is certified;
(2) if the defence advocate considers that such a question arises and the judge has given no indication that he intends to act on his own initiative, he should:
   (a) apply to the judge for a certificate; and
   (b) formulate in writing the question he wishes to be certified;
(3) if the trial judge certifies the question as being fit for appeal, the Crown Court officer will draw up the question certified in the form set out in PD 2004, Annex D, obtain the judge's signature to it, and forward it to the Registrar, whether or not the person to whom the certificate has applied for a certificate;
(4) a copy of the certificate will be forwarded to the person to whom it relates or his legal representative. R.68.2

Exceptional reasons must exist before a certificate is granted: (*R. v Bansal* [1999] Crim.L.R. 484).

Where, in the exceptional case, the question giving rise to an application is discovered after the conclusion of the trial, application will have to be made to the judge at a later date. No time limit is prescribed, but it seems undesirable that a certificate should be granted after the 28 day limit for giving notice of appeal has expired.

If the trial judge is not available, or the time has expired, it will be necessary to apply to the Court of Appeal for leave.

(3A) Appeals by offender in respect of substituted sentence under SOCA 2005, s.74

18–020A A person in respect of whom a reference is made under s.74(3) (also the specified prosecutor, see 18–006, above) is given the right, with leave of CACD, to appeal to that court against the decision of the judge of the Crown Court.

Procedure on such an appeal is governed by SOCA 2005 (appeals under s.74) Order 2006 (SI 2006/2135) Pts 2 and 3, and is similar to that required under CAA 1968.

CAA 1968, s.33(3) (limitation on appeal from CACD) does not prevent a further appeal to the House of Lords/Supreme Court).

(4) Bail pending appeal

18–021 There is no statutory right to bail after conviction; CACD is reluctant to grant bail pending appeal. It is clear that bail will only be granted pending appeal where it appears prima facie on cogent grounds that an appeal is likely to succeed, or where there is a risk that the sentence will have been served by the time the appeal is heard. Even in short sentence cases, the Court is reluctant to grant bail, preferring to expedite the appeal and if necessary to list it at short notice (*R. v Walton* (1979) 68 Cr.App.R. 295; *R. v Shah* (unreported), August 13, 1978, CA).

Bail may be granted, subject to CJPOA 1994, s.25, by CACD or by the Crown Court in a proper case. In no circumstances is it appropriate for a bail application to be made to a member of the court, e.g. on circuit, until a formal application for leave to appeal has been made through the Registrar (*R. v Suggett* (1985) 81 Cr.App.R. 243).

Procedure

18–022 It should be observed that:

(1) where the defence consider that bail should be applied for as a matter of urgency, the application should normally be made in the first instance to the trial judge; CACD may decline to treat an application as urgent if there is no good reason why the application was not so made; PD 2004, IV.50.3–6

(2) the judge may well think it right:

  (a) to hear the application for a certificate in chambers with a shorthand writer or logger present;

  (b) to invite the accused's advocate to submit before the hearing of the application, a draft of the grounds of appeal which he will ask the judge to certify; the advocate for the Crown will be better able to assist the judge at the hearing if the draft ground is sent beforehand to him also;

(3) the first question for the trial judge is then whether there exists a particular and cogent ground of appeal; if there is

no such ground there can be no certificate and if there is no certificate there can be no bail; the judge should not grant a certificate:

(a) with regard to sentence merely in the light of mitigation to which he has, in his opinion, given due weight; or
(b) in regard to conviction on a ground where he considers the chance of a successful appeal is not substantial;

(4) the trial judge should bear in mind that where he refuses a certificate, application may be made to CACD for leave to appeal and for bail.

The length of time which may elapse before the hearing of any appeal is not relevant to the grant of a certificate, but if the judge does decide to grant a certificate, it may be one factor in the decision whether or not to grant bail. A judge who is minded to take this factor into account may find it advisable to have the Crown Court officer contact the Criminal Appeal Office Listing Co-ordinator, in order that he may have an accurate and up-to-date assessment of the likely waiting time. This can be very short. The co-ordinator will require a general account of the weight and urgency of the case.

Bail by the Crown Court

18–023 The judge who tried the case, where the appeal is under CAA 1968, s.1 or s.9, or the judge who passed the sentence in the case of an appeal under s.10 may, in exceptional circumstances grant bail provided:

(1) the case is not one to which CJPOA 1994, s.25 (see 11 BAIL) applies;
(2) the case is not one to which CAA 1968, s.12 (appeal against verdict of not guilty by reason of insanity) s.15 or s.16A (appeal against a finding that the accused was under disability, or that he did the act or made the omission charged against him) apply; and
(3) the judge gives a certificate under CAA 1968, ss.1(2) (question of fact or mixed law and fact) and 11(1A) (fit for appeal against sentence), or under SCA 1981, s.81(1B) that the case is fit for appeal on a ground which involves a question of law alone;
(4) the appellant has not made an application to CACD for bail in respect of the offence or offences to which the appeal relates;
(5) the power is exercised within 28 days from the date of the conviction appealed against, or from the date the

sentence was passed where the appeal is against sentence, or in the case of an order made or treated as made on conviction, from the date of the making of the order.

Conditions; appearance

18–024 Where notice of appeal has not been served in accordance with CAA 1968, s.18(1), it must be a condition of any bail granted at the Crown Court that:

(1) notice be lodged within the prescribed period, and
(2) not later than 14 days from the end of that period, the appellant lodge with the Crown Court the Registrar's certificate to that effect.

The Crown Court may direct the appellant to appear:

(a) if notice is lodged within time, at such time as the CACD requires; or
(b) if notice is not lodged within the period, at such time and place as the Crown Court may require.

The Registrar is empowered to vary conditions of bail granted to the appellant the Crown Court, or by CACD provided the respondent does not object. If the Registrar refuses to do so, the appellant is entitled to have the matter determined by a single judge.

See *R. v Ofori* (1994) 99 Cr.App.R. 219 in relation to recommendations for deportation.

Application to CACD

18–025 Notice of an application to the CACD by the appellant R.68.7
to be granted bail pending the determination of his appeal or pending his retrial is in the form set out in PD 2004, Annex D and, unless notice of appeal or of an application for leave to appeal has previously been given, must be accompanied by such a notice and must be served on the Registrar, save that where notice of such an application is given together with a notice of appeal or notice of application for leave to appeal, it must be served on the Crown Court officer. An application may also be made to the court orally.

Notice in writing of intention to make such an application must, unless CACD or the single judge otherwise directs, at least 24 hours before it is made be served on the prosecutor and on the DPP, if the prosecution was carried on by him or, if the application is to be made by the prosecutor or a constable under BA 1976, s.3(8), on the appellant.

As to bail with condition of surety in CACD see r.68.8; as to the forfeiture of recognisances in respect of failing to appear at CACD, see r.68.9.

(5) CDS funding for appeal

18–026 The position as to CDS funding for the purpose of pursuing an appeal to CACD is as follows:

(1) in the first instance, a person who is represented at the Crown Court under a representation order, and is convicted and sentenced there, is entitled to receive from those assigned to him under that order:
   (a) advice on the question whether there appear to be reasonable grounds of appeal;
   (b) where such grounds exist, assistance in the preparation of, or in giving notice of appeal, accompanied by proper grounds;
   (c) while the question is being considered, assistance in giving notice of appeal or of application for leave to appeal, accompanied by "provisional grounds";

(2) where the trial judge gives his certificate that a case is fit for appeal, any order in force at the Crown Court will include public funding for the purposes of an application to the Crown Court for bail pending appeal;

(3) if notice of appeal is given, or notice of application for leave to appeal as a result of such advice, the facilities under the Crown Court order extend up to, but do not include, the moment when any application for leave is put before the CACD or before a judge, and include the exploration of a reasonable possibility of calling evidence on appeal, if this evidence comes to light almost immediately after the conclusion of the trial (*Practice Note* (1974) 59 Cr.App.R. 158);

(4) if the above arrangements break down, or advice is not, for any reason, available, the Registrar may be asked to intervene and grant public funding.

Where an application for a representation order is refused by the single judge, it will not be granted by the court on a further application for leave, save in exceptional circumstances (*R. v Oates* [2002] 1 W.L.R. 2833 considering the position under ECHR Art.6(3)(c)).

(6) Suspension of RT disqualification

18–027 Where a person disqualified from holding or obtaining a driving licence appeals, or applies for leave to appeal, against his conviction or sentence, the Crown Court, or CACD RTOA 1988, ss.39(1), 40(1), (2), (7) may, if it thinks fit, suspend the disqualification on such terms as it thinks fit.

2. Interlocutory appeals

(1) Appeals under CJA 1987, s.9(11); CPIA 1996, s.35(1)

CJA 1987, s.9(11)

18–028 An appeal lies by either side from an order or ruling made by a judge of the Crown Court at, or for the purposes of, a preparatory hearing in a serious fraud case (see 16 CASE MANAGEMENT), on either: CJA 1987, ss.9(11), (12); CJA 2003, s.310(3)

(1) a question as to the admissibility of evidence; or
(2) any other question of law relating to the case,or
(3) any question as to the joinder or severance of charges

(*Re Gunarwardena, Harbutt & Banks* (1990) 91 Cr.App.R. 55) but not from the trial judge's ruling on a challenge to the prosecution case statement (*R. v Smithson* [1995] 1 Cr.App.R. 14) or from the judge's decision refusing to quash counts on the indictment (*R. v Hedworth* [1997] 1 Cr.App.R. 421) or to the judge's decision whether to order disclosure (*R. v (Interlocutory application; Disclosure) 2006, The Times*, August 1, 2006, CA).

Rule 65 applies, with necessary modifications, to appeals under CJA 2003, s.217 (discharge of jury following tampering) (r.65(11); SI 2006/353). Appeal lies only with the leave of the trial judge or of CACD.

CPIA 1996, Sections 35, 36

18–029 An appeal lies from a ruling of the judge under CPIA 1996, s.31(3) (see 16 CASE MANAGEMENT) but only with his leave or that of CACD. The preparatory hearing may be continued notwithstanding the grant of leave to appeal but the jury will not be sworn until the appeal has been abandoned or determined. CPIA 1996, ss.35, 36

Initiating an appeal

18–030 Proceedings under CJA 1987, s.9(11) and CPIA 1996, s.35(1) are initiated by an application to a judge of the Crown Court for leave to appeal, which must be made orally within two days of the making of the order or ruling to which it relates. R.65.1

Unless the application is made on the occasion of the order or ruling to which it relates, the appellant must serve notice in writing, specifying the grounds of the application, on the Crown Court officer and on all parties to the hearing directly affected by the order or ruling in question. He must also, no later than the day referred to below serve notice of appeal from an order or ruling under s.9(11) or s.31(3) of the 1996 Act or, as the case may be, of an application to CACD for leave to appeal from such a ruling on; the Registrar; the Crown Court officer; and all parties to the preparatory hearing directly affected by the said order or ruling.

The day referred to above is:

(1) the day which occurs seven days after the making of the order or ruling; or
(2) where an application is made to the judge of the Crown Court for leave to appeal under s.31(3) of the 1996 Act as in para.(1), the day which occurs seven days after such application is determined or withdrawn.

The time for giving notice may be extended, before or after it expires, by CACD.

Any notice of appeal or of an application for leave to appeal, or an application to CACD for an extension of time is in the form set out in PD 2004, Annex D.

If notice in writing of an application for leave to appeal was served on the Crown Court, a copy must accompany the notice of appeal or, as the case may be, of an application for leave to appeal required to be served on the Registrar.

Note that:

(a) notice of appeal or of an application for leave to appeal may be given either in respect of the whole or any part of the order to which it relates and must:
    (i) specify any question of law in respect of which the appeal is brought and, where appropriate, such facts of the case as are necessary for its proper consideration;
    (ii) summarise the arguments intended to be put to the CACD; and
    (iii) specify any authorities intended to be cited.
(b) where the judge of the Crown Court has given leave to appeal the notice of appeal must state that fact and specify the grounds on which leave was given;
(c) notice of appeal or of an application for leave to appeal must be accompanied by any documents or other things (or copies thereof) necessary for the proper determination of the appeal or application.

Respondent's notice

18–031 Upon receiving notice of appeal or of an application for leave to appeal, the respondent if he desires to oppose the appeal, must, within seven days of receipt of the notice, serve a notice in the form set out in PD 2004, Annex D on the Registrar; R.65.2

(1) stating the date on which the appellant's notice was received by the respondent;
(2) summarising his response to the arguments of the appellant; and
(3) specifying the authorities which he intends to cite,

and must at the same time serve a copy on the appellant and any other party to the proceedings directly affected by the order or ruling and on the Crown Court officer.

The time for giving notice under this rule may be extended, either before or after it expires, by CACD.

Subsequent procedure in CACD is dealt with in Rr.65.3–10.

CDS funding of appeal; costs

18–032 Public funding may be ordered for the purpose of such proceedings either by the Crown Court or by CACD. As to costs, see POA 1985, ss.16(4A), 18(2); CJA 2003, s.312.

(2) Publicity; CCA 1981: CPIA 1996

18–033 A person aggrieved may appeal to CACD, if the court grants leave, against:

CJA 1988, ss.159(1), (2); CJA 2003, s.41, Sch.3, para.53, s.332, Sch.37, Pt 4

(1) an order under CCA 1981, s.4 or s.11, as amended made in relation to trial on indictment;
(2) an order restricting the access of the public to the whole or any part of a trial on indictment or to any proceedings ancillary to such a trial;
(3) an order restricting the publication of a report of the whole or any part of a trial on indictment or any such ancillary proceedings; and
(4) an order made by the Crown Court under s.58(7) or (8) of CPIA 1996, in a case where the court has convicted a person on trial on indictment.

The decision of CACD is final.

(3) Procedure

Appeal against order restricting reporting of proceedings

18–034 An application for leave to appeal under CJA 1988, ss.159(l)(a), (aa) or (c) must be made within 14 days after the date on which the order was made by: Rr.67.1, (1)–(6)

(1) serving on the Registrar a notice in the form set out in PD 2004, Annex D; and
(2) at the same time serving a copy of the application on the Crown Court officer at the place where the order was made, on the prosecutor and the defendant and on any other interested person.

A prosecutor or a defendant or any interested person may, not later than three days after service of the application, notify the Registrar in writing that he wishes to be made a respondent to the appeal if leave is granted, and must serve a copy of such notice on the applicant.

The period of 14 days referred to above may be extended by CACD or the single judge, before or after it expires, on an application:

(a) made in writing, specifying the grounds of the application, and served on the Registrar; and
(b) a copy of the application being served by the applicant on every person who is to be served with the application.

An application to extend the time will be determined without a hearing, unless CACD or the single judge, as the case may be, directs otherwise. The application for leave to appeal may also be determined without a hearing.

Subsequent procedure in CACD is governed by R.67.1(6)(7).

Appeal against order for proceedings *in camera*

18–035 Where: R.67.2

(1) a prosecutor or a defendant has served a notice under R.16.10(1) of his intention to apply for an order that all or part of a trial be held *in camera* for reasons of national security or for the protection of a witness or any other person; and
(2) a notice has been displayed under R.16.10(2),

a person aggrieved may serve notice on the Registrar in the form set out in PD 2004, Annex D (p.167) that he intends to appeal against any order that may be made on the prosecutor's or defendant's application, serving a copy of such notice on the Crown Court officer at the place where the trial is to take place, on the prosecutor and the defendant and on any other interested person.

Note that:

(a) such notice must be served on the Registrar within seven days of the display of the notice under R.16.10(2); and
(b) where such an order is made at the trial, the notice will be treated as the application for leave to appeal against the order; but
(c) where an order is made at the trial, a person aggrieved who has not served such notice may apply for leave to appeal against the order by serving notice in the form set out in the Practice Direction on the Registrar within 24 hours after the making of the order, serving a copy of such notice on each of the persons who are to be served.

Where an order has been made, and a person aggrieved has served notice under the above provisions the Crown Court officer will forthwith upon the making of the order notify the Registrar of its making, and the applicant for the order must, as soon as practicable, send the Registrar a copy of any transcript or note of the application for the order and of any documents that were in evidence in the Crown Court.

Both the application for leave to appeal and, where leave to appeal is granted, the appeal, will be determined without a hearing. There is no discretion to order an oral hearing. As to the compatability of the proceedings with ECHR Art.6, see *Re Times Newspapers* [2006] Crim.L.R.757.

(4) Trials without a jury

18–036 Once the provisions as to trials without a jury come into force an interlocutory appeal will lie to CACD against an order that a trial proceed (CJA 2003, s.46(3)), or a new trial take place (*ibid* s.46(5)), without a jury, but only with leave of the judge or CACD. CACD may confirm or revoke the order. CJA 2003, s.49

3. Appeals by the Crown against judges' rulings under CJA 2003, Part 9

18–037 CJA 2003, Pt 9, now partially in force, gives to the Crown a right of appeal to CACD against: CJA 2003, s.57

(1) "terminatory" rulings made by the judge in relation to a trial on indictment (s.58); and
(2) certain evidentiary rulings made by the judge in the course of such a trial, (s.62), excepting that the Crown have no right of appeal under these provisions against:
  (a) a ruling that the jury be discharged; or
  (b) a ruling from which an appeal lies to CACD by virtue of any other enactment, e.g. an appeal from a preparatory hearing against a ruling on admissibility of evidence.

The first of these is brought into force (by SI 2005/950) in relation to criminal proceedings committed, transferred or sent for trial, or where a voluntary bill was preferred, **after April 4, 2005**. The second of these rights is not yet in force.

An appeal under these provisions may be brought only with the leave of the judge who made the ruling. CJA 2003, s.57(4)

(1) "Terminatory" rulings

18–038 Right of appeal

CJA 2003, ss.57, 58(1)(2)(13)(14); DVA 2004, s.30

In a case where:

(1) an accused was committed for trial;
(2) proceedings were transferred for trial;
(3) an order was made by a magistrates' court sending the accused for trial under CDA 1998, s.51; or
(4) a voluntary bill was preferred,

on or after April 4, 2005, the Crown may appeal, in respect of a "terminatory" ruling made by the judge in relation to a trial on indictment, at any time (whether before or after the commencement of the trial) before the judge:

(a) starts his summing-up, or
(b) would start his summing-up but for the making of an order under Pt 7 (trial without a jury),

where the ruling relates to one or more offences included in the indictment.

The procedure covers the case both of a ruling which formally terminates a trial and a ruling which is in practice terminating, since, in the absence of a right of appeal, the Crown would offer no further evidence.

The judge's ruling has no effect whilst the Crown is able to take any steps under s.58(4) below.

"Ruling" here includes any decision, determination, direction, finding, notice, order, refusal, rejection or requirement. CJA 2003, s.74(1)

Crown seeking to appeal

18–039 Following the ruling, the Crown must, if they are to appeal in respect of it: CJA 2003, s.58(4)(5)

(1) inform the court that they intend to appeal, or
(2) request an adjournment to consider whether to appeal, and
(3) following the adjournment if granted, inform the court that they intend to appeal.

If the Crown requests an adjournment under (2) the request must be made immediately following the making of the ruling; if it is a ruling of no case to answer it must also be made immediately following the ruling, notwithstanding that the prosecutor also nominates earlier rulings to be the subject of appeal. R.66.2(1)(5)

The judge must grant the request for adjournment unless it is in the interests of justice for the prosecutor to indicate immediately whether or not he intends to apply for leave to appeal. The adjournment will be to the next business day after the day on which the ruling is given unless the interests of justice require a longer adjournment. The Crown Court officer will provide a transcript of the ruling.

Where the ruling: CJA 2003, ss.58(6), (7), (8), (9)

(a) which must be a single ruling, relates to two or more offences,
   (i) any one or more of those offences may be the subject of an appeal, the appeal need not be appealed in so far as it as it affects all the offence; and
   (ii) where the Crown inform the court that they intend to appeal they must, at the same time, inform the court of the offence or offences which they seek to make the subject of the appeal;
(b) is a ruling that there is no case to answer, the Crown may, at the same time inform the court that they intend to appeal, nominate one or more other rulings which relate to the offence or offences the subject of the appeal, and those other rulings will be treated as the subject of the appeal.

If the Crown is to act under ss.58(4), (5) it must agree for an acquittal to follow in respect of those offences the subject of the appeal; the same applies if they fail to obtain leave to appeal or they abandon the appeal before it is determined by CACD.

Application to the judge of the court for leave to appeal

18–040 The prosecutor must inform the judge immediately after the ruling or the adjournment if he intends to seek leave to appeal against a ruling and at the same time he may apply orally for leave to appeal, and before deciding whether or not to grant leave to appeal, the judge must hear oral representations from the defendant. He will then decide whether or not to give leave to appeal on the same day on which an oral application for leave to appeal is made. The judge of the court may extend the period only if it is in the interests of justice to do so. R.66.3

If the judge gives leave to appeal he will issue a certificate in the form set out in PD 2004, Annex D and the court officer must forward that certificate to the Registrar.

Effect on ruling; continuation of proceedings

18–041 The judge's ruling effectively acquitting the accused or otherwise terminating the trial, will not take effect in relation to the offence or offences which are the subject of the appeal whilst the appeal is pursued, and if, and to the extent that the ruling has no effect: CJA 2003, ss.58(10), (11), (12)

(1) any consequences of it have no effect;
(2) the judge may not take any steps in consequence of it; and
(3) if he does, any such steps will be of no effect.

Where the trial involves more than one offence, or more than one accused, but the appeal does not apply to all the offences or all the accused, proceedings in respect of any offence which is or any accused who is, not the subject of an appeal may, at the discretion of the judge, be continued. CJA 2003, s.60

Expedited and non-expedited appeals

18–042 Two alternative appeal routes are provided by s.59; the judge must determine which route the appeal should follow. Where the Crown inform the court that they intend to appeal, the judge must decide whether or not the appeal should be expedited. At the time when the prosecutor informs the judge of the court that he intends to seek leave to appeal against a ruling, he must also make oral representations as to whether or not that appeal should be expedited under CJA 2003, s.59(1). CJA 2003, s.59

Before deciding whether or not the appeal should be expedited, the judge must hear oral representations from the defendant or any interested party. The court officer will provide a copy of the reasons given by the judge, for his decision whether or not the appeal should be expedited, to the prosecutor, the defendant and all interested parties.

The judge may reverse his decision that the appeal should be expedited at any time before notice of appeal or application for leave to appeal is served on the Crown Court under r.66.5(1) and must provide reasons for that reversal in writing to the prosecutor, the defendant and all interested parties.

At any time after notice of appeal or application for leave to appeal has been served on the Registrar under r.66.5(1), the prosecutor or defendant may invite CACD to reverse a judge's decision that the appeal should be expedited and written notice of such an application must be served on: R.66.4

(a) the Registrar;
(b) the court officer;
(c) the prosecutor;
(d) the defendant; and
(e) any interested party.

"Interested party" in this context means a person other than the defendant who: R.66.1

(i) is a party to the proceedings in the Crown Court;
(ii) may be affected by the decision of the trial judge under s.59(1) as to whether or not the appeal should be expedited; and
(iii) is permitted by the trial judge or CACD to make representations on that issue.

In the case of an expedited appeal, he may adjourn the trial; if he decides not to expedite the trial he may either adjourn the trial or discharge the jury, if one has been sworn.

Notice of appeal or application to CACD for leave to appeal

18–043 Subject to R.66.8 in relation to public interest rulings (see 18–045), a notice of appeal (where the judge of the court has granted leave) or notice of application for leave to appeal must be in the form prescribed in PD 2004, Annex D and must be served by the prosecutor on the Registrar, the court officer, the defendant and on any interested party (see 18–042, above): R.66.5

(1) where the judge of the court below has decided that the appeal should be expedited under s.59(1) and that decision has not been subsequently reversed before 5.00pm on the day on which the prosecutor informs the judge of

the court that he intends to seek leave to appeal or, if the prosecutor demonstrates to that judge that it is not practical to do so, before 5.00pm on the next business day; or

(2) in any other case, within seven business days of the day on which the prosecutor informs the judge of the court that he intends to seek leave to appeal.

CACD may extend the period for service either before or after it expires, on application by the prosecutor. The notice must be accompanied by any documents necessary for the proper determination of the appeal or application for leave to appeal including:

(a) a transcript of the ruling which is the subject of the appeal;
(b) the skeleton arguments provided to the judge below by the parties in respect of the issue which gave rise to the ruling; and
(c) if the appeal is to be expedited, a copy of the reasons given by the judge under r.66.4(3).

Subject to r.66.8 (PII appeals) the notice served on the defendant must be accompanied by the form set out in the Practice Direction for the defendant to complete if he wishes to oppose the appeal or application.

Defendant's response

18–044 Upon receiving notice of an appeal or application for leave to appeal, the defendant if he wishes to oppose the appeal or application, must serve his response in the form set out in PD 2004, Annex D on the Registrar, the court officer; the prosecutor; and on any interested party (see 18–042, above): R.66.6

(1) on the next business day after the day on which the notice of appeal or application for leave to appeal is served on the defendant, where the judge of the court has decided that the appeal should be expedited under s.59(1) and that decision has not been subsequently reversed under s.59(4); or
(2) within seven business days of the day on which notice of the appeal or application for leave to appeal is served on the defendant in any other case.

CACD may extend the period of service either before or after it expires.

Public interest rulings

18–045 In any appeal or application for leave to appeal against a public interest ruling, the prosecutor need not describe the material that is the subject of the ruling in the notice of appeal or application for leave to appeal. R.66.8

Where he has reason to believe that to reveal to the defendant or any interested party:

(1) the category of material that is the subject of the public interest ruling would have the effect of disclosing that which he considers should not be disclosed, the prosecutor need not describe the category of the material in the notice of appeal or application for leave to appeal;
(2) the fact that a public interest ruling has been made would have the effect of disclosing that which he considers should not be disclosed, the prosecutor need not serve notice of appeal or application for leave to appeal on the defendant or any interested party as otherwise required, unless CACD otherwise directs.

Where the prosecutor has taken the measures set out in:

(a) (1) above the notice of appeal or application for leave to appeal served on the Registrar must be accompanied by a confidential annexe indicating that the measures have been taken and giving his reasons for taking them;
(b) (2) above, the defendant is not entitled to be present in person at the hearing by CACD of the appeal or application for leave to appeal, or to appear by way of live television link, unless CACD otherwise directs.

Determination of appeal

18–046 On an appeal under s.58, CACD may confirm, reverse or vary any ruling to which the appeal relates, and where it does so must make it clear how the case is to proceed; thus here the appeal relates to: CJA 2003, ss.56(1), 61(2), (3), (4), (5)

(1) a single ruling, and CACD:
  (a) confirms the ruling, it must, in respect of the offence (or each offence which is the subject of the appeal), order that the accused in relation to that offence be acquitted of that offence;
  (b) reverses or varies the ruling, it must, in respect of the offence (or each offence which is the subject of the appeal):
    (i) order that proceedings for that offence be resumed in the Crown Court;

(ii) order that a fresh trial may take place in the Crown Court; or

(iii) order that the accused in relation to the offence be acquitted of the offence, but may not make an order (b)(i) or (ii) above unless it considers it necessary in the interests of justice;

(2) a ruling that there is no case to answer and one or more other rulings, and CACD: CJA 2003, s.61(6), (7), (8)

(a) confirms the ruling that there is no case to answer, it must, in respect of the offence (or each offence which is the subject of the appeal), order that the accused in relation to that offence be acquitted of that offence;

(b) reverses or varies the ruling that there is no case to answer, it must, in respect of the offence (or each offence which is the subject of the appeal), make any of the orders under (1)(b) above, and subject to the same proviso.

(2) Evidentiary rulings (Not yet in force)

Right of appeal

18–047 Once this part of the Act comes into force, then, subject to the condition set out below, the Crown may appeal either a single or two or more "qualifying" evidentiary rulings made by the judge. A "qualifying" ruling is defined as a ruling relating to the admissibility or exclusion of prosecution evidence made in relation to a trial on indictment at any time (whether before or after the commencement of the trial) before the opening of the case for the defence, but may not appeal in respect of: CJA 2003, ss.62(1), (2), (3), (4), (9)

(1) a single ruling, unless it relates to one or more "qualifying offences" (as decribed in CJA 2003, Sch.1, Pt 4 (see 58 APPENDIX A, Pt 1); or

(2) two or more rulings unless each ruling relates to one or more such "qualifying offences" (whether or not it relates to any other offence).

As to the meaning of "ruling", see CJA 2003, s.74(1), above.

Leave to appeal; condition

18–048 An appeal may only be brought with the leave of the judge, or of CACD, which must not be given unless the CJA 2003, ss.63, 65 judge or CACD is satisfied that, in relation to an appeal in respect of:

(1) a single qualifying evidentiary ruling, the ruling significantly weakens the Crown's case in relation to the offence or offences which are the subject of the appeal;
(2) two or more such rulings, the rulings taken together significantly weaken the Crown's case in relation to the offence or offences which are the subject of the appeal.

There is no provision here, as there is in the case of appeals against "terminatory" rulings (see 18–039, above) that the Crown should agree to an acquittal where leave is refused or the appeal abandoned.

Procedure

18–049 If the Crown intends to appeal under this provision, they must, before the opening of the case for the defence, inform the court of: CJA 2003, ss.62(5), (7), (8)

(1) their intention to do so;
(2) the ruling or rulings to which the appeal relates; and
(3) at the same time, of the offence or offences which are the subject of the appeal.

For these purposes the case for the defence opens when, after the conclusion of the evidence for the Crown, the earliest of the following occurs:

(a) evidence begins to be adduced by or on behalf of the accused;
(b) it is indicated to the court that no evidence will be adduced by or on behalf of an accused;
(c) an accused's case is opened, as permitted by CPA 1865, s.2.

In respect of the ruling, or each ruling, to which the appeal relates, the qualifying offence, or at least one of the qualifying offences to which it relates, must be the subject of the appeal; any other offence to which the ruling relates *may*, but need not, be the subject of the appeal. CJA 2003, s.62(6)

Nothing in s.62 affects the rights of the Crown to appeal in respect of an evidentiary ruling under s.58 (above). CJA 2003, s.62(11)

Proceedings may be continued in respect of any offence which is not the subject of the appeal.

Expedited and non-expedited appeals

18–050 Where the Crown inform the court (in accordance with s.62(5) above, the judge must decide whether or not the appeal should be expedited. CJA 2003, s.59

If he decides that it should:

(1) *not* be expedited, he may;
  (a) order an adjournment; or
  (b) discharge the jury, if one has been sworn;
(2) be expedited, he or CACD may subsequently reverse that decision, and if reversed, he may act as in (1) above.

Determination of appeal

18–051 On an appeal under s.62, CACD may confirm, reverse or vary any ruling to which the appeal relates, and, in addition, must, in respect of the offence or each offence which is the subject of the appeal, do any of the following, that is to say order that: CJA 2003, s.66

(1) proceedings for that offence be resumed in the Crown Court;
(2) a fresh trial may take place in the Crown Court for that offence;
(3) the accused in relation to the offence be acquitted of it,

but no order may be made under (3) above, in respect of an offence, unless the Crown have indicated that they do not intend to continue with the prosecution of that offence.

(3) Supplementary

Reversal of rulings: Part 9

18–052 CACD is not entitled to reverse a ruling on an appeal under CJA 2003, Pt 9 unless satisfied that the ruling:

(1) was wrong in law;
(2) involved an error of law or principle; or
(3) was a ruling that it was not reasonable for the judge to have made.

Effect on time limits

18–053 Any period during which proceedings for an offence are adjourned pending the determination of an appeal under Pt 9, is disregarded so far as the offence is concerned, for the purposes of the overall time limit or the custody time limit (under POA 1985, s.22) which applies to the stage which the proceedings have reached when they are adjourned. CJA 2003, s.70

Costs

18–054 Where CACD reverses or varies a ruling on an appeal under the provisions, it may make such order as to the costs to be paid by the accused, to such person as may be named in the order as it considers just and reasonable. POA 1985, s.18(2A); CJA 2003, s.69(3)

Reporting restrictions

18–055 CJA 2003, ss.71 and 72 provide for restrictions on reporting anything of the proceedings associated with the appeal until after the conclusion of the trial, and create offences in respect of infringements of those proceedings.

Retrials

18–056 Special rules under CJA 2003, s.84, govern the retrial of an accused person on an indictment preferred by CACD (see 53 RETRIALS).

B. References to the Court of Appeal by the Attorney-General

1. On a point of law

18–057 Where a person tried on indictment has been acquitted (whether in respect of the whole or part of the indictment) the Attorney-General may, if he desires the opinion of CACD on a point of law which has arisen in the case, refer that point to the court for consideration and their opinion. CJA 1988, s.36

In such a case, the court may hear argument:

(1) by, or by an advocate for, the Attorney-General;
(2) if the acquitted person desires to present argument, by an advocate on his behalf or, with leave, by the acquitted person himself.

If the court thinks fit, it may refer the matter to the House of Lords.

The acquittal at the trial is not affected by the proceedings and steps are taken to protect the anonymity of the acquitted person.

A reference is in writing and must: R.69.1

(a) specify the point of law referred to, and where appropriate such facts of the case as are necessary for the proper consideration of the point of law;
(b) summarise the arguments intended to be put to the court; and

(c) specify the authorities intended to be cited,

but no mention must be made in the reference of the proper name of any person or place which is likely to lead to the identification of the acquitted person. A reference is entitled merely "Reference under s.36 of the Criminal Justice Act 1972", together with the year and number of the reference.

The Registrar will serve notice of the reference on the acquitted person:

(i) informing him that the reference will not affect the trial or any acquittal in that trial; and
(ii) inviting him within such period as may be specified in the notice (being not less than 28 days from the date of service of the notice) to inform the Registrar if he wishes to present any argument to the court and, if so, whether he wishes to present such argument in person or by counsel on his behalf.

The Attorney-General will not be heard until the time for the acquitted person to present his argument has expired. R.69.2

The Attorney-General may withdraw or amend the reference at any time before CACD has begun the hearing or, after that, and until the court has given its opinion, may withdraw or amend the reference by leave of the court and notice of such withdrawal or amendment will be served on the acquitted person on behalf of the Attorney-General. R.69.3

2. Lenient sentences

18–058 Where it appears to the Attorney-General that in the case of an offence of a description specified in an order made by the Home Secretary (see below), or in which sentence is passed on a person for an offence triable only on indictment, or for an offence of a description specified in an order: CJA 1988, ss. 35(3), (9), 36(1); CJPOA 1994, Sch.9, para.34; CSA 1997, Sch.4, para.13; PCC(S)A 2000, s.165, Sch.9, para.102; CJA 2003, s.304, Sch.32, Pt 1, para.46

(1) the sentencing judge in a proceeding in the Crown Court has been unduly lenient; or
(2) the trial judge has:
    (a) erred in law as to his powers of sentencing; or
    (b) failed to impose a sentence required by FA 1968, s.51A(2); PCC(S)A 2000, ss.110(2) or 111(2), or CJA 2003, any of ss.225–228,

the case may be referred to CACD.

Offences are presently specified by SI 2006/1116.

A reference lies in respect of the specification of the minimum term in relation to a life sentence (*R. v Sullivan and Others, The Times*, July 14, 2004, CACD).

On such a reference, CACD may quash any sentence passed on him in the proceeding, and pass in place of it such sentence as it thinks appropriate for the case, and as the court below had power to pass when dealing with the offender.

The Guideline case of *Att.-Gen.'s Reference (No. 4 of 1989) (Brunt)* (1989) 11 Cr.App.R.(S.) 517 makes it clear that:

- where a case is referred CACD may increase a sentence under s.36 only if it considers it unduly lenient, not merely because the sentence is less than CACD would impose;
- a sentence is "unduly lenient" where it falls outside the range of sentences which the judge could reasonably consider appropriate; in that respect, CACD will refer to reported cases and any guidance given in guideline cases;
- CACD has a discretion whether to exercise its powers under the section, even where it considers the sentence unduly lenient; this may be the case where in the light of events since the trial it appears either that the sentence could be justified or that to increase it would be unfair to the offender or detrimental to others for whose well-being the court ought to be concerned.

CA's task under s.36 is to decide whether the judge's sentence, in the light of the material then before him, can properly be characterised as unduly lenient; it is not open to CA to take into account new material which was not available to the sentencing judge, provided that the conclusion that the judge reached was appropriate on the facts before him (*Att.-Gen.'s Reference (No.19 of 2005), The Times*, March 16, 2006).

Definitions

18–059 Note the following definitions:

(1) "sentence" has the same meaning for these provisions as in CAA 1968, except that it does not include an interim hospital order;

(2) "offence triable only on indictment" means an offence punishable only on conviction on indictment; CJA 1988, s.35(9)

(3) for the purposes of these provisions, any two or more sentences are to be treated as passed in the same proceedings if they would be treated as such for the purposes of CAA 1968, s.10. CJA 1988, s.36(3)

Conduct of prosecutor

18–060 Where the prosecutor has been party to a bargain with the defence, or has acquiesced in a bargain between the court and the defence (see 43 INDICATION OF SENTENCE), it may be an abuse of the process to refer a resulting sentence to CACD, albeit that it was too lenient (see, e.g. *Att.-Gen.'s References (Nos. 80 and 89 of 1999) (R. v Thompson and Rodgers)* 2 [2000] Cr.App.R. (S.) 138, CA; *Att.-Gen.'s Reference (No. 44 of 2000) (R. v Peverret), The Times*, October 25, 2000, CA; *Att.-Gen.'s References (Nos. 86 and 87 of 1999) (R. v Webb and Simpson)* [2001] Crim.L.R. 58, CA).

The application

18–061 Notice of application for leave to refer a case to CACD under s.36 must be given within 28 days from the day on which the sentence or the last of any sentences in the case was passed. The sending of the application to the Registrar constitutes the giving of such notice. CJA 1988, s.36, Sch.3, para.1

The application must be in writing, and in addition to specifying the details of the offender, and the dates of conviction and sentence, must state: R.70.1

(1) the judge by whom, and the location of the Crown Court at which the sentence was passed; and
(2) the reason why it appears to the Attorney-General to be unduly lenient.

A reference is entitled "Reference under s.36 of the Criminal Justice Act 1988" together with the year, the number of the application and the name of the offender. R.70.2

Registrar's notice

18–062 As soon as practicable after receiving the application, the Registrar will cause a copy of it to be served on the offender, together with a notice which will:

(1) inform him that the result of the reference could be that the court would quash his sentence, and in place of it pass such sentence as it thought appropriate, and as the court below had power to pass, when dealing with him (including a greater punishment);
(2) inform him of his entitlement:
    (a) to be present though in custody, with leave;
    (b) to reasonable costs out of central funds; and tell him of the court's power to pass sentence though he is not present; and

(3) invite him, within such period as the Registrar may specify, not being less than 14 days from the date of service on him of the notice, to serve notice on the Registrar, if he wishes:
   (a) to apply to the court for leave to be present; and
   (b) to present any argument to the court on the hearing of the application or, if leave is given, of the reference, and whether to present it in person or by counsel on his behalf;
(4) draw his attention to the effect of r.77, governing the supply of documents and exhibits; and
(5) advise him to consult a solicitor as to his position as soon as possible.

The court will not hear any argument by or on behalf of the Attorney-General until the period specified by the Registrar has expired unless the offender agrees, or has indicated that he does not wish to present any argument to the court. R.70.3

The reference

18–063 The reference must be in writing and must summarise the arguments intended to be put before CACD, and specify any authorities intended to be cited. It must be sent to the Registrar, who will, as soon as practicable after receiving it, serve a copy on the offender. R.70.4

If CACD gives leave for the case to be referred to them and are satisfied that the application contains the required information, they may treat the application as the reference.

C. Appeal by way of case stated

18–064 Any order, judgment or other decision of the Crown Court, other than a judgment or other decision relating to trial on indictment, or certain matters under the Betting and Gaming legislation, may be questioned by any party to the proceedings, on the ground that: SCA 1981, s.28

(1) it is wrong in law, or
(2) in excess of jurisdiction,

by applying to the Crown Court to state a case for the opinion of the High Court.

"Decision" means "final decision" and the High Court will not entertain such an appeal unless the Crown Court has reached a final determination (*Loade v DPP* [1989] 3 W.L.R. 1281).

Appeals by way of case stated are not usually an appropriate procedure for appealing against sentence: *Allen v W Yorks Probation Service*, *The Times*, February 20, 2001.

Making the application

18–065 An application under SCA 1981, s.28 to the Crown Court to state a case for the opinion of the High Court must be made in writing to a court officer within 21 days after the date of the decision in respect of which the application is made, stating the ground on which the decision is questioned, a copy being sent to any other party to the proceedings. Rr.64.7(1)–(3)

On receipt of the application the Crown Court officer will forthwith send it to the judge who presided at the proceedings in which the decision was made and the judge: Rr.64.7(1)–(7)

(1) will inform the Crown Court officer whether or not he has decided to state a case, and that officer will give notice in writing to the applicant of the judge's decision;
(2) if he considers the application to be frivolous may refuse to state a case and, if the applicant so requires, will cause a certificate stating the reasons for refusal to be given to him;

If the decides to state a case, the procedure under rr. 64.7(8)–(12) will be followed.

Procedure

18–066 If the judge decides to state a case: R.64.7(8)–(10) (12)

(1) the applicant must, within 21 days of receiving notice of that decision, draft the case and send a copy of it both to the Crown Court officer and to the other parties to the proceedings;
(2) each party to the proceedings in the Crown Court must then, within 21 days of receiving a copy of the draft case:
    (a) give notice in writing to the applicant and to the Crown Court officer that he does not intend to take part in the proceedings in the High Court; or
    (b) indicate in writing on a copy of the draft case that he agrees with it, and send a copy to a court officer; or
    (c) draw up an alternative case and send it, together with the copy of the applicant's case, to the Crown Court officer;
(3) the judge will then consider the applicant's draft case and any alternative draft case sent to the Crown Court officer

under (2)(c) above and will state and sign the case within 14 days after either:

(a) receipt of all the documents required to be sent to the court; or
(b) the expiration of the 21 days referred to in (1) above,

whichever is the sooner.

As to the position where the judge has given a reasoned judgment, see *R. v Blackfriars CC Ex p. Sun World Ltd* [2000] Crim. L.R. 593.

Extension of time

18–067 Any of the time limits referred to in the Rules may be extended, either before or after it expires, by the Crown Court. R. 64.7(14)

The use of the term "Crown Court" as distinct from "judge" in r.26(11), (14) of the previous Rules, dealing with recognisances and extension of time, was held not to require the participation of the magistrates in the decision, but to reflect the possibility that a judge, other than the judge who heard the original application, might consider the application for an extension (*DPP v Coleman* [1998] 2 Cr.App.R. 7).

If the prosecutor applies for an extension of time, the acquitted appellant ought to have an opportunity to make representations (*ibid.*).

R.64.7(15) makes certain adjustments in r.64.7 where a case is stated in accordance with a mandatory order of the High Court.

Form of case: ancillary orders

18–068 A case stated by the Crown Court must state: R.64.7(13)

(1) the facts found by the Crown Court;
(2) the submissions of the parties, including any authorities relied on by them during the course of those submissions;
(3) the decision of the Crown Court in respect of which the application is made; and
(4) the question on which the opinion of the High Court is sought.

The Crown Court, in dealing with such an appeal: R. 64.7(11)

(a) may order the applicant, before the case is stated and delivered to him, to enter into a recognisance before the Crown Court officer, with or without sureties, and in such sums as the court thinks proper having regard to his means, conditioned to prosecute the appeal without delay;

(b) may grant the applicant bail (as may the High Court);

(c) may not (but the High Court may) suspend an RT disqualification pending appeal;

(d) may not grant public funding. The representation order in force in the Crown Court is authority for counsel and solicitor assigned to advise on reasonable grounds of appeal and to make the application for a case to be stated; thereafter an applicant will need to apply to the Commission under AJA 1999, s.12.

Withdrawal of appeal

18–069 An appellant is entitled to withdraw an appeal by case stated without leave of the court (*Collett v Bromsgrove DC* (1996) 160 J.P. 593).

D. Judicial review

18–070 In relation to the jurisdiction of the Crown Court *other than its jurisdiction in relation to trial on indictment*, the High Court has all such jurisdiction to make: SCA 1981, s.29

(1) a mandatory order (CPR 1998, r.54. 1), to compel the Crown Court to exercise its proper jurisdiction;

(2) a prohibiting order, to restrain it from proceeding improperly; and

(3) a quashing order, to quash any order which has been made improperly.

Where an order is jurisdictionally flawed, the High Court may intervene despite the fact that the order relates to a trial on indictment, see *R. v Maidstone CC Ex p Harrow LBC* [2000] 1 Cr.App.R. 117, *R. (Kenneally) v Snaresbrook CC* [2002] 2 W.L.R 1430.

Nature of judicial review

18–071 While judicial review provides a speedy and effective remedy in a proper case, it is a discretionary remedy (see *R. v Peterborough MC Ex p Dowler* [1997] 2 W.L.R 843, *R. v Hereford MC Ex p Rowlands* [1997] 2 W.L.R. 854). Its ambit is restricted; in particular:

(1) the issue of these orders is reserved for simple and straightforward cases; the High Court will not attempt to resolve direct conflicts of evidence on material facts;

(2) the jurisdiction is confined essentially to matters of jurisdiction, thus the proper exercise of a discretion to admit or reject evidence in committal proceedings is not subject to control;
(3) the High Court will not permit the machinery of judicial review to be used as a means of appeal.

It is an abuse of process to attack a finding of fact which has been the basis of a judgment in the Crown Court by means of judicial review (*R. v Knightsbridge CC Ex p. Quinlan*, *The Times*, December 13, 1988).

Application for permission

18–072 Procedure for judicial review is under CPR 1998, r.54. The permission of the High Court must be obtained before a claim for judicial review is made. CPR 1998, r.54

A claim is made by filing a claim form:

(1) promptly; and
(2) in any event not later than three months after the grounds to make the claim first arose (unless any other enactment specifies a shorter time limit), and this time limit may not be extended by agreement between the parties.

Where the decision of the Crown Court to dismiss an appeal is quashed, it is necessary for the case to be relisted before the Crown Court where it will be for a differently constituted court to determine the matter *de novo* (*R. v Leeds CC Ex p. Barlow* [1989] R.T.R. 246).

Applications for judicial review are not usually an appropriate procedure for appealing against sentence: *Allen v W Yorks Probation Service*, *The Times*, February 20, 2001, but see below, 18–084.

Bail; RT disqualification; public funding

18–073 In relation to such proceedings, the Crown Court:

(1) may grant bail to a person who has applied for *certiorari*, or who has applied for leave (so may the High Court);
(2) may not remove an RT disqualification pending the decision of the High Court (but the High Court may);
(3) does not deal with public funding; application must be made to the Commission under AJA 1999, s.12.

Jurisdiction

18–074 By statute (SCA 1981, s.29(6)) an order as to defence public funding made under AJA 1999, s.17, is not a matter relating to trial on indictment. As to what matters fall within the Crown Court's exclusive jurisdiction:

(1) an order for costs made on entering a finding of not guilty under CJA 1967, s.17, is not a matter falling within the exclusion in SCA 1981, s.29(3) (*R. v Wood Green CC Ex p. DPP* [1993] 2 All E.R. 656; *R. v Leicester CC Ex p. CC & E*, *The Times*, February 23, 2001);

(2) the decision of a judge to revoke a previous order discharging a representation order is a matter relating to trial on indictment, and is excluded from the jurisdiction of the High Court (*R. v Isleworth CC Ex p. Willington* [1993] 2 All E.R. 390) as is an order refusing to amend a representation order so as to provide for leading counsel: *R. v Liverpool CC The Times*, February 13, 2001;

(3) while an application to a judge under CJA 1987, s.6(1) for dismissal of transferred charges is not a matter relating to trial on indictment, being analogous to proceedings for the transfer of a case from the magistrates' court for trial in the Crown Court, the jurisdiction to review such an order is likely to be exercised only in exceptional circumstances (*R. v CCC Ex p. Director of SFO* [1993] 2 All E.R. 399);

(4) an order of a judge of the Crown Court staying a trial on the ground of abuse of process is an order relating to trial on indictment (*DPP v Manchester & Ashton CC* [1993] 2 All E.R. 663, HL);

(5) an order deciding which of two or more indictments should be tried first is an order affecting the conduct of the trial (*R. v Southwark CC Ex p. Ward* [1996] Crim. L.R. 123);

(6) arraignment and the conduct of a plea and directions hearing are matters relating to trial on indictment (*R. v Leeds CC Ex p. Hussain* [1995] 3 All E.R. 527);

(7) an order as to disclosure relates to trial on indictment (*R. v Chester CC Ex p. Cheshire CC* [1996] Crim. L.R. 336);

(8) an order under CYPA 1933, s.39 (protecting the anonymity of a child or young person) may, or may not be a matter relating to trial on indictment, depending on the circumstances (see *R. v Manchester CC Ex p. H & D* [2000] 1 Cr.App.R. 262).

No right to judicial review arises in these cases unless, perhaps, the judge acts in a way which was clearly contrary to the statutory provisions (*R. v Maidstone CC Ex p. Harrow LBC* [2000] 1 Cr.App.R. 117, *R. (Kennealy v Snaresbrook CC etc* [2002] 2 W.L.R 1430, *cf. R. v Leicester CC Ex p.*

Commissioners of Customs & Excise, *The Times*, February 23, 2001). As to orders in relation to costs, for example, see *In re Sampson* [1987] 1 W.L.R. 194. The position is not affected by the coming into force of ECHR, see *R. v Canterbury CC Ex p. Regentford Ltd*, *The Times*, February 6, 2001 and also *R. v Leicester CC*; above.

Suspension of disqualification

18–075 Where a person ordered to be disqualified applies to the High Court for a quashing order to remove proceedings in the Crown Court, being proceedings in, or in consequence of which, he was convicted or his sentence was passed, or applies for leave to make such an application, the High Court may, if it thinks fit, suspend the disqualification on such terms as it thinks fit. RTOA 1988, s.40(1), (5), (7)

E. Tainted acquittals

General

18–076 Under CPIA 1996, s.54 provision is made for a form of judicial review in a case where one person has been acquitted of an offence, and another person has been convicted of perverting the course of justice, intimidating witnesses, jurors, etc., under CJPOA 1994, s.51(1) or aiding, abetting, counselling, procuring, suborning or inciting the committing of an offence under s.1 of the Perjury Act 1911, involving interference or intimidation of a juror or a witness (or potential witness) in any proceedings which led to the acquittal.

Need for certificate

18–077 Where it appears to the court before which the person was convicted that there was a real possibility that, but for the interference or intimidation, the acquitted person would not have been acquitted, and that there is no doubt, because of lapse of time or any other reason, that it would not be contrary to the interests of justice to take proceedings against the acquitted person for the offence of which he was acquitted, the court must certify that fact. CPIA 1996, s.54(1), (2), (5)

Certification

18–078 The certification referred to in s.54(2) must be made in the form set out in the Practice Direction Annex D at any time following conviction but no later than: R.40.1, 2

(1) immediately after the court sentences or otherwise deals with that person in respect of the offence;

(2) where the court, being a magistrates' court, commits that person to the Crown Court, or remits him to another magistrates' court, to be dealt with in respect of the offence, immediately after he is so committed or remitted, as the case may be; or
(3) where that person is a child or young person and a judge of the Crown Court, remits him to a youth court to be dealt with in respect of the offence, immediately after he is so remitted.

Subsequent procedure

18–079 The court officer will then, as soon as practicable after the drawing up of the form, serve (as to which see R. 40.3(2)) a copy on: R.40.3(1)

(1) the acquitted person referred to in the certification;
(2) the prosecutor in the proceedings which led to the acquittal; and,
(3) where the acquittal has taken place before a court other than, or at a different place to, the court where the certification has been made, on the clerk of the magistrates' court before which the acquittal has taken place; or the Crown Court officer at the place where the acquittal has taken place.

If the person to be served is acting by a solicitor (as defined in r.40.3(4)), the copy of the form may be served by delivering it, or by sending it by post, to the solicitor's address for service.

The court officer of the court before which an acquittal has taken place will after receipt of a copy of a form recording a certification under s.54(2) relating to the acquittal enter in the register or record a note:

(a) that the certification has been made,
(b) the date of the certification,
(c) the name of the court which has made the certification,
(d) the name of the person whose conviction occasioned the making of the certification, and
(e) a description of the offence of which that person has been convicted.

Where the certification has been made by the same court as the court before which the acquittal has occurred, sitting at the same place, the entry must be made as soon as practicable after the making of the certification. R.40.5

Where a court makes such a certification, the court officer will, as soon as practicable after the drawing up of the form, display a copy at a prominent place within court premises to which place the public has access, for at least 28 days from, the day on which the certification was made, or, as the case may be, the day on which the copy form was received at the court. If the acquittal has taken place before a court other than, or at a different place to, the court which has made the certification, the court officer at the court where the acquittal has taken place must do the same. R.40.6

Application to High Court

18–080 Where a court so certifies, it will be possible to make an application to the High Court for an order quashing the acquittal, and if such an order is made it will be possible to take proceedings against the acquitted person for the offence of which he was acquitted. CPIA 1996, ss.54(3), (4)

See also *Practice Statement (Administrative Court: annual statement)* [2002] 1 W.L.R. 810.

Conditions precedent to order

18–081 The High Court will not be empowered to make such an order unless four conditions are fulfilled. If it appears to the High Court, taking into account all the information before it but ignoring the possibility of new factors coming to light, that: CPIA 1996, ss.54(3), 55

(1) but for the interference or intimidation, the acquitted person would not have been acquitted;
(2) because of lapse of time or for any other reason it would not be contrary to the interest of justice to take proceedings against the acquitted person for the offence of which he was acquitted;
(3) the acquitted person has been given a reasonable opportunity to make written representations to the court; and
(4) the conviction for the administration of justice offence will stand;

the High Court will not make an order if, for instance, the time for giving notice of appeal has not expired or an appeal is pending.

Time limits

18–082 Where an order is made quashing an acquittal and it is proposed to take proceedings against the acquitted person, any time limits within which, by statute, a prosecution must be commenced will run from the making of the order. CPIA 1996, s.56

Entry in records; display of notice

18–083 The court officer at the court:

(1) where an acquittal has taken place will, on receipt from the Administrative Court Office of notice of an order made under CPIA 1996, s.54(3) quashing the acquittal, or of a decision not to make such an order, enter in the records a note of the fact that the acquittal has been quashed, or that a decision has been made not to make such an order, as the case may be; R.40.7(1)

(2) which has made a certification under s.54(2) will, on receipt from the Administrative Court Office of notice of an order made under s.54(3) quashing the acquittal referred to in the certification, or of a decision not to make such an order, enter in the records, in relation to the conviction which occasioned the certification, a note that the acquittal has been quashed by the said order, or that a decision has been made not to make such an order, as the case may be. R.40.7(2)

Where the court officer of a court which has made a certification under s.54(2), or before which an acquittal has occurred to which such a certification refers, receives from the Administrative Court Office notice of an order quashing the acquittal concerned, or notice of a decision not to make such an order, he will, as soon as practicable after receiving the notice, display a copy of it at a prominent place within court premises to which place the public has access. This copy must continue to be displayed at least until the expiry of 28 days from the day on which the notice was received at the court. R.40.8

F. Powers of High Court to vary sentence

18–084 Where a person who has been sentenced for an offence by the Crown Court: SCA 1981, s.43(1), (2)

(1) after being convicted of an offence by a magistrates' court and committed for sentence; or
(2) on appeal against conviction or sentence,

applies to the High Court for a quashing order, then if the High Court determines that the Crown Court had no power to pass that sentence it may, instead of quashing the conviction, amend it by substituting any sentence which the magistrates' court in a case under (2) or the Crown Court in a case under (1) above, had power to impose.

The High Court will, in an exceptional case, quash a sentence imposed by the Crown Court:

(a) where it is plainly demonstrated that in the process of sentencing an error of law has been perpetrated (*R. v Liverpool CC Ex p. Baird* (1985) 7 Cr.App.R.(S.) 437);
(b) which is harsh and oppressive and so far outside the normal sentence imposed for the offence as necessarily to involve an error of law (*R. v St Albans CC Ex p. Cinnamond* [1981] 1 All E.R. 802; *cf. R. v Croydon CC Ex p. Miller* (1987) 85 Cr.App.R. 152); *R. (Sogbesan) v ILCC* [2003] 1 Cr.App.R.(S.) 79;
(c) which is irrational and truly astonishing (*R. v Acton CC Ex p. Bewley* (1988) 10 Cr.App.R.(S.) 105; *R. v Chelmsford CC Ex p. Birchall* (1989) 11 Cr.App.R.(S.) 510); and
(d) where the sentence imposed is "outside the broad area of the lower court's jurisdiction" [*sic*]: *R. v Truro CC Ex p. Adair* [1997] C.O.D. 296, DC; *R. v Southwark CC Ex p. Smith* [2001] 2 Cr.App.R.(S.) 35.

Such sentence begins to run, unless the High Court directs otherwise, from the time when it would have started to run if passed in those proceedings, disregarding any time during which the offender was released on bail pending his application.

Where, on judicial review, the decision of the Crown Court to dismiss an appeal is quashed, it is necessary for the case to be relisted before the Crown Court, where it will be for a differently constituted court to determine the matter *de novo* (*R. v Leeds CC Ex p. Barlow* [1989] R.T.R. 246).

G. Reference to the Criminal Cases Review Commission

18–085 The Criminal Cases Review Commission, set up by CAA 1995, s.8 may refer to CACD the conviction or sentence (not being one fixed by law) of a person convicted on indictment, a verdict of not guilty by reason of insanity and a finding of disability, where a finding that he did the act or made the omission was returned (CAA 1995, s.9; DVA 2004, s.58(1), Sch.10, para.31). Its powers and functions are reviewed in *R. v Criminal Cases Review Commission Ex p. Pearson* [1999] Crim.L.R. 732.

CAA 1995, s.14, as amended by CJA 2003, s.315 contains further provisions relating to such references.

Powers of CACD to order investigation

18–086 On an appeal against conviction, or an application for leave to appeal against conviction CACD (not a single judge) may direct the Commission to investigate and report on any matter if it appears that: CAA 1968, s.23A; CJA 2003, s.313

(1) in the case of an appeal, the matter is relevant to the determination of the appeal, and ought, if possible, to be resolved before the appeal is determined;
(2) in the case of an application for leave to appeal, the matter is relevant to the determination of the application and ought, if possible, to be resolved before the application is determined;
(3) an investigation of the matter is likely to result in the Court being able to resolve it; and
(4) the matter cannot be resolved by the Court without an investigation by the Commission.

In due course the parties will be informed of the results, and the report and any statements, opinions and reports will be made available to them.

H. Appeals to CACD under PCA 2002

(1) Prosecutor's appeal regarding confiscation

Appeal by prosecutor or Director

18–087 The prosecutor or the Director may appeal to CACD where a judge of the Crown Court: PCA 2002, ss.31, 32(1)(4)

(1) makes a confiscation order under PCA 2002, in respect of the order; or
(2) decides not to make a confiscation order, against that decision,

except in the case of an order or decision made by virtue of ss.19, 20 (reconsideration), 27 or 28 (convicted and unconvicted absconders).

The *Explanatory Notes* published by HMSO state that only an appeal on a point of law lies under this section. The post-conviction procedures being mandatory there is no scope for an appeal on the merits; it is otherwise in revaluation cases.

An appeal requires the leave of CACD.

Further appeal lies to the House of Lords/Supreme Court under *ibid*., s.33.

As to appeals to CACD in respect of orders made by the Crown Court in relation to external requests or orders, see PCA 2002 (External Requests and Orders) Order 2005 (SI 2005/3181), Pt 2, or, in regard to the former law, see CJ(IC)A 1990 (Enforcement of Overseas Forfeiture Orders) Order 2005 (SI 2005/3180).

Prosecutor's notice of appeal

18–088 Where the appellant seeks to apply to CACD for leave to appeal under PCA 2002, s.31, he must serve a notice of appeal in the form set out in PD 2004, Annex D (pp.203–207) on the Crown Court officer and on the defendant. As to further procedure in CACD, see Proceeds of Crime Act 2002 (Appeals under Part 2) Order 2003 (SI 2003/82), arts 5–10. Rr.72.1(1), (2), (3)

The notice of appeal served upon the defendant must be accompanied by a notice in the form set out in PD 2004, Annex D (pp.209–211) for him to complete:

(1) informing him that the result of the appeal could be that CACD would increase a confiscation order already imposed on him, make a confiscation order itself, or direct the Crown Court to hold a fresh hearing;
(2) informing him of his right under art.6 of the above Order to be present at the hearing, even though he is in custody; and
(3) inviting him to serve notice on the Registrar if he wishes to apply for leave to be present, or to present any argument on the hearing of the application, and whether he wishes to present it in person or by means of a legal representative.

The notice will also draw to his attention R.71.4 (supply of documentary and other exhibits) and advise the defendant to consult a solicitor as soon as possible.

The appellant must provide a Crown Court officer with a certificate of service stating that he has served the notice of appeal on the defendant in accordance with the Rules, or explaining why he has been unable to effect service.

Respondent's notice

18–089 Where a defendant is served with a notice of appeal under R. 72.1, and wishes to oppose the application for leave to appeal, he must, not later than 14 days after the date on which he received the notice of appeal, serve on the Registrar and on the appellant notice in the same form: R.72.2

(1) stating the date on which he received the notice of appeal;
(2) summarising his response to the arguments of the appellant; and
(3) specifying the authorities which he intends to cite.

The time for giving notice may be extended by the Registrar, a single judge or by CACD. If the Registrar refuses an extension of time, the defendant is entitled to have his application determined by a single judge; if the single judge refuses the extension the defendant is entitled to have his application determined by the court.

Amendment and abandonment of appeal

18–090 The appellant may amend a notice of appeal served under R.72.1 or abandon an appeal under PCA 2002, s.31: R.72.3

(1) without the permission of CACD at any time before the hearing of the appeal has begun; and
(2) with the permission of CACD after the hearing of the appeal has begun,

by serving notice in writing on the Registrar, and where the appellant abandons an appeal under (1) above he must send a copy of the notice to the defendant, a court officer of the court of trial and the magistrates' court responsible for enforcing any confiscation order which the Crown Court has made.

Where the appellant serves a notice amending a notice of appeal he must send a copy of it to the defendant.

Where an appeal is abandoned the application for leave to appeal or appeal will be treated, for the purposes of PCA 2002, s.85 (conclusion of proceedings), as having been refused or dismissed by CACD.

(2) Appeal in relation to restraint orders

General

18–091 There is no appeal against the making of a restraint order. A person dissatisfied with the making of an order must apply to the Crown Court for its variation or discharge. Appeal does, however, lie to CACD where: PCA 2002, ss.43, 44

(1) on an application for a restraint order the court decides not to make one, by the person who applied for the order, against that decision;
(2) an application is made under s.42(3) in relation to a restraint order or an order under s.41(7), by the person

who applied for the order or any person affected by it in respect of the Crown Court's decision on the application,

and CACD may either confirm the order or make such order as it believes appropriate.

Leave is required, and leave will be given only where CACD considers that the appeal would have a real prospect of success or there is some other compelling reason why the appeal should be heard. An order giving leave may limit the issues to be heard and may be made subject to conditions. R.73.1

As to procedure, see 18–094, below.

As to appeals to CACD in respect of orders made by the Crown Court in relation to external requests or orders, see PCA 2002 (External Requests and Orders) Order 2005 (SI 2005/3181), Pt 2, or, in regard to the former law, see CJ(IC)A 1990 (Enforcement of Overseas Forfeiture Orders) Order 2005 (SI 2005/3180).

Effect of appeal

CACRRR 2003, r.10

18–092 Unless CACD or the Crown Court orders otherwise, an appeal under s.43 will not operate as a stay of any order or decision of the Crown Court.

As to procedure, see that prescribed in 18–094 below, which applies to appeals under PCA 2002, ss.43 and 65.

Futher appeal lies to the House of Lords Supreme Court under PCA 2002, s.44.

(3) Appeals in relation to the appointment etc of receivers

18–093 Appeal lies to CACD (PCA 2002, s.65):

(1) if on an application for an order under any of ss.48 to 51 or s.53 (appointment of a receiver) the Crown Court decides not to make one, by the person who applied for the order, against the decision;
(2) if the Crown Court makes an order under any of ss.48 to 51 or s.53 (appointment of a receiver), in respect of the court's decision, by the person who applied for the order or any person affected by the order;
(3) if on an application for an order under s.62 (directions) the Crown Court decides not to make one, by the person who applied for the order, against the decision;
(4) if the court makes an order under s.62 (giving directions), in respect of the court's decision, by the person who

applied for the order, any person affected by the order and the receiver;

(5) against a decision of the Crown Court on an application under s.63 (directions), by
   (a) the person who applied for the order in respect of which the application was made or (if the order was made under s.52 or s.53) the Director;
   (b) any person affected by the court's decision;
   (c) the receiver.

The procedure for initiating an appeal is the same as that in the case of an appeal under s.43, as to which see 18–094, above.

On such an appeal CACD may confirm the decision, or make such order as it believes is appropriate. Further appeal lies to the House of Lords/Supreme Court under s.66.

As to appeals to CACD in respect of orders made by the Crown Court in relation to external requests or orders, see PCA 2002 (External Requests and Orders) Order 2005 (SI 2005/3181), Pt 2, or, in regard to the former law, see CJ(IC)A 1990 (Enforcement of Overseas Forfeiture Orders) Order 2005 (SI 2005/3180).

(4) Procedure

Notice of appeal

18–094 Where an appellant wishes to apply to the CACD for leave to appeal under PCA 2002, s.43 or s.65, he must serve a notice of application in the form set out in PD 2004, Annex D on the Crown Court officer. R.73.2

Unless the Registrar, a single judge or CACD directs otherwise, the appellant must serve the notice, accompanied by a respondent's notice in the form set out in *ibid.* for the respondent to complete on:

(1) each respondent;
(2) any person who holds realisable property to which the appeal relates; and
(3) any other person affected by the appeal,

as soon as practicable and in any event not later than seven days after the notice of appeal is served on a Crown Court officer.

With his notice, the appellant must serve the following documents:

(a) four additional copies of the notice for CACD;
(b) four copies of any skeleton argument;
(c) one sealed copy and four unsealed copies of any order being appealed;

(d) four copies of any witness statement or affidavit in support of the application for leave to appeal;
(e) four copies of a suitable record of the reasons for judgment of the Crown Court; and
(f) four copies of the bundle of documents used in the Crown Court proceedings from which the appeal lies.

Where it is not possible to serve all of these documents the appellant must indicate which documents have not yet been served and the reasons why they are not currently available.

The appellant must provide a Crown Court officer with a certificate of service stating that he has served the notice of appeal on each respondent in accordance with para.(2) and including full details of each respondent or explaining why he has been unable to effect service.

Respondent's notice

18–095 A respondent who wishes to ask the CACD to uphold the decision of the Crown Court for reasons different from or additional to those given by the Crown Court, must serve a respondent's notice on the Registrar, in the form set out in PD 2004, Annex D and where he seeks leave to appeal to CACD he must request it in the notice. R.73.3

The notice must be served on the Registrar not later than 14 days after:

(1) the date the respondent is served with notification that CACD has given the appellant leave to appeal; or
(2) the date the respondent is served with notification that the application for leave to appeal and the appeal itself are to be heard together.

Unless the Registrar, a single judge or CACD directs otherwise, the respondent serving a respondent's notice must serve the notice on the appellant and any other respondent:

(a) as soon as practicable; and
(b) in any event not later than seven days, after it is served on the Registrar.

Amendment and abandonment of appeal

18–096 The appellant may amend his notice of appeal or abandon his appeal without the permission of CACD at any time *before* CACD has begun hearing the appeal; and *with* its permission after the hearing of the appeal has begun, by serving notice in writing on the Registrar. He must give notice to each respondent. R.73.4

I. Appeal by specified prosecutor to CACD Under SOCA 2005, s.74

18–097 A specified prosecutor who has made a reference to a judge of the Crown Court SOCA 2005, s.74(3), has, with the leave of CACD, a right of appeal to that court against the decision of the judge of he Crown Court, either to substitute, or not to substitute a sentence under the provisions of the Act.

CAA 1968, s.33(3) (limitation on appeal from CACD) does not prevent a further appeal to the House of Lords/Supreme Court).

Procedure on such an appeal is governed by SOCA 2005 (Appeals under s.74) Order 2006 (SI 2006/2135) Pts 2 and 3, and is similar to that required of an appellant on an appeal under CAA 1968.

19 CHILDREN AND YOUNG PERSONS

19–001 A number of topics are relevant here as affecting children and young persons, in particular:

1. Juveniles defined (see below);
2. Juveniles as accused persons (see below);
3. The trial of juveniles (19–005, below);
4. Remand of juveniles (19–013, below);
5. Penalties on conviction (19–020, below);
6. Parenting orders (19–030, below);
7. Evidence of children; competency (19–035, below);
8. Restriction on publication (19–041, below);
9. Reparation orders (19–045, below);
10. Youth offender panels (19–048, below)

1. Juveniles defined

CYPA 1933, ss.44(1), 107(1); CJA 1991, Sch.8, para.1(3)

19–002 Young persons under 18 are commonly known as juveniles though the law distinguishes for some purposes between "children" (under 14) and "young persons" (14 to 18). Section 44 (1) of CYPA 1933 provides that every court dealing with a child or young person brought before it, whether as an offender or otherwise, must have regard to the welfare of the child or young person who is brought before it, and shall, in a proper case, take steps for removing him from undesirable surroundings and seeing that proper provision is made for his education and training.

2. Juveniles as accused persons

Jurisdiction

MCA 1980, s.24(1); CJA 2003, s.42

19–003 CJA 2003, s.42 provides that a juvenile charged with an offence other than:

(1) an offence of homicide; or
(2) each of the requirements of FA 1968, s.51A(1) would be satisfied with respect to
   (i) the offence, and
   (ii) the person charged with it, if he were convicted of the offence,

must be dealt with in the youth court unless:

(a) the offence is such as is mentioned in PCC(S)A 2000, s.91(1) and the court considers that, if found guilty, it ought to be possible to sentence him in pursuance of that section; or
(b) he is charged jointly with an adult and the adult court considers it necessary in the interests of justice to commit the cases of both for trial, or to send the case or transfer the case to the Crown Court for trial; or
(c) he is charged jointly with an adult; or
(d) (i) the charge arises out of circumstances connected with an offence with which an adult is charged; or
(ii) an adult is charged with aiding and abetting or procuring an offence by a juvenile; or
(iii) a juvenile is charged with aiding and abetting or procuring an offence by an adult.

In (c) and (d) there is a discretion and it is for the court to determine whether the trial should be in the adult court or the youth court.

Juveniles may be remitted to the youth court from both the Crown Court and the adult magistrates' court, see below.

Juveniles in the Crown Court

19–004 The manner in which juveniles come before the Crown Court is outlined in 15 CASES COMMITTED, TRANSFERRED, SENT FOR TRIAL.

3. Trial of juveniles

General

19–005 PD 2004 IV.39.2–17 apply to the trial of children and young persons (classified as "young defendants") in the Crown Court. The steps which are to be taken to comply with these provisions should be judged in any given case taking account of the age, maturity and development, intellectual and emotional of the young defendant on trial, and of all the other circumstances of the case.

The overriding principle

19–006 Some young defendants accused of committing serious crimes may be very young and very immature when standing trial in the Crown Court. The purpose of such trial is to determine guilt (if that is in issue) and decide the appropriate sentence if the young defendant pleads guilty or is convicted. PD 2004, IV.39.3

The trial process should not itself expose the young defendant to avoidable intimidation, humiliation or distress. All possible steps should be taken to assist him to understand and participate in the proceedings. The ordinary trial process should, so far as necessary, be adapted to meet those ends. Regard should be had to his welfare as required by CYPA 1933, s.44 (see above 19–002).

Before trial

19–007 If a young defendant is indicted jointly with an adult defendant, the judge should, at the plea and directions hearing:

(1) consider whether he should be tried on his own, and should ordinarily so order unless of opinion that joint trial would be in the interests of justice, and would not be unduly prejudicial to the welfare of the young defendant; if he is tried jointly with an adult the ordinary procedures will apply subject to such modifications (if any) as the judge may see fit to order (PD 20, IV.39.4);
(2) consider, and so far as practicable give, directions on the matters covered in paras IV.39.9–15 (below) (*ibid.* IV.39.5);
(3) be ready (if he has not already done so) to give a direction under CYPA 1933, s.39 or, as the case may be, YJCEA 1999, s.45; any such order, once made, should be reduced to writing and copies should on request be made available to anyone affected or potentially affected by it (*ibid.* IV.39.8).

It may be appropriate to arrange that a young defendant should visit, out of court hours and before the trial, the courtroom in which the trial is to be held so that he can familiarise himself with it (*ibid.* IV.39.6).

If any case against a young defendant has attracted or may attract widespread public or media interest, the assistance of the police should be enlisted to try and ensure that he is not, when attending for the trial, exposed to intimidation, vilification or abuse (*ibid.* IV.39.7).

The trial

19–008 To avoid an atmosphere of intimidation where a young defendant is on trial:

(1) the trial should, if practicable, be held in a **courtroom** in which all the participants are on the same or almost the same level (PD 2004, IV.39.9);

(2) the young defendant should normally, if he wishes, be free to sit with members of his **family** or others in a like relationship and in a place which permits easy, informal communication with his **legal representatives** and others with whom he wants or needs to communicate (*ibid.* IV.39.10);

(3) the judge should **explain** the course of proceedings to him in terms he can understand and should remind those representing him of their continuing duty to explain each step of the trial to him and should ensure, so far as practicable, that the trial is conducted in language which he can understand (*ibid.* IV.39.11);

(4) the trial should be conducted according to a **timetable** which takes full account of a young defendant's inability to concentrate for long periods; frequent and regular breaks will often be appropriate (*ibid.* IV.39.12);

(5) **robes and wigs** should not be worn unless the young defendant asks that they should be, or the judge for good reason orders that they should; a person responsible for the young defendant's security where he is in custody should not be in **uniform**, nor should there be a recognisable **police** presence in the courtroom save for good reason (*ibid.* IV.39.13); and

(6) the judge should be prepared to restrict **attendance** at the trial to a small number, perhaps limited to some of those with an immediate and direct interest in the outcome of the trial; he should rule on any challenged claim to attend (*ibid.* IV.39.14).

Where the judge is called upon to exercise his **discretion** in relation to any procedural matter falling within the scope of this practice direction but not the subject of specific reference, such discretion should be exercised having regard to the principles in IV.39.3 (see 19–006, above) (*ibid.* IV.39.16).

Facilities for reporting

19–009 Facilities for reporting the trial (subject to any direction given under CYPA 1933, s.39 or YJCEA 1999) must be provided, but the judge may restrict the number of those attending in the courtroom to report the trial to such number as is judged practicable and desirable. In ruling on any challenged claim to attend the courtroom for the purpose of reporting the trial the judge should be mindful of the public's general right to be informed about the administration of justice in the Crown Court. Where access to the courtroom by reporters is restricted, PD 2004, IV.39.15

arrangements should be made for the proceedings to be relayed, audibly and if possible visually, to another room in the same court complex to which the media have free access if it appears that there will be a need for such additional facilities.

Appeal and committals for sentence

19–010 The practice direction does not in terms apply to appeals and committals for sentence, but regard should be paid to the effect of it if the arrangements for hearing any appeal or committal might otherwise be prejudicial to the welfare of a young defendant. PD 2004, IV.39.17

Screens

19–011 The provision of screens, from behind which a child witness is to give evidence, is a matter within the trial judge's discretion, as in the case of an adult (*R. v Foster* [1995] Crim.L.R. 333). See also 57 SPECIAL MEASURES DIRECTIONS.

Attendance of parent or guardian

19–012 Where a child or young person is charged with an offence or is, for any other reason brought before a court, the court: CYPA 1933, s.34A; CJA 1991, s.56

(1) *may*, in any case; and
(2) *must* in the case of a young person under the age of 16,

require a parent or guardian to attend during all stages of the proceedings, unless and to the extent that the judge is satisfied that it would be unreasonable to do so, having regard to the circumstances of the case.

Reference to a "parent" or "guardian" is a reference to a local authority where the child or young person is in its care, or is provided with accommodation by it in the exercise of its functions referred to its social services committee under the 1970 Act, and to any person with whom he is allowed to live.

4. Remand of juveniles

General

19–013 The judge remanding a child or young person charged with or convicted of one or more offences, sending his case to the Crown Court for trial, or committing him for sentence, which does not release him on bail, must remand or commit him to local authority accommodation (and in the following provisions reference to a "remand" is to be construed as reference to a committal). CYPA 1969, s.23(1); CJA 1991, s.59

"Young person" here means a person who has attained the age of 14 years and is under the age of 17.

The court remanding such a person to local authority accommodation must designate the local authority which is to receive him, and that authority must be:

(1) in the case of a person who is being looked after by a local authority, that authority; and
(2) in any other case, the local authority in whose area it appears to the court that he resides or that one of the offences was committed.

Where a juvenile is so remanded with conditions, and a constable has reasonable grounds for suspecting that he has broken any of those conditions, he may be arrested and taken before a magistrate in a manner similar to that applying in breach of bail (CYPA 1969, s.23A; CJPOA,1994, s.23), see 11 BAIL.

Remand with security requirement

19–014 Where a person is remanded to local authority accommodation, it is lawful for any person acting on behalf of the designated authority to detain him.

CYPA 1969, ss.23(3), (4), (5); CJA 1991, s.60(1); CJPOA 1994, s.20; CDA 1998, ss.97(1), (2); CJA 2003, s.303, Sch.32, para.15

The judge remanding him may, after consultation with the designated authority, require that authority to comply with a security requirement, that is to say, a requirement that the person in question be placed and kept in secure accommodation, though such a requirement is not to be imposed unless that young person:

(1) has attained the age of 12 or is a young person of a description prescribed under CDA 1998, s.97(2) (yet to be prescribed); and
(2) is charged with or has been convicted of a violent or sexual offence, (as listed in CJA 2003, Sch.15, Pts 1 and 2 respectively (see APPENDIX A Pt 2)) or an offence punishable in the case of an adult with imprisonment for 14 years or more; or
(3) has a recent history of absconding when remanded to local accommodation, and is charged or has been convicted of an imprisonable offence alleged or found to have been committed while he was so remanded,

and, in the case of (2) or (3) above, the judge is of the opinion that only such a requirement would be adequate to protect the public from serious harm from him.

If the young person is aged 15 or 16, then the court may remand to a remand centre if no local authority secure

CYPA 1969, ss.23(4), (5A);

accommodation is available, provided the court has been notified that such a centre is available, or to a prison if neither secure accommodation nor a remand centre is available. This is unless the judge is of the opinion that, by reason of his physical or emotional immaturity, or a propensity to harm himself, it would be undesirable for him to be remanded to a remand centre or a prison. CDA 1998, s.90(3)

The local authority is empowered to detain the accused in a secure training centre. CYPA 1969, s.7A; CJPA 2001, s.133

Definitions

19–015 "Secure accommodation" means accommodation which is provided in a community home, a voluntary home or a registered childrens' home for the purpose of restricting liberty and is approved for that purpose by the Home Secretary. CYPA 1969, ss.23(1), (4); CJA 1991, s.59; CJPOA 1994, s.19(1); CDA 1998, s.98(1)

The judge may require the local authority to keep a child or young person in secure accommodation if it has been notified that such accommodation is available for him.

"Sexual offence" and "violent offence" are defined in CJA 2003, Sch.15 (see APPENDIX A, s.2).

Legal representation

19–016 The judge may not impose a security requirement in respect of a child or young peson, nor declare him to be a person eligible for remand centre or prison, if he is not legally represented unless: CYPA 1969, s.23(5A); CDA 1998, s.97(3); SI 1998/2327; CDSA 2006, s.4

(1) he was granted a right to representation funded by the CDS but the right has been withdrawn because of his conduct, or because it appeared that his financial resources were such that he was not eligible to be granted such a right; or
(2) having been informed of his right to apply for a representation order and having had the opportunity to do so, he refused or failed to apply; or
(3) he applied for such representation and the application was refused because it appeared that his financial resources were such that he was not eligible to be granted a right to it.

Explanation in open court

19–017 When imposing a security requirement, the judge must: CYPA 1969, s.23(6); CJA 1991, s.60(6)

(1) state in open court that he is of the opinion set out above; and

(2) explain to the person remanded or committed in open court and in ordinary language why he is of that opinion.

Remand without security requirement

19–018 A judge remanding a person to local authority accommodation without imposing a security requirement may, after consultation with the designated authority: CYPA 1969, ss.23(7), (7A), (8), (9); CJA 1991, s.60(4); CJPA 2001, s.130

(1) subject to CYPA 1969, s.23AA (electronic monitoring), require the person to comply with:
   (a) any conditions as could be imposed under BA 1976, s.3(6) (see 11 BAIL) if he were then being granted bail; and
   (b) any conditions imposed for the purpose of securing the electronic monitoring of his compliance with any other condition imposed; and

   where such conditions are being imposed, must explain in open court and in ordinary language why they are being imposed; and
(2) impose on the authority requirements for securing compliance with any of the above bail conditions, or stipulating that he must not be placed with a named person.

Where a person is remanded to such accommodation, a "relevant court" may: CYPA 1969, ss.23(9), (10), (11); CJA 1991, s.60(1)

(i) on the application of the designated authority impose on that person any such conditions as might be imposed under BA 1976, s.3(6);
(ii) impose on the authority any requirements for securing compliance with the conditions imposed; and
(iii) on the application of the authority or the person remanded, vary or revoke any such conditions.

A "relevant court" for these purposes means the court by which such person was remanded or any magistrates' court having jurisdiction over the place where he is for the time being (CYPA 1969, s.23(12)).

Electronic monitoring

19–019 The judge must not impose an electronic monitoring condition under CYPA 1969, s.23(7)(b) unless the accused: CYPA 1969, s.23AA; CJPA 2001, s.132(2)

(1) has attained the age of 12 years;
(2) is charged with, or has been convicted of:
   (a) a violent or sexual offence;
   (b) an offence punishable in the case of an adult with imprisonment for 14 years or more; or

(c) one or more imprisonable offences which, together with any other imprisonable offences of which he has been convicted in any proceedings, amount, or would amount if he were convicted of the offences with which he is charged, to a recent history of repeatedly committing imprisonable offences while remanded on bail or to local authority accommodation; and provided that:
   (i) the judge has been notified that such arrangements are available, and the necessary provision can be made; and
   (ii) a youth offending team has informed the judge that in its opinion the imposition of such a requirement is suitable in the case of the accused.

The requirement must include a provision making a person responsible for the monitoring.

5. Penalties on conviction

19–020 Special provisions apply to juveniles in relation to punishment on conviction. Custodial sentences are dealt with under 31 DETENTION OF YOUNG OFFENDERS.

Remittal to youth court

19–021 Where a person under 18 is convicted in the Crown Court of an offence other than homicide, the judge, unless he is of opinion that the case is one which can properly be dealt with by: PCC(S)A 2000, s.8(1)(2)(8); CJA 2003, s.41, Sch.3, para.74(2)

(1) an absolute or conditional discharge,
(2) a fine, or
(3) an order under PCC(S)A 2000, s.150, requiring his parent or guardian to enter into recognisances, is required to remit him to a youth court for sentence. This is unless the judge is satisfied that it would be undesirable to do so.

The appropriate youth court will be:

(a) if the offender was sent to the Crown Court under CDA 1998, s.51 or s.51A, a youth court acting for the place where he sent to the Crown Court for trial; or
(b) in any other case, a youth court acting either for the same place as the Crown Court or for the place where the offender habitually resides.

The judge may, subject to CJPOA 1994, s.25 (restrictions on granting bail), give such directions as appear to be necessary with respect to the offender's custody or release on bail until he can be brought before the youth court. The appropriate certificate will be sent to the justices' chief executive (PCC(S)A 2000, s.8(4)).

An offender has no right of appeal against the order of remittal (*ibid.* s.8(5)).

"Undesirable" to remit

19–022 Clearly, it may be "undesirable" to remit an offender to the youth court, where, for example:

(1) the judge who has presided over the trial is likely to be better informed as to the facts and circumstances of the case;
(2) there will be a risk of disparity in sentencing if co-accused are sentenced in different courts on different occasions;
(3) there is the risk of delay, duplication of proceedings and fruitless expense in such a procedure; or
(4) difficulties may be caused in seeking to challenge the proceedings, appeal from the conviction lying to CACD, and against sentence to the Crown Court.

It may be desirable to remit where a report has been sought and the trial judge is likely to be unavailable when it is completed, though this situation can always be avoided by the magistrates who transfer the case to the Crown Court for trial giving directions for the preparation of reports (*R. v Lewis* (1984) 79 Cr.App.R. 94, *per* the Lord Chief Justice).

It is suggested that the only occasion when remittal to a youth court is merited is where the judge has in mind the making of a supervision order, in which circumstances the magistrates may have a more complete knowledge of the local situation.

Financial penalties: (1) general

19–023 While fines, compensation and orders to pay costs may be made against juveniles in much the same way as against adults (see 36 FINES AND ENFORCEMENT), certain differences need to be noticed:

(1) there is no statutory limit on the amount of a fine that may be imposed on a juvenile in the Crown Court, but where the court is limited to magistrates' court powers, the maxima are: MCA 1980, s.36; CJA 1991, s.17(2)
(a) in the case of a young person under 18, £1,000; and

(b) in the case of a child, £250, unless the maximum fine in the case of an adult is less, when that maximum applies;

(2) a juvenile may not be committed to prison in default of payment of a fine or compensation, though a magistrates' court enforcing a Crown Court fine may order him to attend at an attendance centre.

Financial penalties: (2) responsibility of parent or guardian

19–024 Since few juveniles are likely to have the money available to pay fines, compensation or costs, where a person aged under 18 is convicted of an offence for which a fine or an order for costs may be imposed or a compensation order made, and the judge is of the opinion that the case would best be met by such an order, whether or without any other punishment, the judge: PCC(S)A 2000, ss.137(1), (3), (4), (5)

(1) must, in the case of an offender under 16; and
(2) may, in the case of an offender aged 16–17,

order the fine, compensation or costs to be paid by the offender's parent or guardian unless:

(a) that person cannot be found; or
(b) it would be unreasonable, having regard to the circumstances, to make such an order.

This provision is extended to cover a case in which the judge would otherwise order a child or young person to pay a surcharge under CJA 2003, s.161A, as inserted by DVA 2004, s.58(1), Sch.10, para.51.

A similar provision applies in a case where the judge is minded to impose a fine in respect of the breach of certain community and other orders (*ibid.* s.173(3)).

An order should not be made unless the parent or guardian has been given an opportunity of being heard, or has been required to attend and has failed to do so.

Financial penalties: (3) purpose of section 137

19–025 In considering whether to make an order under these provisions, the judge should have regard to the purpose of the section, which is that:

(1) parents should take some responsibility for their childrens' activities and they should take their duties seriously; though

(2) they cannot be held vicariously liable for every act of their child (*Lenihan v West Yorkshire Met Police* (1981) 3 Cr.App.R.(S.) 42); and

(3) it is unreasonable to make an order where a parent has done the best he or she can to keep their child from criminal ways (*R. v Sheffield CC Ex p. Clarkson* (1986) 8 Cr.App.R.(S.) 454) and is in no position to control it (*TA v DPP* [1997] 1 Cr.App.R.(S.) 1).

If the judge observes the principle that compensation orders should be made only in simple and straightforward cases, orders are likely to be rare: see the complications outlined in *Bedfordshire CC v DPP* [1996] 1 Cr.App.R.(S.) 322.

Financial penalties: (4) local authority as "parent or guardian"

19–026 References to a parent or guardian are to be construed as references to a local authority where the child or young person is: PCC(S)A 2000, s.137

(1) one for whom that authority has parental authority; and
(2) in their care; or
(3) provided with accommodation by them in the exercise of any function (in particular those under CA 1989) which stands referred to their social services committee under the Local Authority Social Services Act 1970.

An order remanding a young person into local authority accommodation does not confer parental responsibility (*North Yorkshire County Council v Selby Youth Court JJ* [1994] 1 All E.R. 991).

Financial penalties: (5) orders against local authorities

19–027 The power of a local authority to restrain an offender in its care might be less than that of a parent. It has the same right to assert the unreasonableness of an order as has the parent.

Where the authority has done everything it reasonably and properly can to protect the public from the offender, it is unreasonable to make an order against it (*D v DPP* (1995) 16 Cr.App.R.(S.) 1040).

Where the authority stands *in loco parentis* and the accused juvenile is acquitted, the authority is entitled to a defendant's costs order, where it would be appropriate in the case of the accused: *R. v Preston CC Ex p. Lancashire CC* [1998] 3 All E.R. 765.

Financial penalties: (6) fixing the quantum

19–028 Similar provisions apply to an order against a parent or guardian as apply to financial orders in respect of offenders, and a parent or guardian, other than a local authority, may be required to comply with a financial circumstances enquiry.

PCC(S)A 2000, s.138; CJA 2003, s.304, Sch.32, Pt 1, paras 118, 119; DVA 2004, s.58(1), Sch.10, para.50

Financial penalties: (7) parents, etc. as appellants

19–029 A parent or guardian may appeal to CACD against an order made in the Crown Court as if he had been convicted on indictment and the order was a sentence passed on his conviction.

PCC(S)A 2000, s.137(7)

6. Parenting order

19–030 In any court proceedings where a child or young person is convicted of an offence, or in certain other situations, the judge may make a parenting order in respect of the offender's parent or guardian, provided that he:

(1) is satisfied that such an order would be desirable in the interests of preventing the commission of any further offence by the offender; and
(2) has been notified by the Home Secretary that arrangements for implementing such orders are available in the area in which the parent resides or is to reside.

CDA 1998, ss.8(1) (c), (2), (3); YJCEA 1999, Sch.4, para.26; PCC(S)A 2000, Sch.9, para.194; CJA 2003, s.324, Sch.34, para.1

Such an order requires the parent or guardian:

(a) to comply, for a period not exceeding 12 months, with such requirements as the judge considers desirable in the interests of preventing the repetition or commission of any offence, and as are specified in the order; and
(b) to attend, for a concurrent period not exceeding three months and not more than once in any week, such counselling or guidance sessions as may be specified in directions given by the "responsible officer", who will be an officer of a local probation board, a local authority social worker or a member of a youth offending team,

though a requirement under (b) need not be included where an order has been made in respect of that parent or guardian on a previous occasion.

The Act requires that any requirements included should, as far as is practicable, avoid conflict with a parent's religious beliefs, and interference with the times, if any, at which the offender normally works or attends an educational establishment.

Where directions under an order are to be given by an officer of a local probation board that officer must be one appointed for or assigned to the local justice area within which it appears the child or, as the case may be, the parent or guardian, resides or will reside.

Mandatory order

19–031 Where a person under the age of 16 is convicted of an offence, the judge, after obtaining and considering information about the offender's family circumstances and the likely effect of an order on those circumstances, *must*: CDA 1998, ss.9(1), (2)

(1) make such an order, if satisfied that the above condition is fulfilled; and
(2) if he is not so satisfied, state in open court that it is not so satisfied and why.

Explaining the effects of the order; review

19–032 Whichever the section under which the order is made, the judge has a duty, before making an order, to explain to the parent in ordinary language: CDA 1998, s.9(3)

(1) the effect of the order and of the requirements proposed to be included in it;
(2) the consequences which may follow under s.9(7) if he fails to comply with any of the requirements; and
(3) the power of the court to review the order on the application either of the responsible officer or of the parent.

A judge, on the application of the responsible officer or a parent, may, if he considers it appropriate discharge any order in force, or vary it by: CDA 1998, s.9(5)

(a) cancelling it; or
(b) inserting into it (either in addition or substitution for any of its provisions) any provision which could have been included in the order if he had then the power to make and was exercising that power.

Non-compliance with requirements

19–033 If, while an order is in force, a parent fails to comply with any requirement included in it or specified directions given by the responsible officer, he or she are liable on summary conviction to a fine not exceeding level 3 on the standard scale. CDA 1998, s.9(7)

Variation and discharge

19–034 If, while an order is in force, it appears to the court which made the order, on the application either of the responsible officer or the parent, that it is appropriate to do so, it may: CDA 1998, ss.9(5), (6)

(1) discharge the order; or
(2) vary it by cancelling any provision in it, by inserting, whether in addition to or in substitution for any of its provisions, any provision which could have been included in the order if the court then had power to make it and was executing the power.

Where an application under s.10(5) for the discharge of an order is dismissed, no further application for its discharge may be made by any person except by consent of the court that made the order.

7. Evidence of children

19–035 The evidence of a child:

(1) is to be received unless it appears to the judge that the child is incapable of giving intelligible evidence;
(2) is, in criminal proceedings, to be given unsworn; and
(3) does not, of itself, need to be corroborated.

CJA 1988, s.33A; CJA 1991, s.52(1)

The power of the judge to determine whether a witness is competent to give evidence applies to children as it applies to other persons (see 19–038, below).

The evidence of a child aged 14 or over must be given in solemn form: *R. v Sharman* [1998] 1 Cr.App.R. 406.

The test of admissibility of a child's evidence should primarily depend on the answer to the question "whether a jury could be sure the child had given a creditable and accurate account on the video tape, notwithstanding any breaches of the guidelines? If 'Yes', it was a matter for the jury. If 'No' the interview would be inadmissible" (*R. v Hanton* (unreported EWCA Crim 2009). In *R. v K (Evidence: Child video interview) The Times*, April 10, 2006 CACD observed that that test needed to be more widely promulgated, rather than that in *G v DPP* (1997) 2 Cr.App.R. 78), which stressed the importance of whether passages possibly influenced by others were corroborated by independent evidence, and not to extract from that case the reference to corroborating material being of central importance.

The question of a child's competence ought to be revisited at the conclusion of the child's evidence. It is vitally important that as short a time as possible elapses before any interview with the child after the event, and the hearing at which any cross-examination takes place (*R. v Powell* [2006] Crim.L.R. 780 (3½ yr old child)).

Warning as to very young children

19–036 There is no longer any rule of law requiring corroboration of the unsworn evidence of a child, or any rule of practice to warn of the danger of convicting on such evidence, but it may be appropriate to warn the jury, if there is one, to take particular care with the evidence of a very young child.

Evidence through TV link and by means of video recording

19–037 The special protection for child witnesses is dealt with in 57 SPECIAL MEASURES DIRECTIONS.

Competency of child witnesses: approach

19–038 The object of Parliament in enacting CJA 1991, s.52(2) was to apply to children the ordinary test of competence, regardless of any real or notional additional test previously imposed if they were to give evidence on oath.

Thus:

(1) there is no minimum age for competence;
(2) the question in each case is whether the child is possessed of sufficient intelligence to justify the reception of his evidence, and understands the duty of speaking the truth; this will obviously vary from child to child, the younger the child, the greater the care that needs to be taken before admitting the evidence;
(3) it is a question for the judge to decide; it is well within his capacity to do so, and he requires no expert evidence on the matter;
(4) if the judge finds that the child is able to understand questions, and to answer them in a coherent and comprehensible manner, he has no wider discretion to refuse the evidence (apart from his discretion under PACE 1984, s.78); and
(5) the judge may find it appropriate to remind the child, in the presence of the accused and of the jury: "Tell us all you can remember of what happened. Don't make anything up or leave anything out. That is very important".

(See *R. v Hampshire* [1995] 2 All E.R. 1019; *R. v Z* [1990] 2 All E.R. 971; *DPP v M* [1997] 2 All E.R. 749; *G v DPP* [1997] 2 All E.R. 755).

Restrictions on accused cross-examining in person

19–039 No person charged with an offence as is mentioned below may cross-examine in person a witness who: YJCEA 1999, s.35(1), (2);

(1) is alleged to be the person against whom the offence was committed or a witness to the offence, and SOA 2003, Sch.6, para.4
(2) is a child, or is to be cross-examined after giving evidence in chief by means of a video recording made or in any other way when he was a child.

Section 35 applies to any offence under SOA 2003, Pt 1, kidnapping, false imprisonment, or an offence under the Child Abduction Act 1984, ss.1, 2, any offence under CYPA 1933, s.1 or any other offence which involves an assault on, or injury to, any person.

The prohibition applies not only to the offence to which s.35 applies, but also to any other offence of whatever nature with which that person is charged in the proceedings. YJCEA 1999, ss.38(1), (2), (3); r.31

These restrictions should be explained to the accused by the judge as early in the proceedings as reasonably practicable.

Trial judge's duty

19–040 Where, under this restriction, an accused is prevented from cross-examining a witness in person, the judge must: YJCEA 1999, ss.38(1), (2), (3); r.31

(1) invite the accused to arrange for a legal representative to act for him for the purpose of cross-examining the witness; and
(2) require the accused to notify the court within seven days as to whether a legal representative is to act for him for that purpose and the details of that representative. The court is required to notify all parties of these details.

If the accused declines to be represented or fails to notify the court as required, the judge must consider whether it is necessary in the interests of justice to appoint a legal representative. If he does so, the court will notify all parties of the details of the appointment.

Where under this restriction the accused is prevented from cross-examining a witness in person, the judge must give an appropriate warning to the jury, if there is one, to ensure the accused is not prejudiced: YJCEA 1999, s.39(1)

(a) by any inferences that might be drawn from the fact that the accused has been prevented from cross-examining the witness in person;
(b) where the witness has been cross-examined by a legal representative appointed by the court, by the fact that this has happened rather than the witness being cross-examined by a person acting as the accused's own legal representative.

As to procedure, see generally r.31, and 57 SPECIAL MEASURES DIRECTIONS.

8. Restrictions on publication

CYPA 1933, s.39

19–041 No newspaper report of the proceedings in the Crown Court may reveal the name, address or school, or include any particulars calculated to lead to the identification of any child or young person concerned in the proceedings, either as being the person by or against or in respect of whom the proceedings are taken, or as being a witness therein, nor may any picture be published, except in so far, if at all, as the judge permits. CYPA 1933, s.39; CYPA 1963, ss.57(1), 64(3), Sch.5

The judge has complete discretion as to who to hear on any application (*ibid.*, and see *Re R (Wardship) Restrictions on Publication* [1994] 2 F.L.R. 637). The onus is on the applicant to show cause for restricting publicity (*R. v CCC Ex p. W, B, & C* [2001] 1 Cr.App.R. 2).

It has been suggested that:

(1) the judge should make it clear what the terms of his order are, clearly identifying the relevant children where necessary;
(2) copies of the order should be made available for press representatives to inspect; and
(3) a short notice might be included in the Daily List to indicate that an order has been made. (See *R. v CCC Ex p. Crook* [1995] 2 Cr.App.R. 212.)

The order must, of course, be strictly in accordance with the terms of s.39 (*Ex p. Godwin* (1992) 94 Cr.App.R. 34), and its details must be clear and precise (*Briffett and Another v DPP* (2002) 166 J.P. 66).

CYPA 1933, s.49; proceedings emanating from youth courts

19–042 Similar provisions are enacted in CYPA 1933, s.49 in regard to proceedings in the Crown Court emanating from youth courts (as to the differing emphasis in the sections, see *R. v Lee (A Minor)* 96 Cr.App.R. 188). CYPA 1933, s.49; CJPOA 1994, s.49; CDA 1998, s.119, Sch.8; para.1; PCC(S)A 2000, s.165, Sch.7, para.2(2); CJA 2003, s.304, Sch.32, para.2(3)

In so far as proceedings in the Crown Court are concerned:

(1) on appeal from a youth court; or
(2) in proceedings on appeal from a magistrates' court arising out of proceedings under PCC(S)A 2000, Sch.7 (variation or revocation of supervision order),

no report may be published which reveals the name, address or school of any child or young person concerned in the proceedings, whether as the subject of those proceedings or as a witness, or which includes any particulars likely to lead to his identification (a similar ban applies to pictures) and it is the duty of the judge to announce in the course of the proceedings that this prohibition applies (otherwise it does not).

The prohibition may be expressly dispensed with, to a specified extent, where:

(a) the court is satisfied that it is appropriate to do so for the purpose of avoiding injustice to the child or young person; or
(b) such a person is unlawfully at large, and it is necessary to dispense with the prohibition for the purpose of apprehending him and bringing him before a court or returning him to custody; provided always that
(c) an application for such dispensation is made by or on behalf of the DPP, and notice has been given by him to the child or young person's legal representative.

YJCEA 1999, s.45; proceedings involving persons under 18

19–043 Once YJCEA 1999, s.45 as amended by CA 2003, s.109(1), Sch.8 comes into force the judge in any criminal proceedings (other than one to which CYPA 1933, s.49 applies (see 19–042, above)) will be able, having regard to the welfare of the person concerned, to:

(1) direct that no matter relating to any person concerned in the proceedings, that is:
    (a) a person against whom or in respect of whom the proceedings are taken; or
    (b) (in particular) a witness in the proceedings; be, while he is under the age of 18, included in any publication if it is likely to lead members of the public to identify him as a person concerned in the proceedings;
(2) (or an appellate court will be able) by an "excepting direction" dispense to any extent specified in the direction with the restrictions imposed by (1) above if satisfied that:
    (a) it is necessary to do so in the interests of justice; or
    (b) that their effect is to impose a substantial and unreasonable restriction on the reporting of proceedings; or
    (c) that it is in the public interest to remove or relax that restriction,

but no excepting direction may be given under (b) and (c) by reason only of the fact that the proceedings have been determined in any way or have been abandoned.

The excepting direction may be given at the time the direction under (1) is given, or subsequently, and may be varied or revoked by the judge or by an appellate court.

Other situations

19–044 The CSA 1997, s.45 provides for further situations in which the restrictions may be dispensed with, *viz*, if the judge is satisfied that it is in the public interest to do so, he may dispense with them to any specified extent, in proceedings (for an offence committed after the commencement of the Act) relating to:

CYPA 1933, s.49(4A), (4B); CJA 2003, s.304, Sch.32, para.2(2)

(1) the prosecution or conviction of the offender for the offence;
(2) the manner in which he, or his parent or guardian, should be dealt with in respect of the offence;
(3) the enforcement, amendment, variation, revocation or discharge of any order made in respect of the offence;
(4) where an attendance centre order is made, the enforcement of any rules made under CJA 2003, s.222(1)(d) or (e); and
(5) where a detention and training order is made, the enforcement of any requirements imposed under PCC(S)A 2000, s.103(6)(b),

provided the power is not exercised without affording the parties to the proceedings an opportunity to make representations, and taking them into account.

9. Reparation orders

Making an order

19–045 "Reparation" here means an order to make reparation otherwise than by the payment of compensation.

PCC(S)A 2000, s.73(1), (2), (3), (4), (6); CJA 2003, s.304, Sch.32, Pt 1, para.106

Where a child or young person is convicted of an offence other than one for which the sentence is fixed by law, the judge may make a reparation order requiring the offender to make reparation as specified in the order, to a specified person or persons identified as a victim of the offence, or a person otherwise affected by it, provided that:

(1) he does not pass on him a custodial sentence, or make a community order under CJA 2003, s.177, or a supervision

order including requirements authorised by Sch.6, an action plan order, or a compensation order;
(2) the person to whom reparation is to be made consents; and
(3) the court has been notified by the Home Secretary that arrangements for implementing such orders are available in the area proposed to be named in the order.

The judge must give his reasons if he does not make an order in a case where he has power to do so. PCC(S)A 2000, s.73(5)

Before making an order the judge must obtain and consider a written report by an officer of a local probation board or a local authority social worker or a member of a youth offending team indicating the type of work suitable to the offender, and the attitude of the victim or victims to the requirements proposed to be included in the order.

Requirements of the order

19–046 The requirements specified in the order must be such that, in the judge's opinion, are commensurate with the seriousness of the offence, or the combination of that offence and one or more offences associated with it, and must, so far as is practicable, be such as to avoid any conflict with: PCC(S)A 2000, s.74(1), (2), (8); CJA 2003, s.304, Sch.32, Pt 1, para.106

(1) the offender's religious beliefs; or
(2) the requirements of any (other) community order, or any youth community order, to which he is subject; and

any interference with the times, if any, at which the offender normally works or attends school or any other educational establishment; and the order must not require the offender:

(a) to work for more than 24 hours in aggregate; or
(b) to make reparation to any person without the consent of that person.

The order will name the local justice area in which it appears that the offender resides, or will reside, and any reparation required by the order will be made under the supervision of the responsible officer, and within a period of three months from the date the order is made.

Failure to comply with the order

19–047 Schedule 8 has effect for dealing with the discharge, revocation and amendment of reparation orders. The appropriate court for dealing with these matters is the youth court acting for the local justice area for the time being named in the order. PCC(S)A 2000, s.75, Sch.8, paras 2, 4, 5

Where an action plan (see 21–081) below or a reparation order is in force, and it is proved to the satisfaction of that court.

(1) that an offender has failed to comply with any requirement included in an order; and
(2) that the order was made by the Crown Court,

it may commit him in custody or release him on bail until he can be brought or appear before the Crown Court.

Where such offender is brought before the Crown Court, and it is proved to the judge's satisfaction that he has failed to comply with the requirement in question, he may revoke the order, and deal with him for the offence in respect of which the order was made in any manner in which he could have dealt with him for that offence if the order had not been made, taking into account the extent to which the offender has complied with the order. He may do so, notwithstanding the offender has reached the age of 18 before coming before the court.

The offender must be present in court unless the judge decides to take no action other than to:

(a) revoke the reparation or action plan order; or
(b) cancel a requirement included in the order; or
(c) alter in the order the name of any area; or
(d) change the responsible officer.

10. Youth offender panels

19–048 The power to refer a juvenile to a youth offender panel under PCC(S)A 2000, s.16, is reserved to the magistrates' courts. Jurisdiction will arise in the Crown Court only on appeal, or where an offender is subject to such an order at the time he was convicted in the Crown Court. PCC(S)A 2000, Sch.1, para.14(3)

20 COMMITTALS FOR SENTENCE

20–001 A judge of the Crown Court may need to deal with offenders committed from the magistrates' court for sentence or to be dealt with. The judge's powers in dealing with such persons vary according to the statute under which the committal is made.

Powers of Crown Court on committal for sentence

20–002 The judge's powers vary, according to whether the offender is committed under PCC(S)A 2000, ss.3–4A or under s.6. On a committal under:

(1) **ss.3, 3A and 4**, the judge may deal with the offender in any way in which he could have dealt with him if he had just been convicted of the offence, on indictment, but may not remit him to the magistrates' court (*R. v Isleworth CC Ex p. Buda* [2000] 1 Cr.App.R.(S.) 538); PCC(S)A 2000, s.5; CJA 2003, s.41, Sch.3, para.26

(2) **ss.3B, 3C and 4A**, the judge may deal with the offender in any way in which he could have dealt with him if he had just been convicted of the offence, on indictment; PCC(S)A 2000, s.5A; CJA 2003, s.41, Sch.3, para.27

(3) **s.6**, the judge may deal with him in any way in which the magistrates' court could deal with him if it had just convicted him of the offence, save that; PCC(S)A 2000, s.6; CJA 2003, ss.41, 304, Sch.3, para.28, Sch.32, Pt 1, para.92
   - (a) if the offender is committed in respect of a suspended sentence, the powers in CJA 2003, Sch.12, paras 8 and 9 are exercisable; and
   - (b) where the offender is committed in respect of an offence triable only on indictment in the case of an adult, but which was tried summarily because the offender was under 18 years of age, the judge's powers are to:
     - (i) impose a fine not exceeding £5,000; or
     - (ii) deal with the offender in respect of the offence in any way in which the magistrates' court could have dealt with him if it had just convicted him of an offence punishable with a term of imprisonment not exceeding six months.

Any duty or power which would, apart from these provisions, fall to be discharged or exercised by the magistrates, must not be exercised, but instead, will be discharged or exercised by the judge of the Crown Court.

A magistrates' court may no longer commit an offender to the Crown court for sentence where it assumes jurisdiction in respect of an offence triable either-way, and deals with the offender; only where a plea of guilty is entered in a plea before venue.

Magistrates' powers

20–003 The powers of a magistrates' court to impose a sentence of imprisonment are presently restricted to the imposition of a sentence of six months imprisonment, for a single either-way offence, or to a total of 12 months for two or more such offences imposed consecutively. Once CJA 2003, s.283 comes into force, probably in the autumn of 2007, this maximum will be increased to: MCA 1980, s.32; CJA 2003, s.282

(a) 12 months (51 weeks) in relation a summary offence under an enactment (passed before the coming into force of CJA 2003, s.281) providing a maximum sentence of six months; or
(b) in relation to offences in MCA 1980, Sch.1 (i.e. either-way offences tried summarily), a maximum of 12 months; and
(c) in relation to the summary trial of an offence triable either way (other than a "Schedule offence") 12 months.

A "Schedule offence" is one of those offences contained in MCA 1980, Sch.2 (i.e. criminal damage under CDA 1971, s.1, and aggravated vehicle taking under TA 1968, s.12A where no allegation is made other than damage) where the damage involved does not exceed the prescribed limit.

As to fines in the magistrates' courts, see MCA 1980, ss.24, 32, CJA 1982, s.37(2), PCCA 2000, s.135; as to the fixing of fines by magistrates in relation to an offender's daily disposable income, see CJA 2003, ss.164A, 164B (not yet in force).

Ancillary orders; interim RT disqualification

20–004 Since committal to the Crown Court is an alternative to dealing with the offender, the magistrates' court is not empowered on committal to make any ancillary orders, save that where the magistrates' court: RTOA 1988, s.26(1), (4), (10); RTA 1991, s.25; PCC(S)A 2000, Sch.9, para.119

(1) commits an offender under s.6 or any enactment to which that section applies; and

(2) does not exercise its power or duty to disqualify under RTOA 1988, ss.34, 35 or 36,

it may order him to be disqualified until the Crown Court has dealt with him in respect of the offence.

If the offender is not sentenced within six months of the date of committal, that disqualification lapses. On dealing with the offender, a judge of the Crown Court, if he imposes a disqualification, must reduce the period by the length of the interim disqualification.

Procedure

20–005 On committal for sentence it is the duty of the committing magistrates to ensure that the Crown Court is informed of the facts found, and:

(1) the judge should sentence on the facts found below and should not normally allow any dispute as to the facts to be reopened, but

(2) if an issue does not arise until the case is before the Crown Court, the judge should normally determine the issue on any necessary and available evidence (see 34 FACTUAL BASIS FOR SENTENCE).

Where the offender claims to have raised the matter before the lower court, where the magistrates did not attempt to decide the issue, the judge will need to decide upon the course to be followed, taking into account all the circumstances, including):

(a) the facts of the offence(s) as alleged by each party;

(b) whether, on a balance of probabilities, he is satisfied that the offender raised the issue before the lower court;

(c) the fact that the offender was committed because his record was considered serious enough to justify such a course; and

(d) the delay which remittal to the magistrates' court will cause. (*Munroe v CPS* (1988) 152 J.P. 657).

1. Indication of plea of guilty to serious offence (s.3)

20–006 Once CJA 2003, Sch.3 comes into force, and:

(1) a person aged 18 or over appears or is brought before a magistrates' court on an information charging him with an offence triable either way (unless excluded by MCA 1980, s.17D ("schedule offence")); and

PCC(S)A 2000, s.3; CJA 2003, s.41, Sch.3, paras 22, 55(2)

(2) he, or his representative indicates under MCA 1980, ss.17A or s.17B that he would plead guilty if the offence were to proceed to trial, and
(3) the magistrates' court, proceeding under MCA 1980, s.9(1) convicts him of that offence,

and the magistrates are of opinion that the offence or the combination of the offence and one or more offences associated with it was so serious that the Crown Court should, in the court's opinion have the power to deal with the offender in any way it could deal with him if he had been convicted on indictment, they may commit the offender in custody or on bail to the Crown Court for sentence in accordance with PCC(S)A 200, s.5(1), and where it does so may also commit him in respect of certain other offences (see under s.6, below).

The power may be exercised where the magistrates consider that a *financial* penalty in excess of their powers (£5,000) ought to be imposed (*R. v N Essex JJ. Ex p. Lloyd* [2001] 2 Cr.App.R.(S.) 15).

The magistrates may also commit where they are of opinion that a restriction order under MHA 1983 is required; see MHA 1983, s.43(4); CJA 2003, s.41, Sch.3, para.55(2).

A convicted corporation is treated as an individual aged 18 or over, but the custody and bail provisions do not apply.

If, on appearance before the Crown Court, it appears that the appellant pleaded guilty under a material mistake of fact, the court has a discretion to allow him to change his plea, and if, as a consequence, he pleads not guilty, he may be remitted to the magistrates' court: *R. v Isleworth CC etc* [2000] 1 Cr.App. R.(S.) 538).

2. Dangerous adult offender (s.3A)

20–007 Where, once CJA 2003, Sch.3 comes into force: PCC(S)A 2000, s.3A; CJA 2003, s.41, Sch.3, para.23

(1) on the summary trial of one of those offences specified in CJA 2003, s.224, triable either way, a person aged 18 or over is convicted of an offence, and
(2) it appears to the magistrates' court, in relation to the offence, that the criteria for the imposition of a sentence under CJA 2003, s.225(3) or s.227(2) (dangerous offenders) would be met (see 29 DEALING WITH AN OFFENDER),

the magistrates' court:

(a) must commit the offender in custody or on bail to the Crown Court for sentence in accordance with PCC(S)A 2000, s.5(1), and also
(b) may commit him in respect of certain other offences (see 20–014, below),

though nothing prevents the court from committing a specified offence to the Crown Court for sentence under s.3 (above) if the provisions of that section are satisfied.

In reaching their decision, or taking any step, under this provision:

(i) the magistrates' court is not bound by any indication of sentence given in respect of the offence under MCA 1980, s.20 (mode of trial proceedings); and
(ii) nothing the magistrates' court does under this section may be challenged, or be the subject of any appeal in any court on the ground that it is not consistent with an indication of sentence.

3. Indication of plea of guilty by juvenile (s.3B)

20–008 Where, once CJA 2003, Sch.3 comes into force:

PCC(S)A 2000, s.3B; CJA 2003, s.41, Sch.3, para.23

(1) a person under 18 is brought before a magistrates' court on an information charging him with an offence mentioned in PCC(S)A 2000, s.91; and
(2) he or his representative indicates under MCA 1980, s.24A or, as the case may be, s.24B, that he would plead guilty if the offence were to proceed to trial; and
(3) proceeding as if MCA 1980, s.9(1) were complied with and he pleaded guilty under it, the magistrates convict him of the offence,

then, if the magistrates are of opinion that the offence or the combination of the offence and one or more offences associated with it was so serious that the Crown Court should, in the magistrates' opinion have the power to deal with the offender as if the provisions of PCC(S)A 2000, s.91(3) (detention for grave crimes) applied, they may:

(a) commit the offender in custody or on bail to the Crown Court for sentence in accordance with PCC(S)A 200, s.5A(1), and also
(b) commit him in respect of certain other offences (see under 20–014, below).

As to the power to commit where magistrates are of the opinion that a restriction order under MHA 1983 is required, see MHA 1983, s.43(4); CJA 2003, s.41, Sch.3, para.55(2).

4. Dangerous young offender (s.3C)

20–009 Where once CJA 2003, Sch.3 comes into force:

PCC(S)A 2000, s.3C; CJA 2003, s.41, Sch.3, para.23

(1) on the summary trial of one of those offences specified in CJA 2003, s.224, a person under 18 is convicted of an offence, and
(2) it appears to the magistrates' court, in relation to the offence, that the criteria for the imposition of a sentence under CJA 2003, s.225(3) or s.227(2) (dangerous offenders) would be met (see 29 DEALING WITH AN OFFENDER),

that court:

(a) must commit the offender in custody or on bail to the Crown Court for sentence in accordance with PCC(S)A 2000, s.5A(1), and also
(b) may commit him in respect of certain other offences (see 20–014, below),

though nothing prevents the court from committing a specified offence to the Crown Court for sentence under s.3 (above) if the provisions of that section are satisfied.

(See as to the problems raised by conflicting legislation in this area *CPS v S. E. Surrey YC Ex p. G* [2006] Crim.L.R. 367.)

5. Indication of plea of guilty (s.4)

20–010 Where, once CJA 2003, Sch.3 has come into force:

PCC(S)A 2000, s.4; CJA 2003, s.41, Sch.3, para.24

(1) a person aged 18 or over appears or is brought before a magistrates' court on an information charging him with an offence triable either way (other than a "schedule offence"), and
(2) he, or, where applicable his representative, indicates under MCA 1980, ss.17A, 17B or 20(7) that he would plead guilty if the offence were to proceed to trial, and
(3) the magistrates court, proceeding under MCA 1980, s.91 convicts him of that offence,

then:

(a) if the magistrates have committed him to the Crown Court for one or more offences which, in their opinion are related to the offence, they may commit him in custody or on bail to the Crown Court, to be dealt with in respect of the offence in accordance with s.5(1); or

(b) if that power is not exercisable but the court is still to determine to, or whether to, send the offender for trial under CDA 1998, s.51 or s.51A for one or more related offences:
   (i) it must adjourn the proceedings relating to the offence until after it has made those determinations; and
   (ii) if it sends the offender to the Crown Court for trial for one or more related offences, may then exercise that power.

20–011 In reaching their decision, or taking any step, under this provision:

(1) the magistrates' court is not bound by any indication of sentence given in respect of the offence under MCA 1980, s.20 (mode of trial poceedings); and
(2) nothing the court does under this section may be challenged, or be the subject of any appeal in any court on the ground that it is not consistent with an indication of sentence.

If the power conferred above is not exercisable, but the court still has to determine to, or whether to, send the offender for trial under CDA 1998, s.51 or s.51A (see 15 CASES COMMITTED, TRANSFERRED, SENT, FOR TRIAL) for one or more related offences, it must adjourn the proceedings until after it has made those determinations, and then, if it sends the offender to the Crown Court for trial for one or more related offences, may exercise this power.

If the magistrates' court does not, in committing under s.4, state that it has, in its opinion, power also to commit him under s.3(2) or, as the case may be s.3A(2), the Crown Court may act in accordance with s.5(1) unless he is convicted before it of one or more of the related offences.

6. Indication of guilty plea by juvenile with related offences (s.4A)

20–012 Where, once CJA 2003, Sch.3 has come into force: PCC(S)A 2000, s.4A; CJA 2003, s.41, Sch.3, para.25

(1) a person under 18 appears or is brought before a magistrates' court on an information charging him with an offence mentioned in s.91(1) and

(2) he or his representative indicates under MCA 1980, s.24A, or as the case may be, s.24B, that he would plead guilty if the offence were to proceed to trial; and
(3) proceeding as if MCA 1980, s.9(1) were complied with and he pleaded guily under it, the magistrates convict him of the offence,

then:

(a) if the magistrates have committed him to the Crown Court for one or more offences which, in their opinion are related to the offence, they may commit him in custody or on bail to the Crown Court, to be dealt with in respect of the offence in accordance with s.5A(1); or
(b) if that power is not exercisable but the court has still to determine to, or whether to, send the offender for trial under CDA 1998, s.51 or s.51A for one or more related offences, it:
    (i) must adjourn the proceedings relating to the offence until after it has made those determinations; and
    (ii) may, if it sends the offender to the Crown Court for trial for one or more related offences, then exercise that power.

Where the court under (a) above commits the offender to the Crown Court to be dealt with in respect of the offence, and does not state that, in its opinion, it also has power to commit him under s.3B(2), or as the case may be, ss.3C(2), s.5A(1) will not apply unless he is convicted before the Crown Court of one or more of the related offences. Where s.5A(1) does not apply, the Crown Court may deal with the offender in respect of the offence in any manner in which the magistrates' court could have dealt with him if it had just convicted him of the offence.

Where the magistrates' court commits a person in accordance with PCC(S)A 2000, s.4A(2), it may also commit him in respect of certain other ancillary offences under s.6.

7. Proceeds of Crime Act 2002

20–013 Where an offender is convicted of an offence by a magistrates' court, and the prosecutor asks the court to commit him to the Crown Court with a view to a confiscation order being considered under PCA 2002, s.6, the magistrates' court must commit him to the Crown Court in respect of the

PCA 2002, s.70; CJA 2003, s.41, Sch.3, para.75(4)

offence, and may commit him in respect of any other offence where:

(1) the offender has been convicted of it by the magistrates' court or any other court, and
(2) the magistrates' court has power to deal with him in respect of it.

If a committal is made under this section in respect of an offence or offences, PCA 2002, s.6 applies accordingly, and the committal operates as a committal of the offender to be dealt with at the Crown Court in accordance with PCA 2002, s.71.

If a committal is made under this section in respect of an offence for which (apart from this section) the magistrates' court could have committed the offender for sentence under PCC(S)A 2000, s.3(2) (above) the court must state whether it would have done so.

A committal under this section may be in custody or on bail. PCA 2002, s.71

Where an offender is committed to the Crown Court under s.70 in respect of an offence or offences, then, (whether or not the court proceeds under s.6):

(a) in the case of an offence in respect of which the magistrates' court has stated under s.70(5) that it would have committed the offender for sentence, the judge at the Crown Court must inquire into the circumstances of the case, and may deal with the offender in any way in which he could deal with him if he had just been convicted of the offence on indictment before it; or
(b) in the case of any other offence the judge must inquire into the circumstances of the case, and may deal with the offender in any way in which the magistrates' court could deal with him if it had just convicted him of the offence.

8. Ancillary matters (s.6)

20–014 Where magistrates commit an offender to the Crown Court under: PCC(S)A 2000, s.6; CJA 2003, ss.41, 304, Sch.3, para.28, Sch.32, Pt 1, para.91

(1) the Vagrancy Act 1824, (as amended by SOA 2003, Sch.6, paras 1, 2);
(2) PCC(S)A 2000, ss.3 to 4A (see 20-006–20-012 above);
(3) PCC(S)A 2000, s.13(5) (conditionally discharged offender convicted of further offence),

to be sentenced or otherwise dealt with in respect of an offence, then, if the relevant offence is:

(a) an indictable offence, they may also commit him in respect of any other offence, in respect of which they have power to deal with him (being an offence of which he has been convicted by them or any other court); and
(b) a summary offence, they may commit him in respect of any other offence of which they have convicted him, being either one punishable with imprisonment, or one in respect of which they have a power or a duty to disqualify him under RTOA 1988, ss.34, 35 or 36, or any suspended sentence in respect of which they have power to deal with him (under CJA 2003, Sch.12, para.11(1)).

20–015 **TABLE**. The Table below seeks to identify the powers of the Crown Court in committals under differing provisions.

Committal Powers	Category of Offender	Sentencing Powers	Sentencing Authority
(1) PCC(S)A 2000, s.3; CJA 2003, s.41, Sch.3, para.22	Offender aged 18 or over indicating plea guilty to either-way offence committed because offence(s) so serious as to require Crown Court powers on indictment. A corporation may be committed for sentence and is treated as an individual of not less than 18. Bail/custody does not apply (MCA 1980, s.38(4); CJA 1991, s.25(1)(2)).	Powers on indictment	PCC(S)A 2000, s.5(1)
(2) PCC(S)A 2000, s.3A; CJA 2003, s.41, Sch.3, para.23	Offender aged 18 or over convicted summarily of an offence under CJA 2003, ss.225(3) or 227(2) and categorised as "dangerous adult offender"	Powers on indictment	PCC(S)A 2000, s.5(1)
(3) PCC(S)A 2000, s.3B; CJA 2003, s.41, Sch.3, para.23	Offender under 18 indcating plea of guilty to either-way offence committed because offence(s) so serious as to require Crown Court powers on indictment	Powers on indictment	PCC(S)A 2000, s.5A(1); CJA 2003, s.41, Sch.3, para.23
(4) PCC(S)A 2000, s.3C: CJA 2003, s.35, Sch.3, para.20	Offender under 18 convicted summarily of an offence and categorised as a "dangerous young offender" under CJA 2003, s.226(3) or s.228(2)	Powers on indictment	PCC(S)A 2000, s.5A(1); CJA 2003, s.235, Sch.3, para.20

(5)	PCC(S)A 2000, s.4	Accused not less than 18, charged with offence triable either way, indicating plea of guilty if committed for trial, and accordingly convicted by magistrates, and committed for sentence	Powers on indictment where magistrates certify power to commit under s.3 otherwise magistrates' powers	PCC(S)A 2000, ss.4(5), 5
(6)	PCC(S)A 2000, s.4A; CJA 2003, s.41, Sch.3, para.25	Accused under 18, charged with either way offence and indicating plea of guilty, committed in respect "related offences"	Powers on indictment where magistrates certify power to commit under s.3 otherwise magistrates' powers	PCC(S)A 2000, s.6; CJA 2003, s.41, Sch.3 para.25
(7)	CJA 2003, s.179, Sch.8 para.9(6)	Offender found by magistrates to be in breach of requirement of community order made by Crown Court	May (a) add more onerous require-ments; (b) powers on indictment; (c) in case of persistent failure by 18+ to comply in case of non-imprisonable offence, up to 51 weeks. If (b) – revocation	CJA 2003, s.179, Sch.8, paras 10(1), 10(1) (6)
(8)	PCC(S)A 2000, Sch.3, para.4(4)	Offender found by magistrates to be in breach of relevant youth community order made by the Crown Court	Choice between (a) £1,000 fine; (b) making an attendance centre order; (c) making a curfew order; and (d) revocation and "as if order not made"	PCC(S)A 2000, Sch.3, para.5(1)

(9)	PCC(S)A 2000, Sch.3, para.13(3)	Offender in respect of whom a relevant Crown Court youth community order is in force, committed with a view to its revocation	Revocation	PCC(S)A 2000, Sch.3, para.14
(10)	PCC(S)A 2000, Sch.3, para.11(1), (2)	Offender committed for sentence during currency of relevant youth community order	Choice between (a) simple revocation; and (b) "powers on indictment"	PCC(S)A 2000, Sch.3, para.11(2)
(11)	PCC(S)A 2000, s.6	Offender committed in respect of (1)–(6) and (17) also in respect of other joined offences	Magistrates' powers in respect of ancillary	PCC(S)A 2000, s.7
(12)	MHA 1983, s.43(1)	Offender 14 or over committed with a view to a restriction order being made under MHA 1983, s.41	Choice between (a) making a restriction order; and (b) "magistrates' powers"	MHA 1983, s.43(2)
(13)	PCC(S)A 2000, s.61 Sch.5, para.2(1) (c)	Juvenile offender committed for failure to attend at, or breach of rules at, attendance centre	Revocation and "as if order not made"	PCC(S)A 2000, s.61, Sch.5, para.3
(14)	PCC(S)A 2000, s.66, Sch.7, para.2(1) (c)	Juvenile offender committed in respect of breach of supervision order	Revoke the order and "as if not made"	PCC(S)A 2000, s.66, Sch.7, para.2(4)
(15)	PCC(S)A 2000, s.72, Sch.8	Juvenile offender committed by the youth court for breach of action plan or reparation order	Revocation of the order and "as if not made"	PCC(S)A 2000, s.72, Sch.8, para.2(4), (5)
(16)	BA 1976, s.6(6)	Bail absconder committed because greater punishment required; or (b) more appropriate	Imprisonment for not more than 12 months and/or a fine	BA 1976, s.6(7)
(17)	PCA 2002, s.70	Offender committed with a view to a confiscation order being made	Powers on indictment	PCA 2002, s.71
(18)	PCC(S)A 2000, s.13 (5)	Offender committed for breach of Crown Court condtional discharge	Powers on indictment	PCC(S)A 2000, s.13(6)

21 COMMUNITY SENTENCES

It is important to bear in mind that the provisions of CJA 2003 apply only to offences committed on or after April 4, 2005. In relation to offences committed before that date the former law under PCC(S)A 2000 applies. When dealing with multiple offences, some occurring on one side and others on the other side of the critical date, extreme care needs to be taken in founding the appropriate order on the right statute. If the judge wishes to reserve proceedings for any subsequent breach to the Crown Court he needs to bear in mind that in relation to orders under PCC(S)A 2000 he must so specify, otherwise such proceedings will take place in the magistrates' court. In relation to orders under CJA 2003, the breach proceedings will be reserved to the Crown Court unless the judge directs otherwise.

A. Community sentence under PCC(S)A 2000, s.35

General

21–001 A "community sentence" under PCC(S)A 2000 is defined as one which includes one or more community orders. PCC(S)A 2000, s.33(2)

"Community orders" under the Act are ten in number:

(1) a curfew order (21–055);
(2) a community rehabilitation order (formerly a probation order) (21–004, below);
(3) a community punishment order (formerly a community service order) (21–005, below);
(4) a community punishment and rehabilitation order (formerly a combination order) (21–007, below);
(5) a drug rehabilitation order (21–044, below);
(6) an attendance centre order (21–062, below);
(7) an exclusion order (21–059, below);
(8) a supervision order (21–069, below);
(9) an action plan order (21–081).

None of the powers to make community orders conferred by PCC(S)A 2000, Pt IV is exercisable in respect of an offence for which the sentence is fixed by law, or falls to be imposed under ss.109(2), 110(2) or 111(2) of the Act (required custodial sentences for certain repeat offences by offenders aged 18 or over (*ibid.*, s.34)).

Additional requirements

21–002 Each of these orders is a separate order in its own right, though the objects of some may overlap with those of others, and there are additional requirements, intended to achieve a particular aim, which may be inserted and which may be common to several orders.

Thus requirements may be attached to secure:

(1) curfew;
(2) residence;
(3) participation in activities;
(4) attendance at probation hostels;
(5) mental treatment;
(6) treatment for drug dependency;
(7) abstinence from Class A drugs;
(8) exclusion from particular places or areas.

Many of these orders fall to be dealt with as "youth community orders" under CJA 2003. The principal orders, however, namely (2) (3) and (4) in para.21–001 are dealt with at 21–004 *et seq.*, below.

General restrictions on imposing community sentences

21–003 There is a general restriction on imposing a community sentence on an offender unless the judge is of opinion that the offence, or the combination of the offence and one or more offences associated with it, was serious enough to warrant such a sentence, and where he does pass such a sentence: PCC(S)A 2000, s.35

(1) the particular order or orders comprising or forming part of the sentence must be such as in his opinion is, or taken together are, the most suitable for the offender; and
(2) the restrictions on liberty imposed by the order or orders must be such as in his opinion are commensurate with the seriousness of the offence, or the combination of the offence and the one or more offences associated with it.

A community sentence must not consist of both a community punishment (formerly a community service) order and a community rehabilitation (formerly a probation) order, whether for a single offence or for two or more offence (*Gilding v DPP*, *The Times*, May 20, 1998). Special provisions apply to curfew orders and community punishment orders for persistent petty offenders, see 21–005, below).

Community rehabilitation order

21–004 Where an offender aged 16 or over is convicted of an offence committed **before April 4, 2005** and the judge is of the opinion that supervision is desirable in the interests of: PCC(S)A 2000, ss.41(1)–(3); CJCSA 2000, s.43

(1) securing the offender's rehabilitation; and
(2) protecting the public from harm from him, or preventing the commission by him of further offences,

he may, subject to the general restrictions on making community orders (see 21–003, above) make an order requiring him to be under supervision for a period specified in the order of not less than six months nor more than three years. The order will specify the local justice area in which the offender resides or will reside.

Special provisions apply under PCC(S)A 2000, Sch.4, paras 1 and 2, to offenders residing in Scotland and Northern Ireland. PCC(S)A 2000, s.41(4)–(6)(11)

The order requires an offender:

(a) aged 18 or over at the time of his conviction to be under the supervision of an officer of a local probation board appointed for or assigned to the local justice area specified in the order;
(b) aged under 18 at that time, to be under the supervision either of such an officer or a member of a youth offending team.

In addition, an order may require the offender to comply during the whole or any part of the rehabilitation period with such requirements as the judge, having regard to the circumstances of the case, considers desirable in the interests of:

(i) securing the rehabilitation of the offender; or
(ii) protecting the public from harm from him; or
(iii) preventing the commission of further offences.

Apart from making a compensation order under *ibid.* s.130 (see 23 COMPENSATION), the payment of sums by way of damages for injury or compensation for loss must *not* be included among the additional requirements of an order. PCC(S)A 2000, s.42(1)(3)

Without prejudice to the generality of this provision, Sch.2 to the 2000 Act sets out those requirements authorised by the Act, namely:

- residence, hostels (para.1);
- activities (para.2);
- probation centres (paras 3, 4);
- mental treatment (para.5);

- drug/alcohol dependence (para.6);
- drug/abstinence (PCC(S)A 2000, s.42(2A–F));
- curfew (para.7);
- exclusion (para.8).

References to these requirements in detail will be found at 21–033 *et seq*., below.

Community punishment order

21–005 Where an offender aged 16 or over is convicted: PCC(S)A 2000, ss.46, 59; CJCSA 2000, s.44

(1) of an offence punishable with imprisonment **committed before April 4, 2005**; or
(2) in the case of a persistent petty offender, of any offence committed before that date;

the judge may, subject to the general restrictions governing the making of community orders (see 21–003, above) make a community punishment order, requiring the offender to perform unpaid work.

In the case of (2) above, he must not make an order unless he is satisfied that:

(a) one or more fines imposed on the offender in respect of one or more previous convictions have not been paid; and
(b) if a fine were imposed in an amount which was commensurate with the seriousness of the offence, the offender would not have sufficient means to pay it; and
(c) if he were not so satisfied he would be minded to impose a fine in respect of the offence (PCC(S)A 2000, s.59(1)(2).

An order must not be made, however, unless the judge is satisfied after hearing, if he thinks it necessary, an appropriate officer, that the offender is a suitable person to do work under such an order, and that provision for him to perform the work can be made under arrangements in force in the local justice area in which the offender resides or will reside. PCC(S)A 2000, s.46(4), (6)

A community punishment and rehabilitation order (see 21–007, below), which combines some of the benefits of a community service order with supervision under a probation order, may be more suitable. Since a community sentence may not consist of or include both a separate punishment order and a separate rehabilitation order, whether for a single offence or for two or more offences, a judge wishing to make an order combining the two must make the "combination" order (*Gilding v DPP, The Times*, May 20, 1998).

Special provisions apply under PCC(S)A 2000, Sch.4, para.3, to offenders residing in Scotland and Northern Ireland.

An order is effective from the moment it is pronounced (*Walsh v Barlow* [1985] Crim.L.R. 46; *Thorpe v Griggs* (1984) 6 Cr.App.R.(S.) 286).

Number of hours; consecutive orders; other obligations

21–006 The number of hours to be worked must be specified in the order, and must be in the aggregate, whatever the age of the offender: not less than 40 and not more than 240. Some credit ought to be given for time spent in custody awaiting trial (*R. v Lawrence* (1982) 4 Cr.App.R.(S.) 69). PCC(S)A 2000, s.46(5)

Where convictions for two or more offences are concerned, the judge may direct the hours specified in one to be concurrent with, or consecutive or additional to, the hours specified in another order, although: PCC(S)A 2000, s.46(8)

(1) the hours specified in a single order must not exceed 240; and
(2) the total hours imposed on the same occasion should not exceed 240 hours (*R. v Evans* (1977) 64 Cr.App.R. 127); though
(3) there is nothing to prevent different courts on different occasions from imposing orders which will in effect exceed 240 hours (*R. v Siha* (1992) 13 Cr.App.R.(S.) 588; *cf R. v Anderson* (1989) 11 Cr.App.R.(S.) 417), but it is undesirable; and
(4) it is wrong in principle to impose a consecutive order on an offender already subject to an order, if the effect is to create a combination exceeding 240 hours (*R. v Anderson* (1989) 11 Cr.App.R.(S.) 417); unless there are less than 240 hours yet to be worked under the original order (*R. v Siha* (above)).

In addition to performing for the number of hours specified in the order such work at such times as he may be instructed, the offender has a general obligation to keep in touch with the responsible officer in accordance with such instructions as he is given, and notify him of any change of address. PCC(S)A 2000, s.47(1)(3)

In general (there are exceptions) the work is to be performed within 12 months of the date of the order, but, in any event, unless revoked, it remains in force until the offender has worked the number of hours specified in it.

Community rehabilitation and punishment order

21–007 A community rehabilitation and punishment order (formerly a "combination order") combines the features of both the previous orders. The judge may: PCC(S)A 2000, s.51(1)–(3); CJCSA 2000, s.45

(1) in respect of an offender over the age of 16;
(2) convicted of an offence punishable with imprisonment committed **before April 4, 2005;**
(3) subject to the general restrictions on imposing community orders; and
(4) if he is of opinion that the order is desirable in the interests of:
 (a) securing the rehabilitation of the offender;
 (b) protecting the public from harm from him; or
 (c) preventing the commission by him of further offences,

make a "combination order", requiring him both to:

(i) be under supervision for a specified period of not less than 12 months nor more than three years; and
(ii) perform unpaid work for a specified numberr of hours, being in the aggrergate not less than 40 more more than 100.

Where such an order is made, subject to PCC(S)A 2000, ss.41, 42, 46, 47 and Sch.2 the Act applies to such an order, so far as (1) is concerned, as if it were a community rehabilitation order, and as far as (2) is concerned, as if it were a community punishment order. PCC(S)A 2000, s.651(4)

Additional requirements of mental treatment or treatment for drug or alcohol dependency may be added, with the offender's consent.

Special provisions apply to transfer of the order to Scotland.

B. Community sentence under CJA 2003

Introduction

21–008 CJA 2003, Ch.2 creates, for offenders:

(1) aged 16 or over, a single generic community sentence which combines requirements formerly available under PCC(S)A 2003 under different community orders; and
(2) under 16, a number of separate youth community orders under PCC(S)A 2000 Pt IV, enumerated below.

A "community sentence" means a sentence which consists of or includes: CJA 2003, s.147

(a) a community order, or
(b) one or more youth community orders.

A "youth community order" includes those orders set out at D in 21–053, below:

The clear distinction formerly maintained between custodial and community sentences is blurred by the Act, which provides for some of the community-based requirements of the latter to be attached to sentences of imprisonment of less than 12 months, in the case of a "custody plus order" (40–020) or of "intermittent custody" (40–026) and to an order deferring sentence (see 30 DEFERRING SENTENCE).

Restrictions on making community orders

21–009 Neither a community order nor a youth community order may be made in respect of an offence: for which the sentence: CJA 2003, s.150

(1) is fixed by law;
(2) falls to be imposed under FA 1968, s.51A (required sentences for certain firearms offences);
(3) falls to be imposed under PCC(S)A 2000, s.110(2) or s.111(2) (required sentences for certain repeated offences committed by offenders aged 18 or over, see 40–053); or
(4) falls to be imposed under any of CJA 2003, ss.225–228 (dangerous offenders, see 29–014 *et seq.*, 40–043–40–050 and 31–024–31–027).

In the case of an offender aged 18 or over, no community order under CJA 2003 may be made in respect of an offence committed **before April 4, 2005**.

Pre-sentence drug testing

21–010 Where, in the case of an offender aged 14 or over convicted of an offence, the judge is considering a community sentence, or a suspended sentence, he may, provided that he has been notified that he has that power, for the purpose of ascertaining whether the offender has any specified Class A drug (only heroin and "crack" cocaine have so far been specified) in his body, make an order requiring him to provide, in accordance with his order, specified samples. CJA 2003, s.161(1), (2), (4), (5), (6)

Failure, without reasonable excuse, to comply is punishable with a fine of an amount not exceeding level 4 (see below).

Where the offender has not attained the age of 17, the order must provide for the samples to be provided in the presence of an "appropriate adult" as defined in subs.(8). CJA 2003, s.161(3), (8)

COMMUNITY SENTENCES

Threshold for community sentences

21–011 The judge must not (CJA 2003, s.148) pass a community sentence on an offender unless he is of opinion that subject to s.151(2) the offence, or the combination of the offence and one or more offences associated with it, was serious enough to warrant such a sentence, and where he does pass such a sentence: CJA 2003, s.148

(1) the particular requirement or requirements forming part of the community order must be such as in his opinion is, or taken together are, the most suitable for the offender; and
(2) subject to s.134(2), the restrictions on liberty imposed by the order must be such as in his opinion are commensurate with the seriousness of the offence, or the combination of the offence and one or more offences associated with it.

Where the judge passes a community sentence which consists of or includes one or more youth community orders:

(a) the particular order or orders forming part of the sentence must be such as in his opinion is, or taken together are, the most suitable for the offender; and
(b) the restrictions on liberty imposed by the order or orders must be such as in his opinion are commensurate with the seriousness of the offence, or the combination of the offence and the one or more offences associated with it.

In determining the restrictions on liberty to be imposed by a community order or a youth community order in respect of an offence, the judge may have regard to any period for which the offender has been remanded in custody in connection with the offence or any other offences the charge for which was founded on the same facts or evidence. CJA 2003, s.149

"Remand in custody includes: CJA 2003, s.242(2)

(i) remand or committal to custody by court order;
(ii) remand or committal to local authority accommodation under CYPA 1969, s.23, and being kept in secure accommodation or detained in secure training under s.23(7A); and
(iii) remand, admission or removal to hospital under MHA 1983, ss.35, 36, 38 or 48.

Persistent offender previously fined

21–012 In the case of an offender: CJA 2003, s.151

(1) aged **16 or over convicted of an offence,**

(2) who on three or more previous occasions has, on conviction in the United Kingdom of any offence committed by him after attaining the age of 16, had passed on him a sentence consisting only of a fine, and

(3) despite the effect of s.143(2) the judge would not (apart from that section) regard the current offence, or the combination of the current offence and one or more offences associated with it as being serious enough to warrant a community sentence,

he may make a community order in respect of the current offence instead of imposing a fine, if he considers that, having regard to all the circumstances, including:

(a) the nature of the offences to which the previous convictions relate, and their relevance to the current offence, and

(b) the time that has elapsed since the offender's conviction of each of those offences,

it would be in the interests of justice to do so.

Note that:

- the reference to a court in the United Kingdom includes a reference to a finding of guilt in service disciplinary proceedings (see s.151(4));
- a compensation order and a surcharge under CJA 2003, s.161A (inserted by DVA 2004) do not, for the purpose of these provisions, form part of an offender's sentence (s.151(5); DVA 2004, s.58(1), Sch.10, para.63);
- it is immaterial for the purposes of s.151(1)(b) whether on previous occasions a court has passed on the offender a sentence not consisting only of a fine (s.151(6));
- these provisions do not, of course, limit the extent to which the judge may, in accordance with CJA 2003, s.143(2), treat any previous conviction as increasing the seriousness of the offence.

Approach to community order

21–013 Where an offender aged 18 or over is being sentenced for a non-imprisonable offence or offences, great care is needed in assessing whether a community sentence is appropriate, since failure to comply may result in a custodial sentence. SGC 3, 1.1.10

Having decided (in consultation with the Probation Service where appropriate) that a community sentence is justified, the judge must decide which requirements should be included in the community order. The requirements or orders imposed will have SGC 3, 1.1.11

the effect of restricting the offender's liberty, whilst providing punishment in the community, rehabilitation for the offender, and/or ensuring that the offender engages in reparative activities.

The key issues are:

(a) which requirements to impose;
(b) how to make allowance for time spent on remand; and
(c) how to deal with breaches.

The judge should have the possibility of a possible breach firmly in mind when passing sentence for the original offence. If he is to reflect the seriousness of an offence, there is little value in setting requirements as part of a community sentence that are not demanding enough for the offender; there is equally, on the other hand, little value in imposing requirements that would "set an offender up to fail" and almost inevitably lead to sanctions for a breach.

Seriousness the initial factor

21–014 The guiding principles, in community sentences, are proportionality and suitability. Once the judge has decided that: SGC 3, 1.1.13, 1.1.14

(1) the offence has crossed the community sentence threshold, and
(2) a community sentence is justified,

the initial factor in defining which requirements to include in the sentence should be the seriousness of the offence(s) committed.

This means that;

(a) "seriousness" is an important factor in deciding whether he chooses the low, medium or high range of order (see below); but
(b) having taken that decision, selection of the content of the order within the range will be determined by a much wider range of factors.

Sentencing ranges must remain flexible enough to take account of:

(i) the suitability of the offender,
(ii) his ability to comply with particular requirements, and
(iii) their availability in the local area.

The justification for imposing a community sentence in response to persistent petty offending is the persistence of the offending behaviour rather than the seriousness of the offences being committed. The requirements imposed should ensure that the restriction on liberty is proportionate to the seriousness of the SGC 3, 1.1.14

offending, to reflect the fact that the offences, of themselves, are not sufficiently serious to merit a community sentence.

Information for the judge

21–015 In many cases, a pre-sentence report will be pivotal in helping the judge to decide whether to impose a custodial sentence or to impose a community sentence, and if so, whether particular requirements, or a combination of requirements, are suitable for an individual offender, but the judge must always ensure, especially where there are multiple requirements, that the: SGC 3, 1.1.15

(1) restriction on liberty placed on the offender is proportionate to the seriousness of the offence committed; and
(2) the likely effect of one requirement on another and that they do not place conflicting demands upon the offender.

Having reached the provisional view that a community sentence is the most appropriate disposal, the judge should request a pre-sentence report, indicating:

(a) which of the three sentencing ranges is relevant; and
(b) the purpose(s) of sentencing that the package of requirements is required to fulfil.

These two factors will guide the Probation Service in determining the nature and combination of requirements that may be appropriate and the onerousness and intensity of those requirements. Usually, the most helpful way for the judge to do this is to produce a written note for the report writer, copied on the court file. If it is known that the same tribunal and defence advocate will be present on the day of sentence and a probation officer is present in court when the request is made, it may not be necessary to commit details of the request to writing. However, events may change and it is good practice to ensure that there is a clear record of the judge's request. SGC 3, 1.1.16

There will be occasions when any type of report may be unnecessary despite the intention to pass a community sentence, though this is likely to be infrequent. The judge might consider dispensing with the need to obtain a pre-sentence report for adult offenders, e.g. where: SGC 3, 1.1.17

(i) the offence falls within the *low* range of seriousness; and
(ii) where he is minded to impose a single requirement, such as an exclusion requirement (where the circumstances of the case show that this would be an appropriate disposal without electronic monitoring); and

(iii) the sentence will not require the involvement of the Probation Service.

High, medium and low ranges of sentence

21–016 In order to enable judges to benefit from the flexibility that community sentences provide and also to meet its statutory obligations, any structure governing the use of community requirements must allow the judge to choose the most appropriate sentence for each individual offender. While the judge has a statutory obligation to pass a sentence commensurate with the seriousness of the offence, within the range of sentences justified, he may quite properly consider factors which heighten the risk of the offender committing further offences or causing further harm, with a view to lessening that risk. The extent to which requirements are imposed must be capable of being varied to ensure that the restriction on liberty is commensurate with the seriousness of the offence. SGC 3, 1.1.18

SGC 3, 1.1.19–25 recommend that there should be three sentencing ranges within the community sentence band, based upon seriousness:

(1) low, for those offenders whose offence is relatively minor within the community service band, including persistent petty offenders whose offences only merit a community sentence by virtue of failing to respond to the previous imposition of fines — such offenders would merit a "light touch" approach, for example, normally a single requirement such as a short period of unpaid work, or a curfew, or a prohibited activity requirement or an exclusion requirement (where the circumstances of the case mean that this would be an appropriate disposal without electronic monitoring);
(2) medium; and
(3) high, for those offenders who have only just fallen short of a custodial sentence and for those who have passed the custody threshold but for whom a community sentence would be deemed appropriate.

It is not intended that the offender necessarily progress from one range to the next on each sentencing occasion. The decision as to the appropriate range each time is based upon the seriousness of the new offence(s).

The decision on the nature and severity of the requirements to be included in a community sentence should be guided by:

(a) the assessment of offence seriousness (low, medium or high);

(b) the purpose(s) of sentencing the judge wishes to achieve;
(c) the risk of re-offending;
(d) the ability of the offender to comply; and
(e) the availability of requirements in the local area.

The resulting restriction on liberty must be a proportionate response to the offence that was committed.

In all three ranges there must be sufficient flexibility to allow the sentence to be varied to take account of the suitability of particular requirements for the individual offender and whether a particular requirement or package of requirements might be more effective at reducing any identified risk of re-offending. It will fall to the judge to ensure that the sentence strikes the right balance between proportionality and suitability. SGC 3 seeks to set out (paras 1.1.25–33) a non-exhaustive set of examples. These focus on punishment in the community although SGC recognises that not all packages will necessarily need to include a punitive requirement. There will clearly be other requirements of a rehabilitative nature such as a treatment requirement or an accredited programme which may be appropriate depending on the specific needs of the offender and assessment of suitability. Given the intensity of such intervention it is expected that these will normally only be appropriate at medium and high levels of seriousness, and where assessed as having a medium or high risk of re-offending. In addition, when passing sentence in any one of the three ranges, the court should consider whether a rehabilitative intervention such as a programme requirement, or a restorative justice intervention might be suitable as an additional or alternative part of the sentence. SGC 3, 1.1.23, 24

Where the judge seeks to impose an **electronic monitoring** requirement (it is mandatory in some circumstances) he should bear in mind that it should be used with the primary purpose of promoting and monitoring compliance with other requirements, in circumstances where the punishment of the offender and/or the need to safeguard the public and prevent re-offending are the most important concerns (SGC 3, 1.1.33). See generally 21–014, below.

Recording the sentence

21–017 The fact that there is, under CJA 2003, only one generic community sentence does not mean that an offender who has completed a community sentence and has then re-offended, is to be regarded as ineligible for a second community sentence on the basis that this has been tried and has failed.

Further community sentences perhaps with different requirements may be well be justified.

SGC has suggested that:

(1) the judge, in imposing sentence will wish to be clear about the "purposes" that the community sentence is designed to achieve when setting the requirements; "sharing" those purposes with the offender and the Probation Service will enable them to be clear about the goals that are to be achieved; SGC 3, 1.1.34, 35

(2) if he does not include in the order an express direction that any failure to comply with the requirements of the order is to be dealt with by a magistrates' court, the responsible officer will bring the breach proceedings in the Crown Court; and CJA 2003, s.179, Sch.8

(3) any judge dealing with the matter thereafter must have full information about the requirements which were inserted into the previous community sentence imposed on the offender (including whether it was a low/medium/high level order), and about the offender's response.

This will enable him to consider the merits of imposing the same or different requirements as part of another community sentence. The requirements should be recorded in such a way as to ensure that they can be made available to another court if another offence is committed. SGC 3, 1.1.36

When an offender is required to serve a community sentence, the court records should be clearly annotated to show which particular requirements have been imposed. SGC 3, 1.1.35

Time spent on remand

21–018 The judge will need to consider whether to give any credit for time spent in custody on remand. SGC 3, 1.1.37, 38

The judge should:

(1) seek to give credit for time spent on remand in custody or equivalent status in all cases;

(2) make clear, when announcing sentence, whether or not credit for time on remand has been given; and

(3) explain his reasons for not giving credit where he considers either that this is not justified, would not be practical, or would not be in the best interests of the offender.

Where an offender has spent a period of time spent in custody on remand, there will be occasions where a custodial sentence is warranted but the length of the sentence justified by the seriousness of the offence would mean that the offender would be released immediately.

Under the present framework it may be more appropriate:

(a) to pass a community sentence since that will ensure supervision on release; or
(b) where the custodial sentence would be for 12 months or more, to pass a custodial sentence in the knowledge that licence requirements will be imposed on release from custody; this will ensure that the sentence imposed properly reflects the seriousness of the offence.

Recommendations made by the judge at the point of sentence will be of particular importance in influencing the content of the licence. This will properly reflect the gravity of the offence. SGC 3, 1.1.39, 40

Annex A to SGC 3 gives detail advanced by the Sentencing Advisory Panel (not binding on judges).

Transfer of orders to Scotland and Northern Ireland

21–019 Where the judge considering the making of a community order is satisfied that the offender resides, or will reside when the order comes into force, in Scotland or Northern Ireland, the provisions of CJA 2003, s.180, Sch.9 apply.

21–020 Quick guide to orders

A. **Offenders aged 16 or over** (21–021–21–033)
B. **Requirement available in case of all offenders** (21–033–21–049)
C. **Additional requirements available in case of offenders aged up to 25** (21–050–21–052)
D. **Youth Community orders** (21–053–21–086).

21–021 Where a person aged 16 or over is convicted of an offence, the judge may impose upon him a single "community order", imposing on him any one of the following requirements: CJA 2003, s.177(1)(2)

(1) an unpaid work requirement (as defined by s.199), see 21–034, below);
(2) an activity requirement (as defined by s.201), see 21–036 below;
(3) a programme requirement (as defined by s.202), see 21–037, below;
(4) a prohibited activity requirement (as defined by s.203), see 21–038 below);

(5) a curfew requirement (as defined by s.204), see 21–039 below;
(6) an exclusion requirement (as defined by s.205), see 21–040 below:
(7) a residence requirement (as defined by s.206), see 21–041 below;
(8) a mental health treatment requirement (as defined by s.207), see 21–042 below;
(9) a drug rehabilitation requirement (as defined by s.209), see 21–044 below;
(10) an alcohol treatment requirement (as defined by s.212), see 21–049 below;
(11) a supervision requirement (as defined by s.213), see 21–049 below; and
(12) in a case where an offender is under 25, an electronic monitoring requirement (as defined by s.215), see 21–022, and 21–051 below; and
(13) in a case where an offender is under 25, an attendance centre requirement, (as defined by s.214), see 21–050

though these provisions are subject to CJA 2003, ss.150 (not available where sentence fixed by law) and 218, and to the following provisions of CJA 2003, Ch. 4 relating to particular requirements, namely:

(a) s.199(3) (unpaid work requirement);
(b) s.201(3)(4) (activity requirement);
(c) s.202(4)(5) (programme requirement);
(d) s.203(2) (prohibited activity requirement);
(e) s.207(3) (mental health requirement);
(f) s.209(2) (drug rehabilitation requirement); and
(g) s.212(2)(3) (alcohol treatment requirement).

As to the breach, revocation or amendment of orders, see 14 BREACH, AMENDMENT AND REVOCATION; as to the transfer of orders to Scotland or Northern Ireland, see CJA 2003, Sch.9.

The provisions as to drug treatment and testing orders under PCC(S)A 2000, ss.52–55, are repealed by CJA 2003, Sch.37.

Adding an electronic monitoring requirement

21–022 Where the judge makes an order imposing:

(1) a curfew requirement, or an exclusion requirement, he must also impose an electronic monitoring requirement (as defined by s.215), unless either he is prevented from CJA 2003, s.177(3)

doing so by the non-consent of the proposed supervisor or the unavailability of facilities (s.218(4)), or in the particular circumstances of the case, he considers it inappropriate to do so;

(2) a requirement under (1)–(4), or (7)–(12) above, he may also impose an electronic monitoring requirement unless either he is prevented from doing so by s.215(2) or s.218(4), referred to in (1) or in the particular circumstances of the case, he considers it inappropriate to do so. CJA 2003, s.177(4)

Where the judge makes: R.48.1

(a) a curfew order with an electronic monitoring requirement under CSA 1997, s.3 or under PCC(S)A 2000, ss.37 and 36B; or
(b) a community rehabilitation order with curfew and electronic monitoring requirements under PCC(S)A 2000, s.41, Sch.2, para.7,

the court officer will serve notice of the order on the person in respect of whom it is made by way of pages 1 and 2 of the form set out in the Practice Direction, and will serve notice of the order on the person responsible for electronically monitoring compliance with it by way of the form set out in PD 2004, Annex D. Where any community order additional to the curfew order has been made in respect of the offender, the court officer will serve a copy of the notice on the local probation board or youth offending team responsible for the offender.

Compatibility

21–023 Before making an order imposing two or more different requirements, the judge must consider whether, in the circumstances of the case, the requirements are compatible with each other. CJA 2003, s.178(6)

Completion of order

21–024 An order must specify a date, not more than three years after the date of the order by which all the requirements in it must have been complied with; an order which imposes two or more requirements may also specify an earlier date or dates in relation to compliance with any one or more of them. CJA 2003, s.178(5)

Provisions applying to relevant orders generally

21–025 Certain general provisions apply to "relevant orders" generally, such orders being:

(1) community orders;
(2) custody plus orders (40–020 below);
(3) suspended sentence orders (40–080 below);
(4) intermittent custody orders (40–026 below).

A reference (in CJA 2003, Ch.4) to a requirement being imposed by, or included in, a relevant order is, in relation to a custody plus order when that order comes into force, or an intermittent custody order, a reference to compliance with the requirement being required by the order to be a condition of the licence. CJA 2003, s.196

Duties of responsible officer

21–026 Where a relevant order has effect, it is the duty of the responsible officer (as defined in s.197, except in relation to s.l97(1)(a)):

(1) to make any arrangements that are necessary in connection with the requirements imposed by the order; CJA 2003, s.198
(2) to promote the offender's compliance with those requirements; and
(3) where appropriate, to take steps to enforce those requirements.

Local justice area to be specified

21–027 A community order or suspended sentence order must specify the local justice area in which the offender resides or will reside and in the case of a custody plus order or an intermittent custody order must specify the local justice area in which the offender will reside, in the case of a: CJA 2003, s.216

(1) custody plus order, during the licence period following his release (s.181(3)(b)), or
(2) of an intermittent custody order, during any period during which he is released on licence (s.183(3)).

Avoidance of conflict with religious beliefs, etc

21–028 The judge must ensure, as far as practicable, that any requirement imposed by a relevant order is such as to avoid: CJA 2003, s.217

(1) any conflict with the offender's religious beliefs or with the requirements of any other relevant order to which he may be subject; and
(2) any interference with the times, if any, at which he normally works or attends school or any other educational establishment.

Availability of arrangements in local area

21–029 The judge must not include:

(1) an unpaid work requirement in a relevant order unless he is satisfied that provision for the offender to work under such a requirement can be made under the arrangements for persons to perform work under such a requirement which exist in the local justice area in which he resides or will reside; CJA 2003, s.218

(2) an activity requirement in a relevant order unless he is satisfied that provision for the offender to participate in the activities proposed to be specified in the order can be made under the arrangements for persons to participate in such activities which exist in the local justice area in which he resides or will reside;

(3) an attendance centre requirement in a relevant order in respect of an offender unless the court has been notified by the Home Secretary that an attendance centre is available for persons of his description.

In subsection (5) "place", in relation to an exclusion requirement, includes an area. CJA 2003, s.205

Copies of relevant orders

21–030 The court by which any relevant order is made must forthwith provide copies of the order: CJA 2003, s.219

(1) to the offender,
(2) if the offender is aged 18 or over, to an officer of a local probation board assigned to the court,
(3) if the offender is aged 16 or 17, to an officer of a local probation board assigned to the court or to a member of a youth offending team assigned to the court, and
(4) where the order specifies a local justice area for which the court making the order does not act, to the local probation board acting for that area.

Where a relevant order imposes any requirement specified in the first column of CJA 2003, Sch.14, the court by which the order is made must also forthwith provide the person specified in relation to that requirement in the second column of that Schedule with a copy of so much of the order as relates to that requirement.

Where a relevant order specifies a local justice area for which the court making the order does not act, the court making the order must provide to the magistrates' court acting for that area, a copy of the order, and such documents and information relating to the case as it considers likely to be of assistance to a court acting for that area in the exercise of its functions in relation to the order.

Duty of offender to keep in touch with responsible officer

21–031 An offender in respect of whom a community order or a suspended sentence order is in force must keep in touch with the responsible officer in accordance with such instructions as he may from time to time be given by that officer, and must notify him of any change of address. The obligation is enforceable as if it were a requirement imposed by the order. CJA 2003, s.220

Breach, amendment and revocation

21–032 Action on the breach, amendment and revocation of orders is dealt with at 14 BREACH, AMENDMENT AND REVOCATION.

C. Requirements available in case of all offenders

21–033 CJA 2003, ss.199–214 describes in detail the requirements available in relation to a community order. They are also available in respect of a custody plus order (40–020 below) (when that order comes into force), an intermittent custody order (40–026 below) and a suspended sentence order (40–080 below).

(1) Unpaid work requirement

General

21–034 Under this requirement, the offender is required to perform unpaid work in accordance with s.200 for the number of hours specified in the relevant order being in the aggregate: CJA 2003, s.199(1), (2), (5)

(1) not less than 40,
(2) not more than 300.

Where orders are made in respect of two or more offences of which the offender has been convicted on the same occasion, and each includes such a requirement, the judge may direct that the hours of work specified be concurrent with or in addition to those specified in any other of those orders, provided the number of hours which are not concurrent does not exceed 300.

Under the previous legislation it was held that there was nothing to prevent different courts, on different occasions, from imposing orders which would, in effect, exceed the maximum, but that it was undesirable *(R. v Siha* (1992) 13 Cr.App.R.(S.) 588; *cf. R. v Anderson* (1989) 11 Cr.App.R.(S.) 417).

Such a requirement is not to be included in a community order unless, after hearing an appropriate officer, the judge is satisfied that the offender is a suitable person to perform work under such a requirement.

An "appropriate person for these purposes is:

(a) in the case of an offender aged 18 or over, an officer of a local probation board; and
(b) in the case of an offender under 18, an officer of a local probation board, a local authority social worker or a member of a youth offending team.

Under such a requirement, the offender must perform for the number of hours specified such work at such times as he may be instructed by the responsible officer. CJA 2003, s.189(1), (2), (3)

Subject to Sch.8, para.20 and the power (in Sch.12, para.18) to extend the period, the work must be performed within 12 months, but until it is revoked the order remains in force until the work has been performed under it.

Suspended sentences

21–035 Where a requirement is imposed by a suspended sentence order, the supervision period as defined by s.189(1)(a) continues until the offender has worked under the order for the number of hours specified, but does not continue beyond the end of the operational period as defined by s.189(1)(b)(ii). CJA 2003, s.199(5)

(2) Activity requirement

21–036 Such a requirement requires the offender to do either or both of the following: CJA 2003, s.201(1)(2)(3)(4)(5)

(1) to present himself to a person or persons specified in the order at a place or places specified on such number of days as may be specified;
(2) to participate in such activities specified in the order, on such number of days (not exceeding 60) as may be so specified,

such activities including, in particular, activities having a reparative purpose, but the judge must not include such a requirement in an order unless:

(a) he has consulted:
  (i) in the case of an offender aged 18 or over, an officer of a local probation board;
  (ii) in the case of an offender aged under 18, either an officer of a local probation board or a member of a youth offending team; and
(b) is satisfied that it is feasible to secure compliance with the requirement.

Such a requirement may not be included in an order if compliance with it would involve the co-operation of a person other than the offender and the offender's responsible officer, unless that other person consents to the inclusion. CJA 2003, ss.201(6)–(10)

A requirement of this nature operates to require the offender:

(i) in relation to (1) above, in accordance with instructions from his responsible officer, to present himself at a place or places, being a community rehabilitation centre or other approved place, on the number of days specified in the order and while there, to comply with instructions given by, or under the authority of the person in charge;
(ii) where (2) above is concerned, in accordance with instructions to participate in activities on the number of days specified and, while doing so, to comply with instructions given by, or under the authority of, the person in charge.

Schedule 2 lays down that instructions given should as far as practicable be such as to avoid interference with the times, if any, at which the offender normally works or attends a school or other educational establishment.

(3) Programme requirement

21–037 Such a requirement requires the offender to participate in an accredited programme, that is, a systematic set of activities specified in the order at a specified place on a specified number of days. CJA 2003, ss.202(1)–(5); SI 2005/373

A requirement of this sort must not be included in an order unless:

(1) the accredited programme which the judge proposes to specify has been recommended to him as being suitable for the offender, by:
  (a) in the case of an offender aged 18 or over, an officer of a local probation board; or

(b) in the case of an offender aged under 18, either an officer of a local probation board or a member of a youth offending team, and

(2) the judge is satisfied that the programme will be available at the place proposed to be specified.

A requirement may not be included in an order if compliance with it would involve the co-operation of a person other than the offender and the offender's responsible officer, unless that other person consents to the inclusion.

Under such a requirement, the offender is required: CJA 2003, s.202(6)(7)

(a) in accordance with instructions from his responsible officer, to participate in the accredited programme at the place specified in the order on the number of days specified in the order, and
(b) while there, to comply with instructions given by, or under the authority of the person in charge.

(4) Prohibited activity requirement

21–038 A "prohibited activity requirement", in relation to a relevant order, is a requirement that the offender refrain from participating in activities specified in the order on a specified day or days, or during a specified period. CJA 2003, s.203

The judge may not include a "prohibited activity requirement" in a relevant order unless he has consulted:

(1) in the case of an offender aged 18 or over, an officer of a local probation board;
(2) in the case of an offender aged under 18, either an officer of a local probation board or a member of a youth offending team.

The requirements that may, by virtue of this provision be included in a relevant order include a requirement that the offender does not possess, use or carry a firearm within the meaning of FA 1968.

(5) Curfew requirement

21–039 A "curfew requirement", in relation to a relevant order, means a requirement that the offender remain, for periods specified in the order, at a place so specified. The order may specify different places or different periods for different days, CJA 2003, s.204

but may not specify periods which amount to less than two hours or more than 12 hours in any day, and note that:

(1) a community order or a suspended sentence order (see 40–080) which imposes a curfew requirement must not specify periods falling outside the period of six months beginning with the day on which it is made; and
(2) a "custody plus order" (40–020) which imposes a curfew requirement must not specify a period which falls outside the period of six months beginning with the first day of the licence period as defined by s.181(3)(b); and
(3) an "intermittent custody order" (40–026) which imposes a curfew requirement must not specify a period if to do so would cause the aggregate number of days on which the offender is subject to the requirement for any part of the day to exceed 182 days.

Before making an order imposing a curfew requirement, the judge must obtain and consider information about the place proposed to be specified in the order (including information as to the attitude of persons likely to be affected by the enforced presence there of the offender).

(6) Exclusion requirement

21–040 An exclusion requirement, in relation to a relevant order, means a provision prohibiting the offender from entering a place (or area) specified in the order for a period so specified. Where the order is a community order, the period specified must not be more than two years. CJA 2003, s.205

An "exclusion requirement" may:

(1) provide for the prohibition to operate only during the periods specified in the order, and
(2) specify different places for different periods or days.

(7) Residence requirement

21–041 A residence requirement, in relation to a community order or a suspended sentence order, means a requirement that, during a period specified in the relevant order, the offender reside at a place specified in the order. If the order so provides, a residence requirement does not prohibit the offender from residing, with the prior approval of the responsible officer, at a place other than that specified in the order. CJA 2003, s.206

Before making a community order or suspended sentence order containing a residence requirement, the judge must consider the offender's home surroundings.

The requirement may not specify a hostel or other institution as the place where an offender must reside, except on the recommendation of an officer of a local probation board.

(8) Mental health treatment requirement

21–042 A mental health treatment requirement, in relation to a relevant order, is a requirement that the offender submit, during a period or periods specified in the order, to treatment by or under the direction of a registered medical practitioner or a chartered psychologist (or both, for different periods) with a view to the improvement of the offender's mental condition. CJA 2003, s.207(1)(2)

The treatment required must be one of the following kinds of treatment, specified in the order:

(1) treatment as a resident patient in an independent hospital or care home within the meaning of the Care Standards Act 2000, or a hospital within the meaning of MHA 1983, but not in hospital premises where high security psychiatric services within the meaning of that Act are provided;
(2) treatment as a non-resident patient at such institution or place as may be specified in the order;
(3) treatment by or under the direction of such registered medical practitioner or chartered psychologist (or both) as may be so specified,

but the nature of the treatment is not to be specified in the order except as mentioned above.

The judge may *not*, by virtue of this provision include a mental health treatment requirement in a relevant order unless; CJA 2003, s.207(3)

(a) he is satisfied, on the evidence of a registered medical practitioner approved for the purposes of MHA 1983, s.12, that the mental condition of the offender;
   (i) is such as requires and may be susceptible to treatment, but
   (ii) is not such as to warrant the making of a hospital order or a guardianship order within the meaning of MHA 1983;
(b) he is also satisfied that arrangements have been, or can be made for the treatment intended to be specified in the order (including arrangements for the reception of the

offender where he is to be required to submit to treatment as a resident patient); and

(c) the offender has consented to such a requirement.

While the offender is under treatment as a resident patient in pursuance of a "mental health requirement" of a relevant order, the responsible officer will carry out supervision only to such extent as may be necessary for the purpose of the revocation or amendment of the order. CJA 2003, s.207(4)

Note that:

(i) MHA 1983, s.54(2)(3) has effect with respect to proof for, the purposes of subs.(3)(a) of an offender's mental condition as they have effect with respect to proof of an offender's mental condition for the purposes of MHA 1983, s.37(2)(a); CJA 2003, s.207(5)(6)

(ii) "chartered psychologist" means a person for the time being listed in the British Psychological Society's Register of Chartered Psychologists.

Treatment at place other than that specified in order

21–043 Where the medical practitioner or chartered psychologist by whom or under whose direction an offender is being treated for his mental condition in pursuance of a "mental health treatment requirement" is of the opinion that part of the treatment can be better or more conveniently given in or at an institution or place which: CJA 2003, s.208

(1) is not specified in the relevant order, and

(2) is one in or at which the treatment of the offender will be given by or under the direction of a registered medical practitioner or chartered psychologist,

he may, where the offender consents, make arrangements for him to be treated accordingly.

Such arrangements as are mentioned may provide for the offender to receive part of his treatment as a resident patient in an institution or place notwithstanding that the institution or place is not one which could have been specified for that purpose in the relevant order.

Where such arrangements are made for the treatment of an offender:

(a) the medical practitioner or chartered psychologist by whom the arrangements are made must give notice in writing to the offender's responsible officer, specifying the institution or place in or at which the treatment is to be carried out; and

(b) the treatment provided will be deemed to be treatment to which he is required to submit in pursuance of the relevant order.

(9) Drug rehabilitation requirement

General

21–044 A "drug rehabilitation requirement", in relation to a community order or suspended sentence order, means a requirement that during a period specified in the order ("the treatment and testing period") the offender must: CJA 2003, s.209(1)(2)(7)

(1) submit to treatment by or under the direction of a specified person having the necessary qualifications or experience, with a view to the reduction or elimination of the offender's dependency on or propensity to misuse drugs, and

(2) for the purpose of ascertaining whether he has any drug in his body during that period, provide samples of such description as may be so determined, at such times or in such circumstances as may (subject to the provisions of the order) be determined by the responsible officer or by the person specified as the person by or under whose direction the treatment is to be provided.

"Drug" here means a controlled drug as defined by MDA 1971, s.2.

(CJA 2003, Sch.37 repeals PCC(S)A 2000, s.51 thus abolishing the drug treatment and testing order.)

The judge may *not* impose a "drug rehabilitation requirement" unless: CJA 2003, s.209(2)

(a) he is satisfied:
  (i) that the offender is dependent on, or has a propensity to misuse, drugs; and
  (ii) that his dependency or propensity is such as requires and may be susceptible to treatment;

(b) he is also satisfied that arrangements have been or can be made for the treatment intended to be specified in the order (including arrangements for the reception of the offender where he is to be required to submit to treatment as a resident);

(c) the requirement has been recommended to the court as being suitable for the offender:
  (i) in the case of an offender aged 18 or over, by an officer of a local probation board; or

(ii) in the case of an offender aged under 18, either by an officer of a local probation board or by a member of a youth offending team; and

(d) the offender consents to comply with the requirement.

The treatment and testing period must be at least six months, and the required treatment for any particular period must be treatment as a resident in such institution or place as may be specified in the order, or treatment as a non-resident in or at such institution or place, and at such intervals, as may be so specified, but the nature of the treatment is not to be more precisely specified in the order except in the above provisions. CJA 2003, s.209(3)(4)(6)

A community order or a suspended sentence order imposing a "drug rehabilitation requirement" must provide that the results of tests carried out on any samples provided by the offender in pursuance of the requirement to a person other than the responsible officer are to be communicated to the responsible officer.

Provision for review by court

21–045 A community order or a suspended sentence order imposing a drug rehabilitation requirement may, and must if the treatment and testing period is more than 12 months: CJA 2003, s.210(1)(2)(4)

(1) provide for the requirement to be reviewed periodically at intervals of *not less than one month*,
(2) provide for each review of the requirement to be made, subject to s.211(6) (whereby the offender is excused attendance), at a hearing held for the purpose by the court responsible for the order (a "review hearing"),
(3) require the offender to attend each review hearing,
(4) provide for the responsible officer to make to the court responsible for the order, before each review, a report in writing on the offender's progress under the requirement, and
(5) provide for each such report to include the test results communicated to the responsible officer under s.209(6) or otherwise and the views of the treatment provider as to the treatment and testing of the offender,
(6) provide for each such report to include the test results communicated to the responsible officer under s.209(6) or otherwise and the views of the treatment provider as to the treatment and testing of the offender.

References to the court responsible for a community order or suspended sentence order imposing a "drug rehabilitation requirement" are references, in so far as the Crown Court is concerned, to the court by which the order is made.

Where a community order or suspended sentence order imposing a "drug rehabilitation requirement" has been made on an appeal brought from the Crown Court or from CACD, for the purposes of this provision it is taken to have been made by the Crown Court.

Periodic reviews

21–046 At a review hearing (as defined in s.210(l)) the judge may, after considering the responsible officer's report, amend the community order or suspended sentence order, so far as it relates to the drug rehabilitation requirement, but may *not* amend: CJA 2003, s.211(1)(2)(9)

(1) the "drug rehabilitation requirement" unless the offender consents to comply with the requirement as amended;
(2) any provision of the order so as to reduce the period for which the drug rehabilitation requirement has effect below the minimum i.e. not less than six months, specified in s.209(3); and
(3) except with the offender's consent, any requirement or provision of the order while an appeal against the order is pending.

If the offender fails to consent to the "drug rehabilitation requirement" as proposed to be amended, the judge may: CJA 2003, s.211(3)(4)(9)

(a) revoke the community order, or the suspended sentence order and the suspended sentence to which it relates, and
(b) deal with him, for the offence in respect of which the order was made, in any way in which it could deal with him if he had just been convicted by the court of the offence, and

in relation to (2) after taking into account the extent to which the offender has complied with the requirements of the order, the judge may impose a custodial sentence (where the order was made in respect of an offence punishable with such a sentence) notwithstanding anything in s.152(2).

Effect of progress

21–047 If at a review: CJA 2003, s.211(6)(7)(8)(9)

(1) *hearing* (see s.210(l)(b)) the judge, after considering the responsible officer's report, is of the opinion that the

offender's progress under the requirement is satisfactory, the judge may so amend the order as to provide for each subsequent review to be made by the court without a hearing;

(2) *without a hearing*, the judge, after considering the responsible officer's report, is of the opinion that the offender's progress under the requirement is no longer satisfactory, he may require the offender to attend a hearing at a specified time and place.

At that hearing the judge, after considering the report, may either:

(a) exercise the powers conferred by the section as if the hearing were a review hearing, and
(b) so amend the order as to provide for each subsequent review to be made at a review hearing.

(10) Alcohol treatment requirement

21–048 An "alcohol treatment requirement" in relation to a relevant order is a requirement that the offender submit during a period specified in the order to treatment by or under the direction of a specified person having the necessary qualifications or experience, with a view to the reduction or elimination of the offender's dependency on alcohol. CJA 2003, s.212

Such a requirement may *not* be imposed unless the judge is satisfied:

(1) that the offender is dependent on alcohol, and
(2) that his dependency is such as requires and may be susceptible to treatment, and
(3) the offender consents to its requirements.

The period for which the "alcohol treatment requirement" has effect must be for not less than six months, and must be treatment:

(a) as a resident in such institution or place as may be specified in the order,
(b) as a non-resident in or at such institution or place, and at such intervals, as may be so specified, or
(c) by or under the direction of such person having the necessary qualification or experience as may be specified,

but the nature of the treatment must not be more precisely specified in the order.

(11) Supervision requirement

21–049 A "supervision requirement", in relation to a relevant order requires the offender during the relevant period, to attend appointments with the responsible officer or another person determined by him, at such time and place as may be determined. The purpose of the requirement is to promote the offender's rehabilitation. CJA 2003, s.213

"The relevant period" means, in relation to:

(1) a community order, the period for which the community order remains in force,
(2) a custody plus order (40–020), the licence period (as defined by s.181(3)(b)),
(3) an intermittent custody order (40–026), the licence periods (as defined by s.183(3)); and
(4) a suspended sentence order (40–080), the supervision period (as defined by s.189(l)(a)).

D. Requirements available in the case of offenders aged under 25

(11) Attendance centre requirement

21–050 An "attendance centre requirement", in relation to a relevant order, means a requirement that the offender attend at an attendance centre specified in the relevant order for such number of hours as may be specified, being in the aggregate: CJA 2003, s.214

(1) not less than 12; nor
(2) more than 36.

The judge may not impose an attendance centre requirement unless he is satisfied that the centre to be specified in it is reasonably accessible to the offender concerned, having regard to the means of access available to him and any other circumstances.

The first time at which the offender is required to attend at the attendance centre is a time notified to him by the responsible officer; the subsequent hours are fixed by the officer in charge of the centre, having regard to the offender's circumstances.

An offender may not be required under this section to attend at an attendance centre on more than one occasion on any day, or for more than three hours on any occasion.

(12) Electronic monitoring requirement

21–051 An electronic monitoring requirement, in relation to a relevant order, is a requirement for securing the electronic monitoring of the offender's compliance with other requirements imposed by the order during a period specified in the order, or determined by the responsible officer in accordance with the relevant order. CJA 2003, s.215

Electronic monitoring should be used with the primary purpose of promoting and monitoring compliance with other requirements, in circumstances where the punishment of the offender and/or the need to safeguard the public and prevent re-offending are the most important concerns. SGC 2, 2.1.34

The responsible officer will, before the beginning of the period, notify the offender, the person responsible for the monitoring, and any person falling within (2) above, of the time when the period is to begin.

The judge may not include such a requirement in a relevant order unless the court has been notified by the Secretary of State that electronic monitoring arrangements are available in each relevant area; and is satisfied that the necessary provision for dealing with the offender can be made under the arrangements currently available.

Where:

(1) it is proposed to include in a relevant order such a requirement, but
(2) there is a person (other than the offender) without whose co-operation it will not be practicable to secure that the monitoring takes place, the requirement may *not* be included in the order without that person's consent.

A relevant order which includes an electronic monitoring requirement must include provision for making a person responsible for the monitoring.

21–052 An electronic monitoring requirement, in relation to a relevant order, is to secure by the electronic monitoring, the offender's compliance with other requirements imposed by the order during a period specified in the order, or determined by the responsible officer in accordance with the relevant order. CJA 2003, s.215

Where:

(1) it is proposed to include in a relevant order a requirement for securing electronic monitoring, but
(2) there is a person (other than the offender) without whose co-operation it will not be practicable to secure the monitoring,

the requirement may *not* be included in the order without that person's consent.

Electronic monitoring should be used with the primary purpose of promoting and monitoring compliance with other requirements, in circumstances where the punishment of the offender and/or the need to safeguard the public and prevent re-offending are the most important concerns. SGC 2.2.3.34

A relevant order which includes an "electronic monitoring requirement" must include provision for making a person responsible for the monitoring.

The responsible officer will, before the beginning of the period, notify the offender, the person responsible for the monitoring, and any person falling within (2) above, of the time when the period is to begin.

E. Youth Community Orders

21–053 The new community order under CJA 2003, s.177 will not be available for 16 and 17 year old offenders until April 4, 2007. Until that time such offenders will continue to be dealt with under PCC(S)A 2000, Pt 4, Ch.1. For offenders aged 18 and above the new community order under CJA 2003, s.177 is appropriate.

A "youth community order" for the purposes of PCC(S)A 2000, means any of the following orders:

(1) a curfew order;
(2) an exclusion order;
(3) an attendance centre order;
(4) supervision order;
(5) an action plan order.

A "community sentence" means a sentence which consists of or includes: PCC(S)A 2000, s.33; CJA 2003, s.304, Sch.32, Pt 1, para.95

(a) a community order under CJA 2003, s.177, or
(b) one or more youth community orders.

Electronic monitoring

21–054 Where the judge is informed that monitoring arrangements are available, and that provision can be made under those arrangements, a youth community order may include requirements for securing the electronic monitoring of the offender's compliance with the order. PCC(S)A 2000, s.36B; CJCSA 2000, s.52; CJA 2003, s.304, Sch.32, Pt 1, para.96

However, where there is a person other than the offender without whose co-operation the order will not be practicable, the order must not be made without that person's consent. Further, a requirement must not be included where one is already included, and the order must make an appropriate person responsible for monitoring the requirement.

1. Curfew order

21–055 Where notified that such arrangements are available, the judge, may, subject to the general restrictions on the making of cornmunity orders (see above) make a curfew order, that is to say an order requiring the offender to remain, for specified periods, at a specified place, in respect of an offender aged under 16. PCC(S)A 2000, ss.37(1), (2), 59(3); CJA 2003, s.30, Sch.32, Pt 1, para.97

Preconditions for curfew order

21–056 Before making such an order, the judge will need to: PCC(S)A 2000, s.37(8)–(11); CJCSA 2000, Sch.7, para.162

(1) obtain and consider information about the place proposed to be specified in the order, including information as to the attitude of persons likely to be affected by the enforced presence of the offender there;
(2) obtain and consider a report about his family circumstances and the likely effect of such an order on those circumstances; and
(3) explain to the offender in ordinary language:
  (a) the effect of the order, including any additional requirements relating to electronic monitoring (see below);
  (b) the consequences which may follow under Pt II of Sch.3 should he fail to comply with any of the requirements; and
  (c) that the court has power to review the order on the application of either the offender or the "responsible officer", i.e. the person responsible for monitoring the offender's whereabouts during the specified curfew periods.

A copy of the order will be given to the offender, and to the responsible officer.

Requirements of the order

21–057 An order may specify different places or different periods for different days, but may not specify: PCC(S)A 2000, s.37(3)(4)(5)

(1) periods which fall outside the period of six months beginning with the day on which it is made (three months in

the case of an offender under 16 in respect of an offence committed after January 1, 1998); or

(2) periods of less than two hours or more than 12 hours in any one day.

As far as practicable the requirements of the curfew must be such as to avoid:

(a) any conflict with the offender's religious beliefs or with the requirements of any other community orders to which he may be subject; and
(b) interference with the times, if any, at which he normally works or attends school or other educational establishment.

Amendment, revocation and breach

21–058 PCC(S)A 2000, Sch.3 has effect in relation to the amendment and revocation of orders, and also for dealing with failure to comply with its requirements (see 14 BREACH, AMENDMENT AND REVOCATION).

2. Exclusion orders

21–059 When notified that arrangements for monitoring the offender's whereabouts are available, the judge may, subject to the general restrictions on the making of community orders (see 21–003) make, in respect of an offender aged under 16, an exclusion order, that is to say an order prohibiting him from entering a specified place or area for a specified period not exceeding three months. PCC(S)A 2000, ss.40A(1)–(6), (12); CJCSA 2000, s.46; CJA 2003, s.304, Sch.3, para.100

The order may:

(1) specify different places or areas for different periods or days; and
(2) provide for the prohibition to operate only during the periods specified in the order.

The order must include provision for making a person responsible for monitoring the offender's whereabouts during the periods when the prohibition operates.

Preconditions to making an order

21–060 Before making such an order, the judge must obtain and consider information about the offender's family circumstances and the likely effect of such an order on those cirumstances. PCC(S)A 2000, s.40A(4)(9); CJCSA 2000, s.46

The requirements of an order should be, as far as practicable, such as to avoid any conflict with the offender's religious belief and with the requirements of any other community order to which he is subject, also any interference with the times, if any, at which he normally works or attends school or any other educational establishment.

A copy of the order will be given to the offender and to the responsible officer, and any information about the order which the court considers it appropriate for him to have will be given to any affected person. PCC(S)A 2000, s.40B; CJCSA 2000, s.46

Amendment, revocation and breach

21–061 Schedule 3 to the Act (see 14 BREACH, AMENDMENT AND REVOCATION) has effect in relation to the amendment and revocation of such orders, and also deals with failure to comply with an order. PCC(S)A 2000, s.40B; CJCSA 2000, s.46

3. Attendance centre order

21–062 An attendance centre order may be made where: PCC(S)A 2000, s.60; CJA 2003, s.304, Sch.32, Pt 1, para.102

(1) subject to the general restrictions on the making of community orders (see 21–003) an offender aged under 16 is convicted of an offence punishable with imprisonment; or
(2) the court has power, but for s.89 (restrictions on the imprisonment of young offenders and defaulters) to commit a person aged under 16 to prison in default of payment of any sum of money or for failing to do or abstain from doing anything required to be done or left undone.

Prerequisites of order

21–063 Before an order can be made, the judge must be satisfied that: PCC(S)A 2000, s.60(1), (6)

(1) a centre is available for the reception of persons of this description; and
(2) the centre to be specified is readily accessible to him, having regard to his age, means of access and other circumstances.

Number of hours

21–064 In regard to the aggregate number of hours for which the offender may be required to attend: PCC(S)A 2000, s.60(3)(4)(7)

(1) the minimum is 12, except where the offender is under 14, and the court considers that to be excessive having regard to his age and other circumstances; (10); CJA 2003, s.304, Sch.32, Pt 1, para.102

(2) the maximum is 12 except where the judge is of opinion, having regard to all the circumstances, that 12 hours would be inadequate, in which case, the aggregate must not exceed 24,

and it should be, as far as possible, such as to avoid conflict with his religious beliefs, the requirements of any other community order to which he is subject, and any interference with the hours he normally works, or attends school, etc.

The offender must not be required to attend on more than one occasion on any day or for more than three hours on any occasion.

Two or more orders

21–065 There is nothing to prevent the court making a further order PCC(S)A 2000, while a previous one is still running, and the hours specified in s.69(5) the subsequent order may be determined without regard to the number specified in the previous order, or to the fact that the order is still in effect.

Administrative provisions

21–066 The Crown Court officer is responsible for delivering or sending a copy of the order to the offender and the officer in charge of the centre, and the time of first attendance will be specified in the order. Subsequent times will be fixed by the officer in charge, avoiding interference, where practicable, with the offender's school or working hours. PCC(S)A 2000, s.60(8)(9)(11)

Order made on appeal

21–067 Where an order is made on appeal, it is deemed, if it was made on an appeal brought from a magistrates' court to have been made by that court, and if it was made on appeal from the Crown Court or the CACD, to have been made by the Crown Court. PCC(S)A 2000, Sch.5, para.6

Defaulters: Payment of sum due

21–068 Where a defaulter has been ordered to attend an attendance centre in default of payment of a sum of money, then, on payment of: PCC(S)A 2000, s.60(12)

(1) the whole sum to any person authorised to receive it, the order will cease to have effect;

(2) part of the sum to such person, the total number of hours for which the defaulter is required to attend will be proportionately reduced.

4. Supervision orders

21–069 The most common use of a supervision order in the Crown Court is where an offender under 16 is facing really serious charges, but a package has been put together by the Youth Justice Service which the judge feels has a chance of success and would justify him in not passing what would otherwise have been a custodial sentence.

Making an order

21–070 A supervision order may be made by the Crown Court where: PCC(S)A 2000, s.63(1)(2)(5); CJA 2003, s.304, Sch.32, Pt 1, para.103

(1) a person aged under 16 is found guilty of an offence,
(2) the general restrictions on making community orders are fulfilled, and
(3) the judge is satisfied that the offender will reside in a local authority area (he may be required to reside there under Sch.6, para.l),

placing the offender under the supervision of a local authority designated by the order, an officer of a local probation board or a member of a youth offending team for a period specified in the order.

The order, unless it has been previously revoked, ceases to have effect at the end of the period of three years, or such shorter period as may be specified in it, beginning with the date on which it was made. PCC(S)A 2000, s.63(7)

In making a supervision order, the Crown Court has power to discharge any other such order made by any court.

Requirements

21–071 The requirements which may be included in such an order are set out in PCC(S)A 2000, Sch.6, as amended by CJA 2003, s.304, Sch.32, para.127 and include requirements as to: PCC(S)A 2000, s.63, Sch.6, para.2

(a) residence with a named individual (para.1);
(b) complying with the directions of the supervisor (para.2);
(c) activities, reparation and night restrictions (paras 3, 4);
(d) living in local authority accommodation (para.5);

(e) living with local authority foster-parents;
(f) treatment for mental condition (para.6);
(g) drug testing and treatment (para.6A);
(h) education (para.7).

Provided that as to (c) above, the judge:

(i) has first consulted the supervisor as to the offender's circumstances and the feasibility of securing compliance with the requirements;
(ii) considers the requirements necessary for securing the good conduct of the supervised person or for preventing repetition by him of the same offence or the commission of other offences; and
(iii) if the offender is aged under 16, he has obtained and considered information about his family circumstances and the likely effect of the requirements on such circumstances.

An order may also empower the supervisor to give directions requiring the supervised person to submit to certain requirements.

Directions by supervisor

21–072 An order may empower the supervisor to give directions requiring the offender:

(1) to live at a specified place or places for a specified period or to reside with a named individual who agrees to this requirement;
(2) to present himself to specified persons on dates and at places also specified; and
(3) to participate in specified activities.

A supervisor has a discretion as to how to apply the directions contained in the order.

The total number of days to be spent by the supervised person in complying with directions under the order must not exceed 90 days or such lesser number as specified in the order.

Night restriction order; activities

21–073 The order may require a supervised person: PCC(S)A 2000, s.63, Sch.6, paras 3, 4

(1) to remain for specified periods between 6pm and 6am at a place or places specified in the order. A "night restriction order" of this nature may not, however, be for longer than 10 hours, last for longer than 30 days, nor relate to

any day more than three months from the date of the order; it should normally specify the supervised person's place of residence and does not prevent his leaving if accompanied by his parent, guardian, supervisor or person specified by the court;

(2) to refrain from participating in specified activities.

Local authority accommodation

21–074 Where a supervision order has previously been made in respect of the child or young person which included a night restriction order, a prohibited activities order or a residence order, and: PCC(S)A 2000, s.63, Sch.6, para.5

(1) he is found guilty of an offence:
  (a) committed while that order was in force;
  (b) punishable in the case of an adult with imprisonment; and
  (c) which, in the opinion of the judge, is serious, and,
(2) the judge is satisfied that the behaviour which constituted the offence was due, to a significant extent, to the circumstances in which he was living (unless the original supervision order contained a residence requirement),

then, subject to a prior consultation with the local authority, the order may impose a requirement that the child or young person shall live for a specified period, not exceeding three months, in local authority accommodation.

Local authority foster parents

21–075 Where certain conditions are satisfied, and this provision comes into effect a supervision order will be able to impose a foster parent residence requirement that the offender live for a specified period not exceeding 12 months, with a local authority foster parent. PCC(S)A 2000, s.63, Sch.6, para.5A; ASBA 2003, s.88, Sch.2, para.4(1)(5)

These conditions are that:

(a) the offence is punishable with imprisonment in the case of an offenders aged 18 or over;
(b) the offence, or the combination of the offence and one or more offences associated with it, was so serious that a custodial sentence would not be appropriate (or, where the offender is aged 10 or 11, would not be appropriate if the offender were aged 12 or over); and
(c) the court is satisfied that—
  (i) the behaviour which constituted the offence was due to a significant extent to the circumstances in which the offender was living, and

(ii) the imposition of a foster parent residence requirement will assist his rehabilitation.

The order must designate the local authority, which will be the authority in whose area the offender resides, which is to place him with foster parents.

Such a requirement order must not be imposed unless the court has been notified by the Home Secretary that arrangements for implementing such a requirement are available in the area of the designated authority, and the designated authority has been consulted.

The usual requirements as to legal representation apply.

If at any time while a supervision order imposing a foster parent residence requirement is in force, the supervisor notifies the offender.

Requirement as to mental treatment

21–076 A requirement as to mental treatment may be included in a supervision order if the judge is satisfied on the evidence of a medical practitioner approved for the purposes of MHA 1983, s.12, that the mental condition of the supervised person requires and may be susceptible to treatment but does not warrant a hospital order.

PCC(S)A 2000, s.63, Sch.6, para.6

Requirement as to drug treatment and testing

21–077 A requirement as to drug treatment and testing may be included where the judge is satisfied that the offender is dependent on, or has a propensity to misuse drugs which is such as requires and may be susceptible of treatment.

PCC(S)A 2000, s.63, Sch.6, para.6A; CJA 2003, s.279, Sch.24, para.2

The order may require the offender for a specified period to submit to treatment by or under the direction of a person having the necessary qualifications and experience with a view to the reduction or elimination of the offender's dependency on, or propensity to misuse drugs. The staturory reqirements are considered in *R.* (*Inner London Probation Service v Tower Bridge MC* [2002] 1 Cr.App.R.(S.) 43. See also *R. v Woods & Collins* [2005] Crim.L.R.982.

An order may only be made on the recommendation of an officer of a local probation board, or a member of a youth offending team, and in the case of an offender aged 14 or over, only with his consent.

An order which includes such a requirement, may also include a testing requirement, for the purpose of ascertaining whether the offender has any drug in his body during the treatment period.

Requirement as to education

21–078 Such a requirement may, subject to consultation with the supervisor and the local authority, be included in an order if the judge considers it necessary for securing the good conduct of the supervised person or to prevent him from re-offending. PCC(S)A 2000, s.63, Sch.6, para.7

Breaches, variation and discharge

21–079 Powers to deal with breaches of the requirements of, to vary, and, to discharge, supervision orders are exercised normally by youth courts and other magistrates' courts. These powers extend to resentencing, but not to detention in a young offenders' institution. PCC(S)A 2000, s.65, Sch.7, para.2

Where, however, a supervised person is brought before the Crown Court and it is proved to the satisfaction of the court that he has failed to comply with a requirement in an order made by that court, the judge may revoke the order and deal with him for the offence in respect of which the order was made in any manner in which it could have dealt with him for that offence if it had not made the order.

Order made on appeal

21–080 Where an order is made on appeal, it is deemed, if it was made on an appeal brought from a magistrates' court to have been made by that court, and if it was made by the Crown Court or to the CACD to have been made by the Crown Court. PCC(S)A 2000, s.65, Sch.7, para.28

5. Action plan orders

21–081 Where a person aged under 18 is convicted of an offence other than one for which the sentence is fixed by law, the judge may if he is of opinion that it is desirable to do so in the interests of securing the offender's rehabilitation, or of preventing the commission by him of further offences, and provided: PCC(S)A 2000, s.69(1)(2)

(1) the court has been informed by the Home Secretary that arrangements for implementing such orders are available in the area; and
(2) the offender is not already the subject of such an order; and
(3) the judge does not propose to pass a custodial sentence on him, or to make a community order in respect of him, he may make an action plan order:
    (a) requiring the offender, for a period of three months beginning with the date of the order to comply with a series of requirements with respect to his actions and whereabouts;

(b) naming the petty session area in which it appears that the offender resides or will reside; and
(c) placing him under the supervision for that period of an officer of a local probation board, a local authority social worker or a member of a youth offending team; and
(d) requiring him to comply with any directions given by that officer with a view to the implementation of the plan.

The general restrictions governing the making of community orders apply (see above, 21–003).

Before making an order

21–082 Before making an order, the judge must obtain and consider a report from an officer of a local probation board, local authority social worker or member of a youth offending team indicating: PCC(S)A 2000, s.69(6)

(1) the requirements proposed to be included in the order;
(2) the benefits to the offender that the proposed requirements are designed to achieve;
(3) the attitude of the offender's parent or guardian to the proposed requirements; and
(4) in the case of an offender under the age of 16 information about his family circumstances and the likely effect of the order on those circumstances.

Requirements of the order

21–083 The requirements included in an order (or the directions given by the responsible officer), may require the offender to do all or any of the following: PCC(S)A 2000, s.70; CJA 2003, s.304, Sch.32, para.105

(1) participate in specified activities;
(2) present himself to specified persons at specified times and places;
(3) in a case where the offence committed by the offender is punishable with imprisonment in the case of an adult, attend for specified hours at an attendance centre;
(4) stay away from specified places;
(5) comply with specified arrangements for his education;
(6) make reparation to specified persons identified by the court as victims of the offence or as affected by it (provided that person consents to reparation being made) or to the community at large; and

(7) attend at subsequent hearings fixed by the court under s.71, below.

A drug treatment and testing requirement may be included where the judge is satisfied that the offender is dependent on, or has a propensity to misuse drugs which is such as requires and, may be susceptible of treatment. PCC(S)A 2000, s.70(4B)(4C); CJA 2003, s.279, Sch.24, para.1

The order may require the offender for a specified period to submit to treatment by or under the direction of a person having the necessary qualifications and experience with a view to the reduction or elimination of the offender's dependency on, or propensity to misuse drugs.

The required treatment must be treatment as a:

(a) resident patient in such institution or place as may be specified in the order, or
(b) non-resident at such institution or place, and at such intervals as may be specified, but otherwise the nature of the treatment need not be further specified in the order.

21–084 An order may only be made:

(1) where the judge is satisfied that arrangements have been made or can be made for the treatment intended to be specified in the order (including arrangements for the offender's reception in the case of resident treatment);
(2) the requirement has been recommended to the court as suitable for the offender by an officer of a local probation board, or a member of a youth offending team; and
(3) in the case of an offender aged 14 or over, he has consented to its inclusion.

An order which includes such a requirement, may also include a testing requirement, for the purpose of ascertaining whether the offender has any drug in his body during the treatment period, but again, only where the judge has been notified that such arrangements are in force, and, in the case of an offender aged 14 or over he has consented to its inclusion. This order must specify for each month the minimum number of occasions on which samples are to be provided. The order must provide for the results to be communicated to the responsible officer. PCC(S)A 2000, ss.70(4D)–(4H); CJA 2003, s.279, Sch.24, para.1

Subsequent hearings

21–085 Immediately after making an order, the judge may: PCC(S)A 2000, s.71

(1) fix a further hearing, for a date not more than 21 days after the making of the order; and

(2) direct the responsible officer to make, at that hearing, a report as to the effectiveness of the order and the extent to which it has been implemented.

At that hearing the judge will consider the report, and may, on the application either of the responsible officer or the offender, vary the order by cancelling any provision of it, or by inserting into it (either in addition to or in substitution for any of its provisions) any provision that could have been inserted in it originally.

Failure to comply

21–086 PCC(S)A 2000, Sch.8 has effect for dealing with failure to comply with any requirement, and for varying or revoking any order, see 14 BREACH, AMENDMENT AND REVOCATION.

22 COMPANY OFFICER'S DISQUALIFICATION

22–001 An offender convicted before the Crown Court of: CDDA 1986, ss.1, 2; IA 2000, ss.5, 8, Sch.4, para.2

(1) an indictable offence (IA 1978, Sch.1);
(2) in connection with the promotion, formation, management or liquidation of a company; or
(3) with the receivership or management of a company's property,

may be disqualified from being:

(a) a director, liquidator or manager of a company;
(b) a receiver or manager of a company's property; or,
(c) in any way, whether directly or indirectly, concerned, or taking part in, the promotion, formation or management of a company, without leave of the court, and may not act as an insolvency practitioner.

There is no jurisdiction to limit a disqualification to the holding of a directorship in a public company. The judge should make it clear that the order applies to *all* the categories (a)–(c) (*R. v Ward*, *R. v Howarth*, *The Times*, August 10, 2001).

Company Officer's Disqualification

Rationale behind disqualification

22–002 The rationale behind such an order is to protect the public from persons who, whether for reasons of dishonesty, naivety or incompetence, use or abuse their role as a company director to the detriment of the public (*R. v Millard* (1994) 15 Cr.App.R.(S.) 445; *R. v Edwards* (1998) 2 Cr.App.R.(S.) 213; *R. v Victory* (1999) 2 Cr.App.R.(S.) 102).

"Management of the company" defined

22–003 The words "management of the company" refer to the management of the company's affairs. There is no reason to differentiate between internal and external affairs (*R. v Corbin* (1984) 6 Cr.App.R.(S.) 17; *R. v Austen* (1985) 7 Cr.App.R.(S.) 214; *R. v Georgiou* (1988) 87 Cr.App.R. 207).

The correct test, in deciding whether an offence is in connection with the management of a company, is to decide:

(a) whether the offence has some relevant factual connection with the management,

(b) *not* whether it "relates to the management" *nor* whether it was committed "in the course of managing the company."

(*R. v Goodman* [1993] 2 All E.R. 789).

Terms and length of disqualification

22–004 The order must contain a prohibition in respect of *all* the functions referred to in the section (*R. v Cole and Others* [1998] B.C.L.C. 87). Periods of disqualification of:

(1) over ten years should be reserved for particularly serious cases, which may include those where there has been a previous disqualification;
(2) between six and ten years should be reserved for intermediate cases, and
(3) between two to five years may be imposed in cases which are not particularly serious.

(*R. v Millard* (1994) 15 Cr.App.R.(S.) 445).

A person acting in contravention of such an order is liable on conviction on indictment, to imprisonment for not more than two years or to a fine, or both. The period of disqualification should reflect the level of risk to the public.

Compensation coupled with disqualification

22–005 While the ordinary powers of the Crown Court to order compensation apply, where there are complex financial issues involved, it is probably undesirable to couple such an order with a disqualification of this kind (*R. v Holmes* (1992) 13 Cr.App.R.(S.) 29).

23 COMPENSATION

A. PCC(S)A 2000, s.130

General

23–001 In general, the proper forum in which to claim reparation for loss of, or damage to, property, or for injury to the person, is the High Court or a county court. Powers are, however, conferred on the Crown Court to order compensation in a criminal case, ensuring, so far as is possible, that the offender compensates the victim for his criminal actions, and to help the victim avoid the expense and inconvenience of resorting to civil litigation to recoup damages, but the superior courts have emphasised on a number of occasions, that an order:

(1) is not to enable the offender to "buy himself out" of the ordinary criminal penalty;
(2) is intended as a speedy way of dealing with simple cases in which no great amount is at stake; and
(3) should be made only in the plainest and most straightforward situations, and only where the offender has the means to pay (*Stamp v UDT* (1967) 131 J.P. 177; *R. v Ferguson* (1970) 54 Cr.App.R. 410; *R. v Daly* (1974) 58 Cr.App.R. 333; *R. v Kneeshaw* (1974) 58 Cr.App.R. 439; *R. v Inwood* (1974) 60 Cr.App.R. 70).

Compensation may sometimes be enforced without making a formal order, as where the judge insists on payment of compensation before proceeding to sentence, or where sentence is deferred (see 30 DEFERRING SENTENCE) with a view to the making of reparation.

A magistrates' court has no power to make an order when committing an offender to the Crown Court for sentence (*R. v Brogan* (1974) 60 Cr.App.R. 279).

Power to make order

23–002 Where a person is convicted of an offence, the judge may, subject to certain restrictions, make an order requiring him: PCC(S)A 2000, ss.130(1), (2); CJA 2003, s.304, Sch.32, Pt 1, para.117

(1) to pay compensation for any *personal injury*, *loss* or *damage* resulting from the offence, or any offence taken into consideration on sentence; or
(2) to make payments for funeral expenses or bereavement in respect of a death resulting from any such offence,

other than a death due to an accident arising out of the presence of a motor vehicle on a road, and that order may be made:

(a) in addition to, or in a case where the sentence is not fixed by law, or falls to be imposed under PCC(S)A 2000, ss.109 where appropriate, 110(2) or 111(2), FA 1968, s.51A(2) or CJA 2003, ss.225, 226, 227 or 228, instead of, dealing with him in any other way, and

(b) whether on application or otherwise.

If, on passing sentence, the judge does not make an order, where he is empowered to do so, he must give his reasons. PCC(S)A 2000, s.130(2)

As to compensation for serious default under PCA 2002, s.72 *et seq.*, see 23–028, below.

Definitions

23–003 "Personal injury" or "damage" include shock and anxiety directly occasioned by the offence (*Bond v Chief Constable of Kent* (1982) 4 Cr.App.R.(S.) 314). "Loss" includes the loss suffered by an innocent purchaser of stolen goods (*R. v Howell* (1978) 66 Cr.App.R. 179).

Offences taken into consideration; specimen charges

23–004 Where an offender is convicted on specimen charges, the amount of compensation which may be ordered is limited to that set out in the specimen charges (*R. v Crutchley and Tonks* (1994) 15 Cr.App.R.(S.) 627). The fact that an offender freely admits to having made away with a certain sum does not alter the position, and does not, without the proper procedure being followed (see 59 TICs), mean that those offences are being taken into consideration for that purpose (*R. v Hose* (1995) 16 Cr.App.R.(S.) 682, applying *DPP v Anderson* (1978) 67 Cr.App.R.185).

Damage: Theft Act cases

23–005 In the case of an offence under TA 1968, where the property is recovered, any damage to it occurring while it was out of the owner's possession is to be treated as having resulted from the offence, however and by whomsoever it was caused. If such property is not recovered, the presumption does not apply (*R. v Ahmad* (1992) 13 Cr.App.R.(S.) 212). PCC (S)A 2000, s.130 (5)

In a case of dishonest handling, where the goods are recovered, no order may be made in respect of their permanent loss (*R. v Tyce* (1994) 15 Cr.App.R.(S.) 415).

Road accidents

23–006 An order may only be made in respect of injury or loss or damage (other than that suffered by a person's dependants in consequence of his death) which was due to an accident arising out of the presence of a motor vehicle on a road, if it is in respect of:

PCC(S)A 2000, s.130(6)(7)(8)

(1) damage which is treated under s.130(5) as resulting from an offence under the TA 1968; or
(2) loss or damage for which:
   (a) the offender is uninsured in relation to the use of the vehicle (see *McDermott v DPP* [1997] R.T.R. 474); and
   (b) compensation is not payable under any arrangements to which the Secretary of State is a party.

Where an order is made in respect of such injury, loss or damage, the amount to be paid may include an amount representing the whole or part of any loss of, or reduction in, preferential rates of insurance attributable to the accident.

Where sums are payable by the Motor Insurers' Bureau (MIB), the compensation payable is limited to the amount payable by MIB — i.e. £175 (*DPP v Scott* (1995) 16 Cr.App.R.(S.) 292).

A vehicle exempted from insurance under RTA 1988, s.144, is not "uninsured" for this purpose, nor is a driver uninsured who merely refuses to produce details, but is, in fact, covered (*McDermott v DPP* [1997] R.T.R. 474).

Funeral expenses

23–007 Where an order is made in respect of funeral expenses, it may be made for the benefit of any person who incurred the expense, but an order in respect of bereavement may be made only for the benefit of a person for whose benefit a claim for damages for bereavement could be made under the Fatal Accidents Act 1976, s.1A.

PCC(S)A 2000, s.130(9)(10)

The amount of compensation must not exceed that specified in s.1A(3) of that Act, namely, £3,500.

Criminal Injuries Compensation Board

23–008 Compensation ordered by a criminal court is completely different from the compensation which victims of crime may receive from the Criminal Injuries Compensation Board under CJA 1988, Pt VII. Victims may apply to the Board and receive compensation whether or not the offender is detected or convicted. No award is made unless the appropriate amount exceeds £1,000.

The fact that the victim may be able to get compensation from the Board should not prevent the court making an order in a proper case. Guidelines have been prepared by the Board on the range of compensation which might be payable, and are attached to Home Office Circular 85/1988, but these have not been approved by the Lord Chief Justice.

Approach to making an order

23–009 Before making an order, the judge must:

(1) satisfy himself that injury, loss or damage has resulted from the offence of which the offender has been convicted or is having taken into consideration on sentence;
(2) settle the amount of the injury, loss or damage which the offender may be required to pay; and
(3) consider the means of the offender, giving him or his counsel the opportunity to be heard.

General principles

23–010 The general principles to be followed in making an order were restated in *R. v Miller* (1976) 68 Cr.App.R. 56. Those still relevant are:

(1) first and foremost, that an order should be made only where the legal position is clear;
(2) the order must be precisely drawn and must be related to an offence of which the offender has been convicted, or which he has agreed to have taken into consideration;
(3) the judge must have regard to the offender's means;
(4) the order ought not to be oppressive; and
(5) the fact that the victim to whom compensation is payable has since died does not mean that an order is inappropriate (*Holt v DPP* (1996) 2 Cr.App.R.(S.) 314).

Causation

23–011 There must be a causal connection between the offence committed and the damage done or injury caused. The existence of civil liability is not a prerequisite to making an order in criminal proceedings (*R. v Chappell* (1984) 6 Cr.App.R.(S.) 342). The judge needs to ask himself whether loss or damage can fairly be said to have resulted to anyone from the offence (*R. v Rowiston* (1982) 4 Cr.App.R.(S.) 85, and see *R. v Taylor* (1994) 14 Cr.App.R.(S.) 276; *R. v Guertjens* (1992) 14 Cr.App.R.(S.) 280; *R. v Denness* [1996] 1 Cr.App.R.(S.) 159).

Real issue as to liability

23–012 Where there is a real issue as to the offender's liability to pay compensation, whether in respect of specific offences or specific victims, the question cannot be determined by argument, and the judge will need to hear evidence. It is for the Crown to put forward evidence, so that the offender may have an opportunity to test the basis on which the order is to be made (*R. v Horsham JJ. Ex p. Richards* (1985) 7 Cr.App.R.(S.) 158; *R. v Halliwell* (1991) 12 Cr.App.R (S.) 692).

There are cases in which the issue is unclear, as where, e.g.:

(a) up-to-date medical reports, photographs, etc., need to be provided (*R. v Cooper* (1982 Cr.App.R.(S.) 55);
(b) questions of loss of use arise, which in civil cases are "notoriously open to argument" (*R. v Donovan* (1981) 3 Cr.App.R.(S.) 192); or
(c) where matters of set-off and contribution arise in social security benefit frauds (*Hyde v Emery* (1984) 6 Cr.App.R.(S.) 206),

and such cases should generally be left to the civil courts or the executive to deal with.

A compensation order is not intended to be a precise evaluation of loss, such as takes place in a civil court when damages are awarded. The power to award compensation is a fairly blunt instrument. The remedy for the victim is intended to be speedy, efficacious and cost free (*R. v Williams* [2001] Cr.App.R.(S.) 500).

The amount of compensation payable

23–013 The precise extent of the injury, loss or damage does not need to be established by evidence, but there should be some basis of evidence on which the court can consider what sum is appropriate.

The amount of the compensation must be such as the judge considers appropriate, having regard to the evidence, and to any representations made by, or on behalf of, the offender or the prosecutor. PCC(S)A 2000, s.130(4)

A sum may be added by way of interest equivalent to what the victim would be likely to recover if he proved his claim in the civil courts (*R. v Schofield* (1978) 67 Cr.App.R. 282).

Where no sufficient information is available, or the evidence is unclear, the judge may adjourn until that information is to hand.

The amount ought, in general, to be limited to the judge's assessment of the amount that might have been recovered in a civil action (*R. v Gateway Foodmarkets Ltd* [1997] 2 Cr.App.R. 40).

Offender's means

23–014 Once the judge is satisfied that injury, loss or damage of a certain amount has resulted, he is required to consider the means of the offender before deciding what sum is appropriate.

The policy of making a compensation order is subject to the overriding limitations of:

(1) PCC(S)A 2000, s.130(11) which requires the judge to have regard to the means of the offender, in so far as they are known to the court, both in deciding *whether* to make an order, and in determining the amount; and
(2) the principle set out in *R. v Webb & Davis* (1979) 1 Cr.App.R.(S.) 16 that an order should not be made in such an amount that the offender will have no prospect of paying it within the foreseeable future (*R. v Bradburn* (1973) 57 Cr.App.R. 948; *R. v Bagga* (1989) 11 Cr.App.R.(S.) 497; *R. v Olliver* (1989) 11 Cr.App.R(S.) 10; *R. v Hewitt* (1990–91) 12 Cr.App.R.(S.) 466; *R. v Yehou* [1997] 2 Cr.App.R.(S.) 48).

Offender without means

23–015 It is the offender's duty to put information as to his means before the court and any attempt to mislead entitles the court to infer that he has assets (*R. v Bolden* (1987) 9 Cr.App.R.(S.) 83) and it is the duty of his representatives to verify the accuracy of any statements (*R. v Roberts* (1987) 9 Cr.App.R.(S.) 275). If he fraudulently claims to have means to pay, he has only himself to blame if an order is made (*R. v Dando* [1996] 1 Cr.App.R.(S.) 155).

Difficulties can be avoided if the judge indicates a provisional figure, and asks counsel for the defence to provide information as to the offender's means (*R. v Phillips* [1988] 10 Cr.App.R.(S.) 419).

Where the offender gives no evidence on the matter, and explanations given through counsel are "utterly unconvincing", the judge is entitled to act on the basis of any material put before him by the Crown, drawing appropriate inferences (*R. v Maisey & Houghton* [2001] 1 Cr.App.R.(S.) 98).

Where an offender is clearly without means, a compensation order should not be made on the basis of:

(1) a promise to pay; or

(2) offers by friends and relatives to pay (*R. v Hunt* [1983] Crim.L.R. 250; *R. v Webb* [1979] 1 Cr.App.R.(S.) 16); or
(3) the proposed future sale of the matrimonial home (*R. v Harrison* (1980) 2 Cr.App.R.(S.) 313; *R. v Blackmore* (1984) 6 Cr.App.R.(S.) 244; *R. v Butt* (1986) 8 Cr.App.R.(S.) 216; *R. v Hackett* (1988) 10 Cr.App.R.(S.) 388), but

it is not unreasonable to require the offender to sell other items of property to enable him to pay the compensation (*R. v Workman* (1981) 3 Cr.App.R.(S.) 318), provided the court takes steps to ascertain their value (*R. v Chambers* (1981) 3 Cr.App.R.(S.) 318).

Offender sentenced to custodial sentence

23–016 If a victim is entitled to compensation, an order obviates the necessity for civil proceedings. There is no principle that an order should *not* be made against a person upon whom a custodial sentence is imposed, provided that the judge bears in mind that:

(1) a custodial sentence will deprive the offender of his earning power; and
(2) it may make it difficult for him to find work when he is released; and
(3) by the time he came out he might be in financial difficulty; but

if the offender has sufficient assets, or will have earning capacity upon his release it will often be appropriate to make such an order in such a case (*R. v Love* [1999] 1 Cr.App.R.(S.) 75, *R. v Jorge* [1999] 2 Cr.App.R.(S.) 1).

Compensation preferred to fine

23–017 Where the judge considers it appropriate both: PCC(S)A 2000, s.130(12)

(1) to impose a fine, and
(2) to make a compensation order, but
(3) the offender has insufficient means to satisfy both an appropriate fine and appropriate compensation,

preference must be given to compensation, although a fine may be imposed as well.

Compensation has priority over confiscation

23–018 While there is no objection to the judge imposing both a confiscation order (see 24 CONFISCATION ORDERS)

Compensation

and a compensation order under this section where the amount that may be realised is sufficient, the courts should always be at pains to ensure that so far as possible the victim is compensated, and compensation should be the first priority: *R. v Mitchell* [2001] Crim.L.R. 239.

Payment by parent or guardian

23–019 Where the offender is a juvenile, the judge *must* order his parent or guardian to pay the order, unless he is satisfied that: PCC(S)A 2000, s.137

(1) the parent or guardian cannot be found; or
(2) it would be unreasonable to so order, having regard to the circumstances of the case.

Where the offender has reached the age of 16, this provision has effect as if, instead of imposing a duty on a parent or guardian to pay, it confers a power on the court to make an order. In such a procedure it is the parent or guardian's means which need to be taken into account, not those of the juvenile. (See further 19 CHILDREN AND YOUNG PERSONS.)

Form of order:(1) joint orders

23–020 Where an offender is convicted of a number of offences:

(1) and a number of different victims are involved, a separate order must be made in respect of each offence, in respect of each amount (*R. v Oddy* (1974) 138 J.P. 515; *R. v Inwood* (1974) 60 Cr.App.R. 70);
(2) where there is only one victim, but several offences, one compendious order covering all the amounts, while not desirable, is not objectionable (*R. v Wharton* [1976] Crim.L.R. 320);
(3) where the offender's means are insufficient to meet claims by a number of victims, the amount of any compensation ordered should generally be apportioned pro rata among them, but there may be cases where there are good reasons for departing from this general rule (*R. v Amey* (1983) 147 J.P. 124);
(4) it is technically permissible, though undesirable, to make a joint order against two or more offenders; a separate order should be made in respect of each offender.

Form of order: (2) joint orders; several offenders

23–021 An order is not an additional penalty, which gives rise to adjustment of sentence or to claims of disparity. An order may be made against one or more co-offenders who have assets, and yet not against a third who has none (*R. v Love* [1999] 1 Cr.App.R.(S.) 75).

Where two or more offenders are charged jointly and one claimant establishes a claim against them with regard to one item, each ought, in general, to be ordered to pay in equal proportions, unless one of them is shown to be more directly responsible for the offence, or their ability to pay is markedly different (*R. v Grundy & Moorhouse* [1974] 1 W.L.R. 139).

Order made on appeal

23–022 Where an order is made on appeal, it is deemed, if it was made on an appeal brought from magistrates' court to have been made by that court, and if it was made on appeal from the Crown Court or the CACD, to have been made by the Crown Court. PCC(S)A 2000, s.133(5)

Enforcement of orders

23–023 In general, compensation is treated in the same way, for the purposes of enforcement, as a fine (see 36 FINES AND ENFORCEMENT). As with fines and other money payments due to the court, there is power to allow time for payment, or to order payment by instalments.

The superior courts have said that:

(1) an order ought to be sharp in its effect and not protracted by small amounts over a long period (*R. v Bradhurn* (1973) 57 Cr.App.R. 948; *R. v Daly* (1974) 58 Cr.App.R. 333);

(2) where the offender is sentenced at the same time to a custodial term, the judge should direct the first of any instalments to be paid within a specified time of his release (*R. v Bradburn* (1973) 57 Cr.App.R. 948).

Despite a number of decisions to the contrary, the Court of Appeal said in *R. v Olliver* (1989) 11 Cr.App.R.(S.) 10, that there is no reason in principle why an order to pay a fine by instalments should not extend beyond a period of 12 months, even to a period of two or three years.

As to the functions and powers of the Assets Recovery Agency in respect of the proceeds of crime, see 24–005, below.

No default sentence

23–024 The Crown Court, while it may allow time to pay, and payment of compensation by instalments, has no power to impose a default sentence unless: AJA 1970, s.41(8), Sch.9; PCC(S)A 2000, s.165, Sch.9, para.43

(1) the order is for an amount of £20,000 or more; and
(2) the judge considers that the maximum default term of 12 months available to the collecting magistrates' court (under MCA 1980, Sch.4) is inadequate,

in which case he may order a longer period up to the maximum default term for a fine in the equivalent amount.

Payment under order

23–025 The person in whose favour a compensation order is made is not entitled to receive any sum(s) due to him until the possibility of an appeal on which the order could be varied or set aside has expired, though the power of the Crown Court to give leave to appeal out of time is to be disregarded. PCC(S)A 2000, s.132(1)(3)(5)

Where an order is made in respect of an offence taken into consideration on sentence, that order ceases to have effect if the offender successfully appeals against his conviction for the substantive offence(s), or if the CACD annulls the order.

An offender may appeal against an order as if it were part of the sentence imposed in respect of the offence(s) of which he was convicted.

Compensation out of forfeited property

23–026 Where the court makes an order under PCC(S)A 2000, s.143 (see 38 FORFEITURE, RESTITUTION AND AWARDS) in a case where: PCC(S)A 2000, s.145

(1) the offender has been convicted of an offence which has resulted in a person suffering personal injury, loss or damage; or
(2) any such offence is taken into consideration on sentence; and
(3) the judge is satisfied that, but for the inadequacy of the offender's means, it would have made a compensation order under which he would have been required to pay compensation of an amount not less than a specified amount,

he may also order that any proceeds which arise from the disposal of the property, and which do not exceed the sum specified, be paid to that person.

Such an order will not be effective:

(a) before the expiration of six months from the date on which the forfeiture order was made; or
(b) if a successful application is made under s.1(1) of the Police (Property) Act 1897.

As to the position in relation to a confiscation order made under PCA 2002, Pt 1, see 24 CONFISCATION ORDERS.

Review of order

23–027 At any time before the offender has paid into court the whole amount of any order made, and once there is no further possibility of an appeal, the court responsible for enforcing the order may, on the application of the offender, either discharge or reduce the amount remaining to be paid under the order if it appears that: PCC(S)A 2000, s.133; PCA 2002, s.456, Sch.11, para.37

(1) the injury, loss or damage in respect of which it was made has been held in civil proceedings to be less than it was taken to be for the purposes of the order; or
(2) where the order is in respect of the loss of property, the property has been recovered by the victim; or
(3) the offender's means are insufficient to satisfy in full the compensation order and any confiscation order made in the same proceedings; or
(4) the offender has suffered a substantial reduction in his means which was not expected at the time the order was made, and that they are unlikely to increase for a considerable period (*R. v Palmer* (1994) 15 Cr.App.R.(S.) 550),

provided the consent of a judge of the Crown Court has been obtained.

B. Compensation for serious default: PCA 2002

23–028 PCA 2002 provides for compensation to be paid to a person whose property has been affected by the enforcement of the confiscation legislation. PCA 2002, ss.72(1)–(8)

A judge of the Crown Court may order the payment of such compensation as he believes just:

(1) where, but only where:
  (a) a criminal investigation has been started with regard to an offence and proceedings are not started for the offence; or
  (b) proceedings for an offence are started against a person and:
    (i) they do not result in his conviction for the offence, or
    (ii) he is convicted of the offence but the conviction is quashed or he is pardoned in respect of it; and

Compensation

(2) where (1)(a), above, applies:
   (a) in the criminal investigation there has been a serious default by a person mentioned in subs.(9), and
   (b) the investigation would not have continued if the default had not occurred; and
(3) where (1)(b), above, applies, and
   (a) in the criminal investigation with regard to the offence or in its prosecution there has been a serious default by a person who is mentioned in subs.(9), and
   (b) the proceedings would not have been started or continued if the default had not occurred; and
(4) an application is made by a person who held realisable property and has suffered loss in consequence of anything done in relation to it by or in pursuance of an order under Pt 2 of the Act.

Note that the offence referred to:

(i) in (1) above may be one of a number of offences with regard to which the investigation is started;
(ii) in (2) above may be one of a number of offences for which the proceedings are started.

Application is made in writing and may be supported by a witness statement. It must be lodged in the Crown Court, and served on both the person alleged to be in default and the person by whom the compensation would be payable under s.72(9)(a) (below), or if the compensation is payable out of a police fund under s.72(9)(a), the chief officer of the force concerned. R. 58.10

Source of payment

23–029 Compensation is payable to the applicant as follows. If the person in default was: PCA 2002, s.72(9); CRCA 2005, s.50, Sch.4, para.97

(1) a member, or was acting as a member, of a police force, the compensation is payable out of the police fund from which the expenses of that force are met;
(2) a member of the CPS or was acting on its behalf, the compensation is payable by the DPP;
(3) a member of the SFO, the compensation is payable by the Director of that Office;
(4) a member of, or acting on behalf of, the Revenue and Customs Prosecution Office, the compensation is payable by the DRCP.

Compensation on variation or discharge

23–030 Where the court varies a confiscation order under s.29 or discharges one under s.30, an application may be made to the PCA 2002, s.73

Crown Court by a person who held realisable property and has suffered loss as a result of the making of the order, and the judge may order the payment of such compensation as it believes is just, to the applicant, by the Lord Chancellor.

The application must be in writing, supported by a witness statement giving details of the order made under s.28, the variation or discharge under s.29 or s.30, the realisable property to which the application relates and the loss suffered by the applicant as a result of the making of the order.

These documents must be lodged with the Crown Court, and must be served on the prosecutor or on the Director, where he is appointed the enforcement authority, at least seven days before the date fixed for the hearing unless the Crown Court specifies a shorter period. R. 58.11

24 CONFISCATION ORDERS

Introduction

24–001 The duty of depriving an offender of any benefit he may have received from his crimes and, at the same time, depriving any other person of any benefit derived through the offender, is imposed, under PCA 2002, upon a judge of the Crown Court. The principal means of achieving that object is by a confiscation order. Such an order is made in addition to any other disposal, and does not prevent the judge dealing with the offender in any other way.

PCA 2002 is a consolidating Act; it replaces the dual schemes provided by DTA 1994 and CJA 1988, for the confiscation of the proceeds of drug trafficking and other major crime.

As to enforcement in different parts of the United Kingdom, see SI 2003/333, also rr.57.4–6.

The provisions of PCA 2002, Pt 2, are brought into effect by SI 2003/333, but those provisions relating to confiscation orders and absconding offenders have no effect where the offence or any of the offences was **committed before March 24, 2003** (PCA 2002 (Commencement No. 5 Transitional Provisions, Savings and Amendment) Order, (SI 2003/333)).

The judge **must** determine whether confiscation proceedings are to be held **before** he proceeds to sentence. PCA 2002, s.11

Date is of the essence

24–002 Different procedures apply depending on the date of the commission of the offence.

Thus in the case of:

(1) an **offence committed before November 1, 1995**, CJA 1988, s.71(as amended by CJA 1993 and CJPOA 1994) applies;
(2) **proceedings instituted** on or after February 3, 1995, where the offender was convicted of at least one offence committed before November 1, 1995, CJA 1988, s.71 (as amended by CJA 1993) applies;
(3) a **drug trafficking offence** committed on or before March 23, 2003 (whether the offender was convicted before the Crown Court or committed for sentence under PCC(S)A 2000, s.3, DTA 1994) applies;

(4) **the offence was committed on** any date between (and including) November 1, 1995 and March 23, 2003, CJA 1988, ss.71–83, (as amended by CJA 1993 and PCA 1995) apply;

(5) **the offence was committed** on or after March 24, 2003, PCA 2002 applies.

The law and practice relating to (1)–(4) above is to be found in the 2003 edition of this work under the heading DRUG TRAFFICKING AND CONFISCATION.

If the prosecutor does not rely on a pre-commencement offence for the purposes of the confiscation proceedings, the new law applies (*R. v Aslam* [2005] 1 Cr.App.R.(S.) 116).

Nature of orders under PCA 2002

24–003 Under the Act a judge of the Crown Court may make, in respect of an offence committed after March 24, 2003:

(1) a **confiscation order** (s.6) in respect of a person appearing before the court, for the purpose of recovering from:
  (a) an offender having a "criminal lifestyle" the "benefit" of his "general criminal conduct"; and
  (b) an offender who has been convicted of particular offences, the benefit of his "particular criminal" conduct, (these concepts are defined below); and

(2) a **restraint order** (under s.41), prohibiting the dealing with property, where
  (a) a criminal investigation has been started with regard to an offence; and
  (b) there is reasonable cause to believe that the alleged offender has benefited from his "criminal conduct"; and

he may also appoint a **receiver** to realise any property and to apply the proceeds to discharging any sum due under a confiscation order.

As to (2) see 52 RESTRAINT ORDER; RECEIVERS.

He also has powers (under PCA 2002, Pt 8, Ch 2) to make a number of other orders, in connection with confiscation investigations, as to which see 55 SEARCH AND ACCESS.

Nature of orders

24–004 The provisions of PCA 2002, like those they supercede, though draconian, are not penal in nature; their purpose is to deprive an offender of that which is not rightfully his. "It is notoriously difficult to combat [the drug trafficker's activities] and the dangers that they create for society provide a justification for action out of the ordinary" (*per* the Lord Chief Justice in *R. v Benjafield, etc*. [2001] 2 Cr.App.R. 7).

The power to make travel restriction orders under CJPOA 2001, ss.33–37 in relation to offenders convicted of drug offences (See 60 TRAVEL RESTRICTION) is not affected.

Assets Recovery Agency

24–005 PCA 2002, Pt 1 establishes an Assets Recovery Agency, headed by a Director. References in this section to "the Director" apply to him, and not to the DPP unless otherwise specified. The functions of the Agency include:

(1) providing for confiscation orders in relation to persons who benefit from criminal conduct and for restraint orders to prohibit dealing with property;
(2) allowing for the recovery of property which is or represents property obtained through unlawful conduct or which is intended to be used in unlawful conduct;
(3) making provision about money laundering;
(4) making provision about investigations relating to benefit from criminal conduct or to property which is or represents property obtained through unlawful conduct or to money laundering; and
(5) making provision to give effect to overseas requests and orders made where property is found or believed to be obtained through criminal conduct.

1. Making an order

Jurisdiction

24–006 Proceedings with a view to making a confiscation order under PCA 2002 apply to all offences committed on or after **March 24, 2003** of which the offender has been convicted. There is no limitation on the date of commission of "offences to be taken into consideration". PCA 2002, s.27

An offence committed over a period of two or more days (or during a period of days) is to be taken to have been committed on the first day.

An order may be made only in one of the following three circumstances, namely on:

(1) **conviction** before the Crown Court.
(2) **committal** to the Crown Court in pursuance of PCC(S)A 2000, ss.3, 4 or 6;

(3) **committal** (after conviction in the magistrates' court) to the Crown Court in pursuance of PCA 2002, s.70.

When the offender is committed for sentence under (3) the judge has the following powers:

(a) if at the time of committal the magistrates' court followed the procedure set out in s.70(5) and stated that it would have committed the offender for sentence under PCC(S)A 2000, s.3 he may deal with the offender as if he had just been convicted of the offence on indictment;
(b) if the magistrates' court did not exercise its power under s.70(5) in relation to an either-way offence, or the offence is not an either-way offence, the judge is limited to dealing with the offender in any way in which the magistrates' court could have dealt with him had he been convicted of the offence before it.

In the event that the offender absconds after conviction the judge may proceed to make a confiscation order in his absence.

Obligation to hold s.6 enquiry

24–007 Where the judge is asked: PCA 2002, s.6(1)–(6), (8)

(1) by the **prosecutor** to do so; or
(2) by the **Director of the Assets Recovery Agency**, to do so; or
(3) **decides** that it is appropriate to do so,

he **must** proceed to hold a **"section 6 enquiry"** with a view to making a confiscation order. In the course of that enquiry, the judge must:

(a) decide whether the offender has "a criminal lifestyle" (as defined in PCA 2002, s.75); and
(b) if he decides that the offender has a "criminal lifestyle," decide whether he has "benefited" (as defined in PCA 2002, s.76) from his "general criminal conduct"; and
(c) if he decides that the offender does **not** have a criminal lifestyle, decide whether the offender has benefited from his "particular criminal conduct"; and
(d) if he decides that the offender has benefited from such conduct, decide the "recoverable amount" (as defined in PCA 2002, s.7), and make a confiscation order requiring the offender to pay that amount,

unless he believes that some victim of the offender's conduct has brought, or intends to bring civil proceedings in respect of loss, injury or damage done to him, in which case the judge has a discretion whether or not to make an order.

The offender cannot rely in mitigation on the fact a confiscation order had been made or will be made against him.

Postponement of enquiry

24–008 The judge may require further information before conducting a confiscation proceeding with a view to the making of an order, in which case he may postpone the proceeding for a specified period (not exceeding two years starting with the date of conviction).

Despite postponing proceedings under s.6, the judge may (subject to s.15(2)) **proceed to sentence** the offender in respect of the offence(s) of which he is convicted, but PCA 2002, s.14

(1) he must not, as part of his sentence include a fine, a financial order other than a compensation order under PCC(S)A 2000, s.130, or any of the forfeiture orders set out in the following paragraphs, although,
(2) if the offender is sentenced during the postponement period, the sentence may be varied by adding one of the prohibited orders, within 28 days starting with the last day of the period of postponement.

For the purpose of time limits relating to appeal, sentence is regarded as having been passed on the date of the variation.

The judge must take care, in his sentencing remarks, if he knows that he will be carrying out fact finding exercises in relation to the same offender at a later stage, not to express himself in a manner that may sensibly be perceived to show that he is unlikely to believe anything the offender is likely to tell him. If remarks of that nature are pertinent to explaining his sentence, he will need to recuse himself from conducting any subsequent fact-finding exercise (*R. v Odewale* [2005] Crim.L.R. 581).

Relationship between order and sentence

24–009 The judge may pass sentence for the offence(s) of which the offender has been convicted either **before** making a confiscation order, as where he postpones his duty to conduct a s.6 enquiry (see 24–008 above), or **after** making a confiscation order.

Where he makes an order **before** passing sentence he must take account of the order before imposing a fine, making any PCA 2002, ss.13(1)–(4)

order involving payment by the offender, other than a compensation order under PCC(S)A 2000, s.130; or

(1) a forfeiture order under MDA 1971, s.27;
(2) a deprivation order under PCC(S)A 2000, s.143; or
(3) a forfeiture order under TerrA 2000, s.23.

Subject to the above, the judge may leave the confiscation order out of account in deciding the appropriate sentence for the offender; he may make both a confiscation order and a compensation order, and may leave the amount of the former out of account in making the latter.

Where the judge: PCA 2002, s.13(5), (6)

(a) makes both a confiscation order and a compensation order under PCC(S)A 2000, s.130 against the same offender in the same proceedings; and,
(b) considers that the offender will not have sufficient means to satisfy both the orders in full,

he must direct that so much of the compensation as he specifies is to be paid out of any sums recovered under the confiscation order, the specified amount being that amount he believes will not be recoverable because of the insufficiency of the person's means.

A sentence already imposed may be **varied** within 28 days of the last day of the postponement period (as set out in s.15(3)).

As to the **subsequent reconsideration** of an order, see 24–039 below.

2. Enforcement of order

Time for payment; interest

24–010 The amount ordered to be paid must ordinarily be paid on the making of the order. If the offender asks for time to pay, the judge may: PCA 2002, s.11

(1) allow time for payment within a specified period not exceeding six months from the date on which the order is made; or
(2) where, on the offender's application, he accepts that there are exceptional circumstances, the judge may extend the period to a maximum of 12 months from the date of the order.

An application under (2) may be made after the expiry of the date originally specified, but not after the expiry of the 12 months from the date the order was made.

No extension may be granted unless the prosecutor, or the Director if he was appointed by the enforcement authority, is given an opportunity to make representations.

The period of time allowed for payment runs from the date the order is made, not from the determination of an appeal against the order. It would be wrong as a matter of principle for offenders to be encouraged to believe that the bringing of an appeal would be likely to lengthen the time allowed for payment (*R. v May and Others* [2005] EWCA Crim 367).

Where the amount required to be paid under the order is not paid when it is required to be paid, interest falls to be paid for the period for which it remains unpaid (at the rate for the time being specified in the Judgments Act 1838, s.17, in relation to civil debts), unless: PCA 2002, s.12(3)(4)

(a) an application has been made under s.11(4) for an extension of time,
(b) that application has not been determined by the court, and
(c) the period of 12 months starting with the day on which the confiscation order was made has not ended.

The amount of the interest is to be treated as part of the amount to be paid under the confiscation order.

Fixing default sentence

24–011 The judge **must** fix a term of imprisonment to be served in default of payment, in terms of the table set out in PCC(S)A 2000, s.139(4) (see 36 FINES AND ENFORCEMENT). PCA 2002, ss.35, 36

Questions relating to the serving of the default sentence of enforcement will be dealt with as follows:

(1) if the Director is not appointed to the enforcement authority enforcement is as for a fine imposed by the Crown Court (i.e. PCC(S)A 2000, ss.139(2)–(4) and (9), and ss.140(1)–(4) apply, with modifications disapplying MCA 1980, s.75 (allowing time to pay), s.81 (young offenders), s.85 (remittal of fine) and s.87 (means enquiry);
(2) if the Director is appointed, enforcement is by the Crown Court, as if the amount were a fine.

As to applications by the Director for enforcement, see 24–013 below.

The provisions of PCC(S)A 2000, s.139(3) prevent immediate committal to prison.

If the offender serves a term of imprisonment or detention in default of paying any amount due under a confiscation order, his serving that term does not prevent the confiscation order from PCA 2002, s.38; CJA 2003, s.304, Sch.32, para.141

continuing to have effect so far as any other method of enforcement is concerned.

Enforcement authority; receivers

24–012 For the purposes of enforcement of confiscation orders, etc. PCA 2002 provides that once the judge decides to make an order he must also:

(1) under ss.34–36 appoint an **enforcement authority**, and:
   (a) where the application or appeal in respect of a confiscation order is made by the Director or before the judge makes a confiscation order the Director applies that he be appointed as the enforcement authority, the Director must be appointed; but
   (b) where the prosecutor made the application to proceed with a view to confiscation, or the judge proceeded of his own motion with that end in view, the judge may not appoint the Director to be the enforcement authority unless the Director applied to be so appointed before the judge made the confiscation order;

(2) under ss.50–55 appoint **an enforcement receiver** and confer upon him the relevant power under s.51 or s.53; note that:
   (a) where the judge does not appoint an enforcement authority, on the application of the prosecutor the judge may appoint an enforcement receiver; and
   (b) where the Director is appointed as the enforcement authority, the judge must appoint an "enforcement receiver" as nominated by the Director;

(3) under s.64, appoint a **"management receiver"** (who would have been appointed in connection with a restraint order) and order the transfer to an **enforcement receiver** (as appointed by the Director) all property held by the "management receiver" by virtue of the exercise of his powers in pursuance of any restraint order.

Subsequent application for enforcement

24–013 Where the Director has been appointed the enforcement authority, he may make an ex parte application to a judge of the Crown Court for the issue of a summons against an offender where he believes that: PCA 2002, s.37(1)–(5)

(1) because of the offender's wilful refusal or culpable neglect the order is not satisfied;
(2) the order is not subject to appeal; and

(3) he, the Director, has done all that is otherwise practicable to enforce the order.

If these conditions appear to be satisfied the judge may issue a summons ordering the offender to appear before the court at the time and place specified; if he fails to appear in pursuance of the summons, a warrant may be issued for his arrest.

Where the offender appears in pursuance of the summons or of a warrant and the judge is satisfied that the conditions set out in subs.(1)–(3) are satisfied, he may issue a warrant committing the offender to prison or detention for default in payment of the amount ordered to be paid by the confiscation order.

Committal warrant

24–014 If the amount remaining to be paid under the confiscation order when the warrant is issued is less than the amount ordered to be paid, the court will substitute for the term of imprisonment or detention fixed in respect of the order under PCC(S)A 2000, s.139(2) such term as bears to the original term the same proportion as the amount remaining to be paid bears to the amount ordered to be paid. PCA 2002, s.37(6)–(10)

Where the offender has been committed to prison or detention in pursuance of such a warrant, and payment is made in respect of some or all of the amount remaining to be paid under the order, then, if the whole amount remaining is paid the offender will be released unless he is in custody for another reason; if part-payment is made, the period of commitment will be is reduced so that it bears to the term fixed under PCC(S)A 2000, s.139(2), the same proportion as the amount remaining to be paid bears to the amount ordered to be paid.

3. Section 6 enquiry procedure

Enquiry a precondition

24–015 A s.6 enquiry is a mandatory precondition to the making of a confiscation order. The judge may sentence an offender before making a confiscation order, but: in relation to offences committed:

(1) **on or before March 23, 2003,** if he proceeds to sentence without ruling on whether or not there should be an enquiry, he may not make a confiscation order (*R. v Ross* [2001] Crim.L.R 405);

(2) **on or after March 24, 2003,** he *should consider* whether to make an order or hold an enquiry before moving to sentence, and he *must* do so before he is entitled to

impose a fine, compensation, forfeiture or deprivation of property.

As to his powers of postponement, see 24-037 below.

As to the compatibility of the procedure under the previous legislation with ECHR, Art.6, see *R. v Benjafield and Others*, above.

Statement of information

24–016 Where the judge is to proceed under s.6 in a case where: PCA 2002, s.16

(1) asked by the prosecutor or the Director, to do so, he will be given a statement of information within the period he orders;
(2) he proceeds of his own motion he will order the prosecutor to give him a statement of information, and the prosecutor must do so within the period he orders.

Where the prosecutor or the Director, as the case may be:

(a) believes the offender has a "criminal lifestyle", the statement will be a statement of the matters he believes are relevant in connection with deciding whether the offender has a criminal lifestyle, whether he has benefited from his general criminal conduct; and his benefit from the conduct, and will include such information as he believes is relevant in connection with the making by the judge of any required assumption under s.10, (see 24–030 below) and for the purpose of enabling him to decide if the circumstances are such that he must not make such an assumption;
(b) does not believe that the offender has a criminal lifestyle, the statement will be a statement of matters he believes are relevant in connection with deciding whether the offender has benefited from his "particular criminal conduct," and the benefit from the conduct.

Such a statement must also contain the information prescribed in R.58.2(2) and must be served upon the offender. R.58.1

If the prosecutor or the Director gives the court a statement, he may at any time give a further statement, and must do so if the judge so orders, and within the period ordered.

If the judge makes an order under this section he may at any time vary it by making another.

Offender's response to statement

24–017 Where a statement of information is given to the judge and a copy is served on the offender, the judge may order him: PCA 2002, s.17

(1) to indicate, within the period ordered, the extent to which he accepts each allegation in it; and
(2) so far as he does not accept an allegation, to give particulars of any matters he proposes to rely on.

If the offender:

(a) accepts to any extent an allegation in the statement the judge may treat his acceptance as conclusive of the matters to which it relates for the purpose of deciding the issues referred to in ss.16(3) or (5), (above), as the case may be;
(b) fails in any respect to comply with such an order he may be treated as accepting every allegation in the statement apart from:
    (i) any allegation in respect of which he has complied with the requirement; or
    (ii) any allegation that he has benefited from his general or particular criminal conduct, and

no acceptance under this section that the offender has benefited from conduct is admissible in evidence in proceedings for an offence.

Rule 58.1(3) requires such information be given in writing to the prosecutor or the Director and a copy be given to the court.

An allegation may be accepted or particulars may be given in a manner ordered by the judge. If he makes an order under this provision he may at any time vary it by making another.

Offender providing information

24–018 Where the judge is proceeding under s.6 in a case where: PCA 2002, s.18

(1) he has been asked by the Director or prosecutor to do so; or
(2) he proceeds of his own motion, or he is considering whether to proceed,

he may, for the purpose of obtaining information to help him in carrying out his functions, at any time, order the offender to give him specified information, and such an order may require all, or a specified part, of the information to be given in a specified manner and before a specified date, provided no information given which amounts to an admission by the defendant that he has benefited from criminal conduct is admissible in evidence in proceedings for an offence.

Such information must be given in writing, and a copy must be sent to the prosecutor or to the Director, depending upon which asked the court to proceed under s.6. R.58.1(4)

Where:

(a) the offender fails, without reasonable excuse, to comply with an order, the judge, quite apart from any power he may have to deal with him in respect of a failure to comply with an order under this section, may draw such inference as he believes to be appropriate;
(b) the prosecutor or the Director, as the case may be, accepts to any extent an allegation made by the offender in giving information required by the judge's order, or in any other statement given to the court in relation to any matter relevant to deciding the available amount under s.9, the judge may treat the acceptance as conclusive of the matters to which it relates.

An allegation may be accepted in any manner the judge may order.

If the judge makes an order under these provisions he may at any time vary it by making another.

Aims of the enquiry

24–019 Confiscation under PCA 2002 is by reference:

(1) to the offender's benefit from his "general criminal conduct" where he is shown on conviction to have a "criminal lifestyle"; or
(2) where he does not have such a lifestyle, to his benefit from his "particular criminal conduct".

The judge must therefore investigate and decide:

(a) whether the offender has "a criminal lifestyle" (within the meaning of s.75 as to which see below); and
(b) if he decides that he has, whether he has "benefited" (see 24–021–023) from his "general criminal conduct" (24–022, below); and
(c) if he does *not* have a "criminal lifestyle" whether he has benefited from his "particular criminal conduct" (see 24–022); and
(d) finally, if he has benefited, the "recoverable amount" (see 24–034).

The judge must decide any question arising under subs.(2) above, on a balance of probabilities. PCA 2002, s.6(7)

His enquiry will be preceded by the provision of a statement of information given by the Director or prosecutor, as to which see 24–016.

"Criminal lifestyle"

24–020 An offender has a criminal lifestyle for the purpose of the Act, if the offence, or any of the offences of which he is convicted: PCA 2002, s.75(1), (2), (3), (4), (5), (6)

(1) is a "lifestyle offence" specified in Sch.2 (see APPENDIX A, Section 3);
(2) constitutes conduct forming part of a **course of criminal activity**;
(3) is an offence committed over a period of at least six months and the offender has **benefited** from the conduct which constitutes the offence.

Where the offender has benefited from conduct which constitutes the offence (committed after March 24, 2003), such conduct forms part of a course of criminal activity in two circumstances, namely if where:

(a) in the proceedings in which he was convicted, he was also convicted of three or more other offences (i.e. at least four offences in the same proceeding), each of the three or more of them constituting conduct from which he has also benefited, committed **after March 24, 2003** (SI 2003/333, art.7(4)); or
(b) in the period of six years ending with the day when those proceedings were started (or, if there is more than one such day, the earliest day), he was convicted on at least **two separate occasions** of an offence constituting conduct from which he has benefited notwithstanding that any of those offences were committed before **March 24, 2003** (SI 2003/333, art.7(5));

and in either case the offender obtained "relevant benefit" of not less than £5,000.

Benefit from "general criminal conduct"

24–021 Once the judge has decided that the offender has a criminal lifestyle the next step is to decide whether he benefited from his general criminal conduct.

Relevant benefit is benefit from:

(1) conduct which constitutes the offence;
(2) any other conduct which forms part of the course of criminal activity and which constitutes an offence of which the offender has been convicted; or
(3) conduct which constitutes an offence which has been or will be taken into consideration by the judge (see 62

TICs) in sentencing the offender for an offence mentioned in (a) or (b) of the preceding paragraph.

For the purposes of (3) above it is benefit from:

(a) conduct which constitutes the offence; or
(b) conduct which constitutes an offence which has been or will be taken into consideration by the judge in sentencing the offender for the offence mentioned in (a) or (b) of the preceding paragraph.

Provided that the judge must not take into account benefit from conduct constituting an offence committed **before March 24, 2003** (SI 2003/333, art.7(3)).

As to the assumptions to be made where a criminal lifestyle is proved, see s.10 at 24–031 below.

Definitions

24–022 "Criminal conduct" is defined (in s.76) as conduct which constitutes an offence in England and Wales, or would constitute such an offence if it occurred in England and Wales. PCA 2002, s.76(1), (2), (3)

The **"general criminal conduct"** of an offender is *all* his criminal conduct, and it is immaterial whether:

(1) that conduct occurred before or after the passing of PCA 2002;
(2) property constituting a benefit from that conduct was obtained before or after the passing of the Act; or
(3) it formed the subject of criminal proceedings.

The **"particular criminal conduct"** of the offender is his criminal conduct which constitutes:

(a) the offence or offences concerned;
(b) offences of which he was convicted in the same proceedings as those in which he was convicted of the offence or offences concerned; or
(c) offences which the judge will be taking into consideration in deciding his sentence for the offence or offences concerned,

but conduct which constitutes an offence which was committed **before March 24, 2003**, is not particular criminal conduct under ss.76(3) or 224(3) (SI 2003/333).

Assessing the offender's benefit

24–023 In deciding whether the offender has "benefited" (see below) from conduct, and in deciding the benefit from that conduct, the judge must take account of: PCA 2003, s.8(1), (2), (3), (4)

(1) conduct occurring up to the time he makes his decision; and
(2) property (see 24–025 *et seq.*) obtained up to that time.

Where:

(a) the conduct concerned is general criminal conduct; or
(b) a confiscation order has at an earlier time been made against the offender, and his benefit for the purposes of that previous order was benefit from his general criminal conduct,

then his benefit found at the time the last confiscation order (mentioned in (b) above) was made against him must be taken for the purposes of this section to be his benefit from his general criminal conduct at that time.

Definition of "benefit"

24–024 A person "benefits" from conduct if he obtains property as a result of or in connection with the conduct. If he obtains a pecuniary advantage as a result of or in connection with conduct, he is to be taken to obtain as a result of or in connection with the conduct a sum of money equal to the value of the pecuniary advantage. PCA 2002, s.76(4), (5), (6), (7)

References to "property" or a "pecuniary advantage obtained in connection with conduct" include references to property or a pecuniary advantage obtained both in that connection and some other.

If a person benefits from conduct his benefit is the value of the property obtained.

Under the previous legislation it was said in relation to DTA 1994, s.2(3) that a person's "proceeds" are his gross receipts rather than his net profits (see e.g. *R. v Banks* [1997] Crim.L.R. 235; *R. v Fadden, The Times*, January 26, 1998. See also *R. v Dimsey & Allan* [2000] Crim.L.R.,199 as to unpaid tax).

The liability of a **smuggler** who evades duty which he is liable to pay on importation is a pecuniary advantage obtained rendering him liable to pay a compensation order in the amount of the duty evaded irrespective of the fate of the goods imported and whether or not he would have been profiting from the contraband (*R. v Bakewell* [2006] Crim.L.R. 453 following *R. v Smith (David Cadnam)* [2002] 1 Cr.App.R. 35).

"Property"; general provisions

24–025 "Property" is all property wherever situated and includes: PCA 2002, s.150

(1) money;
(2) all forms of real or personal property; and
(3) things in action and other intangible or incorporeal property.

The following rules apply in relation to property:

(a) property is held by a person if he holds an interest in it;
(b) property is obtained by a person if he obtains an interest in it;
(c) property is transferred by one person to another if the first one transfers or grants an interest in it to the second;
(d) references to property held by a person include references to property vested in his trustee in bankruptcy, permanent or interim trustee (within the meaning of the Bankruptcy (Scotland) Act 1985) or liquidator;
(e) references to an interest held by a person beneficially in property include references to an interest which would be held by him beneficially if the property were not so vested;
(f) references to an interest, in relation to land in England and Wales or Northern Ireland, are to any legal estate or equitable interest or power;
(g) references to an interest, in relation to land in Scotland, are to any estate, interest, servitude or other heritable right in or over land, including a heritable security;
(h) references to an interest, in relation to property other than land, include references to a right (including a right to possession).

"Free" property

24–026 Property is free unless an order is in force in respect of it under:

(a) MDA 1971, s.27;
(b) Criminal Justice (Northern Ireland) Order 1994 (SI 1994/2795 (N.I.15)) Art.11, (deprivation orders);
(c) Proceeds of Crime (Scotland) Act 1995, Pt 2 (forfeiture of property used in crime);
(d) PCC(S)A 2000, s.143;
(e) Terr A 2000, s.23 or s.111 (forfeiture orders);
(f) PCA 2002, ss.246, 266, 295(2) or 298(2).

"Realisable" property

24–027 Realisable property is any free property held by the defendant, and any "free" property (see above) held by the recipient of a "tainted gift". PCA 2002, s.83

Gifts and their recipients

24–028 Where the defendant transfers property to another person for a consideration whose value is significantly less than the value of the property at the time of the transfer, he is to be treated as making a gift, and the property given is to be treated as such share in the property transferred as is represented by the fraction whose: PCA 2002, s.78

(1) numerator is the difference between the two values mentioned above; and
(2) denominator is the value of the property at the time of the transfer.

References to a recipient of a "tainted gift" are to a person to whom the defendant has made the gift.

"Tainted gifts"

24–029 Where:

(1) a decision has *not* been made as to whether the defendant has a criminal lifestyle, or a court has decided that he has such a lifestyle, a gift is said to be "tainted": PCA 2002, ss.77(1)–(5)
   (a) where it was made by him at any time after "the relevant day"; and
   (b) if it was made by him at any time and was of property:
      (i) which was obtained by him as a result of or in connection with his general criminal conduct, or
      (ii) which (in whole or part and whether directly or indirectly) represented in his hands property obtained by him as a result of or in connection with his general criminal conduct;
(2) a court has decided that the defendant does *not* have a criminal lifestyle, a gift is said to be "tainted" if it was made by him at any time after:
   (a) the date on which the offence concerned was committed, or
   (b) if his particular criminal conduct consists of two or more offences and they were committed on different dates, the date of the earliest.

24–030 An offence which is a continuing offence is committed on the first occasion when it is committed. For the purposes of (2)(b) in the preceding paragraph, the defendant's "particular criminal conduct" includes any conduct which constitutes offences which the court has taken into consideration in deciding his sentence for the offence or offences concerned (see 62 TICs). PCA 2002, s.77(6)–(9)

A gift may be a "tainted gift" whether it was made before or after the passing of this Act.

The "relevant day" referred to in (1)(a) in the preceding paragraph, is the first day of the period of six years ending with:

(a) the day when proceedings for the offence concerned were started against the defendant, or
(b) if there are two or more offences and proceedings for them were started on different days, the earliest of those days.

Assumptions to be made in case of "criminal lifestyle"

24–031 Where the judge decides that the offender has a "criminal lifestyle" he *must* make the following four assumptions for the purpose both of deciding: PCA 2002, ss.10(1)–(5)

(1) whether the offender has benefited from his "general criminal conduct" (see 24–022 above), and;
(2) his benefit from that conduct namely:
  (a) **any property transferred** to the offender at any time after the "relevant day" is assumed to have been obtained by him:
    (i) as a result of his "general criminal conduct"; and
    (ii) at the earliest time he appears to have held it;
  (b) **any property held** by the offender at any time after the date of conviction is assumed to have been obtained by him:
    (i) as a result of his "general criminal conduct"; and
    (ii) at the earliest time he appears to have held it;
  (c) **any expenditure incurred** by the offender at any time after "the relevant day" was met from property obtained by him as a result of his "general criminal conduct";
  (d) for the purpose of valuing any **property obtained** (or assumed to have been obtained) by the offender, it is assumed that he obtained it free of any other interests in it;

but the judge must not make a required assumption in relation to particular property or expenditure if that assumption is shown to be incorrect, or if there would be a serious risk of injustice if the assumption were made. The phrase "serious risk of injustice" does not mean hardship to the offender by virtue of the order. The purpose of s.10(6)(b) is not to provide for the exercise of a discretion by the judge in determining whether it PCA 2002, ss.10(6), (7) is fair to make an order, but to ensure a sensible calculation of the benefit and to ensure that the assumptions are not so unreasonable or unjust in respect of the particular offender that they should not be made (*CPS v Jones* [2006] W.L.R.(D) 174). Where he does not make one or more of the required assumptions he must state his reasons, though he must still decide whether the offender has benefited from his general criminal conduct and determine the recoverable amount, albeit without the assistance of those assumptions.

Note that the "relevant day" is the first day of the period of six years ending with:

(i) the day when proceedings for the offence concerned were started against the defendant, or
(ii) if there are two or more offences, and proceedings for them were started on different days, the earliest of those days,

but if a confiscation order mentioned in s.8(3)(c) has been made against the defendant at any time during the period mentioned in subs.(8), then the "relevant day" is the day when the defendant's benefit was calculated for the purposes of the last such confiscation order, and assumption (2) does not apply to any property which was held by him on or before the relevant day.

The "date of conviction" is the date on which the offender was convicted of the offence concerned, or if there are two or more offences and the convictions were on different dates, the date of the latest. PCA 2002, ss.10(8), (9), (10)

Offender having no criminal lifestyle

24–032 Where the judge decides that the offender does not have a "criminal lifestyle" he must go on to decide whether the offender has benefited from his "particular criminal conduct defined at 24–022 above. Conduct which constitutes an offence committed **on or before March 23, 2003** does not come within the definition. SI 2003/333

Assessment of benefit

24–033 For the purpose of deciding the value at any time of property then held by a person, its value is the market value of the property at that time, but if at that time another person holds an interest in the property its value, in relation to such person is the market value of his interest at that time, ignoring any previous charging order made under the enactments referred to in PCA 2002, ss.79–81. PCA 2002, s.8(1)–(4)

Special rules apply to the valuation of property obtained from conduct (s.80), and to "tainted gifts" as defined in ss.77, 144 and 147 (s.81).

Where the conduct concerned is general criminal conduct, the judge must, in order to avoid double counting, deduct the aggregate of the any amounts ordered to be paid under those orders made under the enactments listed in s.8(7) unless an amount has been taken into account for the purposes of a deduction under this provision on an earlier occasion. PCA 2002, s.8(5), (6), (7), (8)

Deciding the "recoverable amount"

24–034 Once the judge has assessed the amount of the offender's benefit, he must make a confiscation order in that amount, unless: PCA 2002, s.7

(1) the offender shows that the "available amount" is less than that assessed benefit; in which case the amount subject to confiscation (the "recoverable amount") is the "available amount" (see below), or a nominal amount, if the available amount is nil, but
(2) a victim of the offender's conduct has started or intends to start civil proceedings (s.6(6)), in which case the amount subject to confiscation is such amount as the judge believes is just, and which does not exceed the assessed benefit, as the case may be.

In calculating the offender's benefit from the conduct concerned, any property in respect of which:

(a) a recovery order is in force under PCA 2002, s.266, or
(b) a forfeiture order is in force under PCC(S)A 2000, s.298(2),

must be ignored.

Where the judge decides the available amount, he must include in the confiscation order a statement of his findings as to the matters relevant for deciding that amount.

"The available amount"

24–035 The "available amount" is the aggregate of: PCA 2002, s.9

(1) the total of the values (at the time the confiscation order is made) of all the **"free property"** (see 24–026 above) then held by the offender;
(2) deducting the total amount payable in pursuance of **obligations** which then have priority; and

(3) adding the total of the values (at that time) of all "tainted gifts" (see 24–029 above).

An obligation "has priority" if the offender has an obligation to pay:

(a) an amount due in respect of a fine or other order of a court which was imposed or made on conviction of an offence and at any time before the time the confiscation order is made, or
(b) a sum which would be included among the preferential debts (within the meaning of the Insolvency Act 1986, s.385) if the defendant's bankruptcy had commenced on the date of the confiscation order or his winding up had been ordered on that date.

Expert evidence

24–036 A party to proceedings PCA 2002, Pt 2 (confiscation orders) who wishes to adduce expert evidence (whether of fact or opinion) in the proceedings must, as soon as practicable: R.57.9

(1) serve on the other parties a statement in writing of any finding or opinion which he proposes to adduce by way of such evidence; and
(2) serve on any party who requests it in writing, a copy of (or if it appears to the party proposing to adduce the evidence to be more practicable, a reasonable opportunity to examine):
   (a) the record of any observation, test, calculation or other procedure on which the finding or opinion is based, and
   (b) any document or other thing or substance in respect of which the observation, test, calculation or other procedure has been carried out.

A party may serve notice in writing waiving his right to be served with any of those matters and, in particular, may agree that the statement mentioned in (1) may be given to him orally and not served in writing.

If a party who wishes to adduce expert evidence in such proceedings fails to comply with this rules he may not adduce that evidence in those proceedings without the leave of the court, except where r.57.10 below applies.

Rule.57.10 provides that if a party has reasonable grounds for believing that the disclosure of any evidence in compliance with r.57.9 might lead to the intimidation, or attempted intimidation, of any person on whose evidence he intends to rely in the proceedings, or otherwise to the course of justice being interfered with, he is not obliged to comply with the above requirements in relation to that evidence, unless a judge of the Crown Court orders otherwise. Thus, where, in accordance with this provision, a party considers that he is not obliged to comply with the requirements imposed by r.57.9 with regard to any evidence in relation to any other party, he must serve notice in writing on that party stating that the evidence is being withheld, and the reason for so doing.

CPR 2005, Pt 57 applies with necessary modifications to the PCA 2002 (External Requests and Orders) order 2005 (SI 2005/3181) in the same way as it applies to the corresponding provisions of PCA 2 (SI 2005/353).

4. Postponement of making order

The act of postponement

24–037 Instead of proceeding under s.6 **before** sentencing the offender for his offence(s), the judge may, on the application of the offender, the prosecutor or the Director (as the case may be) or of his own motion (*R. v Zelzele* [2001] Crim.L.R. 830), postpone the s.6 proceeding, on one or more occasions for up to ("the permitted period") a total of two years from the offender's conviction, or three months from the date on which any appeal against conviction is disposed of if the three months ends more than two years after the date of conviction. There is no limitre exceptional circumstances (see, e.g. *R. v Jagdev, The Times*, July 4, 2002). PCA 2002, s.14(1)–(4), (9); R.58.2

If two or more offences are involved, and the they were on different dates, the date of the offender's conviction is the later of the latest. PCA 2002, s.14(9)

A postponement may be granted without a hearing and for any reason.

It is not enough to adjourn the proceeedings, he must postpone the hearing in terms:

(1) it is not necessary to specify the very date on which the substantive hearing is to begin, still less the day on which any order will be made;
(2) it is sufficient if he gives directions for the service of statements and specifies a date on which the proceedings will next be listed, whether for disposal or for such other

directions as may be necessaary, or for its disposal (*R. v Knights* [2006] Crim.L.R. 171).

The period of postponement may be extended provided the whole period ends before the expiry of the permitted period, unless there are exceptional circumstances. Where the application is made before the permitted period ends, it may be granted even after it ends. PCA 2002, s.14(8)

Effect of postponement

24–038 If the judge postpones s.6 proceedings, he may proceed to sentence the offender for the offence (or any of the offences) concerned, provided that he does not in respect of those offences: PCA 2002, s.15

(1) impose a fine on him,
(2) make one of those orders enumerated in s.13(3) (24–009), or
(3) make a compensation order under PCC(S)A 2000, s.130.

He must take care, in his sentencing remarks, if he knows that he will be carrying out fact finding exercises in relation to the same offender at a later stage, not to express himself in a manner that may sensibly be perceived to show that he is unlikely to believe anything the offender is likely to tell him. If remarks of that nature are pertinent to explaining his sentence, he will need to recuse himself from conducting any subsequent fact-finding exercise (*R. v Odewale* [2005] Crim.L.R. 581).

If he sentences the offender for the offence (or any of the offences) concerned in the postponement period after that period ends, he may vary the sentence by:

(a) imposing a fine on him,
(b) making an order falling within s.13(3) (24–009), or
(c) making a compensation order under PCC(S)A 2000, s.130,

but only within the period of 28 days which starts with the last day of the postponement period. (See under the previous legislation *R. v Davies* [2002] 1 W.L.R. 1806, where the judge had only specified a timetable for exchange of information and had not specified a period of postponement, or adopted the statutory period.)

For the purposes of the time limit for notice of appeal or of application for leave to appeal to CACD, and the time limit for notice of application for leave to refer a case under CJA 1988, s.36 (Attorney-General's reference) sentence is to be regarded as imposed or made on the day on which it was varied.

5. Subsequent reconsideration

General

24–039 The question of making a confiscation order may fall to be considered subsequently as where, for example:

(1) the judge at the original proceedings decided not to enquire under s.6, and it is sought to reconsider the case;
(2) the judge at the original proceedings decided that there was no relevant benefit to the defendant, and it is sought to lead evidence which was not available at the time;
(3) an order was made at the time, but it is sought to lead fresh evidence as to the amount of the benefit;
(4) an order was made at the time, but it is sought to lead fresh evidence as to the available amount, or
(5) the available amount calculated at the time is inadequate to satisfy the order.

An application by the prosecutor or the Director, for reconsideration under ss.19, 20 or 21 is made in writing, giving, amongst other detail, the grounds for the application and an indication of the evidence available to support it. It must be lodged with the Crown Court, and must be served on the offender at least seven days before the date fixed for the hearing of the application. R.58.3

Statement of information

24–040 Where the judge holds a s.6 enquiry, in reconsidering an earlier order (ss.19, 20), or the prosecutor or the Director applies for a reconsideration of the benefit calculated under the original order (s.21): PCA 2002, s.26

(1) the prosecutor or the Director (as the case may be) will give the court a statement of information (see 24–016 above) within the period the judge orders;
(2) s.16 as to such statements (see 24–016 above) will apply accordingly (with appropriate modifications where the prosecutor or the Director applies under s.21);
(3) s.17 as to the offender's response (see 24–017 above) will apply accordingly; and
(4) s.18 as to the offender providing information (see 24–018 above) will apply as it applies in the circumstances mentioned in s.18(1).

Case (1): no s.6 enquiry originally; fresh evidence

24–041 Where an offender was before the Crown Court in the circumstances obtaining under s.6(2) (24–015 above) but PCA 2002, ss.19(1), (2) no judge has proceeded to hold an enquiry under that section, and:

(1) there is evidence which was not available to the prosecutor on the relevant date, and
(2) before the end of the period of six years starting with the date of conviction the prosecutor or the Director applies to a judge of the Crown Court to consider the evidence, and
(3) after considering the evidence the judge believes it is appropriate to proceed under s.6.

He must proceed to hold an enquiry under s.6.

Modifications appropriate to s.19 enquiry

24–042 Where the judge embarks upon such an enquiry, the provisions of the Act apply with certain modifications, thus: PCA 2002, ss.19(3)–(8)

(1) if the offender has already been sentenced for the offence, (or any of the offences) concerned, s.6 has effect as if his "particular criminal conduct" (see 24–022 above) included conduct which constitutes offences which the judge has taken into consideration in deciding his sentence for the offence or offences concerned;
(2) s.8(2) in relation to calculating the offender's "benefit" (see 24–020 and 24–024 above) does not apply; instead the judge must take account of:
    (a) conduct occurring before the "relevant date" (see below);
    (b) property obtained before that date;
    (c) property obtained on or after that date if it was obtained as a result of, or in connection with, conduct occurring before that date.
(3) in relation to s.10 (**assumptions**) (see 24–031 above):
    (a) assumptions (1) and (2) do not apply with regard to property first held by the offender on or after the relevant date;
    (b) assumption (3) does not apply with regard to expenditure incurred by him on or after that date;
    (c) assumption (4) does not apply with regard to property obtained (or assumed to have been obtained) by him on or after that date.
(4) "the recoverable amount" (see 24–034 above) for the purposes of s.6 is such amount as the judge believes is just, but does not exceed the amount found under s.7 (see 24–034 above);

(5) in arriving at the just amount the judge must have regard in particular to:
   (a) the amount found under s.7;
   (b) any fine imposed on the offender in respect of the offence (or any of the offences) concerned;
   (c) any order which falls within s.13(3) (see 24–009) and has been made against him in respect of the offence (or any of the offences) concerned and has not already been taken into account by the judge in deciding what is the free property held by him for the purposes of s.9; and
   (d) any compensation order which has been made against him in respect of the offence (or any of the offences) concerned under PCC(S)A 2000, s.130;

(6) if a compensation order under s.130 has been made against the offender in respect of the offence or offences concerned, ss.13(5) and (6) do not apply.

Note that:

(i) the "relevant date" is, if the judge made a decision not to proceed under s.6, the date of the decision, and if he did not make such a decision, the date of conviction.
(ii) the "date of conviction" is the date on which the offender was convicted of the offence concerned, or if there are two or more offences and the convictions were on different dates, the date of the latest.

Case (2) no benefit found originally; fresh evidence

24–043 Where, in the original s.6 enquiry the judge decided either, that the offender had a criminal lifestyle but had not benefited from his general criminal conduct, or that he did not have a criminal lifestyle and had not benefited from his particular criminal conduct then, if the judge proceeded under s.6 because: PCA 2002, ss.20(1)–(5)

(1) the Director asked him to do so; and
   (a) the Director has evidence which was not available to him when the judge decided that the offender had not benefited from his general or particular criminal conduct; and
   (b) before the end of the period of six years starting with the date of conviction the Director applies to a judge of the Crown Court to consider the evidence; and
   (c) after considering the evidence the judge concludes that he would have decided that the offender had benefited from his general or particular criminal

conduct (as the case may be) if the evidence had been available to him;

(2) the prosecutor asked him to or because he believed it was appropriate for him to do so; and
   (a) there is evidence which was not available to the prosecutor when the court decided that the offender had not benefited from his general or particular criminal conduct; and
   (b) before the end of the period of six years starting with the date of conviction the prosecutor or the Director applies to the Crown Court to consider the evidence; and
   (c) after considering the evidence the judge concludes that he would have decided that the offender had benefited from his general or particular criminal conduct (as the case may be) if the evidence had been available to him,

he must make a fresh decision under ss.6(4)(b) or (c) whether the offender has benefited from his general or particular criminal conduct (as the case may be), and may make a confiscation order under that section.

Modifications appropriate to s.20 enquiry

24–044 Where the judge then proceeds under s.6, if the offender has already been sentenced for the offence (or any of the offences) concerned, s.6 has effect as if his particular criminal conduct included conduct which constitutes offences which the court has taken into consideration in deciding his sentence for the offence or offences concerned. The following modifications also apply: PCA 2002, ss.20(6), (7), (8), (9)

(1) s.8(2) in relation to calculating the offender's benefit (see 24–020–24–030 above) will not apply, and instead the judge must take account of;
   (a) conduct occurring before the date of the original decision that the offender had not benefited from his general or particular criminal conduct;
   (b) property obtained before that date;
   (c) property obtained on or after that date if it was obtained as a result of or in connection with conduct occurring before that date.

(2) in relation to s.10 (**assumptions**) (see 24–031 above):
   (a) assumptions (1) and (2) do not apply with regard to property first held by the defendant on or after the date of the original decision that he had not

benefited from his general or particular criminal conduct;

(b) assumption (3) does not apply with regard to expenditure incurred by him on or after that date

(c) assumption (4) does not apply with regard to property obtained (or assumed to have been obtained) by him on or after that date.

"Recoverable amount": s.20

24–045 "The recoverable amount" (see 24–034 above) for the purposes of a s.6 enquiry conducted under s.20 will be such amount as: PCA 2002, s.20(10), (11), (12), (13)

(1) the court believes is just, but
(2) does not exceed the amount found under s.7.

In arriving at the just amount the court must have regard in particular to:

(a) the amount found under s.7;
(b) any fine imposed on the defendant in respect of the offence (or any of the offences) concerned;
(c) any order which falls within s.13(3) and has been made against him in respect of the offence (or any of the offences) concerned and has not already been taken into account by the court in deciding what is the free property held by him for the purposes of s.9 (see 24–009, above);
(d) any compensation order which has been made against him in respect of the offence (or any of the offences) concerned under PCC(S) A 2000, s.130.

If a compensation order under s.130 has been made against the defendant in respect of the offence or offences concerned, s.13(5) and (6) above do not apply.

The date of conviction is the date found by applying s.19(10) (24–042, above).

Case (3): benefit calculated originally: fresh evidence as to amount

24–046 Where the judge did make a confiscation order at the time, but there is evidence which was not available to the prosecutor or the Director at the relevant time, and the prosecutor or the Director believes that if the court were to find the amount of the offender's benefit in pursuance of this section it would exceed the relevant amount, then where: PCA 2002, s.21(1)(2)

(1) before the end of the period of six years starting with the date of conviction the prosecutor or the Director applies to a judge of the Crown Court to consider the evidence, and
(2) after considering the evidence the judge believes it is appropriate for him to proceed under this provision,

he must make a new calculation of the offender's benefit from the conduct concerned.

Modifications appropriate to s.21 enquiry

24–047 Where the judge holds a s.6 enquiry in accordance with s.21, the following modifications apply: PCA 2002, s.21(4)(5)(6)

(1) if the offender has already been sentenced for the offence (or any of the offences) concerned, s.6 has effect as if his particular criminal conduct included conduct which constitutes offences which the judge has taken into consideration in deciding his sentence for the offence or offences concerned;
(2) s.8(2) in relation to calculating the offender's benefit (see 24–022–24–032 above) does not apply, and the rules applying instead are that the judge must take account of:
   (a) conduct occurring up to the time it decided the offender's benefit for the purposes of the confiscation order;
   (b) property obtained up to that time;
   (c) property obtained after that time if it was obtained as a result of or in connection with conduct occurring before that time.
(3) in applying s.8(5) as to aggregate (see 24–033 above) the confiscation order must be ignored.
(4) in relation to s.10 **(assumptions)** (see 24–031 above):
   (a) assumptions (1) and (2) will not apply with regard to property first held by the defendant after the time the court decided his benefit for the purposes of the confiscation order;
   (b) assumption (3) will not apply with regard to expenditure incurred by him after that time;
   (c) assumption (4) will not apply with regard to property obtained (or assumed to have been obtained) by him after that time.

Position where benefit exceeds relevant amount

24–048 If the amount found under the new calculation of the offender's benefit exceeds: PCA 2002, ss.21(7), (8), (9), (10)

(1) the relevant amount, the judge must make a new calculation of the recoverable amount for the purposes of s.6; and
(2) the amount required to be paid under the confiscation order, the judge may vary the order by substituting for the amount required to be paid such amount as he believes is just.

In applying (1) above, the judge must:

(a) take the new calculation of the offender's benefit; and
(b) apply s.9 (available amount, 24–035 above) as if references to the time the confiscation order is made were to the time of the new calculation of the recoverable amount and as if references to the date of the confiscation order were to the date of that new calculation.

In applying (2) above, the judge must have regard in particular to;

(i) any fine imposed on the offender for the offence (or any of the offences) concerned;
(ii) any order which falls within s.13(3) (see 24–009, above) and has been made against him in respect of the offence (or any of the offences) concerned, and has not already been taken into account by the judge in deciding what is the free property held by the defendant for the purposes of s.9;
(iii) any compensation order which has been made against him in respect of the offence (or any of the offences), concerned under PCC(S)A 2000, s.130;

but in applying subs.(2) above the judge must not have regard to an order falling within (c) above if a court has made a direction under s.13(6) (24–009 above) that payment be made out of the confiscation order.

Supplementary provisions

24–049 Note that:

(1) in deciding under this section whether one amount exceeds another the judge must take account of any change in the value of money; PCA 2002, ss.21(11)–(14)
(2) the relevant time is, when the court calculated the offender's benefit for the purposes of the confiscation order, if this section has not applied previously, or when the court last calculated his benefit in pursuance of this section, if this section has applied previously;

(3) the relevant amount is the amount found as the offender's benefit for the purposes of the confiscation order, if this section has not applied previously, or the amount last found as his benefit in pursuance of this section, if this section has applied previously;
(4) the date of conviction is the date found by applying s.19(10) (24–042, above).

Case (4): order made: reconsideration of available amount

24–050 Where a court has made a confiscation order, and the amount required to be paid was the "available amount" as assessed under s.7(2) (see 24–035 *et seq.* above), the prosecutor, the Director or a receiver appointed under s.50 or s.52 may apply to the Crown Court to make a new calculation of the available amount. PCA 2002, ss.22(1)–(4)

The application must be in writing, and may be supported by a witness statement. There must be lodged with the Crown Court, and must be served on the offender, on the receiver if the prosecutor or the Director is making the application, and a receiver has been appointed under s.50 or s.52, and if the receiver is making the application, on the prosecutor or on the Director if he is appointed the enforcement authority, at least seven days before the date fixed for the hearing unless the Crown Court specifies a shorter period. R.58.4

On the hearing the judge must:

(1) make the new calculation, and in doing so,
(2) apply s.9, in relation to the available amount, as if references to the time the confiscation order is made were a reference to the time of the new calculation and as if references to the date of the confiscation order were to the date of the new calculation.

If the amount found under the new calculation exceeds the relevant amount the judge may vary the order by substituting for the amount required to be paid such amount as he believes is just, but does not exceed the amount found as the defendant's benefit from the conduct concerned.

In deciding what is just he must have regard in particular to; PCA 2002, s.22(5)(6)

(a) any fine imposed on the offender for the offence (or any of the offences) concerned;
(b) any order which falls within s.13(3) (24–009 above) and has been made against him in respect of the offence (or any of the offences) concerned and has not already been

taken into account in deciding what is the free property held by him for the purposes of s.9 (24–026 above); and
(c) any compensation order which has been made against him in respect of the offence (or any of the offences) concerned under PCC(S)A 2000, s.130), but

in deciding what is just regard must not be paid to an order falling within subs.(c) a direction has been made under s.13(6) (see 24–009 above), that it be paid from the confiscation order.

Note that:

(i) in deciding under this section whether one amount exceeds another the judge must take account of any change in the value of money; PCA 2002, ss.22(7), (8), (9)
(ii) the "relevant amount" is the amount found as the available amount for the purposes of the confiscation order if this section has not been applied previously, or the amount last found as the available amount in pursuance of this section, if it has been applied previously;
(iii) the amount found as the defendant's benefit from the conduct concerned is the amount so found when the confiscation order was made, or, if one or more new calculations of his benefit have been made under s.21 (above), the amount found on the occasion of the last such calculation.

Case (5): inadequacy of "available amount": variation of order

24–051 Where a judge has made a confiscation order, the offender, or a receiver appointed under s.50 or s.52, may apply to a judge of the Crown Court to vary the order by substituting a lesser sum. PCA 2002, s.23

The application must be in writing, and may be supported by a witness statement. These must be lodged with the Crown Court, and must be served on the prosecutor or on the Director, where he is appointed the enforcement authority, the offender, if the receiver is making the application, and the receiver if the offender is making the application, at least seven days before the date fixed for the hearing unless the Crown Court specifies a shorter period. R.58.5

On such an application, the judge:

(1) must calculate the available amount, and in doing so he must apply s.9 (24–034 above) as if references to the time the confiscation order is made were to the time of the

calculation and as if references to the date of the order were to the date of the calculation; and

(2) if he finds that the available amount (so calculated) is inadequate for the payment of any amount remaining to be paid under the order, he may vary the order by substituting for the amount required to be paid, such smaller amount as he believes is just.

If a person has been adjudged bankrupt or his estate has been sequestrated, or if an order for the winding up of a company has been made, the judge must take into account the extent to which realisable property held by that person or that company may be distributed among creditors.

The judge may disregard any inadequacy which he believes is attributable (wholly or partly) to anything done by the offender for the purpose of preserving property held by the recipient of a tainted gift (24–029 above) from any risk of realisation under Pt 2 of the Act.

"Company" above, means any company which may be wound up under the Insolvency Act 1986 or the Insolvency (Northern Ireland) Order 1989 (SI 1989/2405 (NI 19)).

Inadequacy of available amount: discharge of order

24–052 Where a judge has made a confiscation order, the designated officer of a magistrates' court may apply to a judge of the Crown Court for the discharge of the order, the amount remaining to be paid under the order being less than £1,000. PCA 2002, s.24

The application must be in writing and must give details of the amount outstanding under the order and the grounds for the application. It must be served on the offender, the prosecutor and any receiver appointed under s.50. The judge may determine the application without a hearing unless one of those persons named above indicates, within seven days after the application was served on him, that he would like to make representations. R.58.6

In dealing with the matter, the judge:

(1) must calculate the available amount, and in doing so it must apply s.9 (24–042 above) as if references to the time the confiscation order is made were to the time of the calculation and as if references to the date of the confiscation order were to the date of the calculation; and

(2) if he finds that the available amount (as so calculated) is inadequate to meet the amount remaining to be paid, and is satisfied that the inadequacy is due wholly to a specified reason or a combination of specified reasons as set out below, he may discharge the confiscation order.

The specified reasons are:

(a) in a case where any of the realisable property consists of money in a currency other than sterling, that fluctuations in currency exchange rates have occurred; and
(b) any reason specified by the Home Secretary by order.

Reconsideration etc: variation of prison term

24–053 Where a judge varies a confiscation order under ss.21, 22, 23, 29, 32 or 33, the effect of the variation is to vary the maximum period applicable in relation to the order under PCC(S)A 2000, s.139(4) and: PCA 2002, s.39

(1) the result is that that maximum period is less than the term of imprisonment or detention fixed in respect of the order under PCC(S)A 2000, s.139(2), the judge must fix a reduced term of imprisonment or detention in respect of the confiscation order under s.139(2) in place of the term previously fixed; or
(2) if (1) is not the case, the judge may amend the term of imprisonment or detention fixed in respect of the confiscation order under PCC(S)A 2000, s.139(2).

If the effect of s.12 is to increase the maximum period applicable in relation to a confiscation order under PCC(S)A 2000, s.139(4), the appropriate person, i.e. the Director if he was appointed as the enforcement authority for the order under s.34; or the prosecutor in any other case may apply to a judge of the Crown Court to amend the term of imprisonment or detention fixed in respect of the order under s.139(2).

Application is made in writing giving the grounds for the application and details of the enforcement measures taken if any. On receipt of the application the court must:

(a) at once send to the offender, and if the Director has not been appointed as the enforcement authority, the magistrates' court responsible for enforcing the order, a copy of the application; and
(b) fix a date, time and place for the hearing and notify the same to the applicant and the offender. R.58.9

If the judge makes an order increasing the default term, the court must, at once, send a copy of the order to the applicant, the offender, the enforcing magistates' court if the Director has not been appointed as the enforcement authority, and, if the offender is in custody at the time of the making of the order, the person having custody of him.

Small amount outstanding: discharge of order

24–054 Where a court has made a confiscation order, and a justices' chief executive applies to the Crown Court for the discharge of the order, the amount remaining to be paid under the order being £50 or less, the judge may discharge the order. PCA 2002, s.25

6. Offender absconding; s.27

Offender convicted or committed

24–055 Where the offender absconds after: PCA 2002, s.27(1)–(4)

(1) (a) he is convicted of an offence or offences in proceedings before the Crown Court;
(b) he is committed to the Crown Court for sentence in respect of an offence or offences under PCC(S)A 2000, ss.3, 4 or 6; or
(c) he is committed to the Crown Court in respect of an offence or offences under s.70 below (committal with a view to a confiscation order being considered); and

(2) the prosecutor or the Director applies to the Crown Court to proceed under this section, and the judge believes it is appropriate for him to do so,

the judge must proceed under s.6 in the same way as he must proceed if the two conditions above are satisfied PCA 2002, ss.27(1)–(4), but if he proceeds under s.6 as applied by this section, Pt 2 has effect with these modifications: PCA 2002, s.27(5)

(i) any person the judge believes is likely to be affected by an order under s.6 is entitled to appear before him and make representations;
(ii) the judge must not make an order under s.6 unless the prosecutor or the Director (as the case may be) has taken reasonable steps to contact the defendant;
(iii) s.6(9) as to the offences concerned applies as if the reference to subs.(2) were to subs.(2) of this section;
(iv) ss.10 (assumptions), 16(4), 17 and 18 as to statements of information are to be ignored; and
(v) ss.19, 20 and 21 in regard to subsequent applications are to be ignored while the defendant is still an absconder.

Once the defendant ceases to be an absconder, s.19 in relation to the reconsideration of his case has effect as if subs.(1)(a) read PCA 2002, s.27(7) "(a) at a time when the first condition in s.27 was satisfied the court did not proceed under s.6." If the judge does not believe it is appropriate for him to proceed under this section, once the defendant ceases to be an absconder s.19 has effect as if subs.(1)(b) read: "(b) there is evidence which was not available to the prosecutor or the Director on the relevant date".

Defendant neither convicted nor acquitted

24–056 Where: PCA 2002, ss.28(1)–(5)

(1) proceedings for an offence or offences are started against a defendant but are not concluded; and
(2) he absconds; and
(3) the period of two years (starting with the day the judge believes he absconded) has ended; and
(4) the prosecutor or the Director applies to a judge of the Crown Court to proceed under this section; and
(5) the judge believes it is appropriate for him to do so,

he must proceed under s.6 in the same way as he is required to proceed if the two conditions mentioned in 24–045 above are satisfied, but if he does so, Pt 2 has effect with these modifications:

(a) any person the judge believes is likely to be affected by an order under s.6 is entitled to appear before him and make representations;
(b) the judge must not make an order under s.6 unless the prosecutor or the Director (as the case may be) has taken reasonable steps to contact the defendant;
(c) s.6(9) as to offences applies as if the reference to subs.(2) were to subs.(2) of this section;
(d) ss.10 (assumptions), 16(4), 17 and 18 (statement of information) and 19 and 20 (reconsideration of case) are to be ignored;
(e) s.21 (reconsideration of benefit) must be ignored while the defendant is still an absconder.

Once the defendant has ceased to be an absconder s.21 has effect as if references to the date of conviction were to: PCA 2002, ss.28(6)(7)

(i) the day when proceedings for the offence concerned were started against him, or
(ii) if there are two or more offences and proceedings for them were started on different days, the earliest of those days.

If the judge makes an order under s.6 as applied by this section, and the defendant is later convicted in proceedings before the

Crown Court of the offence (or any of the offences) concerned, s.6 does not apply so far as that conviction is concerned.

Variation of order

24–057 Where the judge makes a confiscation order under s.6 as applied by s.28, and the defendant ceases to be an absconder, then, if he is convicted of an offence (or any of the offences) mentioned in the last paragraph: PCA 2002, ss.29(1)(2)

(1) if he believes that the amount required to be paid was too large (taking the circumstances prevailing when the amount was found for the purposes of the order), and
(2) he may, before the end of the relevant period apply to the Crown Court to consider the evidence on which his belief is based.

Application must be made in writing and must be supported by a witness statement, giving details of the order made against him, the circumstances in which he ceased to be an absconder, his conviction of the offence or offences concerned and the reason why he believes the amount required to be paid under the order was too large.

The application and the statement must be lodged with the Crown Court and must be served on the prosecutor or on the Director, where he is appointed the enforcement authority, at least seven days before the date fixed for the hearing unless the Crown Court specifies a shorter period. R.58.7

If the judge, after considering the evidence concludes that the defendant's belief is well founded, he:

(a) must find the amount which should have been the amount required to be paid (taking the circumstances prevailing when the amount was found for the purposes of the order), and
(b) may vary the order by substituting for the amount required to be paid such amount as it believes is just.

The "relevant period" is the period of 28 days starting with:

(i) the date on which the defendant was convicted of the offence mentioned in s.28(2)(a), or
(ii) if there are two or more offences and the convictions were on different dates, the date of the latest.

But in a case where s.28(2)(a) applies to more than one offence the court must not make an order under this section unless it is satisfied that there is no possibility of any further proceedings PCA 2002, ss.29(3)(4) being taken in relation to any such offence in respect of which the defendant has not been convicted.

Discharge of order

24–058 Where the judge makes a confiscation order under s.6 as applied by s.28, and the defendant is later tried for the offence or offences concerned and acquitted on all counts, he may apply to the Crown Court to discharge the order, and in such a case the judge must discharge the order. PCA 2002, ss.30(1)(2)

Application is made in writing and must be supported by a witness statement giving details of the order made against him, the date on which he ceased to be an absconder, his acquittal, if he has been acquitted of the offence concerned, and if he has not been acquitted of the offence concerned:

(1) the date on which he ceased to be an absconder;
(2) the date on which the proceedings taken against him were instituted and a summary of the steps taken in the proceedings; and
(3) any indication by the prosecutor that he does not intend to proceed against him.

The application and the statement must be lodged with the Crown Court and must be served on the prosecutor or on the Director, where he is appointed the enforcement authority, at least seven days before the date fixed for the hearing unless the Crown Court specifies a shorter period. R.58.8

If a confiscation order under s.6 as applied by s.28, was made and the defendant ceased to be an absconder, but was not tried and acquitted on all counts, then, if he applies to the Crown Court to discharge the order, the judge may discharge it only if he finds that: PCA 2002, ss.30(3), (4)

(a) there has been undue delay in continuing the proceedings mentioned in s.28(2), or
(b) the prosecutor does not intend to proceed with the prosecution.

If the judge discharges a confiscation order under this section he may make such a consequential or incidental order as he believes is appropriate. PCA 2002, s.30(5)

If the judge orders the discharge of the order, the court must serve notice on the magistrates' court responsible for its enforcement where the Director has not been appointed as the enforcement authority. R.58.8(5)

7. Appeals

Appeal by prosecutor or Director

24–059 The prosecutor or the Director may appeal to CACD where a judge of the Crown Court: PCA 2002, ss.31, 32(1), (4)

(1) makes a confiscation order under PCA 2002, in respect of the order; or
(2) decides not to make a confiscation order, against that decision,

except in the case of an order or decision made by virtue of ss.19, 20 (reconsideration), 27 or 28 (convicted and unconvicted absconders).

The *Explanatory Notes* published by HMSO state that only an appeal on a point of law lies under this section. The post-conviction procedures being mandatory there is no scope for an appeal on the merits; it is otherwise in revaluation cases (see *R. v Bakewell* [2006] Crim.L.R. 453).

An appeal requires the leave of CACD. As to further procedure see 18–087 *et seq*.

Crown Court proceeding afresh after appeal

24–060 Where CACD orders the Crown Court to proceed afresh, the judge of the Crown Court must comply with any directions CACD makes, and if he makes or varies a confiscation order under this section or in pursuance of a direction under this section he must have regard to any:

(1) fine imposed on the accused in respect of the offence (or any of the offences) concerned;
(2) order which falls within s.13(3) (see 24–009) and has been made against him in respect of the offence (or any of the offences) concerned, unless the order has already been taken into account by a court in deciding what is the free property held by the accused for the purposes of s.9.

Ancillary provisions

24–061 Where the Crown Court proceeds afresh under that section in pursuance of a direction by the CACD: PCA 2002, s.32(5)(11)

(1) if a court has already sentenced the defendant for the offence (or any of the offences) concerned, s.6 will have effect as if his particular criminal conduct included conduct which constitutes offences which the court has taken into consideration in deciding his sentence for the offence or offences concerned;

(2) if a compensation order has been made against the defendant in respect of the offence (or any of the offences) concerned under PCC(S)A 2000, s.130, the judge must have regard to it, and s.13(5) and (6) (24–009 above) do not apply;
(3) s.8(2) in relation to benefit (24–023 above) does not apply, and the rules applying instead are that the judge must take account of:
  (a) conduct occurring before the relevant date;
  (b) property obtained before that date;
  (c) property obtained on or after that date if it was obtained as a result of or in connection with conduct occurring before that date.
(4) in s.10 (assumptions, see 24–031 above):
  (a) assumptions (1) and (2) do not apply with regard to property first held by the defendant on or after the relevant date;
  (b) assumption (3) does not apply with regard to expenditure incurred by him on or after that date; and
  (c) assumption (4) does not apply with regard to property obtained (or assumed to have been obtained) by him on or after that date.
(5) s.26 (statement of information) applies as it applies in the circumstances mentioned in subs.(1) of that section.

The relevant date is the date on which the Crown Court decided not to make a confiscation order.

Further appeal lies to the House of Lords/Supreme Court, where similar provisions in respect of a fresh order by a judge of the Crown Court apply. PCA 2002, s.33

8. Commencement and conclusion of proceedings

Proceedings for an offence

24–062 Proceedings for an offence are **started** when: PCA 2002, s.85

(1) a magistrate issues a summons or warrant under MCA 1980, s.1 in respect of the offence;
(2) a person is charged with an offence after being taken into custody without a warrant;
(3) a voluntary bill of indictment is preferred under AJ(MP)A 1933, s.2 in a case falling within subs.(2)(b) of that section (preferment by CACD or a High Court judge).

If more than one time is found under the subsection in relation to proceedings they are started at the earliest of them.

Proceedings are **concluded**:

(1) if the defendant is acquitted on all counts in proceedings for an offence, when he is acquitted;
(2) if the defendant is convicted in proceedings for an offence and the conviction is quashed or the defendant is pardoned before a confiscation order is made, when the conviction is quashed or the defendant is pardoned;
(3) if a confiscation order is made against the defendant in proceedings for an offence (whether the order is made by the Crown Court or CACD):
  (a) when the order is satisfied or discharged, or
  (b) when the order is quashed and there is no further possibility of an appeal against the decision to quash the order;
(4) if the defendant is convicted in proceedings for an offence but the judge decides not to make a confiscation order against him:
  (a) if an application for leave to appeal under s.31(2) is refused, when the decision to refuse is made;
  (b) if the time for applying for leave to appeal under s.31(2) expires without an application being made, when the time expires;
  (c) if on appeal under s.31(2) CACD confirms the judge's decision and an application for leave to appeal under s.33 is refused, when the decision to refuse is made;
  (d) if on appeal under s.31(2) CACD confirms the judge's decision and the time for applying for leave to appeal under s.33 expires without an application being made, when the time expires;
  (e) if on appeal under s.31(2) CACD confirms the judge's decision and on appeal under s.33 the House of Lords/Supreme Court confirms CACD's decision, when the latter confirms the decision;
  (f) if on appeal under s.31(2) CACD directs the Crown Court to reconsider the case, and on reconsideration the judge decides not to make a confiscation order against the defendant, when he makes that decision;
  (g) if on appeal under s.33 the House of Lords/Supreme Court directs the Crown Court to reconsider the case, and on reconsideration the judge decides not to make

a confiscation order against the defendant, when he makes that decision.

In applying any one of the above provisions any power to extend the time for making an application for leave to appeal is to be ignored, as must the fact that a court may postpone making a confiscation order.

Conclusion of applications

24–063 Applications are concluded as follows: PCA 2002, s.86

(1) under ss.19, 20, 27 or 28 in a case where:
  (a) the judge decides not to make a confiscation order against the defendant, when he makes the decision;
  (b) a confiscation order is made against him as a result of the application, when the order is satisfied or discharged, or when the order is quashed and there is no further possibility of an appeal against the decision to quash the order;
  (c) the application is withdrawn, when the person who made the application notifies the withdrawal to the court to which the application was made.

(2) under s.21 or s.22:
  (a) in a case where the judge decides not to vary the confiscation order concerned, when he makes the decision;
  (b) in a case where the judge varies the confiscation order as a result of the application, when the order is satisfied or discharged, or when the order is quashed and there is no further possibility of an appeal against the decision to quash the order;
  (c) in a case where the application is withdrawn, when the person who made the application notifies the withdrawal to the court to which the application was made.

Other interpretative provisions

24–064 A reference to the offence (or offences) concerned must be construed in accordance with s.6(9). PCA 2002, s.88

A "criminal investigation" is an investigation which police officers or other persons have a duty to conduct with a view to it being ascertained whether a person should be charged with an offence.

A "defendant" is a person against whom proceedings for an offence have been started (whether or not he has been convicted).

A reference to "sentencing the defendant for an offence" includes a reference to dealing with him otherwise in respect of the offence.

9. Seizure and forfeiture of cash

Detention of cash

24–065 PCA 2002 empowers an officer of revenue and customs or a constable to seize any cash if he has reasonable grounds for suspecting it to be: PCA 2002, ss.294, 295, 297; SOCA 2005, s.100

(1) recoverable property; or
(2) intended by any person for use in unlawful conduct

or part of it, if it is not reasonably practicable to seize only that part, provided, in either case, the cash to which his suspicion relates. exceeds the minimum amount, i.e. £5,000 (SI 2004/420).

There is nothing to prevent seizure under s.295 of money which has already been seized under e.g. PACE 1984, s.19 (*Merseyside Chief Constable v Hickman and Another, The Times*, April 7, 2006).

As to the meaning of "recoverable property", see PCA 2002, s.240, as to "unlawful conduct" see *ibid.* s.241.

While the officer of revenue and customs or constable continues to have reasonable grounds for his suspicions, the cash may be detained initially for a period of 48 hours (calculated in accordance with s.295(1A)(1B)). The period may be extended on application, by any magistrates' court (SI 2003/638), or a single justice, but not beyond the period of three months beginning with the date of the order, or, in the case if any further order, not beyond as period of two years from the date of the first, provided that, in relation to any cash to be further detained, there are reasonable grounds for suspecting that the cash is:

(a) **recoverable property; or**
(b) **intended to be used in unlawful conduct**, and in either case
 (i) its continued detention is justified while its derivation is further investigated or consideration is given to bringing proceedings (in the UK or elsewhere) against any person for an offence with which the cash is connected, or

(ii) the proceedings against any person for an offence with which the cash is connected have been started and have not be concluded.

Persons affected by the order must be notified of its making.

If, on application by the person from whom the cash was seized, a magistrates' court, is satisfied that the conditions in s.295 for the detention of the cash are no longer met, it may order it to be released. A constable or officer of revenue and customs, after notifying the magistrates' court, may release the whole or any part of the cash if satisfied that its detertion is no longer justified. Unless the cash, or part of it, is required as evidence, it must be paid into an interest-bearing account and any interest on it will be added to it on forfeiture or release. PCA 2002, s.296

Forfeiture

24–066 While cash is detained under s.295, an application for the forfeiture of the whole or any part it may be made to the magistrates' court by HM Revenue and Customs or a constable under s.298 and the court may order forfeiture of the cash or any part of it is satisfied that it is recoverable property or is intended by any person for use in unlawful conduct. Special provisions apply in relation to recoverable property belonging to joint tenants. PCA 2002, s.298

Procedure in the magistrates' court is governed by the Magistrates' Courts (Detention and Forfeiture of Cash) Rules 2002 (SI 2002/2998).

Where an application for forfeiture is made, there is no power to release the cash until the proceedings, (including any appeal) have been concluded.

Appeal against forfeiture

24–067 An appeal lies to the Crown Court *by any party to proceedings* for an order for forfeiture of cash under s.298 who is aggrieved by an order made or a decision not to make such an order. The appeal must be made before the end of the period of 30 days starting with the day on which the court made its order or decision. PCA 2002, s.299; SOCA 2005, s.101

The Crown Court may make any order it thinks appropriate, and if it upholds the appeal, may order the release of the cash.

The proceedings are civil in nature and by way of re-hearing.

10. External Requests; cross-border enforcement

The legislation

24–068 Foreign requests and orders are received by the Home Secretary and forwarded to the appropproiate authority, the CPS, DARA. RCPO or SFO to take court action. Those bodies have a discretion whether or not to proceed. Procedure is under PCA 2002 (External Requests and Orders) Order 2005 (SI 2005/3181), Pt 2, or, in regard to the former law, under the CJ(IC)A 1990 (Enforcement of Overseas Forfeiture Orders) Order 2005 (SI 2005/3180).

The scheme

24–069 The procedure under both Orders is similar. It provides for the registration of external forfeiture orders:

(1) arising from a criminal conviction in the country from which the order is sent; and
(2) concerning relevant property in England and Wales.

Such an order must be an order made by a court in a designated country for the forfeiture and destruction, or the forfeiture and disposal of anything:

(a) in respect of which a "relevant offence" has been committed; or
(b) which was used or intended for use in connection with the commission of such an offence.

A "relevant offence" is defined as one that corresponds to or is similar to an offence under the law of England and Wales.

Such a request is channelled through the Secretary of State to the "relevant Director" being the DPP or DRC, or in certain circumstances the DSFO.

An application by a relevant Director 4(1) to a judge of the Crown Court must include a request to appoint the Director as the enforcement authority, and may be made to a judge in chambers without giving notice to the other party.

The judge's role

24–070 The judge must give effect to an external forfeiture order by registering it where he is satisfied that:

(1) the order was made consequent on the conviction of the person named in the order and no appeal is outstanding in respect of that conviction;

(2) the order is in force and no appeal is outstanding in respect of it;
(3) giving effect to the order would not be incompatible with any of the Convention rights of any persons affected by it; and
(4) the property whose confiscation is specified is not subject to a charge.

Where the judge decides to give effect to an external forfeiture order he must:

(a) register the order in that court; provide for notice to be given to any person affected by it; and
(b) appoint the relevant Director as the enforcement authority for the order.

Only an order registered in the Crown Court may be implemented under the legislation.

There are provisions for cancelling or varying the order, appealing to CACD and HL and the appointment of enforcement receivers.

An order is satisfied when the property specified in it has been forfeited or disposed in accordance with the legislation (art.24).

Procedure

24–071 CPR 2005, rr.59–61 and 71 apply with the necessary modifications to proceedings under SI 2005/3181 as they apply to corresponding proceedings under PCA 2002 (r.57.15 inserted by SI 2006/353).

Cross-border enforcement

24–072 The enforcement in England and Wales of confiscation orders made under the Proceeds of Crime (Scotland) Act 1995, is governed by SI 2001/953.

As to the enforcement in England and Wales of restraint and receivership proceedings from Scotland and Northern Ireland, see SI 2002/3133 and 52 RESTRAINT ORDERS; RECEIVERSHIP).

25 CONTEMPT OF COURT

25–001 The judge has power to punish summarily for "contempt in the face of the court" where that contempt is committed:

(1) in the courtroom, witnessed by the judge;
(2) in the courtroom and reported to the judge;
(3) beyond the courtroom, and even beyond the precincts of the court; where
    (a) it is reported to the judge; and
    (b) relates to proceedings then in progress, or pending before the court.

The judge is entitled to defer until a later date the issue of whether the accused was in contempt of court, and the appropriate punishment (*R. v Santiago* [2005] Crim. L.R. 74). The "real need", i.e. "the urgency to act immediately" expressed in *Balogh v St Albans CC* [1974] 3 All E.R. 283 has been tempered by *Wilkinson v The Official Solicitor* [2003] 1 W.L.R. 1254. See also *Rooney v Snaresbrook CC* (1979) 68 Cr.App.R. 78; *R. v Griffin* (1989) 88 Cr.App.R. 63).

The "real need" for summary action

25–002 The judge must make his own assessment of the need for taking immediate action to deal with an alleged contempt (*R. v Goult* (1983) 76 Cr.App.R. 140). He will need to distinguish between conduct:

(1) which involves disruption of the court, or threats to witnesses or jurors, which should be visited by immediate arrest; and
(2) which is not likely to disturb the trial or affect the verdict or judgment, as this can be dealt with at a later stage of the trial, under the RSC 52, r.5 or on indictment at the instance of the Attorney General though procedure on indictment was ruled inappropriate in *R. v D* [1984] A.C. 778, 792.

Where the contempt proceedings arise in the course of a trial, the judge should ask the jury to withdraw before, e.g. having a witness arrested in court (*R. v Maguire* [1997] 1 Cr.App.R. 61).

Where a contempt is alleged to have taken place without the presence of the judge, the latter has no power to remand the alleged contemnor into custody before the contempt is proved.

Where he wishes to ensure that such a person is not at liberty during the further course of the trial he will have either to adjourn the trial and proceed to deal with the alleged contempt, or arrange for another judge to hear the allegation of contempt (*R. v Stevens & Holmes* (unreported) May 21, 1997 QBD).

Summary procedure

25–003 The jurisdiction is *sui generis*; there is no prosecutor, nor need for a prosecutor or representative of the injured party to initiate the proceedings. The proceedings are not adversarial.

(1) Where the contempt proceedings touch upon a trial in session they must be in open court, and the advocate defending at the trial cannot be excluded (*R. v Coolledge* [1996] Crim.L.R. 749);
(2) where the judge observes the conduct complained of he may act *ex proprio motu*;
(3) where the matter is reported to him, the judge may wish to hear evidence, if necessary on both sides;
(4) the judge identifies the cause of complaint, which ought to be made plain to the contemnor, and the judge selects the witnesses and, subject to rights of cross-examination, investigates the matter, decides on guilt and passes sentence.

There needs to be a speedy disposal of such a case (*Wilkinson v S* [2003] 1 W.L.R. 1254. In *R. v Serumaga*, *The Times*, February 28, 2005 CACD found no material to justify a remand of seven days. There is nothing in AJA 1960, s.13(1) to prohibit the grant of bail to an alleged contemnor (*ibid.*).

Legal representation

25–004 In general, unless a serious contempt is committed in the face of the court, preventing or disrupting its business, the judge should invite the alleged contemnor, but cannot compel him, to be legally represented. This ensures that the judge has the assistance of an advocate in considering his powers in the circumstances of the case (*R. v Tyne Tees TV Ltd*, *The Times*, October 20, 1997). Giving the contemnor the opportunity to apologise is one of the more important aspects of the summary procedure (*R. v Hill* [1986] Crim.L.R. 457; *R. v Moran* (1985) 81 Cr.App.R. 51; *R. v Griffin* (1989) 88 Cr.App.R. 63).

Some common situations

25–005 The most common situations are where witnesses are victimised or threatened, or attempts are made to influence or intimidate jurors. Here there is a "real need" for the judge to intervene, not only to safeguard the dignity of the court, but in the latter case to reassure other jurors waiting their call to court; this sort of contempt is prevalent and calls for a deterrent sentence (*R. v Goult* (1983) 76 Cr.App.R. 140; *R. v Mulvaney* (1982) 4 Cr.App.R.(S.) 106; *R. v Maloney* (1986) 8 Cr.App.R.(S.) 123; *R. v Pittendrigh* (1985) 7 Cr.App.R.(S.) 221); *R. v Edmonds* [1999] 1 Cr.App.R.(S.) 476; *R. v Smith* [2001] 1 Cr.App.R.(S.) 66; *R. v Rogers* [2002] 1 Cr.App.R.(S.) 272).

Where the accused disrupts the proceedings (*R. v Aquarius* (1974) 59 Cr.App.R. 165), or stages an outburst after sentence (*R. v Logan* [1974] Crim.L.R. 609), or abuses the trial judge (*R. v Hill* [1986] Crim.L.R. 457; *R. v McDaniel* (1990–91) 12 Cr.App.R.(S.) 45), the appropriate course is to pass a sentence for contempt consecutive to that for the substantive offence, and not attempt to include a contempt element in the sentence for the substantive offence.

Conduct of legal practitioners

25–006 For the conduct of a legal practitioner to amount to contempt of court, it will need to be scandalous; bad manners, incompetence or discourtesy do not amount to contempt (*Weston v Courts Administrator* [1976] 2 All E.R. 875).

Recalcitrant witnesses

25–007 A number of potential situations may occur here:

(1) Failure to attend may be dealt with by warrant (12 BENCH AND WITNESS WARRANT);
(2) in the case of a witness who attends but declines to testify, it will be a question for the judge whether some positive action is called for in the circumstances. Refusal to answer a question may be dealt with by mere admonition, unless the answer to it is vital;
(3) the judge ought to approach the question only after reflection. Unless there is good reason for dealing with the matter speedily, sentence should be adjourned to the end of the trial, or at least to the end of the prosecution case (*R. v Moran* (1985) 7 Cr.App.R.(S.) 101; *R. v Lewis* (1993) 96 Cr.App.R. 412), so that the witness has a chance to reconsider his position (*R. v Phillips* (1984) 78 Cr.App.R. 88; *R. v Moran* (1985) 81 Cr.App.R. 51; *R. v Leonard* (1984) 6 Cr.App.R.(S.) 279; *R. v Jardine* (1987) 9 Cr.App.R.(S.) 41; *R. v Montgomery* [1995] 2 Cr.App.R. 23; *R. v MacLeod*, [2001] Crim.L.R. 589).

Nature and length of sentence

25–008 The authorities are usefully summarised in *R. v Montgomery* (1995) 16 Cr.App.R.(S.) 274. The following general principles emerge:

(1) an immediate term of imprisonment is the only appropriate sentence to impose on a person aged 18 or over who interferes with the administration of justice, unless the circumstances are wholly exceptional (*R. v Owen* (1976) 63 Cr.App.R. 199);
(2) where victims of, or witnesses to, serious crime refuse to do their duty or succumb to fear of reprisals by refusing to give evidence, there is a failure of law and order. When this occurs it is usually necessary to impose a custodial sentence to mark the gravity of the matter and to stiffen the resolve of other potential witnesses who may similarly be minded to default (*R. v Montgomery,* see above);
(3) while interference with jurors is often visited with higher sentences than refusal to give evidence, there is no rule or established practice to that effect. In the case of a recalcitrant witness, while it is legitimate to have regard to the fact that the maximum sentence for failing to comply with a witness order is three months, this need not inhibit the judge from imposing a substantially longer sentence for a blatant contempt by a witness in the face of the court (*R. v Phillips* (1984) 78 Cr.App.R. 88 and *R. v Jardine* (1987) 9 Cr.App.R.(S.) 41; *R. v Samuda* (1989) 11 Cr.App.R.(S.) 471).
(4) In most cases a moderate term will suffice (*R. v Montgomery* see above).

The judge may order the sentence for contempt to run consecutively to another term, even to a term imposed in a civil court (*R. v Anomo* [1998] Crim.L.R. 356).

Principal factors affecting sentence

25–009 The principal factors affecting sentence are set out in the guideline case of *R. v Montgomery* above, affirmed in *R. v Richardson* [2004] EWCA Crim 758. They are:

(1) the gravity of the offence being tried;
(2) the effect upon the trial;
(3) the contemnor's reasons for refusing to give evidence;
(4) whether the contempt is aggravated by impertinent defiance of the judge (as opposed to a simple refusal (*R. v Leonard* (1984) 6 Cr.App.R.(S.) 279);

(5) the scale of sentences in similar cases;
(6) the antecedents and personal circumstances of the contemnor (*R. v Palmer* (1992) 13 Cr.App.R.(S.) 595); and
(7) whether, e.g. a special deterrent is needed, as where at the beginning of a series of trials it is becoming clear that witnesses are being threatened, or where there is a developing pattern of refusal in relation to certain types of offences or in particular parts of the country.

In the case of a witness refusing to testify, the importance of his evidence ought to be taken into account (*R. v Phillips* (1983) 5 Cr.App.R.(S.) 297).

Young persons

25–010 Apart from a person who commits a bail offence (*R. v Tyson* (1979) 68 Cr.App.R. 314), a person adjudged guilty of contempt of court has not been "convicted of an offence" (*R. v Selby M.C. Ex p. Frame* (1990) 12 Cr.App.R.(S.) 434).

In relation to young offenders:

(1) imprisonment is available only for offenders aged 21 and over; community orders under CJA 2003, s.177 are available in the case of offenders aged 16 or over only;
(2) in the case of a person under 18, there is no power to award a custodial sentence (*R. v Byas* (1995) 16 Cr.App.R.(S.) 869);
(3) in the case of an offender under 16, a fine is probably the only appropriate penalty, though in the case of an offender under 16 an attendance centre order may be appropriate.

Unofficial tape recording of proceedings

25–011 CCA 1981, s.9 governs the unofficial use of tape recorders in court, providing that it is a contempt of court to: PD 2004, I.2.1

(1) use in court, or bring into court for use, any tape recorder or other instrument for recording sound, except with the leave of the judge;
(2) publish a recording of legal proceedings made by means of any such instrument, or any recording derived directly or indirectly from it; and
(3) use any such recording in contravention of any conditions of leave.

These provisions do not apply to the making or use of sound recordings for purposes of official transcripts of the proceedings, upon which the Act imposes no restriction whatever.

The transcript of a permitted recording is intended for the use of the person given leave to make it and it is not intended to be used as, or to compete with, the oficial transcript mentioned in s.9(4). PD 2004, I.2.5

Judge's discretion

25–012 The discretion given to the judge to grant, withhold or withdraw leave to use tape recorders or to impose conditions as to the use of the recording is unlimited, but the following factors may be relevant to its exercise: PD 2004, I.2.2–4

(1) the existence of any reasonable need on the part of the applicant for leave, whether a litigant or a person connected with the press or broadcasting, for the recording to be made;
(2) the risk that the recording could be used for the purpose of briefing witnesses out of court;
(3) any possibility that the use of the recorder would disturb the proceedings or distract or worry any witnesses or other participants.

Consideration should always be given to whether conditions as to the use of a recording made pursuant to leave should be imposed. The identity and role of the applicant for leave and the nature of the subject matter of the proceedings may be relevant to this.

The particular restriction imposed by s.9(1)(b) applies in every case, but may not be present to the mind of every applicant to whom leave is given. It may therefore be desirable on occasion for this provision to be drawn to the attention of those to whom leave is given.

26 COSTS AND TAXATION

1. Introduction

Power to award costs

26–001 The powers enabling a judge to award costs in criminal proceedings are primarily contained in POA 1985, ss.16, 17 and 18, AJA 1999 in relation to funded clients, and in the Regulations made under those Acts, including GR 1986 (SI 1986/1335) as amended. A modern approach to the award of costs in the Crown Court is to be found in PDC 2004, [2004] 2 All E.R. 1070, which took effect from **May 18, 2004**. PDC 2004, I.1.1–I.2.3

POA 1985, by virtue of:

(1) **s.16** makes provision for the award of *defence* costs out of central funds;
(2) **s.17** provides for an award of costs to *private* prosecutors out of central funds;
(3) **s.18** empowers the judge to order a convicted offender, or unsuccessful appellant, to pay costs to the prosecutor;
(4) **s.19(1)** and GR 1986, reg. 3 provide for the award of costs between parties;
(5) **s.19A** provides for the court to disallow, or order a legal or other representative of a party to the proceedings to meet wasted costs;
(6) **s.19B** provides for the court to make a "third party costs order" where there has been serious misconduct by a third party.

As to costs against third parties, see 26–029 below.

In addition, a judge of the Crown Court, as part of the Senior Courts (formerly the Supreme Court), has power under its inherent jurisdiction over officers of the court, to order a solicitor personally to pay costs thrown away.

The judge has the same powers under ss.17 and 18 in relation to the award of costs on committals for sentence, and under s.16 for failure to comply with the conditions of a recognisance, as he has in relation to trials on indictment.

He may also give directions relating to CDS funded costs and Recovery of Defence Costs Orders.

As to costs on **appeals from magistrates' courts**, see 10 APPEALS.

Extent of orders for costs from central funds

26–002 Where a court orders that the costs of an accused, appellant or private prosecutor should be paid from central funds: PDC 2004, I.3.1

(1) the order will be for such amount as the court considers reasonably sufficient to compensate the party for expenses incurred by him in the proceedings;
(2) this will include the costs incurred in the proceedings in the lower courts unless for good reason the court directs that such costs are not included in the order; but
(3) it cannot include expenses incurred which do not directly relate to the proceedings themselves, such as loss of earnings.

Where the party in whose favour the order is CDS funded he will only recover his personal costs (see POA 1985, s.21(4A)(a)).

PDC 2004, Sch.2 (at 26–049, below) sets out the extent of the availability of costs from central funds and the relevant statutory authority.

Amount of costs to be paid

26–003 Except where the judge has directed in an order for costs out of central funds that only a specified sum be paid, the amount of costs to be paid is determined by the Crown Court officer. The judge may, however: PDC 2004, I.4.1, 2, 3

(1) order the disallowance of costs out of central funds not properly incurred; or
(2) direct the Determining Officer to consider whether or not specific items have been properly incurred; and may also
(3) make observations regarding CDS funded costs (for the procedure see 26–034, below).

Where the court orders an offender to pay costs to the prosecutor, orders one party to pay costs to another, disallows or orders a legal or other representative to meet wasted costs, the order for costs must specify the sum to be paid or disallowed.

Where the court is required to specify the amount of costs to be paid, the judge cannot delegate the decision. Where practicable, instructing solicitors should provide the advocate with details of costs incurred at each stage of the proceedings. The judge may require the appropriate officer to make enquiries and inform him of the costs incurred, and may adjourn, if necessary, for enquiries to be made. Special provisions apply in relation to recovery of defence costs orders (see 26–036, below). (As to the extent of the investigation by POA 1985, s.16 and SI 1986/1335, see *R. (Brewer) v Supreme Courts Costs Office, The Times*, August 16, 2006, Q.B.D.).

Quick Guide

2. Defence costs from central funds

Accused not tried or acquitted

26–004 Where a person: PDC 2004, II.2

(1) is not tried for an offence for which he has been indicted, or in respect of which proceedings against him have been sent for trial; or
(2) has been acquitted on any count in the indictment,

the judge may make a "defendant's costs order" in his favour.

As to defence costs on an appeal to the Crown Court, see POA 1985, s.16(3) and 10 APPEALS, in proceedings before the Administrative Court, in CACD, see 18 CHALLENGING THE CROWN COURT.

An order should normally be made whether or not an order for costs between parties is made, unless there are positive reasons for not doing so. For example where the conduct of the accused has brought suspicion on himself and has misled the prosecution into thinking that the case against him was stronger than it was, here the accused may be left to pay his own costs.

The refusal must be based on independent evidence and not simply prosecution evidence that the allegations have been withdrawn. (*Mooney v Cardiff JJ* (2000) 164 J.P. 220.)

The judge, when declining to make a costs order should explain, in open court, that the reason for not making an order does not involve any suggestion that the accused is guilty of any criminal conduct but the order is refused because of the positive reason, which should be identified.

Conviction on some counts, acquittal on others

26–005 Where an accused is convicted of some counts in the indictment but acquitted on others the judge: PDC 2004, II.2.2

(1) may exercise his discretion to make a defendant's costs order; but
(2) may order that only part of the costs incurred be paid;
(3) may make whatever order seems just having regard to the relative importance of the charges and the conduct of the parties generally;
(4) must where he considers it inappropriate that the accused recover all of the costs properly incurred, specify the amount in the order.

Note that:

(a) the judge is entitled to take note of the fact that the accused elected trial on indictment, and if, in his opinion, such election was extravagant and unreasonable, he is entitled to take that fact into consideration in exercising his discretion (*R. v Dawood* [1974] Crim.L.R. 486);
(b) the fact that the judge disagrees with the verdict of a jury is not a ground for refusing costs out of central funds (*Practice Direction* (1959) 43 Cr.App.R. 419);
(c) where the Crown do not proceed because a witness is unavailable an application for costs should normally succeed (*R. v Preston* CC [2001] EWHC Admin 599 (unreported, July 16, 2001));
(d) where a parent or guardian is liable under PCC(S)A 2000, s.171(1) to pay the fine, costs or compensation of a child, the reference to an "accused" in s.16(5)(a) includes such a person (*R. v Preston C* [1998] 3 All E.R. 765);
(e) where the local authority stands *in loco parentis* under PCC(S)A 2000, s.130, and the accused juvenile is acquitted, the authority is entitled to a defendant's costs order, where it would be appropriate in the case of the accused (*R. v Preston CC*, etc., see above).

It does not necessarily follow that because a solicitor has claimed costs under a defendant's costs order that his client cannot make a claim for costs which he has incurred (*R. v Bedlington*, *The Times*, November 30, 2000).

3. Private prosecutor's costs from central funds

26–006 There is no power to order the payment out of central funds of any prosecutor who is a public authority, a person acting on behalf of a public authority or acting as an official appointed by a public authority as defined in the Act. PDC 2004, III.1.1

In the limited number of cases in which a prosecutor's costs may be awarded out of central funds:

(1) an application must be made by the prosecution in each case; and
(2) an order should be made, save where there is good reason for not doing so, as where proceedings have been instituted or continued without good cause; and
(3) the procedure applies to proceedings in respect of an indictable offence, or proceedings before the Administrative Court in respect of a summary offence;
(4) GR 1986, reg. 14(1) extends the provision to certain committals from a magistrates' court.

4. Witness, interpreter or medical evidence

26–007 The costs of attendance of: PDC 2004, IV.1, 2

(1) a witness required by the accused, a private prosecutor or the court, or
(2) an interpreter required because of the accused's lack of English, or
(3) an *oral* report by a medical practitioner,

are allowed out of central funds unless the judge otherwise directs (POA 1985, s.20(3), GR 1986, reg.16(1)). If, and only if, the court makes such a direction can the expense of the witness be claimed as a disbursement out of CDS funds.

A "witness" includes any person properly attending to give evidence, whether or not he gives evidence or is called, but it does not include a character witness unless the judge has certified that the interests of justice require his attendance.

The court may also order the payment out of central funds of such sums as appear to it to be reasonably sufficient to compensate any medical practitioner for the expenses, trouble, or loss of time properly incurred in preparing and making a report on the mental condition of a person accused of murder (see MH(A)A 1982, s.34(5)).

5. Disallowance of items out of central funds

26–008 Where the judge makes an order for costs out of central funds, he: PDC 2004, V.1

(1) *must* direct the appropriate authority to disallow the costs incurred in respect of any items if it is plain that those costs were not properly incurred (such costs are not payable under POA 1985, ss.16(6), 17(1));
(2) *may* direct the appropriate authority to consider or investigate on taxation any items which may have been improperly incurred.

Costs not properly incurred include costs in respect of work unreasonably done, e.g. if the case has been conducted unreasonably so as to incur unjustified expense, or costs have been wasted by failure to conduct proceedings with reasonable competence and expedition. In a plain case it will usually be more appropriate to make a wasted costs order under POA 1985, s.19A (see below). The precise terms of the order for costs and of any direction must be entered on the court record.

The word "improper" in POA 1985, s.19 and GR 1986, reg.3(1) does not denote some grave impropriety but is intended to cover an act or omission which would not have occurred if the party concerned had conducted his case properly (*DPP v Denning* [1991] 3 All E.R. 439).

Procedure

26–009 Where the judge has in mind to give a direction in accordance with (1) or (2), above, he; PDC 2004, V.2, 3

(1) must inform any party whose costs might be affected, or his legal representative, of its precise terms; and
(2) must, in the case of a direction under (1), give a reasonable opportunity to show cause why no direction should be given; and
(3) should, in the case of a direction under (2), inform the party concerned of his rights to make representations to the appropriate authority.

The appropriate authority may consult the court on any matter touching the allowance or disallowance of costs. It is not appropriate for the court to make a direction under (1) above when so consulted.

6. Award against offenders and appellants

General

26–010 A judge may make an order for costs against: PDC 2004, VI.1–7

(1) a person convicted before him, or in dealing with a person in respect of certain orders as to sentence specified in GR 1986, reg.14;
(2) an unsuccessful appellant; and
(3) a person committed by a magistrates' court in respect of the proceedings specified in reg.14(1) and (2).

Where he is satisfied that the offender or appellant has the means and ability to pay he may make such order payable to the prosecutor as he considers just and reasonable (POA 1985, s.18(1); the amount must be specified in the order).

An order under s.18 includes LSC funded costs (POA 1985, s.21(4A)(b)).

In exceptional circumstances costs may be awarded against a non-party (*H Leverton Ltd v Crawford Offshore (Exploration) Services Ltd (in liquidation), The Times*, November 22, 1996).

As to orders in CACD, see 18–054. The Administrative Court is not covered by s.18, but it has complete discretion over all costs between parties in relation to proceedings before it.

Accused electing trial on indictment

26–011 In relation to an accused who elects trial on indictment:

(1) while it is wrong to penalise him merely because he has taken advantage of his constitutional right, nevertheless if he elects and the case is one in which the prosecution costs should fall on him, it is perfectly right that he should suffer a higher penalty as a result of going to the Crown Court (*R. v Hayden* (1974) 60 Cr.App.R. 304, *R. v Yoxall* (1973) 57 Cr.App.R. 263);
(2) in a case which could conveniently have been tried summarily he may be ordered to pay costs on a Crown Court basis (*R. v Bushell* (1980) 2 Cr.App.R.(S.) 77; *R. v Boyle* [1995] Crim.L.R. 514); it is otherwise where the offender pleads guilty at the Crown Court to a lesser offence which could have been tried by the magistrates (*R. v Sentonco* [1996] 1 Cr.App.R.(S.) 174).

The principles were reviewed in *R. v Northallerton MC Ex p. Dove* [2000] 1 Cr.App.R.(S.) 136.

Amount of order

26–012 A number of points may be made:

(1) the order should be fixed having regard to the offender's means, as they are known to the court, and should not exceed a sum, which, having regard to those means, and any other financial order imposed on him, he can reasonably be expected to pay;
(2) the order should never exceed the sum which the prosecution have actually and reasonably incurred;
(3) in the case of an accused brought in at a late stage, it is appropriate to order him to pay his share of the whole costs of the prosecution, as opposed to his share of the costs when he was brought in (*R. v Davies (Cere)* [1999] 2 Cr.App.R.(S.) 356, CA).
(4) if a substantial order for costs is to be made, it is better if it is made in respect of prosecution costs rather than those borne by defence public funds (*R. v Mendey* (1988) 86 Cr.App.R. 102);
(5) in the case of a convicted offender care should be taken to ensure that the order is not out of step with, e.g. any fine he is ordered to pay (see 37 FINES AND ENFORCEMENT) save in the case of a very large fraud, or an offender who is clearly able to pay.

Any person against whom it is proposed to make an order should be given a fair opportunity to adduce any relevant financial information and make any appropriate submissions. As to payment of costs by persons under 18, see 19 CHILDREN AND YOUNG PERSONS.

Offender sentenced to custodial sentence

26–013 It is not generally appropriate to make an order for costs against an offender sentenced to a substantial custodial term unless he has private capital (*R. v Gaston* (1971) 55 Cr.App.R. 88).

7. Costs between parties

(1) Costs incurred as a result of unnecessary or improper act or omission

26–014 The Crown Court may order the payment of any costs incurred as a result of an unnecessary or improper act or omission by or on behalf of any party to the proceedings as PDC 2004,VII.1.1.2

distinct from his legal representative (POA 1985, s.19, GR 1986, reg.3). The judge must hear the parties and may then order all or any part of the costs so incurred by one party to be paid to him by the other party.

As to the meaning of "improper" (see 26–021).

Procedure

26–015 Before making such an order the judge:

(1) must take into account any other order as to costs;
(2) must specify in his order the amount of the costs to be paid;
(3) is entitled to take such an order into account when making any other order as to costs in the proceedings (GR 1986, reg.3(2)–(4)).

Note that:

(a) the order can extend to LSC costs incurred on behalf of any party (POA 1985, s.21(4A)(b)); and
(b) such an order is appropriate only where the failure is that of the accused or the prosecutor; where it is the failure of the legal representative(s), the powers under POA 1985, s.19A (see 26–021), or the Senior (formerly the Supreme) Court's inherent jurisdiction (see 26–033 below) may be exercised.

(2) Restraint, confiscation and receivership proceedings

26–016 Confiscation proceedings are treated for costs purposes as part of the criminal trial. Where a judge is deciding whether to make an order for costs in relation to restraint proceedings, or receivership proceedings, he has a discretion as to: PDC 2004, VII.2.1, 2, 3

(1) whether costs are payable by one party to another;
(2) the amount of those costs; and
(3) when the costs are to be paid.

The general rule is that the judge decides to make an order about costs, the unsuccessful party will be ordered to pay the costs of the successful party, but the judge may make a different order (R.61.19(3)).

CPR 2005 provide for the making of orders in respect of security to be given by a receiver to cover his liability for his

Costs and Taxation

acts and omissions as such (R.60.5), and for orders determining a receiver's remuneration (R.60.6).

In deciding what, if any, order to make about costs, the judge must have regard to all the circumstances, including the conduct of all the parties and whether a party has succeeded on part of an application, even if that party has not been wholly successful.

Types of order

26–017 CPR 2005 set out the types of order which the judge may make as: R.61.19(5)

(1) a proportion of another party's costs;
(2) a stated amount in respect of another party's costs;
(3) costs from or until a certain date only;
(4) costs incurred before proceedings have begun;
(5) costs relating to particular steps in the proceedings;
(6) costs relating to a distinct part of the proceedings; and
(7) interest on costs from or until a certain date including the making of an order.

The list is not exclusive. PDC 2004, VII.2.4, 5, 6

The judge must, where it is practicable, award a proportion (i.e. a percentage) of the costs, or costs between certain dates, rather than making an order relating only to a distinct part or issue in the proceedings. The latter type of order makes it extremely difficult for the costs to be assessed.

Where he orders a party to pay costs, the judge may, in addition, order an amount to be paid on account by one party to another before the costs are assessed. Where he makes such an order, the order should state the amount to be paid and the date on which payment is to be made.

Assessment of costs

26–018 Where the judge makes an order for costs in restraint or receivership proceedings, he may either: PDC 2004, VII.2.7, 8

(1) make an assessment of the costs himself (a summary assessment); or
(2) order assessment of the costs under R.61.20.

If he neither makes an assessment himself nor orders assessment as in (2) above, the order for costs will be treated as an order for the amount of costs to be decided by assessment.

When the judge awards costs to be assessed under R.58.19 he should consider whether to exercise his power to order the paying party to pay such sum as he thinks fit on account of those costs.

In carrying out the assessment of costs, the judge, or the taxing authority, must: PDC 2004, VII.2.9, 10

(a) allow only costs which are proportionate to the matters in issue resolving any doubt which he may have as to whether the costs were reasonably incurred or were reasonable and proportionate in amount in favour of the paying party;
(b) have regard to all the circumstances in deciding whether costs were proportionately or reasonably incurred or proportionate and reasonable in amount, effect being given to any orders for costs which have already been made, and should have regard also to:
   (i) the conduct of all the parties, including in particular conduct before as well as during the proceedings;
   (ii) the amount or value of any property involved;
   (iii) the importance of the matter to all the parties;
   (iv) the particular complexity of the matter, or the difficulty or novelty of the questions raised;
   (v) the skill, effort, specialised knowledge and responsibility involved;
   (vi) the time spent on the case; and
   (vii) the place where, and the circumstances in which work or any part of it was done.

Just disposal of the claim

26–019 The object is to deal with the case justly, which includes, so far as practicable, dealing with it in ways which are proportionate to the amount involved, the importance of the case, the complexity of the issues and the financial position of each party. The relationship between the total of the costs incurred and the financial value of the claim may not be a reliable guide. PDC 2004, VII.2.11–14

The following should be borne in mind:

(1) in any proceedings there will be costs which will inevitably be incurred and which are necessary for the successful conduct of the case; solicitors are not required to conduct litigation at rates which are uneconomic, thus in a modest claim the proportion of costs is likely to be higher than in a large claim, and may even equal or possibly exceed the amount in dispute;
(2) where a hearing takes place, the time taken by the court in dealing with a particular issue may not be an accurate guide to the amount of time properly spent by the

legal or other representatives preparing for the trial of that issue;

(3) CPR 2005 do not apply to assessment of costs in proceedings to the extent that AJA 1999, s.11 (costs in funded cases) applies and statutory instrument made under that Act make different provision.

Remuneration of a receiver

26–020 A receiver may only charge for his services where a judge so directs and specifies the basis on which the receiver is to be remunerated (r.60.6). PDC 2004 VII.2.15

The judge is required, unless he orders otherwise, to award such sum as is reasonable and proportionate in all the circumstances. In arriving at a figure for remuneration he should take into account:

(1) the time properly given by the receiver and his staff to the receivership;
(2) the complexity of the receivership;
(3) any responsibility of an exceptional kind or degree which falls on the receiver in consequence of the receivership;
(4) the effectiveness with which the receiver appears to be carrying out, or to have carried out his duties; and
(5) the value and nature of the subject matter of the receivership.

The judge may, instead of determining the receiver's remuneration himself, refer it to be ascertained by the Crown Court taxing authority. Rules 78.4–78.7 then apply.

8. Legal representatives; wasted costs orders

26–021 POA 1985, s.19A allows the judge to disallow or order the legal or other representative to meet the whole or any part of the wasted costs. PDC 2004, VIII.1.1

Note that:

(1) the order can be made against a person exercising a right of audience or a right to conduct litigation (in the sense of acting for a party in the proceedings);
(2) "wasted costs" are costs incurred by a party (which includes an LSC party) as a result of any improper, unreasonable or negligent act or omission on the part of any representative or his employee, or which, in the light of any such act or omission occurring after they were incurred, the court considers it unreasonable to expect

that party to pay (POA 1985, s.19A(3), PCA 2002, s.89(8)).

There has to be proved improper, unreasonable or negligent conduct (*Ridehalgh v Horsefield* [1994] Ch. 205; *Re Hickman and Rose, The Times*, May 3, 2000). Counsel is responsible for his clerk's errors, in, e.g. not getting him to court, or missing the case in the list (*R. v Rodney (Wasted Costs Order* [1997] 1 Archbold News 2)).

Judge's duty

26–022 The judge has a much greater and more direct responsibility for costs in criminal proceedings than in civil and should keep the question of costs in the forefront of his mind at every stage of the case and ought to be prepared to take the initiative himself without any prompting from the parties. His only concern should be to serve the public interest in the administration of justice (*Harley v McDonald* [2001] 2 W.L.R. 1749 PC). PDC 2004, VIII.1.2

Procedure

26–023 GR 1986, reg.3B requires the judge: PDC 2004, VIII.1.3

(1) to specify the amount of the wasted costs;
(2) before making the order, to allow the legal or other representative and any party to the proceedings to make representations (the party *must* be heard before the order is made (*Re Wiseman*, *The Times*, April 5, 2001);
(3) in making the order, to take into account any other order for costs;
(4) to give reasons for making the order; and
(5) to notify any interested party (which includes the CDS fund and central funds determining authorities) of the order and the amount.

As to postponement, see 26–027 below.

Film Lab Systems International v Pennington [1994] 4 All E.R. 673 and *Medcalf v Mardell* [2003] A.C. 120, both indicate the importance (at least in civil cases) of the judge dealing with the matter at the end of the case, avoiding a position where an advocates conduct of the case is influenced by his self-interest.

The hearing

26–024 A judge contemplating making a wasted costs order should bear in mind the guidance given by CA in *Re a Barrister (Wasted Costs Order) (No. 1 of 1991)* [1993] Q.B. 293, together with the statutory and other rules and recommendations set out by Parliament and PDC 2004. PDC 2004, VIII.1.4

Costs and Taxation

Thus:

(1) there is a clear need for the judge intending to exercise the wasted costs jurisdiction, to formulate carefully and concisely the complaint and grounds upon which such an order may be sought; these measures are draconian and, as in contempt proceedings, the grounds must be clear and concise;
(2) where necessary, a transcript of the relevant part of the proceedings should be available and in accordance with the rules a transcript of any hearing must be made;
(3) an accused involved in a case where such proceedings are contemplated should be present if, after discussion with counsel, it is thought that his interest may be affected, and he should certainly be present if the matter might affect the course of his trial;
(4) GR(A)R 1991 require that before an order can be made, the judge must allow the legal or other representative and any party to the proceedings to make representations; there may be cases where it is appropriate for counsel to be present.

A three stage approach

26–025 A three stage test or approach is recommended where a wasted costs order is contemplated: PDC 2004, VIII.1.4(IV)–(VI)

(1) has there been an improper, unreasonable or negligent act or omission?
(2) as a result have any costs been incurred by a party?
(3) if the answer to (1) and (2) is "yes" should the judge exercise his discretion to disallow or order the representative to meet the whole or any part of the relevant costs, and, if so, what specific sum is involved?

It is inappropriate to propose any settlement that the representative might forego fees. The complaint should be formally stated by the judge and the representative invited to make his own comments. After any party has been heard the judge should give his formal ruling. He must specify the sum to be allowed or ordered; alternatively the relevant available procedure under VIII.1.7 below may be substituted should it be impossible to fix the sum.

CACD guidance

26–026 In *Re P* [2002] 1 Cr.App.R. 207 CACD laid down the following basic principles:

(1) the primary object is not to punish but to compensate, albeit as the order is sought against a non-party, it may, from that perspective be regarded as penal;
(2) because of the penal element a mere mistake is not sufficient to justify an order, there must be a more serious error;
(3) if the allegation is one of serious misconduct or crime, the standard of proof will be higher but otherwise it will be the normal civil standard of proof;
(4) the jurisdiction is a summary jurisdiction to be exercised by the judge who has "tried the case in the course of which the misconduct was committed";
(5) the trial judge may decline to consider an application, for example on the ground that he is personally embarrassed by an appearance of bias, but it will only be in exceptional circumstances that it will be appropriate to pass the matter to another judge; the fact that, in the proper exercise of his judicial function, a judge has expressed views in relation to the conduct of a lawyer against whom an order is sought, does not of itself normally constitute bias or the appearance of bias so as to necessitate a transfer;
(6) fairness is assured if the lawyer alleged to be at fault has sufficient notice of the complaint made against him and a proper opportunity to respond to it.
(7) While the judge is not entitled to delegate his decision, he may require the Crown Court officer to make inquiries and inform him as to the likely amount of the costs incurred. PDC 2004, VIII.1.6

Postponement of making order

26–027 The judge may postpone the making of a wasted costs order to the end of the case if it appears more appropriate to do so, for example because the likely amount is not readily available, there is a possibility of conflict between the legal representatives as to the apportionment of blame, or the legal representative concerned is unable to make full representations because of a possible conflict with the duty to the client. PDC 2004, VIII.1, 7

Relevance of CDS funding

26–028 A wasted costs order should normally be made regardless of the fact that the client of the legal representative concerned is CDS funded. However, where: PDC 2004, VIII.1.8

(1) the judge is minded to disallow substantial costs out of the CDS fund; and

(2) the extent and amount of the costs wasted is not clear;

he may, instead of making a wasted costs order, make observations to the determining authority that work may have been unreasonably done (see PDC 2004, X.1.1. 26–033 below).

9. Award of costs against third parties

Power to make order

26–029 A "third party costs order" is an order as to the payment of all or part of the costs incurred or wasted by any party to the proceedings by a person who is not a party to those proceedings (the third party). PDC 2004, VII.3.1; SI 2004/2408, reg.7

The judge may in respect of misconduct that occurred after **October 18, 2004**. (SI 2004/2408, reg.2), make such an order where:

(1) there has been serious misconduct (whether or not constituting a contempt of court);
(2) by a third party; and
(3) he considers it appropriate having regard to that misconduct, to make such an order against him.

Where the judge makes an order in respect of misconduct occurring on or after that date he must disregard any misconduct which occurred before that date.

The order may be made:

(a) (subject to (c) below), at any time during or after the criminal proceedings;
(b) on the application of any part or of the judge's own initiative (but not otherwise);
(c) during the proceedings only if the judge decides there are good reasons to do so rather than making it after the proceedings, and he must notify the parties and the third party of those reasons and allow them to make representations;
(d) only after allowing the third party and any party to make representations, and the judge may hear evidence.

When making an order the judge may vary or take into account any other order as to costs in respect of the criminal proceedings and may take the third party costs order into account when making any other order as to costs in respect of the criminal proceedings.

The order must specify the amount of costs to be paid in pursuance of it, and the court must notify the third party and any interested party of the order and the amount ordered to be paid.

Application and notice of hearing

26–030 An application for a third party costs order must be in writing, setting out: SI 2004/2408, reg.7

(1) the names and addresses of the applicant, the other parties and of the third party against whom the order is sought;
(2) the date of the end of the criminal proceedings; and
(3) a summary of the facts upon which the applicant intends to rely in making the application, including details of the alleged misconduct of the third party,

and must be sent to the Crown Court officer, who, upon receiving it, must serve copies of it on the third party and the other parties.

Where the judge decides that he might make an order of his own initiative the officer must serve notice in writing accordingly on the third party and the parties, together with a summary of the judge's reasons for considering an order, including details of the alleged misconduct of the third party.

At the same time the officer must serve notice on the parties and the third party of the time and place fixed for the hearing.

At the time notified the judge may proceed in the absence of the third party and of any party if he is satisfied that they have been duly served with the notice, and the copy of the application or, as the case may be the appropriate notice, but may set aside any order if it is later shown that the third party did not receive them.

Appeals

26–031 A third party against whom the judge makes a third party costs order at first instance may appeal to CACD: SI 2004/2408, reg.7

(1) subject to an extension being granted, within 21 days of the order being made,
(2) by the appellant giving notice in writing to the court which made the order,
(3) stating the grounds of appeal, and
(4) serving a copy of the notice of appeal and grounds, including any application for extension of time in which to appeal, on any interested party.

The time limit within which an appeal may be instituted may, for good reason, be extended before or after it expires by a judge of the High Court or Court of Appeal, or by the Registrar.

CACD will give notice of the extension to the appellant, to the court which made the order and to any interested party, and will give notice of the hearing date to the same persons, and will allow the interested party to make representations which may be made orally or in writing. The order may be affirmed, varied or revoked as CACD thinks fit.

Recovery of sums due under a third party costs order

26–032 Where the person required to make a payment in respect of sums due under a third party costs order fails to do so, the payment may be recovered summarily as a sum adjudged to be paid as a civil debt by order of a magistrates' court by the party benefiting from the order, save that where he was receiving services funded for him as part of the Criminal Defence Service or an order for the payment of costs out of central funds was made in his favour, the power to recover shall be exercisable by the Lord Chancellor.

SI 2004/2408, reg.7

10. Solicitors; inherent jurisdiction

26–033 In addition to:

PDC 2004, IX.1.1

(1) the power under GR 1986, reg.3 to order that costs improperly incurred be paid by a party to the proceedings; and
(2) the power under POA 1985, s.19A, to make wasted costs orders,

a judge of the Crown Court, as one of the Senior Courts (formerly part of the Supreme Court) may, in the exercise of his inherent jurisdiction over officers of the court, order a solicitor personally to pay costs thrown away by reason of a serious dereliction of his duty to the court, but:

(a) this power should be used only in exceptional circumstances not covered by the statutory power; *R. v Smith* [1974] 1 All E.R. 651 and *Shaw v Reeves (No. 2)* [1982] 3 All E.R. 1086 emphasise that an order should be made only where the conduct of the solicitor is inexcusable and such as to merit reproof, not where mere mistake, error of judgment or negligence is disclosed; and
(b) no order may be made unless reasonable notice has been given to the solicitor of the matter alleged against him and he is given a reasonable opportunity of being heard in reply.

If the judge considers it necessary to hold such a hearing in chambers, a shorthand note should be kept.

11. CDS funded costs

26–034 Where it appears to a judge sitting in proceedings for which CDS funding has been granted, that: PDC 2004, X.1.1, 2

(1) work may have been unreasonably done, e.g. if the CDS funded person's case may have been conducted unreasonably so as to incur unjustifiable expense; or
(2) costs may have been wasted by failure to conduct the proceedings with reasonable competence or expedition,

he may make observations to that effect for the attention of the appropriate authority, specifying as precisely as possible the item, or items, which the determining officer should consider or investigate on the determination of the costs payable pursuant to the representation order. The precise terms of the observations must be entered in the court record.

This power co-exists with the power to disallow fees when making a wasted costs order. The Criminal Defence Service (Funding) Order 2001 allows the determining officer to disallow the amount of the order from the amount otherwise payable to solicitors and counsel and allows for deduction of a greater amount if appropriate (Sch.1 para.16 of the Funding Order).

Where, the judge:

(a) in proceedings specified in para.1 of Pt II of Sch.1 of the CDS (Funding) Order 2001, where standard fees would otherwise be payable, is dissatisfied with the solicitor's conduct of the case or considers that for exceptional reasons, the fees should be determined by the appropriate authority, he may direct that such determination take place; PDC 2004, X.1.3
(b) has in mind that observations under para.X.l.1 or that a direction under para.X.1.3 should be made, the solicitor or counsel whose fees or expenses might be affected must be informed of the precise terms thereof and of his right to make representations to the appropriate authority and be given a reasonable opportunity to show cause why the observations or direction should not be made. PDC 2004, X.1.4

Where such observations or directions are made the appropriate authority must afford an opportunity to the solicitor or counsel PDC 2004, X.1.5

Costs and Taxation

whose fees might be affected to make representations in relation to them.

Whether or not observations under para. X.1.1 have been made the appropriate authority may consult the judge or the court on any matter touching the allowance or disallowance of fees and expenses, but if the observations then made are to the effect mentioned in para. X.1.1, the appropriate authority should afford an opportunity to the solicitor or counsel concerned to make representations to him. PDC 2004 X.1.6

Very high cost cases

26–035 In proceedings which are classified as a very high costs case (VHCC) as defined in GR 2001, reg.2 (see 17–017) the judge should, at the earliest opportunity, ask the representatives of the LSC funded person whether they have notified the LSC of the case in accordance with GR 2001, reg.23. PDX 2004, X.2.1

If they have not, they should be warned that:

(1) they may not be able to recover the costs;
(2) if the VHCC is one of fraud or serious financial impropriety, that they can be conducted only by a firm which is a member of the specialist fraud panel (see 17–017) and that non-panel firms and the advocates instructed by such firms may not be able to recover their costs.

12. Recovery of defence costs orders

26–036 Recovery of defence costs orders (RDCOs) are created and regulated by RDCOR 2001, made under AJA 1999, s.17. PDC 2004, XI.1.1–6

Where a person receives representation in respect of criminal proceedings funded as part of the CDS, the judge *must* make an order requiring him to pay some or all of the costs of any representation (RDCOR, reg.11), except where a funded accused :

(1) is committed to the Crown Court for sentence;
(2) is appealing to the Crown Court against sentence; or
(3) has been acquitted, other than in exceptional circumstances (RDCOR 2001, reg.4), and also where:
   (a) a funded accused has been acquitted the judge must consider whether it is reasonable in all the circumstances to make an order; and
   (b) a person of modest means properly brings an appeal against conviction (there is no power to make an order on an appeal against sentence — see above) the

> judge should bear in mind that it will not usually be desirable or appropriate to make an order for a significant amount, if to do so would inhibit an appellant from bringing an appeal.

An order may be made up to the maximum of the full costs of the representation in any court (including the magistrates' court) under the representation order and may provide for payment forthwith or in specified instalments (reg.5).

Estimate of costs; accused's resources

26–037 The judge may ask the accused's solicitor to provide an estimate of the total costs which are likely to be incurred under the representation order, though he should bear in mind that whilst the solicitor may have little difficulty in producing an estimate of the costs incurred up to the point of the request, this estimate may not be accurate. In a very high cost case which has been managed under contract, the solicitor will be able to provide accurate figures of all costs incurred to date and to say what costs have been agreed as reasonable for the next stage of the case. PDC 2004, XI.1.7

Note that:

(1) Where an RDCO is made based on this estimate, the accused's solicitor must inform the Commission if it subsequently transpires that the costs incurred were lower than the amount ordered to be paid, and in these circumstances, where the accused has paid the amount ordered, the balance will be repaid to him (RDCOR 2001, reg.14);
(2) an RDCO full costs order may be made at the end of the proceedings;
(3) the appropriate authority will tax the costs incurred under the representation order and the accused will be notified of the RDCO once this is known.

The judge will consider the amount or value of every source of income and capital available to the accused and his partner, but other than in exceptional circumstances, he must not take into account:

(a) the first £3000 of available capital;
(b) the first £100,000 of equity in the principal residence; or
(c) his income, where the gross annual income is less than £25,000.

These limits are subject to annual revision.

Reference to SIU

26–038 Where a representation order has been made or is being considered and: PDC 2004, XI.1.9–11

(1) the accused is being prosecuted by the Commissioners of Revenue and Customs, the SFO, the DTI or the IR; and
(2) the information supplied by the accused suggests that he has sufficient means to pay all the costs incurred in his defence; but
(3) there is some other information which suggests that he has more resources than he has disclosed, for example the type of charge he faces or his reputation,

the appropriate officer may refer the financial resources of the funded accused to the Special Investigation Unit (SIU) at the Legal Services Commission, for a report, which the judge will consider at the end of the case in the same way that the court will provide the judge with a summary of the accused's means. The report is not an application for costs.

The judge may also:

(a) during the proceedings, where further information has come to light which had previously not been disclosed by the accused to the court refer the matter to the SIU, which may then investigate the financial resources of the accused and require him to provide further information or evidence as required;
(b) at the end of the case, where he is considering what order to make, make the order, or if further information is required, adjourn the making of the order and order that any further information which is required should be provided (RDCOR 2001, reg.12);
(c) exercise the power in (b) where further information about the accused's means has come to light during the case; and
(d) where the accused has failed to co-operate either with the court or the SIU, order that further information be provided.

Co-operation of the accused

26–039 The accused is obliged to provide details of his means, or evidence, as is required by the Commission (RDCOR 2001, reg.6), Arrangements are in place to ensure the judge at the first hearing, has available to him, a summary of the means information, or details as to whether or not the accused has provided any information. PDC 2004, XI.1.12–15

Where:

(1) the funded accused does not provide information the judge may order him to do so;
(2) information required under the reulations is not provided the judge may make an RDCO for the full costs of the representation incurred under the representation Order (RDCOR 2001, reg.13);
(3) it appears to the judge that the funded accused has:
    (a) directly or indirectly transferred any resources to another person; or
    (b) another person is or has been maintaining him in any proceedings; or
    (c) any of the resources of another person are or have been made available to him, the value of the resources of that other person may be treated as those of the funded accused. "person" here includes a company, partnership, body of trustees and any body of persons, corporate or not corporate (RDCOR 2001, reg.8);
(4) (a) a person who is required to furnish information or evidence has failed to do so in accordance with RDCOR 2001, and
    (b) the judge considers that there is a real risk that relevant property will be disposed of; or
    (c) at the conclusion of the case, the assessment of costs incurred under the representation order or of the financial resources of the accused has not yet been completed (reg.15),

the judge may make an order prohibiting any person who is required to furnish information or evidence, from dealing with property.

13. Advice on appeal to CACD

26–040 In all cases, the procedure set out in *A Guide to Proceedings in the Court of Criminal Appeal* 1997, published by the Criminal Appeal Office with the approval of the Lord Chief Justice, should be followed. PDC 2004, XX.1.1

14. Enforcement and challenge

Search; time to pay; instalments

26–041 The enforcement of costs is a matter for the appropriate magistrates' court, but where a judge of the Crown Court AJA 1970, s.41(1)(2) makes an order against an accused for the payment of costs, he may:

(1) if the person against whom the costs have been awarded is present in court, order him to be searched and, unless the court otherwise directs, any money found on him will be applied towards payment of the costs;
(2) allow time to pay the sum due under the order; or
(3) direct payment by instalments of such amounts and on such dates as he may specify. PCC(S)A 2000, s.144

Payment by parent or guardian

26–042 Where a young person is found guilty of an offence, the court must order any costs awarded to be paid by the parent or guardian (see 19 CHILDREN AND YOUNG PERSONS).

Appeal against award of costs

26–043 An appeal lies to CACD by an offender convicted on indictment and ordered to contribute towards the costs of the prosecution; no appeal lies by an accused tried on indictment and ordered to contribute towards the costs of his publicly funded defence (*R. v Hayden* (1974) 60 Cr.App.R. 304).

An order for costs made in relation to proceedings on indictment may not be challenged by a quashing order in the High Court.

15. Appeals to a costs judge and further

26–044 The following principles apply to appeals pursuant to GR 1986 as amended the Legal Aid in Criminal and Care Proceedings (Costs) Regulations 1989, and the Criminal Defence Service (Funding) Order 2001. Procedure is governed by PDC 2004, Pt XIII.

(1) Review

26–045 Solicitors and counsel dissatisfied with the costs determined under the above Regulations may apply to the appropriate authority for a review of the determination of them. PDC 2004, XIII.1.1

Such an application must:

(1) be made within 21 days of receipt of the notification of costs payable, although there is power to extend this time;

(2) be made by giving notice in writing to the appropriate authority specifying the items in respect of which the application is made and the grounds of objection, and must be made in such form and manner as the appropriate authority may direct;
(3) state whether the applicant wishes to appear or to be represented, so that he may be informed of the time at which he or his representative may be heard (CR 1986, r.10) and
(4) be accompanied by the particulars, information and documents supplied under reg.6 and any further particulars, etc. required by the appropriate authority.

The appropriate authority will then review the determination in the light of the objections and notify the applicant of his decision. Within 21 days of receiving notification of that decision, the applicant may request the appropriate authority to give his reasons in writing.

(2) Appeal to a Costs Judge

26–046 An applicant dissatisfied with a decision on such a review may appeal to a Costs Judge of the Supreme Court Office by: PDC 2004, XIII.1.1.

(1) giving written notice of appeal in Form A, accompanied by the appropriate fee, made payable to "HM Paymaster-general" within 21 days of receipt of the reasons given for the decision (14 days under rr.16 and 17) or within such longer time as the Costs Judge may direct; setting out the matters specified in PDC 2004, XIII. 1.2, specifying the items in respect of which the appeal is brought and the grounds of objection;
(2) providing detailed grounds of objection in respect of each item;
(3) sending with the notice a copy of the documents prescribed by XIII; and
(4) stating whether he wishes to appear or to be represented, or whether he will accept a decision given in his absence.

Other procedural matters are dealt with in PDC 2004, XIII.2.2–4, XIII.3–2.

An application on the papers may be renewed at an oral hearing (PDC 2003, XIII.3.2).

(As to the extent of the investigation required by POA 1985, s.16 and SI 1986/1335, see *R. (Brewer) v Supreme Courts Costs Office, The Times*, August 16, 2006 Q.B.D.)

(3) Appeal to the High Court

26–047 An appellant desiring to appeal to a judge of the High Court from a decision of the Costs Judge should, within 21 days of the costs judge's decision, request him to certify that a point of principle of general importance (specifying the same) is involved. The appeal can proceed only if such a certificate is granted.

An appeal is initiated by a claim form under CPR Pt 8 in the Queen's Bench Division, within 21 days of the costs judge's certificate, The times may be extended by the costs judge or the High Court.

The procedure is outlined in PDC 2004, XIII.4.2–5.

If he does, the applicant may appeal to the High Court against his decision, the Lord Chancellor being the respondent. The Lord Chancellor may also appeal where dissatisfied with the decision. The appeal is instituted by originating summons in the Queen's Bench Division, and is heard and determined by a single judge whose decision is final. The judge has the same powers as the Determining Officer and the Costs Judge.

16. VAT

26–048 VAT is dealt with in various circumstances relating to costs in criminal cases, see PDC 2004, XIV.

17. Costs from Central Funds and relevant Statutory Authorities: PDC 2004, Sch.2

26–049

Proceedings	Court	Extent of Availability	Authority
Person indicted or sent for trial but not tried	Crown Court	Accused	POA 1985, s.16(2)(a)
Acquittal on indictment	Crown Court	Accused	POA 1985, s.16(2)(b)
Successful appeal to the Crown Court against conviction or sentence	Crown Court	Appellant	POA 1985, s.16(3)
Successful appeal to CACD against conviction or sentence or insanity/disability finding	CACD	Appellant	POA 1985, s.16(4)
Appeal against order or ruling at preparatory hearing	CACD	Appellant	POA 1985, s.16(4A)
Application for leave to appeal to House of Lords	CACD	Appellant	POA 1985, s.16(5)(c)
Attorney-General's reference to CACD on point of law following acquittal	CACD, House of Lords	Acquitted Accused	CJA 1972, s.36(5)
Attorney-General's CACD reference under CJA 1988, s.36 (lenient sentence appeals)	CACD	Convicted Accused	CJA 1988, Sch.3, para.11
Determination of proceedings in a criminal cause or matter in Divisional Court	Divisional Court	Accused in criminal proceedings	POA 1985, s.16(5)(a)
Determination of appeal or application for leave to appeal from CACD or DC	House of Lords	Accused in criminal proceedings	POA 1985, s.16(5)(b) & (c)

Proceedings	Court	Extent of Availability	Authority
Proceedings in respect of an indictable offence	Crown Court	Private prosecutor	POA 1985, s.17(1)(a)
Proceedings before DC or House of Lords	Divisional Court and House of Lords	Private prosecutor	POA 1985, s.17(1)(b)
Criminal cause or matter	All	Defence or private prosecution witness, interpreter & medical practitioner	POA 1985, s.19(3). There are restrictions on what may be paid (GR 1986, regs 18, 19, 20, 21, 24 & 25) e.g. a witness cannot claim for any legal expenses incurred by him in attending court to give evidence or to set aside a witness summons.
Murder case	Crown Court	Medical practitioner	MHA 1982, s.34(5)
Criminal Proceedings (Insanity) Procedure	Crown Court	Person appointed to put the case for defence	POA 1985, s.19(3)(d)
Cross-examination of vulnerable witness	Crown Court	Person appointed to cross-examine	POA 1985, s.19(3)(c)
Compensation of refusal of football banning order	Crown Court on appeal where compensation refused by magistrates	Person against whom notice given (limit £5000)	FSA 1989; FDA 2000, Sch.1
Licensing appeals	Crown Court	Licensing justices	Lotteries & Amusement Act 1976, Sch.3, para.11, GA 1986, Sch.9, para.14(2), LA 1964.

27 COURT SECURITY OFFICERS

General

27–001 Court security officers may be appointed and designated by the Lord Chancellor. An officer must be readily identifiable as such (whether by means of his uniform or badge or otherwise), otherwise he is not to be regarded as acting in the execution of his duty. CA 2003, s.51

It is an offence (s.57) to assault (fine on level 5), resist or willfully obstruct (a fine on level 3) a court security officer acting in the execution of his duty.

Powers of search

27–002 A court security officer, acting in the execution of his duty may search: CA 2003, s.52

(1) any person who is in, or is seeking to enter, a court building, and
(2) any article in the possession of such a person,

such power does not authorise him to require a person to remove any of his clothing other than a coat, jacket, headgear, gloves or footwear.

"Court building," here, means *any* building where the business of any of the courts referred to in CA 2003, s.1, which includes the Senior Courts (formerly the Supreme Court), of which the Crown Court is one, carried on, and to which the public has access.

Powers to exclude, remove or restrain persons

27–003 An officer acting in the execution of his duty may exclude or remove from a court building, or a part of a court building, any person who refuses: CA 2003, s.53

(1) to permit a search under s.52(1), or
(2) to surrender an article in his possession when asked to do so under s.54(1) (below), and may also
    (a) restrain any person who is in a court building, or
    (b) exclude or remove any person from a court building, or a part of a court building,

if it is reasonably necessary to do so to:

(i) enable court business to be carried on without interference or delay;

Court Security Officers

(ii) maintain order; or
(iii) secure the safety of any person in the court building.

An officer acting in the execution of his duty may remove any person from a courtroom at the request of the court.

These powers include a power to use reasonable force, where necessary.

Surrender and seizure of articles

27–004 An officer acting in the execution of his duty, and reasonably believing that an article in the possession of a person who is in, or seeking to enter, a court building, ought to be surrendered on the ground that it may: CA 2003, s.54

(1) jeopardise the maintenance of order in the court building (or a part of it), or
(2) put the safety of any person in the court building at risk, or
(3) be evidence of, or in relation to, an offence,

must ask the person to surrender the article; if that person refuses to surrender the article, the officer may seize it.

Powers to retain articles surrendered or seized

27–005 An officer may retain an article which was: CA 2003, s.55

(1) surrendered in response to a request under s.54(1), or
(2) seized under s.54(2),

until the time when the person who surrendered it, or from whom it was seized, is leaving the court building, but if he reasonably believes that the article may be evidence of, or in relation to, an offence, he may retain it until the time when the person who surrendered it, or from whom it was seized, is leaving the court building, or the end of the permitted period, whichever is later.

The "permitted period" is such period, not exceeding 24 hours from the time the article was surrendered or seized, as will enable the court security officer to draw the article to the attention of a constable.

28 CUSTODY TIME LIMITS

General

28–001 POA 1985 and the regulations made thereunder (SI 1987/299 amended by SI 1999/2744, SI 1999/2743) prescribe time limits during which an accused may be held in custody (and "custody" includes remand, or committal to local authority accommodation) of the magistrates' court or of the Crown Court, in relation to specified stages of the proceedings.

Subject to CJPOA 1994, s.25 (which disapplies these regulations – *R(O) v Harrow CC* [2006] UKHL 42) an accused is entitled to be released on bail where a custody time limit and any extension to it, expires, but his release requires an order of the court. As to the duties of the prosecution (see SI 1987/299, reg.6). Where the prosecution fails to act, the accused will need to apply for bail to the Crown Court or go to the High Court by way of judicial review (*Olotu v Home Office* [1997] 1 W.L.R. 328).

Note that the expiry of a time limit does not necessarily give rise to a breach of ECHR, art 5(3) in relation to trial within a reasonable time (*R.(O) v Harrow CC etc.* [2003] EWHC 868 (Admin) 868).

Objectives

28–002 The objectives of the legislation are to:

(1) ensure that any periods during which an unconvicted person is held in custody awaiting trial are as short as is reasonably and practicably possible;
(2) oblige the prosecution to prepare the case for trial with all due diligence and expedition; and
(3) invest the court with the power and duty to control any extension of the maximum period under the regulations for which such a person may be held in custody awaiting trial.

These are very important objectives, and a judge making a decision on the extension of custody time-limits must be careful to give full weight to all three (*R. v Manchester CC Ex p. McDonald* [1999] 1 Cr.App.R. 409). See further under 16 CASE MANAGEMENT.

CUSTODY TIME LIMITS

Crown Court limits

28–003 Where:

(1) a voluntary bill is preferred against such a person at a Crown Court centre specified in POA (Custody Time Limits) Regulations (SI 1987/299) reg.5(1)–(6A) as amended, the maximum period during which he may be in the custody of the Crown Court in relation to that offence, or any other offence included in the indictment, is 112 days between the time the voluntary bill was preferred, and the start of the trial;

(2) an accused is sent for trial under s.51 of the CDA 1998, the maximum period of custody (reg.5(6B)) between being sent to the Crown Court for an offence is 182 days, less any period previously spent in the custody of the magistrates' court for the relevant offence.

The Regulations are directed towards the offence and not the offender. "Offence" in reg.4(1) is not to be read as "offences"; each offence attracts its own time limit (*R. v Waltham Forest MC Ex p. Lee* (1993) 97 Cr.App.R. 287; *R. v Wolverhampton MC and Stafford CC Ex p. Uppal* (1995) 159 J.P. 86, see also *R. v Maidstone CC Ex p. Clark* [1995] 3 All E.R. 513; *R. v Peterborough CC Ex p. L* [2000] Crim.L.R. 470 and *R. v Leeds CC Ex p. Wardle* [2001] 2 Cr.App.R. 20, HL (where compatibility with ECHR is considered).

Where a case has been sent for trial and the indictment contains counts:

(a) alleging offences which were sent on different occasions, the time limit applies to each count separately;

(b) which were not included in the case sent for trial, the maximum period between the preferment of the bill of indictment, or the addition of the count, and his arraignment is 112 days, less the aggregate of any periods during which, since he was sent for trial, has been in the custody of the Crown Court in relation to an offence for which he was sent for trial.

The "start of the trial"

28–004 The start of a trial on indictment occurs, subject to CJA 1988, s.8 and CPIA 1996, s.28 (preparatory hearings) at the time when a jury is sworn to consider the issue of guilt or fitness to plead or, if the judge accepts a plea before the time when a jury is sworn, when that plea is accepted.

POA 1985, s.22(11), (11A), (11AA); CPIA 1996, s.71; CJA 2003, s.331, Sch.36, Pt 4, para.51

"The time when a jury is sworn" will include the time when that jury would be sworn but for the making of an order CJA 2003, Pt 7 (trials without a jury).

The regime ceases to apply once the trial has started, even if that trial is aborted and a retrial takes place. In the event of the trial being aborted the judge should be vigilant to take steps in fixing a speedy retrial, or, if there are difficulties about such a course, considering the grant of bail or, in an appropriate case, staying the prosecution as an abuse of process (*R. v Leeds CC Ex p. Whitehead* (2000) 164 J.P. 102).

If a preparatory hearing is ordered under: CJA 1988, s.8, or CPIA 1996, s.28 (see 16 CASE MANAGEMENT) the trial starts with that hearing, and arraignment takes place then if it has not taken place before (CJA 1988, s.8, CPIA 1996, s.31).

Note that when DVA 2003 abolished trial by jury of an issue of unfitness to plead raised an arraignment it seems that POA 1985, s.22(11A), in respect of the start of a trial on indictment was not amended.

SI 1987/299, reg.29(5)

Interpretation

28–005 The "maximum period" laid down does not include the day on which custody commenced, and a custody time limit which would otherwise expire on a Saturday, Sunday, Christmas Day, Good Friday or a bank holiday, is treated as expiring on the nearest preceding day which is not one of those days.

Where the limits do not apply

28–006 Where a person:

POA 1985, s.22(5), (6), (6A); CDA 1998, s.43(4), (5)

(1) escapes from the custody of a magistrates' court or the Crown Court before the expiry of a limit which applies in his case; or
(2) having been released on bail in consequence of the expiry of a custody time limit, fails to surrender at the appointed time, or is arrested for breach of bail, and is accordingly at large:
   (a) the period for which the person is unlawfully at large, and
   (b) such additional period (if any) as the court may direct, having regard to the disruption of the prosecution occasioned by:
      (i) the person's escape or failure to surrender; and
      (ii) the length of the period mentioned in (i), must be disregarded so far as the offence in question is concerned for the purposes of the overall

time-limit which applies in his case in relation to the stage which the proceedings have reached at the time of the escape or, as the case may be, at the appointed time.

The fact that the accused is in custody for other matters does not prevent the time-limit running (*R. v Peterborough CC Ex p. L*, see above). Where, following the initial charge(s) on which the accused first appeared before the magistrates, another charge is added, then irrespective of its nature, or when it was added, subject only to the accused being able to show abuse of process, a new custody time-limit is created (*R. v Leeds CC Ex p. Stubley* [1999] Crim.L.R. 822; *R. v Leeds CC Ex p. Wardle* [2001] 2 Cr.App.R. 301, HL).

CJA 2003, Part 9

28–007 Under CJA 2003, Pt 9 (prosecution appeals), any period during which proceedings for an offence are adjourned pending the determination of an appeal will be disregarded, so far as the offence is concerned, for the purpose of the custody time limit which applies to the stage where proceedings have reached when they are adjourned. POA 1985, s.22(6A); CJA 2003, s.70

Expiry of time limit

28–008 On being notified that: SI 1987/299, reg.6(6)

(1) an accused who is in custody pending trial,
(2) has the benefit of a custody time limit under reg.5, and
(3) the time limit is about to expire,

a judge of the Crown Court must grant that person bail in accordance with BA 1976 as modified for the purpose (see 11 BAIL), with effect from the expiry of the limit, subject to a duty to appear before the Crown Court for trial. Where this situation arises, the prosecution will need to decide *before* the expiry of the limit, whether:

(a) to apply for an extension, or further extension, of the time limit; or
(b) to apply for conditions to be attached to the bail granted to the accused.

Application for extension

28–009 An application by the prosecution for the extension, or further extension, of a time limit may be made orally or in writing: SI 1987/299, reg.7

(1) *before* the relevant time-limit has expired (*R. v Peterborough CC Ex p. L*, see above);
(2) by giving, not less than five days before making the application, notice in writing to the accused or his representative, and to the Crown Court officer of his intention to make the application; unless
(3) the accused or his representative informs the Crown that he does not require such notice; or
(4) a judge is satisfied on a balance of probabilities (*Re Craig* (1991) 91 Cr.App.R. 7) that it is not practicable for the prosecution to comply and directs either that the Crown need not comply, or specifies a lesser minmum period.

In the case of an application based on the length and complexity of the case, though reg.7 does not require it, it is good practice to give the grounds in the notice (*R. v CCC Ex p. Marotta* [1998] 10 Arch. News 2). Bail Act considerations have no place under these provisions (*R. v Reading CC* [2002] 1 Cr.App.R. 3).

Successive applications

28–010 It is not:

(1) normally permissible, when an application is refused, for an application to be made to a second judge on the same grounds, but see *R. v Bradford CC Ex p. Crossling, etc.* [2000] 1 Cr.App.R. 463 (where the first judge may have acted on misleading information).
(2) permissible, where the High Court has reviewed a judge's decision, for a further application to be made to a judge of the Crown Court,

(*R. v Peterborough CC Ex p. L,* above; *cf. R. v Leeds CC Ex p. Stubley* [1999] Crim.L.R. 822).

Grounds for extension of period

28–011 A time limit may be extended or further extended by a judge of the Crown Court, *at any time before* its expiry (*R. v Croydon CC Ex p. Commrs of Customs & Excise* [1997] 8 Arch. News 1, DC), but not unless he is satisfied on the balance of probabilities: POA 1985, s.22(3); CDA 1998, s.43(2)

(1) that the need for the extension is due to:
   (a) the illness or absence of the accused, a necessary witness, or a judge;
   (b) a postponement which is occasioned by the ordering by the court of separate trials in the case of two or more accused or two or more offences; or

(c) some other good and sufficient cause; and

(2) that the prosecution has acted with all due diligence and expedition (*R. v Norwich CC Ex p. Parker and Ward* (1993) 96 Cr.App.R. 68; *R. v CCC Ex p. Behbehani* [1994] Crim.L.R. 352; *R. v CCC Ex p. Belle Lane* [1994] Crim.L.R. 352; *R. v Leeds CC Ex p. Briggs (Ronald) (No. 2)* [1998] 2 Cr.App.R. 424).

"Good and sufficient cause", and "due diligence and expedition" are two distinct issues, and require both separate consideration and a separate ruling. "Good cause" will not avail the Crown, if they have not acted with "due expedition" (*R. v CCC Ex p. Bennett*, *The Times*, January 25, 1999).

"Good and sufficient cause" interpreted

28–012 The words are not susceptible of a precise definition (*R. v Norwich CC Ex p. Ricketts* [1990] Crim.L.R. 715). It will be a matter of fact in each case (*McKay White v DPP* [1989] Crim.L.R. 375). See also *R. v Norwich CC Ex p. Cox* (1993) 97 Cr.App.R. 145; *cf. R. v Maidstone CC Ex p. Schultz* (1993) 157 J.P. 601, *R. v Gilligan, R. v Woolwich CC Ex p. Gilligan* [1998] 2 All E.R. 1. Thus:

(1) an almost infinite number of matters may, depending on the facts, constitute such cause, though: e.g.
   (a) the seriousness of the offence, or
   (b) the need to protect the public, or
   (c) the fact that the extension sought is only a short one,
   are not amongst them (*R. v Manchester CC Ex p. McDonald, etc.*, [1999] 1 All E.R. 805); and

(2) matters relevant to the granting or refusing of bail cannot of themselves provide good and sufficient cause for extending a time limit (*R. v Sheffield CC Ex p. Headley* [2000] 2 Cr.App.R. 1).

The unavailability of a suitable judge or court-room, may, in special cases and on appropriate facts, amount to such a cause, see below under "listing difficulties."

"Due diligence and expedition"

28–013 "Due diligence" is not the same as "due expedition". To fulfil the test of "due expedition" it is not enough to show that the prosecuting authorities "are doing their best." The test needs to be measured against some yardstick, or the object of the Act is defeated (*R. v Southampton CC Ex p. Roddie* [1991] Crim.L.R. 619, *R. v Sheffield MC Ex p. Turner*, (1991)

93 Cr.App.R. 180. See also *R. v CCC Ex p. Behbehani* [1994] Crim.L.R. 352).

"All due expedition" requires the diligence and expedition which would be shown by a competent prosecutor conscious of his duty to bring the case to trial as quickly and fairly as possible (*R. v Manchester CC Ex p. McDonald etc* [1999] 1 Cr.App.R. 409, where the cases are reviewed).

Note that:

(1) delay on the part of an independent forensic laboratory is irrelevant to the question whether the Crown has acted with "due expedition", though they should do everything possible to ensure that evidence is available on time (*R. v CCC Ex p. Johnson* [1999] 2 Cr.App.R. 51);
(2) the reference to the Crown having acted "with all due expedition" refers to the time up to the making of the application to extend the limit, not to the issue of whether future delay may be caused by acceding to the application (*R. v Woolwich CC Ex p. Gilligan* [1998] 2 All E.R. 1);
(3) lack of due diligence and expedition will not be fatal if it has no causal connection with the need for an extension (*R. v Winchester CC* [2004] 1 W.L.R. 1623).

Listing difficulties

28–014 While s.22 does not expressly require the Court Service to provide a trial judge and other facilities with all due expedition (*cf. R. v CCC Ex p. Abu-Wadeh*, below) the scheme of the provisions implies a legislative intent that an accused be tried within the time limits laid down (*R. v Stoke-on-Trent CC Ex p. Marden* [1999] 1 Arch. News 2).

The superior courts have held, though reluctantly (*R. v Manchester CC*, above), that the unavailability of a suitable judge, or courtroom in which to try an accused in custody, is capable of amounting to "good and sufficient cause" for extending the time-limits (*R. v CCC Ex p. Abu-Wardeh* [1997] 1 All E.R. 159), though such factors are less likely to be worthy of consideration where the trial is not expected to be long or complex, or one in which the convenience of witnesses has to be arranged, and whose convenience has to be taken into account (*R. v Leeds CC Ex p. Wilson* [1999] Crim.L.R. 738), but:

(1) the judge should approach such grounds with great caution, as there is obviously a danger that the purposes of the statute will be undermined by too readily granting extensions on this basis;
(2) the fact that witnesses are professional investigators does

not make their convenience, particularly with regard to other duties, irrelevant;

(3) where the application is made on the basis that the case clashes with another, the Crown will need to show why the other case requires priority (*R. v Stoke-on-Trent CC Ex p. Marsden* [1999] 1 Arch. News 2; *R. v Croydon YC Ex p. C* [2001] Crim.L.R. 40).

(4) many of the problems which arise in this area can be obviated by fixing an early date for the trial.

Fixing a date

28–015 In *R. v Worcester CC Ex p. Norman* [2000] 3 All E.R. 267, it was said that there is a joint duty on the Crown and on the court to make early arrangements for the fixing of a trial date within the custody time-limits;

(1) ideally, the date should be fixed at the PCMH with the directions then being tailored to the date that has been fixed;

(2) if it is impossible to fix a date at the PCMH the judge should direct that the date be fixed on a date before the expiration of the custody time limit and that the matter should be re-listed in the event of a failure to agree such a date;

(3) if the fixing of a date within the custody time limit is impossible, this should be appreciated at an early date and an application to extend made sooner rather than later, thereby enhancing the prospect of a date being fixed as soon as possible after the expiry of the limit;

(4) if the court fails to take the initiative, it is for the Crown to press for a date within the time-limit, the duty on the defence being to provide the names of witnesses required so that their availability can be ascertained.

The hearing of the application to extend

28–016 Bearing in mind the overriding purposes of the legislation (see 28–002, above) a judge, invested with the power and duty of controlling any extension:

(1) needs to be satisfied, on a balance of probabilities, that both the conditions in s.22(3) are made out, before exercising his discretion;

(2) must not abdicate his responsibility to address the issues by granting the application on the nod, because the parties agree, or because there is no objection to this course (*R. v Manchester CC*, above).

(3) should consider all matters directly and genuinely bearing on the preparation of the case for trial, bearing in mind that:
   (a) the time limit is a maximum not a target; and
   (b) the prosecutor is not required to show that every stage has been completed as quickly and efficiently as is humanly possible, though
   (c) no attention should be paid to excuses such as staff shortages, sickness, etc.;

(4) may need to hear evidence or may, according to the circumstances of the case, be able to rely on information supplied by the advocates. It is for the prosecutor to decide which witnesses to call on the application, and the defence are not entitled to require specific witnesses to be called (*R. v Chelmsford CC* [2002] Crim.L.R. 485);

(5) may, if, but only if, he is so satisfied, exercise his discretion to extend the time-limit. If he is not satisfied he may not, but, if he is satisfied he may, but need not, extend the time-limit (*R. v Manchester CC*, above), and

(6) must give brief reasons for his ruling, indicating the way in which he has reached his conclusions (*R. v Leeds CC Ex p. Briggs* [1998] Crim.L.R. 744).

"Where the judge is considering a *further* extension, he has to consider those matters giving rise to that *further* extension. In relation to delay prior to an earlier extension, while it may relied on by the accused in any challenge, needs to be relied on as the root cause of the need to seek a *further* extension" (*R. (Thomas) v CCC etc., The Times*, August 11, 2006 CACD).

There may be cases where, even though there has been avoidable delay, an extension will not be refused. SI 1987/299, reg.6(1), (2), (3), (4), (5)

Conditions of bail

28–017 An application by the prosecution for conditions to be attached to the bail granted to an accused where the time limits have expired is made:

(1) by giving notice in writing not less than five days before the expiry of the time limit, to the appropriate Crown Court officer and to the accused or his representative;

(2) stating whether or not it intends to ask the Crown Court to impose conditions, and, if it does, the nature of the conditions sought; and

(3) making arrangements for the accused to be brought before the Crown Court within the period of two days preceding the expiry of the time limit.

The Crown need not comply with (1) above if it has given notice of its intention to apply for an extension, or further extension, of the limit; it need not comply with (2) if the judge so directs. If the judge is satisfied that it is not practicable, in all the circumstances, for the prosecution to comply with (1) he may so direct, or specify a lesser minimum period.

On receiving notice that the prosecution intends to ask the court to impose conditions on the grant of bail, the accused or his representative must:

(a) give notice in writing to the Crown Court officer and to the prosecution, that the accused wishes to be represented at the hearing of the application; or
(b) give notice to the appropriate officer, and to the prosecution, stating that the accused does not wish to oppose the application; or
(c) give to the appropriate officer, for the consideration of the Crown Court a written statement of the accused's reasons for opposing the application, sending a copy of the statement, at the same time, to the prosecution.

Appeal to the Crown Court from the magistrates' court

28–018 An appeal brought: R.20.1(1)(2)

(1) by an accused under POA 1985, s.22(7) against a decision of the magistrates' court to extend, or further extend, a time limit imposed by the 1987 Regulations; or
(2) by the prosecution under POA 1985, s.22(8) against a decision refusing to extend or further extend such a time limit,

is commenced by the appellant's giving notice in writing of appeal:

(a) to the designated officer of the magistrates' court which took the decision;
(b) if the appeal is brought by the accused, to the prosecutor, and if the prosecution is being carried on by the CPS, to the appropriate Crown Prosecutor;
(c) if the appeal is brought by the prosecution, to the accused; and
(d) to the Crown Court officer.

28–019 The notice of appeal must state: R.20.1(3)

(1) the date on which the time limit applicable to the case is due to expire; and

(2) if the appeal is brought by the accused under POA 1985, s.22(7), the date on which the time limit would have expired had the magistrates' court decided not to extend, or further extend, the time limit. R.20.1(5)

On receiving the notice of appeal, the Crown Court officer will enter the appeal, and give notice of the time and place of the hearing to the appellant, the other party to the appeal and the clerk to the magistrates' court which took the decision. R.20.1(5)

Without prejudice to the power of the Crown Court to give leave for an appeal to be abandoned (see 10 APPEALS), an appellant may abandon an appeal under these provisions by giving notice in writing to any person to whom the notice of appeal was required to be given, not later than the third day preceding the day fixed for the hearing of the appeal (disregarding any Saturday, Sunday or bank holiday in England and Wales).

Judge's action on allowing appeal

BA 1976, s.3(10); SI 1987/299

28–020 Where:

(1) the Crown successfully appeal a grant of bail by the magistrates' court the judge must stipulate a date (within the powers of the magistrates under MCA 1980, ss.128, 128A and 129) as a remand date on which the accused is to be brought before the magistrates' court (*R. v Manchester MC Ex p. Geza Szakal* [2000] Crim.L.R. 47);
(2) the accused successfully appeals, and is admitted to bail by reason of the expiry of the custody time limit, the judge's powers to impose conditions on the grant are restricted.

There is no power to require a surety for his surrender, or power to require the accused to give security for his surrender under BA 1976, s.3(4), (5). He may be required, however, after (not before) his release, to comply with any other conditions of bail appropriate under s.3(6).

29 DEALING WITH AN OFFENDER

General

29–001 Some general principles governing the sentencing of offenders and the various sentencing options available are, for convenience, set out below in a single composite section preceded by a "road map" referring to the appropriate page in the text.

1. The "Road-map" of sentencing

29–002 Some may find the following "road map" useful in approaching the current maze of sentencing provisions, and deciding where the balance lies between the five declared purposes of sentencing , namely:

(1) punishment;
(2) the reduction of crime (including deterrence);
(3) rehabilitation;
(4) protection of the public; and
(5) reparation.

Once the decision has been made to deal with sentence and not to remit the offender to another court or judge for sentence, (see 29–016–20–020 below), the following "step by step" approach may be useful for assessing:

(a) the seriousness of the offence;
(b) the culpability of the offender; and
(c) the level of actual, intended or foreseeable harm,

thus arriving at a proper and just disposal of the case.

Step 1 — The factual basis for sentence

29–003 Establish a factual basis for sentence, (holding a "Newton" hearing where necessary, see 34 FACTUAL BASIS FOR SENTENCE).

Establish:

(1) the offender's **age** — generally crucial to the sentencing process, (see 29–044 below and 6 AGE OF OFFENDER); in general 18 is the watershed, though in the case of young offenders, (see 31 DETENTION OF YOUNG OFFENDERS), a further breakdown may be necessary;

(2) the **date of the commission of the offence** — also crucial: SI 2005/643 brought into force most of the sentencing provisions of CJA 2003 (except some which are purely procedural or reproduce existing provisions more or less exactly) and these apply only to offences committed on or after **April 4, 2005**. Sentences for offences committed before that date continue to be governed by PCC(S)A 2000 which is expressly saved for this purpose;

(3) the **number** of offences to be dealt with — an offender may be sentenced only on the basis of the offences proved against him by admission or verdict, or which he has asked to be taken into consideration (see 62 TICs) (*R. v Canavan* [1988] 1 Cr. App. R.(S.) 243; *R. v Tovey and Another* [2005] Crim.L.R. 575);

(4) the **seriousness** of the offence(s) (29–021 below);

(5) the **culpability** of the offender; and

(6) the **harm** caused to individuals, to the community or other types of harm (see as to victims' views and impact statements 29–041, 29–042A below);

(7) the prevalence of offence(s) (see 29–046 below); and/or

(8) any mental health disposal (29–066 below).

Step 2 — Mandatory or discretionary? Sentences fixed or prescribed by law

29–004 Certain sentences are fixed, or prescribed by law, thus:

(1) a life sentence (see 45 LIFE SENTENCES);

(2) sentences for dangerous offenders, CJA 2003, s.225 *et seq.*) (see 40 IMPRISONMENT, 31 DETENTION OF YOUNG OFFENDERS);

(3) "automatic" life sentences for 2nd time serious offence PCC(S)A 2000, s.109 (see 40 IMPRISONMENT);

(4) 3rd time domestic burglary. PCC(S)A 2000, s.111 (see 40 IMPRISONMENT);

(5) 3rd time drug trafficking offence, PCC(S)A 2000, s.110 (see 40 IMPRISONMENT);

(6) prohibited weapon FA 1968, s.51A (see 40 IMPRISONMENT, 31 DETENTION OF YOUNG OFFENDERS);

Dangerous offenders

29–005 Dangerous offenders are dealt with differently from ordinary offenders (See 29–014, below). Establish whether the offender qualifies either as an adult or a juvenile dangerous offender, requiring:

(1) a discretionary life sentence; or
(2) an indefinite sentence for public protection; or
(3) where the maximum sentence for the offence carries 10 years or less, an extended sentence?

Step 3 — Aggravating and mitigating features

29–006 Determine the order, or the length of any custodial term contemplated, then adjust it in the light of any aggravating or mitigating factors (*R. v Fraser* (1982) 4 Cr. App. R.(S.) 254).

Previous convictions and offences committed whilst on bail are treated as aggravating factors under CJA 2003, s.143, (see 29–021 below). Other aggravating and mitigating factors are dealt with at 29–007, 29–008, below.

Aggravating factors

29–007 The nature and length of the sentence may be enhanced not only by the facts of the case but by aggravating features in addition to those mentioned above, such as:

(a) the number of offences;
(b) the period of offending ;
(c) any racial or religious element in the offence (29–023 below);
(d) hostility based on victim's sexual orientation or disability (29–024 below);
(e) the impact on the community;
(g) planning and sophistication;
(h) offence(s) were committed while subject to a community order (see 14 BREACH, AMENDMENT AND REVOCATION);
(i) offence(s) committed in contravention of a court order (see 14 BREACH, AMENDMENT AND REVOCATION).

Mitigating and personal factors

29–008 The sentence may be reduced by mitigating factors such as:

(a) good character or lack of previous convictions;
(b) a plea of guilty and the application of the reduction principles (29–025, 28–034, below);
(c) the level of offender's responsibility for offence;
(d) whether offender acting under pressure from others;
(e) clear evidence of contrition and remorse;
(f) offender giving assistance to the authorities (29–036–29–039 below);
(g) lapse of time between offence and sentence;

(h) the length of any remand in custody (29–062, 80–082 below);
(i) the offender's conduct on remand;
(j) restorative justice factors (see *R. v Collins* [2003] EWCA Crim 1687, *R. v Barci* [2003] EWCA Crim 2816, otherwise unreported) and factors such as compensation (see 23 COMPENSATION);

Reports; representation

29–009 In some cases a pre-sentence report may be required by statute (29–067 below); in other cases the judge may derive assistance from:

(1) a pre-sentence, or other report? (29–067–29–073, below);
(2) a medical or psychiatric report (29–074, below);

The latter may be mandatory where the judge has a mental health disposal in contemplation (see 48 MENTALLY DISORDERED OFFENDERS).

It is unsafe to proceed to sentence unless the offender is represented (29–057, below).

Step 4 — Guidelines

29–010 The judge is obliged to have regard to:

(1) any Guideline judgments;
(2) any advice from the SGC;
(3) helpful indications from other reported cases or relevant AGs references.

A judge must have regard to any sentencing guidelines issued by the Sentencing Guidelines Council set up under CJA 2003, s.167, which are relevant in sentencing an offender, to the offender's case, and exercising any other function in relation to the sentencing of offenders, which is relevant to the exercise of that function. CJA 2003, s.172

A guideline is no more than a guideline. It does not affect the judge's powers of sentencing as set out in the legislation, it merely indicates how those powers might be exercised. They are intended to assist the judge to reach a just sentence. They do not alter the law (*R. v Peters* [2005] Crim.L.R. 407).

If the judge decides not to apply a guideline, he must explain why he is not doing so (*R. v Oosthuizen* [2005] Crim.L.R. 979, *R. v Bowering* [2006] Crim.L.R. 361, *R. v Gisbourne* [2006] Crim.L.R. 363). The practice is adopted in *Sentencing — Form of Words* (as to which see 29–085, below).

The Council has a duty to make judges aware of: CJA 2003, s.172A(3)

(a) the sentences imposed by courts in England and Wales;
(b) the cost of different sentences and their relative effectiveness in preventing re-offending;
(c) the resources that are, or are in future likely to be, available for giving effect to sentences imposed by courts in England and Wales;
(d) the manner in which courts sentence offenders or exercise any other function relating to the sentencing of offenders.

The advocate for the Crown ought not to be prevented from advising the judge on the legal aspects of any sentence that he might be contemplating, whether at the judge's invitation or otherwise. He should be immediately familiar with the maximum sentences for the offence(s) which are being dealt with, and with the preconditions for any form of sentence which the judge proposes to impose (see generally *Att.-Gen.'s Ref (No. 7 of 1997)* [1998] 1 Cr. App. R.(S.) 268, *R. (Inner London Probation Service v Tower Bridge MC* [2002] 1 Cr.App.R.(S.) 43).

In particular he must bring to the judge's attention to:

(1) any matters of law relating to sentence; and
(2) any sentencing guideline cases, making copies available to the judge.

(*R. v Pepper & Others The Times*, May 10, 2005, where the authorities are reviewed).

He also has functions in relation to disputed issues of fact (see 34 FACTUAL BASIS FOR SENTENCE).

As to the acceptance or otherwise of pleas, see 41 INDICATION OF SENTENCE. The Attorney-General proposes to issue guidelines on this topic (*R. v Pepper & Others*, above).

If the judge makes an error in sentencing, particularly in relation to his powers, the advocate, whether for the Crown or for the defence, should be alive to the possibility of rectifying the sentence under the slip rule (PCC(S)A 2000, s.155 (see 8 ALTERATION OF SENTENCE)).

Step 5 — Thresholds

29–011 In considering the nature of sentence to be imposed, it is necessary to consider whether:

(1) the case is "so serious" that it crosses the "custody threshold" (29–050–20–053, below);

(2) if the case crosses the custody threshold immediate custody is required;

(3) there are realistic alternatives to a custodial sentence? e.g. deferment of sentence (see 30 DEFERRING SENTENCE);

(4) a "custody plus" order (once it comes into force) be made, i.e. a short-term prison sentence accompanied by community requirements (see 29–065, below);

(5) if a short-term prison sentence is imposed, it should be made "intermittent" (see 40 IMPRISONMENT);

(6) if custody is not appropriate, the case is "serious enough" to cross the "community sentence" threshold (see 29–061–20–064, below);

(7) if it is a case for a community penalty, which community sentence should it be (see 21 COMMUNITY SENTENCES);

(8) if the community sentence threshold is not reached, a lesser sentence is appropriate e.g. a fine (36 FINES AND ENFORCEMENT), compensation (see 23 COMPENSATION), a conditional discharge (see 2 ABSOLUTE AND CONDITIONAL DISCHARGE) or a bind over (see 13 BIND OVER);

(9) orders for deprivation, restitution, or forfeiture of property are appropriate (see 37 FORFEITURE, RESTITUTION AND REWARDS);

(10) a confiscation order under PCA 2002 is appropriate. If so, make the order, or where applicable, take the decision to postpone the confiscation hearing before any other sentence is passed (see 24 CONFISCATION ORDERS);

(11) orders for prosecution and/or defence costs are appropriate (see 26 COSTS AND TAXATION).

Custodial sentences

29–012 Where the judge's decision is that the sentence must be custodial:

(1) how long should the sentence be? (29–054, below) (as to joint conviction with juvenile see *R. v Tyre* (1984) 6 Cr.App.R.(S.) 247);

(2) should the sentence be suspended? (see 29–055, below and 42 IMPRISONMENT):

 (a) for offences committed *before* April 4, 2005, are there "exceptional circumstances" justifying a suspended sentence?

(b) for offences committed *after* April 4, 2005, is a suspended sentence order appropriate (see CJA 2003, ss.189–193 at 40–081, *post*).

(c) in the case of (a) should there be a suspended sentence supervision order?

(3) Do the return to custody provisions (PCC(S)A 2000, s.116) apply (see 40 IMPRISONMENT)?

(4) Are there any breaches of existing court orders to be dealt with? (see 14 BREACH, AMENDMENT AND REVOCATION);

(5) Is there a need for a protective sentence such as an indeterminate sentence for public protection, a "longer than commensurate" sentence or an "extended" sentence? (see 40 IMPRISONMENT);

(6) consider the totality aspect of any custodial sentence (see 40 IMPRISONMENT), whether the several sentences should be; concurrent or consecutive (see 40 IMPRISONMENT); watch "disparity" in the case of several offenders.

(7) is the offender on licence for an offence committed before April 4, 2005, so that the provisions of PCC(S)A 2000, s.116 (**return to prison**) apply? (see 40–093, below).

Time spent on remand must be taken into account; either under CJA 1967, s.67 (offences *before* April 4, 2005), or CJA 2003, s.240 (offences *after* April 4, 2005) (see 29–062, below and 40 IMPRISONMENT).

Step 6 — Ancillary orders

29–013 Consider whether any other additional ancillary order should be attached to the sentence, e.g.

- RT disqualification (see 54 RT DISQUALIFICATION AND ENDORSEMENT)
- anti-social behaviour order, also individual support order (see 9 ANTI-SOCIAL BEHAVIOUR ORDERS)
- company officers (see 22 COMPANY OFFICERS DISQUALIFICATION)
- football banning order (see 37 FOOTBALL BANNING ORDERS)
- licensed premises exclusion order (see 44 LICENSED PREMISES EXCLUSION ORDER)
- recommendation for deportation (see 50 RECOMMENDATION FOR DEPORTATION)
- (harassment) restraining order (see 51 RESTRAINING ORDER (HARASSMENT)

- disqualification from driving for any other offence (under PCC(S)A 2000, s.146, CJA 2003, s.304 (see 54 RT DISQUALIFICATION AND ENDORSEMENT)
- sex offenders notification requirements orders (see 56 SEX OFFENDERS ORDERS)
- travel restriction order
- disqualification from working with children order (see 56 SEX OFFENDERS ORDERS)
- drug abstinence order (see 21 COMMUNITY SENTENCES)
- exclusion from entering a specified place order (see 21 COMMUNITY SENTENCES)
- financial reporting order (SOCA 2005, s.76)
- sexual offences prevention order (SOA 2003, s.104) (see 56 SEX OFFENDERS ORDERS)

In general, unless the statute otherwise permits (e.g. in the case of a confiscation order) all aspects of the sentence, i.e. the principal penalty and any ancillary order, ought to be imposed on the same occasion. In the case of RT disqualifications, however:

(1) there is nothing to prevent the judge from dealing with the substantive part of the sentence on the day of conviction and postponing ancillary questions of endorsement and disqualification until the licence is produced, and any other relevant information is to hand (*R. v Annesley* (1976) 62 Cr.App.R. 113);

(2) a judge who:
   (a) defers sentence in respect of an offence carrying obligatory or discretionary disqualification; or
   (b) adjourns after convicting an offender of such an offence, before dealing with him.

May order him to be disqualified until he has been dealt with for the offence.

Rewards under CLA 1826, ss.28, 29 and commendation(s) should be considered (see 38 FORFEITURE, RESTITUTION AND REWARDS).

Special considerations — dangerous offenders: CJA 2003

29–014 The Criminal Justice Act 2003 (see 40 IMPRISONMENT, 31 DETENTION OF YOUNG OFFENDERS) requires the judge to take the following steps:

(1) Is the current offence a "specified violent or sexual offence" under s.224(2)(a) and Sch.15?

   (a) if the answer is "No", resort to standard sentencing practice.
   (b) if the answer is "Yes", go to question (2);

(2) Does the offender represent a significant risk of causing serious harm by the commission of a further specified offence?
   (a) if the answer is "No", resort to standard sentencing practice.
   (b) if the answer is "Yes", go to question (3);

(3) Is the current offence a serious offence as defined by CJA 2003, s.224(2)(b) (that is the maximum sentence of 10 years or more)?
   (a) if the answer is "No", s.227 applies: where
      (i) the offender is over 18 consider an extended sentence of imprisonment (s.227(1)(a) and (b) and s.227(2));
      (ii) the offender is under 18 consider an extended sentence of detention. (s.228(1)(b) and s.228(2));
      (iii) the judge in both (i) and (ii) above finds that there will be a significant risk of serious harm caused by a future specified offence, he may make assumptions as set out in s.229, in particular under s.229(3), if previously convicted in the UK of one or more relevant offences;
   (b) if the answer is "Yes", s.225 applies where:
      (i) the offender is over 18 and the offence carries a life sentence and the seriousness of the offence merits a life sentence, a life sentence must be passed. Where the offence does not merit a life sentence, an indefinite public protection sentence must be passed and the court must fix a minimum term under PCC(S)A 200, s.82A.
      (ii) the offender is under 18 and the offence carries detention for life and the seriousness of the offence merits a life sentence, a detention for life sentence must be passed (s.226(1)(b) and 226(2)(a), (b))
      (iii) where the offence does not merit a sentence of detention for life and an extended sentence of detention under s.228 is not adequate for the protection of the public, the judge must pass a sentence of indefinite detention for public protection.

In (i) and (ii) above, assumptions under s.229 may be made by the judge in exactly the same way as is set out in (3)(a)(iii) above.

2. Antecedents

29–015 Immediately following the proceedings in the magistrates' court resulting in a case being sent for trial, or committed for sentence to the Crown Court or upon receipt of a notice of appeal from the magistrates' court, the police will: PD 2004, III.27.1–4

(1) prepare the antecedents of the offender (in the form set out in PD 2004, III.27.3);
(2) provide brief details of the circumstances of the last three similar convictions and/or of convictions likely to be of interest to the judge, the latter being judged on a case by case basis, being provided separately and attached to the antecedents;
(3) where the current alleged offence might constitute a breach of an existing order, and it is known that that order is still in force, to enable the judge to consider the possibility of revoking the order, details of the circumstances of the offence leading to its imposition.

Seven copies of the antecedents will be prepared in respect of each accused. Two copies are provided to the CPS direct, the remaining five being sent to the Crown Court. The appropriate officer will send one copy to the defence and one to the Probation Service. Where, following conviction a custodial order is made, one of the court's copies will be attached to the order sent to the prison. PD 2004, III.27.4–7

Note that:

(a) the antecedents must be provided within 21 days of the case being sent to the Crown Court;
(b) any points arising from them must be raised with the police by the defence solicitor as soon as possible and, if there is time, at least seven days before the hearing date so that that the matter can be resolved prior to the hearing;
(c) seven days before the hearing date, the police must check the record of convictions; details of any additional convictions must be provided, using the standard form, and attached to the documents already supplied. Details of any additional outstanding cases must also be provided at this stage.

The antecedents should include dates of release from prior sentences and sentence expiry dates (*R. v Egan, The Times*, March 9, 2004).

3. Remittal, adjournment, deferment

29–016 An offender need not be dealt with on the very day of conviction, nor in every case by the judge before whom he appeared or was convicted.

There is:

(1) a duty in certain circumstances to remit a juvenile offender to the appropriate youth court in (see 29–017, below);
(2) a power to transfer an offender's case, administratively, from one court, or from one circuit, to another, where sentence or another trial is pending, in that court;
(3) a common law power to adjourn, which may be appropriate for:
  (a) the making of enquiries,
  (b) the provision of reports,
  (c) consolidating other outstanding charges, or other co-accused, or
  (d) the making of reparation by the offender (see 23 COMPENSATION);
(4) a statutory power to adjourn for the production of a driving licence (see 54 RT DISQUALIFICATION AND ENDORSEMENT);
(5) certain statutory powers under MHA ss.35, 36 to remand to hospital for a medical examination and report (see 48 MENTALLY DISORDERED OFFENDERS);
(6) power to postpone the making of a confiscation order under PCA 2002, ss.14, 15 (see 24 CONFISCATION ORDERS); and
(7) a statutory power to defer passing sentence for a fixed period, (see 30 DEFERRING SENTENCE).

Where several offenders fall to be sentenced, it is desirable that they should all be sentenced by the same court, and, where practicable, on the same occasion. Where some plead not guilty and their case is adjourned for trial, the sentencing hearing in respect of those any who have pleaded guilty should be adjourned to the conclusion of those trials (*R. v Weekes and Others* (1982) 74 Cr.App.R. 161). As to sentencing a number of offenders, see 29–007 below.

Remittal of juvenile to youth court

29–017 In relation to (1) above, a judge of the Crown Court is under a statutory duty to remit an offender under 18 to a youth court for sentence *unless*: PCC(S)A 2000, s.8

(1) he is satisfied that he can deal with him properly by way of an absolute or conditional discharge, a fine or an order that a parent or guardian enter into a recognisance to take proper care of him and exercise proper control over him, with or without any ancillary order(s) that he has power to make when imposing an absolute or conditional discharge; or
(2) importantly, he is satisfied that it would be undesirable to do so, as to which see 19 CHILDREN AND YOUNG PERSONS.

Outstanding offences; other offenders

29–018 An accused who has a number of indictments, or counts, outstanding against him, should be sentenced on one occasion at the conclusion of all matters on which the Crown intend to proceed. Only in this way will consistency of sentencing be achieved. The problems caused by doing otherwise are obvious (*R. v Bennet* (1980) 2 Cr.App.R.(S.) 96).

In particular, where one offender has undertaken, after pleading guilty, to give evidence at the trial of his co-accused or other criminal confederates, while it is a matter for the judge to decide whether to sentence him before he gives evidence (*R. v Payne* [1950] 1 All E.R. 102), it is generally more sensible to wait until he has given his evidence at the trial of the others (*R. v Weekes* (1982) 74 Cr.App.R. 161).

Adjournment for reports — *R. v Gillam:* a potential trap

29–019 Where the judge adjourns for enquiries to be made or reports to be provided, he should be careful to observe the rules laid down in *R. v Gillam* [1981] Crim.L.R. 55, and the numerous cases which have followed it.

He:

(1) must be careful not to say or do anything which might reasonably create in the offender's mind any expectation that he will adopt a particular option if the reports are favourable; and
(2) should state expressly that:
    (a) he is "keeping his options open"; and

(b) that the grant of bail pending the preparation of a report, is no indication of the nature of any sentence which he has in mind (*R. v Renan* [1994] Crim. L.R. 379),

otherwise CACD has indicated that a sense of injustice, "real or imagined," may be created in the offender's mind, though failure to warn the offender that the court is considering a custodial sentence does not vitiate any subsequent sentence (*R. v Woodin* [1994] Crim.L.R. 72).

Bail or custody

29–020 There is no general presumption in favour of bail after conviction, though it may be granted, (subject to CJPOA 1994, s.25) where:

(1) the offender's case is adjourned for the purpose of enabling enquiries and a report to be made, to assist the court in dealing with him for the offence; or
(2) the offender appears or is brought before the court to be dealt with for breach of the requirements of a community order.

Where an offender's case is adjourned for enquiries or reports, and the offence, or one of the offences, of which he is convicted in the proceedings is punishable with imprisonment, he need not be granted bail if it appears that it would be impracticable to complete the enquiries or to make the report without keeping him in custody. BA 1976, s.4(1) Sch.1, Pt I

4. Determining seriousness

Culpability and seriousness; sentencing guidelines

29–021 The judge must (CJA 2003, s.143(1)–(3)) in relation to all offences whether committed before or after April 4, 2005:

(1) consider the offender's culpability in committing the offence and any harm which the offence caused, was intended to cause or might forseeably have caused, and
(2) when considering the seriousness of
    (a) the current offence committed by an offender who has one or more **previous convictions**, to treat each previous conviction as an aggravating factor if, in the case of that conviction, he considers that it can reasonably be so treated having regard to the nature of

the offence to which the conviction relates and its relevance to the current offence, and the time that has elapsed since the conviction;

(b) an offence committed while the offender was **on bail**, to treat the fact that it was committed whilst he was on bail as an aggravating factor.

A "previous conviction" here, refers to one by a court in the United Kingdom, and a previous finding of guilt in service disciplinary proceedings, but the judge is not prevented from treating a previous conviction by a court outside the United Kingdom as an aggravating feature in any case where he considers it appropriate to do so. CJA 2003, s.143(4), (5)

5. Aggravating and mitigating factors

General; previous convictions — TICs

29–022 In approaching:

(1) the nature of any sentence; or
(2) the length of any custodial term,

the judge should;

(a) first determine the order, or the length of the custodial term which he has in mind, and
(b) then adjust it in the light of any mitigating (or aggravating) factors.

(*R. v Fraser* (1982) 4 Cr.App.R.(S.) 254).

Previous convictions and offences committed whilst on bail are treated as aggravating factors under CJA 2003, s.143, (above, 29–021). Other aggravating and mitigating factors are dealt with below.

When assessing the significance of offences taken into consideration, the judge is likely to attach weight to the demonstrable fact that the offender has assisted the police. Such cooperative behaviour may provide its own early indication of guilt and usually mean that no further proceedings need be started. As with other aspects of sentencing, the way in which the judge deals with offences taken into consideration depends on context. They may add nothing or nothing very much to the sentence he would otherwise have imposed or sometimes they may aggravate the sentence and lead to a substantial increase. This is particularly where the offences show a pattern of criminal activity which suggests careful planning, or if the offences were committed on bail after an earlier arrest (*R. v Miles*, *The Times*, April 10, 2006).

Increase in sentence for racial or religious aggravation

29–023 In considering the seriousness of an offence, whether committed before or after April 4, 2005, other than one under CDA 1998, ss.29 to 32 (racially or religiously aggravated assaults, criminal damage, public order offences and harassment) if the offence was racially or religiously aggravated (within the meaning of CDA 1998, s.28) the judge must treat that as a factor which increases the seriousness of the offence, and must state in open court: CJA 2003, s.145

(1) that it was so aggravated,
  (a) identifying the sentence which would have been appropriate in the absence of racial aggravation; and
  (b) adding an appropriate amount to reflect the element of racial aggravation, and
(2) indicating by how much the sentence has been enhanced to reflect the racial aggravation.

(See *R. v Kelly and Another* [2002] 1 Cr.App.R.(S.) 85).

As to what amounts to "racial" aggravation, contrast the cases of *R. v White* [2001] 1 W.L.R. 1352 and *DPP v Pal* [2000] Crim.L.R. 756. As to where it is not possible to identify which member of a group shouted racist slogans, see *R. v Davies* [2004] Crim.L.R. 677.

In *R. v O'Callaghan* [2005] Crim.L.R. 486. and *R. v McGillivary* [2005] Crim.L.R. 484, it was held that it is not open to the judge to sentence on the basis of racial aggravation unless the offender has been convicted on that basis, though in *R. v Lester* (1976) 63 Cr.App.R. 144) it was said that the Crown might adduce evidence of such aggravation, which was not adduced at the trial, in the course of a Newton hearing. The judge should be careful not to draw any inference that the offence was so aggravated unless he gives notice to the offender and permits him to challenge the inference.

In approaching a racially aggravated sentence it will, in general, be appropriate to adopt a two-tier approach, namely by

(i) first identifying the sentence that would have been appropriate in the absence of racial aggravation; and
(ii) secondly, adding an appropriate amount to reflect the element of racial aggravation,

stating by how much the sentence has been enhanced.

(*R. v Saunders* [2000] 1 Cr.App.R.(S.) 71, considered in *R. v Kelly & Donnelly* [2001] 2 Cr.App.R.(S.) 73), though there may be cases where such an approach is inappropriate, see e.g. *R. v O'Brien* [2003] 2 Cr.App.R.(S.) 66, *R. v Fitzgerald* [2004] 1 Cr.App.R.(S.) 74.

The amount of the enhancement will depend on the circumstances of the particular case (*R. v Morrison* [2001] 1 Cr.App.R.(S.) 5).

Increase in sentences for aggravation related to disability or sexual orientation

29–024 Where the judge is considering the seriousness of an offence committed **on or after April 4, 2005**, in any of the following circumstances, namely, that, at the time of committing the offence, or immediately before or after doing *so* the offender demonstrated towards the victim of the offence hostility based on: CJA 2003, s.146

(1) the sexual orientation (or presumed sexual orientation) of the victim, or
(2) a disability (or presumed disability) of the victim, or
(3) a motivation (wholly or partly) by hostility towards persons who:
   (a) are of a particular sexual orientation, or
   (b) have a disability or a particular disability,

the judge must:

(i) treat the fact that the offence was committed in any of those circumstances as an aggravating factor, and
(ii) state in open court that the offence was committed in such circumstances.

It is immaterial for the purposes of para.(a) or (b) of subs.(2) whether or not the offender's hostility is also based, to any extent, on any other factor not mentioned in that paragraph. "Disability" means any physical or mental impairment.

Where the Crown seeks to adduce evidence of such aggravation, which was not adduced at the trial, the evidence should be adduced after verdict at a Newton hearing. The judge should be careful not to draw any inference that the offence was so aggravated unless he gives notice to the offender and permits him to challenge the inference (see *R. v Lester* (1976) 63 Cr.App.R. 144). The same approach to sentence will apply as in the preceding paragraph.

Reduction in sentence for guilty pleas

29–025 In determining what sentence to pass on an offender who has pleaded guilty to an offence in proceedings before him, or before another court, the judge must take into account: CJA 2003, s.144(1)

(1) the stage in the proceedings at which the offender indicated his intention to plead guilty, and
(2) the circumstances in which this indication was given,

and if the judge then imposes punishment which is less severe than he would othewise have imposed, he must state that fact in open court.

See generally as to this topic, 29–028 *et seq*., below.

In the case of an offence the sentence for which falls to be imposed under PCC(S)A 2000, ss.110(2) or 111(2), (required sentences for certain repeat offences), nothing prevents the judge from imposing a sentence which is not less than 80 per cent of the specified term. CJA 2003, s.144(2)

Savings for power to mitigate, etc.

29–026 In so far as **offences committed on or after April 4, 2005**, are concerned nothing in relation to: CJA 2003, s.166(1), (3)

(1) imposing community sentences (CJA 2003, s.148);
(2) imposing custodial sentences (CJA 2003, ss.152, 153 or 157);
(3) pre-sentence reports and other requirements (CJA 2003, s.140); or
(4) the fixing of fines (CJA 2003, s.164),

prevents the judge from mitigating an offender's sentence by taking into account any such matters as, in his opinion, are relevant in mitigation of sentence, including his power to mitigate:

(a) any penalty included in the offender's sentence by taking into account any other penalty included in that sentence, and
(b) the sentence of an offender convicted of one or more other offences, by applying the "totality principle" (see 42–013).

In particular:

(i) CJA 2003, s.152, does not prevent the judge, after taking into account such matters, from passing a community sentence, even though he is of opinion that the offence, or the combination of the offence and one or more offences associated with it, was so serious that a community sentence could not normally be justified for the offence (CJA 2003, s.166(2)); and

(ii) in the case of a person suffering from a mental disorder within the meaning of MHA 1983, nothing mentioned in the sections referred to in (1)–(4) above, is to be taken as requiring the judge to pass a custodial sentence, or any particular custodial sentence, or as restricting any power (whether under MHA 1983 or otherwise) which enables the judge to deal with an offender in the manner he considers to be most appropriate in all the circumstances. CJA 2003, s.166(5), (6)

6. "Discounts" on sentence

29–027 A tract of cases developed by the CACD has restricted the judge's discretion in passing sentence, by giving an offender the right to expect a discount on the otherwise appropriate sentence, where:

(1) he pleads guilty to the indictment (*R. v Barnes* (1983) 5 Cr.App.R.(S.) 368); the position is now governed by statute (see 29–028, below);
(2) the judge considers that the offence would not have been committed but for the activities of an informer (*R. v Beaumont* (1987) 9 Cr.App.R.(S.) 342; *R. v Chapman* (1989) 11 Cr.App.R.(S.) 222; *R. v Tonnessen* [1998] 2 Cr. App.R.(S.) 328; *R. v Underhill* [1979] 1 Cr.App.R.(S.) 270);
(3) the accused co-operates with the prosecuting authorities, not only by pleading guilty, but by giving information early enough for it to be potentially useful; this is also now covered by statute (see 29–036, below).

Such a discount should reflect the seriousness of the offence, the importance of the information, and the effect, where the informant gives evidence, on his future circumstances (*R. v Wood* [1996] Crim. L.R. 916) and the circumstances of the entrapment or other factors should be expressly mentioned in the judge's sentencing remarks (*R. v Mackey & Shaw* (1993) 14 Cr.App.R.(S.) 53).

(1) Reduction in sentence for a guilty plea

Statutory provisions

29–028 In determining the sentence to be passed on an offender who has pleaded guilty to an offence in proceedings before that or another court, the judge must take into account:

(1) the stage in the proceedings for the offence at which the offender indicated his intention to plead guilty; and
(2) the circumstances in which this indication was given.

If, as a result of taking into account such matters the judge imposes a punishment on the offender which is less severe than he would otherwise have imposed, he must state in open court that he has done so.

In the case of an offence the sentence for which falls to be imposed under PCC(S)A 2000, ss.110(2) or 111(2) (required sentences for certain repeat offences) nothing in that subsection prevents the judge, after taking into account any matter referred to in (1) above, from imposing any sentence which is not less than 80 per cent of that specified in the subsection, i.e. in the case of s.110, five years seven months. SGC Guidelines do not apply (*Att.-Gen.'s Reference (No. 6 of 2006)* [2006] Crim.L.R. 772. CJA 2003, s.144(2) 174(2)(d), (e)

SGC Guideline

29–029 SGC has issued a guideline (SGC 1) making a statement of purpose, and stating a recommended approach to the application of the principle, guidance on determining the level of reduction in an individual case and guidance on whether to withhold a reduction.

The content of this guideline is also intended to assist judges when arriving at the appropriate minimum term for the offence of murder, applying CJA 2003, Sch.21, para.12 (see 48 LIFE SENTENCES).

Statement of Purpose

29–030 A reduction in sentence is appropriate because a guilty plea:

(1) avoids the need for a trial (thus enabling other cases to be disposed of more expeditiously,
(2) shortens the gap between charge and sentence,
(3) saves considerable cost, and,
(4) in the case of an early plea, saves victims and witnesses from the concern about having to give evidence.

It is a separate issue from aggravation and mitigation generally. SGC 1, 2.1, 2

SGC suggests that the judge, in deciding the most appropriate length of sentence and before calculating the reduction for the guilty plea, should:

(a) address separately the issue of remorse, together with any other mitigating features present, such as admissions to the police in interview; and

(b) reflect in the sentence the implications of any other offences that the offender asks to be taken into consideration on sentence.

The reduction should then be applied to any of the punitive elements of the sentence; it has no impact on the decisions in relation to ancillary orders.

Where an offence crosses the threshold for the imposition of a community or custodial sentence, application of the reduction principle may properly form the basis for imposing a fine or discharge rather than a community sentence, or an alternative to an immediate custodial sentence. Where the reduction is applied in this way, the actual sentence imposed incorporates the reduction. SGC 1, 2.3–06

Application of the Reduction Principle

29–031 SGC 1, 3.1. recommends that the judge should:

(1) decide the sentence for the offence(s), taking into account any other offences which have been formally admitted (see 59 TICs);
(2) select the amount of the reduction by reference to a prescribed sliding scale;
(3) apply that reduction to the sentence he has decided on; and
(4) state, when pronouncing sentence, what the sentence would have been if there had been no such reduction.

Determining the level of deduction

29–032 SGC 1, 4.1, 2 recommends that the level of reduction should be:

(1) a proportion of the total sentence imposed, the proportion being based upon the stage in the proceedings at which the guilty plea was entered;
(2) save where PCC(S)A 2000, s.152(3) as amended by (CJA 2003, s.144(2) applies, (i.e. required sentences for certain offences) the level of the reduction is to be gauged on a sliding scale generally ranging from:
  (a) a maximum of one third (where the guilty plea was entered at the first reasonable opportunity in relation to the offence for which sentence is being imposed),
  (b) reducing to a maximum of one quarter (where a trial date has been set), and to
  (c) a maximum of one tenth (for a guilty plea entered at the "door of the court" or after the trial has begun).

The level of reduction should reflect the stage at which the offender indicated a willingness to admit guilt to the offence for which he is eventually sentenced.

Decisions on sentence do not and should not, however, involve a mathematical exercise resulting from arithmetical calculations. The SGC seem to have lost sight of the fact the judge in a criminal case has the heavy responsibility of making a balanced analysis of the requirements of both mercy and justice in each individual case, reflecting the sometimes conflicting aggravating and mitigating features of it. Mathematics does not supply the answer to that most sensitive and difficult of judicial responsibilities (see *R. v Martin*, *The Times*, June 6, 2006).

Note also:

(i) the maximum reduction is to be given only where the offender indicated willingness to admit guilt at the first reasonable opportunity; when this occurs will vary from case to case (see Annex 2 for illustrative examples);
(ii) where the admission of guilt comes later than the first reasonable opportunity, the presumption is that the reduction for a guilty plea will be less than one third.
(iii) where the plea of guilty comes very late, it is still appropriate to give some reduction.
(iv) if, after pleading guilty there is a Newton hearing and the offender's version of the circumstances of the offence is rejected, this should be taken into account in determining the level of reduction.
(v) if a not guilty plea was entered and maintained for tactical reasons (such as to retain privileges whilst on remand), a late guilty plea should attract very little, if any, discount. SGC 1, 4.3

Where one of two accused pleads guilty, e.g. at the practice direction hearing, and the second six weeks later, the latter cannot expect the same discount as the former (*R. v McDonald* [2002] 1 Cr.App.R.(S.) 138).

Withholding a reduction

29–033 SGC in the draft guideline addresses certain special cases recommending, e.g.:

(1) **dangerousness** — where the judge determines that a longer than commensurate, extended, or indeterminate sentence is required for the protection of the public, the

minimum custodial term, but not the protection of the public element of the sentence, should be reduced to reflect the plea;

(2) **offender caught "red-handed"** — since the purpose of giving credit is to encourage those who are guilty to plead at the earliest opportunity, there is no reason why credit should be withheld on these grounds alone; the normal sliding scale applies;

(3) **maximum penalty thought to be too low** — the judge is bound to sentence for the offence with which the offender has been charged, and to which he has pleaded guilty; he cannot remedy perceived defects (e.g. an inadequate charge or maximum penalty) by refusal of the appropriate discount;

Note also that in the case of:

(a) two or more summary only offences, where the maximum sentence available is six months imprisonment and the sentence for each offence should be reduced to reflect the guilty plea, it may be appropriate for the sentences to be ordered to run consecutively to each other. The overall sentence would not undermine the general principle that the maximum sentence should not be imposed following a guilty plea, since the decision whether or not to make the individual sentences concurrent or consecutive will follow the normal principles that apply to that decision;

(b) an offender under 18 where the offence is one which would but for the plea have attracted a sentence of long-term detention in excess of 24 months under PCC(S)A 2000, s.91, a detention and training order of 24 months might be imposed.

Spelling it out

29–034 Both PCC(S)A 2000, s.152(2) and CJA 2003, s.144(1) requires the judge, in determining sentence on an offender who has pleaded guilty, to take into account:

(1) the stage in the proceedings for the offence at which the offender indicated his intention to plead guilty (*R. v Hussain* [2002] Crim.L.R. 327); and

(2) the circumstances in which his indication was given (*R. v Fearon* [1996] 2 Cr.App.R.(S.) 25; *R. v Aroride* [1999] 2 Cr.App.R.(S.) 406).

If the judge then imposes a sentence which is less severe than it would otherwise have been, he must state in open court that he has done so (*R. v Hastings* [1996] 1 Cr.App.R.(S.) 167); if he withholds a discount he must refer expressly to s.152(3) and explain why he is doing so.

As to the attitude of the CACD where the judge fails to state that he has taken the plea into consideration, see *R. v Wharton*, *The Times*, March 27, 2001, considering *R. v Bishop* [2000] 1 Cr.App.R.(S) 432.

(2) Agents provocateurs

29–035 Where the judge takes the view that the offence would not have been committed save for the activities of an informer, he may, if he thinks fit, give a discount on sentence (*R. v Beaumont* (1987) 9 Cr.App.R.(S.) 342; *R. v Chapman* (1989) 11 Cr.App.R.(S.) 222; *R. v Tonnessen*, [1998] 2 Cr.App.R.(S.) 328; *R. v Underhill* [1979] 1 Cr.App.R.(S.) 270).

Using test letters to establish the guilt of postal employees suspected of theft of mail does not come within this principle (*R. v Ramen* (1988) 10 Cr. App. R.(S.) 334; nor does the use of test purchases by undercover officers in relation to drug dealing (*R. v Springer* [1999] 1 Cr.App.R.(S.) 217; *R. v Mayeri* [1999] 1 Cr.App.R.(S.) 304).

(3) Assistance by accused: reduction in sentence

General

29–036 Offenders need to know that it is worth their while disclosing the criminal activities of others for the benefit of the law-abiding public in general (*R. v Sivan* (1988) 10 Cr.App.R.(S.) 282). To this end, and within the time limits specified below, the judge will need to tailor any sentence on any offender who has given such assistance to the authorities, punishing him for his offences, while at the same time rewarding him as far as is possible for the help he has given. The common law position is as shown in the previous edition of this work.

Information relevant to the offender's assistance should be put before the judge in the form of a document from a senior member of the police or other law-enforcement agency. A document of this kind although supplied by a police officer is supplied at the request of the accused. It follows that the judge must rely very heavily on the greatest possible care being taken in compiling such a document. Thus:

(1) except in very unusual circumstances, it will not be necessary or desirable for a document of this kind to contain details which will attract a public interest immunity application;
(2) if such a document does contain information which attracts a public interest immunity consideration, the usual rules about the conduct of such an application apply. It will be a case in which the defence could and should be told of the public interest immunity application;
(3) in the absence of any consideration of public interest immunity, a document of this kind should be shown to the defence, who will discuss its contents with the offender. On general principles, an offender is entitled to see documents put before the sentencing judge. There should not normally be any question of evidence being given or of an issue being tried on the question of the extent of the information provided;
(4) if the offender wishes to disagree with the contents of such a document, it is not appropriate for there to be cross-examination of the police officer. The officer is not a Crown witness. It will be possible in an appropriate case for an offender to ask for an adjournment to allow further consideration to be given to the preparation of the document. Otherwise, his remedy is not to rely on the document;
(5) the judge will normally disregard such a document if asked by the offender to do so. In such a case he will not be minded to entertain any submission that the offender has given valuable assistance to the police;
(6) if the judge does take the documents into consideration, he should say no more than that he has taken into consideration all the information about the defendant with which he had been provided.

(*R. v X* [1999] 2 Cr.App.R. 125.)

SOCA 2005, Pt 2, Ch.2

29–037 Under SOCA 2005, Pt 2, Ch.2, where an offender: SOCA 2005, s.73(1), (2)

(1) following a plea of guilty,
(2) is either convicted of an offence in proceedings in the Crown Court or is committed to the Crown Court for sentence, and

(3) has, pursuant to a written agreement made with a specified prosecutor (within the meaning of s.71(4)), assisted, or offered to assist the investigator or prosecutor in relation to that or any other offence,

the judge may, in determining what sentence to pass on the offender take into account the extent and nature of the assistance given or offered.

If he passes a sentence which is less than it would have passed but for the assistance given or offered, the judge: SOCA 2005, s.73(3), (4)

(a) must state in open court:
 (i) that he has passed a lesser sentence than he would otherwise have passed, and
 (ii) what the greater sentence would have been but
(b) need not do so if he thinks that it would not be in the public interest to disclose that the sentence has been discounted; but in such a case he must give written notice of the matters specified in (a) and (b) to both the prosecutor and the offender.

If s.73(3) above does not apply by virtue of s.73(4), then CJA 2003, ss.174(1)(a) and 270 (requirement to explain reasons for sentence or other order) do not apply to the extent that the explanation will disclose that a sentence has been discounted in pursuance of this provision. SOCA 2005, s.73(7)

Note that in this provision: SOCA 2005, s.73(8)

- a reference to a sentence includes, in the case of a sentence which is fixed by law, a reference to the minimum period an offender is required to serve, and a reference to a lesser sentence must be construed accordingly;
- a reference to imprisonment includes a reference to any other custodial sentence within the meaning of PCC(S)A 2000, s.76.

Each of the following is a specified prosecutor: the DPP, the DRCP, the DSFO, the DPP for Northern Ireland, and any prosecutor designated for the purpose by one of those.

An agreement with a specified prosecutor may provide for assistance to be given to that prosecutor or to any other prosecutor (s.73(9)).

An offender receiving such a discounted sentence, and who either fails to any extent to give assistance in accordance with the agreement; or having given the assistance in accordance with the agreement, in pursuance of another written agreement gives or agrees to give further assistance, may have his sentence referred back to court, see 8 ALTERATION OF SENTENCE.

Nothing in any enactment which: SOCA 2005, s.73(5)

(1) requires that a minimum sentence be passed in respect of any offence or an offence of any description, or by reference to the circumstances of any offender (whether or not the enactment also permits the court to pass a lesser sentence in particular circumstances), or
(2) in the case of a sentence which is fixed by law, requires the court to take into account certain matters for the purposes of making an order which determines or has the effect of determining the minimum period of imprisonment which the offender must serve (whether or not the enactment also permits the court to fix a lesser period in particular circumstances),

affects the power of a court to act under this provision.

If, in determining what sentence to pass on the offender, the judge takes into account the extent and nature of the assistance given or offered as mentioned above, that does not prevent the court from also taking account of any other matter which it is entitled by virtue of any other enactment to take account of for the purposes of determining, the sentence, or in the case of a sentence which is fixed by law, any minimum period of imprisonment which an offender must serve. SOCA 2005, s.73(6)

A balancing act

29–038 The extent of the discount given will ordinarily depend on the value of the help given. Value is a function of quality and quantity. In dealing with such a case the judge must balance, on the information before him:

(1) the nature and effect of the assistance given; if the information is:
    (a) unreliable, vague, lacking in practical utility or already known to the authorities, no identifiable discount need be given or, if given, may be minimal;
    (b) is accurate, particularised, useful in practice and hitherto unknown to the authorities, enabling serious criminal activity to be stopped and serious criminals brought to book, the discount may be substantial;
(2) the degree of assistance provided, e.g. whether the offender is prepared to back up his information by testifying or expressing willingness to testify, or making a witness statement incriminating a co-accused, particularly

where such conduct leads to the co-accused's conviction or his plea of guilty;

(3) the degree of risk to which the offender exposes himself or his family to personal jeopardy.

Procedure

29–039 Information relevant to the agreement between the prosecutor, and such assistance given by the offender in pursuance of it, should be put before the judge in the form of a written document from the specified prosecutor's staff. There should be no need to see the judge in chambers.

Certain propositions relating to the former non-statutory procedure (see *R. v X* [1999] 2 Cr.App.R. 125) are still relevant, in that:

(1) except in very unusual circumstances, it will not be necessary or desirable for the document to contain details which will attract a public interest immunity application;
(2) if the document does contain such information the usual rules about the conduct of such an application apply. It will be a case in which the defence could and should be told of the public interest immunity application;
(3) in the absence of any consideration of public interest immunity, the document should be shown to the defence, who will discuss its contents with the offender. On general principles, an offender is entitled to see documents put before the sentencing judge. There should not normally be any question of evidence being given or of an issue being tried on the question of the extent of the information provided;
(4) if the offender wishes to disagree with the contents of such a document, it will be possible in an appropriate case for an offender to ask for an adjournment to allow further consideration to be given to the preparation of the document.

7. Other Factors Affecting Sentence

Prison overcrowding

29–040 CJA 2003, s.152(2) provides that the judge must not pass a custodial sentence unless he is of opinion that the offence is so serious that neither a fine alone nor a community sentence can be justified. Where a custodial sentence is imposed, s.153(2) requires that it be for the shortest term commensurate with the seriousness of the offence.

When deciding whether, having regard to the seriousness of the offence, a community sentence can be justified, the judge will have regard to the importance, on the facts of the particular case, of imposing a sentence that will encourage the reformation and rehabilitation of the offender and thereby the reduction of crime.

When prisons are overcrowded the result is to hinder or prevent the valuable work of rehabilitation that a prison should normally provide. For that reason, the fact that prisons are overcrowded can be a relevant factor where the judge's decision is on the cusp, so that there is a real issue as to whether a community sentence can be justified rather than a custodial sentence. Prison overcrowding also makes it all the more important that the judge comply with the requirements of ss.152 and 153 above (*Att.-Gen.'s Reference (No. 11 of 2006)*, *The Times*, March 28, 2006 CA).

Views of victim

29–041 The damaging and distressing effects of a crime on the victim clearly represent an important factor in the sentencing decision, and those effects may include the anguish and emotional suffering of the victim or, in a case of death, the surviving close family (*R. v Nunn* [1996] Crim.L.R. 210), but

(1) the sentence imposed by the court cannot *depend* upon the views of the victim of the offence; it is for the judge to assess the impact of the offence(s) on the particular victim though where:
   (a) the sentence passed may actually aggravate the victim's distress, this may be a consideration; and
   (b) the victim's forgiveness may be treated as showing that the harm done by the offender is less than would otherwise be the case (see *R. v Roche* [1999] Crim.L.R. 339);

(2) the judge needs to balance the victim's views with the nature of the offence and the particular facts of the case (*R. v Nunn* [1996] Crim.L.R. 210, *R. v Hayes The Times*, April 5, 1999, *R. v Roche*, above); and

(3) the judge is entitled to receive evidence of the psychological effects of the offence on the victim.

Victims' personal statements

29–042 A victim's personal statement given to the prosecutor may help to identify whether the victim has a particular need for information, support or protection. The judge may take the statement into account when determining sentence. As to the Victims' Advocate Scheme, see below. PD 2004, III.28.1, 2

If the judge is presented with a victim's personal statement the following approach should be adopted:

(1) the statement and any evidence in support should be considered and taken into account prior to passing sentence;
(2) evidence of the effects of an offence on the victim contained in the victim's personal statement or any other statement, must be in proper form, that is made in the form of a witness statement made under CJA 1967, s.9, or as an expert's report, and served upon the accused's solicitor or on the accused if he is not represented, prior to sentence;
(3) except where inferences can properly be drawn from the nature of the offence or the circumstances surrounding it, the judge ought not to make assumptions unsupported by evidence about the effects of an offence on the victim;
(4) the judge should pass what he considers to be the appropriate sentence having regard to the circumstances of the offence and of the offender, taking into account, so far as he considers it appropriate, the consequences to the victim; and
(5) the judge should consider whether it is desirable in pronouncing the sentence to refer to the evidence provided on behalf of the victim.

The opinions of the victim or the victim's close relatives as to what the sentence should be are therefore not relevant, unlike the consequence of the offence on them. Victims should be advised of this; if, despite the advice, opinions as to sentence are included in the statement, the judge should pay no attention to them. There are two recognised exceptions to this rule, namely where:

(a) the sentence passed may actually aggravate the victim's distress, and
(b) the victim's forgiveness may be treated as evidence that the damage done by the offender is less than would normally be the case (see the cases reviewed in *R. v Roche* [1999] 2 Cr.App.R.(S.) 105);

Victims' Advocate Scheme

29–042A In respect of cases of murder and manslaughter (excluding death by dangerous driving) charged **on or after April 24, 2006**, a Protocol issued by the President of the QBD on May 3, 2006 provides for a scheme (now being piloted) which allows the family of the victim an opportunity to make a "family impact statement" (FIS) in open court after the offender's conviction and before the judge proceeds to sentence about the effect of the crime on the family. PD 2004, III.28.1.2 (29–042, above) continues to apply.

The family is entitled to choose whether that statement is made by:

(1) a CPS prosecutor;
(2) an independent advocate (at public expense); or
(3) a lay "friend" and

may choose whether the statement be in the form of:

(a) a written document put before the judge;
(b) oral testimony by the maker; or
(c) a statement read out in court by any of those persons in (1)–(3) above.

The contents of the statement must be brought to the attention of the accused.

In so far as procedure is concerned, the prosecutor will serve the FIS at the PMCH together with the preferred mode of presentation.

In relation to procedure:

(i) a decision should ordinarily be taken at the PCMH as to the method by which the victim's family prefers to present the statement, though, where appropriate that choice may be changed at a later stage with the judge's leave;
(ii) the judge will ordinarily accede to the family's choice unless there are good reasons for not doing so; where there is a disagreement between family members as to who will make the statement, the judge will decide;
(iii) where a written statement is made the judge will need to indicate that he has received and read it;
(iv) where an oral statement is made it is given by a witness from the witness box, that witness:
   - will be examined by the CPS, independent advocate or lay friend;
   - may be cross-examined, where appropriate, on behalf of the offender.

The judge will intervene to prevent questions which go beyond the effect of the murder/manslaughter on the victim's family.

Offender's medical condition

29–043 The guideline case of *R. v Bernard* [1997] 1 Cr.App.R.(S) 135 makes it clear that in relation to the CACD:

(1) a medical condition, which may at some time in the future affect either the offender's life expectancy or the prison's ability to treat him, is not generally a reason to interfere with an otherwise appropriate sentence;
(2) if the offender is HIV positive or otherwise has a reduced life expectancy, this should not generally affect the sentence;
(3) where the offender has a serious medical condition and it is not easily treatable in prison, he is not automatically entitled to a lesser sentence;
(4) in exceptional circumstances, the offender's serious medical condition might enable the court to reduce the sentence as an act of mercy.

Age

29–044 The age of an offender ought to be taken into account on sentence:

(1) it will almost always be appropriate to impose on a young offender a shorter sentence than would be appropriate in the case of an adult, and
(2) where deterrence may be a factor in the case of an adult, it is necessary to balance that aspect against the youth of the offender (*R. v Marriott* (1995) 16 Cr.App.R.(S.) 428) but
(3) in the case of very serious offences, however, the room for reduction is limited, indeed there may be none at all (*R. v Dodds, The Times*, January 28, 1997).

As to offenders of advanced age, see *R. v W (Sentencing; Age of defendant), The Times*, October 26, 2000.

Foreign jurisdictions; deportation, etc.

29–045 The level of sentence which might be imposed in other jurisdictions is irrelevant *R. v Maguire* [1997] 1 Cr.App.R.(S.) 130.

The fact that the offender will eventually be deported is not a matter which goes to reducing the length of a sentence of imprisonment. There are procedures at the end of a sentence for considering whether the Home Secretary will adopt a recommendation to deport: *R. v Chen (Siao Bing) and Others, The Times*, April 17, 2001.

As to foreign offenders serving sentences in English prisons, that is a comparatively small consideration where deterrent sentences are merited (*ibid.*).

Prevalence of offence

29–046 The prevalence of offences of a particular class, and public concern about them, is relevant to the seriousness of an offence before the court (*R. v Cunningham* [1993] Crim.L.R. 149; *R. v Cox* [1993] Crim.L.R. 152).

Amount and purity of drugs

29–047 In regard to assessing the amount and purity of drugs in reference to sentence, see *R. v Morris* [2001] 1 Cr.App.R.(S.) 87.

8. Choice of disposal

29–048 The form of sentence imposed on an offender will depend upon the factors outlined above, and the objective which the judge has in view, bearing in mind any restrictions placed upon his discretion, in particular by PCC(S)A 2000, as amended by CJA 2003.

The traditional object of the criminal law in sentencing is the *punishment* of offenders, the statute creating the offence providing a punitive penalty of a fine and/or imprisonment, the latter translating into one of the forms of detention for young offenders in the case of persons under 21.

Where the judge seeks:

(1) to **punish**, the appropriate custodial sentence, be it imprisonment or one of those forms of detention provided for young offenders, as the case may be, will be apposite, or a financial penalty:

(2) merely to **mark the conviction**, and no more, an absolute discharge may be appropriate;

(3) to encourage the offender **not to offend again**, there are available four forms of preventive or conditional sentences:

- (a) a bind-over under JPA 1361, where breach involves forfeiture of a specific sum;
- (b) a common law bind-over, the breach of which may also involve a fresh sentence; and
- (c) a conditional discharge, which permits a court to act on a breach, but does not involve a specific sentence on the breach; and
- (d) a suspended sentence of imprisonment;

(4) **to rehabilitate** the offender, he is likely to go for a community order to which a whole range of requirements with various aims may be added; (some of these may also be added to a short term sentence of imprisonment, or a named youth community order, as appropriate. A detention and training order (see 31 DETENTION OF YOUNG OFFENDERS), though punitive, is intended to have a regime which is, at the same time, "constructive", with an emphasis on discipline and education;

(5) to deal with a person who requires **treatment** for a specified mental disorder, hospital and guardianship orders under MHA 1983 may be made, or treatment requirements may be added to a community order.

(6) to keep **dangerous offenders** out of circulation, the appropriate provisions of PCC(S)A 2000 and CJA 2003 will be appropriate.

A good working rule is not to mix sentences which fall into established and different categories (*R. v McElhorne* [1983] Crim.L.R. 487).

9. Discretionary Custodial Sentences

29–049 Custodial sentences, for the purposes of PCC(S)A 2000, Pt V are, in relation to an offender: PCC(S)A 2000, s.76(1), (2); CJA 2003, s.304, Sch.3, Pt 1, para.108

(1) **imprisonment** (other than a committal or attachment for contempt of court or any kindred offence), as to which see PCC(S)A 2000, s.89(1)(a);

(2) **detention for public protection** under CJA 2003, s.226 in relation to **offences committed on or after April 4, 2005;**

(3) **detention under CJA 2003, s.228,** in relation to **offences committed on or after April 4, 2005;**

(4) **detention in a young offender institution** under PCC(S)A 2000, s.96;

(5) **detention under** PCC(S)A 2000, **s.90 or 91;** or

(6) **detention and training order under** PCC(S)A 2000, s.100.

Different considerations govern different types of custodial sentence, but the imposition of any of them is subject to:

(a) the offence(s) "qualifying" for a custodial sentence (see 29–050, below);

(b) the offender's age (see 6 AGE OF OFFENDER);

(c) unless unnecessary, the availability of a pre-sentence report (see 29–067, below); and
(d) in general, the offender being legally represented (see 29–057, below).

So complex are many of the interlocking provisions governing the question of custodial sentences, that it is in this field particularly, that judges "should not be slow to invite assistance from prosecuting counsel", nor should they be "affronted" where the latter offers such assistance on the relevant provisions and authorities (*Att.-Gen.'s Reference (No. 7 of 1997)* [1997] Crim.L.R. 908).

Restrictions on imposing discretionary custodial sentences

29–050 Where a person is convicted of an offence **committed on or after April 4, 2005**, punishable with a custodial sentence, other than one fixed by law, or falling to be imposed under PCC(S)A 2000, ss.109 where still appropriate, 110(2) or 111(2), or any of CJA 2003, ss.225–228 the judge must not pass a custodial sentence on the offender unless he is of the opinion that the offence, or the combination of the offence, and one or more offences "associated" with it, is "so serious" that neither a fine alone nor a community sentence can be justified for it; although nothing prevents the judge from passing a custodial sentence on an offender who; CJA 2003, s.152

(1) fails to express his willingness to comply with a requirement which it is proposed to include in a community order, and which requires an expression of such willingness; or
(2) he fails to comply with an order under CJA 2003, s.161(2) (pre-sentence drug testing).

"Seriousness" for the purposes of s.152

29–051 The Act is silent as to when an offence is so "serious" that only a custodial sentence is justified; it is a subjective test. Obviously a crime which is deliberate and premeditated, and causes personal or mental injury, is usually more serious than one which is spontaneous and unpremeditated, causing only financial loss. Lawton L.J.'s approach in *R. v Bradbourn* in respect of the previous legislation was deprecated by CACD in *R. v Howells* [1999] 1 Cr.App.R. (S) 335. Of course:

(1) the judge is not bound to impose a custodial sentence just because the offence "qualifies"; he is still required to

consider whether, having regard to mitigating circumstances, such a sentence is appropriate;

(2) the fact that a court imposed a community sentence for an offence, does not prevent it "qualifying" for a custodial sentence if the offender is in breach of the order (*R. v Bray* (1991) 12 Cr.App.R.(S.) 705; *R. v Webster* (1990) 12 Cr.App.R.(S.) 760; *R. v Oliver & Little* [1993] 2 All E.R. 9).

In considering the seriousness of an offence, the judge;

(a) may take into account the offender's *previous convictions*, and/or any failure of his to respond to previous sentences;
(b) may take into account the *prevalence* of offences of a particular class, and public concern about them (*R. v Cunningham* (1992) Cr.App.R.(S.) 444; *R. v Cox* (1993) 96 Cr.App.R. 464); and
(c) must treat as aggravating factors those matters stated at 29–022 above.

"Associated offences" for the purposes of s.152

29–052 "Associated" in relation to an offence is to be read in accordance with PCC(S)A 2000, s.161(1) (CJA 2003, s.305). Under that section an offence is said to be "associated" with another for this purpose if: PCC(S)A 2000, s.161(1)

(1) the offender is convicted of it in the proceedings in which he is convicted of the other offence, or, (although convicted of it in earlier proceedings) he is sentenced for it at the same time as he is sentenced for the other offence; or
(2) he admits the commission of it in the proceedings for which he is sentenced for that other offence and asks the judge to take it into consideration (see 62 TICs) in sentencing him for that offence.

It follows that:

(a) an offence in respect of which a suspended sentence was passed (*R. v Crawford* (1993) 14 Cr.App.R.(S.) 782), or a conditional discharge was made (*R. v Godfrey* (1993) 14 Cr.App.R. 804) on a *previous* occasion; or
(b) an uncharged offence, not represented by a sample count, and not taken into consideration on sentence,

are not "associated" offences.

Offences not qualifying for s.152

29–053 If none of the offences with which he is dealing qualifies for a custodial sentence in this sense, the judge can impose only a community sentence or a financial penalty. Where the offences with which he is dealing are of differing gravity, some "qualifying", others not:

(1) he is not prevented from passing custodial sentences in respect of the offences not qualifying (*R. v Mussell* (1990) 12 Cr.App.R.(S.) 607; *R. v Oliver & Little* [1993] 2 All E.R. 9); but
(2) he ought not, in general, to pass consecutive sentences for such offences, or make the overall sentence longer by reference to them (*R. v Oliver & Little*, above).

Where an offender has been made the subject of a probation order by a court having full knowledge of the relevant matters, it will generally be bad sentencing practice for a court dealing with him *subsequently* for an offence committed *before* the order was made, to impose a custodial sentence (*R. v Duporte* (1989) 11 Cr.App.R.(S.) 116).

Length of discretionary sentence

29–054 In the case of a custodial sentence other than one fixed by law or falling to be imposed under CJA 2003, s.225 or 226, for an offence **committed on or after April 4, 2005**, then, subject to: CJA 2003, s.153

(1) FA 1968, s.51A,
(2) PCC(S)A 2000, ss.109 where still appropriate, 110(2) and 111(2) (required sentences for certain repeat offences), and
(3) CJA 2003, ss.227(2) and 228(2) (dangerous offenders)

the custodial sentence must be for the shortest time (not exceeding the permitted maximum) that is, in the judge's opinion commensurate with the seriousness of the offence, or the combination of the offence and one or more offences associated with it.

Suspending a sentence of imprisonment

29–055 A judge passing a sentence of imprisonment, or, in the case of an offender aged at least 18 but under 21, detention in a young offender institution, for a term of at least 14 days but not more than 12 months in respect of an offence **committed on or after April 4, 2005**, in accordance with CJA 2003, s.181 may order:

(1) the offender to comply during a specified supervision period with one or more of the requirements falling within s.190(1) and specified in the order; and
(2) that the sentence of imprisonment will not take effect unless:
 (a) during the supervision period the offender fails to comply with a requirement imposed under (1) above; or
 (b) during the "operational period" specified in the order, the offender commits in Great Britain another offence (whether or not punishable with imprisonment).

(See 40 IMPRISONMENT.)

Pre-sentence drug testing

29–056 Under CJA 2003, s.161 (not yet in force), where an offender aged 14 or is over convicted of an offence, and the judge is considering passing a suspended sentence on him, he may (provided that he has been notified that he has that power), for the purpose of ascertaining whether the offender has any specified Class A drug (only heroin and crack/cocaine have so far been specified) in his body, make an order requiring him to provide, in accordance with his order, specified samples. CJA 2003, s.161(1)–(6)

Failure, without reasonable excuse, to comply is punishable with a fine of an amount not exceeding level 4 (see 37–004, below).

Where the offender has not attained the age of 17 the order must provide for the samples to be provided in the presence of an "appropriate adult" as defined in subs.(8). CJA 2003, s.161(3), (8)

10. Legal representation

29–057 A judge must not, on conviction on indictment, or on committal for sentence:

(1) pass an immediate sentence of imprisonment (other than a committal for contempt or any kindred offence) on an offender who has not previously been sentenced to such imprison-ment by a court in the United Kingdom; or
(2) pass a sentence of detention on a young offender under s.90, 91 or 96; or
(3) make a detention and training order,

unless the offender has had the assistance of counsel or a solicitor to represent him in the proceedings at some time after he is found guilty and before sentence, except where:

(a) he was granted a right to representation funded by the CDS but the right has been withdrawn because of his conduct, or because it appeared that his financial resources were such that he was not eligible to be granted such a right; or PCC(S)A 2000, s.83 CDSA 2006, s.4
(b) having been informed of his right to apply for a representation order and having had the opportunity to do so, he refused or failed to apply; or
(c) he applied for such representation and the application was refused because it appeared that his financial resources were such that he was not eligible to be granted a right to it.

A breach of these provisions renders any subsequent sentence unlawful, and a nullity (*R. v Wilson* (1995) 16 Cr.App.R.(S.) 997).

Difficulties arise where an offender "sacks" his solicitor and/or counsel, or they withdraw between conviction and sentence. Under the representation order, an offender has the right to be represented by solicitor and counsel of his choice and who are willing to act, unless and until that order is withdrawn (*R. v Kirk* (1983) 76 Cr.App.R. 194; *R. v Harris* [1985] Crim.L.R. 244; *R. v Dimech* [1991] Crim.L.R. 846; *R. v Stowell* [2006] Crim.L.R. 760). Faced with a recalcitrant offender, the proper course is for the judge to revoke the representation order before proceeding to sentence (*R. v Wilson*, above). (See also 17 CDS FUNDING.)

11. Community Sentences

29–058 Community sentences, for the purposes of CJA 2003, Part 12, are, in relation to an **offence committed on or after April 4, 2005**, those which consist of: CJA 2003, s.147

(1) a community order, as defined by s.177 (see 21 COMMUNITY SENTENCES); or
(2) one or more youth community orders, as to which see above, 21–053 *et seq*.

A number of individual requirements may be added to an order under (1) above, as to which see 21 COMMUNITY SENTENCES, above 21–021. Some of these may also be added to a "custody plus" order, to an "intermittent custody order and to a suspended sentence imposed under CJA 2003, as to all of which see 40 IMPRISONMENT.

Community sentences for offences committed before April 4, 2005, are dealt with under PCC(S)A 2000, and consist principally of a community rehabilitation order. a community punishment order and the combination of the two, to which additional requirements may be added, see 21 COMMUNITY SENTENCES.

No community sentence where sentence fixed by law, etc.

29–059 No community order or youth community order may be made in respect of an offence **committed on or after April 4, 2005**, for which the sentence; CJA 2003, s.150

(1) is fixed by law;
(2) falls to be imposed under FA 1968, s.51A (required sentences for certain firearms offences);
(3) falls to be imposed under PCC(S)A 2000, ss.109 where still appropriate, 110(2) or 111(2) (required sentences for certain repeated offences committed by offenders aged 18 or over); or
(4) falls to be imposed under any of CJA 2003, ss.225–228 (requirement to impose custodial sentences for certain offenders posing risk to public).

Pre-sentence drug testing

29–060 Under CJA 2003, s.161 (not yet in force), where an offender aged 14 or is over convicted of an offence, and the judge is considering passing a community sentence, (or a suspended sentence), on him, he will be able (provided that he has been notified that he has that power), for the purpose of ascertaining whether the offender has any specified Class A drug (only heroin and crack/cocaine have so far been specified) in his body, make an order requiring him to provide, in accordance with his order, specified samples. CJA 2003, s.161(1), (2), (4), (5), (6)

Where the offender has not attained the age of 17 the order must provide for the samples to be provided in the presence of an "appropriate adult" as defined in subs.(8). CJA 2003, s.161(3), (8)

General restrictions on imposing community sentences

29–061 In relation to offences **committed on or after April 4, 2005**, the judge may not pass a community sentence on an offender unless he is of opinion that, subject to s.151(2) below the offence, or the combination of the offence and one or more offences associated with it, was serious enough to warrant such CJA 2003, s.148

a sentence, and where he does pass such a sentence:

(1) the particular requirement or requirements forming part of the community order must be such as in his opinion is, or taken together are, the most suitable for the offender, and
(2) subject to s.134(2) below, the restrictions on liberty imposed by the order must be such as in his opinion are commensurate with the seriousness of the offence, or the combin- ation of the offence and the one or more offences associated with it.

Where the judge passes a community sentence which consists of or includes one or more youth community orders,

(a) the particular order or orders forming part of the sentence must be such as in his opinion is, or taken together are, the most suitable for the offender, and
(b) the restrictions on liberty imposed by the order or orders must be such as in his opinion are commensurate with the seriousness of the offence, or the combination of the offence and the one or more offences associated with it.

As to the recommended approach to such an order see 21 COMMUNITY SENTENCES.

Where an offender falls to be sentenced for two or more offences, one or more of which were committed before and some after, April 4, 2005, sentences on the differing counts fall to be passed under different provisions and take differing forms, e.g. where the offender is to be sentenced for two such offences, one pre- and one post-, commencement, and the judge seeks to deal with him by means of a community punishment order under the old law, he will need to make in respect of the post commencement offence, a community order under CJA 2003 with a requirement for unpaid work.

Time spent on remand

29–062 In determining the restrictions on liberty to be imposed by a community order or a youth community order in respect of an offence **committed on or after April 4, 2005**, the judge may have regard to any period for which the offender has been remanded in custody (as defined in CJA 2003, s.242(2)) in connection with the offence or any other offences the charge for which was founded on the same facts or evidence. CJA 2003, s.149

Persistent offender previously fined

29–063 Under CJA 2003, s.151 (not yet in force) where an offender: CJA 2003, s.151

(1) aged 16 or over convicted of an offence,
(2) who on three or more previous occasions has, on conviction in the United Kingdom of any offence committed by him after attaining the age of 16, has had passed on him a sentence consisting only of a fine, and
(3) despite the effect of s.143(2) the judge would not (apart from that section) regard the current offence, or the combination of the current offence and one or more offences associated with it as being serious enough to warrant a community sentence,

he may make a community order in respect of the current offence instead of imposing a fine, if he considers that, having regard to all the circumstances, including:

(a) the nature of the offences to which the previous convictions relate, and their relevance to the current offence, and
(b) the time that has elapsed since the offender's conviction of each of those offences

it would be in the interests of justice to make such an order.

Note that:

- the reference to a court in the United Kingdom includes a reference to a finding of guilt in service disciplinary proceedings (see s.151(4))
- a compensation order does not, for the purpose of these provisions, form part of an offender's sentence (s.151(5))
- it is immaterial for the purposes of s.151(1)(b) whether on previous occasions a court has passed on the offender a sentence not consisting only of a fine (s.151(6))
- these provisions do not, of course, limit the extent to which the judge may, in accordance with CJA 2003, s.143(2), treat any previous conviction as increasing the seriousness of the offence.

Meaning of associated offence for s.161

29–064 "Associated" in relation to an offence bears the interpretation given it by PCC(S)A 2000 s.161 (CJA 2003, s.305). Thus an offence is associated with another offence if: CC(S)A 2000, s.161(10)

(1) the offender is convicted of the other offence, or (although convicted of it in earlier proceedings) is sentenced for it at the same time as he is sentenced for the other offence; or
(2) the offender admits the commission of it in the proceedings in which he is sentenced for the other offence, and requests the judge to take it into consideration in sentencing him for that offence (see 59 TICs).

12. Combining community requirements with short-term prison sentence

29–065 In imposing a term of imprisonment of less than 12 months, the judge may, in certain circumstances (for which see 40 IMPRISONMENT), make either a "custody plus order" under CJA 2003, s.181 (not yet in force), or an "intermittent custody order" under s.183 (now being piloted in named courts), to which he may attach certain community requirements (as to which see 40 IMPRISONMENT).

Intermittent custody is an alternative to immediate full-time custody and must meet all the criteria of such a sentence. It term is not continuous. But interspersed by periods when the offender is released into the community on temporary licence. Such a sentence can be imposed only with the consent of the offender. SGC 1, 2.3.6, 7

13. Mental Health Disposal

29–066 In the case of an offender who is not so mentally disordered as to be absolved from criminal responsibility for his actions, but is nevertheless in need of psychiatric treatment, a judge may, in certain circumstances, remand to hospital for treatment accused persons who are waiting to be tried, as well as those waiting to be sentenced. Those who have been convicted may be:

(1) sent to a hospital under an interim hospital order, or a hospital order;
(2) made the subject of a guardianship order; or
(3) made the subject of a community order with a mental health treatment requirement.

As to the procedure to a verdict of not guilty by reason of insanity or a finding of disability, see 63 UNFITNESS TO PLEAD.

The judge in considering whether to make a hospital order or an interim hospital order, may ask the Regional Health Authority to assist in identifying an appropriate hospital for a particular offender. In some cases a hospital order may be made in conjunction with a restriction order (see generally 48 MENTALLY DISORDERED OFFENDERS).

14. Reports

Pre-sentence report: (1) need for

29–067 For the purposes of forming any such opinion as is mentioned in CJA 2003, ss.148(1), (2)(a), (b) or (3)(b), 152(2) or 153(2), the judge is obliged to take into account all such information as is available to him about the circumstances of the offence, and the offence or offences associated with it including any aggravating or mitigating factors. In forming such opinion as is mentioned in CJA 2003, s.148(2)(a) or (3)(a), he may take into account any information about the offender which is before him. CJA 2003, s.156(1), (2)

He must, unless in the circumstances of the case he is of the opinion that it is unnecessary to do so obtain and consider a pre-sentence report before

(1) in the case of a custodial sentence, forming any such opinion as is mentioned in CJA 2003, ss.152(2), 153(2), 225(1)(b), 226(1)(b), 227(1)(b) or 228(1)(b)(i); or
(2) in the case of a community sentence, forming any such opinion as is mentioned in CJA 2003, ss.148(1), (2)(b) or (3)(b) or any opinion as to the suitability for the offender of the particular requirement or requirements to be imposed by the community order. CJA 2003, s.156(3), (4)

Offenders under 18

29–068 In a case where; CJA 2003, s.156(4), (5)

(1) an offender is aged under 18, and
(2) the offence is not triable only on indictment, and
(3) there is no other offence associated with it which is triable on indictment only, the judge is not entitled to say it is unnecessary to obtain a report, unless;
   (a) there exists a previous report, or reports, and
   (b) he considers the information contained in that report or the most recent, if there is more than one.

In *R. v Atkins*, *The Times*, January 4, 2002, it was suggested that it might be desirable to require a pre-sentence report in all cases involving young offenders, even if a custodial sentence was inevitable.

Basic considerations

29–069 Quite apart from statute, in all cases where a judge is contemplating sending an offender to prison for the first time, other than perhaps for an extremely short period of time, it should be the invariable practice that a pre-sentence report be obtained. *R. v Gillette*, *The Times*, December 3, 1999 suggests that is always necessary, but in *R. v Armsaramah* [2001] 1 Cr.App.R.(S.) 133, CACD disagreed and see *R. v ILCC Ex p. Mentesh* [2001] Cr.App.R.(S.) 467. *Gillette* does not need to be followed in every case.

No report; effect

29–070 A custodial sentence is not invalidated by a breach of the provisions, but any court dealing with an appeal will need to obtain and consider a report if one were not obtained in the court below unless, it is satisfied that the lower court was justified in finding it unnecessary, or itself finds it unnecessary to do so. CJA 2003, s.156(6), (7)

The same *caveat* applies in relation offenders under 18 (CJA 2003, s.159, below) respecting disclosure of pre-sentence reports, applies.

Pre-sentence report: (2) adequacy and availability

29–071 It is for the judge to decide whether a report available to him is adequate for sentencing purposes, and constitutes compliance with PCC(S)A 2000, s.162, and if he considers a further report necessary he may call for one (see *R. v Okinikan* (1993) 96 Cr.App.R. 431).

A degree of care needs to be taken in the assessment of pre-sentence reports, since great importance is likely to be given to them, especially by inexperienced judges. Much of the material contained in them offends the cardinal rules of criminal evidence.

There is a deal of self-serving information contributed by the offender and his family, frequent hearsay drawn from former reports by other officers and other material on the file, and opinion evidence contributed by persons not necessarily qualifying as "experts" on the required level. There tends to be a bias towards non-custodial recommendations, and sometimes there is prejudice created by incompatibility between the officer reporting and the offender.

National guidelines seek to correct a frequently found lack of objectivity (see e.g. *R. v James* (1981) 3 Cr.App.R.(S.) 233).

Note that:

(1) the judge is not obliged to ensure that every detail advanced by the defence is checked and confirmed;
(2) where "fresh and highly relevant" material is raised for the first time in the report, the judge ought to discuss the implications with both parties (*R. v Cunnah* [1996] 1 Cr.App.R.(S.) 393), and there may be need for a fact-finding exercise (see 34 FACTUAL BASIS FOR SENTENCE).

Mentally disordered offenders

29–072 Before sentencing an offender who is, or appears to be, mentally disordered within the meaning of MHA 1983, to a custodial sentence, other than one fixed by law, the judge must, in addition to the requirements as to pre-sentence reports: CJA 2003, s.157

(1) obtain and consider a medical report, made orally or in writing by a medical practitioner approved for the purpose under MHA 1983, s.12, unless he is of opinion that it is unnecessary to do so; and
(2) consider any information before the court relating to his mental condition (whether given in a medical report, a pre-sentence report or otherwise), and the likely effect of such a sentence on that condition and on any treatment which may be available for it.

Nothing in CJA 2003, ss.148, 152, 153 or 157, 156 or 164: CJA 2003, s.166(1), (5), (6)

(a) requires the judge to pass a custodial sentence, or any particular custodial sentence, on a mentally disordered offender; or
(b) restricts his power to deal with such an offender in a more appropriate way under MHA 1983 or otherwise, to deal with such an offender in the manner he considers to be the most appropriate in all the circumstances.

Disclosure of pre-sentence reports

29–073 A "pre-sentence report" is defined by statute, and differs from other reports, such as those of local probation boards and members of youth offending teams (see s.160). The term is restricted to reports which: CJA 2003, s.158

(1) are made or submitted by an appropriate officer (as defined), with a view to assisting the court in determining the most suitable method of dealing with the offender; and
(2) contain information as to *such matters as may be prescribed* by Rules.

Where the court obtains a pre-sentence report, other than a report given orally in court, a copy must be given to: CJA 2003, s.159(1), (2)

(a) the offender or his counsel or solicitor, and
(b) any parent or guardian of an offender under 18, who is present in court; and
(c) to the prosecutor, that is to say, the person having conduct of the proceedings in respect of the offence.

Note that:

(i) if the offender is aged under 18 and it appears to the judge that the disclosure to the offender or to any parent or guardian of his of any information contained in the report would be likely to create a risk of significant harm to the offender, a complete copy of the report need not be given to the offender or, as the case may be, to that parent or guardian; CJA 2003, s.159(4)
(ii) if the prosecutor is not of a description prescribed by order made by the Home Secretary (below), a copy of the report need not be given to him if the judge considers that it would be inappropriate for him to be given it; CJA 2003, s.159(5)
(iii) in relation to an offender aged under 18 for whom a local authority have parental responsibility and who is in their care, or is provided with accomodation by them in the exercise of any social services functions, references to his parent or guardian are to be read as references to the authority. CJA 2003, s.159(6)

The Pre-Sentence Report Disclosure (Prescription of Prosecutors) Order 1998 (SI 1998/191) prescribes a Crown Prosecutor, any other person acting on behalf of the Crown Prosecution Service or a person acting on behalf of the Commissioners of Revenue and Customs, the Secretary of State for Social Security, and the Director of the Serious Fraud Office.

Other reports

29–074 Where a report by an officer of a local probation board or a member of a youth offending team is made to any court (other than to a youth court) with a view to assisting the court in determining the most suitable method of dealing with any person in respect of an offence, and the report does not qualify as a pre-sentence report, a copy of the report must be given: CJA 2003, s.160

(1) to the offender or his counsel or solicitor, and
(2) if the offender is aged under 18, to any parent or guardian of his who is present in court.

In relation to:

(a) an offender aged under 18, where it appears to the judge that disclosure to the offender or to any parent or guardian of his of any information contained in the report would be likely to create a risk of significant harm to the offender, a complete copy of the report need not be given to the offender, or as the case may be, to that parent or guardian;
(b) an offender aged under 18 for whom a local authority have parental responsibility and who is in their care, or is provided with accommodation by them in the exercise of any social services functions, references in this section to his parent or guardian are to be read as references to the authority.

15. Financial penalties

29–075 Where a person is convicted on indictment of any offence other than an offence: CJA 2003, s.163

(1) for which the sentence is fixed by law; or
(2) falls to be imposed under PCC(S)A 2000, ss.109 where still appropriate, 110(2) or 111(2) (required sentence for certain repeat offences); or
(3) falls to be imposed under any of the sections CJA 2003, ss.225–228 (dangerous offenders),

the judge, if not precluded from sentencing an offender by his exercise of some other power, may impose a fine:

(a) instead of, or
(b) in addition to,

dealing with him in any other way in which he has power to deal with him, subject to any enactment requiring the offender to be dealt with in a particular way. As to surcharges, see 36 FINES AND ENFORCEMENT.

Proper approach to financial penalty

29–076 The amount of any fine fixed must be such as, in the judge's opinion, reflects the seriousness of the offence, but in fixing the amount, he must: CJA 2003, s.164

(1) in the case of an individual offender, inquire into his financial circumstances; and
(2) whether the offender is an individual or other person, take into account the circumstances of the case including, amongst other things, the financial circumstances of the offender, so far as they are known, or appear to him,

and (2) above applies whether it has the effect of increasing or reducing the amount of the fine.

The judge may, before sentencing, make a financial circumstances order under CJA 2003, s.162, and where the offender fails to comply or otherwise fails to co-operate in an enquiry into his financial circumstances, the judge may make such order as he thinks fit. CJA 2003, ss.163, 164(5)

16. The Machinery of Sentence

Presence of offender

29–077 As a general rule, the court must sentence an offender for every separate offence of which he is convicted.

The offender must be physically present in court where:

(1) he is sentenced to a custodial sentence; or
(2) a road traffic disqualification is imposed on him, unless, in this latter case:
   (a) the court has adjourned after conviction; and
   (b) he has been notified of the time and place for the resumption of the hearing, and the reason for the adjournment, and he fails to appear.

Where several offenders fall to be sentenced, it is desirable that they should all be sentenced by the same court. Where one pleads not guilty and his case is adjourned for trial, sentences on those who plead guilty should be adjourned to the conclusion of his trial (*R. v Weekes and Others* (1982) 74 Cr.App.R. 161). Care must be taken in dealing with a number of co-offenders to differentiate between them according to the mitigating or aggravating factors affecting each one of them.

Offences taken into consideration

29–078 The offender may, at this stage, admit other offences, and may ask for them to be taken into consideration. The procedure outlined in 59 TICs must be carefully followed.

Credit of remand periods: general

29–079 In relation to **sentences passed on or after April 4, 2005**, where: CJA 2003, s.240(1)–(4)

(1) an offender is sentenced to imprisonment for a term in respect of an offence committed after the section comes into force; and
(2) he has been remanded in custody (see 29–081, below) in connection with the offence or a related offence, that is to say any other offence, the charge for which was founded on the same facts or evidence,
(3) whether or not he has also been remanded in custody in connection with other offences or has also been detained in connection with other matters,

the judge may direct that the number of days for which the offender was remanded in connection with the offence or a related offence count as time served as part of the sentence unless, and to the extent, that any Rules made by the Home Secretary provide otherwise, or he is of opinion that it is just in all the circumstances of the case not to give a direction.

The judge must state in open court, where he:

(a) gives such a direction: CJA 2003, s.240(5)
    (i) the number of days for which the offender was remanded in custody, and
    (ii) the number of days in relation to which the direction is given, and
(b) does not give a direction or gives such number of days less than that for which the offender was remanded in custody: CJA 2003, s.240(6)
    (i) that his decision is in accordance with the Rules, or
    (ii) that he is of the opinion mentioned above, stating what the circumstances are.

Where the judge is considering departing from the usual practice of making a direction under s.243(3) he must inform the defence advocate, thus giving him the opportunity of addressing him and seeking to persuade him that the circumstances are not such that as to justify the remand period spent in custody not counting as part of the sentence (*R. v Barber*, *The Times*, April 4, 2006).

Sentencing — Form of Words (see 29–085, below) suggests that the judge, in giving his explanation of the sentence should use a form of words directing, on the information before him that:

- [all/none or only x] remand days count towards the sentence;
- if not all remand days are to count, that this is because
    — on those/other days the offender was serving a sentence, and/or

— those/other days count towards a sentence to which the instant sentence will run consecutive, and/or
— he does not regard it as just that those/other days should count, for reasons which he explains

Under the Remand in Custody (Effect of Concurrent and Consecutive Sentences of Imprisonment) Rules, 2005 (SI 2005/2054) no direction should be made if, while on remand, the offender was also serving another sentence of imprisonment and was not released on licence, nor where the judge imposes a sentence to be served consecutively to a sentence to which CJA 1967, s.67 applies.

Supplementary

29–080 Note that: CJA 2003, s.240(7)–(10)

(1) a suspended sentence:
  (a) is to be treated as a sentence of imprisonment when it takes effect under Sch.12, para.8(2)(a) or (b); and
  (b) is to be treated as being imposed by the order under which it takes effect;
(2) the term of imprisonment to which an offender has been sentenced (that is to say, the reference to his "sentence"), includes consecutive terms and terms which are wholly or partly concurrent are to be treated as a single term if:
  (a) the sentences were passed on the same occasion, or
  (b) where they were passed on different occasions, the person has not been released under CJA 2003, Ch. 6 at any time during the period beginning with the first and ending with the last of those occasions;
(3) where an offence is found to have been committed over a period of two or more days, or at some time during a period of two or more days, it shall be taken for the purposes of subs. (1) to have been committed on the last of those days.
(4) this section applies to a determinate sentence of detention under PCC(S)A 2000, s.91 or CJA 2003, s.228 as it applies to an equivalent sentence of imprisonment.
(5) a sentence of imprisonment does not include a committal in default of payment of any sum of money, other than one adjudged to be paid on conviction.

CJA 2003, s.240(3) does not apply in relation to a day for which an offender was remanded in custody:

(a) if on that day he was serving a sentence of imprisonment (and it was not a day on which he was on licence under CJA 2003, Pt 1, Ch.6 or CJA 1991, Pt 2) or;
(b) where the term of imprisonment referred to in s.240(1) is ordered to be served consecutively on another term of imprisonment, if the length of that other term falls to be reduced by the same day by virtue of CJA 1967, s.67.

(The Remand in Custody (Effect of Concurrent and Consecutive Sentences of Imprisonment) Rules (SI 2005/2054).)

Meaning of "remand in custody"

29–081 References in CJA 2003, ss.240, and 241 to an offender's being "remanded in custody" are references to his being: CJA 2003, s.242(2)

(1) remanded in, or committed to, custody by an order of a court;
(2) remanded or committed to local authority accommodation under CYPA 1969, s.23 and placed and kept in secure accommodation or detained in a secure training centre pursuant to arrangements under CYPA 1969, s.23(7A);
(3) remanded, admitted or removed to hospital under MHA 1983, ss.35, 36, 38 or 48.

Under the previous law it was held that a person is in police detention for this purpose at any time when he is in police detention under PACE 1984, and at any time he is detained under s.14 of the Prevention of Terrorism (Temporary Provisions) Act 1989.

The periods for which an offender is in the custody of the court for the orderly and efficient conduct of the trial (see 29–079, above) are not to be credited: *Burgess v SoS*, *The Times*, November 14, 2000.

Special rules apply to detention and training orders (see 31 DETENTION OF YOUNG OFFENDERS).

Certain general principles were enuanciated in respect of the previous law, thus:

(a) the same remand period cannot be taken into account twice in relation to separate periods of imprisonment imposed on different occasions for different offences which are not ordered to run concurrently or consecutively (*R. v Home Secretary Ex p. Kitaya, The Times*, January 20, 1988);
(b) where an offender is remanded at the same time for related offences, which are subsequently tried and he

is sentenced separately, time spent on remand not credited against the first sentence may be credited against the second (*R. v Governor of Haverigg Prison Ex p. McMahon, The Times*, September 24, 1997);

(c) time on remand in relation to offences for which the sentences are later quashed on appeal does not count towards a later sentence for a different offence for which the accused was on remand at the same time (*R. v Governor of Wandsworth Prison Ex p. Sorhaindo, The Times*, January 5, 1999).

In respect of young offenders, see *R. v M (Young Offender; Time Spent in Custody)* [1999] 1 W.L.R 485; *R. v Home Secretary Ex p. Furber* [1998] 1 All E.R. 23.

Persons extradited to the United Kingdom

29–082 In the case of an extradited prisoner, that is a fixed term prisoner who: CJA 2003, s.243

(1) was tried for the offence in respect of which his sentence was imposed:
   (a) after having been extradited to the United Kingdom, and
   (b) without having first been restored or had an opportunity of leaving the United Kingdom; or
(2) was for any period kept in custody while awaiting his extradition to the United Kingdom,

s.240 has effect as if the days for which he was kept in custody while awaiting extradition were days for which he was remanded in custody in connection with the offence, or any other offence the charge for which was founded on the same facts or evidence.

Where the offender has prolonged the period spent in custody by resisting extradition or left the jurisdiction deliberately to avoid apprehension, he need not be allowed the whole of the period (*R. v Howard* [1996] 2 Cr.App.R.(S.) 419; *R. v Andre and Burton* [2002] 1 Cr.App.R.(S.) 24); *R. v Lodde & Lodde The Times*, March 8, 2000).

17. Spelling it out

29–083 Apart from those offences for which the sentence is fixed by law (provision for which is made in s.270, or falls to be imposed under FA 1968, s.51A, or under PCC(S)A 2000, ss.109 where still appropriate, 110(2), 111(2) (required sentences for CJA 2003, s.174

certain repeated offences), the judge, in passing sentence on an offender, must:

(1) state in open court, in ordinary language and in general terms, his reasons for deciding on the sentence passed; and
(2) explain to the offender in ordinary language;
   (a) the effect of the sentence;
   (b) where the offender is required to comply with any order forming part of the sentence, the effects of non-compliance with the order;
   (c) any power, on the application of the offender or any other person, to vary or review any order forming part of the sentence, and
   (d) where the sentence consists of or includes a fine, the effects of failure to pay that fine.

Where any sentencing guidelines are relevant to the sentence, the judge must refer to them. And where his sentence is of a different kind, or outside any range, normally appropriate for the offence, state his reasons for deciding on a sentence of a different kind or outside that range.

In particular, he must:

(i) in relation to a custodial sentence, where the duty in s.152(2) is not excluded by subs. (1)(a) or (b) or (3), state that he is of the opinion referred to in s.152(2) and why he is of that opinion;
(ii) in relation to a community sentence, if the case does not fall within s.151(2) state that he is of the opinion that s.148(1) applies and why he is of that opinion;
(iii) where as a result of taking into account any matter referred to in s.144(1), he imposes a punishment on the offender which is less severe than the punishment he would otherwise have imposed, state that fact; and
(iv) in any case, mention any aggravating or mitigating factors which he has regarded as being of particular importance.

Effect of custodial sentences

29–084 The judge must in passing a custodial sentence, explain the practical effect of the statutory provisions governing the particular term, and ensure that it is understood not only by the offender, but also by any victim and by any member of the public present in court, or "who reads a full report of the proceedings" (see *R. v Hennessey* [2000] Crim. L.R. 602).

PD 2002 made it clear that the judge:

(1) may give the explanation in terms of his own choosing—no form of words is prescribed; but
(2) must ensure that the explanation is clear and accurate; and
(3) must, in any event, continue to give such explanations:
    (a) as are required in other respects by statute; and
    (b) as he considers necessary, of any ancillary orders relating to matters such as disqualification, confiscation, compensation and costs, etc., and

should bear in mind that where terms imposed are consecutive, or wholly or partly concurrent, they are to be treated as a single term.

As to the general requirement to spell out the effect of an accused's plea of guilty see 29–034, above.

Forms of words

29–085 In complying with CJA 2003, s.174 (29–083, above) and other individual statutes requiring the statement in ordinary language of particular facets of the sentencing process, forms of words are suggested both in PD 2004, Annex C and in *Sentencing — Forms of Words* issued by the JSB, the latest edition of which is dated January 2006. The former covers (1) short term prisoner not subject to licence (total term less than 12 months); (2) short term prisoner subject to licence (total term of 12 months and less than four years); (3) long term prisoner (total term of four years or more); and (4) discretionary life sentence. The JSB document covers a wide range of sentences. CJA 1991, s.51(2)

18. Procedure after Sentence

Suspending sentence pending appeal

29–086 There is no obligation on a court to suspend the operation of any sentence or order where an offender gives notice of appeal, but:

(1) it is the usual practice not to enforce a fine pending the result of any appeal;
(2) there is a power, but no obligation, to suspend a disqualification from driving (RTA 1988, s.39; MCA 1980, s.113(1));
(3) there is a power but no obligation, to grant bail to a person sentenced to a custodial term.

A compensation order (see 23 COMPENSATION), and in certain cases, restitution orders (see 38 FORFEITURE, CONFISCATION AND RESTITUTION), are suspended until the expiration of the time for appeal has expired, or, where notice is given, until the determination of the appeal.

19. Rescission and alteration

29–087 Ordinarily, a sentence imposed or other order made by the Crown Court when dealing with an offender, takes effect from the beginning of the day on which it is imposed, unless the judge otherwise directs, but:

(1) as a court of record, the Crown Court has an inherent jurisdiction to rectify mistakes in its record (*R. v Saville* [1981] Q.B. 12); and, more importantly
(2) a sentence or order may be varied or rescinded under PCC(S)A 2000, s.151(1), (2), (3), within the statutory time limit (PCC(S)A 2000, s.155); and
(3) a reduced sentence passed in pursuance of an offender's agreement to give information to the authoritites may be reviewed under SOCA 2005, s.74, when it comes into force.

(See 8 ALTERATION OF SENTENCE.)

30 DEFERRING SENTENCE

Introduction

30–001 The judge may defer passing sentence on an offender until such date as he may specify, not being more than six months after the date of deferment is announced, for the purpose of enabling the court, or any other court to which it falls to deal with him, to have regard in dealing with him, to:

PCC(S)A 2000, s.1(1), (3), (4); CJA 2003, s.278, Sch.23, para.1

(1) his conduct after conviction (including, where appropriate, his making reparation for his offence); or
(2) any change in his circumstances,

but the power to defer is excercisable only

(a) where the offender consents,
(b) the judge is satisfied, having regard to the nature of the offence and the character and circumstances of the offender that it would be in the interests of justice to exercise the power, and
(c) in relation to offences committed **on or after April 4, 2005** the offender undertakes to comply with any requirements to his conduct during the period of the deferment that the judge considers it appropriate to impose.

The requirements may be activities such as reparation to the community.

The court dealing with sentence on the due date may take into consideration the extent to which the offender has complied with any requirements imposed under (b) above.

PCC(S)A 2000, s.1(3); CJA 2003, s.278, Sch.23, para.1

Nothing in these provisions affects the judge's power:

PCC(S)A 2000, s.1(8); CJA 2003, s.278, Sch.23, para.1

(i) to bind over an offender to come up for judgment (see 13 BIND OVER), or
(ii) to defer passing sentence for any other purpose for which he may lawfully do so.

30–002 Where the passing of sentence is deferred under these provisions, it may not be deferred again under the same provisions, though where sentence has been deferred in respect of one or more offences and the magistrates' court deals with the offender by committing him to the Crown Court under PCC(S)A 2000, s.3 the judge's power to deal with him includes the same power of deferring sentence on him as if he had just been convicted of the offence or offences on indictment.

PCC(S)A 2000, ss.1(4), 1D(3); CJA 2003, s.278, Sch.23, para.1

Deferment does not imply that the offence or offences were "not so serious that a non-custodial sentence cannot be justified". The judge may consider that a custodial sentence is justified, and yet defer, having regard to the offender's circumstances (*R. v Bray* (1991) 12 Cr.App.R.(S.) 705).

Approach to new provisions

30–003 SGC 3, 1.2.6 suggests that a deferred sentence is likely to be used in very limited circumstances. Such a sentence enables the judge to review the conduct of the offender before passing sentence, having first prescribed certain requirements. It also provides several opportunities for an offender to have some influence as to the sentence passed on him, as it:

(1) tests his commitment not to re-offend;
(2) gives him an opportunity to do something where progress can be shown within a short period;
(3) provides him with an opportunity to behave or refrain from behaving in a particular way that will be relevant to sentence.

Given the new power to require undertakings and the ability to enforce those undertakings before the end of the period of deferral, SGC 3, 1.2.7 recommends that the decision to defer sentence should be predominantly for a small group of cases at either the custody threshold or the community sentence threshold where the judge considers that there would be particular value in giving the offender the opportunities listed because, if the offender complies with the requirements, a different sentence will be justified at the end of the deferment period. This could be a community sentence instead of a custodial sentence or a fine or discharge instead of a community sentence. It may, rarely, enable a custodial sentence to be suspended rather than imposed immediately.

The judge may impose any conditions during the period of deferment that he considers appropriate. These may be:

(a) specific requirements as set out in the provisions for community sentences; or
(b) requirements that are drawn more widely.

The latter should be specific, measurable conditions so that the offender knows exactly what is required and the court can assess compliance; the restriction on liberty should be limited to ensure that the offender has a reasonable expectation of being able to comply whilst maintaining his or her social responsibilities (SGC 3, 1.2.8).

The requirements which may be imposed by virtue of (b) above include requirements as to the offender's residence during the whole or any part of the period of deferment. PCC(S)A 2000, s.1A(1); CJA 2003, s.278, Sch.23, para.1

Appointment of supervisor

30–004 Where an offender has agreed to comply with any such requirements, as is mentioned in (b) above, the judge may appoint: PCC(S)A 2000, s.1A(2)–(4); CJA 2003, s.278, Sch.23, para.1

(1) an officer of a local probation board, or:
(2) any other person whom the court thinks appropriate in relation to him, to act as a supervisor, provided that that person consents.

The supervisor's duty is to:

(a) monitor the offender's compliance with the requirements; and
(b) provide the court to which it falls to deal with the offender in respect of the offence in question with such information as the court may require relating to the offender's compliance with the requirements.

Administrative provisions

30–005 Where sentence is deferred under these provisions the appropriate officer will forthwith give a copy of the order, setting out any requirements imposed: PCC(S)A 2000, s.1(5), CJA 2003, s.278, Sch.23, para.1

(1) to the offender,
(2) where an officer of a local probation board has been appointed to act as his supervisor, to that board, and
(3) where any other person has been appointed to act as his supervisor, to that person.

The procedure

30–006 In order to avoid the problems that often arise from the exercise of the power to defer sentence the judge should note that:

(1) if he intends to exercise his power under s.1 he should use the word "defer", while if he intends to impose, e.g. a common law bind over, or merely to adjourn, he should avoid the use of the expression "defer" altogether (*R. v Fairhead* (1975) 61 Cr.App.R. 102);
(2) sentence may be deferred only with the offender's consent; the judge should therefore ask him expressly if he consents to the deferment, and undertakes to comply with such requirements as are proposed (*R. v McQuaide* (1974) 60 Cr.App.R. 239).

Spelling it out

30–007 Given the need for clarity in the mind of the offender and the possibility of sentence by another court, the judge should: SGG 2, 2.2.9–2.2.10

(1) give a clear indication of the sentence he would be minded to impose if he had not decided to defer sentence;
(2) ensure that the offender understands the consequences of failure to comply with the requirements during the deferral period;
(3) make clear the consequence of not complying with any requirements; and
(4) indicate the type of sentence he would be minded to impose,

though under the pre-2003 provisions it was said that only a judge who is sure that he will deal with the case on the date to which sentence is deferred should give any hint as to the probable outcome of the case (*R. v Johnson* (1981) 145 J.P. 491).

A judge who sits regularly at a particular location should reserve to himself the duty of dealing with the case on the date to which it is deferred, otherwise he ought to leave a note of his reasoning, or arrange for a transcript to be available at the point of sentence (*R. v Jacobs* (1976) 62 Cr.App.R. 116).

Ancillary orders; RT disqualification

30–008 Deferment being, in effect, a species of adjournment, there is no power to make any other order, other than:

(1) a restitution order; or
(2) a road traffic disqualification (see below).

(*R. v Dwyer* (1974) 60 Cr.App.R. 39.)

No power to remand: process

30–009 No question of remand arises and therefore no question of bail. Where the passing of sentence is deferred, and it is proposed to deal with him on the date originally specified, then, if the offender does not appear on the day, a summons may be issued requiring him to appear before the court at a time and place specified, or a warrant may be issued to arrest him and bring him before the court at a time and place specified in the warrant. PCC(S)A 2000, s.1(16)(7), CJA 2003, s.278, Sch.23, para 1

Appeal and review

30–010 Deferment of sentence ranks as a "sentence" for the purposes of CAA 1968, s.50 (*Att.-Gen.'s Reference (No. 22 of 1992)* [1993] 14 Cr.App.R.(S.) 435; *Att.-Gen.'s Reference (Nos 36 and*

38) [1999] Crim.L.R. 236. As such it may be referred to CACD by the Attorney-General for review (see 18 CHALLENGING THE CROWN COURT) under CJA 1988, s.36(10) if it appears to him to be unduly lenient (see *Att.-Gen.'s Reference (No. 22 of 1992)* above).

Breach of undertakings; sentence on due date

General

30–011 A significant change made by CJA 2003 is, in relation to offences committed **on or after April 4, 2005**, the provision enabling a court to deal with an offender before the end of the period of deferment. For example if the court is satisfied that the offender has failed to comply with one or more requirements imposed in connection with the deferment, the offender may be brought back before the court and the court may proceed to sentence.

Breach of undertaking(s)

30–012 A court which has deferred passing sentence on an offender under PCC(S)A 2000, s.1 may, whether the offence for which sentence was deferred was committed **before or after April 4, 2005**, deal with him before the end of the period of deferment where:

PCC(S)A 2000, s.1B; CJA 2003, s.278, Sch.23, para. 1

(1) sentence was deferred;
(2) the offender undertook to comply with one or more requirements imposed under s.1(3)(b) in connection with the deferment; and
(3) a person appointed to act as a supervisor in relation to the offender has reported to the court that the offender has failed to comply with one or more of those requirements; and
(4) he appears or is brought before the Crown Court, and the judge is satisfied that he has failed to comply with one or more requirements imposed in connection with the deferment.

To bring him before the court, the Crown Court may issue:

(a) a summons requiring the offender to appear before the court at a time and place specified in the summons; or
(b) a warrant to arrest him and bring him before the court at a time and place specified in the warrant.

Conviction of further offence

30–013 A court which has deferred passing sentence on an offender may deal with him before the end of the period of deferment if during that period he is convicted in Great Britain, whether **before or after April 4, 2005**, of any offence. PCC(S)A 2000, s.1C; CJA 2003, s.278, Sch.23, para. 1

Where a court has, under PCC(S)A 2000, s.1 deferred passing sentence on an offender in respect of one or more offences and:

(1) during the period of deferment the offender is convicted in England or Wales of any offence ("the later offence"), then,
(2) whether or not the offender is sentenced for the later offence during the period of deferment), the court which passes sentence on him for the later offence may also, if this has not already been done,
(3) deal with him for the offence or offences for which passing of sentence has been deferred, except that:
   (a) this power must not be exercised by a magistrates' court if the court which deferred passing sentence was the Crown Court; and
   (b) a judge of the Crown Court, in exercising that power in a case in which the court which deferred passing sentence was a magistrates' court, must not pass any sentence which could not have been passed by a magistrates' court in exercising that power.

Where a court which has deferred passing sentence on an offender proposes to deal with him under these provisions before the end of the period of deferment, it may issue a summons requiring him to appear at a time and place specified, or a warrant to arrest him and bring him before the court at a time and place specified.

Powers on due date

30–014 Where the passing of sentence on an offender has been deferred, the power of the judge under that section to deal with the offender at the end of the period of deferment and any power in relation to the breach of an undertaking under s.1B(1) or a further conviction under s.1C(1) or of any other court which deals with him under s.1C(3); PCC(S)A 2000, s.1D(2), (3); CJA 2003, s.278, Sch.23, para.1

(1) is a power to deal with him, in respect of the offence for which passing of sentence has been deferred, in any way in which the original court could have dealt with him if it had not deferred passing sentence; and

(2) where;

(a) the passing of sentence on an offender in respect of one or more offences has been deferred under s.1; and

(b) a magistrates' court deals with him in respect of the offence or any of the offences by committing him to the Crown Court under PCC(S)A 2000, s.3 the power of the Crown Court to deal with him includes the same power to defer passing sentence on him as if he had just been convicted of the offence or offences on indictment before the court.

It should be noted that under the previous legislation:

(i) it was not necessary that the offender be dealt with exactly on the date originally specified; there was nothing to prevent the court adjourning or postponing the hearing of the matter, provided there is no further deferment (*R. v Ingle* (1974) 59 Cr.App.R. 306); but

(ii) if sentence was deferred to a date after the expiry of the six month period, the court was deprived of its jurisdiction (*R. v W London Stipendiary Magistrate Ex p. Watts, The Times*, May 30, 1987);

(iii) it was desirable that the judge who passed sentence should be the same as the judge who deferred sentence in the first place, but if that was not possible the second judge should be fully apprised of the first judge's views (*R. v Gurney* [1974] Crim.L.R. 472);

(iv) the advocate who represented the offender on the earlier occasion should, if possible, appear for him on the date when sentence is to be passed (*R. v Ryan* [1976] Crim.L.R. 508).

30–015 The purpose of deferment must be ascertained, and the judge needs to determine if the offender has substantially conformed or attempted to conform with the proper expectations of the judge who deferred. If he has, then he may legitimately expect that an immediate custodial sentence will not be imposed. If he has not, the judge should be careful to state with precision in what respects he has failed (*R. v George* (1984) 79 Cr.App.R. 26). He should not be influenced by proceedings which are pending but incomplete (*R. v Aquilina* (1989) 11 Cr.App.R.(S.) 431).

DEFERRING SENTENCE

Nature of sentence on deferred date

30–016 On the day on which the sentence originally deferred is dealt with, the judge is bound to approach the matter on a fair consideration of the offender's progress, if any, during the period of deferment. Thus:

(1) it is wrong to imprison the offender if he has fulfilled that which was required of him (*R. v Gilby* (1975) 61 Cr.App.R. 112; *R. v Head* (1976) 63 Cr.App.R. 157; *R. v Smith* (1979) 1 Cr.App.R.(S.) 339); and

(2) if the report made to the court is not unfavourable, a substantial custodial sentence is probably not appropriate.

31 DETENTION OF YOUNG OFFENDERS

Introduction

31–001 An offender under 18 years of age may not be sentenced to imprisonment nor may he be committed to prison for any reason other than that of:

(1) remanding him in custody;
(2) committing him in custody for sentence; or
(3) sending him for trial under CDA 1998, s.51 *et seq*.

Note that;

(a) an offender's age is deemed to be that which it appears to the court to be on the date of conviction (*R. v Danga* (1992) 13 Cr.App.R.(S.) 408) after considering any available evidence;
(b) it is not proper to adjourn after conviction for the purpose only of the offender reaching the age of 18 before being sentenced (*Arthur v Stringer* (1987) 84 Cr.App.R. 361);
(c) where an offender is convicted on a date before reaching a birthday relevant to his sentence, and is then sentenced on another date, after that "milestone" birthday has passed, he falls to be sentenced as if he were still under that age (*R. v Danga* [1992] 1 Q.B. 476; *R. v Robinson* (1993) 14 Cr.App.R.(S.) 448); and
(d) a sentence will not be invalidated because it is later discovered that the offender is of a different age (*R. v Brown* (1989) 11 Cr.App.R.(S.) 263).

CACD has said that CYPA 1933, ss.44(1) and 107(1) (regarding the welfare of the child) does not prevent the judge from considering other matters, such as general deterrence, but that a deterrent sentence should not be passed upon a juvenile unless the court has weighed most carefully in the balance, deterrence on one side and individual treatment for the rehabilitation of the offender on the other.

Interval between date of offence and sentence

31–002 Where, between the date of:

(1) the commission of the offence, and
(2) conviction,

the offender has crossed a relevant age threshold, the starting point in considering sentence is the sentence that he would have been likely to have received at the time of the commission of the offence. Whilst other factors may need to be considered, there would need to be good reason for departing from that starting point, although clearly, particularly where a long interval has elapsed between points (1) and (2) above, circumstances may have changed significantly, e.g. the offender may have revealed himself to be a dangerous criminal, or the tariff may have been increased.

The judge is entitled to take such factors into account and:

(a) may impose a sentence higher than that which would have been imposed at the date of the offence; but
(b) will seldom need to consider passing a sentence beyond the maximum which he could have passed on the date of the commission of the offence.

(*R. v Ghafoor* [2003] 1 Cr.App.R.(S.) 84, *R. v L M* [2003] Crim. L.R. 203.)

A. Available custodial sentences

31–003 Custodial sentences for this age group, recognised and governed by PCC(S)A 2000, Pt V, Ch. 2 as amended by CJCSA and CJA 2003, Pt 12, Ch. 5 are six in number, namely:

(1) for offenders aged 18–20, the normal sentence in lieu of imprisonment is **detention in a young offender institution** under PCC(S)A 2000, s.96;
(2) for offenders under 18, the normal sentence is a **detention and training order** under PCC(S)A 2000, s.100;
(3) for offenders under 18 convicted of certain grave crimes, **detention** under PCC(S)A 2000, s.91;
(4) protective sentences for **dangerous offenders** under 18, in relation to **offences committed on or after April 4, 2005**, detention for life or for public protection under CJA 2003, s.226;
(5) protective sentences for offenders under 18, for specified violent or sexual **offences committed on or after April 4, 2005**, an **extended sentence** under CJA 2003, s.228;
(6) in the case of a person under 18 convicted of murder, **detention during HM Pleasure** under PCC(S)A 2000, s.90; and

different considerations govern different types of custodial sentence, but the imposition of any of them is subject, like any other custodial sentence:

(a) to the offence(s) "qualifying" for a custodial sentence (see 29 DEALING WITH AN OFFENDER);
(b) to the offender's age (see 6 AGE OF OFFENDER);
(c) unless unnecessary, to the availability of a pre-sentence report (see 29 DEALING WITH AN OFFENDER); and
(d) the offender being legally represented (see 29 DEALING WITH AN OFFENDER).

Custody for life and detention of defaulters and contemnors aged 18–20 under PCC(S)A 2000, s.108, were abolished by CJCSA 2000, s.75, Sch.8, from a date to be appointed; this date has not yet been appointed.

Those defaulters, etc. who would previously have been detained under PCC(S)A 2000, s.108 are now likely to be made the subject of an attendance centre order (see 21 COMMUNITY SENTENCES).

Spelling it out

31–004 Special care needs to be taken, in the case of young offenders, to indicate at the point of sentence the exact provisions which are being applied. In such cases, one of the most common reasons for appeals against sentence being allowed is the judge's failure to specify exactly what powers he is exercising (see *R. v Venison* (1993) 15 Cr.App.R.(S.) 624; *R. v Edgell* (1994) 15 Cr.App.R.(S.) 509; *R. v Anderson* (1991) 13 Cr.App.R.(S.) 325).

B. Detention in Young Offender Institution

31–005 The ordinary custodial sentence (i.e. leaving aside ss.90, 91, and 93) for an offender aged at least 18 but under 21: PCC(S)A 2000, s.96

(1) who is convicted of an offence punishable with imprisonment in the case of a person aged 21 or over; and
(2) where the prerequisites for a custodial sentence, (see 29 DEALING WITH AN OFFENDER) are present,

is detention in a young offender institution.

Sections 96–98 are to be repealed by CJCSA 2000, s.75, Sch.8 (no day has yet been appointed).

Length of term

31–006 As far as the length of the term is concerned: PCC(S)A 2000 s.97(1), (2), (3)

(1) the maximum term is the same as the maximum term of imprisonment which the judge may impose for the offence; and

(2) the minimum term which may be ordered is 21 days, applying not to the totality, but to each separate sentence (*R. v Kent YC Ex p. K* (*a Minor*) [1999] Crim.L.R. 168).

The authorities show that what has become the customary discount for a plea of guilty should be given under the provisions (*R. v Stewart* (1983) 5 Cr.App.R.(S.) 320; *R. v George* (1993) 14 Cr.App.R.(S.) 12) and the maximum should not be imposed on a plea of guilty unless the offender had no realistic defence to the charge (*R. v Bright* (1987) 9 Cr.App.R.(S.) 329).

Consecutive sentences

31–007 Subject to the statutory maxima set out above, a young offender: PCC(S)A 2000, s.97(4)

(1) convicted of more than one offence for which he is liable to such a term; or
(2) serving such a term, and convicted of one or more further offences for which he is so liable,

may be sentenced to consecutive terms, as if they were sentences of imprisonment.

If he is: PCC(S)A 2000, s.97(5)

(a) serving such a term; and
(b) is aged 21 or over; and
(c) is convicted of one or more further offences for which he is liable to imprisonment,

he may be sentenced, subject to PCC(S)A 2000, s.84 (restrictions on consecutive sentences for released prisoners) to imprisonment to run consecutively to the term(s) of detention.

Suspending a term

31–008 Although not possible under PCC(S)A 2000, CJA 2003, ss.189–194, (as implemented by SI 2005/950) allows, in respect of **offences committed on or after April 4, 2005**, a term of youth custody of at least 14 days but not more than 12 months to be suspended in the case of an offender aged 18–21, provided it contains a community requirement. Suspension does not apply in the case of pre-commencement offences.

See generally 40 IMPRISONMENT.

C. Detention and training order

31–009 The ordinary custodial sentence (subject to PCC(S)A 2000, ss.90 and 91, and CJA 2003, ss.226 and 228) to be passed on a offender aged under 18 where: PCC(S)A 2000, ss.100(1), (2), (3) 102103;CJA 2003, s.304,

(1) he is convicted of an offence which is punishable with imprisonment in the case of a person aged 21 or over; and Sch.32, Pt 1, para.111
(2) the judge is of opinion that CJA 2003, s.152(2) (the general restriction on custodial sentences) applies, or the case falls within CJA 2003, s.152(3) (persistent offender), see below,

is a detention and training order, which provides a period of detention and training, followed by a period of supervision.

The judge must not make such an order in the case of an offender:

(a) under the age of 15 at the time of his conviction, unless he is of opinion that he is a persistent offender;
(b) under the age of 12 at that time, unless:
  (i) he is of opinion that only a custodial sentence would be adequate to protect the public from his further offending; and
  (ii) the offence was committed on or after such date as the Home Secretary may appoint.

The judge is entitled (by virtue of CYPA 1963, s.29(1)) to impose a detention and training order on an offender who was aged 17 at the date he committed an offence, even though he has attained the age of 18 by the date on which sentence is imposed (*Aldis v DPP* [2002] Crim.L.R. 434). A young person aged 15 at the time of conviction may be sentenced to a detention and training order even though he was 14 at the time of the commission of the offence (*R. v T* [2004] EWCA 2199).

There is no power to impose an extended sentence under PCC(S)A 2000, s.85 with a detention and training order—there is no licence period (*R. v B* [2005] Crim.L.R. 488).

What amounts to a "persistent offender"

31–010 "Persistent offender" is not defined in the Act, nor is it to be interpreted by reference to the government circular *Tackling Delays in the Youth Justice System* (*R. v Thomas* [2001] 1 Cr.App.R.(S.) 415). The currently understood meaning of the words should be applied to the facts of the case: *R. v S (A)* [2001] 1 Cr.App.R.(S.) 18 (a series of offences over two days).

Their application is best left to the good sense of the judge (*R. v Dexter* [2001] 1 Cr.App.R.(S.) 389).

Note that it is not necessary to come within the definition that:

(1) the offender should have previous convictions (*R. v Smith* [2001] 1 Cr.App.R.(S.) 62) or that

(2) he should have committed a string of offences, either of the same or a similar character (*R. v B*, above); or
(3) his failure to address his offending behaviour arises by his failure to comply with previous orders (*ibid.*); and

account may be taken of offences in respect of which he has been formally cautioned (*R. v D* [2001] Crim.L.R. 864), (and no doubt, reprimanded under CDA 1998, s.650).

Term of order

31–011 The term of an order must: PCC(S)A 2000, s.101(1), (2), (3), (5), (8)

(1) be for 4, 6, 8, 10, 12, 18 or 24 months, and
(2) not exceed 24 months, taking into account any period for which the offender has been remanded in custody in connection with the offence, or any other offence the charge for which was founded on the same facts or evidence; and
(3) not exceed the maximum term of imprisonment that the judge could, in the casese of an offender aged 21 or over, impose for the offence.

Consecutive terms may be imposed, each for one of the terms set out in (1) above, though the aggregate does not amount to one of those specified (*R. v Norris* [2001] 1 Cr.App.R.(S.) 116), but it is not permissible to pass a number of shorter terms and aggregate them into a term of four months (*R. v Kent YC Ex p. Kingwell* [1999] 1 Cr.App.R.(S.) 263).

Where the offence is a summary offence, and the maximum term of imprisonment that a court could (in the case of an offender aged 18 or over) impose for the offence is 51 weeks (see 40 IMPRISONMENT) the term of detention and training must not exceed six months. PCC(S)A 2000, s.101(2A); CJA 2003, s.249

Discount for plea

31–012 When reflecting a plea of guilty (see 29 DEALING WITH AN OFFENDER) in the sentence, it is appropriate for the judge, where the offender is:

(1) not liable to a term of detention under PCC(S)A 2000, s.91, to reduce the term of the detention and training order below the maximum available term, unless there are proper grounds for not allowing a discount (*R. v Kelly* [2002] 1 Cr.App.R.(S.) 11); and
(2) liable to such a term, the discount may properly be reflected by imposing a detention and training order for the maximum term (*R. v March* [2002] Crim.L.R. 509).

Time spent in custody

31–013 The judge must, in fixing the term of the order, take into account time spent in custody in connection with the offence. He should indicate his intention to make such an order, so that he can be informed of any period spent in custody or on remand before considering the length of term (*R. v Haringey YC Ex p. A, The Times*, May 30, 2000; *R. v Davis, The Times*, December 20, 2000).

In relation to this type of order:

(1) the judge is not bound to reflect mathematically all such time in the sentence passed;
(2) it is neither appropriate nor desirable in determining the period of such an order that a precise reflection should be given for a day or two spent in custody (*R. v ILCC Ex p. N & S* [2000] Crim.L.R. 871); but
(3) if a significant time has been spent in custody, a matter of weeks or months, the proper approach is to reduce the otherwise appropriate term to reflect that period;
(4) how the judge reflects *longer* periods in custody will depend on the circumstances, including;
   (a) the apparent impact, if any, of the period of custody on the offender;
   (b) the length of time spent in custody; and
   (c) the relationship between the period spent in custody and the period of detention and training contemplated (*R. v Fieldhouse & Watts* [2000] Crim.L.R. 1020).

In *Fieldhouse* it was said that while no rule of general application can be devised where, for instance, one month has been spent in custody, this is the equivalent of a two month term, thus if the term otherwise contemplated is:

(i) four months, such a period may result in a non-custodial sentence being passed;
(ii) up to 12 months, the period spent in custody may result in the imposition of a term at the next level down; or
(iii) 18–24 months, the period spent on remand may have no effect.

In that case a 24 month order was upheld despite a plea of guilty and a significant period spent in custody. (See also *R. v AD* [2000] Crim.L.R. 867; *R. v ILCC Ex p. I, The Times*, May 12, 2000.)

References to "remand in custody"

31–014 The reference in s.101(8) to an offender being remanded in custody, is a reference to his being held in a police PCC(S)A 2000, s.101(11), (12);

station, his being remanded in or committed to custody by an order of the court, his being remanded or committed to local authority accommodation under CYPA 1969, s.23, and placed and kept in secure accommodation or detained in a secure training centre or being remanded, admitted or removed to hospital under MHA 1983, ss.35, 36, 38 or 48. CJCSA 2000, s.133(3)

A person is in "police detention" for the purposes of s.23(7) where he is in police detention at any time under PACE 1984, or at any time when he is detained under the Prevention of Terrorism (Temporary Provisions) Act 1989, s.14.

Consecutive terms

31–015 Where the offender: PCC(S)A 2000, s.101(3), (7)

(1) is convicted of more than one offence for which he is liable to an order; or
(2) is already subject to such an order and is convicted of one or more further offences for which he is liable to an order,

the judge has the same power to pass consecutive terms as if they were sentences of imprisonment, save that, while there is no requirement that the total term add up to one of the periods specified in s.101(1) (*R. v Norris* [2001] Crim.L.R. 48):

(a) an order must not be made in respect of an offender the effect of which would be that he would be subject to detention and training orders for an aggregate which exceeds 24 months; and
(b) if the aggregate term to which he would otherwise be subject, does exceed 24 months, the excess will be treated as remitted.

The judge may, when imposing consecutive detention and training orders, whose individual terms are taken from the list in subs.(1), agree to an aggregate term taken from the list, i.e. any even number of months between four and 24. This gives him some measure of discretion in arriving at terms which reflect the varying culpability of different offenders involved in the same case (*R. v B* [2001] Crim.L.R. 80).

There is no power to order a detention and training order to run consecutively to a sentence under s.91: *R. v Hayward* [2001] Crim.L.R. 236.

Improper combinations

31–016 A detention and training order may not be imposed to run concurrently with a term of detention under PCC(S)A 2000, s.91 (see 31–019): *R. v Hayward* [2001] 2

Cr.App.R.(S.) 31; and the converse also applies (*R. v Lang* [2001] 2 Cr.App.R.(S.) 39).

New offences during currency of the order

31–017 Where: PCC(S)A 2000, s.105

(1) after his release and before the date on which the term of the order ends, the offender commits an offence punishable with imprisonment in the case of a person aged 21 or over; and
(2) whether before or after that date he is convicted of that "new offence" the judge of the court by or before which he is convicted may, whether or not the judge passes any other sentence on him, order him to be detained in such secure accommodation as the Home Secretary may determine for the whole or any part of the period which:
   (a) begins with the date of the judge's order; and
   (b) is equal in length to the period between the date on which the new offence was committed, or the last of the days if it was committed over several, and the date on which the order would end.

The term will, as the judge directs, be served either before and be followed by, or concurrently with, any sentence imposed for the offence, and in either case will be disregarded in determining the appropriate length of that sentence.

D. Detention during HM Pleasure

31–018 Where a person convicted of murder, or of any other offence the sentence for which is fixed by law as life imprisonment, appears to the court to have been under 18 at the time the offence was committed, the judge must (notwithstanding anything in PCC(S)A 2000 or any other Act) sentence him to be detained during Her Majesty's Pleasure. PCC(S)A 2000, ss.82A, 90; CJCSA 2000, s.60).

See 45 LIFE SENTENCES.

E. Offenders under 18—certain grave offences—s.91

31–019 Where: PCC(S)A 2000, s.91; SOA 2003, ss.289, 304, Sch.32, Pt 1, para.110

(1) an offender under 18 is convicted on indictment of an offence:
   (a) punishable in the case of a person aged 21 or over with imprisonment for 14 years or more, not being an offence the sentence for which is fixed by law;

Detention of Young Offenders

(b) under SOA 2003, s.3 (sexual assault); or
(c) under SOA 2003, s.13 (child sex offences committed by children or young persons); or
(d) under SOA 2003, s.25 (sexual activity with a child family member); or
(e) under SOA 2003, s.26 (inciting a child or family member to engage in sexual activity); or

(2) an offender under 18 is convicted on indictment of an offence, under FA 1968 s.5(1)(a), (ab), (aba), (ac), (ad), (ae), (af) or (c) (prohibited weapons) or under FA 1968, s.5(1A), and the offence was committed when he was 16 or over, and the judge is of the opinion mentioned in s.51A(2);

(3) an offender aged at least 14 but under 18 is convicted of an offence under:
(a) RTA 1988, s.1 (causing death by dangerous driving); or
(b) RTA 1988, s.3A (causing death by careless driving while under the influence of drink or drugs), and

(4) the judge is of the opinion that neither a community sentence nor a detention and training order is suitable,

he may, subject to the general restrictions on passing custodial sentences set out in CJA 2003, ss.152 and 153, sentence the offender to be detained for such period as he may specify, not exceeding the maximum term of imprisonment with which the offence is punishable in the case of a person aged 21 or over.

In general:

(i) unless the offence merits a sentence *longer than two years*, and the criteria under s.91 are met, a term of detention and training should be imposed, and
(ii) if such is not permitted, then a non-custodial sentence should be passed (*R. (M) v Waltham Forest YC & DPP etc.* 166 JP 453, *R. (W) v Southampton YC etc.* [2003] 1 Cr.App.R.(S.) 87).

Where FA 1968, s. 51A (below) applies, the sentence must be for at least the required minimum term, but not exceeding the maximum term of imprisonment with which the offence is punishable in the case of a person aged 21 or over. PCC(S)A 2000, s.91(5); CJA 2003, s.289(3)

Such an offender is liable to be detained in such place as the Home Secretary may direct or arrange.

Guideline cases

31–020 An order is primarily applicable to cases where the judge contemplates a sentence of at least two years; anything less than that should be dealt with by a detention and training order.

If the 24-month limit on detention and training orders is intended to ensure that offenders under 18 are not sentenced to lengthy periods of detention where this can be avoided, the judge ought to think long and hard before passing a sentence which exceeds this limit. However, the co-existence of the powers contained in s.91 recognise the "unwelcome but undoubted fact" that some crimes committed by offenders of this age merit sentences of detention in excess of 24 months.

The following principles are to be deduced from *Fairhurst* [1986] 1 W.L.R. 1374*; R. v Wainfur* [1996] Crim.L.R. 674; *R. v Mills* [1997] 3 All E.R. 780; and *R. v Manchester City YC Ex p. D* [2002] Crim.L.R. 149.

(1) a sentence of detention under s.91 should not be passed simply because a 24-months' term seems to be on the low side for the particular offence; the 24-month limit should not be exceeded unless the offence is clearly one calling for a longer sentence;

(2) if the judge is minded to impose an sentence of, e.g. four years under s.91 but is persuaded by mitigation that the circumstances justify a significant reduction, to e.g. 2½ years
  - (a) while he ought not to exceed the 24-month limit without careful thought;
  - (b) if he concludes that a longer sentence, even if not a much longer sentence, is called for, he should impose what he considers the appropriate period under s.91;

(3) if, on a plea of guilty to an offence falling within s.91 the judge imposes a sentence of 24-months under s.100, where, but for the plea, detention under s.91 for a longer period would have been ordered, he should state this fact expressly.

CACD now accepts that where an offender is convicted of a number of offences, for some of which detention under s.91 is available but for others it is not, the judge should sentence under s.91 where available and make the rather dubious order of "no separate penalty" (really a magistrates' courts order) in respect of those offences not qualifying (*R. v JC, Marcus Artrh* [2005] 1 Cr.App.R.(S.) 10).

Length of sentence

31–021 The offender may be sentenced to be detained for a determinate period not exceeding the maximum term of imprisonment with which the offence is punishable in the case of an offender of 21 or over, as may be specified in the order.

Note that:

(1) the judge will need to have in mind the period during which danger is capable of arising from the offender's activities, without imposing a term which leaves the offender without hope (*R. v Storey* (1973) 57 Cr.App.R. 840; *R. v Bryson* (1974) 58 Cr.App.R. 464);

(2) if the offence carries life imprisonment in the case of an offender of 21, and the doctors cannot indicate the period required, protection of the public should be secured by custody for life under s. 94 (*R. v Nightingale* (1984) 6 Cr.App.R.(S.) 65).

The term should not exceed that which would be passed on an offender over 18, or over 21, for the same offence(s) (*R. v Burrowes* (1985) 7 Cr.App.R.(S.) 106).

In *R. v AM and Others* [1998] 2 Cr.App.R. 57, CACD upheld a single sentence of detention under s.91 in respect of one offence, making the length commensurate with the gravity of all the offences, and passing no separate penalty (a doubtful practice) for the other offences.

Prescribed minimum sentences for certain firearms offences

FA 1968, s.51A; PCC(S)A 2000, s.91; CJA 2003, s.287

31–022 Where a person is convicted of certain offences under FA 1968, s.5, **committed on or after April 4, 2005**, the judge must impose in the case of an offender aged under 18 when convicted, a sentence of detention under s.91 for at least three years (with or without a fine), unless he is of opinion that there are exceptional circumstances relating to the offence or to the offender which justify his not doing so.

Where an offence is found to have been committed over a period of two or more days, or at some time during a period of two or more days, it is to be taken to have been committed on the last of those days.

Combination of sentences

31–023 It is generally undesirable that sentences of detention under s.91 and secure training orders under s.100 be imposed, either consecutively to, or concurrently with, each other (*R. v*

Gaskin (1985) 7 Cr.App.R.(S.) 28; *R. v McKenna* (1985) 7 Cr.App.R.(S.) 348).

However, it is not always possible to avoid this. Thus:

(1) terms of detention under s.91 and those under s.100 may be served in different establishments and it is generally undesirable to impose terms *concurrent* under both sections;
(2) the judge minded to impose *concurrent* terms under the two sections, should make sure that no administrative difficulty will result before doing so;
(3) where some of the offences fall within s.91 and others are "associated" but do not fall within the section, it will usually be preferable to impose a term under s.91 which takes account of the associated offence or offences, and to impose "no separate penalty" for the lesser offences; and
(4) there is no power to order a detention and training order to run consecutively to a sentence under s.91. (*R. v Hayward* [2001] Crim.L.R. 236.)

F. Protective Sentences

31–024 CJA 2003, in s.226 (detention for public protection) and s.228 (extended sentences) replicate for offenders under 18 the provisions of ss.225 and 227 in relation to offenders aged 18 and over. The principles governing these sentences are dealt with at length in 40 IMPRISONMENT, at 40–043–40–051.

32 DISCLOSURE OF UNUSED MATERIAL

A. General

Introduction

32–001 While it is vital that obligations of disclosure are properly discharged by both the prosecution and the defence, the judge's active hands-on oversight of the process is an important safeguard against any potential miscarriage of justices. The judge needs to have clearly in mind that:

(1) consideration of irrelevant unused material may consume wholly unjustifiable and disproportionate amounts of time and public resources, undermining the overall performance and efficiency of the criminal justice system; and
(2) unused prosecution material falls to be disclosed if, and only if, it satisfies the test for disclosure regime applicable to the proceedings in question, subject to any overriding public interest considerations.

The regime applicable to the case will depend on the date on which the particular criminal investigation started, thus where the criminal investigation commenced:

(a) **before April 1, 1997**, the common law applies, as set out in *R. v Keane* (1994) 99 Cr.App.R. 1:
(b) **on or after April 1, 1997, but before April 4, 2005**, the test under CPIA 1997, before amendment by CJA 2003, applies, with separate tests for disclosure of unused prosecution material at the primary and secondary stages (the latter following service of a defence statement by the accused), supported by the Code of Practice (SI 1997/1033) issued under CPIA 1996, s.23(1);
(c) **on or after April 4, 2005**, the "enhanced" provisions test set out in CPIA 1996, as amended by CJA 2003, Pt V apply, providing a single test for the disclosure of unused material, supported by the 2005 Code of Practice (SI 2305/985).

There may be circumstances where an investigation is commenced before April 4, 2005 and further offences are committed after that date. In such a situation the original disclosure scheme under the Act will apply to the original investigation and the enhaced provisions to the fresh offences.

CPIA 1996 s.13 identifies the stage(s) at which the prosecutor is required to disclose material and the formalities relating to defence statements, the time limits applicable to defence disclosure being set out in SI 1997/684.

Regard must be had to the Attorney-General's Guidelines on disclosure (April 2005), though they do not have the force of law (*R. v Brown* [1995] 1 Cr.App.R. 191); see also *Disclosure: A Protocol for the Control and Management of Unused Material in the Crown Court*, issued by the Court of Appeal in 2006, in the light of which the text in this section has been updated. This is referred to in the text merely as *Protocol*.

CPR 2005, Pt 25 sets out the procedures to be followed in applying to the court in relation to both sensitive and non-sensitive unused material; *ibid.* Pt 3 is relevant in respect of the judge's general case managemernt powers, as is PD 2005.

The concept of fairness

32–002 The concept of fairness recognises that:

(1) there are interests other than those of the accused that need to be protected, including those of victims and witnesses who might otherwise be exposed to harm; the scheme of CPIA 1996 seeks to protect those interests;
(2) where there are fears for the safety of a prosecution witness, the prosecutor may be justified in not providing the defence with copies of audio and video tapes, but instead providing transcripts of the tapes and confining them to inspection of the tapes under controlled conditions (*R. v DPP Ex p. J.* [2000] 1 W.L.R. 1215, DC);
(3) material should not be disclosed which overburdens the participants in the trial process, diverts attention from the relevant issues, leads to unjustifiable delay, and is wasteful of resources;
(4) disclosure is a continuing process throughout the proceedings, up to the stage when any final appeal is determined.

In order to facilitate the extent of such disclosure, and to narrow the issues in respect of which it is necessary to call evidence, the accused is required to make advance disclosure of the general nature of his defence and of any expert evidence upon which he proposes to rely. The "equality of arms" principle in ECHR requires close attention to the appropriate rules: see e.g. *Dowsett v UK* [2003] Crim.L.R. 890; *Edwards & Lewis v UK* [2003] Crim.L.R. 891.

B. The application of the common law

32–003 The common law rules on disclosure as set out in *R. v Keane* (1994) 99 Cr.App.R. 1:

(1) continue to apply where a case does not fall within CPIA 1996;
(2) govern disclosure prior to the stage when the Act applies, ie to cases where the the criminal investigation started before April 1, 1997; and
(3) govern the judge's decision in relation to disclosure of sensitive material for which public interest immunity is claimed.

The Crown Court (CPIA 1996) (Disclosure) Rules 1997 govern the procedure to be followed when an application is made for non-disclosure on the grounds of public interest immunity (Pt II). In so far as ECHR is concerned, *Rowe and Davis v UK* [2000] Crim.L.R. 584 did not criticise the procedure used in Pt II applications, which has now been further approved by the CACD in *R. v Davis*; *R. v Rowe*; *R. v Johnson* (1997) 97 Cr.App.R. 110.

C. The Criminal Procedure and Investigations Act 1996

Application of the Act

32–004 CPIA 1996 applies to cases reaching the Crown Court by any of the recognised methods, set out in *ibid.* s.1(2), as amended by CDA 1998, Sch.8. i.e.

- committal under MCA 1980, ss.6(1) or 6(2);
- transfer under CJA 1987, s.4 or CJA 1991, s.53;
- documents containing evidence served on the accused in accordance with SI 2005/902, where the matter has been sent to the Crown court purusant to CDA 1998, ss.51 or 51A;
- where a matter has been added to the indictment in accordance with CJA 1988, s.40 or;
- where a voluntary bill has been preferred under AJ(MP)A 1933, s.2(2)(b) or POA 1985, s.22B(3)(a).

Initial duty of prosecutor to disclose

32–005 In relation to cases in which a criminal investigation began **after April 4, 2005**, CJA 2003, Pt 5, replaces the previous two-stage test, with a new objective single test for the disclosure of unused prosecution material to the defence. CPIA 1996, s.3(1); CJA 2003, s.32

DISCLOSURE OF UNUSED MATERIAL

The former duty of secondary disclosure by the prosecutor is replaced with a revised continuing duty to disclose material that meets the new test, and he is specifically required to review the prosecution material on receipt of the defence statement, and to make further disclosure as required by his continuing duty.

In relation to criminal investigations begun **before April 4, 2005**, the former two-tier procedure applies.

The prosecutor is required to:

(1) disclose to the defence any prosecution material which has not previously been disclosed and which might reasonably be considered as capable of undermining the case for the prosecution against the accused, or of assisting the case for the accused; or
(2) give the accused a written statement that there is no such material.

"Prosecution material" for the purposes of both primary and secondary disclosure by the proseution is defined as material which: CPIA 1996, ss.3(2), 7(3)

(a) is in the prosecutor's possession and came into his possession in connection with the case for the prosecution against the accused; or
(b) in pursuance of the code of practice, he has inspected in connection with the case for the prosecution against the accused.

At common law, information affecting only the credibility of a defence witness did not need to be disclosed (*R. v Brown* [1995] 1 Cr.App.R. 191) unless it also contained evidence favourable to the accused (*R. v Mills* [1998] 1 Cr.App.R. 43). See as to the disclosure of previous convictions *R. v Vasilou* [2000] Crim. L.R. 845; the fact that a witness giving evidence can expect to receive a reward at the conclusion of the trial ought to be disclosed (*R. v Allan* (2004) 148 SJ 1032).

Although no specific time limit is prescribed, the prosecutor must act under this provision as soon as is "reasonably practicable" after the: CPIA 1996, s.13(1); CJA 2003, s.332, Sch.37, Pt 4

(a) accused pleads not guilty;
(b) accused is committed or transferred for trial;
(c) accused is sent for trial under CDA 1998, s.51;
(d) court includes a count in the indictment; or
(e) bill of indictment is preferred,

depending on the manner in which the matter comes before the Crown.

When a case is sent to the Crown Court under CDA 1998, s.51, the rules (SI 2000/3305) allow the prosecutor 70 days from the date on which the case was sent (50 days where the accused is in custody) within which to serve the *evidence* on which the charge or charges are based. These time limits may be extended or varied at the court's direction.

Where the prosecutor acts under s.3 above and before doing so the prosecutor was given a document in pursuance of a provision included by virtue of s.24(3), in a Code operative under Pt II of the Act, he must give that document to the accused at the same time as he acts under s.3. CPIA 1996, s.4; CJA 2003, s.332, Sch.37, Pt 4

Case management

32–006 The Protocol (see 32–001, above) makes it clear that the judge has a duty to enforce the statutory scheme. He needs to consider at any preliminary hearing whether it is practicable for the prosecution to comply with primary or initial disclosure at the same time as service of the s.51 papers, or whether disclosure ought to take place after a certain interval but before the matter is listed for a PCMH.

It is important if the listing of the PCMH is to be an effective one, that:

(1) the defence have a proper opportunity to read the case papers and to consider the initial or primary disclosure,
(2) with a view to the timely drafting of a defence case statement where the matter is to be contested) before the matter is listed for a PCMH.

If the nature of the case does not allow service of the evidence and initial or primary disclosure within the 70, or if applicable 50, days (or such other period as directed by the magistrates' court):

(a) the prosecution advocate at the preliminary Crown Court hearing, or further hearing prior to the PCMH, must be made aware of the problems, why and how the position has arisen so as to be able to assist the judge as to what revised time limits are realistic;
(b) the prosecution advocate should make any foreseeable difficulties clear as soon as possible at the Crown Court preliminary hearing (where there is one); or
(c) failing this, where such difficulties arise or have come to light after directions for service of case papers and disclosure have been made, the prosecution should notify the court and the defence promptly,

in advance of the PCMH date, and prior to the date set by the judge for the service of the material.

In order to ensure that the listing of the PCMH is appropriate, the judge should not impose time limits for service of case papers or initial/primary disclosure unless and until he is confident that the prosecution advocate has taken the requisite instructions from those who are actually going to do the work specified. It is better to impose a realistic timetable from the outset than to set unachievable limits. Reference should be made to CPR 2005, Pt 3 and the PD 2005 in this respect.

Timetable; directions and further directions

32–007 The provisions set out in the preceding paragraph are likewise appropriate where directions, or further directions, are made in relation to prosecution or defence disclosure at the PCMH. Failure to consider whether the timetable is practicable may dislocate the court timetable and can even imperil trial dates.

Thus:

(1) at the PCMH all the advocates must be fully instructed about any difficulties the parties may have in complying with their respective disclosure obligations, and must be in a position to put forward a reasonable timetable for resolution of them;
(2) where the judge gives directions in the light of such inquiry, extensions of time should not be given lightly or as a matter of course. If extensions are sought, then an appropriately detailed explanation must be given;
(3) it is not sufficient merely for the prosecutor to say that the papers have been delivered late by the police or other investigator: the judge will need to know why they have been delivered late;
(4) likewise, where the accused has been dilatory in serving a defence statement after the prosecutor has complied with his duty to make primary or initial disclosure, or has purported to do so, it is not sufficient for the defence to say that insufficient instructions have been taken for service of this within the 14-day time limit: the judge will need to know why sufficient instructions have not been taken, and what arrangements have been made for the taking of such instructions; delays and failures by the defence are as damaging to the timely, fair and efficient hearing of the case as delays and failures by the prosecution, and judges should identify and deal with all such failures firmly and fairly;

(5) as part of any timetabling exercise the judge should set a date by which any application by the defence for disclosure, if there is to be one, should be made and should require the defence to indicate in advance of the cut-off date what documents they are interested in and from what source; in appropriate cases, the judge should require justification of any request.

Questions of disclosure must be decided by the prosecutor, and the assistance of the judge should only be sought if a question can properly be decided by him, most obviously where questions of public interest immunity are involved (*R. v B* [2000] Crim.L.R. 500).

The judge should not allow the prosecutor to abdicate his statutory responsibility for reviewing the unused material by the expedient of allowing the defence to inspect (or providing the defence with copies of) everything on the schedules of non-sensitive unused prosecution material, irrespective of whether that material, or all of that material, satisfies the relevant test for disclosure.

Where that test is satisfied it is for the prosecutor to decide the form in which disclosure is made. Disclosure need not be in the same form as that in which the information was recorded. Guidance on case management issues relating to this point was given by Rose LJ. in *R. v CPS* (*Interlocutory Application under sections* 35/36 CPIA) [2005] EWCA Crim.2342.

The statement must be given during the period which, by virtue of s.12, is the "relevant period" for this section.

Compulsory disclosure by accused: (1) general

32–008 In relation to criminal investigations begun **after April 4, 2005**, CJA 2003, Pt 5, requires the accused to provide a more detailed defence statement than the previous legislation required. Where the prosecutor has complied, or purported to comply with the initial duty on him, the accused is required to give a defence statement both to the court and and to the prosecutor:

CPIA 1996, s.5(1), (5); CJA 2003, s.331, Sch.36, Pt 3, para. 22, s.332, Sch.37, Pt 4

(1) setting out the nature of his defence (but see *R. v Tibbs* [2001] 2 Cr.App.R. 309, *R. v Wheeler* (2000) 164 J.P. 565);
(2) indicating the matters on which he takes issue with the prosecution; and
(3) setting out, in respect of each such matter, the reason why he takes issue with the prosecution.

As to the contents of such a statement, see 32–014, below.

Compulsory disclosure by accused: (2) cross-service of statement

32–009 Where there are other accused in the proceedings and the court so orders, the accused will be obliged to give a defence statement to each other accused specified by the court, but this provision is not yet in force. CPIA 1996, s.5 (5A), (5B), (5C), (5D); CJA 2003, s.33

The court may make an order either of its own motion or on the application of any party.

A defence statement that has to be given:

(1) to the court and the prosecutor (under subs.(5)) must be given during the period which, by virtue of s.12, is the relevant period for this section;
(2) to a co-accused (under subs.(5A)) must be given within such period as the court may specify.

Compulsory disclosure by accused: (3) time limits

32–010 Service of the defence statement is a critical stage in the disclosure process, and timely service of the statement will allow for the proper consideration of disclosure issues well in advance of the trial date.

Defence disclosure must be: DTLR 1997, r.2

(1) made within 14 days of the date upon which the prosecutor complies, or purports to comply, with the requirements of initial disclosure; and
(2) extended, if the judge so orders, by as many days as he (entirely at his own discretion) specifies.

There may be cases where it is simply not possible to serve a proper defence case statement within the 14 day time limit; well founded defence applications for an extension of time under (2) above may be granted in a proper case. It may be proper to put the PCMH back by a week or so, to enable a sufficient defence case statement to be filed and considered by the prosecutor. As to the contents of such a statement, see 32–014, below.

The judge may extend the period only if an application is made by the accused before the end of that period which: DTLR 1997, r.3

(a) states that the accused believes, on reasonable grounds, that it is not possible for him to give a defence statement under ss.5 or 6 of the Act during the limitation period;
(b) specifies the grounds for so believing; and
(c) specifies the number of days by which he wishes the period to be extended.

The judge must not make an extension order unless satisfied that the accused cannot reasonably give or, as the case may be, could not reasonably have given, such a statement during the limitation period.

Compulsory disclosure by accused: (4) application to extend the time limits

32–011 Notice of application for extension of the time limits must be made in writing to the Crown Court officer within the time limit; a copy of the notice being served at the same time on the prosecutor. The notice must specify, in addition to the matters set out in (a), (b) and (c) of the preceding paragraph, the date of service of the copy notice on the prosecutor. DTLR 1997, r.8

Compulsory disclosure by accused: (5) prosecutor's representations

32–012 The prosecutor may make representations to the court concerning the application in writing within 14 days of the service of the defence notice. Where such representations are received, or on the expiration of 14 days from service of the defence notice, the judge will consider the application to extend the defence time limit and may do so on the papers or at a hearing.

If a hearing is held, the:

(1) court must give notice of it to the prosecutor and to the applicant;
(2) hearing is with notice; and
(3) prosecutor and the applicant are entitled to make representations to the court.

A copy of any order made by the court must be served on the prosecutor and the applicant. Before the extension order has expired, the judge may, on application by the accused (following the same procedure), further extend the period at his discretion. There is no limit to the number of times this procedure may be repeated.

Voluntary disclosure by accused

32–013 Where the prosecutor complies with his duty of initial disclosure under s.3 above, or purports to comply with it, the accused may give a defence statement to the prosecutor, and if he does so, must give one to the court. CPIA 1996, s.6, Sch.25, Pt 2, paras 10, 26, Pt 3

If the accused gives such a statement, he must give it during the period which is, by virtue of s.12 the relevant period.

Contents of defence statement;

32–014 A purported defence case statement which is little more than reiteration of the accused's plea, i.e., an assertion that he is not guilty, is not a defence statement under the Act. A defence statementsmust comply with the requisite formalities set out inCPIA 1996, ss 5(6) and (7) or s. 6A as applicable (*R. v Patrick Bryant* [2005] EWCA Crim.2079 (per Judge LJ. at para.12).

Where the **pre-April 2005** regime applies under CPIA 1996, the accused must, in his defence statement, set out the nature of his defence in general terms, indicating the matters upon which he takes issue with the prosecutor and setting out, in relation to each matter, why issue is taken. Any alibi defence relied upon must comply with the formalities in s.5(7)(a) and (b).

Where the enhanced requirements for defence disclosure apply under s.6A of the Act, i.e. where the case involves a criminal investigation commencing on **or after April 4,** 2005, the defence statement must spell out in detail,

(1) the nature of the accused's defence, including any particular defences on which he intends to rely,
(2) the matters of fact on which he takes issue with the prosecution,
(3) in the case of each such matter, why he takes issue with the prosecution, and
(4) any point of law (including any point as to the admissibility of evidence) or abuse of process which he wishes to take, and any authority on which he intends to rely for that purpose.

A defence statement purporting to be given under s.5, 6 or 6B above, or a statement of the kind mentioned in s.6B(4) on behalf of an accused by his solicitor will, unless the contrary is proved, be deemed to be given with the authority of the accused. CPIA 1996, s.6E(1), (2), (3); CJA 2003, s.36

Alibi defence

32–015 Where an alibi defence is relied upon: CPIA 1996, s.6A; CJA 2003, s.33 (1), (2)

(1) in relation to the **pre-April 4, 2005** regime, the particulars must comply with s.5(7) (a) and (b) of the Act;
(2) and the **enhanced provisions apply** under s.6A, the particulars given must comply with s.6(2)(a) and (b) of the Act, and the defence statement must give particulars which include:

(a) the name, address and *date of birth* of any witness the accused believes is able to give evidence in support of the alibi, or as many of those details as are known to the accused when the statement is given;

(b) any information in the accused's possession which might be of material assistance in identifying or finding any such witness in whose case any of the details mentioned in paragraph (a) are not known to the accused when the statement is given,

These latter provisions (i.e. (2) above) do not apply in relation to offences in to which the criminal investigation began **before July 15, 2005**.

"Evidence in support of an alibi" is evidence tending to show that by reason of the presence of the accused at a particular place or in a particular area at a particular time he was not, or was unlikely to have been, at the place where the offence is alleged to have been committed at the time of its alleged commission.

The judge's functions

32–016 The Protocol (see 32–001, above) makes it clear that where there are disclosure failings on the party of the defence or the prosecution, the judge should, in exercising appropriate oversight, pose searching questions to the parties and, having so and having explored the reasons for default, should give clear directions to ensure that such failings are addressed and remedied well in advance of the trial date.

The judge must insist that the defence case statement is served by the due date, and he should then examine it with care to ensure that it complies with the formalities required by the Act (see 32–014, 015, above) bearing in mind that:

(1) if the material does not weaken the prosecution case or strengthen that of the accused, there is no requirement to disclose it;
(2) for this purpose the parties' respective cases should not be restrictively analysed, but they must be carefully analysed, to ascertain the specific facts the prosecution seek to establish and the specific grounds on which the charges are resisted;
(3) the trial process is not well served if the defence are permitted to make general and unspecified allegations and then seek far-reaching disclosure in the hope that material may turn up to make them good;
(4) neutral material or material damaging to the accused need not be disclosed and should not be brought to the attention of the court.

(*R. v H & C* [2004] 2 Cr.App.R.10 HL).)

Where:

(a) no defence case statement, or no sufficient case statement, has been served by the PCMH, the judge should make a full investigation of the reasons for this failure to comply with the mandatory obligation under CPIA 1996, s.5(5).

(b) there is no, or no sufficient, defence statement by the date of PCMH, or any pre-trial hearing where the matter falls to be considered, the judge must consider whether the defence should be warned, pursuant to CPIA 1996, s.6E(2) (see below), that an adverse inference may be drawn at the trial. In the usual case, where s.6E(2) applies and there is no justification for the deficiency, such a warning should be given.

Section 6E(2) referred to above provides that in relation to a criminal investigation begun **after April 4, 2005** (SI 2005/950), if it appears to the judge at a pre-trial hearing that an accused has failed to comply fully with ss.5, 6B or 6C, so that there is a possibility of comment being made or inferences drawn under s.11(5), he must warn the accused accordingly. This is the ultimate sanction for a failure in disclosure by the accused.

The judge must, of course, be alert to ensure that accused persons do not suffer because of the faults and failings of their lawyers, but there must be a clear indication to the professions that if justice is to be done, and if disclosure is to be dealt with fairly in accordance with the law, a full and careful defence case statement is essential.

Updated disclosure by accused (not yet in force)

32–017 Where the accused has, before the beginning of the relevant period determined under s.12, given a defence statement under ss.5 or 6: CPIA 1996, s.6B; CJA 2003, s.33(3)

(1) he must during that period give to the court and the prosecutor an "updated defence statement;" to assist the management of the trial; and

(2) such statement must comply with the requirements imposed by or under s.6A above, by reference to the state of affairs at the time when the statement is given; and

(3) where there are other accused in the proceedings and the court so orders, the accused must also give an updated defence statement, within such period as may be specified by the court, to each other accused so specified.

The court may make an order under (3) either of its own motion or on the application of any party.

Notification of intention to call defence witnesses (not yet in force)

32–018 As part of the updated notice by the accused, he is required to serve, on the court and the prosecutor, before the trial, details of any witnesses (other than himself) whom he intends to call, and also details of all experts instructed, including those not called to give evidence. A Code of Practice will govern police interviews with the defence witnesses disclosed.

CPIA 1996, s.6C; CJA 2003, s.34

The notice must indicate, subject to the extent to which such details have already been given under s.6(2), whether he intends to give or call any evidence at trial and, if so:

(1) giving the name, address and date of birth of each proposed witness (other than the accused himself), or as many of those details as are known to the accused when the notice is given; and
(2) providing any information in the accused's possession which might be of material assistance in identifying or finding any proposed witness in whose case any of the details mentioned in (1) are not known to the accused when the notice is given.

Details do not have to be given under this provision to the extent that they have already been given under s.6A(2) above.

Notice must be given during the period which, by virtue of s.12, is the relevant period for this section.

If, following the giving of a notice under this section, the accused:

(a) decides to call a person who is not included in the notice as a proposed witness, or decides not to call a person who is so included, or
(b) discovers any information which, under (1) and (2) above, he would have had to include in the notice if he had been aware of it when giving the notice,

he must give an appropriately amended notice to the court and the prosecutor.

Notification of names of experts instructed by accused (not yet in force)

32–019 If the accused instructs a person with a view to his providing any expert opinion for possible use as evidence at the trial of the accused, he must, unless the name and address of

CPIA 1996, s.6D; CJA 2003, s.35

such person have already been given under s.6C, give to the court and the prosecutor a notice specifying the person's name and address. Notice must be given during the period which, by virtue of s.12, is the relevant period.

Disclosure by accused: copies to jury

32–020 The judge in a trial before a judge and jury: CPIA 1996, s.6E(4), (5), (6); CJA 2003, s.36

(1) may, whether of his own motion or on application of a party, and where he is of opinion that seeing a copy of the defence statement would help the jury to understand the case or to resolve any issue in the case, direct that the jury be given a copy of any defence statement, and
(2) if he does so, may direct that it be edited so as not to include references to matters evidence of which would be inadmissible.

The reference here, to "a defence statement" is a reference, where the accused has given:

(a) only an initial defence statement (that is, a defence statement given under ss.5 or 6), to that statement;
(b) both an initial defence statement and an updated defence statement (that is, a defence statement given under s.6B), to the updated defence statement;
(c) both an initial defence statement and a statement of the kind mentioned in s.6B(4), to the initial defence statement.

These provisions do not affect an alleged offence into which a criminal investigation has not begun **before July 15, 2005**.

Continuing duty of prosecutor to disclose

32–021 At all times in relation to an alleged offence into which a criminal investigation has begun **on or after July 15, 2005**: CPIA 1996, s.7A; CJA 2003, s.37

(1) after the prosecutor has complied with s.3 or purported to comply with it, and
(2) before the accused is acquitted or convicted or the prosecutor decides not to proceed with the case concerned.

the prosecutor must keep under review the question whether at any given time taking into account the state of affairs at that time (including the case for the prosecution as it stands at that time (and, in particular, following the giving of a defence statement), there is prosecution material which:

(a) might reasonably be considered capable of undermining the case for the prosecution against the accused or of assisting the case for the accused, and
(b) has not been disclosed to the accused,

the prosecutor must disclose it to the accused as soon as is reasonably practicable (or within the period mentioned in sub-s.(5)(a), where that applies).

Where the accused gives a defence statement under ss.5, 6 or 6B, and if as a result of that statement:

(i) the prosecutor is required by this section to make any disclosure, or further disclosure, he must do so during the relevant period under s.12, but
(ii) he should only disclose material in response to such a request if the material meets the appropriate test for disclosure and if declines to make disclosure he will during that period give to the accused a written statement to that effect, and the matter must proceed to a formal hearing under s.8 (see below, 32–022).

For the purposes of these provisions "prosecution material" is material which is in the prosecutor's possession and came into his possession in connection with the case for the prosecution against the accused, or which, in pursuance of a code operative under Pt 2 of the Act, he has inspected in connection with the case for the prosecution against the accused.

Subsections (3) to (5) of s.3 (method by which prosecutor discloses) apply for the purposes of this section as they apply for the purposes of that.

Material must not be disclosed under this section to the extent that the court, on an application by the prosecutor, concludes it is not in the public interest to disclose it and orders accordingly, or to the extent that it is material the disclosure of which is prohibited by RIPA 2000, s.17.

Application by accused for disclosure: (1) notice

32–022 Where the accused has given a defence statement under ss.5, 6 or 6B and the prosecutor has complied with s.7A(5) or has purported to comply with it or has failed to comply with it, if the accused has at any time reasonable cause to believe that: CPIA 1996, s.8; CJA 2003, s.38

(1) there is prosecution material which is required to be disclosed under s.7A to be disclosed to him; and

(2) that material has not been disclosed to him,

he may apply to the court for an order requiring the prosecutor to disclose such material to him. The procedure for making such an application is set out in CPR 2005, r.25(6).

It must be made by notice in writing to the court, and to the prosecutor at the same time, specifying: R.25.6

- (a) the material to which the application relates;
- (b) that the material has not been disclosed to the accused;
- (c) the reason why the material might be expected to assist the applicant's defence as disclosed by the defence statement; and
- (d) the date on which notice of application was served on the prosecutor.

The prosecutor must give notice, in any event, to the court within 14 days of service of notice of application by the accused that:

- (a) he wishes to make representations concerning the material to which the application relates, specifying the substance of those representations; or if he does not so wish,
- (b) he is willing to disclose that material.

CJA 2003, s.38 above has no effect in relation to alleged offences into which a criminal investigation began **before July 15, 2005**.

Application by accused for disclosure: (2) dealing with the application

32–023 An application is to be dealt with by the trial judge or, if the trial has not started, the judge designated to conduct the trial or, if none has been designated, by a judge designated for the purposes of determining the application. R.25.6

It may be dealt with at a hearing or on the papers, as the judge sees fit, unless the prosecutor has given notice that he wishes to make representations, in which case there must be a hearing on notice at which both parties may make representations. On an application by the prosecutor, the judge may give leave for the matter to be determined in the absence of the accused and his legal representative.

The consideration of detailed defence requests for specific disclosure (so-called 'shopping lists') otherwise than in accordance with r.25.6, is wholly improper. Likewise, defence requests for specific disclosure of unused prosecution material in purported pursuance of CPIA 1996, s.8 and r.25.6, which are not referable to any issue in the case identified by the defence case statement, should be rejected. The judge should require an application to be made under s.8 and in compliance with r.25.6 before considering any order for further disclosure. Any practice of making a blanket order for disclosure is inconsistent with the statutory framework laid down by the Act (*R. v H and C* (above)).

A copy of any order made by the judge must be served on the prosecutor and the applicant.

Methods of disclosure

32–024 Where primary or secondary disclosure by the prosecutor is required, and CPIA 1996, ss.3(3), (4), (5), 5, 7(4)

(1) the material consists of information which has been recorded in any form:
  - (a) the prosecutor discloses it by securing that a copy is made of it and that the copy is given to the accused; or
  - (b) if, in the prosecutor's opinion, that is not practicable or is not desirable, by allowing the accused to inspect it at a reasonable time and a reasonable place, or by taking steps to secure that he is allowed to do so, and a copy may be in such form as the prosecutor thinks fit and need not be in the same form as that in which the information has already been recorded.

(2) the material consists of information which has not been recorded, the prosecutor ` discloses it by securing that it is recorded in such form as he thinks fit and taking either of the disclosure steps set out in (a) and (b) above.

(3) the material does not consist of information, the prosecutor discloses it by allowing the accused to inspect it at a reasonable time and a reasonable place or by taking steps to secure that he is allowed to do so.

The above provisions, i.e. CPIA 1996, s.3(3)–(5) do not apply in relation to disclosure required by ss.3, 7 or 9, if the Sexual Offences (Protected Material) Act 1997, s.3(1) applies in relation to that disclosure (*ibid.* s.9(2)).

Where material has been seized and retained by the police, but not examined by the disclosure officer or the prosecutor, the Attorney-General's guidelines require that a s.9 statement must be included in the sensitive schedule describing the material in CPIA 1998, s.3(6), (7) general terms and justifying its not having been examined. Permission must be given to the defence to inspect the material.

Material must not be disclosed under these provisions to the extent that it is:

(a) material the disclosure of which is prohibited by RIPA 2000, s.17; or
(b) a judge, on the application of the prosecutor, decides that it is not in the public interest to disclose it (see 32–031, below) and orders accordingly.

Prosecutor's failure to observe time limits

32–025 The prosecutor's failure to act: CPIA 1996, s.10; CJA 2003, s.331, Sch.36, Pt 3, para.7

(1) where he purports to act under s.3 after the end of the period which, by virtue of s.12 is the relevant period for ss.3, or 12
(2) where he purports to act under s.7A(5) after the end of the period which by virtue of s.12 is the relevant period for s.7A,

does not, on its own, constitute grounds for staying the proceedings for abuse of process (see 3 ABUSE OF PROCESS), but his failure may constitute such grounds if it involves such delay by him that the accused is denied a fair trial.

Faults in disclosure by accused; comment

32–026 The trial judge or any other party may make such comment as appears appropriate, and the judge or jury may draw such inferences as appear proper in deciding whether the accused is guilty of the offence concerned, in three different sets of circumstances: CPIA 1996, s.11; CJA 2003, s.39

The **first set** of circumstances is where the accused:

(1) fails to give an initial defence statement;
(2) gives an initial defence statement, but does so after the end of the period which is the relevant period for s.5 by virtue of s.12;
(3) is required by s.6B to give an updated statement or a statement of the kind mentioned in s.6B(4) but fails to do so;
(4) gives an updated statement, or a statement of the kind mentioned in s.6B(4) but does so after the end of the period which is the relevant period for s.6B by virtue of s.12;
(5) sets out inconsistent defences in his defence statement;
(6) at his trial;

(a) puts forward a defence which was not mentioned in his defence statement or is different from any defence set out in that statement;
(b) relies on matter which, in breach of the requirements imposed by or under s.6A, was not mentioned in his defence statement;
(c) adduces evidence in support of an alibi without having given particulars of the alibi in his defence statement; or
(d) calls a witness to give evidence in support of an alibi without having complied with s.6A(2)(a) or (b).

32–027 The **second case** is where s.6 applies, the accused gives an initial defence statement, but:

(1) gives the initial defence statement after the end of the period which, by virtue of s.12, is the relevant period for s.6, or
(2) does any of the things mentioned in paras (3) to (6) above.

The **third case** (not yet in force) is, and here commentary by another party under subs.(5)(a) may be made *only with the leave of the court*, is where the accused:

(a) gives a witness notice but does so after the end of the period which, by virtue of s.12, is the relevant period for s.6C, or
(b) at his trial calls a witness not included, or not adequately identified, in a witness notice.

Where the accused puts forward a defence which is different from any defence set out in his defence statement, then in doing anything under subs.(5) or in deciding whether to do anything under it, the judge must have regard in taking or deciding whether to take either of the above courses of action to:

(i) the extent of the difference in the defences; and
(ii) whether there is any justification for it.

A person may not be convicted of an offence solely on an inference drawn under subs.(5). Where the accused calls a witness whom he has failed to include, or to identify adequately, in a witness notice, in doing anything under subsection (5) or in deciding whether to do anything under it the judge must have regard to whether there is any justification for the failure.

Interpretation

32–028 In these provisions: CJA 2003, s.39(11), (12)

(a) "initial defence statement" means a defence statement given under s.5 or 6;
(b) "updated defence statement" means a defence statement given under s.6B;
(c) a reference simply to an accused's "defence statement" is a reference, where he has given:
  (i) only an initial defence statement, to that statement;
  (ii) both an initial and an updated defence statement, to the updated defence statement;
  (iii) both an initial statement and a statement of the kind mentioned in s.6B(4), to the initial defence statement.
(d) a reference to evidence in support of an alibi must be construed in accordance with s.5;
(e) "witness notice" means a notice given under s.6C.

D. Public interest immunity (PII)

(1) General

32–029 There is provision in the Code of Practice for the police "disclosure officer" to list on a sensitive schedule any material which he believes it is not in the public interest to disclose, and the reasons for that belief. The schedule must include a statement that the disclosure officer believes the material is sensitive.

Examples are material:

(1) relating to national security;
(2) received from the intelligence and security agencies;
(3) relating to intelligence from foreign sources which reveals sensitive intelligence gathering methods, given in confidence;
(4) which relates to the use of a telephone system and which is supplied to an investigator for intelligence purposes only;
(5) relating to the identity or activities of informants, or undercover police officers or other persons supplying information to the police who may be in danger if their identities are revealed;
(6) revealing the location of any premises or other place used for police surveillance or the identity of any person allowing a police officer to use them for surveillance;

(7) revealing, directly or indirectly, techniques and methods relied on by a police officer in the course of a criminal investigation, e.g. covert surveillance techniques or other methods of detecting crime;
(8) disclosure of which might facilitate the commission of other offences or hinder the prevention and detection of crime;
(9) comprising internal police communications such as management minutes;
(10) upon the strength of which search warrants were obtained;
(11) containing details of persons taking part in identification parades;
(12) supplied to an investigator during a criminal investigation which has been generated by an official of a body concerned with the regulation or supervision of bodies corporate or of persons engaged in financial activities, or which has been generated by a person retained by such a body; or
(13) supplied to an investigator during a criminal investigation which relates to a child or young person and which has been generated by a local authority social services department, an Area Child Protection Committee or other party contacted by an investigator during the investigation.

Disclosure

32–030 In exceptional circumstances, where an investigator considers that material is so sensitive that its revelation to the prosecutor by means of an entry on the sensitive schedule is inappropriate, as where the material would be likely to lead directly to the loss of life, or directly threaten national security the existence of the material must be revealed to the prosecutor separately.

In such circumstances:

(1) the responsibility for informing the prosecutor lies with the investigator who knows the detail of the sensitive material;
(2) the investigator should act as soon as reasonably practicable after the file containing the prosecution case is sent to the prosecutor; and
(3) he must ensure that the prosecutor is able to inspect the material so that he can assess whether it needs to be brought before a court for a ruling on disclosure.

The judge's role

32–031 The judge:

(1) must give detailed consideration to the material sought to be withheld in the context of the prosecution and defence cases,
(2) must identify the public interest in question and assess the prejudice claimed to ensure that any derogation from the full disclosure rule was the minimum necessary to secure the required protection;
(3) may (CPIA 1996, ss.3(6), 7(5), 8(5), 9(8)) order that it is not in the public interest to disclose material, and if he does so, the material must not be disclosed by the prosecutor (the common law rules as to whether disclosure is in the public interest, summarised in the cases set out below, continue to apply);
(4) must (CPIA 1996, s.15(3), (4); CJA 2003, s.331, Sch.36, Pt 3, para.31) without need of any application by the accused, throughout the trial keep under review the question whether, at any given time, it is still not in the public interest to disclose material affected by his order and.
(5) must, in making his decision, undertake a balancing exercise between the competing interests of non-disclosure in the public interest and fairness to the accused.

If the disputed material may prove the accused's innocence or avoid a miscarriage of justice, then the balance comes down resoundingly in favour of disclosing it (*R. v Keane,* above). The cases were reviewed in *R. v H* [2004] 2 W.L.R. 335 HL.

The interests of justice include allowing an accused to put forward a tenable case in its best light (*R. v Agar* (1990) 90 Cr.App.R. 318).

Material damaging to the defendant is not disclosable and should not be brought to the court's aittention.

Procedure

32–032 The procedure relating to so-called "Pt II applications" has has been incorporated into CPR 2005, r.25 the relevant parts of which are set out below.

Thus:

(1) a prosecutor's notice of application under CPIA 1996, ss.3(6), 7A(8) or 8(5) i.e. in the ordinary case (Type 1) is served on the Crown Court officer of the Crown Court,

and on the accused, and must specify the nature of the material to which it relates (25.1(1)(2)(3));

(2) where the prosecutor has reason to believe that to reveal to the accused the nature of the material to which the application relates would have the effect of disclosing that which he contends should not, in the public interest, be disclosed (i.e. Type 2), there is no need to specify in the notice of application the nature of the material, but they must still notify the accused that an application has been made (r.25.(4));

(3) in the exceptional case (Type 3) where the prosecutor has reason to believe that to reveal to the accused the fact that an application is being made would have the effect of disclosing that which he contends should not, in the public interest, be disclosed, the notice need not be served on the accused, and may be served on the trial judge or if the application is made bfore the start of the trial, on the judge, if any, who has been designated to conduct the trial, instead of on the appropriate officer of the court (r.251(5), (6));.

(4) the Crown Court officer, on receiving such an application will refer it, if the trial has started, to the trial judge, or if received before the start of the trial, to the judge designated to conduct the trial or, if no judge has been designated, to a judge designated for the purpose (r.25.2(1), (2)), and will give written notice to the parties and any person claiming to have an interest in the material, of the date and time of the hearing, unless the judge orders otherwise (r.25.2(3));

(5) applications are determined by the trial judge, the judge who has been designated to conduct the trial if the trial has not started or, if no judge has been designated, by a judge designated for the purpose of hearing the application.

(6) the hearing is *inter partes*, and both prosecutor and accused are entitled to make representations to the court (r.25.2(3), (4)) unless the prosecutor applies to make representations in the absence of the accused, when the judge may sit in his absence and in the absence of his legal representatives;

(7) where the application is made under (2) or (3) above, the hearing is *ex parte*; and only the prosecutor may make representations (r.25.2(5)). There is nothing in the Rules, however, to prevent the judge giving the accused or his legal representative an opportunity to outline the defence

case in order to assist the judge in making his decision as to what is and what is not material to the defence case (if it is not already clear from the Defence Statement). The judge may well wish to adopt such a course in order to avoid any possible breach of ECHR Art.6(1) (see *Jaspar v U.K.; Fitt v. UK* (above)).

The Protocol (see 32–001, above) suggests that the prosecution should be alert to the possibility of disclosing a statement in redacted form by, for example simply removing personal details. This may obviate the need for a P 11 application, unless the redacted material in itself would also satisfy the test for disclosure. Documents may be summarised, or the prosecutor may make an admission under CJA 1967, s.10, about the substance of the material.

Except where the material is very short or where it is of such sensitivity that do so would be inappropriate, the prosecution should have supplied securely sealed copies to the judge beforehand, together with a short statement of the reasons why each document is said to be relevant and fulfils the disclosure test and why it is said that its disclosure would cause a real risk of serious prejudice to an important public interest; in undertaking this task, the use of merely formulaic expressions is to be discouraged. In any case of complexity a schedule of the material should be provided showing the specific objection to disclosure in relation to each item, leaving a space for the decision.

The application, even if held in private or in secret, should be recorded. The judge should give some short statement of reasons; this is often best done document by document as the hearing proceeds.

If the judge concludes that it is in the public interest that an item of sensitive material be disclosed to the accused, it will be necessary to disclose the material if the case is to proceed.

The prosecutor who made the initial assessment of materiality and the judge who ruled that material need not be disclosed must both be alert to recognise the emergence of a new situation which might affect the balance between the conflicting interests. For this reason, the judge who is to conduct the trial should also conduct the PII/non-disclosure hearing (*R. v Davis, Johnson and Rowe*, above) which has been considered by the European Court of Human Rights, *sub nom. Rowe & Davis v UK* (1997) Cr.App.R. 110).

The approach to disclosure

32–033 When any issue of derogation from the golden rule arises, the judge must address a series of questions:

(1) What is the nature of the material which the prosecution seek to withhold? He must consider this in detail.
(2) Is the material such as may weaken the prosecution case or strengthen the defence? If "No", disclosure should not be ordered. If "Yes", disclosure should be ordered in full.
(3) Is there a chance of serious prejudice to an important public interest ? If so, what, if any, disclosure of the material should be ordered? If not full disclosure should be ordered.
(4) If the answer to (2) and (3) is "Yes", can the accused's interests be protected without disclosure, or should disclosure be ordered to an extent which will give adequate protection to the public interest in question and also afford adequate protection to the interests of the defence?
(5) Do the measures proposed in answer to (4) represent a derogation necessary to protect the public interest, or should he order such greater disclosure as will represent the minimum derogation from the golden rule of full disclosure? If limited disclosure is ordered pursuant to (4) or (5), may the effect be to render the trial process, viewed as a whole, unfair to the accused?
(6) If "Yes", then fuller disclosure should be ordered even if this leads, or may lead the prosecution to discontinue the proceedings so as to avoid having to make disclosure.
(7) If the answer to (6) when first given is "No", does that remain the correct situation once evidence is adduced and the defence advanced? It is important that the answer to (6) should not be treated as final, but as a provisional, answer which the judge must keep uinder review.

(*R. v H & C* [2004] 2 Cr.App.R. 10 HL.)

Appointment of special advocate

32–034 In *R. v H* (above) HL suggested that the power of the judge to appoint a special advocate to represent the accused on an application only in exceptional cases where it might be necessary in the "interests of justice". Such such an appointment ought not be ordered unless and until the judge was satisfied that no other course would adequately meet the overriding requirement of fairness to the accused.

Other persons claiming interest

32–035 Where an application is made by the prosecutor under ss.7A(8) or 8(5), 14(2) or 15(4) and a person claiming to have an interest in the material:

CPIA 1996, s.16; CJA 2003, s.331, Sch.36, Pt 3, para.32

(1) applies to be heard by the court; and
(2) shows that he was involved (whether alone or with others) in the prosecutor's attention being brought to the material,

the judge must not make an order unless that person has been given an opportunity to be heard. Where the prosecutor has reason to believe that a person who was involved (whether alone or with others and whether directly or indirectly) in the prosecutor's attention being brought to any material to which an application relates may claim to have an interest in that material, he must give notice in writing to—

(a) the person concerned of the application, and
(b) the Crown Court officer or, as the case may require, the judge,

of his belief and the grounds for it. The procedure is then in accordance with r.25.5.

Emergence of new situation

32–036 It was not suggested that the procedure set out in *Davis, Johnson & Rowe* offended ECHR Art. 6(1), but it was made clear that where competing interests, including the safety of witnesses, arise, only such measures restricting the rights of the defence (including the principle of equality of arms) "which are strictly necessary" are permissible. In *Jaspar v UK*; *Fitt v UK* [2000] Crim.L.R. 584), where the procedures set out in *Davis, Johnson & Rowe* were followed, the trial judge gave the defence as much information regarding the nature of the withheld evidence as possible without disclosing what it was, and the defence accepted an invitation by the judge to outline the defence case to him. It was held there was no breach of Art. 6(1). See also *PG and JH. v UK* [2002] Crim.L.R. 308.

Public interest; review

32–037 After a judge has made an order as above, the trial judge must keep under review, until the accused is acquitted or the prosecutor decides not to proceed with the case, the question whether, at any given time it is still not in the public interest to disclose material affected by the order. CPIA 1996, s.16; CJA 2003, s.331, Sch.36, para.29, 31

There is no need for any application, but the accused may apply to the judge for a review of the question, if at any time the judge considers that it is in the public interest to disclose material to any extent, he will so order, and take steps to inform the prosecutor of his order.

Review of non-disclosure order: application by accused

32–038 If an application is made by the accused it is made by notice in writing to the Crown Court officer, specifying the reason why the accused believes the court should review the question whether it is still not in the public interest to disclose the material affected by the order. A copy of the notice must be served on the prosecutor at the same time as it is sent to the court officer. The court officer will refer it, if the:

(1) trial has started, to the trial judge; or
(2) application is received before the start of the trial either:
  (a) to the judge who has been designated to conduct the trial, or
  (b) if no judge has been designated for that purpose, to the judge who made the order to which the application relates.

The judge to whom the application is referred will consider whether the application may be determined without a hearing and may so determine it if he thinks fit, but no application may be determined by the judge without a hearing if it appears to him that there are grounds on which he might conclude that it is in the public interest to disclose material to any extent.

Ordinarily the hearing of an application is *inter partes* and the accused and the prosecutor are entitled to make representations, but:

(i) where after hearing the accused's representations the prosecutor applies to the judge for leave to make representations in the absence of the accused, the judge may for that purpose sit in the absence of the accused and any legal representative of his; and
(ii) subject to r.25.5(4), where the order to which the application relates was made following an application of which the accused was not notified under r.25.1(3) or (4), the hearing must be *ex parte* and only the prosecutor is entitled to make representations.

The Crown Court officer will give notice in writing to the prosecutor, to the accused and, where appropriate, to any person claiming to have an interest in the material to which the application relates who has applied under s.16(b) of the 1996 Act to be heard by the court, of the date and time when and the place where the hearing of an application to which this rule applies will take place and of any order which is made by the court following its determination of the application (R.25.4).

(2) Material held by other agencies

General

32–039 There is no specific procedure for the disclosure of unused material held by third parties in criminal proceedings, although the procedure under CP(AW)A 1965, s.2 MCA 1980, s.97 is often used in order to effect such disclosure. The test applied under both Acts, however, is not the test to be applied under the CPIA 1996, whether in the original or enhanced form. These two provisions require that the material in question to is material evidence, i.e. immediately admissible in evidence in the proceedings (see *R. v Reading JJ. Ex p. Berkshire CC* [1996] 1 Cr.App.R. 239, *R. v Derby MC Ex p. B* [1996]1 Cr.App.R. 385 and *R. v Alibhai and Others* [2004] EWCA Crim. 681) (Protocol, see 32–001, para.52.)

Material held by other government departments or Crown agencies is not prosecution material for the purposes of CPIA 1996, ss.3(2) or 8(4) but under the Attorney-General's updated guidelines (paras 51 *et seq*.,) where it is suspected that a non-government agency or other third party has material which might be disclosable if it were in the possession of the prosecution and it is appropriate to seek access to that material, the prosecution should take steps to obtain it. If a request for access by the prosecution is refused by the third party and if the requirements of CP(AW)A 1965, s.2 are complied with, the prosecutor should apply for a witness summons requiring a representative of the third party to produce the material to the court.

Social services files

32–040 Where material is held by a third party such as a local authority, a social services department, hospital or business, the prosecutor may seek to make arrangements to inspect the material with a view to applying the relevant test for disclosure to it and determining whether any or all of the material should be retained, recorded and, in due course, disclosed to the accused. In considering the latter, the investigators and the prosecution will establish whether the holder of the material wishes to raise P 11 issues, as a result of which the material may have to be placed before the court. CPIA 1996, s.16 gives such a party a right to make representations to the court.

Where the third party in question declines to allow inspection of the material, or requires the prosecution to obtain an order before handing over copies of the material, the prosecutor will need to consider whether it is appropriate to obtain a witness summons under CP(AW)A 1965, s.2, though this is only appropriate where the statutory requirements are satisfied, and where the prosecutor considers that the material may satisfy the test for disclosure. *R. v Alibhai and Others*, above makes it clear that the prosecutor has a "margin of consideration" in this regard.

Where the third party in question declines to allow inspection of the material, or requires the prosecution to obtain an order before handing over copies of the material, the prosecutor will need to consider whether it is appropriate to obtain a witness summons under CP(AW)A 1965, s.2 where the statutory requirements are satisfied, and where the prosecutor considers that the material may satisfy the test for disclosure. *R. v Alibhai and Others*, above makes it clear that the prosecutor has a "margin of consideration" in this regard (Protocol, see above 32–001, paras 53–55).

Objections by third party

32–041 The third party may have a duty to assert confidentiality, or the right to privacy under Art.8 of the ECHR, where requests for disclosure are made by the prosecution, or anyone else. Where issues are raised in relation to allegedly relevant third party material, the judge must:

(1) ascertain whether inquiries with the third party are likely to be appropriate, and, if so, identify who is going to make the request, what material is to be sought, from whom is the material to be sought and within what time scale must the matter be resolved;

(2) consider what action would be appropriate in the light of the third party failing or refusing to comply with a request, including inviting the defence to make the request on its own behalf and, if necessary, to make an application for a witness summons.

The judge should be aware that a summons can only be issued where the document(s) sought would be admissible in evidence. While it may be that the material in question may be admissible in evidence as a result of the hearsay provisions of CJA 2003, ss.114 to 120). It is this that determines whether an order for production of the material is appropriate, rather than the wider considerations applicable to disclosure in criminal proceedings (see *R. v Reading JJ.* (above); *R. v Derby MC*, (above).

Any directions made (for instance, the date by which an application for a witness summons with supporting affidavit under CP(AW)A 1965, s.2 should be served) should be put into writing at the time. Any failure to comply with the timetable must immediately be referred back to the court for further directions, although a hearing will not always be necessary.

Where the prosecution do not consider it appropriate to seek such a summons, the defence should consider doing so, where they are of the view (notwithstanding the prosecution assessment) that the third party may hold material which might undermine the prosecution case or assist that for the defendant, and the material would be likely to be "material evidence" for the purposes of the 1965 Act. The judge at the PCMH should specifically enquire whether any such application is to be made by the defence and set out a clear timetable.

Relevance of material

32–042 The court, by issuing a witness summons to produce the documents, can only require disclosure of relevant or "material" documents. On the authorities:

(1) to be material such documents must not only be relevant to the issues arising in the criminal proceedings, but also admissible in evidence;
(2) documents desired merely for the purpose of cross-examination are not admissible in evidence;
(3) the applicant must satisfy the court that there is a real possibility that the documents are likely to be material; and
(4) the procedure is not to be used as a fishing expedition (*R. v Reading JJ.*, above; *R. v Derby MC, supra*).

It is then for the judge, doing a balancing exercise, to decide whether the public interest in maintaining the confidentiality of those documents and the public interest in seeing that justice is done, requires the documents to be disclosed or withheld (*R. v Higgins* [1996] 1 F.L.R. 137).

Procedure

32–043 An application must identify the documents sought and why they are said to be material evidence, particularly where attempts are made to access the medical reports of those who allege that they are victims of crime. Victims do not waive the confidentiality of their medical records, or their right to privacy under Art.8 of the ECHR, by the mere fact of making a complaint against the accused.

The procedure is as follows:

(1) the possessor of the documents must first decide whether or not they are relevant;
(2) the assistance of the judge should only be sought if a question can properly be decided by him, most obviously where questions of public interest immunity are involved: *R. v B* [2000] Crim.L.R. 50;
(3) if the judge is to be involved, it will be for him either to accept the assertion of the possessor or to look at the documents himself. That decision is to be taken at his discretion, judicially exercised;
(4) the judge should be alert to balance the rights of victims against the real and proven needs of the defence. As a public authority, he must ensure that any interference with the ECHR art.8 rights of those entitled to privacy is in accordance with the law and necessary in pursuit of a legitimate public interest; general and unspecified requests to trawl through such records should be refused;
(5) if the possessors' claim that the documents are irrelevant is suspect or implausible, the judge will no doubt look at them himself, or he may regard assistance from an independent and competent member of the Bar as being sufficient.
(6) a verbatim record must be kept of any *ex parte* application (*R. v Turner* (1995) 2 Cr.App.R. 94).

If material is held by any person in relation to family proceedings (e.g. where there have been care proceedings in relation to a child, who has also complained to the police of sexual or other abuse) then an application has to be made by that person to the family court for leave to disclose that material to a third party, unless the third party, and the purpose for which disclosure is made, is approved by Rule 10.20A(3) of the Family Proceedings Rules 1991 (SI 1991/1247). This would permit, for instance, a local authority, in receipt of such material, to disclose it to the police for the purpose of a criminal investigation, or to the CPS, in order for the latter to discharge any obligations under CPIA 1996 (Protocol, see 32–001, above para.62).

Costs

32–044 There is power to award costs in favour of local authorities out of public funds only where the court orders under CP(AWA) 1965, s.2C that the witness summons shall be of no effect (see 12 BENCH AND WITNESS WARRANT).

E. Confidentiality

General

32–045 If an accused is given, or allowed to inspect, a document or other object under CPIA 1996, ss.3,4, 7*A*,14 or 15, he must not disclose it, or any information recorded in it, except: CPIA 1996, s.17; CJA 2003, s.331, Sch.6, Pt 3, para.33

(1) in connection with the proceedings for whose purposes he was given the object or document, or allowed to inspect it; or
(2) with a view to the taking of further criminal proceedings (e.g. by way of appeal) in connection with those proceedings.

The accused's use or disclosure of any such object or information is limited in relation:

(a) to an object, the extent to which it has been displayed to the public in open court; or
(b) to information, the extent to which it has been communicated to the public in open court; or
(c) both to an object and information, with permission of the court, use or disclosure for the purpose and to the extent specified by the judge.

The procedure is governed by r.26.1–3.

Contravention

32–046 Any contravention by the accused of the restrictions on use or disclosure is a contempt of court, punishable in the Crown Court by imprisonment not exceeding two years or a fine or both.

While nothing in the Rules affects the judge's power to make an order of committal or to impose a fine of his own motion against a person guilty of a contempt under the Act, the procedure prescribed by r.26.4. is as follows:

(1) an application for an order of committal, or for the imposition of a fine may be made by the prosecutor, or by any other person claiming to have an interest in the object, or in any information recorded in an object, the use or disclosure of which is alleged to contravene s.17 of the Act.
(2) the application is made by notice in writing to the officer of the Crown Court sitting at the same place as that in which the Crown Court sat or is sitting to conduct the proceedings for whose purposes the object mentioned in para.(1) above was given or inspected.
(3) the application must set out the name and a description of the applicant, the name, description and address of the

person sought to be committed or fined, and the grounds on which his committal or the imposition of a fine is sought and must be supported by an affidavit verifying the facts.

(4) subject to para.(5) below, the notice, accompanied by a copy of the affidavit in support, must be served personally on the person sought to be committed or fined; and

(5) the judge may dispense with service of the notice if he is of the opinion that it is necessary to do so in order to protect the applicant or for another purpose identified by him.

Procedure on committal, etc., hearing

32–047 Except with the leave of the judge hearing the application, no grounds may be relied upon at the hearing save those set out in the notice referred (R.26.4(16)).

The person sought to be committed or fined may give oral evidence on his own behalf (R.26.4(17)). In principle:

(1) proceedings must be heard in open court (r.26.4(14)), although

(2) proceedings may be heard in private r.26.4.(15))where the object or information, the use or disclosure of which is alleged to contravene, is an object or information which is, or forms part of, material in respect of which a Pt II application was made, whether or not the judge made an order that the material be not disclosed; provided that

where the judge hears the proceedings in private he must nevertheless, if he commits any person to custody or imposes a fine on him in pursuance of the Act, state in open court the name of that person, the period specified in the order of committal or the amount of the fine imposed, or both.

Orders

32–048 The judge making an order of committal may:

(1) by order, suspend the execution of the order of committal for such period, or on such terms or conditions, as he may specify; the applicant for the order of committal must then, unless the judge otherwise directs, serve on the person against whom it is made a notice informing him of the making and the terms of the order;

(2) on the application of any person committed to custody for a contempt under the Act, discharge him;

(3) on finding an accused guilty of such contempt, order that any object disclosed to the accused be forfeited and dealt with in any such manner as he may order; this includes the power to order the object to be destroyed or to be given to the prosecutor or placed in his custody for such period as the judge may specify. He will give an opportunity to anyone found guilty of such a contempt, or to any other person claiming to have an interest in any object disclosed to the accused which is the subject matter of the contempt proceedings, to be heard;

(4) order any copy of the object in the possession of the accused convicted of such a contempt to be forfeited and dealt with in such manner as he may order.

As to the procedure relating to forfeiture, see r.26.5.

33 EUROPEAN COURT

33–001 Under the EEC Treaty, Art. 177, the European Court of Justice has jurisdiction, among other things, to give preliminary rulings concerning the interpretation of the Treaty, the validity or interpretation of Acts of the institutions of the Community, and the interpretation of the statutes of bodies established by an act of the Council, where these statutes so provide.

Where a question of such nature is raised before any court or tribunal of a member state, then it may, if it considers that a decision on a question of law is necessary to enable it to give judgment, request the Court of Justice to give a ruling.

The Crown Court is a "court or tribunal" falling within Art.177, and a judge of the Crown Court has a discretion to refer a question if he considers it "necessary" to enable him to give judgment.

Courses open to the court

33–002 The European Communities Act 1972 requires Community law to be treated as a question of law, not one of fact which requires proof by a skilled witness. It is ordinarily applied like any domestic law. If a question of interpretation arises, and the judge is satisfied that there is a real doubt as to the law, which must be settled before the case is decided, three courses are open to him:

(1) usually, particularly in trials on indictment, he may decide the question himself, leaving an appellate court to refer any question to the European Court;
(2) in an appeal from a magistrates' court, he may state a case for the opinion of the High Court, leaving that court to refer any question to the European Court; or
(3) he may refer the matter himself to the European Court.

This last option, which is likely to be impracticable in most cases in the Crown Court, is not an appeal. The European Court does not decide the case; it gives a ruling, binding on all courts in the Community.

Approach to reference

33–003 Ordinarily, a court should exercise considerable caution before referring a question of Community law, and should certainly not do so before all the evidence has been called, and there is no possibility of an acquittal on the facts. It is better for the judge to form his own view, and if his decision is questioned, the appellate court will usually be in a better position to assess the appropriateness of, and to formulate, the question to be referred (*R. v Plymouth JJ. Ex p. Rogers* [1982] Q.B. 863).

Procedure

33–004 An order referring a case: R.75.1

(1) may be made by the judge of his own motion or on application by a party to the proceedings;
(2) must set out in a schedule the request for the preliminary ruling, and the judge may give directions as to the manner and form in which the ruling is to be prepared;
(3) a copy must be sent to the senior master of the Supreme Court (QBD) for onward transmission; and
(4) the proceedings in the Crown Court must be adjourned until the preliminary ruling has been given.

The reference should be drafted as clearly and precisely as possible, since it will have to be translated into other official languages by the European Court's translators. It should include a statement of reasons which is succinct, yet sufficiently complete to give a clear understanding of the facts and legal context of the main proceedings, and in particular, should include:

(a) a statement of the facts which are essential to a full understanding of the main proceedings;
(b) an exposition of any national law which may be applicable;
(c) a statement of the reasons which have prompted the court to refer the question(s) to the European Court; and
(d) where appropriate, a summary of the parties' arguments,

so as to put the Court in a position to give an answer which will be of assistance.

The order for reference should be accompanied by copies of any documents needed for a proper understanding of the case, particularly the text of any applicable English provisions. The order and any relevant documents should be sent directly to the European Court by registered post, addressed to: The Registry, Court of Justice of the European Communities, L-2925 Luxembourg.

See also *Practice Direction (ECJ reference procedure)* [1999] 1 Cr.App.R. 452), PD 2004, I.10.1.

34 FACTUAL BASIS FOR SENTENCE; NEWTON HEARING

34–001 As far as possible an offender should be sentenced on a basis which accurately reflects the facts of the individual case; a different set of circumstances is likely to arise depending upon whether there has been a trial or sentence follows a plea of guilty.

(1) Conviction following trial

General

34–002 Where a an offender is convicted after a trial:

(1) the factual basis for sentence may be derived from the evidence called at the trial, but
(2) the judge must be careful to sentence only for those offences:
   (a) to which the offender has pleaded guilty; or
   (b) of which the offender has been convicted at the trial, or any other trial where sentence is pending and falls to be dealt with; or
   (c) which the offender formally asks to be taken into consideration, as to which see 59 TICs.

Where an issue arises as to sentence on which no evidence was called at the trial, the judge may hold a Newton hearing (see 34–013 below) to determine the matter (*R. v Finch* (1993) 14 Cr.App.R.(S.) 226).

Clearly, where the prosecution does not proceed on a count or counts, the judge must pass sentence on the basis that the offender is not guilty on that or those counts.

Interpreting the verdict

34–003 Problems may arise in interpreting the jury's verdict. In particular:

(1) if the verdict can be explained only on one view of the facts, the judge must adopt that view as the basis for sentence;
(2) if more than one view of the facts is consistent with the verdict, the judge may form his own view in the light of the evidence given;

(3) if the verdict leaves open an important issue which may affect sentence, the judge must decide where the truth lies.

(*R. v Solomon and Another* (1984) 6 Cr.App.R.(S.) 120; *R. v McGlade* (1991) 12 Cr.App.R.(S.) 105; *R. v Martin* [2002] 2 Cr.App.R.(S.) 34.)

(2) Conviction following plea of guilty

General

34–004 Where sentence is passed following a plea of guilty, the basis for the sentence is to be derived from the prosecution case, which includes the facts disclosed in the witness statements of the prosecution and the facts outlined by the prosecution advocate, unless the plea is tendered and accepted on an agreed basis.

Where:

(1) a plea of guilty is tendered on a specific basis, the facts will appear from any agreed statement of facts reached between the prosecution and the defence; and
(2) a dispute arises as to the facts:
   (a) outlined by the prosecution, or
   (b) where there has been a trial with a jury, to be deduced from a simple verdict of guilty by the jury,

it is for the judge to resolve the issue.

Crown's obligation to state facts in open court

34–005 To enable the public and the press to know the circumstances of an offence of which the accused has been convicted and for which he is being sentenced, in relation to each offence to which the offender has pleaded guilty, the prosecution must state the facts in open court before sentence is passed. PD 2004 III.26.1

While he is not obliged to pass sentence on the least serious version of the facts (*R. v Solomon* [1984] Crim.L.R. 433), the judge should give the offender the benefit of any doubt (see *R. v Stosiek* (1982) 4 Cr.App.R(S.) 205). Other than in a case of murder reduced to manslaughter (see *R. v Frankum* [1984] Crim.L.R. 434) it is inappropriate for the judge to take a "special verdict" (*R. v Larkin* [1943] K.B. 174).

At this stage, or immediately before sentence, the offender may ask for other admitted offences, not the subject of the indictment, or of committal from the magistrates' court, to be taken into consideration on sentence. As to the procedure, see 59 TICs.

Resolution of disputes; duty on defence

34–006 In *R. v Underwood* [2004] Crim.L.R. 1049 where CACD re-stated the principles, and the general guidance appropriate to this last situation, the court recognised three common scenarios. The prosecution may:

(1) accept and agree the offender's account of the disputed facts;
(2) reject the offender's version; or
(3) lack the evidence to dispute positively the offender's version.

CACD stated that where there is a difference between the prosecution evidence and the factual basis on which the offender intended to plead guilty, responsibility for taking the initiative and alerting the prosecutor to the disputed areas rests with the defence.

It is generally sensible to agree to a request for a hearing when asked for one by any advocate, and not to indicate any provisional view formed on the papers.

Unless a disputed fact is proved by the prosecution to the satisfaction of the judge, it ought not to count in passing sentence (*R. v Kerrigan* (1993) 14 Cr.App.R.(S.) 179). The judge will need to direct himself that the offender's account must be accepted unless it is proved to be untrue (*R. v Ahmed* (1984) 6 Cr.App.R.(S.) 391).

If the factual dispute is not clarified, the CACD will approach the sentence on the facts tendered by the offender (*R. v Brown* (1981) 3 Cr.App.R.(S.) 250; *R. v McFarlane* (1995) 16 Cr.App.R.(S.) 315).

Judge acting of his own motion

34–007 The judge is entitled, however, of his own motion, on a plea of guilty:

(1) to make known any concerns he may have about any matter revealed by the state of the evidence before him; and
2) to insist on holding a Newton hearing to determine disputed facts notwithstanding prior agreement between prosecution and defence as to the facts (*R. v Beswick* [1996] 2 Cr.App.R. 427).

Where appropriate, he may:

(a) decline to accept the plea, and in an appropriate case direct trial by a jury; or

(b) hear submissions, and then form his own view of the facts, in which case, if there is a substantial conflict, he is bound to accept the version given by the accused; or

(c) if he is not prepared to sentence on the accused's version, conduct his own hearing, and after considering evidence on both sides if tendered, come to his own decision on the facts.

Accused's version accepted

34–008 Where there is an agreed basis of plea it should be written down and signed by both advocates; where it is not signed by both advocates, the judge is entitled to ignore it; if the prosecution disputes the offender's version, the areas of dispute should be identified so as to focus the judge's attention on the precise facts in dispute (*R. v Underwood* (see 34–006, above)).

The signed agreement made available to the judge before the start of the prosecution opening and, if possible, before the judge is invited to approve the acceptance of any plea or pleas. Only on that basis can both prosecution and defence be confident of knowing how the case will be opened and only on that basis can the judge be confident of knowing the basis on which he is asked to sentence and whether it will be necessary to conduct a fact-finding inquiry (*R. v Smith* [2002] 1 Cr.App.R.(S.) 386).

The judge may not pass sentence on the basis that the offender's culpability is greater than that accepted by the Crown, unless he inquires into the matter and hears evidence (*R. v Newton* (1983) 77 Cr.App.R. 13; *R. v Oakley* [1997] Crim.L.R. 607).

Prosecution not in a position to gainsay accused's version

34–009 Where the prosecution have no evidence to dispute the offender's account then, particularly if the facts relied on by the offender arise from his own personal knowledge and depend on his own account of the facts, they should not normally agree that account unless it is supported by other material (*R. v Underwood* (see 34–006, above)).

Neither the prosecution, nor the judge, is bound to agree facts because the prosecution cannot gainsay the accused's version.

Accused's version rejected

34–010 If the prosecution reject the accused's version:

(1) the areas of dispute should be identified in writing and

(2) the document should focus the judge's attention on the precise fact or facts which are in dispute,

leaving the judge to decide whether or not to hold a Newton hearing.

Newton hearing

34–011 After submissions, the judge must decide how to proceed; he is not bound by any agreement as to the plea, and is entitled to insist that any evidence relevant to the facts in dispute be called. Whatever view may be formed by the Crown on any proposed basis of the plea is conditional on the judge agreeing to it (*R. v Underwood*, 34–006 above). The judge is entitled to expect counsel for the Crown to assist him in reaching the true facts by testing the evidence and the Crown is not bound by any agreement reached with the other side which is merely conditional until it has received the judge's approval.

A decision to hold a hearing does not give rise to a ground for the offender to change his plea.

Where necessary:

(1) relevant evidence should be called by the prosecution and defence, particularly where the issue arises from facts which are within the exclusive knowledge of the offender;
(2) the offender should be called, if willing, to give evidence; if he does not give evidence then, subject to any explanation offered, the judge may draw such inference as he sees fit.

The judge may reject the evidence called by the prosecution or by the offender or his witnesses, even if the prosecution has not called contradictory evidence; but his reasons should be explained in a judgment (*R. v Underwood*).

Where procedure inappropriate

34–012 There will be occasions when a Newton hearing will be inappropriate;

(1) some issues, particularly where the offender denies committing a specific criminal offence, will require a jury's verdict;
(2) the judge may not make findings of fact and pass sentence on a basis that is inconsistent with pleas to counts already approved by the court; particular care is needed in relation to a multi-count indictment involving one offender or an indictment involving a number of accused where there was a joint enterprise. The judge, while reflecting the individual basis of pleas, must bear in mind the seriousness of the joint enterprise in which all were involved;

(3) matters of mitigation are not normally dealt with by way of a Newton hearing but it is always open to the judge to allow an offender to give evidence as to matters of mitigation (*R. v Underwood*).

Also:

(a) where the sentence would be the same whatever version the judge adopts, there is no need to go through the procedure (*R. v Bent* (1986) 8 Cr.App.R.(S.) 19);
(b) where the offender's account is manifestly false or implausible, the judge is not obliged to go through the "Newton" procedure (*R. v Hawkins* (1985) 7 Cr.App.R.(S.) 351; *R. v Bilinski* (1988) 86 Cr.App.R.(S.) 146; *R. v Walton* (1987) 9 Cr.App.R.(S.) 107; *R. v Mudd* (1988) 10 Cr.App.R.(S.) 22; *R. v Palmer* (1993) Cr.App.R.(S.) 123; *cf. R. v Satchell* [1996] Crim.L.R.351);
(c) the procedure is not appropriate for determining whether an offender has committed offences other than those to which he has pleaded or has had taken into consideration (*R. v Huchison* (1972) 56 Cr.App.R. 307) or which were not included in the indictment (*R. v Eubank* [2001] Crim.L.R. 495);
(d) where the hearing involves the assessment of identification evidence, the judge must direct himself in accordance with the *Turnbull* guidelines (see 62 TURNBULL GUIDELINES).

Conduct of the hearing

34–013 In deciding the factual basis for sentence, the judge is not bound by the rules of admissibility applicable to a trial of the issue of guilt. In particular:

(1) in conducting a Newton hearing, he is entitled to take into account evidence which he has heard in the separate trials of co-accused (*R. v Smith* (1988) 87 Cr.App.R.393) but he should bear in mind that that evidence was not the subject of cross-examination by the accused who pleaded guilty, and the latter should be permitted to give evidence if he so desires (*R. v Winter* [1997] Crim.L.R.66); and
(2) he is not obliged to accept the version given by the accused, and indeed he may draw adverse inferences from his conduct (*R. v Ghandi* (1986) 8 Cr.App.R.(S.) 391).

In coming to his decision, he may have regard to the accused's previous convictions (*R. v Walton* (1987) 9 Cr.App.R.(S.) 107).

Special provisions apply to committals for sentence (see 20 COMMITTALS FOR SENTENCE).

Effect on sentence

34–014 If:

(1) the issues at the hearing are resolved entirely in the offender's favour, credit for his guilty plea should not reduced;
(2) the offender is disbelieved, having required prosecution witnesses to be called (see e.g. *R. v Stevens*, below), or if he shows no insight into the consequences of his offence and no genuine remorse, the discount may be reduced.

There may be exceptional circumstances in which the entitlement to credit for his plea may be entirely dissipated as a result of a hearting, and in such a case the judge should explain why (*R. v Underwood*, 34–006 above).

The judge is entitled to withold the full credit he might otherwise have given for a plea of guilty where the offender insists on a hearing and the victim of a sexual assault is compelled to give evidence (*R. v Stevens* (1986) 8 Cr.App.R.(S.) 297), but it is wrong for him to give the offender no credit at all for his plea (*R. v Hassall* [2000] 1 Cr.App.R.(S.) 67).

The judge needs to make it quite clear in his sentencing remarks what facts he is accepting (*R. v Gillespie* [1998] Crim.L.R.13).

35 FINANCIAL REPORTING ORDERS

Introduction

35–001 Where a person is convicted in the Crown Court of certain specified offences the judge may make a financial reporting order in respect of him, but only if he is satisfied that the risk of that person committing another such offence is sufficiently high to justify doing so. SOCA 2005, ss.76(1)–(3)

The specified offences are:

(1) an offence under any of the following provisions of TA 1968:
s.15 (obtaining property by deception),
s.15A (obtaining a money transfer by deception),
s.16 (obtaining a pecuniary advantage by deception),
s.20(2) (procuring execution of valuable security, etc.),

(2) an offence under either of the following provisions of TA 1978.
s.1 (obtaining services by deception),
s.2 (evasion of liability by deception),

(3) any offence specified PCA 2002, Sch.2 ("lifestyle offences"). SOCA 2005, ss.76(5)–(7)

The order comes into force when it is made, and has effect for the period specified in it, beginning with the date on which it is made, and in the case of a Crown Court order the period must not exceed:

(a) if the person is sentenced to imprisonment for life, 20 years,
(b) otherwise, 15 years.

Effect of order

35–002 A person in relation to whom an order is made must: SOCA 2005, ss.79(1)–(6)

(1) make a report, in respect of: SOCA 2005, ss.79(7), (8)
  (a) the period of a specified length beginning with the date on which the order comes into force; and
  (b) each subsequent period of that length beginning immediately after the end of the previous period;

(2) set out in each report, in the specified manner, such particulars of his financial affairs relating to the period in question as may be specified;

(3) include any specified documents with each report;

Financial Reporting Orders

(4) make each report within the specified number of days after the end of the period in question;
(5) make each report to the specified person.

Rules may provide for the maximum length of the periods which may be specified; "specified" means specified by the court in the order.

A person who without reasonable excuse includes false or misleading information in a report, or otherwise fails to comply with any requirement of this section, is guilty of an offence. SOCA 2005, s.79(10)

Variation and revocation of order

35–003 An application for variation or revocation of an order may be made by either the person in respect of whom it was made, or the specified person to whom reports are to be made under it. The application must be made to the court which made the order, but if the order was made on appeal, the application must be made to the court which originally convicted the person in respect of whom the order was made. If (in either case) that court was a magistrates' court, the application may be made to any magistrates' court acting in the same local justice area as that court. SOCA 2005, s.80

Verification and disclosure

35–004 SOCA 2005, s.81 provides for the specified person, i.e. the person to whom reports under a financial reporting order are to be made, to verify the accuracy of any report made.

36 FINES AND ENFORCEMENT

Introduction

36–001 Financial penalties may be said to be three in number, namely: a fine, a compensation order, and an order to pay the costs of the prosecution. Although fines and other financial penalties do not restrict the offender's liberty in quite the same way as a community or custodial sentence, they deprive the offender of money and therefore the ability to spend that money in other ways.

The general power

36–002 Where a person is convicted on indictment of any offence other than an offence: CJA 2003, s.163

(1) for which the sentence is fixed by law; or
(2) falls to be imposed under PCC(S)A 2000, ss.109 where still appropriate, 110(2) or 111(2); or
(3) falls to be imposed under any of CJA 2003, ss.225–228,

the judge, if not precluded from sentencing an offender by his exercise of some other power, may impose a fine:

(a) instead of, or
(b) in addition to,

dealing with him in any other way in which he has power to deal with him, subject to any enactment requiring the offender to be dealt with in a particular way.

On appeal from a magistrates' court, the powers of the Crown Court are those of the magistrates.

A person guilty of attempting to commit an offence is liable on conviction on indictment to any penalty to which he would have been liable on conviction for the full offence. CAA 1981, s.4(1)(b)

Duty to order payment of surcharge

36–003 Once DVA 2004, s.14 comes into force, a judge dealing with an offender for one or more offences must also, except as below, order him to pay a surcharge in such amount as is prescribed by the Home Secretary. The exceptions are where the judge dealing with an offender considers: CJA 2003, s.163A; DVA 2004, s.14

(1) that it would be appropriate to make a compensation order, but

(2) that the offender has insufficient means to pay both the surcharge and appropriate compensation,

in which case he must reduce the surcharge accordingly (if necessary to nil).

For the purposes of this provision the judge does not "deal with" a person if he:

(a) discharges him absolutely, or
(b) makes an order under MHA 1983 in respect of him.

An order may provide for the amount to depend on:

(i) the offence or offences committed,
(ii) how the offender is otherwise dealt with (including, where the offender is fined, the amount of the fine),
(iii) the age of the offender.

This is not to be read as limiting CJA 2003, s.330(3) (power to make different provision for different purposes, etc.).

The standard scale

36–004 Where reference is made to the "standard scale" of fines, the standard scale is as follows: CJA 1982, s.37; CJA 1991, s.17(1)

Level on the scale	*Amount of fine*
1	£200
2	£500
3	£1,000
4	£2,500
5	£5,000

Proper approach to financial penalty

36–005 The amount of any fine fixed must be such as, in the judge's opinion, reflects the seriousness of the offence, but in fixing the amount, he must: CJA 2003 ss.164(3), (4)

(1) in the case of an individual offender, inquire into his financial circumstances; and
(2) whether the offender is an individual or other person, take into account the circumstances of the case including, amongst other things, the financial circumstances of the offender, so far as they are known, or appear to him,

and (2) above applies whether it has the effect of increasing or reducing the amount.

It is wrong to impose a fine upon an offender of substantial means for an offence for which one of lesser means would go to prison (*R. v Lewis* [1965] Crim.L.R. 121); conversely it is wrong to imprison an offender because he is unable to pay a substantial fine (*R. v Reeves* (1972) 56 Cr.App.R. 366);

In applying subs.(3), the judge must not reduce the amount of a fine on account of any surcharge he orders (once that provision has come into effect) the offender to pay under CJA 2003, s.161A, except to the extent that he has insufficient means to pay both. CJA 2003, s.164(4A); DVA 2004, s.14

Ability to pay means

36–006 The overriding principle in relation to the imposition of a fine is that the fine imposed should be within the offender's ability to pay.

It should be remembered that:

(1) it is wrong to scale up a fine in the case of an unusually affluent offender (*R. v Fairbairn* (1980) 2 Cr.App.R.(S.) 315);
(2) it may be necessary to scale down an otherwise appropriate fine if the sum is more than the offender can be fairly required to pay within a reasonable time; and
(3) despite a number of pronouncements to the contrary, CACD in *R. v Olliver* (1989) 11 Cr.App.R.(S.) 10, said that there was no reason in principle why an order to pay a fine by monthly instalments should not extend for two or even three years.

Clearly, unless the circumstances warrant it, an offender should not be fined more heavily merely because he has elected trial by jury; this is a matter which can be dealt with by an order for costs (*R. v Jamieson* (1974) 60 Cr.App.R. 318).

A fine should not, of course, be imposed on the basis that someone other than the offender is going to pay it on his behalf (*R. v Baxter* [1974] Crim. L.R. 611) let alone on the basis that the public should be reimbursed for any possible claim made on the Criminal Injuries Compensation Board (*R. v Roberts* (1980) 2 Cr.App.R. (S.) 121).

Fines imposed on large **corporations** for breach of health and safety at work legislation ought to be significant if they are to penalised financially (*R. v P & O Ferries (Irish Sea)* (unreported)).

Financial circumstances order

36–007 Where an individual offender is convicted of an offence, the judge may, before sentencing him, make a financial CJA 2003, s.162

circumstances order, requiring him to give to the court, within a specified period, such statement of his financial circumstances as the judge may require. Failure to comply is an offence.

Parents and guardians

36–008 For the enforcement of fines in respect of juvenile offenders against parents and guardians, see 19 CHILDREN AND YOUNG PERSONS.

Time to pay: instalments

36–009 Where the judge imposes a fine he may make an order: PCC(S)A 2000, s.139(1)

(1) allowing time for the payment of the amount of the fine;
(2) directing payment of that amount by instalments of such amounts and on such dates as may be specified in the order,

and he must fix a term of imprisonment in default of payment, but no person may on the occasion when a fine is imposed on him by the Crown Court be committed to prison or detention unless:

(a) in the case of an offence punishable with imprisonment, he appears to the court to have sufficient means to pay forthwith;
(b) it appears to the judge that he is unlikely to remain long enough at a place of abode in the UK to enable the payment of the fine to be enforced by other methods; or
(c) on the occasion when the fine is imposed, the judge sentences him to an immediate prison sentence, custody for life, or detention in a young offender institution for that or another offence, or so sentences him for an offence in addition to forfeiting his recognisance, or he is already serving a sentence of custody for life or a term of: imprisonment or detention.

Approach to order

36–010 When imposing a fine payable by instalments, with imprisonment in default, the proper course is for the judge to:

(1) impose the fine;
(2) fix an appropriate term in default of the *whole* amount; and
(3) make such an instalment order as he thinks fit (*R. v Cooper* (1982) 4 Cr.App.R.(S.) 55; *R. v Power* (1986) 8 Cr.App.R.(S.) 8).

Maximum terms in default

36–011 The maximum periods of imprisonment or detention under s.108, are: PCC(S)A 2000, s.139(4)

An amount not exceeding £200	7 days
An amount exceeding £200 but not exceeding £500	14 days
An amount exceeding £500 but not exceeding £1,000	28 days
An amount exceeding £1,000 but not exceeding £2,500	45 days
An amount exceeding £2,500 but not exceeding £5,000	3 months
An amount exceeding £5,000 but not exceeding £10,000	6 months
An amount exceeding £10,000 but not exceeding £20,000	12 months
An amount exceeding £20,000 but not exceeding £50,000	18 months
An amount exceeding £50,000 but not exceeding £100,000	2 years
An amount exceeding £100,000 but not exceeding £250,000	3 years
An amount exceeding £250,000 but not exceeding £1 million	5 years
An amount exceeding £1 million	10 years

Custodial sentence and default terms

36–012 Where a person liable for the payment of a fine is sentenced to, or is serving, or is otherwise liable to, serve a term of imprisonment, the judge may order that any default term shall not begin to run until after the end of the first-mentioned term, nor is this power restricted by any enactment authorising the Crown Court to deal with an offender in any way the magistrates might have dealt with him or could deal with him. PCC(S)A 2000, s.139(5), (7); CJCSA 2000, Sch.7, Para.195

Where both the maximum sentence of imprisonment and a fine have been imposed for an offence, a further sentence of imprisonment may be imposed for default in payment of the fine (*R. v Carver* (1955) 39 Cr.App.R. 27);

Improper combinations

36–013 A fine may be imposed in addition to any other penalty except that a fine may not be imposed for the same offence as that on which the court makes an an order for conditional or absolute discharge (see 2 ABSOLUTE AND CONDITIONAL DISCHARGE).

Coupling a fine with a custodial sentence

36–014 Insofar as combining an immediate custodial sentence with a fine is concerned, while this may be permissible:

(1) it must be clear that the offender has the resources to arrange for payment even though he is to be in custody (*R. v Fairbairn* (1980) 2 Cr.App.R.(S.) 315);
(2) if this is not clear, then a fine ought not to be added (*R. v Maund* (1980) 2 Cr.App.R.(S.) 289); and
(3) it is appropriate if the general circumstances of the case show that the offender will continue to have access to the proceeds of his crime (*R. v Benmore* (1983) 5 Cr.App.R.(S.) 468).

Coupling a fine with an order for costs

36–015 The judge may both impose a fine and order the offender to pay the costs of the prosecution in an appropriate case. The principles governing such an order were reviewed in *R. v Northallerton MC Ex p. Dove* [2000] 1 Cr.App.R.(S.) 136.

(1) The judge must have regard to the means of the offender, and it is quite wrong to impose a very small fine and a very heavy order for costs—the two must go in step (*R. v Whalley* (1972) 56 Cr.App.R. 304; see *R. v Firmston* (1984) 6 Cr.App.R.(S.) 189, *R. v Nottingham JJ Ex p. Fohmann* (1987) 84 Cr.App.R. 316, *R. v Jones* (1988) 10 Cr.App.R.(S.) 95, *cf. R. v Boyle* (1995) 16 Cr.App.R.(S.) 927).
(2) While there is no requirement that the costs should stand in any arithmetical relationship to the fine, the costs should not in the ordinary way be grossly disproportionate to the fine.

Personal search of offender

36–016 A judge of the Crown Court may, where: PCC(S)A 2000, s.142; DVA 2004, s.58(1), Sch.10, para.53

(1) any person has been fined, or has had a recognisance forfeited;
(2) any person is made the subject of an order for costs, or compensation;
(3) a parent or guardian is ordered to pay a fine, costs or compensation;
(4) the Crown Court orders any person to pay a surcharge under CJA 2003, s.151A (see 37–003 above); or
(5) an appellant from the magistrates' court is liable to pay any sum by virtue of an order made by the Crown Court or the magistrates' court,

order that person, if before him, to be searched, and any money found on him may be applied towards the payment of any sum owing, the balance being returned.

Enforcement by magistrates' court

36–017 The enforcement of Crown Court fines is a matter for the appropriate magistrates' court. PCC(S)A 2000, s.140

37 FOOTBALL BANNING ORDERS

Introduction

37–001 Under the Football Spectators Act 1989, as amended by the Football (Disorder) Act 2000, a judge of the Crown Court may, in dealing with an offender convicted of certain types of offences, make a banning order, by which the offender is required to report himself to a designated police station at a time when a specified football match is taking place. As to the compatibility of such an order with ECHR, Art.7 see *Gough v Derbyshire Chief Constable*, *The Times*, July 19, 2001.

Where an offender is:

FSA 1989, ss.14, 14A; F(D)A 2000, s.2; ASBA 2003, s.86(4)

(1) convicted before the Crown Court of a "relevant" offence (defined in Sch.1); or
(2) committed to the Crown Court for sentence for such an offence,

the judge may, in addition to:

(a) imposing a sentence in respect of the relevant offence, or
(b) discharging him conditionally (in spite of the provisions of PCCA 2000, ss.12 and 14),

make a banning order in relation to him, and *must* make such an order if satisfied that there are reasonable grounds to believe that making a banning order would help to prevent violence or disorder (both of which expressions are defined in *ibid.*, s.14C) at or in connection with any regulated football matches.

For the purpose of deciding whether to make an order the judge may consider evidence led by the prosecution and the defence, and it is immaterial whether such evidence would have been admissible in the proceedings in which the offender was convicted.

If he is not so satisfied he must state that fact in open court, and give his reasons.

Declaration of relevance

37–002 Before making an order, the court must make a "declaration of relevance", by determining in relation to any offence under the provisions of Sch.1, whether it is "relevant" in the sense that it is related to football matches (s.14(9)). An offence committed on a train while returning from a football match is not "relevant" to the match (*R. v O'Keefe* [2004] 1 Cr.App.R.(S.) 67).

Ordinarily the judge is not entitled to make such a declaration unless it is shown that the Crown gave notice to the offender at least five days before the first day of the trial that it proposed to relate the offence to football matches, to a particular football match or to particular football matches. However, in any particular case, he may make a declaration: FSA 1989, s.23

(1) notwithstanding the fact that notice was not given as required; provided
(2) the accused consents to waive that notice; or
(3) the judge is satisfied that the interests of justice do not require "more notice" to be given.

Appeal lies to CACD against the making of a declaration of relevance, and if the declaration is reversed, the banning order will be quashed. FSA 1989, s.23(4)

Surrender of passport

37–003 A banning order must, unless it appears to the judge that there are exceptional circumstances, impose a requirement as to the surrender in accordance with the Act, in connection with regulated football matches outside the United Kingdom, of the offender's passport. FSA 1989, s.14A(3)(4); F(D)A 2000, s.2

If it appears to the judge that there are exceptional circumstances, he must state them in open court.

Effect of banning order

37–004 The judge must, on making an order, explain the effect of it in ordinary language to the offender, the effect being that: FSA 1989, s.14E; F(D)A 2000, s.2

(1) he report initially to the police station specified in the order within five days, beginning on the day the order is made (special rules apply where he is in custody, see *ibid.* ss.14E (5), (6), amended by CJA 2003, s.304, Sch.32, Pt 1, para.57);
(2) he surrender his passport in an appropriate case; and
(3) subject to any exemption, he report on the occasion of any "regulated" football matches when required to do so, to the police station so specified at the time, or between the times, specified in the notice by which the requirement is imposed.

Failure, without reasonable excuse, to report or to comply with conditions is a summary offence punishable with a fine not exceeding level 5 on the standard scale, or 51 weeks FSA 1989, ss.14G, 21C; F(D)A 2000, s.2; CJA 2003, s.304, Sch.32, para.57

imprisonment or both. The judge may, if he thinks fit, impose additional requirements.

Period of ban

37–005 A banning order has effect for a period beginning with the day it is made, being neither more than the maximum nor less than the minimum. FSA 1989, s.14F; F(D)A 2000, s.2

Where:

(1) it is made under s.14A in addition to a sentence of imprisonment taking immediate effect, the maximum is ten years and the minimum six years;
(2) in any other case where it is made under s.14A, the maximum period is five years and the minimum three; and
(3) it is made on complaint to the magistrates' court under s.14B, the maximum is three years and the minimum two years.

Administrative provisions

37–006 The order will specify the police station at which the offender is to report initially and the Crown Court officer will: FSA 1989, s.18(1)(2)

(1) give a copy of the order to the offender and, as soon as reasonably practicable, send a copy to the enforcing authority and the officer responsible for the police station at which the offender is to report initially; and
(2) if the offender is sentenced to or is serving a custodial sentence, send a copy to the governor of the prison or other person to whose custody he is committed.

Application to terminate

37–007 Where the order has had effect for at least two-thirds of the period determined under s.14F, the offender may apply to the court by which it was made to terminate it. FSA 1989, s.14H; F(D)A 2000, s.2

On such an application the judge may:

(1) having regard to:
    (a) the offender's character,
    (b) his conduct since the order was made,
    (c) the nature of the offence which led to it, and
    (d) any other circumstances,

either terminate the order from a specified date or refuse the application; and

(2) order the offender to pay all or any part of the costs of the application.

Where an application is refused, no further application in respect of the order, may be made within a period of six months beginning with the date of the refusal.

38 FORFEITURE, RESTITUTION AND AWARDS

1. Forfeiture (deprivation) order

38–001 The general power of forfeiture or deprivation, which applies to all criminal offences, overlaps the narrower specific powers provided by various statutes, to which reference should be made, if appropriate.

The general power

38–002 Subject to certain restrictions (see below) a general power is given to deprive an offender of his rights in property where he is convicted of an offence, and: PCC(S)A 2000, s.143

(1) the judge is satisfied that any property which:
  (a) has been lawfully seized from him; or
  (b) was in his possession, or under his control at the time when he was apprehended for the offence, or when the summons in respect of it was issued,
    (i) has been used for the purpose of committing, or facilitating the commission of, any offence; or
    (ii) was intended by him for that purpose; or

(2) the offence (or an offence which the court has taken into consideration) consists of unlawful possession of property which:
  (a) has been lawfully seized from him; or
  (b) was in his possession, or under his control at the time when he was apprehended for the offence, or when the summons in respect of it was issued.

"Facilitating the commission of an offence" includes, for this purpose, the taking of any steps after it has been committed, for the purpose of disposing of any property to which it relates or of avoiding apprehension or detection. PCC(S)A 2000, s.143(8)

Such an order may be made whether or not the judge also deals with the offender in any other way in respect of the offence of which he has been convicted, and without regard to any restrictions on forfeiture in any enactment contained in an Act passed before July 29, 1988. PCC(S)A 2000, s.143(4)

Order only in straightforward cases

38–003 An order should be made only in the most straightforward of cases, and only upon the offender's admission, or on a specific finding by the court (*R. v Troth* [1980] R.T.R. 389). There may be cases where the order will have a disproportionately severe effect on an offender and should not be made (*R. v Tavernor* [1976] R.T.R. 242).

Where a number of offenders are equally guilty, it is wrong to make an order in relation to one accused only (*R. v Ottey* (1984) 6 Cr.App.R.(S.) 163) but it may be fair and proper to reflect the differing levels of participation (*R. v Burgess* [2001] 2 Cr.App.R.(S.) 2).

It is desirable that the judge, on making such an order, should make an express finding on the basis on which it is made (*R. v Ranasinghe* [1999] 2 Cr.App.R.(S.) 366).

Serious road traffic offences

38–004 Where a person commits an offence: PCC(S)A 2000, s.143(6), (7), (7A); PRA 2002, s.56(5), (6)

(1) under RTA 1988 which is punishable with imprisonment; or
(2) of manslaughter; or
(3) under OPA 1861, s.35 (furious or wanton driving),

and the offence consists of:

(a) driving, attempting to drive or being in charge of a vehicle; or
(b) failing to comply with a requirement under RTA 1988, s.7 (failure to provide specimen for analysis or for a laboratory test) or s.7A (failing to allow a specimen to be subjected to a laboratory test) in the course of an investigation into whether the offender had committed an offence while driving, attempting to drive or in charge of a vehicle; or
(c) failing, as the driver of a vehicle, to comply with RTA 1988, s.170(2), (3) (duty to stop and give information or to report accident).

the vehicle is said to be regarded for the purposes of s.143(1), above, and s.144(1)(b), below, as used for the purpose of committing the offence, and for committing any offence of aiding, abetting, counselling or procuring the commission of the offence.

As to the power of a constable to seize and dispose of vehicles driven without a licence or insurance, see RTA 1988, ss.165A, 165B inserted by SOCA 2005, s.152.

Effect of order

38–005 The effect of an order is that, apart from depriving the offender of his rights, if any, in the property, it enables the PCC(S)A 2000, ss.143(4), 144 property to be taken into the custody of the police, if not already in their possession, and the Police (Property) Act 1897, s.69 then applies, with certain modifications, leaving any third party or other claimant to make a claim within the six months under the Act.

Restrictions on use of section 143

38–006 As forfeited property has some financial value, the court must, in considering whether to make an order, have regard to: PCC(S)A 2000, s.143(5)

(1) the value of the property; and
(2) the likely financial and other effects on the offender (taken together with any other order the court contemplates making).

Note also that:

(a) the power is applicable to all offences, including those to which a narrower specific statutory power applies (e.g. drugs and firearms, as to which see below) (*R. v O'Farrell* (1988) 10 Cr.App.R.(S.) 74);
(b) the power does not extend to depriving an offender of his rights in real property (*R. v Khan* [1982] 3 All E.R. 969);
(c) the order is confined to the use, etc. of the property by the offender, not, e.g. by a person to whom drugs are supplied (*R. v Slater* (1986) 150 J.P.N. 734);
(d) the order is punitive in nature, and must be looked on as part of the sentence. The "totality principle" is therefore appropriate and it may be necessary to adjust other parts of the sentence (*R. v Priestley* [1996] Crim.L.R. 356).

Procedure and evidence

38–007 An order may be made only:

(1) where the Crown prove that the requirements of the section are fulfilled (*R. v Kingston-upon-Hull JJ. Ex p. Hartung* [1981] R.T.R. 262; *R. v Pemberton* (1982) 4 Cr.App.R.(S.) 328); or
(2) on an admission by the accused or a precise finding of fact by the judge (*R. v Troth* [1980] R.T.R. 389, *R. v Ball* [2003] Crim.L.R. 122);
(3) in the most straightforward cases, where the judge has given a warning of his intention, and a prior opportunity

is given for representations to be made (*R. v Powell* [1985] Crim.L.R. 330, *R. v Ball*, above); and

(4) in the case of a number of joint offenders, against all rather than against one only (*R. v Ottey* (1984) 6 Cr.App.R.(S.) 163).

Application for benefit of victim

38–008 Where the judge makes an order in a case where: PCC(S)A 2000, s.145

(1) the offender has been convicted of an offence which has resulted in a person suffering personal injury, loss or damage; or
(2) any such offence is taken into consideration on sentence; and
(3) but for the inadequacy of the offender's means he would have made a compensation order under which he would have been required to pay not less than a specified amount,

he may also order that any proceeds which arise from the disposal of the property and which do not exceed a sum he specifies, shall be paid to that person.

An order of this kind is not effective:

(a) before the end of the period specified in s.144(1)(a);
(b) if a successful application under the Police (Property) Act 1897, s.1(1) has been made.

Firearms offences

38–009 An order as to the forfeiture or disposal of a firearm or ammunition found in the possession of an offender may be made, where the offender: FA 1968, s.52(1)

(1) is convicted of an offence under the Firearms Act 1968 (other than one under s.23(3) or an offence relating specifically to air weapons); or
(2) is convicted of an offence for which he is sentenced to imprisonment or detention in a young offender institution; or
(3) has been ordered to enter into a recognisance to keep the peace and/or be of good behaviour, a condition of which was that he should not carry a firearm; or
(4) is subject to a probation order containing a requirement that he shall not possess, use or carry a firearm.

Where a firearm is forfeited, it may be seized and detained by a constable. FA 1968, s.52(3)

Drugs offences

38–010 Where a person is convicted of an offence:

MDA 1971, s.27(1), (2); CJA1988, s.70; PCA 2002, s.456, Sch.11, para.5

(1) under MDA 1971; or
(2) an offence specified in PCA 2002, Sch.2, para.1 (drug trafficking offences); or
(3) so far as it relates to that paragraph, Sch.2, para.10,

and anything is shown to the satisfaction of the court to relate to the offence, the judge may order it to be forfeited and either destroyed or dealt with in such other manner as he may order. If a person claiming to be the owner, or to be otherwise interested in the property, applies to be heard, an order must not be made unless an opportunity is given to him to be heard.

A number of broad principles were laid down in the cases of *R. v Cuthbertson* (1980) 144 J.P. 366; *R. v Ribeyre* (1982) 4 Cr.App. R.(S.) 165; *R. v Marland & Jones* (1986) 82 Cr.App.R. 134; *R. v Churcher* (1986) 8 Cr.App.R.(S.) 94; *R. v Cox* (1986) 8 Cr.App. R.(S.) 384; *R. v Llewellyn* (1985) 7 Cr.App.R.(S.) 225, thus:

(a) the order is concerned with forfeiture and not with restitution, compensation or the redress of unlawful enrichment;
(b) the order is apt to deal only with things which are tangible in the sense that physical possession may be taken of them by order of the court; "anything" includes money (*R. v Beard* [1974] 1 W.L.R. 1549);
(c) it is necessary to connect the specific thing forfeited with a particular offence to which it relates (and see *R. v Morgan* [1977] Crim.L.R. 488); working capital for future deals may be forfeited under the general power in PCC(S)A 2000, s.143 (*R. v O'Farrell* (1988) 10 Cr.App.R. (S.) 74); and
(d) the offender ought to be permitted to adduce any material tending to show that the thing in question is not related to the offence.

Public Order Act 1986

38–011 A court by which a person is convicted of an offence under ss.19, 21, 23, 29B, 29C, 29E or 29F of the Act in relation to racial or religious hatred, or . . . s.18 relating to the display of racially offensive written material, must order to be forfeited any written material or recording (as defined in s.29) produced and shown to be written material or a recording to which the offence relates.

POrA 1986, ss.25, 33; RHA 2006, Sch.

The order does not take effect until the ordinary time for appeal has expired, or, if an appeal is initiated, until it is finally determined or abandoned.

Terrorism Act 2000

38–012 Where a person is convicted of an offence under the Terrorism Act 2000, the judge may order the forfeiture under: Terr A 2000, s.23

(1) s.15(1) or (2) or 16, of any money or other property which:
   (a) at the time of the offence he had in his possession or under his control; and
   (b) at that time, he intended should be used, or has reasonable cause to suspect might be used, for the purposes of terrorism;
(2) s.15(3), of any money or other property which:
   (a) at the time of the offence he had in his possession or under his control; and
   (b) at that time, he intended should be used, or has reasonable cause to suspect might be used, for the purposes of terrorism;
(3) s.17, of any money or other property:
   (a) to which the arrangement in question related; and
   (b) which at that time, he intended should be used, or has reasonable cause to suspect might be used, for the purposes of terrorism;
(4) s.18, of the money or other property to which the arrangement in question related; and
(5) ss.15–18, of any money or other property which is wholly or partly, and directly or indirectly, received by any person as a payment or reward in connection with the commission of the offence.

Where a person other than the convicted person claims to be the owner of, or otherwise interested in, anything which can be forfeited under s.23, he must be given an opportunity to be heard before the order is made.

Provisions are made in s.29 for an appeal against the order.

Game Act 1831

38–013 CJPOA 1994, Sch.9, para.4 contains provisions for forfeiting vehicles in the possession or under the control of poachers.

2. Restitution order

General

38–014 A restitution order should be made only where the title to property is abundantly clear; in any other case an applicant should be left to seek his remedies under the Police

(Property) Act 1897, or in the civil courts (*R. v Ferguson* (1970) 54 Cr.App.R. 410).

An order may, however, be made where: PCC(S)A 2000, s.148(1), (2), (10), (11)

(1) goods have been stolen and a person is convicted with reference to the theft (whether or not stealing is the gist of the offence); or
(2) the court takes such an offence into consideration on determining sentence.

The words "stolen" and "theft" refer also to offences of obtaining property by deception, blackmail, and handling property obtained by deception and blackmail.

"Goods" includes, unless the context otherwise requires, all kinds of property within the meaning of TA 1968 except land, and includes things severed from the land by stealing.

An order may be made in respect of money owed by the Crown.

Nature of order

38–015 Whether or not the passing of sentence is deferred in other respects, the judge may make an order: PCC(S)A 2000, ss.148(2), 149(2)

(1) ordering any person having possession of the goods to restore them to a person entitled to recover them from him;
(2) on the application of a person entitled to recover from the offender any other goods, directly or indirectly representing those in (1) above, as being the proceeds of any disposal or realisation of the whole or part, or of goods representing them, that those other goods be delivered or transferred to the applicant; and
(3) ordering that a sum not exceeding the value of the goods in (1) above be paid out of any money of the offender, taken out of his possession on apprehension, to any person who, if the goods were in the possession of the offender, would be entitled to recover them from him.

Orders under (2) and (3) above may be combined provided the person in whose favour the orders are made does thereby recover more than the value of the goods.

Where an order is made under (1) above, and it appears that the offender has sold the goods to another who acted in good faith, or has borrowed money from that other on their security, the court may order to be paid to that person, out of the money of the offender taken from his possession on apprehension, a sum not exceeding the price paid or the amount owed. No application is necessary. PCC(S)A 2000, s.148(4)

Note that in relation to (3) above:

(a) money found in the offender's possession after his arrest may be seized (*R. v Ferguson* (above)); but
(b) not money found on him before his arrest (*R. v Hinde* (1977) 64 Cr.App.R. 213).

It is not necessary to show that the money was the proceeds of the crime, only that it belonged to the offender (*R. v Lewis* [1975] Crim.L.R. 353). The magistrates have no power to make a restitution order when committing an offender to the Crown Court for sentence (*R. v Blackpool JJ. Ex p. Charlson* [1972] 1 W.L.R. 1456).

Procedure

38–016 No order should be made unless, in the judge's opinion, the relevant facts appear from: PCC(S)A 2000, s.148(5), (6); CJA 2003, s.41, Sch.3, para.74(5)

(1) evidence given at the trial, or the "available documents"; together with
(2) any admissions made by or on behalf of any person, in connection with the proposed exercise of the court's powers.

The "available documents" include any written statements or admissions which were made for use, and would have been admissible, as evidence at the trial, and such documents as were served on the offender in pursuance of regulations made under CDA 1998, Sch.3, para.1 (sending for trial).

Evidence given after sentence is not "evidence given at the trial" (*R. v Church* (1971) 55 Cr.App.R. 65).

A representation order ought to be made where complex matters of restitution fall to be decided.

3. Confiscation orders

38–017 These are governed by the provisions of PCA 2002, see 24 CONFISCATION ORDERS.

4. Forfeiture of seized cash

38–018 As to forfeiture of seized cash, see above 24 CONFISCATION ORDERS at 24–065.

5. Sheriff's Awards; Crown Court Commendations

38–019 A judge of the Crown Court may, where a person appears to have been active in or towards the apprehension of a person later charged with an *indictable* offence, order the sheriff of the county in which the offence was committed, to pay a reward of such sums as seem to him to be just and reasonable.

CLA 1826, s.28; CLA 1967, s.10; CA 1971, s.56(1), Sch.8, SOCA 2005, s.111, Sch.7, Pt 3, para.39

This is an important power and the Senior Master has recently commented as follows:

(1) there are no fetters on this power; any suggestions that there is no money in the budget etc, ought to be discounted; the 1826 Act does not allow for such intervention by the executive;
(2) an award is not intended to be compensatory but to be sufficient to reflect the public's appreciation of the recipient's bravery;
(3) many of the awards made are, in the light of modern day standards, extremely mean; it is suggested that a sum of £350 might be the bottom line save for small children, and that an award of £500 would not be over-generous;
(4) once an award is made, a cheque is drawn by the Crown Court officer and sent to the High Sheriff for presentation;

The Crown Court also issues from time to time a certificate of commendation, where the judge identifies a person who has merited commendation for conduct not coming within CLA 1826. Such certificates are intended to supplement the existing system.

39 FORMALITIES AND OATHS

39–001 As to the use of the Welsh language in courts in Wales, see *Practice Direction (Criminal; Consolidated)* [2002] 3 All E.R. 904, paras 22, 23.

1. Arraignment

"A . . . . . B . . . . . you stand indicted for that you, on the . . . . day of . . . . (e.g. stole) . . . . . How say you A . . . . B . . . . . are you guilty or not guilty?"

2. Challenge to jurors

"A . . . . . B . . . . . , the names that you are about to hear called are the names of the jurors who will try you. If, therefore, you wish to object to them, or to any of them, you must do so as they come to the Book to be sworn and before they are sworn, and your objection shall be heard."

3. Jurors' oath or affirmation

(a) On trial

The oath to be taken by jurors is:

(i) "I swear by Almighty God that I will faithfully try the defendant(s), and give a true verdict according to the evidence."

Any person who objects to being sworn will be permitted to make his solemn affirmation instead. The words of the affirmation are:

(ii) "I do solemnly, sincerely and truly declare that I will faithfully try the defendant(s), and give a true verdict according to the evidence."

(b) Defendant standing mute

"I swear by Almighty God (or I solemnly, sincerely and truly declare and affirm) that I will well and truly try whether A . . . . B . . . . . , the defendant, who stands charged with . . . . . is mute of malice (or will not answer directly to the indictment wilfully and of malice), or by the Visitation of God, and a true verdict give according to the evidence."

4. Charge to the jury

"Members of the Jury, the defendant A . . . . . B . . . . . stands indicted for that he, on the . . . . day of . . . . (e.g. stole) . . . .

To this indictment he has pleaded not guilty, and it is your charge to say, having heard the evidence, whether he be guilty or not guilty."

5. Witness' oath or affirmation

"I swear by Almighty God (or I solemnly, sincerely and truly declare and affirm) that the evidence I shall give shall be the truth, the whole truth, and nothing but the truth."

As to questioning a witness who desires to affirm, see *R. v Mehrban* [2002] 1 Cr.App.R. 40.

6. Witness under 18

"I promise before Almighty God to tell the truth, the whole truth, and nothing but the truth."

7. Interpreter's oath or affirmation

"I swear by Almighty God (or I solemnly, sincerely and truly declare and affirm) that I will well and faithfully interpret, and true explanation make, of all such matters and things as shall be required of me, according to the best of my skill and understanding."

(For the form of oath in Welsh, see *Welsh Courts (Oaths & Interpreters) Rules 1943* S R & O, 1943 No. 683, as amended by SI 1959/1507, SI 1972/97). PD 2004, IV.42.4

8. Jury retiring: bailiff's oath

"I shall keep this jury together in some private and convenient place; I shall suffer none to speak to them, neither shall I speak to them myself, touching the trial held here this day, without leave of the court, unless it be to ask them if they are agreed upon their verdict."

Note: CJPOA 1994, s.43, amending JA 1974, s.13, allows the jury, if the judge thinks fit and so permits, to separate at any time, whether before or after they have been directed to consider their verdict.

9. Voir dire

"I swear by Almighty God (or I solemnly, sincerely and truly declare and affirm) that I will true answer make to all such questions as may be asked of me."

10. Intermediary declaration

(See 57 SPECIAL MEASURES DIRECTIONS.)

"I solemnly, sincerely and truly declare that I will well and faithfully communicate questions and answers and make true explanation of all matters and things as shall be required of me according to the best of my skill and understanding."

11. Person accompanying witness into remote TV room

"I swear by almighty God to adhere to the instructions given by the learned judge and to observe them fully."

For procedure see 57 SPECIAL MEASURES DIRECTIONS, 57–013.

40 IMPRISONMENT

Quick guide:

1. General

Introduction

40–001 A sentence of imprisonment may be imposed only where:

(1) **the offender** is (except under CJA 2003, s.225, below, where the minimum age is 18) aged 21 or over at the date of conviction; and
(2) **the offence** for which the term is to be imposed:
(a) carries imprisonment, and
(b) "qualifies" for a custodial sentence.

Where a person is convicted of an offence punishable with a custodial sentence, other than one fixed by law, or falling to be CJA 2003, s.152

imposed under PCC(S)A 2000, ss.109(2), 110(2) or 111(2), or any of CJA 2003, ss.225–228, a sentence of imprisonment may not be imposed on the offender unless the judge is of the opinion that the offence, or the combination of the offence, and one or more offences "associated" with it, is "so serious" that neither a fine alone nor a community sentence can be justified for it.

Nevertheless, nothing prevents the judge from passing a custodial sentence on an offender who fails to:

(a) express his willingness to comply with a requirement which it is proposed to include in a community order, and which requires an expression of such willingness; or
(b) comply with an order under CJA 2003, s.161(2) (pre-sentence drug testing), when that provision comes into force.

As to offenders under 21, see 31 DETENTION OF YOUNG OFFENDERS.

As to the need for a pre-sentence or medical report, and for legal representation, see 29 DEALING WITH AN OFFENDER.

2. Nature of term

Date of commission of offence

40–002 The nature of a sentence of imprisonment will depend crucially on whether the offence for which it is to be imposed was **committed before, or on or after, April 4, 2005;** in relation to life sentences (see 45 LIFE SENTENCES) and minimum sentences for firearms offences other dates may be crucial.

Categories of sentence

40–003 A sentence if imprisonment may be:

- a normal determinate sentence;
- a sentence fixed by law;
- a required minimum sentence under PCC(S)A 2000, ss.110(2) or 111(2), or under FA 1968, s.15A: or
- a "protective" sentence (see 40–004 below).

Where the sentence of imprisonment is for a period of less than 12 months and the offence for which is imposed was **committed on or** after April 4, 2005, it may be accompanied by an "intermittent-custody order" under CJA 2003, ss.183–188 (see 40–026, below).

Once the provisions of CJA 2003, ss.181, 182 come into force (probably autumn 2007), a sentence of less than 12 months will have to be accompanied by a "custody plus order" (see 40–020 below).

As to the effect of the different sentences of imprisonment, (see 40–020 below).

A number of general topics in relation to sentence of imprisonment, such as aggravating and mitigating factors, "discounts", and the requirement of reports before sentence, being common to other sentencing options, are dealt with in 29 DEALING WITH AN OFFENDER.

"Protective" sentences; dangerous offenders

40–004 What may be termed "protective" sentences fall to be imposed on dangerous offenders. The nature of the particular sentence to be imposed will depend upon whether the offence for it is to be imposed was **committed before, or on or after April 4, 2005**.

In relation to offences **committed**:

(1) **before April 4, 2005**, such sentences are:
  - (a) a longer than normal sentence under PCC(S)A 2000, ss.79, 80 (40–037 below) for serious "violent" or serious "sexual" offences;
  - (b) a required minimum or "automatic" life sentence under PCC(S)A 2000 s.109(1) (40–053 below) for an offender committing a second "serious offence"; and
  - (c) an extended sentence (extended as to the licence period) under PCC(S)A 2000, s.85 (40–041 below) for an offender convicted of "violent" or sexual offences;

(2) **on or after April 4, 2005**, such sentences are:
  - (a) an indefinite term for the protection of the public, under CJA 2003, s.225 (40–044 below) in respect of a dangerous offender; and
  - (b) an extended term (similar to (1)(c) above, under CJA 2003, s.228 (40–046 below) in respect of "violent" or "sexual" offences.

As to the effect of these sentences, see 40–043 below.

The sentences under (1) above continue to apply in respect of offences **committed before April 4, 2005**, but have no application to offences committed after that date.

Commencement of sentence

40–005 Any sentence imposed, or other order made, by the Crown Court when dealing with an offender, takes effect from PCC(S)A 2000, ss.154, 155; CJA 2003, the beginning of the day on which it is imposed unless the judge otherwise directs. s.304, Sch.32, para.121

Note that:

(1) a sentence or other order varied under SCA 1981, s.47 (see 8 ALTERATION OF SENTENCE), takes effect from the beginning of the day on which it was originally imposed unless the judge otherwise directs; but
(2) the judge has no power under that section, or otherwise, to antedate the commencement of the sentence (*R. v Gilbert* (1974) 60 Cr.App.R. 220; *R. v Whitfield* [2002] 2 Cr.App.R.(S.) 44).

3. Length of term: discretionary sentences

Approach to custodial sentence

40–006 Where a custodial sentence is appropriate:

(1) it is a general principle that the offender may be sentenced only in respect of offences:
   (a) proved against him, whether by a plea of guilty, or by a guilty verdict on indictment; or
   (b) admitted by him, where he asks for them to be taken into consideration on sentence (*R. v Kidd* [1998] 1 All E.R. 42 (specimen or sample counts), see 59 TICs);
(2) apart from a case in which the sentence is fixed by law, or falls to be imposed under PCC(S)A 2000, ss.109–111 (required sentences for certain certain repeat offences, under CJA 2003, s.225 (dangerous (offenders), or under FA 1968, s.51A (minimum sentences for certain firearms offences), the sentence must be commensurate with the seriousness of the offence; but
(3) in the case of a "violent" or "sexual" offence, the sentence may be extended as to its licence period under PCC(S)A 2000, s.85 (40–041) or CJA 2003, s.227 (40–046) as the case may be;
(4) in the case of a sentence of less than 12 months, the term must be expressed in weeks, and must be:
   (a) for at least 28 weeks, and
   (b) not more than 51 weeks in respect of any one offence; and

the judge must pay due regard to the statutory maxima (40–007 below), the regularly expressed views of CACD, and of the Sentencing Guidelines Council (SGC) established under CJA 2003, s.167.

Where a judge passes a custodial sentence other than one of those mentioned in (2) above, the custodial term must be for the shortest term (not exceeding the permitted maximum, see below) that in the judge's opinion is commensurate with the seriousness of the offence, or the combination of the offence and one or more offences associated with it.

Statutory maximum

40–007 The maximum term provided by statute for a particular offence ought to be reserved for the most serious type of case (*R. v Byrne* (1975) 62 Cr.App.R. 159), and should not be imposed where there is substantial mitigation (*R. v Markus* [1974] 3 W.L.R. 645; *R. v Thompson* [1980] 2 Cr.App.R.(S.) 242; *R. v Cade* (1984) 6 Cr.App.R.(S.) 28), and

(1) where the statutory maximum is altered by a provision taking effect:
   (a) after the commission of the offence, but
   (b) before sentence, the former maximum should govern the sentence unless there is a clear indication to the contrary (*R. v Penwith Ex p. Hay* (1979) 1 Cr.App.R. (S.) 265; *R. v Cairns* [1998] Crim.L.R. 141; *R. v Hobbs* [2002] 2 Cr.App.R.(S.) 22);

(2) where the facts of the offence of which the offender has been convicted fall clearly within the definition of another offence with a lesser maximum, it may be appropriate to approach the sentence with the lower maximum in view—this is particularly apposite in dealing with sexual offences (see, e.g. *R. v Quayle* (1993) 14 Cr.App.R.(S.) 726; *R. v Blair* 1996] 1 Cr.App.R.(S.) 336);

(3) the judge is always entitled to take into account prevalence and public concern (*R. v Cunningham* (1993) 14 Cr.App.R.(S.) 444);

The maximum sentence should not normally be imposed on an offender who has pleaded guilty (see 29 DEALING WITH AN OFFENDER).

4. Concurrent or consecutive

40–008 In passing sentence, the judge:

(1) must pass a separate sentence on each count of the indictment; it is wrong to impose a comprehensive sentence covering all of them together;

(2) has a general power to order that sentences run concurrently (*R. v Torr* (1966) 50 Cr.App.R. 73), and may

(3) (subject to PCC(S)A 2000, s.84 as to prisoners released on licence) order one term to commence at the expiration of a previous sentence imposed by any court in England and Wales, and this is so whether the sentences are passed in respect of separate counts contained in one indictment, or of counts in different indictments (*R. v Greenberg* [1943] 1 K.B. 381);

(4) ought not to order one sentence to run *partly* concurrently and *partly* consecutively to another (*R. v Salmon* [2003] 1 Cr.App.R.(S.) 85).

This topic is fully dealt with in 29 DEALING WITH AN OFFENDER.

Released prisoners

40–009 The judge, in sentencing a person to imprisonment (including a sentence of detention under PCC(S)A 2000, s.91 or CJA 2003, s.228) may **not** order or direct that the term commence on the expiry of any sentence from which the offender has been released early on licence. CJA 2003, s.265

General points

40–010 A number of general points may be made in respect of consecutive sentences:

(1) consecutive sentences should not ordinarily be imposed:
   (a) in respect of offences which arise out of a single incident (*R. v Jones* (1980) 2 Cr.App.R.(S.) 152), though there may be exceptional circumstances (see *R. v Wheatley* (1983) 5 Cr.App.R.(S.) 417; *R. v Dillon* (1983) 5 Cr.App.R.(S.) 439; *R. v Lawrence* (1989) 11 Cr.App.R.(S.) 580); or
   (b) where offences form part of a series committed against the same victim over a short period of time.

(2) where there are convictions on two or more indictments, it is bad practice to make part of a sentence on the second indictment consecutive to a sentence on the first (*R. v Mills* (1969) 53 Cr.App.R. 294).

(3) where a very long sentence is passed, no useful purpose is generally served by imposing a short consecutive sentence for a different offence (*R. v Smith* (1981) 3 Cr.App.R.(S.) 201).

Otherwise, see generally 29 DEALING WITH AN OFFENDER.

Spelling it out

40–011 Where he passes on an offender more than one term of imprisonment, the judge should state in the presence of the PD 2004, I.8.1

offender whether the terms are to be concurrent or consecutive. Should this not be done, the court officer should ask him, before the offender leaves court, to do so.

If the offender is at the time of sentence, already serving two or more consecutive terms of imprisonment and the judge intends to increase the total period, he should use the expression "consecutive to the total period of imprisonment to which you are already subject". PD 2004, I.8.2

Particular cases

40–012 CACD has indicated that;

- where an offender commits **further offences while on bail** awaiting trial or sentence for earlier offences, the sentences for the subsequent offences ought to be consecutive to those for the earlier offences (*R. v Young* (unreported) March 16, 1973; *R. v Hunnybun* (unreported) November 23, 1979);
- where an offender is convicted of a substantive offence and also of an **assault upon an officer**
  - — if the assault is part and parcel of the substantive offence it may be treated as aggravating that offence and concurrent sentences may be passed (*R. v Kastercum* (1972) 56 Cr.App.R. 298; *R. v Wellington* (1988) 10 Cr.App.R.(S.) 384); but
  - — if the assault is in the course of an effort to escape, the offender should be sentenced for the substantive offence independently, a consecutive term being imposed for the assault (*R. v Kastercum*, above; *R. v Gormley* [1973] R.T.R. 483; *R. v Fitter* (1983) 5 Cr.App.R.(S.) 168).
- where an offender **burgles** with intent to steal, and in the course of the offence **uses violence on an occupant** who interrupts him, the offences do not form part of the same transaction and a consecutive term ought to be imposed for the assault (*R. v Bunch* (unreported) November 6, 1971; *R. v Jones*, December 15, 1975).
- where an offender is sentenced to a custodial term for an offence, a sentence for **attempting to pervert the course of justice** in relation to that offence ought normally to be made consecutive (*Att.-Gen.'s Ref (No. 1 of 1990)* (1990) 12 Cr.App.R.(S.) 245).
- where an offender **carries a firearm** with intent when pursuing his criminal activities, a consective sentence should be imposed in respect of the firearm (*R. v Jaffier* [2004] 2 Cr.App.R.(S.) 41);

- in imposing a **life sentence**, it is pointless to make it consecutive to a fixed term which the offender is serving (*Jones v DPP* (1962) 46 Cr.App.R. 129). A determinate sentence cannot be made consecutive to a life term (*R. v Foy* (1962) 46 Cr.App.R. 290);
- where serious offences are **committed in prison** a sentence consecutive to that which the prisoner is already serving should be imposed;
- there may be other **exceptional circumstances** where a consecutive sentence is justified (e.g. indecent assault and threats to kill arising from the same circumstances (*R. v Fletcher* [2002] Crim.L.R. 591).

The totality principle

40–013 Wherever consecutive sentences are imposed, while there is nothing to prevent the aggregate from exceeding the maximum for any one of them (*R. v Blake* (1961) 45 Cr.App.R. 292) it is the final duty of the judge to ensure (particularly in the case of young offenders (*R. v Morgan* (1972) 56 Cr.App.R. 181) that the totality of the terms is not:

(1) excessive or unjust in relation to the types of offence committed; or
(2) unsuitable to the offender (*R. v Bocskei* (1970) 54 Cr.App.R. 519).

(See also *R. v Reeves* (1980) 2 Cr.App.R.(S.) 35; *R. v Millen* [1980] 2 Cr.App.R.(S.) 357; *R. v Stevens* [1997] 2 Cr.App.R.(S.) 180; *R. v Cooper* (1984) 5 Cr.App.R.(S.) 295.)

5. Ancillary orders

Custodial sentence combined with fine

40–014 It may be appropriate to combine a financial penalty with an immediate custodial sentence where:

(1) there is reason to believe that the offender has assets which he has not disclosed (*R. v Michel* (1984) 6 Cr.App.R.(S.) 379; *R. v Benmore* (1983) 5 Cr.App.R.(S.) 468);
(2) there is reason to believe that a substantial amount of stolen property remains available for the offender's benefit on release (*R. v Chatt* (1984) 6 Cr.App.R.(S.) 75); and
(3) exceptionally, the maximum custodial term is not an adequate penalty (*R. v Garner* (1986) 82 Cr.App.R. 27).

Recommending licence conditions

40–015 In respect of offences **committed after April 4, 2005**, except in the case of a sentence of: CJA 2003, s.238

(1) detention for juveniles under PCC(S)A 2000, s.91; or
(2) a term under CJA 2003, s.228 (dangerous offenders)

the judge who sentences an offender to a term of imprisonment for 12 months or more in respect of an offence, may, when passing sentence, recommend to the Home Secretary (who is bound to have regard to such a recommendation) particular conditions which, in his view, should be included in any licence granted to the offender on his release. Such a recommendation is not part of the sentence.

The conditions are those which impose on an offender:

(a) a requirement that he reside at a certain place;
(b) a requirement relating to his making or maintaining contact with a person;
(c) a restriction relating to his making or maintaining contact with a person;
(d) a restriction on his participation in, or undertaking of, an activity;
(e) a requirement that he participate in, or co-operate with, a programme or set of activities designed to further one or more of the purposes referred to in s.250(8) of the Act;
(f) a requirement that he comply with a curfew arrangement;
(g) a restriction on his freedom of movement (which is not a requirement referred to in subpara.(f));
(h) a requirement relating to his supervision in the community by a responsible officer. SI 2005/950

6. Length of term served; relevance to sentence

40–016 CJA 1991, ss.32–39 abolished remission, and replaced it with a system under which all prisoners released before the end of their sentences remained at risk of having their sentences re-activated if they offended again. It replaced parole with a system of discretionary early release for those serving four years or more. It restricted an offender's liberty throughout the entire term imposed by the court to ensure that:

(1) at least half of that term was served in custody; and

(2) offenders sentenced to 12 months or more were supervised by officers of a local probation board, whether or not they are granted parole.

CJA 2003, repeals CJA 1991, ss.32–51, and substitutes for the division into sentences of less and those of more than four years, a division beween those of less than 12 months, and those of 12 months and over. CJA 2003, ss.244, 245

With effect from **April 4, 2005**, CJA 2003, Pt 12 makes a distinction between:

(a) a fixed term prisoner sentenced to a determinate sentence of imprisonment for a term of 12 months or more (or a determinate sentence of detention under PCC(S)A 2000, s.91); he qualifies for release automatically after half his sentence has been served, (unless he misbehaves in prison), and serves the remainder of his sentence in the community; he is liable to recall to custody throughout the whole period;

(b) an offender serving a sentence of imprisonment for a term less than 12 months (other than one to which an "intermittent custody order" relates) qualifies for release at the end of the "custodial period" (expressed in weeks) stated by the judge;

(c) an offender serving a sentence of imprisonment to which an "intermittent custody order" relates, qualifies for a release at the end of any part of the term which is not a licence period, if not recalled under s.254;

(d) an offender serving two or more concurrent sentences, is governed by rules under CJA 2003, ss.263(2) and 264(2);

(e) an offender classified as a "dangerous offender" by the judge imposing the sentence is released only on a direction by the Parole Board (i.e. when it is safe to do so);

(f) an offender serving an extended sentence under CJA 2003, ss.227, 228 qualifies for release automatically at the end of (one-half) of the "appropriate custodial term", if the Parole Board has not authorised his earlier release. CJA 2003, s.247

For the special rules governing life sentences, see 45 LIFE SENTENCES.

SGC 3, 2.1.2 points out that under the new framework (see above) the impact of a custodial sentence will be more severe since the period in custody and under supervision will be for the whole of the sentence term imposed by the judge. These requirements will be set shortly before release by the Home Secretary (with advice from the Probation Service) but the judge may make recommendations at the sentencing stage on the content of those requirements (SGC 3, 2.1.3). The conditions that the Home Secretary may attach to a licence are to be prescribed by order.

7. Sentences of 12 months or more

Length of term

40–017 Judges need to be aware that:

(1) a fixed term custodial sentence of 12 months or more under the new frame-work (40–016 above) will increase the sentence actually served (whether in custody or in the community) by up to one third; and

(2) SGC recommends that in order to maintain consistency between the lengths of sentence under the former framework and the new, the judge imposing a fixed term custodial sentence of 12 months or more for an offence **committed on or after April 4, 2005**, should consider reducing the overall length of the sentence that would have been imposed under the former provisions (by no more than one quarter). SGC 3, 2.1.7

Spelling it out

40–018 The changes in the nature of custodial sentences for offences **committed on or after April 4, 2005**, require changes in the way the sentence is pronounced (see 29 DEALING WITH AN OFFENDER).

The judge in imposing such a sentence (other than for a "dangerous offender" (see 40–043 *et seq.*) needs to spell out the practical implications of the sentence being imposed, so that offenders, victims and the public alike all understand.

He should state clearly, at the point of sentence:

(1) the way in which the sentence has been calculated;
(2) how it will be served;
(3) that the sentence is in two parts, one in custody and one under supervision in the community.
(4) that the sentence does not end when the offender is released from custody;

(5) that non-compliance with licence requirements imposed in the second half of the sentence is likely to result in a return to custody.

Licence conditions

40–019 In respect of offences **committed on or after April 4, 2005,** the judge imposing a prison sentence of 12 months or more (other than for a "dangerous offender") may recommend conditions that should be imposed by the Probation Service on release from custody, though any such recommendations do not form part of the sentence and they are not binding on the Probation Service. CJA 2003, ss.238(1)

As a matter of practice (SGC points out at 3, 2.1.1–14) the judge is not likely to know with any certainty at the point of sentence to what extent the offender's behaviour may have been addressed in custody or what the offender's health and other personal circumstances might be on release, so that it will be difficult, especially in the case of longer custodial sentences, for him to make an informed judgment about the most appropriate licence conditions to be imposed on release. The Probation Service is best placed to make the decision at the point of release.

It may, however be helpful for the judge to:

(1) indicate any areas of an offender's behaviour about which he has the most concern; and
(2) make suggestions about the types of intervention whether this, in practice, takes place in prison or in the community.

A curfew, exclusion requirement or prohibited activity requirement might be suitable conditions to recommend for the licence period. The judge might also wish to suggest that the offender should complete a rehabilitation programme, for example for drug abuse, anger management, or improving skills such as literacy and could recommend that this should be considered as a licence requirement if the programme has not been undertaken or completed in custody.

The Probation Service ought to have due regard to any such recommendations and the final decision on licence conditions will need to build upon any interventions during the custodial period and any other changes in the offender's circumstances.

The involvement of the Probation Service at the pre-sentence stage will clearly be pivotal. A recommendation on the likely post-release requirements included in a pre-sentence report will assist the judge in making his decision on the overall length of the sentence although any recommendation would still have to be open to review when release is being considered.

8. Sentences of less than 12 months; "custody plus order"

40–020 "Custody plus," replaces all short prison sentences of less than 12 months (with the exception of "intermittent custody" for which see 40–026, below), and is available for all offenders aged 18 or over. CJA 2003, ss.181,182

Once the judge has decided that neither a fine alone nor a community sentence is justified, and the offence is not so serious as to merit a sentence of 12 months or more, the appropriate sentence in this age bracket is a custody plus order.

The order is made up of:

(1) a short period of up to three months (expressed in weeks) in custody, to fulfil the punishment purpose of the sentence, followed by
(2) a longer period, of a minimum of six months (expressed in weeks), on licence under supervision in the community, to fulfil the reparation and crime prevention purposes of the sentence.

The judge must, at the time of sentence:

(a) fix the lengths of the two parts, and
(b) attach to the supervision part of the sentence, such specific requirements, based upon those available under the generic community sentence (see 21 COMMUNITY SENTENCES) as he considers desirable so as to address the offender's rehabilitative needs.

A custody plus order ranks as a custodial sentence, but the requirements imposed during the licence period increase the scope of the sentence to include reparation and rehabilitation. The judge has a wide discretion and will need to achieve a balance between the punitive and the rehabilitative part of the sentence, based on the seriousness of the offence and the requirements of the offender.

Once the judge has decided to impose a custody plus order, he may order the sentence to be suspended, or may order, where the necessary provisions are available locally, and with the consent of the offender, whether the term may be served intermittently. If neither of these considerations is appropriate the term must be served immediately.

SAP recommends to the SGC that any appropriate reduction for a guilty plea may be applied to any or all of the punitive elements of a custody plus order, according to the circumstances.

IMPRISONMENT

This may include suspending the sentence or making a community order.

Statutory provisions

40–021 The term of a sentence of imprisonment for less than 12 months, unless the judge makes an "intermittent custody order" under CJA 2003, s.183 (see 40–026, below) must: CJA 2003, s.181(1)(2)

(1) be expressed in weeks;
(2) be for at least 28 weeks;
(3) not be for more than 51 weeks in respect of any one offence, and
(4) not exceed the maximum term permitted for the offence.

In passing sentence for such an offence, the judge must: CJA 2003, s.181(2), (3) (5), (9)

(a) specify the "custodial period," which must be
  (i) at least 2 weeks; and
  (ii) in respect of any one offence not more than 13 weeks, at the end of which the offender is to be released on licence; and
(b) unless the sentence is suspended by order require the licence to be granted subject to conditions requiring the offender's compliance during the remainder of the term ("the licence period") or any part of it, with one or more specified (community) requirements falling within s.182(1) (see 40–022, below).

In determining the term of the sentence and the length of the custodial period, the judge must ensure that the licence period is at least 26 weeks in length. CJA 2003, s.181(6)

Where two or more terms of imprisonment are passed in accordance with these provisions, to be served consecutively; CJA 2003, s.181(7)

  (i) the aggregate length of the terms of imprisonment will have to be not more than 65 weeks, and
  (ii) the aggregate length of the custodial periods will have to be not more than 26 weeks. (CJA 2003, s.181(7)).

A "custody plus order" which specifies two or more requirements may, in relation to any requirement, refer to compliance within a specified part of the licence period. CJA 2003, s.181(8)

Licence conditions

40–022 The requirements which may be imposed are, with four exceptions, those that are available under a community CJA 2003, s.181(1), (2)

order (see 21 COMMUNITY SENTENCES) or a suspended sentence order (see 40–086, below) and are subject to similar restrictions to those imposed under a community order.

The four requirements which may be included in a community order, or a suspended sentence order but are excluded from a custody plus order are:

(1) a residence requirement (which is a standard licence requirement);
(2) a mental health treatment requirement
(3) a drug rehabilitation requirement and
(4) an alcohol treatment requirement

Where the judge makes a custody plus order requiring a licence to contain: CJA 2003, s.182(3), (4)

(a) a curfew requirement or an exclusion requirement he **must**; and
(b):

- an "unpaid work requirement",
- an "activity requirement",
- a "programme requirement";
- a "prohibited activity requirement",
- a "residence requirement",
- a "supervision requirement", or
- an "attendance centre requirement,"

he **may** also: require the licence to contain an electronic monitoring requirement (as defined by s.215) unless:

(i) he is prevented from doing so by ss.215(2) (no facilities) or 218(4) (no consent of supervisor), or
(ii) in the particular circumstances of the case, he considers it inappropriate to do so.

Before making a custody plus order requiring a licence to contain two or more different requirements falling within subs.(1), the judge will need to consider whether, in the circumstances of the case, the requirements are compatible with each other. CJA 2003, s.182(5)

Guidelines

40–023 SAP in their recommendations to the SGC recommend that the judge, having decided to impose a custody plus order, must:

(1) begin by determining the overall term of the order (within the 28–51 week range), being the shortest term commensurate with the seriousness of the offence; and then
(2) go on to determine the length of the custodial period (within the two–13 week range), being, again, the shortest term commensurate with the seriousness of the offence; and then
(3) go on to impose suitable licence requirements and decide whether these are to be complied with during part or all of the licence period.

In relation to consecutive sentences of custody plus, the judge should calculate for each individual offence the overall term of the order that is commensurate with its seriousness. If the combined sentence exceeds the statutory limit, the combined elements of the sentence must be reduced, to ensure that the length of the custodial term is commensurate with the totality of the criminal conduct. The judge will then need to consider whether the onerousness of the licence requirements adequately reflects the seriousness of the multiple offending and the likelihood of re-offending.

When imposing a custody plus order to be served concurrently with, or consecutive to, a sentence of 12 months or more, the judge, while he may in passing sentence sensibly recommend interventions which may be useful, ought to make it clear that the requirements ultimately to be imposed in the licence, are a matter for prison authorities and the probation service.

Where, owing to the period of time spent on remand, an offender is eligible for immediate release, SAP recommends that the judge should still impose a custody plus order to mark the seriousness of the offence, unless he considers a community order more appropriate in the circumstances and more likely to reduce the risk of re-offending. Where the offender has spent more timer in custody on remand than the custodial period of the custody plus order, the judge may wish to consider whether the length and severity of the licence period should be reduced.

Suggested requirements

40–024 It is for the judge to decide the nature and number of requirements to attach to the order; the SAP in their recommendations to the SGC suggested that the judge should be guided by the seriousness of the offence, dividing offences into categories as follows:

(1) **low seriousness** — offences just crossing the custody threshold, should carry an overall term of 28 weeks, a

custody period of two weeks, and a maximum of two requirements, one of which will normally be a supervision requirement, the other being selected from 40–60 hours unpaid work, an activity requirement of up to 20 days, a prohibited activity requirement, an attendance center requirement (if available), a programme requirement, a curfew requirement of up to 12 hours a day for a few weeks, or an exclusion requirement lasting a few weeks or until the end of the order, depending upon its purpose;

(2) **medium seriousness** — offences falling obviously within the custody plus category, should carry an overall term of 29–40 weeks, a custody period of three–9 weeks with a variable licence period and, in general, no more than two licence requirements of which one will normally be a supervision requirement, the other(s) being selected from 60–80 hours unpaid work, up to 30 days of activity, a prohibited activity requirement, a programme requirement, a curfew requirement of up to 12 hours a day for two–three months, or an exclusion requirement lasting a few months or until the end of the order, depending upon its purpose;

(3) **high seriousness** — offences only just falling below the 12 months threshold, should carry an overall term of 41–51 weeks, a custodial period of 10–13 weeks and a variable licence period and two or more requirements, one of which will normally be a supervision requirement, the other(s) being selected from 80–100 hours unpaid work, an activity requirement of up to 60 days, a programme requirement, a curfew requirement of up to 12 hours a day for four–six months, or an exclusion order lasting until the end of the custody plus order.

In regard to (2) and (3) above, SAP recommend that the increased seriousness of the order be satisfied by increasing the period of time for which the requirements are imposed, rather than by imposing additional requirements.

Breach, amendment and revocation

40–025 As to breach, amendment and revocation of the requirements of a custody plus order, see 14 BREACH, AMENDMENT AND REVOCATION.

9. "Intermittent custody" order

General

40–026 Where:

(1) CJA 2003, ss.183–186 are in force in a particular location of the Crown Court; and
(2) the offence for which the senterce falls to be imposed was **committed on or after April 4, 2005**,

the judge may order that the custodial part of a sentence be served intermittently, enabling an offender to maintain his job, family ties or education (all of which have been shown to play a part in reducing re-offending).

The intention of the Act is that the custodial periods will be served in short blocks of a few days at a time, while the licence period runs between the blocks (and may continue after the last custodial period). SGC 3.2.3.6, 7 emphasise that:

(a) intermittent custody must be imposed only for offences that have crossed the custodial threshold;
(b) the sentence is intended to be an alternative to immediate full-time custody and must therefore meet all the criteria that apply to such a sentence, including the requirement to ensure that the sentence is for the shortest term commensurate with the seriousness of the offence;
(c) the effect of the sentence is to intersperse periods during which the offender is released on temporary licence in the community;
(d) such a sentence may be imposed only if the offender **consents** to serving the custodial part of the sentence intermittently; and
(e) the judge must make sure that the relevant resources are available in the local area and must consult the Probation Service to confirm that the offender is an appropriate candidate for such a sentence.

As to the views of SGC on the type of case for which such a sentence is appropriate, see 40–028, below.

Judge's powers

40–027 Where the judge passes a sentence of imprisonment for a term which, expressed in weeks: CJA 2003, s.183(1), (2), (4), (5), (6)

(1) is for at least 28 weeks,
(2) is for not more than 51 weeks in respect of any one offence, and

(3) does not exceed the maximum term permitted for the offence; and,
(4) the number of custodial days is at least 14; and
(5) in respect of any one offence not more than 90,

then, *provided the offender has agreed* to serve the custodial part of the proposed sentence intermittently, during the parts of the sentence that are not to be licence periods, the judge may:

(a) specify the number of days that the offender must serve in prison under the sentence before being released on licence for the remainder of the term, and
(b) make an "intermittent custody order"
  (i) specifying periods during which the offender is to be temporarily released on licence before he has served that number of days in prison, and
  (ii) requiring any licence to be granted subject to conditions requiring the offender's compliance during the licence periods with one or more of the requirements falling within s.182(1), above, and specified in the order.

The "licence period" in relation to a term of imprisonment to which an intermittent custody order relates, means any period during which the offender is released on licence by virtue of s.183(1)(a) or (b)(i); "the number of custodial days", in relation to a term of imprisonment to which an intermittent custody order relates, means the number of days specified under subs. 183(1)(a).

Where sentence appropriate

40–028 SGC is of the opinion that intermittent custody is not intended to be used for: SGC 3, 2.3.9 SGC 3, 2.3.10

(1) sex offenders; or
(2) those convicted of serious offences of either violence or burglary;
(3) other offences which by their nature would make intermittent custody inappropriate;

Public safety should always be the paramount consideration.

SGC is also of opinion that the circumstances of the offender are likely to be the determining factor in deciding whether an intermittent custody order is appropriate, i.e. where the custody threshold has been crossed and where suspending the custodial sentence or imposing a non-custodial sentence have been ruled out. Suitable candidates for weekend custody might include:

offenders who are full-time carers, or are in employment, or in education.

SGC 3, 2.3.11 recommends that the judge:

(a) before considering such a sentence be satisfied that a custodial sentence of less than 12 months is justified and that neither a community sentence nor a suspended sentence is appropriate;
(b) when imposing a custodial sentence of less than 12 months, should always consider whether it would be appropriate to sentence an offender to intermittent custody; primary considerations being public safety, the suitability of the offender and the availability of such a sentence;
(c) should strive to ensure that the intermittent custody provisions are applied in a way that limits discrimination and they should, in principle, be considered for all offenders.

It further suggests that the relevant steps in the decision-making process should be for the judge to ask himself whether: SGC 3, 2.3.11

(i) the custody threshold been passed;
(ii) if so, it is unavoidable that a custodial sentence be imposed;
(iii) if so, that sentence can be suspended, bearing mind that he would have imposed a custodial sentence if the power to suspend had not been available;
(iv) if not, it can be served intermittently;

if not, the judge should impose a sentence which takes immediate effect for the term commensurate with the seriousness of the offence.

Length of term; consecutive terms

40–029 SGC suggests (3, 2.3.13) that the demands made on the offender by such a sentence will generally be greater than for a custodial sentence to be served immediately in full: CJA 2003, s.183(7)(8)(9)

(1) the disruptive effect on family life;
(2) the psychological impact of going in and out of custody; and
(3) the responsibility on the offender to travel to and from the custodial establishment on many occasions,

combine to make the sentence more onerous.

For those reasons it suggests that once the judge has decided that an offender should be sent to prison and has determined the length of the sentence, he should reduce the overall length of the sentence because it is to be served intermittently.

Where the judge exercises his powers in respect of two or more terms of imprisonment that are to be served consecutively:

(a) the aggregate length of the terms of imprisonment must not be more than 65 weeks, and
(b) the aggregate of the numbers of custodial days must not be more than 180.

Ancillary provisions

40–030 The Home Secretary may, by order, require a court, in specifying licence periods under subs.(1)(b)(i), to specify only periods:

(1) of a prescribed duration,
(2) beginning or ending at prescribed times, or
(3) including, or not including, specified parts of the week.

An intermittent custody order which specifies two or more requirements may, in relation to any requirement, refer to compliance within such licence period or periods, or part of a licence period, as is specified in the order.

Pre-conditions on power to make order

40–031 The judge may not make an "intermittent custody order" in respect of an offender unless; CJA 2003, s.184

(1) the court has been notified by the Home Secretary that arrangements for implementing such orders are available in the area proposed to be specified in the order; and
(2) (a) he has consulted an officer of a local probation board,
(b) the court has received from the Home Secretary notification that suitable prison accommodation is available for the offender during the custodial periods, and
(c) it appears that the offender will have suitable accommodation available to him during the licence periods.

Licence conditions

40–032 CJA 2003, s.185(1)(b) has effect subject to s.218 and to the following provisions of Ch.4 limiting the power to require the licence to contain particular requirements: CJA 2003, s.183(8), (9)

(1) unpaid work requirement (s.199(3)),
(2) activity requirement (s.201(3) and (4)),

(3) programme requirement (s.202(4) and (5)), and
(4) prohibited activity requirement (s.203(2)).

CJA 2003, s.182(3)–(5) (licence conditions) have effect in relation to an intermittent custody order as they have effect in relation to a custody plus order, when the latter comes into force.

An "intermittent custody order" which specifies two or more requirements may, in relation to any requirement, refer to compliance within such licence period or periods, or part of a licence period, as is specified in the order.

SGC suggests (3, 2.3.12) that since a primary objective of being able to serve a custodial sentence intermittently is to enable offenders to continue to fulfil existing obligations in the community, and since the time spent in custody is utilised extensively for activities, experience has so far shown that additional, similar, requirements to be completed whilst on licence are not practical, though requirements such as curfews, prohibited activity and exclusion requirements might be appropriate in a particular case.

Breach, amendment, etc.

40–033 As to breach, amendment and revocation of the requirements of an intermittent custody order, see 14 BREACH, AMENDMENT AND REVOCATION.

10. "Protective" sentences under PCC(S)A 2000

Introduction

40–034 In relation to offences **committed before April 4, 2005**, discretionary and automatic life sentences, longer than commensurate sentences and extended sentences continue to be available. An offender being sentenced for offences committed both before and after April 4 is required to be sentenced by reference to two different regimes. It will generally be preferable to pass sentence on the later offences by reference to the new regime. The "protective" sentences prescribed under PCC(S)A are applicable only to offences **committed before April 4, 2005**, and are three in number:

(1) a longer than normal sentence under PCC(S)A 2000, ss.79, 80 for serious "violent" or serious "sexual" offences;
(2) a required minimum or "automatic" life sentence under PCC(S)A 2000 s.109 (40–053 below) for an offender committing a second "serious offence"; and

(3) an extended sentence (extended that is to the licence period) under PCC(S)A 2000, s.85 for an offender convicted of "violent" or sexual offences.

New "protective" sentences are introduced by CJA 2003, applicable to offences **committed after April 4, 2005**.

(a) "Sexual" and "violent offences"

"Sexual offences"

40–035 "Sexual" offences include offences under: PCC(S)A 2000, s.161(2); SO(A)A 2000, s.6; SOA 2003, Sch.6, para.43(4)

- SOA 1956 (except under ss.30, 31, or 33–36);
- MHA 1959, s.128;
- Indecency with Children Act 1960;
- TA 1968, s.9 (burglary with intent to rape);
- CLA 1977, s.54;
- Protection of Children Act 1978;
- An offence under any provision of SOA 2003, Pt 1, except ss.52, 53, or 71;
- CLA 1977, s.1 (conspiracy to commit any of the above); or
- Criminal Attempts Act 1981 (attempting to commit such offences.

Attempted rape is a "sexual offence" for this purpose: *R. v Robinson* (1993) 14 Cr.App.R.(S.) 559.

"Violent offences"

40–036 "Violent offences" are offences which lead or are intended or likely to lead, to a person's death or to physical injury to a person, and include offences which are required to be charged as arson, whether or not they would otherwise fall within the definition. PCC(S)A 2000, s.161(3)

The term has been narrowly defined, thus:

(1) the terms of the count on which the offender stands convicted must "necessarily establish" that the offence led, or was intended or likely to lead, to a person's death or serious injury (*R. v Murray* (1994) 15 Cr.App.R.(S.) 567; *R. v Cochrane* (1994) 15 Cr.App.R.(S.) 708; *R. v Bibby* (1995) 16 Cr.App.R.(S.) 127; *R. v Szczerba* [2002] Crim.L.R. 429) even if only indirectly (see *R. v Zosco* (1994) 16 Cr.App.R.(S.) 354);

(2) the following offences have been held to be "violent offences":

(a) robbery, where committed with an unguarded blade (*R. v Cochrane*, above; *R. v Johnson* [1998] 1

Cr.App.R.(S.) 126) but not where committed with an unloaded gun (*R. v Touriq Khan* (1995) 16 Cr.App.R.(S.) 180), or with an imitation firearm (*R. v Palin* (1995) 16 Cr.App.R.(S.) 888); it will always be a question of fact for the judge to decide whether a particular instance of robbery constitutes a violent offence (*R. v Grady* [2000] 2 Cr.App.R. 468);

(b) false imprisonment (*R. v Watford* (1994) 15 Cr.App.R.(S.) 730; *R. v Waller* [1994] Crim.L.R. 863), and attempting to abduct a child contrary to the Child Abduction Act 1984 (*R. v Newsome* [1997] 2 Cr.App.R.(S.) 69; distinguishing *R. v Wrench* [1996] I Cr.App.R.(S.) 145);

(c) attempted arson (*R. v Guirke* [1997] 1 Cr.App.R.(S.) 170);

(3) in relation to threats to kill, these may or may not amount to a "violent offence", depending on the circumstances of the case (see *R. v Richart* (1995) 16 Cr.App.R.(S.) 977; *R. v Ragg* [1995] Crim.L.R 664; *R. v Etcheils* [1995] Crim.L.R. 754).

The same offence may be both a "sexual offence" and a "violent offence" (*R. v Robinson* (1993) l4 Cr.App.R.(S.) 448 (attempted rape)).

(b) Longer than normal sentences: PCC(S)A 2000, s.80(2)(b)

Basic considerations

40–037 A custodial sentence other than one fixed by law, or falling to be imposed under PCC(S)A 2000, s.109(2) and subject to ss.10 (2) and 111(2)) (required sentences for certain repeat offences) may be, in relation to an offence **committed before April 4, 2005** for such longer term, not exceeding the statutory maximum, as is, in the judge's opinion, necessary to protect the public from serious harm from the offender but the subsection applies only where: PCC(S)A 2000, s.80(2)(b)

(1) the circumstances of the offence(s);
(2) the nature and circumstances of previous offences;
(3) medical or other evidence about the offender; or
(4) a combination of these and other sources,

give rise to a belief that there is a substantial risk of his committing "violent" or "sexual offences" in the future (*R. v Crow*

Pennington [1994] Crim.L.R. 958*; R. v Henshaw* [1996] 2 Cr.App.R.(S.) 31). The judge needs to consider both the facts of the case before him, and the background of the offender, in order to decide whether there is that element of dangerousness which clearly creates a risk of really serious harm to the public *(R. v Harper & Sabin, The Times*, October 12, 1998; *R. v T* [2000] Crim.L.R. 866).

It follows that:

(a) the offence before the court must be a "violent" or "sexual offence" (see 40–035 and 40–036 above);

(b) there must be a basis for the inference (which may be founded on previous convictions, medical evidence or both (*R. v Fawcett* (1995) Cr.App.R.(S.) 55)) that the offender will commit one or more such offences in the future (*R. v Walsh* [1994] Crim.L.R. 701; *R. v Ely* (1994) 15 Cr.App.R.(S.) 1881; *R. v Bowler* (1994) 15 Cr.App.R.(S.) 78; *R. v Nicholas* (1994) 15 Cr.App.R.(S.) 381; *R. v Swain* (1994) 15 Cr.App.R.(S.) 765; *R. v Drabble* (1996) 2 Cr.App.R.(S.) 322); and

(c) in the case of a "violent" offence, there must be a basis for believing that the offences show a tendency to cause death or personal injury, whether physical or psychological (*R. v Gardiner* [1994] Crim.L.R. 539: *cf. R. v Ely*, above) to a particular individual or small group of individuals *(R. v Hashi* (1995) 16 Cr.App.R.(S.) 121);

(d) the absence of previous convictions does not, of itself, prevent the application of the subsection; the offender's opportunity for committing similar offences in the future needs to be considered (*R. v L* (1994) 15 Cr.App.R.(S.) 501).

The provision does not apply where the offence is an isolated one, and the inference in (b) above cannot be drawn (*R. v Thomas* [1995] Crim.L.R. 174, *R. v Mumtaz Ali* [1995] Crim.L.R. 303; *R. v Samuels* [1995] Crim.L.R. 443), nor apparently does it apply where the offence against the group mentioned in (c) above is confined to the family circle (*R. v L* (1994) 15 Cr.App.R.(S.) 501).

The power is exercisable only in relation to an individual offence, not where consecutive terms are imposed, in relation to the whole sentence. Where the power is exercised in relation to one offence, however, there is nothing to prevent the judge passing a consecutive sentence in relation to an offence for which it is not exercised, and the total may exceed the maximum sentence for the offence, provided the totality principle is not infringed: *R. v B, The Times*, December 31, 1998.

The correct approach

40–038 Before passing a longer than normal sentence under for an offence **committed before April 4, 2005**, the judge:

(1) must intimate to counsel his intention of invoking the subsection, to give a counsel an opportunity to make submissions (*R. v Baverstock* (1993) 14 Cr.App.R.(S.) 471; *R. v Bacon* [1995] Crim.L.R. 575);
(2) must fully investigate the facts, and make such express findings of fact which enable him to conclude, e.g. that the offence is a "violent" offence (*R. v Oudkerk* [1994] Crim.L.R. 700; *R. v Touriq Khan* [1994] Crim.L.R. 862);
(3) may need, unless he can draw valid inferences from the terms of the indictment or the evidence, to conduct a fact-finding exercise (see 35 FACTUAL BASIS FOR SENTENCE) *R. v Cochrane* (1994) 15 Cr.App.R.(S.) 708.

In determining the appropriate sentence, the judge must balance the need to protect the public against the need to ensure that the totality of the sentence is not out of proportion to the nature of the offence (*R. v Mansell* (1994) 15 Cr.App.R.(S.) 771; *R. v Webb* [1995] Crim.L.R. 965; *R. v Gabbidon & Bramble* [1997] Crim.L.R. 137; *R. v de Silva* [2000] Crim.L.R. 502); *R. v Wilson* [2000] Crim.L.R. 503.) This is particularly important where the ordinary sentence is likely (as in a case of armed robbery) to contain an element designed to protect the public.

The judge should:

(a) first determine the ordinary sentence commensurate with the offence, leaving out of account at this stage, any element of enhancement to protect the public: and then
(b) increase that term by the factor of from 50–100 per cent (see *R. v Chapman* [2000] Cr.App.R.(S.) 377; *R. v Smith* [2001] 2 Cr.App.R.(S.) 160), needed to protect the public from serious harm (it must be serious harm (*R. v JT* [2001] 1 Cr.App.R.(S.) 205); but must
(c) ensure that the longer term does not exceed the permitted maximum for the offence (*R. v Walters* [1997] 2 Cr.App.R.(S.) 87; *R. v Campbell* (1997) 1 Cr.App.R.(S.) 119); then

(d) impose the sentence, pointing out clearly and in straight-forward terms, what he considers to be the serious harm in question. (He is in any event obliged to state in open court, in ordinary language. the *effect* of the sentence.)

Consecutive or concurrent

40–039 Different divisions of CACD have come to differing conclusions as to whether a longer than normal sentence may be made consecutive to another sentence, whether imposed previously or on the same occasion. In *R. v Everleigh* (2002) 1 Cr.App.R.(S.) 32, reviewing the cases, it was said that two basic principals emerge:

(1) it is inappropriate for such a sentence to be made consecutive to another sentence passed on the same occasion, because it is intended that the sentence itself protect the public from serious harm, without the need of adding any other penalty; but
(2) there is nothing objectionable, indeed it may be beneficial, to order such a sentence to run consecutively to a previous sentence of imprisonment.

The power is exercisable only in relation to an individual offence not, where consecutive terms are imposed, in relation to the whole sentence (*R. v B, The Times*, December 31, 1998).

Mitigating factors

40–040 While mitigating factors, such as a plea of guilty, the impulsive nature of the offence or the offender's limited intelligence, will not carry the usual weight where the subsection is invoked, for the overriding factor is the protection of the public (*R. v Bowler* (1994) 15 Cr.App.R.(S.) 78), these factors should not be ignored.

Thus:

(1) the minimum custodial term, but not the public protection element should be reduced to reflect a plea of guilty; and
(2) some account must be taken of the age of the offender, for in the case of an older offender, the risk to the public may diminish with time, and in the case of a young offender, protection of the public needs to be balanced against the added risk presented when he is released from a crushingly long sentence.

Unless the offender qualifies for a life sentence a determinate term ought to be imposed under PCC(S)A 2000 s.2(2)(b) (*R. v*

Chapman (1994) 15 Cr.App.R.(S.) 844; *R. v Spear* (1995) 16 Cr.App.R.(S.) 469). The criteria for the imposition of a discretionary life sentence are not affected by s.2(2)(b) (*R. v Helm* [1995] Crim.L.R. 441; *R. v Roche* [1995] Crim.L.R. 442).

(c) Sentence extended for licence purposes; PCC(S)A 2000, s.85

General

40–041 Where the judge:

(1) proposes to impose a custodial sentence for a "violent" or, "sexual" offence **committed after September 30, 1998** and **before April 4, 2005**; and PCC(S)A 2000, s.85(1)(2)(8)

(2) considers the period, if any, for which the offender would otherwise be subject to licence, would not be adequate for the purpose of preventing the commission by him of further offences, and securing his rehabilitation,

he may pass upon him an "extended sentence" that is a custodial sentence extended for licence purposes, replacing the normal licence period by a licence which will endure to the end of the extended licence period (*R. v Barker* [2001] Crim. L.R. 147).

He must not, however, in respect of a "violent offence" pass an extended sentence unless the custodial portion of the sentence is more than four years (see *R. v Langstone* [2001] 2 Cr.App.R.(S.) 98).

The length of such a sentence must be a term equal to the aggregate of:

(a) the custodial *term*—i.e. the term of the custodial sentence which he would have imposed otherwise than under this provision; and

(b) the extension period—i.e. a further period, for which the offender is to be subject to a licence, and which is of such length as the judge considers necessary for the purpose of (2) above.

Provided that in the case of: PCC(S)A 2000, s.85(3), (4), (5)

(i) a "sexual" offence, the extension period does not exceed 10 years;

(ii) a "violent" offence, the extension period does not exceed five years and the custodial term is not less than four years; and

(iii) the term of any extension period does not exceed the maximum permitted for the offence.

There is nothing to prevent the imposition of such a sentence where the sentence would otherwise have been such as to result in the offender's immediate release: *R. v Ajaib* [2000] Crim.L.R. 770.

In *R. v Barker* [2001] Crim.L.R. 147 CACD suggested that there was no prohibition in law on the imposition of two or more such extended sentences consecutively, but see *R. v Cridge* [2000] 2 Cr.App.R.(S) 477 as to the practical difficulties involved in such a course.

Approach to sentence

40–042 The purpose of an extended sentence under s.85(1)(b) is to prevent the commission of further offences and to secure rehabilitation of the offender. It is not to protect the public from serious harm; that is the role of the longer than commensurate sentence under s.80.

The judge should approach sentence in the case of a "violent" or "sexual" offender in three stages (*R. v Nelson* (2002) 1 Cr.App.R.(S.) 134).

He should:

(1) decide on the sentence which would be commensurate with the offence; then
(2) decide whether a longer period in custody is needed to protect the public from serious harm from the offender and, if so, whether a longer than commensurate custodial sentence is required; and
(3) decide where the appropriate custodial sentence would be for four years or more, whether that sentence, commensurate or longer than commensurate, is adequate to prevent the commission by the offender of further offences and secure his rehabilitation. If not, an extended sentence is called for.

It is not appropriate to reduce the custodial sentence because an extended licence period is being imposed: *R. v Nelson* [2001] Crim.L.R. 498; see also *Att.-Gen.'s Reference (No. 39 of 2002), The Times*, July 11, 2002.

Note also (*R. v Pepper and Others* [2005] EWCA Crim 1181) that:

(a) when imposing sentences for several offences, the judge should always identify the offence(s) to which the extended sentence was intended to relate, thus focussing on whether the sentence complies with the statutory criteria, considering particularly:

(i) whether the offence was committed before or after **September 30, 1998**;

(ii) the need not to exceed the maximum sentence for the offence; and

(iii) the fact that different restrictions applied top sexual (not more than 10 years) and violent (not less than four not more than five) offences;

(b) when minded to impose such a sentence the judge should always invite submissions from the advocates.

The minimum custodial term, but not the public protection element, should be reduced to reflect a plea of guilty.

11. "Protective" sentences for dangerous offenders: CJA 2003, Pt 12, Ch.5

(a) General

Introduction

40–043 Specified violent or sexual offences committed **on or after April 4, 2005**, attract the new mandatory sentencing provisions relating to the protection of the public from dangerous offenders, contained in CJA 2003, ss.224 to 229, being:

(1) a sentence of life imprisonment;
(2) imprisonment (or in the case of a juvenile detention) for public protection; or
(3) an extended sentence.

It should be noted that, in relation to offences committed before April 4, 2005, discretionary life sentences, automatic life sentences, longer than commensurate sentences and extended sentences continue to be available. An accused being sentenced for offences committed both **before and after April 4, 2005** must be sentenced by reference to the two different regimes. It will generally be preferable to pass sentence on the later offences by reference to the new regime, imposing no separate penalty for the earlier offences. But this may not be possible if the later offences are less serious than the earlier ones.

Care should be taken to ensure that a continuing offence which, as initially indicted, **straddled April 4, 2005** is indicted, if necessary by amendment, so that sentence can properly be passed by reference to the new and/or old regime as appropriate.

In the case of (2) the offender is released at a date determined by the Parole Board, and remains on licence for at least 10 years.

In the case of (3) from the half-way point of the custodial period, the offender may be released if the Parole Board determines it is safe to do so, but release will not be automatic until the end of the custodial period. The offender remains on licence for the unexpired period of the original sentence, if any, and for the extended period designated by the judge when imposing sentence.

To qualify for one of the new sentences, the offender must be convicted of a "specified offence", that is one of the 153 categories of violent or sexual offences listed in CJA 2003, Sch.15, Pts I or 2 (see APPENDIX A, SECTION 2). Violent offences range from murder to affray and threats of various kinds and sexual offences from rape to exposure. SOA 1956, which is referred to in identifying offences numbered 66 to 92 of Pt 2 of the Schedule, was repealed on May 1, 2004. Thus while one of the new sentences may not be imposed in relation to any of the offences under that Act: offences committed under it may be relevant to the assessment of "dangerousness" under s.229.

If, in relation to a dangerous offender, the requirements of MHA 1983 (see 48 MENTALLY DISORDERED OFFENDERS) are satisfied the judge may dispose of the case under *ibid.* s.37 (hospital order) as amended by CJA 2003, Sch.32, para.38(b) (see 48–004 *et seq.*).

When offenders are to be sentenced for several offences only some of which are specified, the judge who imposes an indeterminate sentence under ss.225 or 226 or an extended sentence under ss.227 or 228, for the principal offences, should generally impose a shorter concurrent sentence for the other offences. In the case of a specified offence where there is a risk of serious harm, the sentence for such other offence must be an extended sentence where the principal offence is a serious offence (s.227(2)).

Although there is no statutory prohibition on the imposition of **consecutive indeterminate sentences** or the imposition of an indeterminate sentence consecutive to another period of imprisonment, it is undesirable to impose such sentences; the same principle applies to sentences of life imprisonment and to sentences of detention for life or for public protection (*R. v O'Brien and Others, The Times*, August 30, 2006).

Serious offence: life sentence or imprisonment for public protection

40–044 Where:

(1) an offender aged 18 or over is convicted of a "serious" offence on or after April 4, 2005; and CJA 2003, s.225

(2) the judge is of opinion that there is a "significant risk" to members of the public of serious harm occasioned by the commission by him of further "specified" offences, CJA 2003, s.225 applies and if:

(a) the offence is one in respect of which the offender would, apart from s.225 be liable to imprisonment for life; and

(b) the judge considers that the seriousness of the offence, or of the offence and one or more offences associated with it, is such as to justify the imposition of a sentence of imprisonment for life (i.e. a discretionary life sentence, as to which see 45 LIFE SENTENCES);

the judge must impose a sentence of imprisonment for life; and

(3) a case does not fall within (2) above, the judge must impose a sentence of imprisonment for public protection, i.e. a sentence of imprisonment for an indeterminate period, subject to the provisions of CSA 1997, Ch.2, Pt 2, as to the release of prisoners and the duration of licences.

As to the fixing of a minimum term, see 40–045, below.

An offence for which a sentence is imposed under s.225 is not to be regarded as an offence the sentence for which is fixed by law.

The provisions of s.225 are mirrored in s.226 in relation to offenders under 18 at the time of conviction (see 31 DETENTION OF YOUNG OFFENDERS).

The minimum term

40–045 The procedure for fixing a minimum term in relation to these new sentences should be as before the Act in relation to discretionary and automatic life sentences. The court, taking into account the seriousness of the offence or the combination of the offence and one or more offences associated with it:

(1) must identify the notional determinate sentence which would have been imposed if a life sentence or imprisonment for public protection had not been required; this should not exceed the maximum permitted for the offence;

(2) half that term should normally then be taken, and from this should be deducted time spent in custody or on remand (see PCSA 2000, s.82A as amended; CJA 2003, s.240.) There will continue to be exceptional cases where

more than half may be appropriate (see *R. v Szczerba* [2002] 2 Cr.App.R.(S.) 387 paras 31 to 34.

As previously, when the offender has served the period specified he may require the Home Secretary to refer his case to the Parole Board who may direct his release if "satisfied that it is no longer necessary for the protection of the public" that he should be confined. If released, he will remain on licence indefinitely, save, as we have indicated, when the sentence was imprisonment for public protection and the Home Secretary makes an order, after 10 years, that the licence should cease to have effect. In calculating the minimum term, an appropriate reduction should be allowed for a plea of guilty (see 29 DEALING WITH AN OFFENDER and care should be taken not to incorporate in the notional determinate sentence an element for risk which is already covered by the indeterminate sentence (*R. v Lang*, above).

In the case of both an indeterminate sentence required for public protection and an extended sentence the minimum custodial term, but not the public protection element should be reduced to reflect a plea of guilty.

Certain violent or sexual offences; extended sentence

40–046 Where:

(1) a person aged 18 or over is convicted of a "specified offence", other than a "serious offence (where s.225, above, applies), committed after April 4, 2005; and CJA 2003, s.227
(2) the judge considers that there is a significant risk to members of the public of serious harm occasioned by the commission by the offender of further "specified offences";

the judge must impose on the offender an extended sentence of imprisonment, i.e. a sentence of imprisonment the term of which is equal to the aggregate of:

(a) the appropriate custodial term; and
(b) a further period ("the extended period") for which the offender is to be subject to a licence and which is of such length as the judge considers necessary for the purpose of protecting members of the public from serious harm occasioned by the commission of him of further "specified offences".

The "appropriate custodial term" (see (a) above) means a term of imprisonment, not exceeding the statutory maximum term permitted for the offence and which is the term which apart from s.227 would be imposed in compliance with CJA 2003, s.143(2) (i.e. the shortest term commensurate with the offence (see above, 40–006) and where that term would be as term of less than 12 months, then 12 months.

The extension period must not exceed:

(i) five years in the case of a specified violent offence; and
(ii) eight years in the case of a specified sexual offence.

The term of the extended sentence of imprisonment passed under s.227 in respect of an offence must not exceed the maximum term permitted for the offence.

The provisions of s.227 are mirrored in s.228 in relation to offenders under 18 at the time of conviction (see 31 DETENTION OF YOUNG OFFENDERS).

The custodial term must be the shortest term commensurate with the seriousness of the offence or the offence and other offences associated with it (s.153(2)), save that, if the commensurate term would be less than 12 months, 12 months must be imposed (s.227(3)(b)). The extension period must be of such length as the judge considers necessary to protect the public from serious harm by the commission of further specified offences (s.227(2)(b) *but* must not exceed five years for a violent offence or eight years for a sexual offence. The extended sentence must not exceed the maximum permissible for the offence (s.227(4) and (5)). It will not usually be appropriate to impose consecutive extended sentences, whether the principal offence is serious or merely specified (*R. v Nelson* [2002] 1 Cr.App.R.(S.) 134).

It is to be noted that, in contrast to an extended sentence under PCSA 2000, s.85 (which is repealed by the CJA 2003, Sch.37, Pt 7) the new sentence does not apply to offences punishable with 10 years or more. This means that most sexual offences under SOA 2003 are outwith these provisions.

Until CJCS 2000, s.74 is brought into force, applying imprisonment to those aged 18 or over, the sentence for 18 to 20 year olds should continue to be expressed as "custody for life" or "detention in a Young Offender Institution".

Some parts of the judgment in *R. v Nelson* [2002] 1 Cr.App.R.(S.) 134 may continue to be of help, though the judgment must be read in the light of the new statutory provisions. Thus it was said in that case that the judge should approach the matter in three stages:

- decide on the sentence which would be comensurate with the offence;
- consider whether a longer period in custody was necessary to protect the public from serious harm from the offender; and
- consider whether the sentence was adequate to protect the public from the commission of further offences by the offender, and

impose an extended sentence.

The purpose of imposing an extended sentence was to prevent further offending and to secure rehabilitation; it was not to protect the public from serious harm (that was the purpose of PCC(S)A 2000, s.80(2)(b)).

It is not appropriate to reduce the custodial term because an extended licence period is imposed (*ibid.*).

In passing sentence the judge must take care to identify the offence or offences to which the extended sentence is intended to apply (*R. v Pepper and Others*, *The Times*, May 10, 2005).

Definitions

40–047 For the purposes of CJA 2003, Pt 12, Ch.5 an offence is: CJA 2003, s.224

(1) a **"specified offence"** if it is

  (a) a specified violent offence, that is an offence specified in CJA 2003, Sch.15, Pt 1 (at APPENDIX A, SECTION 2); or
  (b) a specified sexual offence, that is an offence specified in CJA 2003, Sch.15, Pt 2 (at APPENDIX A, SECTION 2);

(2) a **"serious offence"** if, and only if it is,

  (a) a "specified offence", and
  (b) apart from s.225, punishable in the case of a person aged 18 or over with imprisonment for life or imprisonment for a determinate period of 10 years or more (or in the case of an offender aged 18 but under 21, custody for life);

(3) a **"relevant offence"** (see s.229(4) if it is:

  (a) committed in England and Wales that is a specified offence,
  (b) committed in Scotland that is specified in Sch.12,
  (c) committed in Northern Ireland that is specified in Sch.13, or

(d) specified in CJA 2003, Schs.11, 12 or 13, and is constituted by an act or omission outside the United Kingdom.

"Serious harm" means death or serious personal injury, whether physical or psychological. This is a concept familiar since CJA 1991 s.2(2)(b) and pre–2004 decisions of CACD continue to be relevant to its assessment. For example, as was said in *R. v Bowler* 15 Cr.App.R.(S.) 78, sexual assaults which are relatively minor physically may lead to serious psychological injury; and downloading indecent images of children may cause serious psychological injury to a child arising not only from what the child has been forced to do but also from the knowledge that others will see what they were doing, see for instance *R. v Collard* [2004] Crim.L.R. 757 (*R. v Lang*, above).

A "specified" offence may or may not be a "serious" offence (s.224). It will be serious if it is punishable, in the case of a person aged 18 or over, with 10 years' imprisonment or more (s.224(2)(b)).

If serious, it may attract:

(1) life imprisonment; or
(2) imprisonment for public protection for an adult (s.225) or detention for life or detention for public protection for an offender under 18 on the day of conviction (s.225).

It will attract such a sentence if the judge is of opinion that there is a "significant risk" to members of the public of serious harm by the commission of further specified offences (ss.225(1), 226(1)). Indeterminate sentences should not be imposed for the commission of relatively minor offences.

"Members of the public" seems to be an all-embracing term. It is wider than "others", which would exclude the offender himself. In *R. v Lang* CACD saw no reason to construe it so as to exclude any particular group, for example prison officers or staff at mental hospitals, all of whom, like the offender, are members of the public. In some cases, particular members of the public may be more at risk than members of the public generally, for example when an offender has a history of violence to cohabitees or of sexually abusing children of cohabitees, or, where the offender has a particular problem in relation to a particular woman.

The judge, when considering the seriousness of an offence committed by an offender who has **previous convictions** must treat each previous conviction as an aggravating factor if, CJA 2003, s.143

in the case of that previous conviction, he considers that it can reasonably be so treated, having regard in particular to the nature of the offence to which the conviction relates and its relevance to the current conviction and the time that has elapsed since the conviction. This provision requires the court to look beyond the instant offence (and any offences associated with it) in order to see whether there are aggravating factors which he should have in mind when assessing the seriousness of that instant offence. Section 143(3) requires him to consider commission of an offence on bail as an aggravating factor, when considering the seriousness of that offence.

Dangerousness; its assessment

40–048 Where a person has been convicted of a "specified offence" and the judge has to assess under any of sections 225–228 whether there is a "significant risk" to members of the public of serious harm occasioned by the commission by the offender of further such offences, then if, at the time when that offence was committed, the offender: CJA 2003, s.229

(1) (a) was aged under 18; or
   (b) had not been convicted in any part of the UK of any "relevant offence" (see above, 40–047).
   the judge, in making his assessment:
   (i) *must* take into account all such information as is available to him about the nature and circumstances of the offence;
   (ii) *may* take into account any information which is before him about any pattern of behaviour of which the offence forms part; and
   (iii) *may* take into account any information about the offender which is before him;

(2) (a) was aged 18 or over; and
   (b) had been convicted in any part of the UK of one or more "relevant offence" (see above, 40–047), the judge must **assume** that there is such a risk unless, after taking into account:
   (i) all such information as is available to him about the nature and circumstances of each of the offences;
   (ii) where appropriate, any information which is before him any about pattern of behaviour of which any of the offences forms part; and
   (iii) any information about the offender which is before him.

> he considers that it would be unreasonable to conclude that there is such a risk.

When ss.229 and 224 are read together, unless the information about offences, pattern of behaviour and the offender to which regard must be paid show a significant risk of serious harm (defined by s.224 as death or serious injury) from further offences, it will usually be unreasonable to conclude that the assumption applies (*R. v Lang*, above).

Significant risk

40–049 Significant risk must be shown in relation to two matters:

(1) the commission of further specified, but not necessarily serious, offences; and
(2) the causing thereby of serious harm to members of the public.

If there is a significant risk of both, either a life sentence or indeterminate imprisonment for public protection must be imposed on an adult (s.225(2)(3)).

It must be:

(a) a life sentence if the offence is one for which the offender is liable to life imprisonment and the seriousness of the offence, or of the offence and one or more offences associated with it, is such as to justify imprisonment for life (s.225(2));
(b) it must be imprisonment for public protection (s.225(3)).

In relation to those under 18, there are similar provisions in relation to detention for life and detention for public protection subject, in the latter case, an additional criterion by reference to the adequacy of an extended sentence under s.228 (s.226(2)(3)).

In *R. v Lang* CACD considered that Parliament, in referring in ss.225(2)(b) and 226(2)(b) to the seriousness of an offence or offences being "such as to justify" imprisonment or detention for life, thereby making such a sentence mandatory, was intending to adopt the criteria for the imposition of a discretionary life sentence in *R. v Chapman* [2000] 1 Cr.App.R.(S.) 77 (see 48–023, below). This construction is supported by s.143(1) which requires the judge, when considering the seriousness of any offence, to consider the offender's culpability and "any harm which the offence caused, was intended to cause or might foreseeably have caused". This language clearly requires consideration of the culpability of the defendant as well as the seriousness of the offence and therefore involves consideration of dangerousness.

For all practical purposes, imprisonment and detention for public protection are exactly the same as a life sentence, though there may be exceptional cases where the offence itself is so serious that an indeterminate sentence is justified by the seriousness of the offence irrespective of the risk to the public (PD 2004, IV.47 and imprisonment or detention for public protection.

Factors in the assessment: *R. v Lang*

40–050 The most critical part of the "labyrinthian" provisions in ss.225(1) and 226(1) is the assessment of two matters which must be shown before life imprisonment or imprisonment for public protection becomes obligatory, that is the commission of a further specified offence and the causing of serious harm thereby.

In *R. v Lang* CACD considered that the following factors should be borne in mind when a judge is assessing significant risk.

Firstly, **the risk identified must be significant**, this is a higher threshold than mere possibility of occurrence and can be taken to mean (OED) "noteworthy, of considerable amount or importance."

Secondly, in assessing the risk of further offences being committed, **the judge should take into account:**

(1) the nature and circumstances of the current offence;
(2) the offender's history of offending including not just the kind of offence but its circumstances and the sentence passed, details of which the prosecution must have available, and
(3) whether the offending demonstrates any pattern; social and economic factors in relation to the offender including accommodation, employability, education, associates, relationships and drug or alcohol abuse; and the offender's thinking, attitude towards offending and supervision and emotional state. Information in relation to these matters will most readily, though not exclusively, come from antecedents and pre-sentence and medical reports. The judge will be guided, but not bound by, the assessment of risk in such reports. A judge who contemplates differing from the assessment in such a report should give both advocates the opportunity of addressing the point.

Thirdly, if **the foreseen specified offence** is:

(1) serious, there will clearly be some cases, though not by any means all, in which there may be a significant risk of serious harm. For example, robbery is a serious offence, but it can be committed in a wide variety of ways many of which do not give rise to a significant risk of serious harm. Judges should guard against assuming there is a significant risk of serious harm merely because the foreseen specified offence is serious. A pre-sentence report should usually be obtained before any sentence is passed which is based on significant risk of serious harm. In a small number of cases, where the circumstances of the current offence or the history of the offender suggest mental abnormality on his part, a medical report may be necessary before risk can properly be assessed;

(3) is not serious, there will be comparatively few cases in which a risk of serious harm will properly be regarded as significant. The huge variety of offences in Sch.15 includes many which, in themselves, are not suggestive of serious harm. Repetitive violent or sexual offending at a relatively low level without serious harm does not of itself give rise to a significant risk of serious harm in the future. There may, in such cases, be some risk of future victims being more adversely affected than past victims, but this, of itself, is unlikely to give rise to significant risk of serious harm.

Fourthly, in relation to the **rebuttable assumption** in s.229(3) gives rise, the judge is accorded a discretion if, in the light of information about the current offence, the offender and his previous offences, it would be unreasonable to conclude that there is a significant risk; the judge is expected, albeit starting from the assumption, to reach a reasonable conclusion in the light of the information before him. The assumption will be rebutted, if at all, as an exercise of judgment: the statute includes no reference to the burden or standard of proof. It will usually be unreasonable to conclude that the assumption applies unless information about the offences, pattern of behaviour and offender show a significant risk of serious harm from further offences.

In relation to offenders under 18 and adults with no relevant previous convictions at the time the specified offence was committed, the judge's discretion under s.229(2) is not constrained by any initial assumption such as, under s.229(3), applies to adults with previous convictions. It is still necessary, when sentencing young offenders, to bear in mind that, within a shorter time than adults, they may change and develop. This and their level of maturity may be highly pertinent when assessing what their future conduct may be and whether it may give rise to significant risk of serious harm.

In relation to a particularly young offender, an indeterminate sentence may be inappropriate even where a serious offence has been committed and there is a significant risk of serious harm from further offences (see *R. v D* [2005] EWCA Crim 2282).

The judge should usually, and in accordance with CJA 2003, s.174(1)(a) give reasons for all his conclusions: in particular, that there is or is not a significant risk of further offences or serious harm; where the assumption under s.229(3) arises for making or not making the assumption which the statute requires unless this would be unreasonable; and for not imposing an extended sentence under ss.227 and 228. He should, in giving reasons, briefly identify the information which he has taken into account.

The "appropriate custodial term"

40–051 The "appropriate custodial term" means a term of imprisonment which:

(1) is the term that would (apart from these provisions) be imposed in compliance with CJA 2003, s.153(2) (i.e. the shortest term commensurate with the seriousness of the offence); or
(2) where the term that would be so imposed is a term of less than 12 months, a term of 12 months; provided that in the case of:
   (a) a specified "violent offence", the extension period does not exceed five years;
   (b) a specified sexual offence, the extension period does not exceed eight years, and
   (c) the term of any extension period does not exceed the maximum permitted for the offence.

It is the aggregate which is not to exceed the maximum term for the offence: *ibid.*, *R. v Langstone* [2001] 2 Cr.App.R.(S.) 98.

Approach to sentence

40–052 Under the previous legislation it was said that the judge should approach the matter in three stages;

(1) decide on the sentence which would be comensurate with the offence;

(2) consider whether a longer period in custody was necessary to protect the public from serious harm from the offender; and

(3) consider whether the sentence was adequate to protect the public from the commission of further offences by the offender, and

impose an extended sentence (*R. v Nelson* [2002] 1 Cr.App.R. (S.) 134).

The purpose of imposing an extended sentence was to prevent further offending and to secure rehabilitation; it was not to protect the public from serious harm (that was the purpose of PCC(S)A 2000, s.80(2)(b)).

It is not appropriate to reduce the custodial term because an extended licence period is imposed (*ibid.*).

In passing sentence the judge must take care to idenity the offence or offences to which the extended sentence is intended to apply (*R. v Pepper and Others The Times*, May 10, 2005).

12. Required sentences for certain repeat offences

(1) Mandatory ("automatic") life sentence for second serious offence

40–053 Where: PCC(S)A 2000, s.109(1), (2), (4); SOA 2003, Sch.8, para.43(3)

(1) a person is convicted of a "serious offence" **committed after October 1, 1997** and **before April 4, 2005**; and

(2) he was over 18 when that offence was committed, and had been convicted in any part of the UK of another "serious offence",

the judge must impose:

(a) where the offender is 21 or over when convicted—a sentence of imprisonment for life; or

(b) where he is under 21 at that time—a sentence of custody for life under s.94; unless of opinion

(c) that there are exceptional circumstances relating to either of the offences or to the offender, which justify his not doing so.

The new sentences for dangerous offenders (CJA 2003, Ch.5) apply where the relevant offence is committed on or after April 4, 2000.

Approach to sentence

40–054 In approaching the question of sentence, the judge needs:

(1) to determine whether the two serious offences which trigger the statutory assumption contained in s.109 are present; and if they are

(2) to assess the extent to which the offender is a real risk to the public, bearing in mind that the burden is on the offender of displacing the statutory assumption by showing exceptional circumstances.

In the guideline case of *R. v Buckland* [2000] 2 Cr.App.R.(S) 217 it was pointed out that:

(a) the section was founded on an assumption that those who had been convicted of two qualifying serious offences presented such a serious and continuing danger to public safety that they should be liable to indefinite incarceration and, if released, should be liable indefinitely to recall to prison. Where such a danger did exist, the judge would be justified in imposing the statutory sentence, even if exceptional circumstances were found to exist;

(b) however, if exceptional circumstances were found, and the evidence suggested that the offender did not present a serious and continuing danger to public safety, the court might be justified in imposing a lesser penalty.

Meaning of "conviction"

40–055 Care needs to be taken in identifying what is a "conviction". In relation, for example, to probation orders under the former legislation, and supervision orders (*R. v Frost* [2001] Crim.L.R. 143).

There is no age requirement in respect of the first offence; it is only the second offence which must be committed after the commencement date: *R. v Offen and Others* Crim.L.R. 63; *R. v Buckland* 2 Cr.App.R.(S.) 217. The proviso of "exceptional circumstances" applies to both offences (*R. v Offen*, above).

Such a sentence is not to be regarded as "a sentence fixed by law". The judge is bound to have regard to the circumstances relating to the offences or to the offender. Where he does not impose a mandatory life sentence, he must state in open court his opinion, and the nature of the exceptional circumstances. PCC(S)A 2000, s.109(3)

A hospital order may not be made in respect of a mentally disordered offender as an alternative to such a sentence though a hospital direction under MHA 1983, s.45A (inserted by CSA 1997, s.46) may (see MHA 1983, s.71(1); CSA Sch.4, para.12(1), and 48 MENTALLY DISORDERED OFFENDERS).

Meaning of "serious offences"

40–056 "Serious offences" are defined as any of the following committed in England and Wales; PCC(S)A 2000, s.109(5)–(7); SOA 2003, s.139, Sch.6, para.43(3)

(1) an attempt, conspiracy or incitement to commit murder;
(2) soliciting murder (OAPA 1861, s.4);
(3) manslaughter (see *R. v Richards* [2002] Crim.L.R. 144);
(4) an offence under OAPA 1861, s.18 (see *R. v Richards*, above);
(5) rape (*R. v Wood* [2001] Cr.App.R.(S.) 20 (non-consensual buggery is not rape, *ibid*. *R. v Cochrane* (1994) 15 Cr.App.R.(S.) 708) or an attempt to commit rape);
(6) intercourse with a girl under 13 (SOA 1956, s.5);
(7) rape, assault by penetration under SOA 2003, ss.1 or 2;
(8) causing a person to engage in sexual activity without consent, under SOA 2003, s.4 where the activity caused involved penetration within *ibid*., s.4(4)(a) to (d);
(9) rape of a child under 13, assault on a child under 13 by penetration, under SOA 2003, s.5 or 6;
(10) causing or inciting a child under 13 to engage in sexual activity under SOA 2003, s.8, where an activity involving penetration within s.8(3)(a) to (d) was caused;
(11) sexual activity with a person with a mental disorder impeding choice, under SOA 2003, s.30, where the touching involved penetration within s.30(3)(a)–(d);
(12) causing or inciting a person with a mental disorder impeding choice to engage in sexual activity, under SOA 2003, s.31, where an activity involving penetration within s.31(3)(a)–(d) was caused;
(13) an attempt to commit an offence within any of paras (7) to (12) above;
(14) offences under the Firearms Act 1968, ss.16, 17, 18; and
(15) robbery, where at the time of the commission of the offence, the offender had in his possession a firearm or imitation firearm within the meaning of that Act.

An *attempt* to commit a "serious offence" is not in itself a serious offence, except in the case of attempted murder and attempted rape; attempted robbery is not a "serious offence" (*R. v Buckland* [2000] Crim.L.R. 307).

An offender has not committed the "serious" offence of robbery while in possession of a firearm or imitation firearm unless there is included in the indictment a count charging him with an offence under FA 1968 and a guilty verdict or plea on that count (*R. v Murphy* [2002] Crim.L.R. 674). See also *R. v Benjafield & Anor* [2004] 1 Cr.App.R.(S.) 52.

Subsection 109(5) merely identifies what offences are serious in order to determine whether s.109(1) applies so as to trigger the application of the provisions. It has no part to play in the determination of whether there are "exceptional circumstances" to displace the statutory assumption (*R. v Richards*, above).

"Exceptional circumstances"

40–057 These provisions create a statutory assumption that an offender convicted of two qualifying offences presents such a serious and continuing danger to the safety of the public that he should be liable to indefinite imprisonment. It is for the sentencing judge to assess the extent to which the offender poses a real risk to the public, in which case his release will be deferred. The issue must be addressed in every case: *R. v Offen* [2001] 2 Cr.App.R.(S.) 10; see also *R. v McDonald* [2001] 2 Cr.App.R.(S.) 127; *R. v Close* [2002] 1 Cr.App.R.(S.) 16; *R. v Craig* [2002] 1 Cr.App.R.(S.) 74; *R. v Baff* [2003] 2 Cr.App.R.(S.) 37.

The principles in *Offen* should be applied in both *pre-Offen* and *post-Offen* cases (*R. v Fletcher, R. v Smith* [2001] Crim.L.R. 833). If it can be shown that the statutory assumption is displaced because there is, in fact, no need to protect the public from the offender, then the position is "exceptional" and s.109(2) has no application. Where there is no significant risk of danger to the public by way of either violent or sexual offences, the case is to be regarded as an exception to the norm (*R. v Stark* [2002] 2 Cr.App.R.(S.) 104; *R. v Fletcher & Smith* [2002] 1 Cr.App.R.(S.) 82; followed in *R. v Magalhaes* [2005] Crim.L.R. 144 disapproving *R. v Richards* [2002] 2 Cr.App.R.(S.) 26).

The sentence is not to be regarded as a "sentence fixed by law"; the judge is bound to take into account the circumstances of the offence and of the offender.

The burden of proving exceptional circumstances, and thus displacing the assumption, is on the accused (*R. v Faulkner*) [2002] 1 Cr.App.R.(S.) 133).

The meaning of "exceptional"

40–058 "Exceptional" is to be construed as an ordinary English word; it is not a term of art *(R. v Kelly* [1999] 2 Cr.App.R.(S.) 176; *R. v Buckland* [2000] 2 Cr.App.R.(S.) 217; *R. v Williams* [2000] Crim.L.R. 597; *R. v McDonald* [2001] 2 Cr.App.R.(S.) 127; *R. v Kelly (No. 2)* [2002] 1 Cr.App.R.(S.) 85; *R. v Turner (No. 2)*

[2002] 1 Cr.App.R.(S.) 160). To be "exceptional" a circumstance need not be unique or unprecedented or very rare, but it cannot be one which is regularly or routinely encountered.

The position under s.109(2) is not be equated with that pertaining to the consideration of a discretionary life sentence: see 48 LIFE SENTENCES. The statutory assumption remains in place; the burden of displacing it is on the offender. Whether that burden is satisfied depends on all the facts and the evidence (*R. v Turner* [2002] Crim.L.R. 218 considering *R. v Kelly* [1999] 2 Cr.App.R.(S.) 176; *R. v Buckland* [2000] 2 Cr.App.R.(S.) 217: *R. v Offen* [2001] 2 Cr.App.R.(S.) 10; *R. v McDonald* [2001] 2 Cr.App.R.(S.) 127; *R. v Kelly (No. 2)* [2001] 1 Cr.App.R.(S.) 85).

The fact that the two offences are of a different nature, or that a long period elapsed between the offences during which the offender committed no other offences, may, but will not necessarily, reflect on the degree of risk to the public which he constitutes *(R. v Turner* [2002] Crim.L.R. 218). The same is true of two differing crimes, or the age of the offender (see the anomaly identified in *R. v Frost* [2001] Crim.L.R. 143).

40–059 Since the purpose of the legislation is for a life sentence to be passed in circumstances where it was not previously imposed (see *R. v Harvey* [2000] Cr.App.R.(S.) 368), it follows that the following circumstances do not constitute "exceptional" circumstances so as to displace the statutory assumption:

(1) the youth of the offender at the time of the first offence, a long interval between the offences (even a crime-free one) or the different nature of the offences;
(2) the comparatively short sentence passed for the first offence (*Att.-Gen.'s Reference (No. 53 of 1998*) [1999] 2 Cr.App.R. 185);
(3) the fact that the first offence attracted only a short sentence, or that in the case of a joint enterprise there may be disparity between the sentences imposed on different offenders—"it is a disparity consequent on an Act of Parliament" (*R. v McKay* [1999] Crim. L.R. 755);
(4) the gap between the commission of the first offence and the instant offence (*R. v Kelly*, above; *R. v Turner* [2000] Crim.L.R. 492);
(5) the offender's acute mental illness at the time of the offence (*R. v Newman* [2000] Crim.L.R. 309).

Provocation may or may not give rise to "exceptional circumstances" displacing the statutory assumption (*cf. R. v Sanderson*

(1993) 14 Cr.App.R.(S.) 361; *R. v Huntley* (1993) 14 Cr.App.R. (S.) 795; *R. v Turner*, above). In *R. v Newman*, above, mental illness was held not to be an exceptional circumstance.

In *R. v Stephens* [2000] Crim.L.R. 402 it was held that failure to warn the offender of his liability to these provisions was capable of amounting to an "exceptional circumstance".

The specified period

40–060 As in the case of any mandatory life sentence, the judge must specify the minimum period to be served, and the manner in which he arrives at it. Unless the offender would qualify for a discretionary life sentence (see 45 LIFE SENTENCES) it is this period, rather than the automatic life sentence, which is likely to determine the date of his release.

(2) Minimum seven years for third Class A drug trafficking offence

40–061 Where: PCC(S)A 2000, s.110(1), (2), (5), (6); CJA 2003, s.304, Sch.32 Pt 1, para.114

(1) an offender is convicted of a Class A drug trafficking offence committed after October 1, 1997; and
(2) at the time the offence was committed, the offender was 18 or over and had been convicted in any part of the UK of two other Class A drug trafficking offences; and
(3) one of those had been committed after he had been convicted of the other,

the judge must impose upon an offender an appropriate custodial sentence for a term of at least seven years, that is, in the case of:

(a) an offender who is 21 or over, a sentence of at least seven years' imprisonment; or in the case of
(b) an offender under 21, a sentence of at least seven years' detention in a young offender institution,

unless he is of opinion that there are particular circumstances relating to any of the offences or to the offender, which would make that sentence unjust in all the circumstances.

A hospital order may be made in respect of a mentally disordered offender as an alternative to such a sentence, or a hospital direction under MHA 1983, s.45A (inserted by CSA 1997, s.46) and see 48 MENTALLY DISORDERED OFFENDERS. MHA 1983, s.87(1); CSA 1997, Sch.4, para.12(2)

Definitions

40–062 "Class A drug trafficking offences", as the term implies, means a drug trafficking offence committed in respect of PCC(S)A 2000, s.110(5); PCA 2002, s.456, Sch.11, para.37

a Class A drug, and for this purpose "Class A drug" has the same meaning as in MDA 1971; "drug trafficking offence" means an offence which is specified in:

(1) PCA 2002, Sch.2, para.1, or
(2) so far as it relates to that paragraph, para.10 of that Schedule.

The approach to "unjust"

40–063 In *R. v Harvey* [2000] 1 Cr.App.R.(S.) 368, the CACD rejected an approach to the section based on the contention that a sentence passed under the section which was manifestly excessive on the facts of the case was "unjust."

Discount for plea

40–064 Nothing prevents the judge under this section, after taking into account any matters referred to in PCC(S)A 2000, s.152, from imposing a sentence which is not less than 80 per cent of the minimum mandatory sentence (see *R. v Brown* [2000] Crim.L.R. 496; *R. v Hickson* [2002] 1 Cr.App.R.(S.) 298).

(3) Minimum three years for third domestic burglary

40–065 Where:

PCC(S)A 2000, s.111(1), (2), (5), (6); CJCSA 2000, Sch.7, para.191; CJA 2003, s.304, Sch.32, Pt 1, para.115

(1) an offender is convicted of a domestic burglary (i.e. a burglary committed in respect of a building or part of a building which is a dwelling) **committed after November 30, 1999**; and
(2) at the time when that burglary was committed, he was 18 or over and has been convicted in England or Wales of two other domestic burglaries; and
(3) one of those other burglaries was committed after he had been convicted of the other and both of them were **committed after November 30, 1999**,

the judge must impose a sentence of imprisonment for a term of at least three years, except where he is of opinion that there are particular circumstances which:

(a) relate to any of the offences or to the offender, and
(b) would make it unjust to do so in all the circumstances.

Attempted burglary is not burglary (*R. v Maguire* [2003] 2 Cr.App.R.(S.) 10).

Prescribed sequence

40–066 The sequence of events required before an offender qualifies for such as sentence is as follows:

(1) he must have committed a first offence of burglary;
(2) he must have been convicted of that offence; then
(3) he must have committed a second offence of burglary, and then
(4) he must have been convicted of that second offence; then
(5) he must have committed a third offence of burglary.

(*R. v Hoare* [2004] Crim.L.R. 594).

See as to a Gilham situation *R. v Gibson* [2004] Crim.L.R. 592.

Proof of conviction

40–067 In respect of qualifying offences, a certificate from the sentencing court is sufficient proof. PCC(S)A 2000, s.113

Miscellaneous

40–68 Note that:

(1) In relation to required sentences, a person convicted under Service Law, where the corresponding civil offence qualifies under s.110–111, these provisions apply as if he had been convicted in England and Wales of the corresponding civil offence; PCC(S)A 2000, s.114
(2) where an offence is found to have been committed over a period of two or more days, or at some time during a period of two or more days, it will be taken for the purposes of ss.110–111 to have been committed on the last of those days; PCC(S)A 2000, s.115
(3) failure to warn the offender of his liability to these provisions is capable of amounting to an "exceptional circumstance" (*R. v Stephens* [2000] Crim.L.R. 402).

12 Prescribed minimum sentences for certain firearms offences

40–069 Where a person is convicted of certain offences under FA 1968, s.51, the judge *must* impose an appropriate custodial sentence, that is, in the case of an offender **convicted after January 22, 2004**: FA 1968, s.51A; CJA 2003, s.287

(1) aged 18 or over when convicted (but see below), a sentence of imprisonment;
(2) aged under 18 at that time, a sentence of detention under PCC(S)A 2000, s.91,

for at least the required mimimum term (with or without a fine), being:

(a) five years in the case of an offender aged 18 or over when he committed the offence, or
(b) three years in the case of an offender under 18 at that time

unless he is of opinion that there are exceptional circumstances relating to the offence or to the offender which justify his not doing so.

Despite the wording of the Act, CACD pointed out in *R. v Campbell* [2006] Crim.L.R. 654 be no alternative "minimum" of a term of detention in a young offender instititution. The judge must therefore assess the proper sentence leaving out the "minimum" specification.

Where an offence is found to have been committed over a period of two or more days, or at some time during a period of two or more days, it is to be taken to have been committed on the last of those day.

The minimum sentence is not applicable unless the offender is *convicted* of the offence; possession of a firearm without there being any offence included in the indictment is not sufficiemnt (*Att.-Gen.'s Reference (No. 114 of 2004)* [2005] Crim.L.R. 312).

Cases in which exceptional circumstances can be said to arise are likely to be rare (*R. v Jordan and Others* [2005] Crim.L.R. 312) but see *R. v Blackall* [2005] Crim.L.R. 875 (paraplegic offender); *R. v Mehmet* [2005] Crim.L.R. 875 (early plea, good character, no criminal intention, no ammunition) and *R. v Rehman and Another* [2005] Crim.L.R. 878 (early plea, good character, cooperation with the authorities, public employment).

The Act does not permit of a discount on the minimum sentence for a plea of guilty (*R. v Jordan and Others* [2005] Crim.L.R. 313).

CACD has said that circumstances are exceptional for the purposes of s.51A(2) if the minimum five year term would be an arbitrary and disproportionate sentence (*R. v Rehman, The Times*, September 27, 2005).

13. Suspending a sentence

General

40–070 A sentence of imprisonment may, in certain circumstances, be suspended, but the judge's powers, and the nature and effect of the sentence will depend on whether the offence was committed:

(1) **before April 4, 2005**, in which case PCC(S)A 2000, s.118–s.124 apply; or

(2) **on or after April 4, 2005**, when the provisions of CJA 2003, ss.189–194 apply.

(a) PCC(S)A 2000, ss.118–124

Powers

40–071 A judge passing a sentence of imprisonment for: PCC(S)A 2000, s.118(1)–(5)

(1) a term of not more than **two years**;
(2) an offence committed before the **April 4, 2005**,

may order that the sentence shall not take effect unless:

(a) during a period specified in the order, the offender commits in Great Britain another offence punishable with imprisonment; and thereafter
(b) a court having power to do so orders under s.119 that the sentence take effect, provided that a sentence must not be suspended unless the judge is of opinion that:
  (i) the case is one in which a sentence of imprisonment would have been appropriate even without the power to suspend it (*R. v English* (1984) 6 Cr.App.R.(S.) 60; *R. v Fletcher* (1991) 12 Cr.App.R.(S.) 671); and
  (ii) that the exercise of the power can be justified by the *exceptional circumstances* of the case.

The period specified must not be less than one year or more than two, beginning with the date of the order.

Consecutive or concurrent

40–072 It is for the judge suspending the sentence to decide whether one or more terms are to run concurrently or consecutively *(Practice Direction* (1962) 46 Cr.App.R. 119). A suspended sentence passed cannot be made consecutive to another suspended sentence which is not brought into effect *(R. v Blakeway* (1969) 53 Cr.App.R. 498).

Need for exceptional circumstances

40–073 It is crucial to the amended provisions of s.118, that the judge must not impose a suspended sentence unless he is of the opinion that the exercise of the power can be justified by the exceptional circumstances of the case *(R. v Okinikan* (1993) 96 Cr.App.R. 431; *R. v Sanderson* (1993) 14 Cr.App.R. 361).

CACD (in *R. v Okinikan*) declined to lay down any definition of "exceptional circumstances"; they will inevitably depend on the facts of each individual case. CACD pointed out, however, that taken on their own or in combination, good character, youth and an early plea of guilty were not exceptional circumstances justifying a suspended sentence; they are common features of many cases. See also *Att.-Gen.'s Reference (No. 5 of 1993)* (1994) 15 Cr.App.R.(S.) 201; *R. v Dhanji Gorasia* [2002] 1 Cr.App.R.(S.) 84; *R. v Smith* [2002] 1 Cr.App.R.(S.) 258).

While many offenders claim that they intend to take treatment for, e.g. a drug addiction, and there is nothing exceptional in that, it may be an exceptional circumstance where an offender has taken "vigorous, persistent and determined" action to obtain treatment (*Att.-Gen.'s Reference (No. 34 of 1999)* [2000] 1 Cr.App.R.(S.) 322.)

Time spent in custody

40–074 The ordinary rules as to crediting time spent in custody on remand apply to suspended sentences, but a suspended sentence is treated as: PCC(S)A 2000, s.87(8), (9)

(1) a sentence of imprisonment when it takes effect under s.119; and
(2) as imposed by the order under which it takes effect.

Combinations; ancillary orders

40–075 The purpose of suspending a sentence of imprisonment is to avoid sending an offender to prison, it is therefore bad sentencing practice to impose: PCC(S)A 2000, s.118(5)

(1) on the same occasion, an immediate term in respect of one offence and a suspended term in respect of another (*R. v Sapiano* (1968) 52 Cr.App.R. 674);
(2) a suspended sentence on an offender already serving an immediate term for another offence (*R. v Hammond* [1969] Crim.L.R. 500).

A judge imposing a suspended sentence on an offender for an offence under PCC(S)A 2000, may not impose a community sentence on him in respect of that or any other offence, but he must consider whether the circumstances of the case are such as to warrant in addition the imposition of a fine or the making of a compensation order.

As to combining a suspended sentence supervision order, see 40–078 below.

Activation; obligation to deal with order

40–076 Where an offender is convicted of an offence punishable with, imprisonment during the period of a suspended sentence, and either he; PCC(S)A 2000, s.119(1), (2)

(1) he is so convicted by or before a court having power under s.120 to deal with him in respect of the suspended sentence; or
(2) subsequently appears or is brought before such a court

then, unless the sentence has already taken effect, that court must consider his case and the judge must deal with him by one of the following methods:

(a) by ordering that the suspended sentence take effect with the original term unaltered;
(b) by ordering that the sentence take effect with the substitution of a lesser term for the original term;
(c) by varying the original order by substituting for the period specified in it an operational period expiring not later than two years from the date of the variation; or
(d) by expressly making "no order" with respect to the suspended sentence.

An order under (a) must be made unless the judge is of opinion that it would be unjust to do so in view of all the circumstances, including the facts of the subsequent offence, and where he is of that opinion he must state his reasons.

Any question as to whether an offender has committed an offence within the operational period of a suspended sentence is to be determined by the judge, not by the verdict of a jury. PCC(S)A 2000, s.119(5)

The Crown Court officer will notify the original court of the method adopted to deal with its suspended sentence. PCC(S)A 2000, s.119(6)

Concurrent or consecutive

40–077 Where the judge orders that a suspended sentence take effect, with or without any variation of the original term, he may, subject to PCC(S)A 2000, s.84 (restrictions on consecutive sentences for released prisoners) order that the sentence: PCC(S)A 2000, s.119(3), (4)

(1) take effect immediately; or
(2) commence on the expiry of another term of imprisonment passed on the offender by another court.

For the purposes of any enactment conferring rights of appeal, an order made with respect to a suspended sentence is treated as a sentence passed on the offender by that court for the offence for which the suspended sentence was passed. A suspended sentence passed on appeal is treated as if it was passed by the court in which the offender was originally sentenced. PCC(S)A 2000, ss.119(8), 220(3)

Suspended sentence supervision order

40–078 Where: PCC(S)A 2000, s.122(l)–(3)

(1) a judge passes on an offender a suspended sentence of more than six months for a single offence, or
(2) a subsequent judge dealing with an offender under s.119 deals with an offender by varying the operational period of a sentence or by making no order,

he may make a suspended sentence supervision order placing the offender under the supervision of a supervising officer for a period specified in the order, being a period not exceeding the operational period of the suspended sentence, though in a case under (2) above, only where;

(a) he makes it in place of such an order made originally, or
(b) if the court which passed the original sentence could have made an order but did not do so.

The order will specify the local justice area in which the offender resides or will reside, and the supervising officer will be an officer of a local probation board with whom the offender is required to keep in touch, and to notify any change of address. The order may be amended by a magistrates' court if the offender changes or proposes to change his address. PCC(S)A 2000, s.122(5)(6)

Copies of the order will be given by the Crown Court officer to a probation officer assigned to the court and copies will be sent to the designated officer of the magistrates' court specified in the order.

The order ceases to have effect if, before the end of the period specified in it a court orders the suspended sentence passed in those proceedings to take effect under s.119 or the order is revoked under s.124(1) or is replaced under s.122. PCC(S)A 2000, s.124(4)

Breach of the order; revocation; amendment

40–079 Breaches of a suspended sentence supervision order are dealt with in the magistrates' court. The order may be revoked on the application of the offender or the supervising officer: PCC(S)A 2000, s.124(1)(3)

(1) if it was made by the Crown Court and includes a direction reserving the power of revoking it to that court, by the Crown Court; or
(2) in any other case, by a magistrates' court acting for the local justice area for the time being specified in the order.

Amendments may be made by the magistrates' court.

(b) CJA 2003, ss.189–194

Character of new provisions

40–080 The suspended sentence created by CJA 2003, ss.189–194 applies in respect of offences **committed after April 4, 2005**. It differs in several respects from that under the previous legislation, being designed to be more widely available and to be more effective in controlling offending behaviour. In particular:

(1) it applies only to short term sentences of imprisonment, i.e. terms of at least 14 days but not more than 12 months;
(2) a term of detention in a young offender institution may be suspended where an an offender is aged 18 but under 21;
(3) the power is not restricted to "exceptional circumstances"; and
(4) in place of an ancillary suspended sentence supervision order, the suspension of the custodial part of the sentence is on condition that the offender undertake specified activities in the community.

Thus:

(a) the custodial term may be activated not only by the commission of a further offence during the operational period, but also by a breach of the terms of suspension; and
(b) the judge has a discretionary power to review the order from time to time.

Subject to any provision to the contrary contained in CJA 1967, PCC(S)A 2000 or any other enactment passed or instrument made under any enactment after December 31, 1967, a suspended sentence which has not taken effect under CJA 2003, Sch.12, para.8 is to be treated as a sentence of imprisonment for the purposes of all enactments and instruments made under enactments (CJA 2003, s.189(6); SI 2005/543).

Statutory provisions

40–081 A judge passing a sentence of imprisonment (or in the case of a person aged at least 18 but under 21, detention in a young offender institution) a term of at least 14 days but not more than 12 months for an offence **committed on or after April 4, 2005**, may order: CJA 2003, s.189(1)(2)(7)

(1) the offender to comply during a specified supervision period with one or more of the requirements falling within s.190(1) and specified in the order; and

(2) that the sentence of imprisonment (or detention in a young offender institution) is not to take effect unless:
   (a) during the supervision period the offender fails to comply with a requirement imposed under (1) above; or
   (b) during the "operational period" specified in the order, the offender commits in Great Britain another offence (whether or not punishable with imprisonment).

Where two or more sentences imposed on the same occasion are to be served consecutively, the power conferred by subs.(1) is not exercisable in relation to any of them unless the aggregate of the terms of the sentences does not exceed 65 weeks.

There is no need for "exceptional circumstances" as contained in PCC(S)A 2000 ss.118–124 unless sentence is being passed in respect of a pre-commencement offence. In respect of pre-commencement offences, the aggregate of the terms may be up to two years instead of 12 months.

Note that:

(i) the supervision period and the operational period must each be a period of not less than six months and not more than two years beginning with the date of the order. CJA 2003, s.189(3)(4)

(ii) the supervision period must not end later than the operational period.

A judge passing a suspended sentence on any person for an offence may not impose a community sentence in his case in respect of that offence or any other offence of which he is convicted by or before the court or for which he is dealt with by the court. CJA 2003, s.189(5)

Pre-conditions to suspension

40–082 A suspended sentence being a sentence of imprisonment, it is subject to the same criteria as a sentence of imprisonment which is to commence immediately. The judge must therefore be satisfied that the custody threshold has been passed and that the length of the term is the shortest term commensurate with the seriousness of the offence. SGC 3, 2.2.6

There are similarities under CJA 2003 between a suspended sentence and a community sentence. In both cases, in that requirements may be imposed during the supervision period, and the judge may respond to a breach by imposing a custodial sentence. The crucial difference is that the suspended sentence is a prison sentence and is appropriate only for an offence that SGC 3, 2.2.10

passes the custody threshold and for which imprisonment is the only option; a community sentence may be imposed for an offence that passes the custody threshold where the court considers that to be appropriate.

The judge, if minded to impose a suspended sentence

(1) must already have decided that a prison sentence is justified; and
(2) should also have decided the length of sentence that would be the shortest term commensurate with the seriousness of the offence if it were to be imposed immediately;
(3) should not, having decided to suspend the sentence impose a longer term than he would have if the sentence were to take effect immediately. SGC 3, 2.2.12

SGC has recommended that the judge ask himself whether:

(a) the custody threshold has been passed;
(b) if so, is is unavoidable that a custodial sentence be imposed;
(c) if so, that sentence can be suspended;
(d) if not, the sentence can be served intermittently.

If not, the judge should impose a sentence which takes immediate effect for the term commensurate with the seriousness of the offence. SGC 3, 2.2.11

Length of term

40–083 A prison sentence which is suspended should be for the same term which would have applied if the offender were being sentenced to immediate custody, and in assessing the length of the operational period, the judge should have in mind:

(1) the relatively short length of the sentence being suspended; and
(2) the advantages to be gained by retaining the opportunity to extend the operational period at a later stage (see 14 BREACH, AMENDMENT AND REVOCATION).

The operational period of a suspended sentence should reflect the length of the sentence being suspended. As an approximate guide an operational period of up to:

(a) 12 months might normally be appropriate for a suspended sentence of up to six months; and
(b) 18 months might normally be appropriate for a suspended sentence of up to 12 months. SGC 3, 2.2. 10–13

The ordinary rules as to crediting time spent in custody on remand apply to suspended sentences, but a suspended sentence is treated as a sentence of imprisonment when it takes effect under s.119 and is "imposed" by the order under which it takes effect.

Consecutive or concurrent

40–084 Under the previous legislation it was for the judge suspending the sentence to decide whether one or more terms are to run concurrently or consecutively (Practice Direction (1962) 46 Cr.App.R. 119). A suspended sentence passed could not be made consecutive to another suspended sentence which was not brought into effect (*R. v Blakeway* (1969) 53 Cr.App.R. 498).

Combinations; ancillary orders

40–085 Since the whole purpose of suspending a sentence of imprisonment is to avoid sending an offender to prison, it is bad sentencing practice to impose:

(1) on the same occasion, an immediate term in respect of one offence and a suspended term in respect of another (*R. v Sapiano* (1968) 52 Cr.App.R. 674);
(2) a suspended sentence on an offender already serving an immediate term for another offence (*R. v Hammond* [1969] Crim.L.R. 500).

Imposition of requirements by suspended sentence order

40–086 The requirements which may be imposed under s.190(1)(2) are those numbered (1)–(13) at 21–021 (see 21 COMMUNITY SENTENCES) subject to the restrictions of ss.150 and 218 and the provisions as to particular requirements stated in that paragraph. CJA 2003, s.190(1), (2)

As to electronic monitoring, see 40–088, below.

Selection of requirements

40–087 The particular requirement(s) will need to ensure that they properly address those factors that are most likely to reduce the risk of re-offending. SGC 3, 2. 2. 14

Whilst:

(1) the offence for which a suspended sentence is imposed is generally likely to be more serious than one for which a community sentence is imposed;
(2) the imposition of the custodial sentence is a clear punishment and deterrent.

Because of the very clear deterrent threat involved in a suspended sentence:

(a) requirements imposed as part of that sentence should generally be less onerous than those imposed as part of a community sentence; and
(b) a judge who seeks to impose onerous or intensive requirements on an offender should reconsider his decision to suspend a term of imprisonment and consider whether a community sentence might be more appropriate.

Before making a suspended sentence order imposing two or more different requirements falling within subs.(1), the court must consider whether, in the circumstances of the case, the requirements are compatible with each other. CJA 2003, s.190(5)

Electronic monitoring requirement

40–088 The judge's powers to make an electronic monitoring requirement when imposing a suspended sentence are the same as where he makes a community order, as to which see above, 21–022 in 21 COMMUNITY SENTENCES. CJA 2003, s.190(3), (4)

Breach, amendment and revocation

40–089 Breach, amendment and revocation of the order is dealt with under CJA 2003, Sch.12, for which see 14 BREACH, AMENDMENT AND REVOCATION. As to transfer to Scotland and Northern Ireland, see CJA 2003, Sch.13.

Power to provide for review of suspended sentence order

40–090 A suspended sentence order may:

CJA 2003, s.191(1), (2), (3), (5)

(1) provide for the order to be reviewed periodically at specified intervals,
(2) provide for each review to be made, subject to s.173(3), at a review hearing held for the purpose by the judge,
(3) require the offender to attend each review hearing, and
(4) provide for the responsible officer to make to "the court responsible for the order", before each review, a report on the offender's progress in complying with the community requirements of the order.

This provision does not apply in the case of an order imposing a drug rehabilitation requirement, provision for such a requirement to be subject to review being made by CJA 2003, s.210.

"The court responsible for a suspended sentence order" is:

(a) where a court is specified in the order in accordance with subs.(4), to that court;
(b) in any other case, to the court by which the order is made.

A suspended sentence order made on an appeal brought from the Crown Court or from CACD is deemed for this purpose to have been made by the Crown Court.

Periodic reviews of suspended sentence order

40–091 At a review hearing the judge may, after considering the responsible officer's report, amend the community requirements, or any provision of the order, which relates to those requirements, but: CJA 2003, s.192(1), (2), (3)

(1) may not amend the community requirements of the order so as to impose a requirement of a different kind unless the offender **consents** to that requirement,
(2) may not amend a mental health treatment requirement, a drug rehabilitation requirement or an alcohol treatment requirement unless the offender **consents** to comply with the amended requirement,
(3) may amend the supervision period only if the period as amended complies with s.189(3) and (4),
(4) may not amend the operational period of the suspended sentence, and
(5) except with the offender's consent, may not amend the order while the order is being appealed.

For the purposes of s.192(2)(a) a community requirement falling within any paragraph of s.190(1) is of the same kind as another community requirement if they fall within the same paragraph of s.190(1), and an electronic monitoring requirement is a community requirement of the same kind as any requirement falling within s.190(1) to which it relates.

Conduct of review hearing

40–092 If:

(1) before a review hearing is held the judge, after considering the responsible officer's report, is of the opinion that the offender's progress in complying with the community requirements of the order is satisfactory, he may order that no review hearing is to be held at that review; and CJA 2003, s.192(4), (8)
(2) before a review hearing is held, or at a hearing, the judge, after considering that report, is of that opinion, it may CJA 2003, s.173(5), (6), (7), (8)

amend the suspended sentence order so as to provide for each subsequent review to be held without a hearing. If

(a) at a review held without a hearing the judge, after considering the responsible officer's report, is of the opinion that the offender's progress under the order is no longer satisfactory, he may require the offender to attend a hearing at a specified time and place;
(b) at a review hearing the judge is of the opinion that the offender has without reasonable excuse failed to comply with any of the community requirements of the order, he may adjourn the hearing for the purpose of dealing with the case under CJA 2003, Sch.12, para.8;
(c) at a review hearing the judge may amend the suspended sentence order so as to vary the intervals specified under s.199(1).

Return to prison, PCC(S)A 2000, s.116

40–093 In relation to offences committed **before April 4, 2005**, an offender may still returned to prison under s.116, despite that section's repeal by CJA 2003 (*R. v Drewett* [2006] Crim.L.R. 770) where he: PCC(S)A 2000, s.116(1)–(4), 10 11

(1) has been serving a determinate sentence of imprisonment, detention under s.91, or detention in a young offender institution, which he began serving **on or after October 1, 1992**; and
(2) is released on licence under CJA 1991 Pt II; and
    (a) commits, before the date on which he would, but for his release, have served his sentence, an offence punishable with imprisonment, and
    (b) is convicted, whether before or after that date, of the new offence before the Crown Court, or is committed to the Crown Court by the magistrates under s.116(3)(b)

whether or not the judge passes any other sentence on him, and he may be ordered to be returned to prison for the whole or any part of the period which:

(i) begins with the date of the order; and
(ii) is equal in length to the period between the date on which the new offence was committed, and the date on which he would otherwise have served his sentence in full.

A sentence of imprisonment for these purposes does not include a committal for contempt of court or any kindred offence.

As a matter of good sentencing practice, the judge should expressly identify those offences which he considers give rise to an order under section 116 *(R. v Divers* [1999] 2 Cr.App.R.(S.) 421).

The fact that the prisoner has been recalled to prison on revocation of a licence is no bar to the judge making an order in relation to the same sentence *R. v Sharkey* [2000] 1Cr.App.R. 409 disapproving: *R. v Governor of HMP Elmley, etc*. (1999) 2 Cr.App.R.(S.) 165; and see *R. v Cawthorn* [2001] 1 Cr.App.R.(S.) 130. The power is available in respect of a prisoner released on licence; it is not available in respect of an offender who commits an offence following an escape from prison *(R. v Mathews and Jacobs* [2002] EWCA Crim. 677).

As to difficulties raised by this section, see *R. v Howell* [2006] Crim. L.R. 763.

The object of the section

40–094 The power is discretionary and no iron rules can be laid down which might pervert the exercise of the discretionary power, but the Lord Chief Justice in *R. v Blades* (1999) T.L.R. 688, stressed that:

(1) it was relevant that an offender in that position had, by definition, previously committed an offence for which he had been sentenced to imprisonment, and had been released on licence before that sentence had fully been served;
(2) the purpose of a licence was to give an offender an opportunity to live a law-abiding existence instead of remaining in prison for the full term of the nominal sentence. It was clearly understood that if further offences were committed before the expiry of the original term he was liable to be returned to prison;
(3) the commission of a further offence during the licence period shows that he has not availed himself of the opportunity to live a law-abiding existence and has not taken advantage of the probationary opportunity offered;
(4) There was a public interest in making quite clear to offenders and to the public in general that, if an offender committed a further serious offence while on licence there was a real, not simply a theoretical, price to pay.

The nature of the term

40–095 The period of return is taken to be a sentence of imprisonment for the purposes of CJA 1991, Pt II, served either before and followed by, or concurrently with, as the judge directs, the sentence imposed for the new offence, and in either case is disregarded in determining the appropriate length of that sentence. PCC(S)A 2000, s.116(6)–(7)

Section 116 provides that the period for which the offender is returned to prison "begins with the date of the order." Where the judge makes an order in respect of several offences each must begin on that date, and must accordingly run concurrently with each other (*R. v Divers* [1999] 2 Cr.App.R.(S.) 421).

Note that:

(1) where the new offence was committed over a period of, two or more days, or at some time during a period of two or more days, it is to be taken as having been committed on the last of those days; PCC(S)A 2000, s.116(8)

(2) for the purposes of any enactment conferring rights of appeal in criminal cases, an order for return is to be treated as a sentence passed for the new offence, and PCC(S)A 2000, s.116(9)

(3) the sentence for the return and the sentence for the new offence constitute a single term (*R. v Taylor* [1998] 1 All E.R. 357).

Juvenile offenders

40–096 In the case of a young offender aged 15–17, s.116(6)(c) (which provides that the period imposed is to be disregarded in determining the length of the new sentence) "is not sufficiently specific" to create an exception to CJA 1982, s.1B(4) which restricts the sentence to be imposed on an offender of that age to 12 months (24 months under CJPOA 1994) *(R. v Foran* [1996] 1 Cr.App.R.(S.) 149; *R. v F* & S [2000] Crim.L.R. 113).

Committal for sentence

40–097 Where an offender is committed to the Crown Court under s.38, for an offence committed during the currency of a previous sentence, the judge may make an order under s.116 despite the fact that the offender was not committed under s.116(3)(b). Section 42(1) confers power on the court to deal with the offender in any manner in which it could have dealt with him if he had just been convicted on indictment: *R. v Stephenson* [1999] 1 Cr.App.R.(S.) 177.

Sentences served in Scotland

40–098 Where a short-term or a long-term prisoner sentenced by a court in Scotland is released before the date on which he would have served his sentence, and he commits another offence punishable with imprisonment and is brought before the Crown Court, the judge may, instead of making any other order in respect of the plea or finding, refer the case to the court in Scotland which imposed the original sentence, sending to it such particulars as are relevant. PCC(S)A 1993, s.16

Approach to an order

40–099 The judge, in contemplating a s.116 order, will need to establish:

(1) the period of the sentence originally imposed; and
(2) the date on which the offender was released on licence, in order to determine whether the new offence was committed within the term of the original sentence; and
(3) the *quantum* remaining from the original sentence on the day the new offence was committed.

Once he has established that he has power to make an order under s.116, he must, in deciding whether to exercise that power:

(a) decide what is the appropriate sentence for the *new* offence — the possibility of an order under s.116 being disregarded at this stage; then
(b) in deciding whether an order under s.116 should be made, have regard to:
  (i) any progress made by the offender since his release on licence (*R. v Taylor* [1998] 1 Cr.App.R.(S.) 312; and
  (ii) the nature and gravity of the new offence, and whether it calls for a custodial sentence; and finally
(c) having regard to the *totality* of the sentence, decide:
  (i) whether he should make an order under s.116;
  (ii) whether the term imposed under s.116 should be served concurrently with the sentence for the new offence(s); and
  (iii) if the term under s.116 is to b be served *before* the sentence(s) for the new offence(s), how long it should be (*R. v Taylor*, above).

41 INDICATION OF SENTENCE

General

41–001 A judge dealing with a case may be asked by the accused to give, and if asked is entitled to give, an indication, which should ordinarily be as to the maximum sentence he would pass on the accused if a plea of guilty were to be tendered at the stage at which the indication is sought (*R. v Goodyear* [2005] 3 All E.R. 117). The procedure takes place in public in open court, in the presence of the accused, with both sides represented, and the proceedings are recorded in full. Ordinarily such proceedings will take place at the plea and case management hearing.

The potential advantages of such a practice include, first and foremost, that the accused himself can make a better informed decision whether to plead, or not. Experience tends to suggest that this would result in an increased number of early guilty pleas, which a consequent reduction in the number of trials, and the number of cases which are listed for trial, and then, to use current language, "crack" at the last minute, usually at considerable inconvenience to those involved in the intended trial, and in particular, victims and witnesses (*ibid.*).

Properly applied, there may be a reduced number of sentences to be considered by the Attorney-General, and where appropriate, referred to CACD as unduly lenient. In short, an increase in the efficient administration of justice will not impinge on the defendant's entitlement to tender a voluntary plea (*ibid.*).

The following principles are to be extracted from the judgment.

Limits on practice

41–002 The judge should not give an advance indication of sentence unless one has been sought by the accused. He is, however, always entitled:

(1) if he sees fit, to exercise the power recognised in *R. v Turner* (1970) 54 Cr.App.R. 352 to indicate, that the sentence, or type of sentence, would be the same, whether the case proceeded as a plea of guilty or went to trial with a resulting conviction; though given the guidance published by the Sentencing Guidelines Council on the credit to be given for a guilty plea, this will be unusual;

(2) in an appropriate case to remind the defence advocate that the accused is entitled to seek an advance indication of sentence.

Where appropriate, there must be an agreed, written basis of plea. Unless there is, the judge should refuse to give an indication: otherwise he may become inappropriately involved in negotiations about the acceptance of pleas, and any agreed basis of plea.

Discretion to refuse indication

41–003 In whatever circumstances an advance indication of sentence is sought, the judge retains an unfettered discretion to refuse to give one. It may indeed be inappropriate for him to give any indication at all. In particular he may consider that if he were to give a sentence indication at the stage when it is sought, he would not properly be able to judge the true culpability of the accused, or the differing levels of responsibility between accused. From a practical standpoint this is a very important consideration.

Also he may:

(1) consider that, for a variety of reasons, the accused is already under pressure (perhaps from a co-accused), or vulnerable, and that to give the requested indication, even in answer to a request, might create additional pressure;
(2) be troubled that the particular accused may not fully have appreciated that he should not plead guilty unless in fact he is guilty;
(3) be concerned, in a case involving a number of accused, that an indication given to one who seeks it, may itself create pressure on another.

There will be cases where the judge considers that the application is nothing less than a "try on" by an accused who intends or is likely to plead guilty in any event, seeking to take a tactical advantage of the changed process; in such a case he will probably refuse to say anything at all, and indeed, a guilty plea tendered after such tactical manoeuvering may strike him as a plea tendered later than the first reasonable opportunity for doing so, with a consequent reduction in the discount for the guilty plea.

Instead of refusing to give an indication, the judge is entitled to reserve his position until such time as he feels able to give one, for example, until a pre-sentence report is available. There will be cases where a psychiatric or other report may provide valuable insight into the level of risk posed by the accused, and if so, he may justifiably feel disinclined to give an indication at the stage when it is sought.

Again, the judge may not be sufficiently familiar with the case to give an informed indication, and if so, he may defer doing so until he is.

Reasons for decision

41–004 In a case:

(1) of an outright refusal, the judge will probably conclude that it is inappropriate to give his reasons;
(2) where he has in mind to defer any indication, he may choose to explain his reasons, and further indicate the circumstances in which, and when, he would be prepared to respond to a request for a sentence indication.

If at any stage the judge refuses to give an indication (as opposed to deferring it) it remains open to the accused to seek a further indication at a later stage. Once the judge has refused to give an indication, however, he should not normally initiate the process, except, where it arises, to indicate that the circumstances had changed sufficiently for him to be prepared to consider a renewed application for an indication.

Binding effect of indication

41–005 An indication, once given, is binding and:

(1) remains binding on the judge who has given it; and
(2) binds any other judge who becomes responsible for the case.

If, after a reasonable opportunity to consider his position in the light of the indication, the accused does not plead guilty, the indication ceases to have effect.

In straightforward cases, once an indication has been sought and given, there should not be an adjournment for the plea to be taken on another day. The judge who has given an indication should, wherever possible, deal with the case immediately. If that is not possible, any subsequent hearings should be listed before him. If this is not possible, and another judge deals with the case, while he has his own sentencing responsibilities, judicial comity as well as the expectation aroused in the accused that he will not receive a sentence in excess of that which the first judge indicated, requires that the subsequent judge should not exceed the earlier indication.

INDICATION OF SENTENCE

The Defence position

41–006 Subject to the judge's power to give an appropriate reminder to the advocate for the accused, the process of seeking a sentence indication should normally be started by the accused.

Whether or not the judge has given an appropriate reminder, the accused's advocate should not seek an indication without written authority, signed by his client, indicating that he wishes to seek an indication.

The advocate is personally responsible for ensuring that his client fully appreciates that:

(1) he should not plead guilty unless he is guilty;
(2) any sentence indication given by the judge remains subject to the right of the Attorney-General, where it arises, to refer an unduly lenient sentence to CACD;
(3) any indication given by the judge reflects the situation at the time when it is given, and that if a "guilty plea" is not tendered in the light of that indication the indication ceases to have effect;
(4) any indication which may be given relates only to the matters about which an indication is sought; certain steps, like confiscation proceedings, follow automatically, and the judge cannot dispense with them, nor, by giving an indication of sentence, create an expectation that they will be dispensed with.

In the unusual event that the accused is unrepresented, he is entitled to seek a sentence indication of his own initiative. There will be difficulties in either the judge or prosecuting counsel taking any initiative, and informing an unrepresented accused of this right. That might too readily be interpreted as or subsequently argued to have been improper pressure.

Some basic principles

41–007 The following basic principles still hold good: PD 2004, IV.1–5

- an advocate must be free to give the accused the best advice he can and, if need be, in strong terms; it will often include advice that a guilty plea, showing an element of remorse, is a mitigating factor which may enable the court to impose a lesser sentence than would otherwise be the case;
- the advocate will, of course, emphasise that the accused must not plead guilty unless he has committed the acts constituting the offence charged;

- the accused, having considered the advocate's advice must have complete freedom of choice whether to plead guilty or not guilty.

No plea bargaining

41–008 the defence should not seek an indication while there is any uncertainty between the prosecution and the defence about:

(1) an acceptable plea or pleas to the indictment, or
(2) any factual basis relating to the plea.

Any agreed basis should be reduced into writing before an indication is sought. Where there is a dispute about a particular fact which counsel for the accused believes to be effectively immaterial to the sentencing decision, the difference should be recorded, so that the judge can make up his own mind.

The judge should never be invited to give an indication on the basis of what would be, or what would appear to be a "plea bargain". He should not be asked or become involved in discussions linking the acceptability to the prosecution of a plea or basis of plea, and the sentence which may be imposed. He is not conducting nor involving himself in any plea bargaining. In short, he is not to be asked to indicate levels of sentence which he may have in mind depending on possible different pleas. Thus, for example, he should refuse to give an indication based on the possibility that the defendant might plead guilty to OAPA 1861 s.18, alternatively s.20, alternatively s.47.

The Prosecution

41–009 There are a number of specific matters for which the prosecution advocate is responsible.

Thus:

(1) If there is no final agreement about:
  (a) the plea to the indictment, or
  (b) the basis of plea, and

  the defence nevertheless seeks an indication, which the judge appears minded to give, the prosecuting advocate should remind him of the guidance given in the preceding paragraphs that an indication of sentence should not normally be given until the basis of the plea has been agreed, or the judge has concluded that he can properly deal with the case without the need for a Newton hearing;
(2) if an indication is sought, the prosecution advocate should enquire whether the judge is in possession of, or

has had access to, all the evidence relied on by the prosecution, including any:

(a) personal impact statement from the victim of the crime (see above, 29–042) and

(b) information of relevant previous convictions recorded against the accused.

(3) if the process has been properly followed the prosecution advocate will need to do no more, before the judge gives any indication, than:

(a) to draw the judge's attention to any minimum or mandatory statutory sentencing requirements;

(b) where he would be expected to offer assistance with relevant guideline cases, or the views of the Sentencing Guidelines Council, to invite the judge to allow him to do so; and

(c) where it applies, to remind the judge that the position of the Attorney-General to refer any eventual sentencing decision as unduly lenient is not affected.

The prosecuting advocate should not say anything which may create the impression that the sentence indication has the support or approval of the Crown.

As to the acceptance of pleas by the Crown, see *Att.-Gen.'s Guidelines on the Acceptance of Pleas* [2001] 1 Cr.App.R. 425.

Duties of Crown prosecutors

41–010 CCP 2004, para.10 lays down that Crown Prosecutors should only accept the accused's plea if they think the court is able to pass a sentence that matches the seriousness of the offending, particularly where there are aggravating features. Crown Prosecutors must never accept a guilty plea just because it is convenient. In considering whether the pleas offered are acceptable, prosecutors need to ensure that the interests of the victim and, where possible, any views expressed by the victim or victim's family, are taken into account when deciding whether it is in the public interest to accept the plea. However, the decision rests with the prosecutor.

Particular care must be taken when considering pleas which would enable the accused to avoid the imposition of a mandatory minimum sentence. When pleas are offered, Crown Prosecutors must bear in mind the fact that ancillary orders can be made with some offences but not with others.

Where a case is listed for trial, and the view is taken that it is appropriate to accept a plea to a lesser offence, or to a reduced number of offences, or to offer no evidence, the prosecutor should speak to the victim and his family so that the position can be explained and their views taken into account in the decision-making process. They should be kept informed, and any decisions taken should be explained to them.

Effect on CJA 1988, s.36

41–011 If the prosecution advocate has addressed his responsibilities, the discretion of the Attorney-General to refer a sentence will be wholly unaffected by the advance sentence indication process. If a sentence indication has been given in accordance with these guidelines, before referring the eventual sentencing decision to CACD the Attorney-General's decision would no doubt reflect that the accused had indeed pleaded guilty in response to the sentence indication, properly sought from and given by the judge.

There should be no question of the judge giving a preliminary indication, followed by comments on it by the prosecution advocate, with the judge then reconsidering his indication, and perhaps raising it to a higher level, with the defence advocate then making further submissions to persuade the judge, after all, to reduce his indication.

If nothing else, such a process would smack of precisely the kind of bargaining process that should be avoided.

If the prosecuting advocate, contrary to the above guidance, has said or done anything which may indicate or convey support for or approval of the sentence indicated, the question whether the sentence should nevertheless be referred to CACD as unduly lenient, and the decision of CACD whether to interfere with and increase it, will be examined on a case by case basis, in the light of everything said and done by the advocate for the Crown.

(See also *Att.-Gen.'s Refs (Nos 80 and 81 of 1999) (R. v Thompson and Rodgers)* [2000] 2 Cr.App.R.(S.) 138; *Att.-Gen.'s Refs (Nos 86 and 87 of 1999 (R. v Webb & Simpson)* [2001] Crim.L.R. 58, *R. v Mohammed)* [2003] 1 Cr.App.R.(S.) 57); but cf. *Att.-Gen.'s Ref (No. 19 of 2004)*[2005] 1 Cr.App.R.(S.) 18).

Appeal against sentence

41–012 The accused's right to apply for leave to appeal against sentence if, for example, insufficient allowance has been made for matters of genuine mitigation, remains unaffected.

Indication to be sought at earliest opportunity

41–013 A sentence indication should normally be sought at the plea and case management hearing. In cases "sent" to the

Crown Court under CDA 1998, s.51, or transferred under CJA 1987, s.4 or CJA 1991, s.53, this is usually the first opportunity for the accused to plead guilty and therefore the moment when the maximum discount for the guilty plea will be available to him.

This does not, however, rule out the accused's entitlement to seek an indication at a later stage, or even, in a rare case, during the course of the trial itself.

Notice in complex cases

41–014 Since the judge is most unlikely to be able to give an indication, even if it is sought, in a complicated or difficult case, unless issues between the prosecution and the defence have been addressed and resolved, in such a case:

(1) no less than seven days' notice in writing of an intention to seek an indication should normally be given in writing to the prosecution, and to the court;
(2) if an application is made without notice when it should have been given, the judge may conclude that any inevitable adjournment ought to have been avoided and that the discount for the guilty plea should be reduced accordingly.

The fact that notice has been given, and any reference to a request for a sentence indication, or the circumstances in which it was sought, is inadmissible in any subsequent trial.

Procedure at hearing

41–015 The hearing should normally take place:

(1) in open court,
(2) in the presence of the accused;
(3) with both sides represented;
(4) being recorded in full.

There should not be any opening by the prosecution at this stage, or any mitigation plea by the defence. That must be postponed until after the accused has pleaded guilty.

Generally speaking the process ought to be very short, the judge bearing in mind that the accused and the public are present, and that the judge may be the trial judge, and that he is simply deciding whether to respond, and if so how, to a request that he give an indication of the maximum sentence he would pass if the accused pleaded guilty at that stage. Since the case may yet proceed as a trial, and if it does, no reference may be made to the request for a sentence indication, reporting restrictions should normally be imposed, to be lifted if and when the accused pleads or is found guilty.

If the process is properly followed, there should be very little need for the judge to involve himself in the discussions with the advocates, although obviously he may wish to seek better information on any aspect of the case which is troubling him. Even where the judge gives an indication the Attorney-General may refer the sentence to CACD as too lenient.

42 JURISDICTION

General

42–001 The Crown Court is part of the Senior Courts (that is the pre-2007 Supreme Court). It is a superior court of record. Its jurisdiction is exercisable by: SCA 1981, ss.1(1), 8(1), 45(1); CA 2003, s.65(1)

(1) any judge of the High Court;
(2) any circuit judge or recorder; and
(3) subject to, and in accordance with, the provisions of SCA 1981, ss.74 and 75(2), a judge of the High Court, a Circuit Judge, a Recorder or, a District Judge (Magistrates' Courts), sitting with not more than four lay magistrates.

and any such persons, when exercising the jurisdiction of the Crown Court, are judges of the Crown Court.

Note that:

(a) during the period of his appointment, a Deputy District Judge (Magistrates' Courts) is be treated for judicial purposes as if he were a District Judge (Magistrates' Courts). CA 2003, s.24(5)
(b) when the Crown Court sits in the City of London it is known as the Central Criminal Court, and the Lord Mayor of the City and any alderman of the City is entitled to sit as a judge of the Central Criminal Court and any judge of the High Court, or any circuit judge or Recorder; SCA 1981, s.8(2)
(c) a lay magistrate is not disqualified from acting as a judge of the Crown Court for the reason only that proceedings are not at a place within the area for which he was appointed, or because the proceedings are not related to that area in any way. SCA 1981, s.8(2).

Jurisdiction

Judges, etc. as justices of the peace

42–002 A Circuit judge, a Deputy Circuit Judge, a Deputy Judge of the High Court, a Judge of the High Court, and a Recorder have the powers of a justice of the peace who is a District Judge (Magistrates' Courts) in relation to criminal causes and matters each of the holders of such office is qualified to sit as a member of a youth court. CA 2003, s.66(2), (3)

From the explanatory notes to s.66 it was clearly envisaged that the power was intended to enable a judge of the Crown

Court to deal with a summary offence attached. The power is clearly wider than that and has been used by judges in the Crown Court to rectify errors of procedure. See e.g. *R. v Ashton* where a judge *acting as a District Judge (Magistrates' Courts)* e.g. quite properly (a) conducted mode of trial proceedings where these had been omitted, and (b) committed an accused to the Crown Court for sentence where that was appropriate. In the latter case, it was held that there was no statutory impediment prevent him *in his capacity as a judge of the Crown Court* from passing sentence on an accused so committed.

Any matter required under r.6.1 to be recorded in the magistrates' court's register, should be recorded by the clerk in the Crown Court records, ensuring that there is an accurate and accessible record of any decision or other important feature of the proceedings (*R. v Ashton*).

In *R. v Ashton* CACD stressed that in most instances when there has been a procedural failure, it will be unnecessary for s.66 to be used to carry out a process of rectification. Instead, the matter should be approached on the principles set out in *Soneji* and *Sekhon* (see above, 16–014) which will normally obviate the need to go through such procedural steps.

General jurisdiction

42–003 Subject to the provisions of SCA 1981, the Crown Court exercises: SCA 1981, s.45(2), (3)

(1) all such appellate and other jurisdiction as is conferred upon it by that or any other Act; and
(2) all such jurisdiction as was exercisable by it immediately before the commencement of that Act (i.e. January 1, 1972);

and its jurisdiction includes all such powers and duties as were exercisable by it, or fell to be performed by it, immediately before that date.

CA 1971, s.8 and Sch.1 conferred on the Crown Court all appellate and other jurisdiction conferred on courts of quarter session, or on any committees of such courts. SCA 1981, s.45(4)

Subject to CP(AW)A 1965, s.8, the Crown Court has, in relation to the attendance and examination of witnesses, any contempt of court, the enforcement of its orders and all other matters incidental to its jurisdiction, the like powers, rights, privileges and authority of the High Court.

Jurisdiction on indictment; practice and procedure

42–004 All proceedings on indictment are brought before the Crown Court, and its jurisdiction with respect to such proceedings includes jurisdiction: SCA 1981, s.46(1)

(1) in proceedings on indictment in England and Wales for offences wherever committed, and in particular;
(2) in proceedings on indictment for offences within the jurisdiction of the Admiralty of England.

SCA 1981 continues in effect all enactments and rules relating to procedure in connection with indictable offences, and in particular preserves: SCA 1981, s.79(1), (2)

(a) the practice by which, on any one indictment, the taking of pleas, the trial by jury and the pronouncement of judgment may respectively be by or before different judges;
(b) the release, after respite of judgment, of a convicted person on recognisance to come up for judgment if called on, but meanwhile to be of good behaviour;
(c) the manner of trying any question relating to the breach of a recognisance; and
(d) the manner of execution of any sentence on conviction, or the manner in which any other judgment or order given in connection with trial on indictment may be enforced.

The provisions of the Act relating to the Crown Court's appellate jurisdiction are dealt with under **10** APPEALS. The court's powers to grant bail are dealt with under 11 BAIL.

Sittings of the Crown Court

42–005 In relation to the business of the Crown Court:

(1) any business may be conducted at any place in England or Wales, and the sittings of the court at any place may be continuous or intermittent or occasional; SCA 1971, s.78
(2) judges may sit simultaneously to take any number of different cases in the same or different places, and may adjourn cases from time to time; and
(3) the places at which the court sits and the days and times at which the court sits at any place are matters to be determined in accordance with directions given by the Lord Chief Justice.

The Crown Court is a single court and those who sit in it sit merely from time to time as judges of the court. There is nothing which prevents a case which is part-heard at one location or before one judge, from being adjourned to a later date in contemplation of its being reheard before a different court. There is no principle which retains a case within the so-called "seisin" of an individual judge (*R. v Dudley CC Ex p. Smith* (1974) 58 Cr.App.R. 184).

Composition of the Crown Court

42–006 All proceedings in the Crown Court are heard and disposed of before a single judge of the court, except in relation to courts comprising lay magistrates. Where a judge of the High Court, a Circuit Judge, a Recorder or, once CA 2003, s.65 is in force a District Judge (Magistrates' Courts), sits with lay magistrates, he presides, and: SCA 1981, s.73(1), (3)

(1) the decision of the Crown Court may be by a majority; and
(2) if the members of the court are equally divided, the presiding judge Recorder, etc. has a second and casting vote.

Where a situation arises during the course of the proceedings which involves an interlocutory decision, it must be dealt with by the court as then constituted, i.e. including the magistrates.

On a question of law the magistrates will obviously defer to the views of the presiding judge (*R. v Orpin* (1974) 59 Cr.App.R. 231). See generally 10 APPEALS.

Business in chambers

42–007 A judge of the Crown Court may exercise the following jurisdiction, sitting in chambers: R.16.11

(1) hearing applications for bail;
(2) issuing a summons or warrant;
(3) hearing any application relating to procedural matters preliminary or incidental to criminal proceedings in the Crown Court, including applications relating to CDS funding;
(4) jurisdiction under:
    (a) R.12.2 (listing first appearance of accused sent for trial);
    (b) R.28.3 (application for witness summons);
    (c) R.63.2(5) (extending time for appeal against decision of magistrates' court);
    (d) R.64.7 (application to state a case for consideration of High Court);
(5) hearing an application undert YJCA 1999, s.41(2) (evidence of complainant's sexual history);

(6) hearing applications under POA 1985, s.22(3) (extension or further extension of a custody time limit);
(7) hearing an appeal brought by an accused under POA 1985, s.22(7) against a decision of the magistrates' court to extend or further extend a time limit, or by the prosecution under s.22(8) against the magistrates' refusal to extend or further extend such a limit;
(8) hearing an appeal under B(A)A 1993, s.1 (against grant of bail by the magistrates' court;
(9) hearing appeals under CJA 2003, s.16, (against condition of bail imposed by magistrates' court.

Note that in relation to applications for bail, except in the case of an application made by the prosecutor or a constable under BA 1976, s.3(8), the applicant is not entitled to be present on the hearing of the application unless the Crown Court gives him leave to be present. R.19.18(5)

An application to vary the place of trial (see 7 ALLOCATION AND DEPLOYMENT OF BUSINESS) must be heard in open court.

Hearings in camera

42–008 If in any proceedings, a prosecutor or accused has served notice under R.16.10 of his intention to apply for an order that all or part of a trial be held in camera, an application relating to a witness in those proceedings need not identify the witness by name and date of birth. R.16.9

Application to hold trial in camera

42–009 Where a prosecutor or an accused intends to apply for an order that all or part of a trial be held in camera for reasons of national security or for the protection of the identity of a witness or any other person, he must, not less than seven days before the date on which the trial is expected to begin serve a notice in writing to that effect on the Crown Court officer and the prosecutor or the accused as the case may be. On receiving such notice, the court officer will forthwith cause a copy to be displayed in a prominent place within the precincts of the Court. R.16.10(1), (2)

An application by a prosecutor or an accused who has served such a notice: R.16.10(3)

(1) must, unless the Court orders otherwise, be made in camera; and
(2) if an order is made, the trial must be adjourned until whichever of the following is appropriate:

(a) 24 hours after the making of the order, where no application for leave to appeal from the order is made; or
(b) after the determination of an application for leave to appeal, where the application is dismissed; or
(c) after the determination of the appeal, where leave to appeal is granted.

43 JURY MANAGEMENT

General

43–001 CJA 2003, s.321 and Sch.33 make considerable amendments to the Juries Act 1974, in relation to the qualifications for jury service in s.1, and other matters. Mentally disordered persons and persons disqualified from service are listed in JA 1974, Sch.1, substituted by CJA 2003, s.321, Sch.33, para.15.

A number of matters arise in relation to the management of the jury, and of potential jurors.

These are:

(1) excusal from jury service;
(2) challenges to the jury or individual jurors;
(3) difficulties during the trial;
(4) separation before verdict;
(5) discharge and appeal therefrom.

Excusal and deferment of attendance

43–002 A person summoned for jury service may, subject to s.9A(1A) below, show to the satisfaction of the Crown Court officer that there is good reason:

JA 1974, ss.9(2), 9A; CJA 1988, s.120; CJA 2003, s.321, Sch.33, paras 3–12

(1) why he should be excused from attending, in which case the Crown Court officer may excuse him; or
(2) why his attendance should be deferred, in which case that officer may defer his attendance,

though in a case under (2), if an application has been granted or refused, the powers may not be exercised again in respect of the same summons. Special provisions apply under ss.9(2A) and 9(2B) to serving naval, military or airforce personnel, both in relation to excusal and deferment.

Where it appears to the Crown Court officer that a juror attending may be unable to act as such on account of physical disablity or of insufficient knowledge of English, he may refer the matter to a judge (JA 1974, s.9B and see *R. v Osman* [1996] 1 Cr.App.Rep. 126).

Reasons for excusal

43–003 There will be circumstances in which a juror should be excused, as for instance:

(1) where he or she is personally concerned with the facts of the particular case, or is closely connected with a party or prospective witness; or

(2) on grounds of personal hardship or conscientious objection to jury service.

Any person who appeals to the court against a refusal by the appropriate officer to excuse him from service must be given an opportunity to make represention in suppport of his appeal. PD 2004, IV.42.3

A conscientious objection arising from religious beliefs is unlikely, by itself, to amount to a good reason for excusal unless, possibly, it would prevent the potential juror from properly fulfilling his duties (see *R. v Guildford CC Ex p Siderfin* [1989] 3 All E.R. 73).

As to the position of serving police officers and persons employed by the CPS, see *R. v Adrolkov and Others, The Times,* August 18, 2005.

Effect of CJA 2003, s.321

43–004 The effect of CJA 2003, s.321 was to remove certain categories of persons from those previously ineligible for jury service (the judiciary and others concerned with the administration of justice) and certain other categories ceased to be eligible for excusal as of right (such as Members of Parliament and medical professionals).

PD 2004, IV.42.1–3 (as amended by [2005] 1 W.L.R. 1361, while emphasising that jury service is an important public duty which individual members of the public are chosen at random to undertake, and that normal presumption is that everyone, unless mentally disordered or disqualified, will be required to serve when summoned to do so, point out, however, that:

(1) the legislative change has meant an increase in the number of jurors with professional and public service commitments; and the trial judge must continue to be alert to the need to exercise his discretion to adjourn a trial, excuse or discharge a juror should the need arise;

(2) whether or not an application has already been made to the jury summoning officer for deferral or excusal it is also open to the person summoned to apply to the court to be excused; such applications must be considered with common sense and according to the interests of justice. An explanation should be required for an application being much later than necessary;

(3) where a juror appears on a jury panel, it may be appropriate for a judge to excuse the juror from that particular case where the potential juror is personally concerned

with the facts of the particular case or is closely connected with a prospective witness;

(4) where the length of the trial is estimated to be significantly longer than the normal period of jury service, it is good practice for the trial judge to enquire whether the potential jurors on the jury panel foresee any difficulties with the length and if the judge is satisfied that the jurors' concerns are justified he may say that they are not required for that particular jury; this does not mean that the judge must excuse the juror from sitting at that court altogether as it may well be possible for the juror to sit on a shorter trial at the same court;

Excusal in the course of the trial

43–005 Where a juror unexpectedly finds himself in difficult professional or personal circumstances during the course of the trial, jurors should be encouraged to raise such problems with the trial judge. This might apply, for example, to a parent whose child-care arrangements unexpectedly fail or a worker who is engaged in the provision of services the need for which can be critical or Member of Parliament who has deferred his jury service to an apparently more convenient time, but is unexpectedly called back to work for a very important reason. Such difficulties would normally be raised through a jury note in the normal manner.

In such circumstances:

(1) the judge must exercise his discretion according to the interests of justice and the requirements of each individual case;

(2) the judge must decide for himself whether the juror has presented a sufficient reason to interfere with the course of the trial; if the juror has presented a sufficient reason, in longer trials it may well be possible to adjourn for a short period in order to allow the juror to overcome the difficulty. In shorter cases it may be more appropriate to discharge the juror and to continue the trial with a reduced number of jurors. The power to do this is implicit in JA 1974, s.16(1);

(3) in unusual cases (such as an unexpected emergency arising overnight) a juror need not be discharged in open court.

The good administration of justice depends on the co-operation of jurors who perform an essential public service. All applications for excusal should be dealt with sensitively and sympathetically and the trial judge should always seek to meet the interests of justice without unduly inconveniencing any juror. PD 2004, IV.42.3

Appeal to the judge

43–006 A person summoned for jury service may appeal in accordance with the provisions of r.39.2 (as amended by SI 2006/353), against any refusal of the Crown Court officer to excuse him or to defer his attendance. The appeal is commenced by the appellant's giving notice in writing of the appeal to the appropriate court officer of the Crown Court, specifying the matters upon which the appellant relies as providing good reason why he should be excused from attending in pursuance of the summons or why his attendance should be deferred. R.39.2

The judge may not dismiss such an appeal unless the appellant has been given an opportunity of making representations.

Where the appeal is decided in the absence of the appellant, the appropriate court officer of the will notify him of the decision without delay.

Principle of a Random Jury

43–007 The residual discretion of a judge at common law to discharge a juror in order to ensure a fair trial has never been held to include a discretion to influence the overall composition of the jury, as by discharging a jury drawn from a particular section of the community (see *R. v Tarrant*, *The Times*, December 29, 1997). Fairness, in relation to this aspect of the trial, is achieved by the principle of random selection. That residual discretion may be exercised:

(1) even in the absence of objection by either party;
(2) on grounds that would found a challenge for cause;
(3) for instance, where a juror is not likely to be able or willing to perform his duties; and
(4) for instance, where the juror is infirm, hard of hearing, or whose attendance at a long trial would be burdensome (*R. v Mason* [1981] Q.B. 881 at 887).

That common law discretion has now been confirmed by JA 1974, s.10 (see also PD 2004 IV.42) expressly providing for excusal, at the judge's discretion, on grounds of "personal hardship or conscientious objection to jury service."

This discretion does not envisage excusal on more general grounds such as race, religion, political beliefs or occupation.

Racial, etc. cases

43–008 Applications are sometimes made to the trial judge where the case involves an accused of a particular racial or ethnic group, and where it is suggested that the jury should consist, either wholly or partly, of that same particular racial or ethnic group. The trial judge has no discretion to interfere in that way with the composition of the panel, or of an individual jury (see *R. v Danvers* [1982] Crim.L.R. 680, *R. v Broderick* [1970] Crim.L.R. 155, *R. v Ford* (1989) 89 Cr.App.R. 278).

Note that:

(1) the mere fact that a juror is, for instance, of a particular race, or holds a particular religious belief, cannot be made the basis for a challenge for cause on the ground of bias, or on any other ground;
(2) there is no principle of the criminal law that a jury should be racially balanced (*R. v McCalla* [1986] Crim.L.R. 335);
(3) the trial judge's inherent discretion, in the absence of any challenge, to exclude from the jury a person who is obviously incompetent to act (*R. v Mason* (1980) 71 Cr.App.R. 157), is not to be exercised so as to undermine the random nature of the jury, or to influence its overall composition (*R. v Ford*, above).

Challenge for cause

43–009 A challenge may be made for cause, to the panel or part panel, or, more usually, to an individual juror. The judge should require the advocate to make plain immediately which form of challenge he is pursuing, and must decide whether to hear the challenge in chambers, *in camera*, or in open court. CJA 1988, s.118(2)

A record should be made of all proceedings, and in every case the fact of the challenge and the court's decision on it should be entered in the court record.

Challenge to panel or part panel

43–010 An advocate seeking to challenge the panel or part panel on the basis of its composition, should submit his written grounds for the challenge, before any jurors in waiting are called into court—these grounds should be put on the court record. The judge should ensure that counsel understands the position, namely that:

(1) the composition of the panel is the responsibility of the Lord Chancellor; and
(2) challenge will only be entertained if the summoning officer has acted consciously and deliberately in breach of his duty to summon the panel on a random basis.

If the right is not immediately exercised, it is lost.

Prima facie grounds

43–011 If it appears to the judge that there are prima facie grounds on which the challenge could be supported, the summoning officer should be asked to appear and answer the challenge. If the grounds are contested, the judge must determine, after hearing evidence, whether it is borne out, the burden is on the challenger to satisfy the court on a balance of probabilities.

Result of determination

43–012 If the challenge is:

(1) overruled, the jury should be called into court in the normal way, and the judge should make no further reference to the challenge; or
(2) upheld, the trial should be adjourned until a new panel can be produced.

Challenge to individual juror

43–013 Challenges are made when 12 jurors have been called into the box:

(1) at the time when the juror is sworn (*R. v Morris* (1991) 93 Cr.App.R. 102), but
(2) before he is sworn.

The accused should be informed of his right of challenge.

Indication of challenge

43–014 If a challenge is indicated, the juror should be asked to leave the jury box while the rest of the selected jurors are sworn—subsequent challenges should be dealt with in the same way. If the advocate can state the grounds of challenge without prejudicing his client in the eyes of the jury, or embarrassing the juror concerned, the judge may be able to deal with the matter in open court, briefly and informally.

Need for hearing

43–015 Where it is not possible to deal with the matter informally, the sworn jurors should be asked to retire to their room in the charge of the jury bailiff, and the remainder of the panel should be asked to leave court for the time being; the challenged juror should be kept outside, in the care of an usher, but close by in case it is necessary to question him.

The judge will decide whether:

(1) to hear the challenge in open court; or
(2) to exclude the public and press.

If the grounds of the challenge make it desirable in the interests of justice, and of the challenged juror, to close the court, the judge should announce that that court will sit "as in chambers" and the public and press should be asked to leave the court.

Challenges should not be heard in the judge's room.

Hearing the challenge

43–016 If the ground of challenge appears prima facie valid and the facts are contested, the judge must decide the facts. The burden of proof is on the party challenging, on a balance of probabilities.

The judge may:

(1) hear evidence on the *voir dire*;
(2) question the juror; and
(3) permit advocates to ask questions directed to the particular ground of challenge alleged.

Before there can be any right under (3) to question a juror, a prima facie foundation of fact must be laid (*R. v Chandler (No. 2)* (1964) 48 Cr.App.R. 143, *R.v Broderick* [1970] Crim.L.R. 155. *cf. R. v Kray* (1969) 53 Cr.App.R. 412).

The questioning of jurors, whether orally or in a witness questionnaire, where there is no suggestion that they might have an interest in the case, should be avoided save in the most exceptional circumstances (*R. v Andrews* ([1999] Crim.L.R. 156). Speculative questions, seeking to establish the basis for challenge on different grounds, are not permissible.

Decision on the facts

43–017 If the challenge is:

(1) allowed, the juror should be discharged and a fresh juror called to take his place when the remainder of the jury return; or
(2) disallowed, the judge should caution the juror not to disclose to the others any of the matters considered at the hearing of the challenge, and not to allow the fact of the challenge to influence him in any way.

Order under CCA 1981, s.4(2)

43–018 Where matters raised in the challenge might prejudice the trial, the judge should consider making an order under CCA 1981, s.4(2), restricting publication.

Jury problems during the trial; bias, friction, etc.

Guidance to jurors

43–019 PD 2004 IV.42.5, 6 makes it clear that the judge should ensure that the jury is alerted to the need to bring any concerns about fellow jurors to his attention at the time, and not to wait until the case is concluded. At the same time, it is undesirable to encourage inappropriate criticism of fellow jurors, or to threaten jurors with contempt of court.

Therefore:

(1) the judge should take the opportunity, when warning the jury of the importance of not discussing the case with anyone outside the jury, to add a further warning, which should be tailored to the case, and to the phraseology used in the usual warning;
(2) the effect of the further warning should be that it is the duty of jurors to bring to the judge's attention, promptly, any behaviour among the jurors or by others affecting the jurors, that causes concern;
(3) the point should be made that, unless that is done while the case is continuing, it may be impossible to put matters right;
(4) the judge should consider, particularly in a longer trial, whether a reminder on the lines of the further warning is appropriate prior to the retirement of the jury. PD 2004, IV.42.7,8

In the event that such an incident does occur, the judge should have regard to the remarks of Lord Hope in *R. v Connors & Mirza*, above at paras 127 and 128 and consider the desirability of preparing a statement that could be used in connection with any appeal arising from the incident to CACD (PD 2004, IV.42.9 and see also *Practice Direction (Guide to Jurors)* [2004] 1 W.L.R. 655).

Discharge of juror(s)

43–020 The trial judge has an inherent discretion to discharge a juror or jurors in the course of the trial: JA 1974, s.16

(1) through illness or incapacity of continuing to act, provided the number of jurors does not fall below 9 (see *R. v Hambery* (1977) 65 Cr.App.R. 233);
(2) in a case where, after enquiry, it is shown that a juror has been approached (*R. v Blackwell* [1995] 2 Cr.App.R. 625, *R. v Oke* [1997] Crim.L.R. 898, *R. v Appiah* [1998] Crim.L.R. 134);

(3) where it is alleged that dissension is being caused in the jury room (*R. v Orgles* (1994) 98 Cr.App.R. 185, *R. v Farooq* [1995] Crim.L.R. 169).

Where it is alleged that a juror or jurors is or are unable to fulfil their duty, the particular juror may be questioned without the presence of the jury as a whole, but where dissension is alleged, and therefore the inability of the jury as a whole to fulfil their duty, the whole jury ought to be present.

While discharge is a matter within the discretion of the judge, it is sensible, and good practice, to canvas their views on the matter (*R. v Richardson* [1979] 3 All E.R. 247, and *R. v Bryan* [2002] Crim.L.R. 240).

As to the judge's duties, see *R. v Azam* [2006] Crim.L.R. 776.

Discharge of jury as a whole

General

43–021 The trial judge has a discretion to discharge the whole jury from giving a verdict. This position may be reached in a number of ways:

(1) where it clear that the jury is not able to arrive at a verdict;
(2) where there is a "real danger", from anything said or done in the course of the trial, that the jury may be prejudiced against the accused (*R. v Sawyer* (1980) 71 Cr.App.R. 283, *R. v Spencer* (1986) 83 Cr.App.R. 277, *R. v Gough* (1992) 95 Cr.App.R. 433);
(3) in the case of an irregularity as where:
    (a) an accused's bad character is inadvertently disclosed (*cf. R. v Weaver* (1967) 51 Cr.App.Rep. 77, *R. v Blackford* (1989) 89 Cr.App.R. 239);
    (b) where one accused pleads guilty and the prosecution propose to continue the trial of co-accused (*R. v Fredrick* (1990) Crim.L.R. 403); or
    (c) the judge deals with a recalcitrant witness for contempt before the trial is completed (*R. v Maguire* [1997] 1 Cr.App.R. 61);
(4) in the case of misconduct by a juror; or
(5) where a juror's personal knowledge of the accused emerges in the course of the trial (*R. v Hood* [1968] 2 All E.R. 56).

As to the position where the contempt is by the accused in a deliberate attempt to abort the trial, see *R. v Russell* [2006] Crim.L.R. 862.

Separation of jury during consideration of verdict

43–022 CJPOA 1994, s.43 amends JA 1974, s.13 by permitting the jury, if the court thinks fit and so permits, to separate at any time, whether before or after they have been directed to consider their verdict. This gives the judge unfettered discretion to allow the jury to separate at any time.

A direction along the following lines should be given to a jury if they are allowed to separate during consideration of their verdict:

(1) they must decide the case on the evidence and arguments they have seen and heard in court and not on anything they may have seen or heard or may see or hear outside the court;
(2) that the evidence has been completed and it would be wrong for any juror to seek for or receive further evidence or information of any sort about the case;
(3) that they must not talk to anyone about the case save to other members of the jury and then only when they are deliberating in the jury room; and that they must not allow anyone to talk to them about the case unless that person is a juror and he or she is in the jury room deliberating about the case; and
(4) that when they leave court they should try to set the case they are trying on one side until they return to court and retire to their jury room to resume their deliberations.

(*R. v Oliver* [1996] 2 Cr.App.R. 514; *R. v Hunt* [1998] Crim.L.R. 343.)

Enquiry into verdict

43–023 Where there has been no ambiguity, procedural defect or dissent at the time when the verdict is delivered, an inquiry into that verdict will not be authorised on the basis, e.g. of a subsequent allegation by one of the jurors that the verdict was not in fact unanimous: *R. v Lewis*, *The Times*, April 26, 2001 (*Gregory v UK* (1997) 25 E.H.R.R. 577 and *Sanders v UK* (2000) 8 B.H.R.C. 279 distinguished). The court will not inquire as to what went on in the jury room (CCA 1981, s.8(1) *Miah and Akhbar* [1997] 2 Cr.App.R. 12 followed, *R. v Qureshi* [2002] Crim.L.R. 62).

The authorities establishing this principle are not affected by the implementation of HRA 1998 (*R. v Young* [1995] 2 Cr.App.R. 379; *R. v Ellis and Deheer* [1922] 2 K.B. 113; *Nanan v The State* [1986] A.C. 860; *R. v Lewis* [2001] EWCA Crim 749 considered).

In dealing with such a matter;

(1) the judge must apply his mind to the correct principles laid down by European authority;
(2) to accept what the jurors say without determining whether it is correct, or hearing the accused's account which disputes the jurors' account, is a failure to ascertain the circumstances and to consider whether a fair-minded observer would conclude that there was a real possibility of bias.

(*R. v Brown (Robert Clifford)* [2002] Crim.L.R. 409, following *R. v Medicaments (No. 2)* [2001] 1 W.L.R. 700.)

Power to rectify mistake in verdict

43–024 Where the jury have made a mistake, and the interests of justice so require, the trial judge has a discretion to set aside the discharge of the jury before they have separated or seen or heard anything which they should not have seen or heard, in order to let them deliberate further. This is provided that the mistake is brought to his notice without delay.

See *Igwemma v Chief Constable of Greater Manchester*, *The Times*, July 20, 2001 *cf. R. v Tantram*, *The Times*, July 20, 2001.

44 LICENSED PREMISES EXCLUSION ORDER

44–001 Where any court by or before which a person is convicted of an offence committed on licensed premises is satisfied that in committing that offence he resorted to violence, or offered or threatened to resort to violence, the judge *may in addition* to:

LP(E)A 1980, s.1; PCC(S)A 2000, s.165, Sch.9, para.60

(1) any sentence which is imposed in respect of the offence of which he is convicted; and
(2) a community order, or an order discharging him conditionally or absolutely;

make an **exclusion order** prohibiting him from entering those premises or any other licensed premises which the court may specify by name and address without the express consent of the licensee, his servant or agent, for such period, of not less than three months or more than two years, as may be specified. Such an order cannot stand alone.

The order continues in force for the period specified unless it is terminated earlier.

Note that:

(a) the order is designed for those who make a nuisance of themselves in public houses, to the annoyance of other customers and the danger of the landlord, not for persons of otherwise clean record (*R. v Grady* (1990) 12 Cr.App.R. (S.) 152).
(b) there is no need for an application to be made; the trial judge may make an order of his own motion;
(c) if there is to be an application it is undesirable that it should be made by a person who is not a victim or a party in the case. An interested third party ought to make an approach to the prosecuting authority (*R. v Penn* (1996) 2 Cr.App.R.(S.) 214);
(d) the name of each appropriate premises should be included in the same order; there is no need for a separate order in respect of each premises (*ibid.*).

Penalties for non-compliance

44–002 A person who enters premises in breach of such an order commits an offence and is liable on summary conviction to a fine of £1,000 or to imprisonment for 51 weeks or both.

LP(E)A 1980, ss.2, 3; SI 1984/447; CJA 2003, s.244(2), Sch.19, para.25

A court before which a person is so convicted must consider whether the order should continue in force and may, if it thinks fit, terminate the order, or vary it by deleting the name of any specified premises, but the order is not otherwise affected by a person's conviction for such an offence.

The licensee of any premises is entitled to expel a person under the Act.

45 LIFE SENTENCES

Life sentence—meaning

45–001 A life sentence means: CJA 2003, s.277

(1) a sentence of imprisonment for life;
(2) a sentence of detention during HM Pleasure; and
(3) a sentence of custody for life passed before the commencement of CJCSA 2000, s.61(1) (which abolishes that sentence).

Where appropriate

45–002 Life *imprisonment* is appropriate in four different circumstances. It is:

(1) **a mandatory life sentence**, the sentence fixed by law (in the case of an offender aged 21 or over convicted of murder);
(2) **the maximum discretionary sentence** which the judge may impose where there is evidence that the offender is likely to commit grave offences in the future (*R. v Bellamy* [2001] 1 Cr.App.R.(S.) 34); and
(3) **the maximum discretionary sentence** which the judge may impose for public protection under CJA 2003, s.226 in relation to offences committed **on or after April 4, 2005**;
(4) **the required "automatic life sentence"** under PCC(S)A 2000, s.109, for repeat serious **offences committed after October 1, 1997 and before April 4, 2005**.

It is unsuitable to impose on an offender:

(a) already serving a custodial term, a life sentence to commence on the expiry of that term—it should take effect immediately (*R. v Jones* (1962) 46 Cr.App.R. 129);
(b) disproportionate fixed terms for other offences, to run concurrently with a life sentence, thus restricting the chances of the offender's release (*R. v Nugent* (1984) 6 Cr.App.R.(S.) 93; R. *v Daniels* (1984) 6 Cr.App.R.(S.) 8);
(c) a determinate sentence to run consecutively to a life sentence (*R. v Foy* (1962) 46 Cr.App.R. 290).

Automatic life sentences under PCC(S)A 2000, s.109 will be abolished by CJA 2003, s.332, Sch.37, Pt 7 when that repeal is brought into force.

Mandatory or discretionary

45–003 On conviction for murder, an offender aged

(1) 21 years or over *must* be sentenced to **life imprisonment**,
(2) 18–20 *must*, (until the abolition of that sentence comes into effect), be sentenced to **custody for life**, and
(3) 18 or under at the date of the offence *must* be sentenced to **detention at Her Majesty's pleasure**.

In appropriate circumstances, a judge *may* pass a **discretionary life sentence**.

Since November 30, 2000, the minimum term under (3) has been set by the trial judge, as it was, and is, for adults subject to a discretionary life sentence, by virtue of PCC(S)A 2000, s.82A.

The court *vis à vis* the Parole Board

45–004 The release of a prisoner serving a life sentence is a matter for the Parole Board; there is a clear division of functions in relation to such sentences. Thus:

(1) the judge specifies the period which the offender should serve by way of punishment and deterrence; and
(2) the Parole Board decides whether the offender continues to represent a danger to the public.

CJA 2003, Pt 12, Ch. 7, already in force, empowers the judge, rather than the executive, as formerly, to set the minimum term to be served by a person convicted of murder, determined by reference to a new statutory framework set out in Sch.21. Once the minimum term has expired, the Parole Board will consider the offender's suitability for release and, if appropriate, direct his release. See generally *R. v Sullivan and Others, The Times*, July 14, 2004 CACD.

A. Mandatory life sentences

45–005 CJA 2003, s.269 together with other relevant sections relating to life sentences apply to murders committed from **December 18, 2003**, when those sections came into force.

In dealing with murders committed **prior to December 18, 2003**, care must be taken to ensure that the transitional arrangemends applying to offences committed before that date are followed; these are set out in PD 2004, IV.49, below, and apply to murders committed **after May 31, 2002** and **before December 18, 2003** (see 45–015 below). **Before May 31, 2002**, the minimum term was fixed by the Home Secretary, as to which see Lord Bingham's letter at 45–016, below.

(1) Setting the minimum term

The practice direction

45–006 Since December 18, 2003, when CJA 2003, s.269 came into force, a judge passing a mandatory life sentence must either announce in open court: PD 2004, IV.49.2

(1) the minimum term the offender must serve before the Parole Board may consider release on licence under the provisions of CSA 1997, s.28 (as amended by CJA 2003, s.275); or
(2) **a "whole life order"** in that the seriousness of the offence is so exceptionally high that the early release provisions should not apply at all.

In setting the minimum term the judge must set the term he considers appropriate taking into account: PD 2004, IV.49.3

(a) the seriousness of the offence; and
(b) the effect of any direction which he would have given under CJA 2003, s.240 (crediting periods of remand in custody—see 29 DEALING WITH OFFENDERS) if he had sentenced him to a term of imprisonment.

In considering the seriousness of the offence he must have regard to the general principles set out in Sch.21 and any other guidelines issued by the Sentencing Guidelines Council which are relevant to the case and not incompatible with the provisions of Sch.21. As to reduction in sentence for a guilty plea, see 45–028 below. Although it is necessary to have regard to it, it is always permissible not to apply the guidance if the judge considers that there are reasons for not following it. If the guidance is not being applied the judge should give his reason for not doing so. For example, it is necessary to have regard to the need to do justice in the particular case. However, if he departs from any of the starting points given in Sch.21 he is under a duty to state his reasons.

LIFE SENTENCES

Where the offender was 21 or over when he committed the offence and the judge is of opinion that, because of the seriousness of the offence (or of the combination of the offence and one or more offences associated with it), that the offender should spend the rest of his life in prison, he must order that the early release provisions are not to apply to the offender. CJA 2003, s.269(4)

Transitional provisions

45–007 In relation to an offence committed before December 18, 2003, when s.269 came into force, where it falls to a judge to pass a mandatory life sentence, he may not make an order: CJA 2003, s.276, Sch.22

(1) under s.269(2), specifying a minimum term which, in his opinion, is greater than the Home Secretary would have been likely to notify under the previous practice (as mentioned in Sch.22, para.2(a)); and
(2) under s.269(4), unless he is of opinion that under the previous practice the Home Secretary would have been likely to give a notification falling within Sch.22, para.2(b).

Duty to give reasons

45–008 In making an order under the above provisions, the judge must state in open court, in ordinary language, his reasons for deciding on the order made, and in giving his reasons must, in particular state: CJA 2003, s.270

(1) which of the starting points in CJA 2003, Sch.21 (below) he has chosen, and his reason for doing so, and
(2) his reasons for any departure from that starting point.

Starting points

45–009 The "minimum term", in relation to a mandatory life sentence, means the part of the sentence to be specified in an order under s.269(2) (see Transitional Provisions, para.(1)). CJA 2003, s.269(5), Sch.21, paras 1, 4

1. A **whole life order**, where the early release provisions should not apply, that is an order under s.269(4), see Transitional Provisions para.(2) will be appropriate where:

(1) the judge considers that the seriousness of the offence, (or the combination of the offence and one or more offences associated with it) is exceptionally high, and
(2) the offender was aged 21 or over when he committed the offence.

Cases that would normally fall within (1) include:

(a) the murder of two or more persons, where each murder involves any of the following:

(i) a substantial degree of premeditation or planning,
(ii) the abduction of the victim, or
(iii) sexual or sadistic conduct,

(b) the murder of a child (i.e. under 18) if involving the abduction of the child or sexual or sadistic motivation,
(c) a murder done for the purpose of advancing a political, religious or ideological cause, or
(d) a murder by an offender previously convicted of murder.

2. **30 years** will be the appropriate starting point where:

(1) the case does not fall within (1) above, but the judge considers that the seriousness of the offence or the combination of the offence and one or more offences associated with it is particularly high, and
(2) the offender was aged 18 or over when he committed the offence.

Cases that (if not falling within para.4(1) above) would normally fall within para.2 include:

(a) the murder of a police officer or prison officer in the course of his duty,
(b) a murder involving the use of a firearm or explosive,
(c) a murder done for gain (such as a murder done in the course or furtherance of robbery or burglary, done for payment or done in the expectation of gain as a result of the death),
(d) a murder intended to obstruct or interfere with the course of justice,
(e) a murder involving sexual or sadistic conduct,
(f) the murder of two or more persons,
(g) a murder that is racially or religiously aggravated (CDA 1998, s.28) or aggravated by sexual orientation (CJA 2003, s.146(2)(a)(i),(b)(i)), or
(h) a murder falling within para.1 committed by an offender who was aged under 21 when he committed the offence. (*ibid.*, para. 5).

Sadism need not be sexual to justify a 30-year term (*Att.-Gen.'s Reference (Nos 108 and 109 of 2005) The Times*, February 22, 2006).

3. **15 years** will be the appropriate starting point where the offender was aged 18 or over when he committed the offence and the case does not fall within paras 1 or 2 above (*ibid.*, para.6);

4. **12 years** is the appropriate starting point where the offender was aged under 18 when he committed the offence (*ibid.*, para.7).

Aggravating and mitigating factors

45–010 Having chosen a starting point, the judge must take into account any aggravating or mitigating factors, to the extent that he has not allowed for them in his choice of starting point. CJA 2003, s.269(5), Sch.21, paras 8, 9, 10

Detailed consideration of aggravating or mitigating factors may result in a minimum term of any length (whatever the starting point), or in the making of a whole life order.

Aggravating factors (additional to those mentioned in paras 4(2) and 5(2)) that may be relevant to the offence of murder include:

(1) a significant degree of planning or premeditation,
(2) the fact that the victim was particularly vulnerable because of age or disability,
(3) mental or physical suffering inflicted on the victim before death,
(4) the abuse of a position of trust,
(5) the use of duress or threats against another person to facilitate the commission of the offence,
(6) the fact that the victim was providing a public service or performing a public duty, and
(7) concealment, destruction or dismemberment of the body.

Mitigating factors that may be relevant to the offence of murder include:

(1) an intention to cause serious bodily harm rather than to kill,
(2) lack of premeditation,
(3) the fact that the offender suffered from any mental disorder or mental disability which (although not falling within MHA 1959, s.2(1), lowered his degree of culpability,
(4) the fact that the offender was provoked (for example, by prolonged stress) in a way not amounting to a defence of provocation,
(5) the fact that the offender acted to any extent in self-defence,
(6) a belief by the offender that the murder was an act of mercy, and
(7) the offender's age.

Nothing in these provisions restricts the application of CJA 2003,

(a) s.143(2) (previous convictions),
(b) s.143(3) (bail), or
(c) s.144 (guilty plea).

Application of s.269 and Sch.21; (1) the first step

45–011 Where the offender is 21 or over, the first step is to choose one of three starting points, *viz.*, "whole life", 30 years or 15 years. Where the 15 year starting point is chosen, the judge must have in mind that this starting point encompasses a very broad range of murders. It should not be assumed (*R. v Sullivan and Others*, above) that Parliament intended to raise all minimum terms that would previously have had a starting point of less than 15 years. CJA 2003, s.269(5), Sch.21, paras 11,12 PD 2004 IV.49.4

Where:

(1) the offender was 21 or over at the time of the offence, and the judge takes the view that the murder is so grave that the offender ought to spend the rest of his life in prison, the appropriate starting point is a "whole life order", the effect of which is that the early release provisions of CSA 1997, s.28 will not apply; such an order should only be specified where the judge considers that the seriousness of the offence (or the combination of the offence and one or more other offences associated with it) is exceptionally high. Schedule 21, para.4(2) (above) sets out examples of cases where it will normally be appropriate to take the "whole life order" as the appropriate starting point; PD 2004, IV.49.5

(2) the offender is aged 18 to 20 and commits a murder that is so serious that it would require a whole life order if committed by an offender aged 21 or over, the appropriate starting point will be 30 years; PD 2004, IV.49.6

(3) a case is not so serious as to require a "whole life order" but where the seriousness of the offence is particularly high and the offender was aged 18 or over when he committed the offence the appropriate starting point, is 30 years. Schedule 21, para.5(2) (above) sets out examples of cases where a 30 year starting point will normally be appropriate if they do not require a "whole life order"; PD 2004, IV.49.7

(4) the offender was aged 18 or over when he committed the offence and the case does not fall within Sch.21, paras 4(1) or 5(1) the appropriate starting point is 15 years. PD 2004, IV.49.8

Note that:

(a) 18 to 20 year olds are only the subject of the 30 year and 15 year starting points; PD 2004, IV.49.9

(b) the appropriate starting point when setting a sentence of detention during HM Pleasure for an offender under 18 when he committed the offence is always 12 years. PD 2004, IV.49.10

The second step

45–012 After choosing a starting point, the second step is to take account of any aggravating or mitigating factors which would justify a departure from the starting point. Additional aggravating factors (other than those specified in paras 4(1) and 5(1)) are listed at Sch.21, para.10 (above). Examples of mitigating factors are listed at *ibid.*, para.11. Taking into account the aggravating and mitigating features the judge may add to or subtract from the starting point to arrive at the appropriate punitive period. PD 2004, IV.49.11

The third step

45–013 The third step is to consider:

(1) the effect of PCC(S)A 2000, s.151(1) (or when it is in force CJA 2003, s.143(2)) in relation to previous convictions;
(2) PCC(S)A 2003, s.151(2) (or when it is in force CJA 2003, s.143(3)) where the offence was committed whilst on bail; and
(3) the effect of PCC(S)A 2000, s.152 (or when in force, CJA 2003, s.144) where the offender has pleaded guilty.

The judge should then take into account what credit the offender would have received for a remand in custody under CJA 2003, s.240, but for the fact that the mandatory sentence is one of life imprisonment. Where the offender has been remanded in custody in connection with the offence or a related offence the judge should have in mind that no credit will otherwise be given for this time when the offender will be considered for early release. The appropriate time to take it into account is when setting the minimum term. The court should normally subtract the time for which the offender was remanded in custody in connection with the offence or a related offence from the punitive period it would otherwise impose in order to reach the minimum term. PD 2004, IV.49.12

As to reduction in sentence for a guilty plea, see 45–028 below.

Conclusion

45–014 Following these calculations the judge should have arrived at the appropriate minimum term to be announced in open court. As para.9 of Sch.21 makes clear, the judge retains ultimate discretion and may arrive at any minimum term from any starting point. The minimum term is subject to appeal by the offender under CJA 2003, s.271 and to review on a reference by the Attorney-General under CJA 2003, s.272. PD 2004, IV.49.13

(2) Transitional arrangements; offences committed before December 18, 2003

(For the position in relation to murders committed after 31 May 2002, see (3) below.)

A fourth step

45–015 Where the judge passes a sentence of mandatory life imprisonment for an offence committed before December 18, 2003, he should take a fourth step in determining the minimum term in accordance with s.276 and Sch.2. PD 2004, IV.49.14

Before setting the minimum term he must check whether the proposed term is greater than than that which the Home Secretary would probably have notified under the practice before September 2002. PD 2004, IV.49.15

R. v Sullivan and Others, The Times, July 14, 2004:

(1) gives detailed guidance as to the correct approach to this practice and a judge passing a mandatory life sentence where the murder was committed prior to December 18, 2003 is advised by PD 2004, IV.49.16 to read that judgment before proceeding;

(2) the practical result of the judgment is that in sentences where the murder was committed before May 31, 2002, the best guide to what would have been the practice of the Home Secretary is the letter sent to judges by Lord Bingham on February 10, 1997 (the relevant parts of which are set out below). PD 2004, IV.49.17

Lord Bingham:

(a) stated that the fact that an offender was under the influence of drink or drugs at the time of the killing, is so common that he would regard it as neutral. But not in the not unfamiliar case in which a married couple, or two derelicts, or two homosexuals, inflamed by drink, indulge in a violent quarrel in which one dies, often against a background of long-standing drunken violence, when he would tend to recommend a term somewhat below the norm; and PD 2004, IV.49.20

(b) said that given the intent necessary for proof of murder, the consequences of taking life and the understandable reaction of relatives of the deceased, a substantial term will almost always be called for, save perhaps in a truly venial case of mercy killing. While a recommendation of a punitive term longer than, say, 30 years will be very rare indeed, there PD 2004, IV.49.21

should not be any upper limit. Some crimes will certainly call for terms very well in excess of the norm.

Lord Bingham's practice

45–016 The practice of Lord Bingham C.J. (as set out in his letter of February 10, 1997) was to take 14 years as the period actually to be served for the "average", "normal" or "unexceptional" murder. Examples of factors he outlined as capable, in appropriate cases of mitigating the normal penalty were: PD 2004, IV.49.18

(1) youth,
(2) age (where relevant to physical capacity on release or the likelihood of the offender dying in prison),
(3) subnormality or mental abnormality,
(4) provocation (in a non-technical sense), or an excessive response to a personal threat,
(5) the absence of an intention to kill,
(6) spontaneity and lack of premeditation (beyond that necessary to constitute the offence: e.g. a sudden response to family pressure or to prolonged and eventually insupportable stress,
(7) mercy killing, and
(8) a plea of guilty or hard evidence of remorse or contrition.

He then listed the following factors as likely to call for a sentence more severe than the norm: PD 2004, IV.49.19

(1) evidence of a planned, professional, revenge or contract killing,
(2) the killing of a child or a very old or otherwise vulnerable victim,
(3) evidence of sadism, gratuitous violence, or sexual maltreatment, humiliation or degradation before the killing,
(4) killing for gain (in the course of burglary, robbery, blackmail, insurance fraud, etc.),
(5) multiple killings,
(6) the killing of a witness or potential witness to defeat the ends of justice,
(7) the killing of those doing their public duty (policemen, prison officers, postmasters, firemen, judges, etc.),
(8) terrorist or politically motivated killings,
(9) the use of firearms or other dangerous weapons, whether carried for defensive or offensive reasons,
(10) a substantial record of serious violence, and
(11) macabre attempts to dismember or conceal the body.

(3) Murder committed after May 31, 2002 and before December 18, 2003

45–017 For the purpose of a sentence where the murder was committed after May 31, 2002 and before December 18, 2003, the judge should apply the Practice Statement handed down on May 31, 2002 reproduced at paras IV.49.23–33 below. This statement replaces the single normal tariff of 14 years by a higher and a normal starting point of respectively 16 (comparable to 32 years) and 12 years (comparable to 24 years). These starting points have then to be increased or reduced because of aggravating or mitigating factors such as those below. It is emphasised that they were no more than a starting point. PD 2004, IV.49.22 PD 2004, IV.49.23

The normal starting point of 12 years

45–018 Cases falling within this starting point will normally involve the killing of the victim, arising from a quarrel or loss of temper between two people known to each other. It will not have the characteristics referred to in para.49.26. Exceptionally, the starting point may be reduced because of the sort of circumstances described in the next paragraph. PD 2004, IV.49.24

The normal starting point may be reduced because the murder is one where the offender's culpability is significantly reduced, for example, because: PD 2004, IV.49.25

(a) the case came close to the borderline between murder and manslaughter; or
(b) the offender suffered from mental disorder, or from a mental disability which lowered the degree of his criminal responsibility for the killing although not affording a defence of diminished responsibility;
(c) the offender was provoked (in a non-technical sense), such as by prolonged and eventually unsupportable stress; or
(d) the case involved an over reaction in self-defence; or
(e) the offence was a mercy killing.

These factors could justify a reduction to 8/9 years (equivalent to 16/18 years).

The higher starting point of 1/16 years

45–019 The higher starting point will apply to cases where the offender's culpability was exceptionally high or the victim was in a particularly vulnerable position. Such cases will be characterised by a feature which makes the crime especially serious, such as:

(a) the killing was "professional" or a contract killing;

(b) the killing was politically motivated;
(c) the killing was done for gain (in the course of a burglary, etc.);
(d) the killing was intended to defeat the ends of justice (as in the killing of a witness or potential witness);
(e) the victim was providing a public service;
(f) the victim was a child or was otherwise vulnerable;
(g) the killing was racially aggravated;
(h) the victim was deliberately targeted because of his or her religion or sexual orientation;
(i) there was evidence of sadism, gratuitous violence or sexual maltreatment, humiliation or degradation of the victim before the killing;
(j) extensive and/or multiple injuries were inflicted on the victim before the killing;
(k) the offender committed multiple murders.

Variation of the starting point

45–020 Whichever starting point is selected in a particular case, it may be appropriate for the trial judge to vary the starting point upwards or downwards, to take aggravating or mitigating factors which relate to either the offence or the offender in the particular case, into account. PD 2004, IV.49.27

Aggravating factors relating to the offence can include: PD 2004, IV.49.28

(a) the fact that the killing was planned;
(b) the use of a firearm;
(c) arming with a weapon in advance;
(d) concealment of the body, destruction of the crime scene and/or dismemberment of the body;
(e) particularly in domestic violence cases, the fact that the murder was the culmination of cruel and violent behaviour by the offender.

Aggravating factors relating to the offender will include the offender's previous record and failures to respond to previous sentences, to the extent that this is relevant to culpability rather than to risk. PD 2004, IV.49.29

Mitigating factors relating to the offence will include: PD 2004, IV.49.30

(a) an intention to cause grievous bodily harm, rather than to an intent to kill;
(b) spontaneity and lack of pre-meditation.

Mitigating factors relating to the offender may include: PD 2004, IV.49.3

(a) the offender's age;

(b) clear evidence of remorse or contrition;
(c) a timely plea of guilty (see 45–028 below).

Very serious cases

45–021 A substantial upward adjustment may be appropriate in the most serious cases, for example, those involving a substantial number of murders, or if there are several factors identified as attracting the higher starting point present. In suitable cases the result might even be a minimum term of 30 years (equivalent to 60 years) which would offer little or no hope of the offender's eventual release. In cases of exceptional gravity, the judge, rather than setting a whole life minimum term, may state that there is no minimum period which could properly be set in that particular case. PD 2004, IV.49.32

Among the categories of case referred to in para.lV.49.26 some offences may be especially grave. These include cases in which the victim was performing his duties as a prison officer at the time of the crime or the offence was a terrorist or sexual or sadistic murder or involved a young child. In such a case, a term of 20 years and upwards could be appropriate. PD 2004, IV.49.33

In following this guidance, judges should bear in mind the conclusion of CACD in *Sullivan* that the general effect of both these statements is the same. While Lord Bingham does not identify as many starting points, it is open to the judge to come to exactly the same decision irrespective of which was followed. Both pieces of guidance give the judge a considerable degree of discretion. PD 2004, IV.49.34

As to the position where contempt is by the accused in a deliberate attempt to abort the trial, see *R. v Russell* [2006] Crim.L.R. 862.

(4) Announcing the minimum term

45–022 Having gone through the three (or four) steps outlined above, the judge then has a duty under CJA 2003, s.270, to state in open court, in ordinary language, his reasons for deciding on the minimum term or for passing a whole life order. PD 2004, IV.49.35

In order to comply with this duty he should state clearly the minimum term he has determined.

In doing so, he must: PD 2004, IV.49.36

(1) state which of the starting points he has chosen and his reasons for doing so;
(2) where he has departed from that starting point due to mitigating or aggravating features state the reasons for that departure and any aggravating or mitigating features which have led to that departure;

(3) at that point also declare how much, if any, time is being deducted for time spent in custody;
(4) then explain that the minimum term is the minimum amount of time the prisoner will spend in prison, from the date of sentence, before the Parole Board can order early release. If it remains necessary for the protection of the public, the prisoner will continue to be detained after that date;
(5) state that where the prisoner has served the minimum term and the Parole Board has decided to direct release, he will remain on licence for the rest of his life and may be recalled to prison.

Where the offender was 21 or over when he committed the offence and the judge considers that the seriousness of the offence is so exceptionally high that a "whole life order" is appropriate, he should state clearly his reasons for reaching this conclusion. He should also explain that the early release provisions will not apply. PD 2004, IV.49.37

(5) Discretionary life sentences: criteria

45–023 The criteria governing the imposition of a *discretionary* life sentence are essentially the same whether the form of such a sentence is one of imprisonment, custody for life under PCC(S)A 2000 s.93 or detention for life under s.91 (*R. v Turton* (1986) 8 Cr.App. R.(S.) 174; *R. v Hall* (1986) 8 Cr.App.R.(S.) 458; *R. v Kelly* (1987) 9 Cr.App.R.(S.) 181; *R. v Silson* (1987) 9 Cr.App.R.(S.) 282; *R. v Powell* (1989) 11 Cr.App.R.(S.) 113), or, presumably, CJA 2003, ss.225 and 226; (and see PD 2004, para.IV.47.1–6, below).

The sentence is imposed only in the most exceptional circumstances (*R. v Wilkinson* (1983) 5 Cr.App.R.(S.) 105), particularly in cases where the offender is subject, in a marked degree, to mental instability. With few exceptions, it is reserved for offenders:

(1) who satisfy the criteria of PCC(S)A 2000, s.80(2)(b) as being in a mental state which makes them dangerous to the public (*R. v Picker* (1970) 54 Cr.App.R.330; *R. v Headley* (1979) 1 Cr.App.R.(S.) 158; *R. v Meek* (1995) 16 Cr.App.R.(S.) 1003), but
(2) who cannot be dealt with under the provisions of MHA 1983 (see 48 MENTALLY DISORDERED OFFENDERS).

For these reasons a life sentence is appropriate where:

(a) the offence or offences of which the offender stands convicted are, in themselves, grave enough to warrant a very long sentence; or
(b) the nature of the offences or the offender's history show that he is a person of unstable character likely to commit such offences again in the future; *and*
(c) his *mental instability or psychiatric illness* is of a kind that requires constant supervision and reassessment; and
(d) if such offences, particularly the major sexual offences or offences of violence, are committed in the future, the consequences to others may be specially injurious.

(*R. v Hodgson* (1968) 52 Cr.App.R. 113; *R. v Wilkinson* (1983) 5 Cr.App.R.(S.) 105; *Att.-Gen.'s Reference (No. 34 of 1992 (Oxford))* [1994] 15 Cr.App.R.(S.) 167; *Att.-Gen.'s Reference (No. 32 of 1996 (Whittaker))* [1997] 1 Cr.App.R.(S.) 261; *R. v Chapman* [2000] 1 Cr.App.R. 77). In the case of a personality, rather than a mental, disorder, a long determinate sentence may be appropriate (*cf. R. v Chapman* (1994) 15 Cr.App.R.(S.) 844; *R. v Spear* (1995) 16 Cr.App.R.(S.) 242; *R. v Trowbridge* [2002] 2 Cr.App.R.(S.) 38).

Wherever a life sentence is contemplated, counsel should be asked to address the judge on the question (*R. v Mac Dougall* (1983) 5 Cr.App.R.(S.) 78; *R. v J* (1992) 14 Cr.App.R.(S.) 506).

Medical evidence

45–024 As to the matters raised in paras (b)–(d) above, there should be a medical report (*R. v De Havilland* (1983) 5 Cr.App.R.(S.) 109), but since the judge must ultimately decide the sentence, there may be cases where a report is not necessary (*R. v Birch* (1987) 9 Cr.App.R.(S.) 509; *Att.-Gen.'s Reference (No. 32 of 1996)* [1996] Crim.L.R. 917; *R. v Cobb* [2001] Crim.L.R. 924; *R. v Powell and Horsford* [2001] Crim.L.R. 925). As to persistent paedophiles, see *R. v Hatch* [1997] 1 Cr.App.R.(S.) 22.

Offender eligible for hospital order

45–025 Where the pre-conditions for a hospital order (see 48 MENTALLY DISORDERED OFFENDERS) are satisfied, and a bed is available in a secure hospital, the judge should make a hospital order instead of imposing a discretionary life sentence (*R. v Mitchell* [1997] 1 Cr.App.R.(S.) 90) (*R. v Fleming* (1993)

14 Cr.App.R.(S.) 151 to be disregarded)), unless, in *abnormal circumstances* the judge decides to impose a life sentence in such a case, where he considers the offender's culpability so great that a hospital order cannot be justified (*R. v Fairhurst* [1996] 1 Cr.App.R.(S.) 242, *cf. R. v Watson* [2004] Cr.App.R. (S.) 35). It is not proper to impose a life sentence merely to frustrate the offender's premature release by a Mental Health Review Tribunal (*ibid.*).

For a recent example, see *R. v IA* [2006] 1 Cr.App.R.(S.) 91.

The minimum term

45–026 PCC(S)A 2000, s.82A empowers the judge when passing a sentence of life imprisonment, where such a sentence is *not fixed by law*, to specify the period which must be served before the offender may require the Secretary of State to refer his case to the Parole Board. The discretionary life sentence therefore falls into two parts:

(1) that period which consists of the period of detention imposed for punishment and deterrence, taking into account the seriousness of the offence; and
(2) the remaining part of the sentence, during which the offender's detention will be governed by considerations of risk to the public.

The judge is not obliged by statute to make use of this provision when passing a discretionary life sentence, but he should do so, save in the very exceptional case (under s.82A(14)) where he considers that the offence is so serious that the offender should spend the rest of his life in prison, irrespective of the risk to the public. In such a case, the judge should make that clear in open court when passing sentence. PD 2004, IV.47.1–3

Approach to the minimum term

45–027 In cases where the judge must specify the relevant period under s.82A, he should allow the accused's advocate to address him as to the appropriate length of the period. Where he proposes not to specify such a period, the accused's advocate should be allowed to address him as to the appropriateness of that course of action. PD 2004, IV.47.4

In specifying the relevant part of the sentence, the judge should have regard to the specific terms of s.82A and should indicate the reasons for reaching his decision as to the length of the relevant period. PD 2004, IV.47.5

Whether or not the the judge orders that s.82A should apply, he must not, following the imposition of a discretionary life PD 2004, IV.47.6

sentence, make a written report to the Home Secretary through the Lord Chief Justice as was the practice until February 8, 1993.

Reduction for plea of guilty

45–028 There are important differences between the usual fixed term sentence and the minimum term set following the imposition of the mandatory life sentence for murder. The most significant of these is that a reduction for a plea of guilty in the case of murder will have double the effect on time served in custody when compared with a determinate sentence. This is because a determinate sentence provides, in most circumstances, for the release of the offender on licence half way through the total sentence whereas in the case of murder a minimum term is the period in custody before consideration is given by the Parole Board to whether release is appropriate.

Given this difference, the special characteristic of the offence of murder and the unique statutory provision of starting points, careful consideration needs to be given to:

(1) the extent of any reduction; and
(2) the need to ensure that the minimum term properly reflects the seriousness of the offence.

Whilst the general principles continue to apply (both that a guilty plea should be encouraged and that the extent of any reduction should reduce if the indication of plea is later than the first reasonable opportunity), the process of determining the level of reduction is different. SGC 1, 6.4, 6.5

Approach to reduction

45–029 SGC 1, 6.5 recommends the following approach:

(1) Where the judge determines that there should be a *whole life* minimum term, there will be no reduction for a guilty plea;
(2) in other circumstances:
    (a) the judge must weigh carefully the overall length of the minimum term taking into account other reductions for which offenders may be eligible so as to avoid a combination leading to an inappropriately short sentence;
    (b) where it is appropriate to reduce the minimum term having regard to a plea of guilty, the maximum reduction will be one sixth;
    (c) in the special circumstances of a conviction for murder, even where a minimum term of over 30 years

(but not whole life) is fixed, the reduction should never exceed five years;

(d) the sliding scale will apply so that, where it is appropriate to reduce the minimum term on account of a guilty plea, the maximum reduction (one sixth or five years whichever is the less) is only available where there has been an indication of willingness to plead guilty at the first reasonable opportunity, with a maximum of 5 per cent for a late guilty plea;

(e) the judge should then review the sentence to ensure that the minimum term accurately reflects the seriousness of the offence taking account of the statutory starting point, all aggravating and mitigating factors and any guilty plea entered.

Announcing the minimum term

45–030 When a judge gives in public his decision as to the minimum term a prisoner is required to serve, he should: PD 2004, Annex C

(1) make clear how that term is calculated;

(2) normally commence by indicating what he considers would be the appropriate determinate sentence suitable for punishment and deterrence;

(3) then explain that it is necessary to calculate a minimum term so that it will be known when the prisoner's case should be referred to the Parole Board; and finally;

(4) explain that if a prisoner is released on licence, still, for the remainder of his life, he can be recalled to prison if he does not comply with the terms of his licence.

46 LIVE LINKS

Introduction

46–001 A "live link" enables a witness other than accused to give evidence, usually by means of CCTV, from a place outside the court building, instead of having to attend court in the usual manner. CJA 2003, Pt 8, once in force extends the present provisions in relation to young persons, under YJCEA 1999, see 19 CHILDREN AND YOUNG PERSONS.

"Live link" for the purposes of the Act means a live television link or other arrangement by which a witness, while at a place in the United Kingdom which is outside the building where the proceedings are being held, is able to see and hear a person at the place where the proceedings are being held and to be seen and heard by the accused, the judge and the jury (if there is one), legal representatives acting in the proceedings, and any interpreter or other person appointed by the court to assist the witness. CJA 2003, s.56(2)(3)(4)

The extent (if any) to which a person is unable to see or hear by reason of any impairment of eyesight or hearing is to be disregarded.

46–002 A witness (other than the accused) may, if the judge so directs, give evidence through a live link in: CJA 2003, s.51(1), (2), (3), (4), (5)

(1) an appeal to the Crown Court arising out of a summary trial,
(2) a trial on indictment, and
(3) a hearing before the Crown Court which is held after the accused has entered a plea of guilty, and

the judge may give such a direction either on an application by a party to the proceedings, or of his own motion, but may authorise such a course only where:

(a) he is satisfied that it is in the interests of the efficient or effective administration of justice for the witness to give evidence in the proceedings through a live link, e.g. from his place of work,
(b) he has been notified that suitable facilities are available in the area in which it appears that the proceedings will take place.

The responsibility for ensuring that facilities are in place is that of the prosecutor. The withdrawal of any such a notification will not affect a direction given under this section before that withdrawal.

In deciding whether to give a direction, the judge must consider all the circumstances of the case, some of the more important being: CJA 2003, ss.51(6), (7), (8)

- the availability of the witness,
- the need for the witness to attend in person,
- the importance of the witness's evidence to the proceedings,
- the views of the witness,
- the suitability of the facilities at the place where the witness would give evidence through a live link, and
- whether a direction might tend to inhibit any party to the proceedings from effectively testing the witness's evidence.

The judge must state in open court his reasons for refusing an application for a direction under the section.

Effect of direction; rescission

46–003 Where the judge gives a direction for a witness to give evidence through a live link, the witness must give all his evidence through the live link unless the direction is rescinded. The judge may rescind a direction if it appears to him to be in the interests of justice to do so, on an application by a party to the proceedings, or of his own motion, but no application may be made by a party unless there has been a material change of circumstances since the direction was given, e.g. where problems arise with the technology after a direction has been given. CJA 2003, ss.52(1), (2)

Where the judge does rescind the order, the witness ceases to be able to give evidence through the live link, but this does not prevent the judge from giving a further direction under s.51 in relation to him.

The judge must state in open court his reasons for rescinding a direction, or for refusing an application to do so.

Other powers

46–004 Nothing in CJA 2003, Pt 8 is to be regarded as affecting any power of a judge: CJA 2003, s.56(5)

(1) to make an order, give directions or give leave of any description in relation to any witness (including the accused), or
(2) to exclude evidence at his discretion (whether by preventing questions being put or otherwise).

Warning to jury

46–005 Where, as a result of a direction under s.51, evidence has been given though a live link, the judge may give the jury (if there is one) such directions as he thinks necessary to ensure that the jury give the same weight to the evidence as if it had been given by the witness in the courtroom or other place where the proceedings were held. CJA 2003, s.54

Witness outside the United Kingdom

46–006 Any party may apply for leave under CJA 1988, s.32(1) for evidence to be given through a live television link by a witness who is outside the United Kingdom. Such an application and any matter relating to it may be dealt with by the judge in chambers.

The procedure is as follows:

(1) the application is made by giving notice in writing, in the form set out in the Practice Direction, within 28 days after the date of the committal of the accused, or, as the case may be, the giving of a notice of transfer under CJA 1987, s.4(l)(c), or of the service of copies of the documents containing the evidence on which the charge or charges are based under CDA 1998, Sch.3, para.1, or of the preferring of a voluntary bill in relation to the case;
(2) the period of 28 days may be extended by the Crown Court, either before or after it expires, on an application made in writing, specifying the grounds of the application; the court officer shall notify all the parties of the decision of the Crown Court;
(3) any notice must be sent to the Crown Court officer and at the same time a copy thereof must be sent by the applicant to every other party to the proceedings;
(3) any party receiving a copy of a notice must, within 28 days of the date of the notice, notify the applicant and the court officer, in writing, whether or not:
  (a) he opposes the application, giving his reasons for any such opposition; and
  (b) he wishes to be represented at any hearing;
(4) once the period in (3) above has expired the judge will determine whether an application under para.(1) is to be dealt with:
  (a) without a hearing; or
  (b) at a hearing at which the applicant and such other party or parties as the court may direct may be represented;

Live Links

   (c) and the court officer shall notify the applicant and, where necessary, the other party or parties, of the time and place of any such hearing;
(5) the court officer will notify all the parties of the judge's decision in relation to an application under para.(1) and, where leave is granted, the notification will state:
   (a) the country in which the witness will give evidence;
   (b) if known, the place where the witness will give evidence;
   (c) where the witness is to give evidence on behalf of the prosecutor, or where disclosure is required by CPIA 1996, s.5(7) (alibi) or by rules under PACE 1984, s.81 (expert evidence), the name of the witness;
   (d) the location of the Crown Court at which the trial should take place; and
   (e) any conditions specified by the Crown Court in accordance with the paragraph below.

The judge dealing with an application under para.(1) may specify that as a condition of the grant of leave the witness should give the evidence in the presence of a specified person who is able and willing to answer under oath or affirmation any questions the trial judge may put as to the circumstances in which the evidence is given, including questions about any persons who are present when the evidence is given and any matters which may affect the giving of the evidence. R.30

Terrorism cases

46–007 The Protocol on terrorism cases (see 16 CASE MANAGEMENT, 16–062) provides that unless a judge otherwise directs all Crown Court hearings prior to the trial will be conducted by video link for all accused in custody.

47 MAJORITY VERDICT

Judge's direction

47–001 It is important that all those trying indictable offences should so far as possible adopt a uniform practice when complying with JA 1974, s.17, both in directing the jury in summing-up and also in receiving the verdict or giving further directions after retirement. So far as the summing-up is concerned, it is inadvisable for the judge, or indeed for advocates, to attempt an explanation of the section for fear that the jury will be confused. Before the jury retire, however, the judge should direct them in some such words as the following: PD 2004, IV.46.1

> *"As you may know, the law permits me, in certain circumstances, to accept a verdict which is not the verdict of you all. Those circumstances have not as yet arisen, so that when you retire I must ask you to reach a verdict upon which each one of you is agreed. Should, however, the time come when it is possible for me to accept a majority verdict, I will give you a further direction."*

Taking the verdict

47–002 It is not generally desirable that the jury be told the actual time which must elapse before they may return a majority verdict (*R. v Porter* [1996] Crim.L.R.126). Thereafter the practice should be as follows: PD 2004, IV.46.2–8

(1) should the jury return BEFORE two hours and 10 minutes since the last member of the jury left the jury box to go to the jury room (or such longer time as the judge thinks reasonable) has elapsed (see s.17(4)), they should be asked, in respect of each count separately:

(a) "Have you reached a verdict upon which you are all agreed? Please answer 'yes' or 'no'."

(b) (i) if unanimous, or on those counts where it is unanimous, is this verdict to be accepted.

(ii) if not unanimous, or on those counts where not unanimous—the jury should be sent out again for further deliberation with a further direction to arrive, if possible, at a unanimous verdict.

(2) should the jury return, (whether for the first time or subsequently) or be sent for AFTER the two hours and 10 minutes (or the longer period) has elapsed then questions

(a) and (b) above should be put to them, and if it appears that they are not unanimous, they should be asked to retire once more and told that they should continue to endeavour to reach a unanimous verdict but that, if they cannot the judge will accept a majority verdict (as in s.17(4)), i.e. the verdict of 10 out of 11 or 12 jurors, or 9 out of 10 jurors.

(3) when the jury FINALLY return, they should be asked, separately on each count:
   (i) "Have at least 10 (or 9 as the case may be) of you agreed upon your verdict?"
   (ii) if "yes", "What is your verdict? Please answer only 'Guilty' or 'Not Guilty'."
   (iii) if "Not Guilty", accept the verdict without more ado;
   (iv) if "Guilty", is that the verdict of you all, or by a majority?"
   (v) if "Guilty by a majority"—"How many of you agreed to the verdict and how many dissented?"

Recording the time; further deliberations

47–003 At whatever stage the jury return, before question (a) above, is asked, the senior Crown Court officer present will state in open court, for each period when the jury was out of court for the purpose of considering their verdict(s), the time at which the last member of the jury left the jury box to go to the jury room, and the time of their return to the jury box, and will additionally state in open court the totals of such periods. PD 2004, IV.46.5

If there is an error in procedure, e.g. in timing, the judge has a discretion to correct that error by a further direction (*R. v Shields* [1997] Crim.L.R. 758).

If the jury is not able to agree on a verdict by the requisite majority, the judge, in his discretion, may either ask them to deliberate further or discharge them from giving a verdict.

Multiple count indictment

47–004 Where there are several counts (or alternative verdicts) left to the jury the above practice will, of course, need to be adapted to the circumstances. PD 2004, IV.46.7

Thus:

(1) the procedure will have to be repeated in respect of each count (or alternative verdict);
(2) the verdict being accepted in those cases where the jury is unanimous; and
(3) the further direction in para.46.3 being given in cases in which it is not unanimous;

(4) should the jury in the end be unable to agree on a verdict by the required majority (i.e. if the answer to the question in para.46.4(a) be in the negative) the judge in his discretion will either ask them to deliberate further or discharge them. See *R. v Noah* (2004) S.J. 1249.

Application to other verdicts

47–005 JA 1974, s.17 applies also to verdicts other than "Guilty" or "Not Guilty", e.g. to: PD 2004, IV.46.8

(1) special verdicts under the CP(I)A 1964;
(2) verdicts under that Act as to fitness to be tried; and
(3) special verdicts on findings of fact.

Accordingly in such cases the questions to jurors will have to be suitably adjusted.

A majority verdict which does not comply with the statutory language is not a proper majority verdict (*R. v Bateson* (1970) 54 Cr.App.R. 11; *R. v Barry* [1975] 1 W.L.R. 1190; *R. v Austin* [2003] Crim.L.R. 426).

48 MENTALLY DISORDERED OFFENDERS

Introduction

48–001 A variety of powers is available to deal with offenders who:

(1) are not so mentally disordered as to be absolved from criminal responsibility for their actions; but
(2) are nevertheless in need of psychiatric treatment.

A judge may, in certain circumstances, remand to hospital for treatment an accused person awaiting trial, as well as those waiting to be sentenced.

A convicted offender may be:

(a) sent to a hospital under an interim hospital order, or a hospital order;
(b) made the subject of a guardianship order; or
(c) made the subject of a community order with a requirement that he undergo psychiatric treatment.

In some cases a hospital order may be made in conjunction with a restriction order.

Although some offenders receive treatment in prison, the judge has no control over the allocation of offenders to prisons which are able to provide treatment, nor is it correct sentencing practice to pass a sentence of imprisonment on the assumption that the offender will receive psychiatric treatment in prison.

It should be noted that:

(i) the psychiatric facilities which the courts may use for their purposes are the same as those provided by the NHS for treatment of non-offender patients;
(ii) with the exception of the four "medical hospitals" (Broadmoor, Rampton, Moss Side and Park Lane) which provide treatment in conditions of the highest security, any given psychiatric hospital will, as a general rule, admit patients only from a particular catchment area, from which each prospective patient must come, or with which he must have some connection;
(iii) different hospitals specialise in the treatment of different forms of mental disorder, so that

in respect of any one catchment area there are likely to be at least two hospitals, one providing treatment for mental illness, and one providing treatment for mental handicap; for this reason the consent of the hospital is required before the judge may order admission; and

(iv) where the judge has in mind making a hospital order or an interim hospital order, Regional Health Authorities are required to assist in identifying an appropriate hospital for a particular offender.

1. Disposal on special verdict or finding of disability

48–002 The position in relation the judge's powers on a special verdict being returned that the accused is not guilty by reason of insanity, or findings being recorded that the accused is under a disability and that he did the act or made the omission charged against him are dealt with under 63 UNFITNESS TO PLEAD/INSANITY.

2. Disposal on conviction on indictment

Approach to sentence

48–003 The judge, in approaching sentence in a case involving a degree of mental disorder should take the following step (*R. v Birch* (1990) 90 Cr.App.R. 78, at p.87):

(1) if a period of compulsory detention is not, or may not, be apposite, he should consider the possibility of a community order with a requirement of in- or out-patient treatment;

(2) otherwise, he will need to satisfy himself that the preconditions for making a hospital order are satisfied; here he acts on the evidence of the doctors, and if left in doubt may use the provisions of ss.38 and 39 to make an interim order;

(3) if he is satisfied that the preconditions for a hospital order are made out, he will have to decide whether to make such an order or whether "the most suitable way of disposing of the case" is to impose a sentence of imprisonment;

(4) he must then consider whether the further condition imposed by s.41 is satisfied, in which case he may make a restriction order; he is not obliged to do so, and may again consider sending the offender to prison, either for life or for a fixed term (*R. v Speake* (1957) 41 Cr.App.R. 222);

(5) if he decides on a restriction order, he must then choose between an unlimited order or one for a fixed term; and

(6) he must choose between an order without restriction, which may enable the author of a serious act of violence to be at liberty within months of the making of the order, and a restriction order which may lead to the offender being detained, in some cases, for a longer period than if he had been given a custodial sentence; it is, moreover, a choice which depends upon the prognosis, the ultimate responsibility for which is left to the judge.

Hospital order

48–004 Where a person is convicted before the Crown Court of an offence punishable with imprisonment, other than an offence for which the sentence is fixed by law, the judge may make a hospital order authorising his admission to, and detention in, a specified hospital.

MHA 1983, s.37(1); CJA 2003, s.304, Sch.32, Pt 1; CJA 2003, s.332, Sch.37, Pt 5, para.38

In the case of an offence the sentence for which would otherwise fall to be imposed under:

(1) FA 1968, s.51A(2) (minimum term for certain firearms offences); or

(2) PCC(S)A 2000, ss.109 where still appropriate, 110(2) or 111(2) (minimum term for certain repeat offences); or

(3) any of CJA 2003, ss.225–228 (dangerous offenders),

(read in accordance with CJA 2003, s.305(4)) there is nothing to prevent the judge from making a hospital order.

Such an order allows the offender to be taken to the specified hospital and detained there until he is discharged by the hospital authorities or by a Mental Health Review Tribunal.

Preconditions for hospital order

48–005 Before a hospital order may be made, the judge must be:

(1) dealing with an offender for an imprisonable offence;

(2) satisfied on the written or oral evidence of two medical practitioners (at least one of whom is approved for the purposes of s.12 of the Act) that:

(a) the offender is suffering from mental illness, psychopathic disorder, mental impairment or severe mental impairment; and
(b) the mental disorder from which the offender is suffering is of a nature or degree which makes it appropriate for him to be detained in a hospital for medical treatment; and
(c) in the case of a psychopathic disorder or mental impairment, the treatment is likely to alleviate or prevent the deterioration of his condition;

(3) satisfied there is a place available for the offender at the hospital to be specified in the order; and
(4) of the opinion, having regard to all the circumstances, including the nature of the offence and the character and antecedents of the offender, and to other available methods of dealing with him, that the most suitable method of disposing of the case is by means of a hospital order.

The gravity of the offence committed is not material save that it may indicate a need for special treatment (*R. v Eaton* [1976] Crim. L.R. 390).

An offender should always be represented where the court is contemplating such an order (*R. v Blackwood* (1974) 59 Cr.App.R. 170).

Effect of hospital order

48–006 Once the offender is admitted to hospital pursuant to such an order, unless it is accompanied by a restriction order under s.41, his position is almost exactly the same as if he were a civil patient. In effect:

(1) he passes out of the penal system and into the hospital regime;
(2) neither the judge nor the Home Secretary has any say in his disposal;
(3) like any other mental patient, he may be detained only for a period of six months, unless the authority to detain is renewed. If it expires without being renewed the patient may leave.

Furthermore:

(a) he may be discharged at any time by the hospital managers or the "responsible medical officer";
(b) if he absconds or is absent without leave and is not retaken within 28 days he is automatically discharged at the end of that period (s.18(5)); and

(c) if he is allowed continuous leave of absence for more than six months, he cannot be recalled (s.17(5)).

Restriction order: s.41

48–007 A restriction order is an order which accompanies a hospital order in cases where the judge considers that for the protection of the public from serious harm, the offender should not be released from hospital without careful consideration by either the Home Secretary or a Mental Health Review Tribunal. The order prevents the offender from being discharged, granted leave of absence or transferred to another hospital without the approval of the Home Secretary. In certain circumstances a restricted patient may be discharged by a Mental Health Review Tribunal. HO 1990

Preconditions for restriction order

48–008 The judge may, where he makes a hospital order in respect of an offender, also make a restriction order, ordering that the offender be subject to special restrictions, provided that:

(1) having regard to the nature of the offence, the antecedents of the offender, and the risk of his committing offences if set at large, he considers it necessary for the protection of the public from serious harm to do so; and
(2) at least one of the medical practitioners whose evidence is taken into account has given evidence orally before the court.

Such order may be made either without limit of time, or during such period as may be specified in the order. In the ordinary case, where punishment as such is not intended and the object is that the offender should receive treatment and be at large again as soon as he can safely be discharged, a restriction order is not appropriate (*R. v Morris* (1961) 45 Cr.App.R. 185); but a restriction order ought to be made, where the judge considers that the public needs to be protected:

(a) in cases of violence or the more serious sexual offenders, particularly if the offender has a record of such offences or there is a history of mental disorder involving violent behaviour (*R. v Gardiner* (1967) 51 Cr.App.R. 187; *R. v Birch* (1989) 11 Cr.App.R.(S.) 202); and
(b) in the case of the anti-social pest who requires treatment under a hospital order (*R. v Toland* (1974) 58 Cr.App.R. 453; *R. v Royse* (1981) 3 Cr.App.R.(S.) 58).

The section places the responsibility of making a restriction order on the judge if, in his opinion, it is necessary for the protection of the public; the fact that all the medical witnesses advise against it does not mean that it is wrong in principle; but there must be evidence on which to base such an order (*R. v Courtney* [1988] Crim.L.R. 130).

In certain, circumstances, as an alternative to recommending a restriction order under s.41, the responsible medical officer may make a "supervision application" to the Health Authority under s.25A (inserted by s.1 of the Mental Health (Patients in the Community) Act 1995) which provides limited "teeth", including recall to hospital.

Effect of restriction order

48–009 In marked contrast with the regime under the ordinary hospital order, is an order coupled with a restriction on discharge pursuant to s.41. Such an order is not a separate means of disposal; it has no existence independently of the hospital order to which it relates. It does, however, fundamentally affect the circumstances in which the patient is detained. Thus:

(1) the offender is no longer regarded simply as a patient whose interests are paramount;
(2) the control of the patient is not handed over unconditionally to the hospital authorities; and
(3) the interests of the public are safeguarded by transferring responsibility for discharge from the medical officer and the hospital managers, to the Home Secretary or a Mental Health Review Tribunal.

Approach to restriction order

48–010 The judge is required to assess not the seriousness of the risk that the accused will reoffend, but the risk that if he does so the public will suffer serious harm. In *R. v Birch* (above) where the principles were reviewed, CACD was of the opinion that:

(1) the harm need not be limited to personal injury;
(2) the harm need not relate to the public in general, it suffices if a single person or category of persons is at risk; and
(3) the potential harm must however be serious; a high possibility of a recurrence of minor offences is not enough.

The decision whether to make an order is one for the judge; he may make an order even where the medical witnesses do not advise it (*R. v Royse* (1981) 3 Cr.App.R.(S.) 58; *cf. R. v Reynolds*, *The Times*, November 1, 2000). The seriousness of the offence is only one of the factors which he is required to take into consideration.

A minor offence by an offender who is shown to be mentally disordered and dangerous may be the subject of a restriction order; conversely, a serious offence committed by an offender adjudged to have a low risk of re-offending may lead to a restriction order being made (*R. v Courtney* (1987) 9 Cr.App.R.(S.) 404; *R. v Khan* (1987) 9 Cr.App.R.(S.) 455).

A restriction order should not be imposed merely to mark the gravity of the offence (though this is a factor in the assessment of risk), or as a means of punishment, since a hospital order is not intended for that purpose.

In all but the most exceptional cases, a restriction order should be without limit of time (*R. v Gardiner*, above).

Restriction order after committal by magistrates

48–011 Where an offender is committed to the Crown Court by a magistrates' court, with a view to a restriction order being made, the judge must enquire into the circumstances of the case, and:

MHA 1983, s.43(1)(2); PCC(S)A 2000, s.165, Sch.9, para.91

(1) if he has power under s.41 to do so, and the offence is punishable on summary conviction with imprisonment, he may make a hospital order with or without a restriction order (see *R. v Avbunudje* (1999) 2 Cr.App.R.(S.) 189); or
(2) if he does not make such an order, he may deal with the offender in any other manner in which the magistrates could have dealt with him.

The Crown Court has the same powers to make orders under ss.35, 36 and 38 as in the case of a person convicted before it.

MHA 1983, ss.43(1), (3); PCC(S)A 2000, s.165, Sch.9, para.91

Restriction order; ancillary provisions

48–012 In making a restriction order, then:

(1) if the doctors are able to assert confidently that recovery will take place within a fixed period, the order may be limited to that period; but
(2) if the prognosis of successful medical treatment cannot be certain, the safer course is to make an order without limit of time (*R. v Gardiner* (1967) 51 Cr.App.R. 187).

Where a restriction order is made, the judge should ascertain that the hospital to which the offender is to be admitted has the facilities for his safe custody (*R. v Cox* (1968) 52 Cr.App.R. 106). In addition:

(a) arrangements may be made for his admission to hospital in any part of the country where a vacancy exists; and
(b) the judge may give such directions as he thinks fit for his conveyance to a place of safety and his detention there, pending his admission to hospital within 28 days.

(*R. v Marsden* (1968) 52 Cr.App.R. 301).

Custodial sentence as an alternative

48–013 The choice of a custodial sentence as an alternative to a hospital order coupled with a restriction order may arise where:

(1) the offender is dangerous and no suitable secure hospital accommodation is available;
(2) the judge is of the opinion that notwithstanding the offender's mental disorder, there was an element of culpability in the offence deserving of punishment, as where there is no connection between his disorder and the offence, or his responsibility, though diminished, is not extinguished, though even here a custodial sentence may not be appropriate (see, e.g. *R. v Mbatha* (1985) 7 Cr.App.R.(S.) 373).

Hospital and limitation directions

48–014 Such an order is appropriate in the case of an offender convicted of an offence, before the Crown Court, the sentence for which is not fixed by law, and: MHA 1983, s.45A; CSA 1997, s.46; PCC(S)A 2000, Sch.11, para.1; CJA 2003, s.304, Sch.32, Pt 1, para.38, s.307, Sch.37, Pt 4

(1) the judge considers making a hospital order in respect of him before deciding to impose a sentence of imprisonment ("the relevant sentence");
(2) the judge is satisfied, on the written or oral evidence of two registered medical practitioners, that:
    (a) the offender is suffering from a psychopathic disorder;
    (b) the mental disorder from which he is suffering is of a nature and degree which makes it appropriate for him to be detained in a hospital for medical treatment; and

(c) such treatment is likely to alleviate or prevent a deterioration of his condition.

The judge may, in such circumstances give both of the following directions: a hospital direction, that the offender, instead of being removed to and detained in prison, be removed to and detained in a specified hospital, and a limitation direction, that the offender be subject to the special restrictions imposed by s.41, but the latter direction should not be given unless one of the medical practitioners has given oral evidence before the court. Similar provisions as to admission, etc., apply as in the case of a hospital order.

A hospital direction has effect as a transfer direction under MHA 1983, s.47 and a limitation direction as a restriction direction under *ibid*. s.49.

Guardianship order

48–015 An alternative to a community order under CJA 2003, Pt 12 with a requirement of treatment may be, in some cases, a guardianship order which places the offender under the guardianship either of the local authority social services department, or of some person approved by the local authority (such as a relative). The conditions for the making of a guardianship order are essentially the same as those for a hospital order. HO 1990

The judge will need to be satisfied: MHA 1983, s.37(1), (2), (6); PCC(S)A 2000, s.165, Sch.9, para.90(2)

(1) in the case of an offender who has attained the age of 16, that the mental disorder is of a nature or degree which warrants his reception into guardianship; and
(2) that the local authority or other person is willing to receive him into guardianship.

The order gives the guardian power to require the offender to live at a specified place, to attend specified places at specified times for treatment, occupation, education or training, and to allow access to any doctor, approved social worker or other person specified. The disadvantage is that there is no sanction available to the court in the event of non-compliance as there is in the case of a community order. HO 1990

Improper combination of sentence

48–016 When making a hospital or guardianship order, the judge may not, in addition: MHA 1983, s.37(8); CDA 1998, s.119, Sch.8, para.54; PCC(S)A 2000, s.165, Sch.9,

(1) pass a sentence of imprisonment, impose a fine, or make a community order within the meaning of CJA 2003, Pt 12; or

(2) make an order under PCC(S)A 2000, s.150, binding over the parent or guardian of a juvenile offender. para.90; CJA 2003, s.251, Sch.21, Pt 1, para.24

Remand to hospital for reports

48–017 The judge may remand to hospital, for reports on his mental condition, a person who: MHA 1983, s.35(1), (2)

(1) is awaiting trial for an offence punishable with imprisonment; or
(2) has been arraigned for such an offence but has not yet been sentenced or otherwise dealt with for that offence.

Before doing so, however, the judge must:

(a) be satisfied on the written or oral evidence of a registered medical practitioner, that there is reason to suspect that the person is suffering from mental illness, psychopathic disorder, mental impairment or severe mental impairment; and
(b) be of the opinion that it would be impracticable for a report on his mental condition to be made if he were remanded on bail; and
(c) be satisfied on the oral or written evidence of the medical practitioner who would be responsible for making the report (or of some other person representing the managers of the hospital) that arrangements have been made for his admission to that hospital within the seven days beginning with the date of the remand. MHA 1983, s.35(3), (4)

Remand conditions; absconding

48–018 When a person is remanded to hospital under these provisions:

(1) the remand, or further remand, must be for not more than 28 days at a time, or for more than 12 weeks in all, and the Crown Court may terminate the remand at any time if it appears appropriate to do so; MHA 1983, s.35(7)
(2) the Crown Court may further remand, beyond the 28 days, if it appears, on the written or oral evidence of the responsible medical officer, that a further remand is warranted; MHA 1983, s.35(5)
(3) such further remand may be granted without the need for the patient to be brought before the court, provided he is represented by an advocate who is given an opportunity of being heard; and MHA 1983, s.35(6)

(4) the patient is entitled to obtain, at his own expense, an independent medical report, and to apply to the judge, on the basis of it, for his remand to be terminated. MHA 1983, s.35(7)

If a person absconds from a hospital to which he has been remanded, or while being conveyed to or from that hospital, he may be arrested and brought before the court that remanded him. A judge may thereupon terminate the remand and deal with him in any way in which he would have dealt with him if he had not been remanded.

Remand to hospital for treatment

48–019 The judge may, instead of remanding in custody: MHA 1983, ss.36(1), (2), (3), 54(1)

(1) a person in custody awaiting trial before the court for an offence punishable with imprisonment (other than an offence for which the sentence is fixed by law); or
(2) a person who, at any time before sentence, is in custody in the course of a trial before that court for such an offence,

remand him to a hospital specified by the court if he is satisfied, on the written or oral evidence:

(a) of two registered medical practitioners that he is suffering from mental illness or severe mental impairment of a nature or degree which makes it appropriate for him to be detained in a hospital for medical treatment; and
(b) of the medical practitioner who would be in charge of his treatment, or a representative of the hospital managers, that arrangements have been made for his admission within a period of seven days beginning with the date of the remand.

It should be noted that:

(i) where the judge has remanded under these provisions, he may further remand if it appears on the written or oral evidence of the responsible medical officer that a further remand is warranted; MHA 1983, s.36(4)
(ii) the power of further remand may be exercised without that person being brought before the court, provided he is represented by an advocate who is given an opportunity of being heard; MHA 1983, s.36(5)
(iii) a person must not be remanded, or further remanded under these provisions, for more than 28 days at a time, or for more than 12 weeks in all; a judge may MHA 1983, s.36(6)

at any time terminate the remand if it appears appropriate to do so; and

(iv) a person remanded under these provisions is entitled to obtain, at his own expense, an independent medical report from a medical practitioner chosen by him, and to apply to the court on the basis of it, for his remand to be terminated. MHA 1983, s.36(7)

The same provisions in relation to an absconder apply as they do under s.35(9) and (10) above.

Interim hospital order

48–020 Where a person is convicted before the Crown Court of an offence punishable with imprisonment (other than an offence the sentence for which is fixed by law), and the judge is satisfied, on the written or oral evidence of two registered medical practitioners, at least one of whom is employed at the hospital which is to be specified in the order that: MHA 1983, ss.38(1), (3), (4), 54(1)

(1) the offender is suffering from mental illness, psychopathic disorder, mental impairment or severe mental impairment; and
(2) there is reason to suppose that the mental disorder from which the offender is suffering is such that it may be appropriate for a hospital order to be made in his case; and
(3) the judge is satisfied on the written or oral evidence of the medical practitioner who would be in charge of his treatment, or of some other representative of the hospital managers, that arrangements have been made for his admission within the period of 28 days beginning with the date of the order,

he may, before making a hospital order, or dealing with him in some other way, make an interim hospital order authorising his admission to such hospital as is specified and his detention there.

An interim hospital order remains in force for such period not exceeding 12 weeks as the judge may specify in making the order, but may be renewed for further periods of not more than 28 days at a time, if it appears, on the written or oral evidence of the responsible medical officer, that such continuation is warranted. No order may continue in force for more than 12 months in all, and the judge must terminate the order: MHA 1983, s.38(5); CSA 1997, s.49

(a) if he makes a full hospital order in respect of the offender; or

(b) after considering the written or oral evidence of the responsible medical officer, he decides to deal with the offender in some other way.

The power of renewing an interim hospital order may be exercised without the offender being brought before the court if he is represented by counsel who is given an opportunity of being heard. The same provisions apply in relation to persons absconding from hospital, etc., as apply in the case of ss.35 and 36 (see above). MHA 1983, s.38(7)

Information from Health Authorities

48–021 Where a court is minded to make a hospital order, or an interim hospital order, in respect of any person, it may request the Regional Health Authority for the region in which that person resides or last resided, or any other appropriate Regional Health Authority to furnish the court with such information as it has, or can reasonably obtain, with respect to the hospital or hospitals in its region or elsewhere at which arrangements could be made for the admission of that person. In Wales, such a request should be addressed to the Secretary of State. MHA 1983, s.39

Power to specify hospital

48–022 CSA 1997, s.47 provides that any power to specify a hospital which is conferred by s.37 (provided a restriction order under s.41 is made), s.45A or CP(IUP)A 1991, Sch.1, para.1 (where the judge has given a direction), includes power to specify a hospital unit.

Adding a restraining order: SOA 1997

48–023 Where the judge:

(1) imposes a sentence of imprisonment, makes a hospital order or makes a guardianship order in respect of a person convicted of a sexual offence to which SOA 1997, Pt I applies; or SOA 1997, s.5A; CJCSA 2000, Sch.5

(2) orders that a person who has been found not guilty of such an offence by reason of insanity, or to be under disability, and to have done the act charged against him in respect of the offence, be admitted to hospital, or makes a guardianship order against him,

he may, if satisfied that it is necessary to do so in order to protect the public in general, or any particular members of the public, make a restraining order in respect of that person, prohibiting him from doing anything prescribed in it.

The person subjected to the order may, if he was convicted of the offence, appeal against it as if it were a sentence passed for the offence, and in the other circumstances, as if he had been convicted of the offence and the order were a sentence passed on that conviction. The order may be varied or discharged by the Crown Court.

Reports by medical practitioners

48–024 A report in writing by a medical practitioner, or a person representing the managers of a hospital, may be received in evidence without proof of the signature of the person concerned, and without proof that he has the requisite qualifications or authority, or is of the requisite description of medical practitioner, but the court may require the signatory to be called to give evidence.

MHA 1983, s.54(3); CSA 1997, Sch.4, para.12

Where, in pursuance of a direction of the court, any such report is tendered in evidence otherwise than by or on behalf of the person who is the subject of the report then:

(1) if that person is represented by an advocate or solicitor, a copy of the report must be given to that advocate or solicitor;
(2) if that person is not represented, the substance of the report must be disclosed to him or, if he is a child or young person, to his parent or guardian if present in court; and
(3) except where the report relates only to his admission to hospital, that person may require the signatory of the report to be called to give oral evidence and evidence to rebut that contained in the report may be called by or on behalf of that person.

As to the expenses of any such practitioner see 26 COSTS AND TAXATION.

Community order with medical treatment requirement

48–025 Where punishment is inexpedient, the court may consider making a community order within the meaning of CJA 2003, Pt 12 order with a requirement of medical treatment (see 21 COMMUNITY SENTENCES).

49 MITIGATION: DEROGATORY ASSERTIONS

General

49–001 Where:

(1) a person has been convicted of an offence, and a speech in mitigation is made by him or on his behalf before a judge of the Crown Court determining what sentence should be passed on him in respect of the offence; or CPIA 1996, s.58

(2) sentence has been passed on a person in respect of an offence and a submission relating to the sentence is made by him or on his behalf, before the Crown Court hearing an appeal against the sentence, and

there are substantial grounds for believing:

(a) that an assertion forming part of the speech or submission is derogatory to a person's character (for instance because it suggests that his conduct is, or has been, criminal, immoral or improper); and

(b) that the assertion is false, or that the facts asserted are irrelevant to the sentence; and

(c) that the assertion was not made at the trial at which the person was convicted of the offence, or during any other proceedings relating to the offence,

the court may, as soon as is reasonably practicable after making the determination on sentence, make an order under s.58(8), in relation to the assertion, prohibiting its publication. Where it appears to the court that there is a real possibility of such an order being necessary this order may be made before the court has made its determination on sentence, under s.58(7).

Orders under s.58(8) and s.58(7)

49–002 An order under s.58(7), made in anticipation of an order under s.58(8) being made, may be revoked at any time, and in any event ceases to have effect when the court makes a determination with regard to sentencing. An order under s.58(8) may be made whether or not one under s.58(7) was made. An order under s.58(8) may also be revoked at any time, and in any event ceases to have effect at the end of a period of 12 months beginning with the day on which it was made.

Appeal

49–003 Appeal lies in respect of making such an order where a person has been convicted on indictment (see 18 CHALLENGING THE CROWN COURT).

50 RECOMMENDATION FOR DEPORTATION

General

50–001 Subject to certain limitations (see below), a judge sentencing an offender:

(1) aged 17 or over,
(2) who is not a British citizen within the meaning of the British Nationality Act 1981,
(3) for an offence punishable with imprisonment,

may impose, as part of the sentence, but ancillary to any other principal sentence, a recommendation to the Home Secretary that the offender be deported from the UK.

The recommendation ought to be considered by the Home Secretary in deciding whether or not to make a deportation order.

Preconditions for order

50–002 Before making a recommendation for deportation, the judge must be satisfied that: IA 1971, ss.3(6), 6(1)–(3)

(1) the offender is not a British citizen and has no right of abode;
(2) the offender is 17 or over;
(3) the offence is punishable with imprisonment;
(4) the offender has been given not less than seven days clear notice in writing of the court's intention.

As to how the matter should be approached, see 50–005, below.

The fact that the offender has no right of abode does not mean that it ia obligatory to make a recommendation for deportation upon completion of a custodial sentence; it must always depend upon the circumstances (*R. v Wong* [2005] EWCA Crim 296).

There are techical differences between the approach to the deportation of EC citizens and non EC citizens (see below).

Commonwealth citizens

IA 1971, s.7(1); SI 1972/1514; IAA 1999, s.169, Sch.14, para.46; CJA 2003, s.304, Sch.32, para.16

50–003 A British citizen, or any citizen who has a "right of abode" in the UK (IA 1971, s.2), may not be the subject of a recommendation for deportation, nor may a citizen of a Commonwealth country or of the Republic of Ireland, where the judge is satisfied that the offender:

(1) was such at the coming into force of the Act on January 1, 1973; and
(2) was ordinarily resident in this country at that time; and
(3) has been ordinarily resident here for the five years immediately preceding his conviction, although
(4) any part of that five years during which he was undergoing imprisonment or detention by virtue of a sentence passed on conviction in the UK, Channel Islands or the Isle of Man, and for which he was imprisoned or detained for six months or more, is excluded from the period.

Note that:

(a) "ordinary residence" is a matter of fact and degree; mere temporary absence will not create a gap in "ordinary" residence; and
(b) illegal residence *ab initio* cannot amount to "ordinary residence" (*R. v Bangoo* [1976] Crim.L.R. 746).

EC nationals

50–004 EC Nationals who are in the UK exercising their right of free movement under the Treaty of Rome, in the course of their employment, or as dependants of someone who is here in the course of employment, may be deported only where the requirements of Community Law, as interpreted by the Court of Justice, are satisfied. Directive 2004/38/EC [2004] O.J. L229/35 which came into force on April 30, 2006, confers on EU citizens and their families enhanced rights to reside within the territory of member states.

The provisions of the Treaty, Council Directive 64/221 EC made under it, and certain rulings of the Court of Justice (see, e.g. (1980) 2 C.M.L.R. 208) oblige a court considering such a recommendation to note, *inter alia*, that:

(1) no recommendation should be made without full enquiry (*R. v Kraus* (1982) 4 Cr.App.R.(S.) 113);
(2) the judge may act where the offender's record, taken together with the offence committed, indicates it is likely that he will offend again — this is a very important consideration (*R. v Compassi* (1987) Cr.App.R.(S.) 270, *R. v Spura* (1988) 10 Cr.App.R.(S.) 376);
(3) the existence of a previous conviction is not, in itself, a basis for making a recommendation;
(4) the judge must be satisfied that the offender's continued presence in the UK represents "a genuine and sufficiently serious threat to the requirements of public policy affect-

ing one of the fundamental interests of society" (*R. v Escauriaza* (1987) 9 Cr.App.R.(S.) 542; *R. v Soura* (1988) 10 Cr.App.R.(S.) 376) which indicates that the requirements of EC law are not substantially different from the principles enunciated in *R. v Nazari* (see below);

(5) reasons for the recommendation must be given both to the Home Secretary and to the offender (*Ex p. Dannenberg* [1984] 2 All E.R. 481; *R. v Frank* (1992) 13 Cr.App.R. 500, *R. v Bozat* [1997] 1 Cr.App.R.(S.) 270).

Non-EC nationals

50–005 The question of making a recommendation in relation to an offender who is not an EC national, must be decided independently of the offender's status under IA 1971 (*R. v Nunu* (1991) 12 Cr.App.R.(S.) 752). *R. v Benabbas* [2006] 1 Cr.App.R.(S) 94, re-affirms the distinction drawn between immigration-related cases, and cases where offences are committed by a person unlawfully in the country (see below).

The judge must consider only whether the offence committed justifies the conclusion that the offender's continued presence in the country is contrary (i.e. a "detriment") to the public interest (*R. v Carmona* [2006] Crim.L.R. 657).

R. v Nazari (1981) 71 Cr.App.R. 87 still provides the classic test, namely that in examining "detriment" the judge should consider:

(1) the nature and seriousness of the offence, which is generally indicated by the sentence imposed (*R. v Carmona, supra*);
(2) the likelihood of its being repeated, or of other offences being committed,
(3) the broad picture and such evidence as is available;

The mere fact that the offender is living on social security benefits is not a reason for regarding his continued presence as a deteriment (*R. v Serry* (1980) 2 Cr.App.R.(S.) 336).

Contrary to earlier decisions (see *R. v Cravioto* (1990) 12 Cr.App.R.(S.) 71; *R. v Odendaal* (1992) 13 Cr.App.R.(S.) 341) CACD in *R. v Carmona*, above stated that in recommending the deportation of a convicted offender, it was *not* for the judge to consider the effect on his family (or on his rights under ECHR), where the offence justified a recommendation. The judge is not equipped to undertake such an assessment, which is a matter for the Home Secretary, or for the Asylum and Immigration Tribunal if a deportation order is made.

The judge is not concerned with the political systems which operate in other countries. It is inappropriate for him to express a view about such a matter. He has no knowledge beyond common knowledge which may be wrong. These are matters for the Home Secretary (*R. v Altawel* (1981) 3 Cr.App.R.(S.) 28).

Relevance of immigration status

50–006 *R. v Benabbas* [2006] 1 Cr.App.R(S) 94 reviewed the cases in detail and restated the principle that where the offender's presence on this country:

(1) is lawful and regular, the *Nazari* approach (above) involves a relatively straightforward exercise, i.e. balancing the aggravation of the offender's wrong-doing, present, past and potential against any mitigation which may be put forward;
(2) is illegal or irregular, the position may be more complicated, varying from:
  (a) a lawful entrant who overstays his permit to the
  (b) unlawful entrant who gains entry by fraudulent means; and also because the illegality or irregularity may be either:
    (i) the essence of the offence; or
    (ii) entirely irrelevant to it

While a recommendation ought not to be made simply because of the irregularity or illegality of status, rather than on the *Nazari* principle, it is justified where, e.g. entry is by the use of a forged passport, since there is a detriment to the public interest which undermines confidence in the system.

As to "sham" marriages for the purpose of establishing a right of abode, see *R. v Ahemed* [2006] 1 Cr.App.R(S) 78 distinguishing *R. v Aziz* [2004] EWCA Crim. 1700.

Giving reasons

50–007 The recommendation is part of the sentence and CJA 2003, s.174 applies to it, requiring the judge to give, in general terms, and in ordinary language the reasons for his decision, the bald statement "that your continued presence in this country is contrary to the public interest" without giving reasons, may not be sufficient (see *R. v Mohammed Ahsan* [2006] EWCA Crim 826).

51 RESTRAINING ORDER (HARASSMENT)

Making of order on conviction

51–001 A judge sentencing or otherwise dealing with an offender convicted under PHA 1997 ss.2 or 4 may: PHA 1997, s.5

(1) as well as sentencing him or dealing with him in any other way;
(2) make a restraining order, for the purpose of protecting the victim of the offence, or any other person mentioned in the order, from further conduct which amounts to harassment, or will cause fear of violence,

by preventing him from doing anything described in the order, for a specified period or until further order. When DVA 2004, s.58(1), Sch.10, para.43 comes into force, the judge will be able to make an order whatever the nature of the offence (the words "under PHA 1997, ss.2 or 4" in (1) above being omitted).

Breach of the order without reasonable excuse is an offence punishable on conviction on indictment with five years' imprisonment.

Requirements of order

51–002 In making an order the judge should:

(1) bear in mind that the purposes of an order is to prohibit particular conduct with a view to protecting the victim(s) of the offence and preventing further offences under ss.2 or 4 of the Act;
(2) ensure that the order is expressed and drawn up in clear and precise terms so that there is no doubt as to what the offender is prohibited from doing; and
(3) in including terms in the order have regard to considerations of proportionality, i.e. whether any term is proportionate and necessary to achieve the aim set out in (1).

(*R. v Debnath* [2006] Crim.L.R. 450.)

Breach and sentence

51–003 In sentencing for such a breach, the judge should consider:

(1) whether there was a history of disobedience to court orders;

(2) whether the seriousness of the particular conduct proved, (which may range from violence, to threats, to letters of affection);
(3) whether there had been persistent misconduct or merely a solitary instance of misbehaviour;
(4) the effect on the victim;
(5) the degree of future risk and whether the victim requires protection;
(6) the offender's mental health; and
(7) any plea of guilty, remorse shown, etc.

(*R. v Liddle and Others* [1999] 3 All E.R. 816.)

Order on acquittal

51–004 An order may be made even where an accused is acquitted of an offence if the judge considers that it is necessary to do so to protect a person from harassment by him, and in such a case, both prosecution and defence may lead further evidence. PHA 1997, s.5A; DVA 2004, s.12

Where CACD allows an appeal against conviction, it has power to remit the case to the Crown Court to consider whether an order ought to be made.

An appeal against such an order lies as if the person made subject to it had been convicted of the offence in question by the court which made the order, and the order had been made under s.5 above.

52 RESTRAINT ORDERS; RECEIVERS

A. Restraint orders

The jurisdiction to make restraint orders and to appoint receivers under PCA 2002, is transferred by the Act from the High Court to the Crown Court. The enforcement in England and Wales of restraint and receivership proceedings from Scotland and Northern Ireland, is governed by SI 2002/3133.

Making a restraint order

52–001 Where any of the five pre-conditions set out in para.52–003 below is satisfied, the judge may make a restraint order prohibiting any specified person from dealing with any realisable property held by him. "Dealing with property" includes removing it from England and Wales. PCA 2002, s.41(1), (9)

Such an order is analogous to a *Mareva* injunction, (now known as a "freezing" order." The object of the order, like that of a Mareva injunction is "to strike a balance at an interlocutory stage between keeping assets available to satisfy a final order, if and when one is made, and meeting the reasonable requirements of their owner in the meantime"(*Re Peters* [1988] 3 All E.R. 46; *per* Nourse L.J. at 51), preventing "the dissipation of realisable property which may become subject to a confiscation order".

A number of points may be made:

(1) unlike a confiscation order (see above 24 CONFISCATION ORDER) a restraint order is not a final order made on conviction of an offender; it is pre-emptive and provisional in operation, and is intended to prevent the dissipation of assets until the court is in a position, if satisfied that it is right so to do, to make a confiscation order;
(2) an order may be made when any one of the conditions set out in PCA 2002, s.40 is satisfied; it may be granted at a stage before there has been any determination of whether or not the person in respect of whose property it is made has been guilty of criminal conduct, let alone whether or not he has benefited from such conduct;
(3) the judge is concerned solely with the preservation of assets at a time when it cannot be known whether an accused will be convicted or not thus he must seek to strike a balance between:

(a) keeping the assets of the person against whom it made available to satisfy any confiscation order which may be subsequently made; and
(b) meeting that person's reasonable requirements in the meantime.

(4) the grant of an order is discretionary; the judge must proceed on the basis of statements made *ex parte* on behalf of the prosecutor; he cannot assume that a confiscation order under the Act will be made in due course; the order takes effect immediately it is made, before intimation to the specified person;

Where there are several accused it may be appropriate to make orders in respect of each to protect, as against each other, the whole sum which is said to represent the proceeds of the offence(s) (*In Re Peters, above, R. v Jennings* [2006] 1 W.L.R. 182).

As to the particularities of the order, see 52–004 below.

The powers under s.41 do not have effect where they would otherwise be exercisable by virtue of a condition in PCA 2002, s.189(2) or (3) (Northern Ireland) being satisfied, and the offence mentioned in s.40(2)(a) or 40(3)(a), as the case may be, was committed **before March 24, 2003** (SI 2003/333).

If :

(a) a judge makes a restraint order, and PCA 2002, s.41(6), (7)
(b) the applicant for the order applies to the judge for him to do so, (whether as part of the application for the restraint order or at any time afterwards),

the judge may make such order as he believes to be appropriate for the purpose of ensuring that the restraint order is effective (see *DPP v Scarlett* [2001] 1 W.L.R. 515 — judge ordering repatriation of monies in foreign bank).

The application

52–002 An order may be made: PCA 2002, s.42

(1) on an *ex parte* application made in chambers, but
(2) only on the application of the prosecutor, the Director or an accredited financial investigator (accredited by the Director in accordance with PCA 2002, s.3).

Application is made without notice, but must be made in writing and must be supported by a witness statement giving the grounds for the application, and; R.59.1

(a) to the best of the witness's ability full details of the realisable property in respect of which the applicant is seeking the order, specifying the person holding that property;

(b) the grounds for, and full details of any application for any ancillary order under s.41(7) for the purpose of ensuring that the restraint is effective; and

(c) where the application is made by an accredited financial investigator (see below), a statement that he has been authorised under PCA 2002, s.68 to make the application.

An application for the appointment of a management receiver or an enforcement receiver under r.60.1 may be joined with an application under r.61 for a restraint order, or an application under r.22 for the conferral of powers on a receiver. R.61.2

Preconditions for restraint order

52–003 The five conditions which justify the making of an order are that: PCA 2002, s.40

(1) a criminal investigation has been started in England and Wales with regard to an offence, and there is reasonable cause to believe that the alleged offender has benefited from his criminal conduct;

(2) proceedings for an offence have been started in England and Wales and not concluded, and there is reasonable cause to believe that the alleged offender has benefited from his criminal conduct;

(3) an application by the prosecutor or the Director for subsequent reconsideration of an order has been made under ss.19, 20, 27 or 28 of the Act and not concluded (see above 24–062), or the judge believes that such an application is to be made, and there is reasonable cause to believe that the offender has benefited from his criminal conduct;

(4) an application by the prosecutor or the Director has been made under s.21 for reconsideration of the benefit and not concluded (see above 24–062), or the judge believes that such an application is to be made, and there is reasonable cause to believe that the court will decide under that section that the amount found under the new calculation of the offender's benefit exceeds the relevant amount (as defined in that section);

(5) an application by the prosecutor or the Director has been made under s.22 for a reconsideration of the available amount, and not concluded, (see above 24–062) or the judge believes that such an application is to be made, and

Restraint Orders; Receivers

there is reasonable cause to believe that the court will decide under that section that the amount found under the new calculation of the available amount exceeds the relevant amount (as defined in that section),

but condition (2) above, is not satisfied if the judge believes that there has been undue delay in continuing the proceedings, or the prosecutor does not intend to proceed, and the same applies if an application as mentioned in conditions (3) (4) and (5) above has been made.

If condition (1) is satisfied;

(a) references in this Part to the defendant (or offender) are to the alleged offender;
(b) references in this Part to the prosecutor are to the person the judge believes is to have conduct of any proceedings for the offence;
(c) section 77(9) has effect as if proceedings for the offence had been started against the offender when the investigation was started.

Particularities of the order

52–004 The order may: PCA 2002, s.41(2)

(1) provide that it applies to;
   (a) all realisable property held by the specified person whether or not the property is described in the order;
   (b) realisable property transferred to the specified person after the order is made;
(2) be made subject to exceptions, and an exception may in particular; PCA 2002, s.41(3), (6)
   (a) make provision for reasonable living expenses and reasonable legal expenses (see 52–007 below);
   (b) make provision for the purpose of enabling any person to carry on any trade, business, profession or occupation;
   (c) be made subject to conditions,
   but an exception to a restraint order must not make provision for any legal expenses which;
      (i) relate to an offence which falls within subsection (5), and
      (ii) are incurred by the defendant or by a recipient of a tainted gift.

The offences falling within subsection (5) are the offence mentioned in section 40(2) or (3) if preconditions (1) or (2) of s.40

(as the case may be) are satisfied, and the offence (or any of the offences) concerned, if preconditions (3) or (4) are satisfied).

An order must include a statement that disobedience of the order, either by a person to whom it is addressed, or by any other person, may be contempt of court, and details of the possible consequences of being held in contempt must be included. It is the duty of the applicant to serve copies of the order and of the witness statement made in support, on the defendant and any person prohibited from dealing with realisable property by the order, and to notify any person whom he knows to be affected by the order, of its terms. R.59.2

Charges; seizure

52–005 Charging orders are abolished by PCA 2002, but s.41(8) provides that a restraint order is not to affect property for the time being subject to a charge under:

- DTA 1986, s.9;
- CJA 1988, s.78;
- CJ(Confiscation) (NI) Order 1990 (SI 1990/2588 (N.I. 17)), Art.14
- DTA 1984, s.27;
- Proceeds of Crime (NI) Order 1996 (SI 1996/1299 (N.I. 9)), Art. 32.

Where a restraint order is in force a constable or a customs officer may seize any realisable property to which it applies to prevent its removal from England and Wales. Property so seized will be dealt with in accordance with the directions of the court which made the order. PCA 2002, s.45

Terms of the order; exceptions

52–006 It is suggested that its terms need careful consideration, since an order may cause serious hardship to the subject of it. Save in exceptional cases its terms should not go beyond what is required to prevent dissipation of the assets; the order does not, and properly does not, prevent the meeting of ordinary and reasonable expenditure (*Re Peters*, above).

The civil courts have generally insisted upon adequate provision being made in the order for the specified person's reasonable living expenses (see s.41(3)(a) in the preceding paragraph). See also *Re Peters*, above. An order ought, ordinarily, from the moment it is granted on the *ex parte* application, to contain a provision for such expenses unless good reason is shown why this should not be done in the particular case. It may be convenient for the prosecutor, when applying for the order, to insert such an exception into the draft order sought; or, if he does not, he should come before the judge prepared to explain why, in the circumstances of the case, it would be inappropriate to include such a provision; and the circumstances relied upon ought to be set out in the application.

In a case where it is known that the specified person carries on a trade, business, profession or occupation, a similar approach should be taken, in line with the provisions in s.41(3)(b) of the Act.

Approach to living and legal expenses

52–007 In a case on the similar Scottish provisions of the Act (*MA v WMM for a Restraint Order* September 22, 2005) a number of points were made in relation to "reasonable living expenses":

(1) it will generally be appropriate to put a limit in the order;
(2) consistent with the principle that a person not convicted of any offence should not unreasonably be made to incur expenditure in coming to court, the limit should err on the side of generosity, though at the *ex parte* stage it may not be possible to fix the appropriate limit with any accuracy;
(3) the applicant may, of course, once the order is granted, attempt to reach agreement with the specified person as to the appropriate level of expenditure to be permitted by the exception to the order; if agreement is reached, the order may be varied by consent; if not, either party may apply to the court;
(4) the expression "reasonable living expenses" may cover the payment of ordinary debts as they fall due, though a separate exception may be required here; if there is any uncertainty about this, an application may be made to the court;

As to policing the exception, s.41(3)(c) permits the judge to impose conditions. He might require the specified person, as a condition of making an exception allowing payment of reasonable living expenses, to take certain steps designed to enable the prosecutor to be aware of the level and type of expenditure and apply to the court if he considers that it goes beyond what is permissible. There might be a condition to require the specified person to identify the accounts from which he habitually makes payment of his ordinary living expenses. There may be other appropriate conditions. Alternatively, the specified person might be required to establish a separate account into which certain sums can be paid and from which payments can be made consistent with the order.

In relation to costs, i.e. reasonable legal expenses (see s.41(3)(a)), the judge is not entitled (see s.41(4)) to make an exception to allow the specified person to pay the legal expenses of defending the criminal case brought against him, but he may, in making a restraint order, include an exception allowing the specified person to incur legal expenses in connection with the restraint order itself.

General procedural provisions

52–008 A number of general provisions contained in CPR 2005 may be noticed in relation to restraint and receivership proceedings.

(1) applications in restraint and receivership proceedings are dealt with without a hearing, unless the judge orders otherwise; proceedings may be heard in chambers; R.61.3,4

(2) as far as evidence in the proceedings is concerned:

(a) the judge may control it by giving directions as to the issues on which he requires evidence, the nature of that evidence and the way in which it is to be placed before him; he may exclude evidence that would otherwise be admissible, and may limit cross-examination; R.61.5

(b) any fact which needs to be proved by the evidence of a witness may be proved, unless the judge orders otherwise, by his evidence in writing; a party may apply for leave to cross-examine, and if it is granted and the witness fails to attend, his evidence may not be used without the judge's permission; R.61.6

(c) a party may apply to the court to issue a witness summons requiring a witness to attend or to produce documents to the court; r.28.3 applies; R.61.7

(d) hearsay evidence may be admitted without the duty to give notice required by CEA 1995, s.2(1). R.61.8

As to costs in such proceedings, see r.61.19–61.22.

Hearsay evidence

52–009 Evidence must not be excluded in restraint proceedings on the ground that it is hearsay (of whatever degree); CEA 1995, ss.2 to 4 apply in relation to them as those sections apply in relation to civil proceedings. PCA 2002, s.46

Note that for the purposes of this section:

(1) "restraint proceedings" are proceedings for a restraint order; for the discharge or variation of such an order; and on an appeal under ss.43 or 44;

(2) "hearsay" is a statement which is made otherwise than by a person while giving oral evidence in the proceedings and which is tendered as evidence of the matters stated.

Nothing in s.46 affects the admissibility of evidence which is admissible apart from that section.

Obligations in relation to exercise of powers

52–010 In relation to the powers conferred on a judge by ss.41 to 60 and 62 to 67, below and to the powers of a receiver appointed under ss.48, 50 or 52, there is a general obligation to exercise them: PCA 2002, s.59(1)–(3)

(1) with a view to the value for the time being of realisable property being made available (by the property's realisation) for satisfying any confiscation order that has been or may be made against a defendant;
(2) *in a case where a confiscation order has not been made*, with a view to securing that there is no diminution *in* the value of such property;
(3) without taking account of any obligation of the defendant or a recipient of a tainted gift, if the obligation conflicts with the object of satisfying any confiscation order that has been or may be made against the defendant;

and they may be exercised in respect of a debt owed by the Crown, subject to the following rules:

(a) the powers must be exercised with a view to allowing a person other than the defendant or a recipient of a tainted gift to retain or recover the value of any interest held by him;
(b) in the case of realisable property held by a recipient of a tainted gift, the powers must be exercised with a view to realising no more than the value or the time being of the gift;
(c) in a case where a confiscation order has not been made against the defendant, property must not be sold if the judge so orders.

The judge may order it not to be sold, if, on an application by the defendant, or by the recipient of a tainted gift, he decides that the property cannot be replaced. Such an order may be revoked or varied. PCA 2002, s.69(4), (5)

Discharge and variation

52–011 An application to discharge or vary a restraint order or an order under s.41(7) may be made to the Crown Court by PCA 2002, s.42(2)–(7)

the person who applied for the order, or by any person affected by it, and on such application the court may discharge the order, or vary it.

Where the condition in s.40 which was satisfied was that:

(1) proceedings were started or an application was made, the judge must discharge the order on the conclusion of the proceedings or of the application (as the case may be).
(2) an investigation was started or an application was to be made, the judge must discharge the order if within a reasonable time proceedings for the offence are not started or the application is not made, as the case may be.

Application for;

(a) discharge or variation by a person affected by the order is made in terms of r.59.3;
(b) variation of the order by the person who applied for the order is made in terms of r.59.4; and
(c) discharge of the order by the person who applied for it in terms of r.59.5.

Appeal to CACD

52–012 There is no appeal against the making of a restraint order. A person dissatisfied with the making of an order must apply to the Crown Court for its variation or discharge. PCA 2002, ss.43, 44

Appeal does, however, lie to CACD where:

(1) on an application for a restraint order the court decides not to make one, by the person who applied for the order, against that decision;
(2) an application is made under s.42(3) in relation to a restraint order or an order under s. 41(7), by the person who applied for the order or any person affected by it in respect of the Crown Court's decision on the application,

and CACD may either confirm the order or make such order as it believes appropriate. Leave is required, and leave will be given only where CACD considers that the appeal would have a real prospect of success or there is some other compelling reason why the appeal should be heard. An order giving leave may limit the issues to be heard and may be made subject to conditions (r 73.1). See further 18 CHALLENGING THE CROWN COURT.

Registration

52–013 The Registration Acts, as defined in s.48(2) apply in relation to: PCA 2002, s.47(1)–(3)

(1) restraint orders as they apply in relation to orders which affect land and are made by the court for the purpose of enforcing judgments or recognisances;
(2) applications for restraint orders as they apply in relation to other pending land actions,

but no notice may be entered in the register of title under the Land Registration Act 2002 in respect of a restraint order.

The person applying for a restraint order is treated for the purposes of s.57 of the Land Registration Act 1925 (inhibitions) as a person interested in relation to any registered land to which the application relates, or a restraint order made in pursuance of which the application relates. PCA 2002, s.47(4)

B. Receivers

52–014 A judge of the Crown Court is empowered under the provisions of PCA 2002, to appoint receivers of property in three instances.

Receivers perform two quite different functions under the Act:

(1) "**management receivers**" manage property pending a defendant's conviction (and sometimes afterwards);
(2) "**enforcement receivers**" dispose of such property to satisfy a confiscation order.

The appointment of a receiver before trial is essentially to safeguard the defendant's assets rather than to maximise the amount which may be available to meet any future confiscation order (*Re Peters* [1988] 3 All E.R. 46).

1. Management receivers

52–015 Where:

(1) a restraint order is made, and PCA 2002, ss.48(1), (2), 49(1), (2)
(2) the applicant for that order applies to a judge for an order (whether as part of the application for the restraint order or at any time afterwards),

the judge may by order appoint a receiver in respect of any realisable property to which the restraint order applies, and on the application of the person who applied for the restraint order, may confer on him, in relation to any such property to which the restraint order applies, powers to:

(a) take possession of the property;
(b) manage or otherwise deal with it;
(c) commence, carry on or defend any legal proceedings in respect of it; and
(d) realise so much of it as is necessary to meet the receiver's remuneration and expenses,

provided the property is not for the time being subject to a charge under any of those provisions mentioned above and may further, (s.49(3)(4)) by order confer on the receiver power to enter any premises in England and Wales and to:

(i) search for or inspect anything authorised by the judge;
(ii) make or obtain a copy, photograph or other record so authorised; and
(iii) remove anything which the receiver is required or authorised to take possession of in pursuance of a court order.

As to procedure, see rr.60.1, 60.2 at 52–020 below.

The judge may also by order authorise the receiver, for the purpose of the exercise of his functions, to hold property, enter into contracts, use and be used, employ agents, execute powers of attorney, deeds or other instruments and take any other steps the judge thinks appropriate.

Persons having possession of realisable property

52–016 The judge may order any person who has possession of realisable property to which the restraint order applies to give possession of it to the receiver. PCA 2002, s.49(5), (6), (7)

The judge may:

(1) order a person holding an interest in realisable property to which the restraint order applies to make to the receiver such payment as the court specifies in respect of a beneficial interest held by the defendant or the recipient of a tainted gift; and
(2) may (on payment being made) by order transfer, grant or extinguish any interest in the property,

provided that the property is not for the time being subject to a charge under any of those provisions mentioned at 52–080 above.

The judge must not: PCA 2002, s.49(8)(9)

(a) confer the power to manage the property under s.49(2)(b) or to realise property to meet the receiver's expenses under s.49(2)(d), or

(b) exercise the power conferred on it under (1) above in respect of property,

unless he gives persons holding interests in the property a reasonable opportunity to make representations to it. The judge may order that any power conferred under this section be subject to such conditions and exceptions as he specifies.

"Managing or otherwise dealing with property" includes: PCA 2002, s.49(10)

(i) selling it, or any part of it or interest in it;
(ii) carrying on or arranging for another person to carry on any trade or business the assets of which are or are part of the property;
(iii) incurring capital expenditure in respect of the property.

2. Enforcement receivers

52–017 In the case of a confiscation order made but not satisfied, and not subject to appeal, (e.g. an order falling to be enforced in the magistrates' court) a judge may, on the application of the prosecutor, appoint a receiver in respect of realisable property, and if he does so, he may, on the prosecutor's application, by order, confer on the receiver: PCA 2002, ss.50, 51(1), (2), (3)

(1) in relation to the realisable property, the powers to:
   (a) take possession of it;
   (b) manage or otherwise deal with it;
   (c) realise it in such manner as the judge may specify; and
   (d) commence, carry on or defend any legal proceedings in respect of it; provided it is not for the time being subject to a charge under any of the enactments set out at 54–008, above.
(2) the power to enter any premises in England and Wales and:
   (a) search for or inspect anything authorised by the judge;
   (b) make or obtain a copy, photograph or other record of anything so authorised; and
   (c) remove anything which the receiver is required or authorised to take possession of in pursuance of a court order.

The judge may also authorise the receiver, for the purpose of the exercise of his functions to hold property, enter into contracts, PCA 2002, s.51(4), (5) use and be used, employ agents, execute powers of attorney, deeds or other instruments and take any other steps the court thinks appropriate.

"Managing or otherwise dealing with property" includes: PCA 2002, s.51(10)

(i) selling the property or any part of it or interest in it;
(ii) carrying on or arranging for another person to carry on any trade or business the assets of which are or are part of the property;
(iii) incurring capital expenditure in respect of the property.

As to procedure, see rr.60.1, 60.2 at 52–020 below.

Persons having possession of realisable property

52–018 The judge may order any person who has possession of realisable property to give possession of it to the receiver; and may: PCA 2002, ss.51(6), (7)

(1) order a person holding an interest in realisable property to make to the receiver such payment as he specifies in respect of a beneficial interest held by the defendant or the recipient of a tainted gift;
(2) (on payment being made) by order transfer, grant or extinguish any interest in the property, unless the property is for the time being subject to a charge under any of the enactments set out at 52–005.

The judge must not: PCA 2002, ss.51(8), (9)

(a) confer the power to manage or to realise property, or
(b) exercise the power conferred on him by (1) and (2) above, in respect of property,

unless he gives persons holding interests in the property a reasonable opportunity to make representations. He may order that a power conferred by an order under this section is subject to such conditions and exceptions as he specifies.

3. Director's receivers

52–019 Where a confiscation order is made, and the Director is appointed as the enforcement authority for the order (under s.34) then unless: PCA 2002, s.52(1)–(5)

(1) the order was made by CACD, and

(2) when the Crown Court comes to proceed under this section the confiscation order has been satisfied,

the judge *must* make an order for the appointment of a receiver in respect of realisable property, conferring power on the Director to nominate that person, the order taking effect when the Director does so.

Where this section applies, s.50 in relation to the appointment of management receivers does not apply. The Director will nominate the receiver only where, at the time he does so, the confiscation order is not satisfied, and not subject to appeal.

The person nominated may be a member of the staff of the Agency; or a person providing services under arrangements made by the Director. PCA 2002, s.52(6), (7)

The powers conferred on such a receiver by s.53 are the same as those conferred on an enforcement receiver under s.50, as to which see 52–017 above. The provisions of ss.51(6)–(9) as to persons having possession of realisable property (see 54–016, above), are repeated in ss.53(6)–(9).

The judge may also authorise the receiver, for the purpose of the exercise of his functions, to hold property, enter into contracts, use and be used, employ agents, execute powers of attorney, deeds or other instruments, and take any other steps the judge thinks appropriate.

As to procedure, see rr.60.1, 60.2 below.

3. Procedure

Appointment of receiver

52–020 An application for the appointment of a management receiver under s.48(1) or an enforcement receiver under s.50(1) is made as follows under r.60.1. R.60(1)

The application may be made without notice if:

(1) the application is joined with an application for a restraint order under r.59.1;
(2) the application is urgent; or
(3) there are reasonable grounds for believing that giving notice would cause the dissipation of realisable property which is the subject of the application.

It must be in writing and must be supported by a witness statement giving:

(a) the grounds for the application;
(b) full details of the proposed receiver;

(c) to the best of the witness's ability, full details of the realisable property in respect of which the applicant is seeking the order, and specifying the person holding that realisable property;
(d) where the application is made by an accredited financial investigator, a statement that he has been authorised to make the application under s.68; and
(e) if the proposed receiver is not a member of staff of the ARA, the CPS, the Commissioners for Revenue & Customs and the applicant is asking the court to allow the receiver to act;
  (i) without giving security; or
  (ii) before he has given security or satisfied the court that he has security in place, explain the reasons why that is necessary.

Where the application is for the appointment of an enforcement receiver, the applicant must provide the Crown Court with a copy of the confiscation order made against the defendant.

The application and witness statement must be lodged with the Crown Court, and except where notice of the application is not required to be served, the application and witness statement must *be* lodged with the Crown Court and served on the defendant, any person who holds realisable property to which the application relates; and any other person whom the applicant knows to be affected by the application, at least seven days before the date fixed by the court for hearing the application, unless the Crown Court specifies a shorter period.

If the court makes an order for the appointment of a receiver, the applicant must serve copies of the order and of the witness statement made in support of the application on such persons.

Conferment of powers

52–021 An application to the court for the conferral of powers on a management receiver under s.49(1), an enforcement receiver under s.51(1) or a Director's receiver under s.53(1) is made as follows under the procedure in r.60.2. The application may be made without notice if the application is to give the receiver power to take possession of property and: R.60.2

(1) the application is joined with an application for a restraint order under r.59.1;
(2) the application is urgent; or
(3) there are reasonable grounds for believing that giving notice would cause the dissipation of the property which is the subject of the application.

The application must be made in writing and supported by a witness statement which must:

(a) give the grounds for the application;
(b) give full details of the realisable property in respect of which the applicant is seeking the order and specifying the person holding that realisable property; and
(c) where the application is made by an accredited financial investigator, include a statement that he has been authorised to make the application under s.68.

Where the application is for the conferral of powers on an enforcement receiver or Director's receiver, the applicant must provide the Crown Court with a copy of the confiscation order made against the defendant.

The application and witness statement must be lodged with the Crown Court, and except where notice of the application is not required to be served, the application and witness statement must be served on the defendant; any person who holds realisable property in respect of which a receiver has been appointed or in respect of which an application for a receiver has been made, any other person whom the applicant knows to be affected by the application, and the receiver (if one has already been appointed), at least seven days before the date fixed by the court for hearing the application, unless the Crown Court specifies a shorter period.

If the judge makes an order for the conferral of powers on a receiver, the applicant must serve copies of the order on those persons.

Miscellaneous

52–022 As to the giving of security by a receiver, see r.60.5; as to sums remaining in the hands of receivers, see r.24, as to remuneration, see r.26, as to accounts, see r.27 and as to non-compliance by receiver, see r.28, as to distress and forfeiture, see r.29.

4. Application of sums received

By enforcement receivers

52–023 Sums in the hands of an enforcement receiver (s.50), being the proceeds of the realisation of property (under s.51), or sums other than those in which the defendant holds an interest, are applied: PCA 2002, s.54(1)–(5)

(1) in payment of such expenses incurred by a person acting as an insolvency practitioner as are payable by virtue of s.432;
(2) in making any payments directed by the Crown Court; and
(3) on the defendant's behalf towards satisfaction of the confiscation order.

If the amount payable under the confiscation order has been fully paid and any sums remain in the receiver's hands he will distribute them among such persons who held, or hold, interests in the property concerned, (i.e. the proceeds of realisation and other sums mentioned above), as the Crown Court directs, and in such proportions as it directs.

Before making any direction the judge must give persons who held, or hold interests in the property concerned a reasonable opportunity to make representations.

The receiver will apply sums as mentioned in (3) above by paying them to the designated officer of the magistrates' court responsible for enforcing the confiscation order as if the amount ordered to be paid were a fine on account of the amount payable under the order.

By the magistrate's court

52–024 Where the designated officer of the magistrates' court receives sums on account of the amount payable under a confiscation order (whether the sums are received under s.54 or otherwise), receipt reduces the amount payable under the order, but he must apply them in payment of such expenses incurred by a person acting as an insolvency practitioner as are payable under s.432, and are not already paid under s.54(2)(a). PCA 2002, s.55

If he received the sums under s.54 he must next apply them in payment of the remuneration and expenses of:

(1) any management receiver (s.48), to the extent that they have not been met by virtue of the exercise by that receiver of a power conferred under s.49(2)(d); and
(2) the enforcement receiver appointed under s.50,

unless the receiver is a member of the staff of the CPS or of the Commissioners for Revenue & Customs, it being immaterial whether he is a permanent or temporary member or he is on secondment from elsewhere. If a direction was made (under s.13(6), see 23 COMPENSATION) for an amount of compensation to be paid out of sums recovered under the confiscation order, he will next apply the sums in payment of that amount.

If any amount remains after he makes those payments, the amount will be treated for the purposes of JPA 1997, s.60 as if it were a fine imposed by a magistrates' court.

By director's receivers

52–025 Sums which are in the hands of the director's receiver (s.52) which are either the proceeds of the realisation of property under s.53, or sums (other than those) in which the defendant holds an interest, will be applied as follows: PCA 2002, s.56

(1) in payment of such expenses incurred by a person acting as an insolvency practitioner as are payable by virtue of s.432;
(2) in making any payments directed by the Crown Court;
(3) on the defendant's behalf towards satisfaction of the confiscation order by being paid to the Director on account of the amount payable under it.

If the amount payable under the confiscation order has been fully paid and any sums remain in the receiver's hands he will distribute them among such persons who held (or hold) interests in the property concerned (i.e. the property mentioned above) as the Crown Court directs, and in such proportions as it directs. Before making such a direction the judge must give persons who held (or hold) interests such property a reasonable opportunity to make representations.

By the Director

52–026 Where the Director receives sums on account of the amount payable under a confiscation order (whether the sums are received under s.56 or otherwise), receipt reduces the amount payable under the order, but he must apply the sums received as follows: PCA 2002, s.57

(1) in payment of such expenses incurred by a person acting as an insolvency practitioner as are payable by virtue of s.432, but are not already paid under s.56(2)(a);
(2) if he received the sums under s.56, in payment of the remuneration and the expenses of any:
  (a) management receiver appointed under s.48, to the extent that they have not been met by virtue of the exercise by that receiver of a power conferred under s.49(2)(d);
  (b) director's receiver appointed under s.52, unless he is a member of the staff of the Agency or a person providing services for the Director; and

(3) if a direction was made (under s.13(6)) for an amount of compensation to be paid out of sums recovered under the confiscation order, in payment of that amount.

Seized money

52–027 Where money is held by a person,

(1) in an account maintained by him with a bank or a building society; or PCA 2002, s.67
(2) which has been seized by a constable under PACE 1984, s.19 and is held in an account maintained by a police force with a bank or a building society; or
(3) which has been seized by an officer of revenue and customs under PACE 1984, s.19 as applied by an order made under s.114(2) of that Act, and is held in an account maintained by the Commissioners for Revenue & Customs with a bank or a building society, and
  (a) a restraint order has effect in relation to the property; or
  (b) a confiscation order is made against the person by whom the money is held; or
  (c) the Director has not been appointed as the enforcement authority for the confiscation order;
  (d) a receiver has not been appointed under s.50 in relation to the money;
  (e) any period allowed under s.11 for payment of the amount ordered to be paid under the confiscation order has ended.

A magistrates' court may order the bank or building society to pay the money to the designated officer of the magistrates' court on account of the amount payable under the confiscation order.

Failure to comply with an order may result in the defaulting bank or building society being fined; for the purposes of MCA 1980, the sum will be treated as adjudged to be paid by a conviction of the court.

5. Applications for directions

52–028 A receiver appointed under ss.48, 50 or 52 may apply to a judge of the Crown Court for an order giving directions as to the exercise of his powers, as may any person affected by action taken by the receiver and any person who may be affected by action the receiver proposes to take. On such an PCA 2002, s.62

application the judge may make such order as he believes is appropriate.

The procedure on such an application (and on applications under s.63(1) for the discharge or variation of orders relating to receivers) is as follows.

The application must be made in writing and lodged with the Crown Court. It must also be served on the following persons (except where they are the person making the application);

(1) the person who applied for appointment of the receiver;
(2) the defendant;
(3) any person who holds realisable property in respect of which the receiver has been appointed;
(4) the receiver; and
(5) any other person whom the applicant knows to be affected by the application,

at least seven days before the date fixed by the court for hearing the application, unless the Crown Court specifies a shorter period.

If the judge makes an order for the discharge or variation of an order relating to a receiver under s.63(2), the applicant must serve copies of the order on any persons whom he knows to be affected by the order.

6. Discharge and variation

Variation and discharge of orders under ss.52 and 53

52–029 The following persons may apply to a judge of the Crown Court to vary or discharge an order made under any of ss.48 to 53: PCA 2002, s.63

(1) the receiver;
(2) the person who applied for the order or (if the order was made under ss.52 or 53) the Director;
(3) any person affected by the order.

The procedure is that stated in the preceding paragraph in relation to an application for directions.

On such application the judge may discharge or vary the order, but in the case of an order under ss.48 or 49 in relation to management receivers:

(a) if the condition in s.40 which was satisfied was that proceedings were started or an application was made, the judge must discharge the order on the conclusion of the proceedings or of the application (as the case may be);

(b) if the condition which was satisfied was that an investigation was started or an application was to be made, the court must discharge the order if within a reasonable time proceedings for the offence are not started or the application is not made (as the case may be).

As to when applications and other proceedings are commenced or concluded, see 24 CONFISCATION ORDERS.

Management receivers: discharge

52–030 Where: PCA 2002, s.64

(1) a management receiver stands appointed under s.48 in respect of realisable property, and
(2) a judge appoints an enforcement receiver under s.50, or makes an order for the appointment of a director's receiver under s.52,

he will order the management receiver to transfer to the other receiver all property held by him by virtue of the powers conferred on him by s.49, other than that which he holds by virtue of the exercise by him of his power under s.49(2)(d), but in a case where the court makes an order under s.52 appointing a director's receiver, his order to transfer such property does not take effect until the order under s.52 takes effect.

Where the management receiver complies with the order he is discharged from his appointment under s.48, and from any obligation under this Act arising from his appointment.

Where this section applies the judge may make such a consequential or incidental order as he believes appropriate.

7. Restrictions on dealing with property

Restraint orders

52–031 Where a restraint order is made: PCA 2002, s.58

(1) no distress may be levied against any realisable property to which the order applies except with the leave of a judge of the Crown Court and subject to any terms he may impose;
(2) if the order applies to a tenancy of any premises, no landlord or other person to whom rent is payable may exercise any right of forfeiture by peaceable re-entry in relation to the premises in respect of any failure by the tenant to comply with any term or condition of the tenancy, except

with the leave of a judge and subject to any terms he may impose;

(3) if any court in which proceedings are pending in respect of any property is satisfied that a restraint order has been applied for or made in respect of the property, that court may either stay the proceedings or allow them to continue on any terms it thinks fit, provided it gives an opportunity to be heard to the applicant for the restraint order, and any receiver appointed in respect of the property under ss.48, 50 or 52.

Enforcement receivers

52–032 Where an enforcement receiver is appointed under s.50 in respect of any realisable property: PCA 2002, s.59

(1) no distress may be levied against any realisable property to which the order applies except with the leave of a judge of the Crown Court and subject to any terms he may impose;

(2) if the order applies to a tenancy of any premises, no landlord or other person to whom rent is payable may exercise any right of forfeiture by peaceable re-entry in relation to the premises in respect of any failure by the tenant to comply with any term or condition of the tenancy, except with the leave of a judge and subject to any terms he may impose;

(3) if any court in which proceedings are pending in respect of any property is satisfied that an order under s.50 appointing a receiver in respect of the property has been applied for or made, the judge may either stay the proceedings or allow them to continue on any terms he thinks fit, but before exercising any such power must give an opportunity to be heard to the prosecutor, and the receiver (if the order under s.50 has been made).

Director's receivers

52–033 Where a director's receiver is appointed under s.52 in respect of any realisable property and the order has taken effect: PCA 2002, s.60

(1) no distress may be levied against any realisable property to which the order applies except with the leave of a judge of the Crown Court and subject to any terms he may impose;

(2) if the order applies to a tenancy of any premises, no landlord or other person to whom rent is payable may exercise

any right of forfeiture by peaceable re-entry in relation to the premises in respect of any failure by the tenant to comply with any term or condition of the tenancy, except with the leave of a judge and subject to any terms he may impose;

(3) if a court (whether the Crown Court or any other court) in which proceedings are pending in respect of any property is satisfied that an order under s.52 for the appointment of a receiver in respect of the property has taken effect, the court may either stay the proceedings or allow them to continue on any terms it thinks fit, but before exercising such power must give an opportunity to be heard to the Director, and the receiver.

C. Appealing restraint orders, etc.

Appeal to CACD

52–034 There is no appeal against the making of a restraint order. A person dissatisfied with the making of an order must apply to the Crown Court for its variation or discharge. PCA 2002, ss.43, 44

Appeal does, however, lie to CACD where:

(1) on an application for a restraint order the court decides not to make one, by the person who applied for the order, against that decision;

(2) an application is made under s.42(3) in relation to a restraint order or an order under s.41(7), by the person who applied for the order or any person affected by it in respect of the Crown Court's decision on the application,

and CACD may either confirm the order or make such order as it believes appropriate.

Leave is required, and leave will be given only where CACD considers that the appeal would have a real prospect of success or there is some other compelling reason why the appeal should be heard. An order giving leave may limit the issues to be heard and may be made subject to conditions. R.73.1

See further 18 CHALLENGING THE CROWN COURT.

Financial investigators; applications and appeals

52–035 In relation to applications under ss.41, 42, 48, 49 or 63, or appeals under ss.43, 44, 65 or 66, an accredited financial investigator must not make such an application or bring such an appeal unless he is one of the following, or is authorised for the purpose by one of the following: PCA 2002, s.68

(1) a police officer who is not below the rank of superintendent,
(2) an officer for Revenue & Customs who is not below such grade as is designated by the the Commissioners for Revenue & Customs as equivalent to that rank,
(3) an accredited financial investigator who falls within a description specified in an order made for the purposes of this paragraph by the Home Secretary under s.453.

If such an application is made or appeal brought by an accredited financial investigator any subsequent step in the application or appeal or any further application or appeal relating to the same matter may be taken, made or brought by a different accredited financial investigator who falls within subs.(3).

If:

(a) an application for a restraint order is made by an accredited financial investigator, and
(b) a court is required under s.58(6) to give the applicant for the order an opportunity to be heard, the court may give the opportunity to a different accredited financial investigator who falls within subs.(3).

52–036 A reference to the offence (or offences) concerned must be construed in accordance with s.6(9). PCA 2002, s.88

A "criminal investigation" is an investigation which police officers or other persons have a duty to conduct with a view to it being ascertained whether a person should be charged with an offence.

A "defendant" is a person against whom proceedings for an offence have been started (whether or not he has been convicted).

A reference to "sentencing the defendant for an offence" includes a reference to dealing with him otherwise in respect of the offence.

D. External Requests

The legislation

52–037 PCA 2002 (External Requests and Orders) Order 2005 (SI 2005/3181), and in regard to the former law, CJ(IC)A 1990 (Enforcementy of Overseas Forfeiture Orders) Order 2005 (SI 2005/3180) make provision for "restraint orders" on dealing with property situated in England and Wales specified in a request by an overseas authority.

Such a request is channelled through the Secretary of State to the "relevant Director" being the DPP or DRC, or in certain circumstances the DSFO.

The scheme

52–038 The procedure under both Orders is similar. On an application by a relevant Director 4(1), a judge of the Crown Court, on being satisfied that:

(1) a relevant property in England and Wales is identified in the request (other than property already subject to a charge) ;
(2) a criminal investigation or proceedings for an offence have been started in the country from which the request is made; and
(3) it appears to the judge that there are reasonable grounds for believing that as a result of the investigation or those proceedings an external forfeiture order may be made against the person named in the request,

may make a restraint order, prohibiting any specified person from dealing with relevant property which is identified in the request and specified in the order, other than property subject to a charge (see above 24–026).

The order may be made subject to exceptions (see above 52–006) and be made subject to conditions When the judge makes an order, and the applicant applies to him either then or afterwards, he may also make such further orders for the purpose of ensuring that the restraint order is effective. There is also power, on application, to discharge or vary a restraint order, a right of appeal by either side to CA and HL, and a power to appoint a management receiver.

Procedure

52–039 CPR 2005, rr.59–61 and 71 apply with the necessary modifications to proceedings under SI 2005/3181 as they apply to corresponding proceedings under PCA 2002 (r.57.15 inserted by SI 2006/353).

53 RETRIALS

General

53–001 Certain specialties of evidence and procedure apply to retrials ordered under:

(1) CAA 1968, and
(2) CJA 2003, Pt 10.

A. Retrial under CAA 1968, s.7

Arraignment

53–002 A person who is retried for an offence in pursuance of an order made by CACD under CAA 1968, s.7 is tried on a fresh indictment preferred by direction of that court. CAA 1968, s.8

As to bail pending retrial, see Criminal Appeal Rules 1968, rr.3, 4. Special rules apply in relation to persons subject to mental health procedures (see CAA 1968, s.8(3), (3A)). CACD may make orders as to the custody of the exhibits pending the retrial.

CACD has no power, on ordering a retrial, to order that the retrial take place within a specified time limit less than the two months allowed by CAA 1968, s.8(1) (*R. v Khan* [2001] 4 Archbold News 3) but after the end of two months from the date of the order, such person:

(1) may not be arraigned on an indictment preferred in pursuance of such a direction unless CACD gives leave; and
(2) such person is entitled to apply to CACD to set aside the order and to direct the trial court to enter a judgment of acquittal of the offence for which he was ordered to be retried.

In dealing with an application, whether under (1) or under (2) CACD may either grant leave to arraign or set aside the order for retrial and direct a judgment and verdict of acquittal.

The procedure is provided by r.68.31.

CACD will not give leave to arraign in these circumstances unless satisfied that:

(a) the prosecution has acted with all due expedition (*R. v Coleman* (1992) 95 Cr.App.R. 345, *R. v Horne* *The Times*, February 27, 1992); and

(b) that there is good and sufficient cause for a retrial in spite of the lapse of time since the order under s.7 was made.

The words "with all due expedition" are not to be equated with "all due diligence and expedition" required under POA 1985 (see 28 CUSTODY TIME LIMITS); the former is a less exacting test (*R. v Jones* [2003] 1 Cr.App.R. 20).

Evidence

53–003 Evidence given at a retrial must be given orally if it was given orally at the original trial, unless: CAA 1968, Sch.2, paras 1, 1A; CJA 2003, s.131

(1) all the parties to the retrial agree otherwise;
(2) CJA 2003, s.116 applies (admissibility of hearsay evidence where a witness is unavailable); or
(3) the witness is unavailable to give evidence, otherwise than as mentioned in s.116(2) and CJA 2003, s.114(1)(d) applies (admission of hearsay evidence under residual discretion).

CDA 1998, Sch.3, para.5 (use of depositions) does not apply at a retrial to a deposition read as evidence at the original trial.

The prosecution may be permitted to adduce evidence on a retrial of statements made on oath by the accused at the original trial, to show that he had lied (*R. v Binham* [1991] Crim.L.R. 774).

Sentence

53–004 Where a person ordered to be retried is again convicted on retrial, the judge may pass in respect of the offence any sentence authorised by law: CAA 1968, Sch.2, para.2; CFA 2003, s.131

(1) not being a sentence of greater severity than that passed on the original conviction; and
(2) notwithstanding that, on the date of conviction on retrial, the offender has ceased to be of an age at which such a sentence could otherwise be passed.

Where imprisonment or other detention is imposed in such a case, the sentence begins to run from the time when a like sentence passed at the original trial would have begun to run; but in computing the term of his sentence or the period for which he may be detained thereunder, the judge must have regard to any time:

(a) before the offender's conviction on retrial which would have been disregarded in computing that term or period if the sentence had been passed at the original trial and the original conviction had not been quashed; and
(b) during which he was released on bail under CAA 1968, s.8(2).

CJA 2003, s.240 (crediting of remand periods—see 29 DEALING WITH OFFENDERS).

B. Retrial for serious offences under CJA 2003, Pt 10

53–005 CJA 2003, Pt 10 provides a limited exception to the common law double jeopardy rule by permitting retrials in respect of a number of specified very serious offences, whenever committed, where there has been an acquittal and new and compelling evidence comes to light. The police are empowered to re-investigate the case, and the prosecutor is enabled to apply to CACD for the acquittal to be quashed and for a retrial to take place.

The provisions came into force on **April 4, 2005**. The Act sets out measures relating to the re-investigation of such offences, provisions as to arrest, charge and bail and custody; and the procedure for making applications to CACD for retrial. See also the Criminal Justice Act 2003 (Retrial for Serious Offences) Rules, 2005 (SI 2005/679) in relation to procedure in CACD.

General

53–006 Where:

(1) a person has been acquitted, whether before or after the passing of CJA 2003: CJA 2003, ss.76, 77
  (a) of a "qualifying offence" in proceedings:
    (i) on indictment in England and Wales,
    (ii) on appeal against conviction, verdict or finding on indictment in England and Wales, or
    (iii) on appeal from a decision of such an appeal; or
  (b) in proceeedings elsewhere than in the UK of an offence under the law of the place where the proceedings were held, if the commission of the offence as alleged would have amounted to, or included, the commission in the UK or elsewhere of a "qualifying offence"; and

(2) there is new and compelling evidence, within the meaning of s.78 that that person is guilty of the qualifying offence; and
(3) in all the circumstances it is in the interests of justice for such an order to be made, then, with the written consent of the DPP, the prosecutor may apply to CACD, in the case of (1) for an order quashing that person's acquittal in England and Wales and ordering his retrial for the qualifying offence, and in the case of (2) for a determination whether the acquittal is a bar to that person being retried in England and Wales for the offence, and if it is, for an order that it should not be a bar.

Not more than one application may be made in relation an acquittal.

Definitions

53–007 A person acquitted of an offence in proceedings under the above provisions is treated for the purposes of that provision as also acquitted of any qualifying offence of which he could have been convicted in the proceedings because of the first mentioned offence being charged in the indictment, except an offence: CJA 2003, s.75(2)

(1) of which he has been convicted, or
(2) of which he has been found not guilty by reason of insanity, or
(3) in respect of which, in proceedings where he has been found to be under a disability (as defined by CP(I)A 1964, s.4), a finding has been made that he did the act or made the omission charged against him.

"Qualifying offences" are those set out in CJA 2003, Sch.5, Pt 1, but do not include references to an offence which, at the time of the acquittal was the subject of an order under ss.77(1) or (3) above. CJA 2003, s.75(3), (8)

Conduct punishable under the law in force elsewhere than in the UK is an offence under that law for the purposes of s.62(4) however it is described in that law. CJA 2003, s.75(5)

Consent of DPP

53–008 The written consent of the DPP is required before any application may be made to CACD. He may give his consent only if satisfied that: CJA 2003, s.76(3), (4)

(1) there is evidence as respects which the requirements of s.65 (as to new and compelling evidence) appear to be met, and
(2) it is in the public interest (within the meaning of s.65) for the application to proceed.

Determination by CACD

53–009 A retrial will be ordered only where CACD is satisfied that the requirements of: CJA 2003, s.77

(1) s.78 as to new and compelling evidence; and
(2) s.79 as to the interests of justice

are met, otherwise the application will be dismissed.

Where CACD determines that the acquittal is a bar to the person being tried for the qualifying offence, it must, if satisfied that the provisions of ss.78 and 79 are met, make the order applied for, or otherwise make a declaration to the effect that the acquittal is a bar to the person being tried for the offence.

Where CACD determines that the acquittal is not a bar to the person being tried for the qualifying offence, it will make a declaration to that effect (see, e.g. *R. v Dunlop, The Times*, September 14, 2006 CACD).

"New and compelling" evidence

53–010 In relation to "new and compelling" evidence that the acquitted person is guilty of the qualifying offence: CJA 2003, s.78(1), (2), (3)

(1) evidence is "new" if it was not adduced in the proceedings in which the person was acquitted (nor, if those were appeal proceedings, in earlier proceedings to which the appeal related);
(2) evidence is "compelling" if:
 (a) it is reliable,
 (b) it is substantial, and
 (c) in the context of the outstanding issues, it appears highly probative of the case against the acquitted person.

Note that: CJA 2003, s.78(4), (5) (6), (7)

(i) "the outstanding issues" are the issues in dispute in the proceedings in which the person was acquitted and, if those were appeal proceedings;
(ii) any other issues remaining in dispute from earlier proceedings against the acquitted person;
(iii) for the purpose of this provision, it is irrelevant whether any evidence would have been admissible in earlier proceedings against the acquitted person.

RETRIALS

The "interests of justice"

53–011 The "interests of justice" for the purposes of these provisions, are to be determined having regard, in particular, to: CJA 2003, s.79

(1) whether existing circumstances make a fair trial unlikely;
(2) for the purposes of that question and otherwise, the length of time since the qualifying offence was allegedly committed;
(3) whether it is likely that the new evidence would have been adduced in the earlier proceedings against the acquitted person but for a failure by an officer or a prosecutor to act with due diligence, and
(4) whether, since those proceedings or, if later, since the commencement of CJA 2003, Pt 10, any officer or prosecutor has failed to act with due diligence or expedition.

A reference to an "officer or prosecutor" includes a reference to a person charged with corresponding duties under the law in force elsewhere than in England and Wales, and where the earlier prosecution was conducted by a person other than officer or prosecutor, (3) above applies in relation to that person as well as in relation to a prosecutor.

Application by the prosecutor

53–012 The prosecutor may apply under s.76(1) for the quashing of an acquittal in England and Wales, or under s.76(2) in the case of a person acquitted elsewhere than in the United Kingdom for a determination that that acquittal is no bar to a trial in England and Wales, or if it is, for an order that it should not be such a bar.

The double jeopardy bar does not ordinarily apply to cases which have been discontinued for reasons other than acquittal.

A prosecutor seeking to make a s.76 application must serve notice of that application in the form set out PD 2004, Annex D (pp.105, 106) on the Registrar and the acquitted person, be accompanied, where practicable by: R.41.2

(1) relevant witness statements which are relied upon as forming new and compelling evidence of guilt of the acquitted person as well as any relevant witness statements from the original trial;
(2) any unused statements which might reasonably be considered capable of undermining the application or of assisting an acquitted person's application to oppose that application (under r.41.3);
(3) a copy of the indictment and paper exhibits from the original trial;

(4) copies of the transcript of the summing up and any other relevant transcripts from the original trial; and
(5) any other documents relied upon to support the application,

and file with the Registrar a witness statement or certificate of service which exhibits a copy of that notice.

An application may be abandoned by the prosecutor before the hearing by serving notice in the form set out in the Practice Direction on the Registrar and the acquitted person. R.41.16

Response of the acquitted person

53–013 An acquitted person seeking to oppose a s.76 application must serve a response in the form set out in PD 2004, Annex D on the Registrar and the prosecutor which: R.41.3

(1) indicates if he is also seeking an order under s.80(6) of the Criminal Justice Act 2003 for:
   (a) the production of any document, exhibit or other thing, or
   (b) a witness to attend for examination and to be examined before CACD; and
(2) exhibits any relevant documents.

The acquitted person must serve that response not more than 28 days after receiving notice under r.41.2, although CACD may extend the period for service under para.(2), either before or after that period expires.

Examination of witnesses or evidence by the Court of Appeal

53–014 An application may be made to CACD by a party at least 14 days before the day of the hearing of the s.76 application, in the form set out in PD 2004, Annex D for an order under s.80(6) for: R.41.4

(1) the production of any document, exhibit or other thing; or
(2) a witness to attend for examination and to be examined before CACD,

sending it to the Registrar with a copy sent to each party to the application.

Such application will need to set out the reasons why the order was not sought from the Court when;

   (a) the notice was served on the Registrar under r.41.2, if the application is made by the prosecutor; or

(b) the response was served on the Registrar under r.41.3, if the application is made by the acquitted person.

If CACD makes an order under s.80(6) of its own motion or on application from the prosecutor, it will serve notice and reasons for that order on all parties to the s.76 application.

Reporting restrictions

53–015 CJA 2003, ss.59 and 70 provide for restrictions on reporting anything done under ss.62–68, and create offences in respect of infringements of those proceedings. See, e.g. *In re D (Acquitted person: Retrial), The Times*, March 6, 2006.

Effect of determination

53–016 Where CACD:

(1) quashes an acquittal under CJA 2003, s.77(1); or
(2) declares an acquittal to be no bar to a prosecution, under *ibid*. s.77(3),

any subsequent trial will be on an indictment preferred by direction of CACD, and arraignment must take place within two months from the date of the order, unless CACD allows a longer period.

CACD will not extend the period unless satisfied that:

(a) the Crown has acted with due expedition (see above in relation to retrial under CAA 1968, s.7); and
(b) there is good and sufficient cause for trial despite the lapse of time since the order under s.77 was made. CJA 2003, s.84(1), (2), (3)

The determination of the application may be given at the conclusion of the hearing, or may be reserved. Notice will be given by the Registrar to the parties. Where CACD orders a retrial, the Registrar will serve notice on the Crown Court officer of the appropriate court. R.41.13

Where the accused is not arraigned within the time limits, he may apply to CACD in the form set out in the Practice Direction, to set aside the order and:

(i) for any direction required for restoring an earlier judgment and verdict of acquittal of the qualifying offence, or
(ii) in the case of a person acquitted elsewhere than in the UK, for a declaration to the effect that the acquittal is a bar to his being tried for the qualifying offence. CJA 2003, s.84(4); R.41.14

The prosecutor must ensure that arraignment takes place within two months of that on which CACD ordered a retrial. If the acquitted person has not been arraigned before the end of two months after that date, the prosecutor may apply, by serving the form set out in PD 2004, Annex D on the Registrar, for leave to arraign. (R.41.5). The acquitted person may apply to CACD to set aside the order. CJA 2003, s.84(5)

An indictment under (1) or (2) may relate to more than one offence, or more than one person, and may relate to an offence which, or a person who, is not the subject of an order or declaration under s.77.

Evidence on retrial

53–017 The trial will take account of all the evidence in the case. The evidence given must be given orally if it was given orally at the original trial, unless: CJA 2003, s.84(6), (7)

(1) all the parties to the trial agree otherwise,
(2) CJA 2003, s.116 (witness unavailable) applies, or
(3) the witness is unavailable to give evidence, otherwise than as mentioned in CJA 2003, s.116(2), and s.114(1)(d) (interests of justice).

At a trial pursuant to an order under s.77(1), CDA 1998, Sch.3, para.5 (use of depositions) does not apply to a deposition read as evidence at the original trial.

The prosecution may be permitted to adduce evidence on a retrial of statements made on oath by the accused at the original trial, to show that he had lied (*R. v Binham* [1991] Crim.L.R. 77).

C. Bail under CJA 2003, Pt 10

Bail and custody before application

53–018 The Act recognises that it may take some time for the police and the Crown to formulate the case for CACD, but this time should not be disproportionate. The power to remand in custody or on bail is given to the Crown Court. CJA 2003, s.88(4), (5)

Where a person appears or is brought before the Crown Court in accordance with s.88(1) or (2), the judge may either:

(1) grant bail for him to appear, if notice of application is served on him under s.80(2), before CACD at the hearing of that application, or
(2) remand him in custody to be brought before the Crown Court under s.89(2).

Where bail is granted under this provision, it may be revoked, and the person may be remanded in custody as referred to in (2) above.

If, at the end of the "relevant period" that is:

(a) the period of 42 days beginning with the day on which he is granted bail or remanded in custody, or CJA 2003, s.88(6), (7)
(b) that period as extended or further extended under s.88(8) below,

no notice of application under CJA 2003, s.76(1) or (2) in relation to that person has been given under s.80(1), that person:

(i) if on bail subject to a duty to appear, ceases to be under that duty and to any conditions of that bail, or
(ii) if in custody on remand under ss.88(4)(b) or (5) must be released immediately without bail.

As to applications for bail, see r.41.7.

Procedure; hearing in the Crown Court

53–019 Rules 19.18, 19.22 and 19.23 (see 11 BAIL) apply where a person is to appear or be brought before the Crown Court pursuant to CJA 2003, s.88 or 89 as if they were applications under r.19.18(1), with one modification namely the substitution for r.19.18 of "here a person is to appear or be brought before the Crown Court pursuant to CJA 2003, s.88 or 89 the prosecutor must serve notice of the need for such a hearing on the court officer". R.41.5

Where a person is to appear or be brought before the Crown Court pursuant to s.88 or 89 the judge may order that the person shall be released from custody on entering into a recognisance, with or without sureties, or giving other security before the Crown Court officer, or any other person authorised by virtue of MCA 1980, s.119(1) to take a recognisance where a magistrates' court having power to take the recognisance has, instead of taking it, fixed the amount in which the principal and his sureties, if any, are to be bound.

The court officer will forward a copy of any record made in pursuance of BA 1976, s.5(1) to the Registrar.

Extension of the "relevant period"

53–020 A judge may, on the application of the prosecutor, extend or further extend the "relevant period" until a specified date, but only where he is satisfied that: CJA 2003, s.88(8)

(1) the need for the extension is due to some good and sufficient cause; and
(2) the prosecutor has acted with all due diligence and expedition.

As to "good and sufficient cause" and "diligence and expedition" see 3 ABUSE OF PROCESS).

Further provisions regarding bail and custody in the Crown Court.

The prosecutor may only apply to extend or further extend the relevant period before it expires and that application must be served on the Crown Court officer and the acquitted person. R.41.6

Bail and custody before hearing

53–021 Where notice of application is given under CJA 2003, s.80(1), then in relation to the person to whom that application relates, if he: CJA 2003, s.89(1), (2), (3) (4), (5)

(1) is in custody under s.88(4)(b) or (5) he must be brought before a judge of the Crown Court as soon as practicable and, in any event within 48 hours after the notice is given;
(2) is not in custody under s.88(4)(b) or (5) the Crown Court may, on application by the prosecutor, issue:
   (a) a summons requiring him to appear before CACD at the hearing of the application, or
   (b) a warrant for his arrest,

and a warrant may be issued at any time even though a summons has previously been issued.

The summons, or a subsequent direction of the Crown Court may specify the time and place at which that person must appear, and the time and place may be varied from time to time by a direction of the Crown Court.

A prosecutor's application for a summons or a warrant under s.89(3)(a) or (b) must be served on the court officer and the acquitted person (R.41.6(2)).

Appearance before the Crown Court

53–022 A person arrested under a warrant under s.89(3)(b) must be brought before a judge of the Crown Court as soon as practicable and in any event within 48 hours after his arrest (and SCA 1981, s.81(5) giving the magistrates' court as an alternative, does not apply). CJA 2003, s.89(6), (7) (8), (9)

The judge must, where a person is brought before him under either s.89(2) or (6) either:

(1) remand him in custody to be brought before CACD at the hearing of the application, or
(2) grant bail for him to appear before the CACD at the hearing.

Bail granted by the Crown Court may be revoked, and the person remanded in custody in accordance with s.89(7)(b).

Revocation of bail

53–023 Where bail is revoked under CJA 2003, Pt 10, and the person concerned is not before the Crown Court when his bail is revoked, a judge must order him to surrender himself forthwith to the custody of the court, and where he surrenders in compliance with that order, the judge must remand him in custody. CJA 2003, s.91(1), (2)

Procedure in CACD

53–024 The procedure in CACD is governed by Rr.41.7–41.12. As to applications by the DPP under CJA 2003, s.82, to restrict publication, see rr. 41.8–41.9.

54 RT DISQUALIFICATION AND ENDORSEMENT

Introduction

54–001 An offender convicted of certain offences may be disqualified from driving a mechanically propelled vehicle and from holding or obtaining a driving licence.

Disqualification:

(1) to some extent serves a basic public protection purpose, where the offender's conduct has proved a danger to other road users; and
(2) in most cases, is intended to punish misuse, or careless use of vehicles and to deter both the offender and others from indulging in it.

Disqualification is part of the basic penalty imposed by the court for the offence, but it is an ancillary order and must be attached to the sentence; it cannot stand alone (but see 54–011 below).

Length of disqualification

54–002 The law provides no limit to the length of a disqualification beyond any minimum prescribed period, but:

(1) very long periods should be avoided unless the offender is a menace to other road users (*R. v Rickeard* [1975] R.T.R. 104; *R. v Davitt* [1974] Crim.L.R. 719), since such offenders are particularly likely to commit offences of driving while disqualified which they might not, were the term shorter;
(2) there is no rule that an offender who is sent to prison and also disqualified has the right to have the period of disqualification coincide, more or less automatically, with the period he has to serve; the nature of the offence, his antecedents, and the extent to which he will be handicapped by not being able to drive on his release, are all matters which need to be taken into consideration (*R. v Hansel* (1982) 4 Cr.App.R.(S.) 368);
(3) as to disqualification for life, see *R. v Buckley* (1994) 15 Cr.App.R.(S.) 695.

All disqualifications now run from the date of imposition, and must be concurrent; there cannot be consecutive periods.

The references in the text in bold type emphasise matters found by CACD to be ignored or not sufficiently appreciated in the Crown Court (see, in particular, *R. v Kent* (1983) 77 Cr.App.R. 120).

Situations in which disqualification arises

54–003 An offender may be disqualified: PCC(S)A 2000, s.147, RTOA 1988, ss.34, 35; RTA 1991, s.29, Sch.4, para.95; AVTA 1992, s.3(2)

(1) where a vehicle has been used for the purpose of crime (i.e. a non-road traffic offence);
(2) on conviction of an offence which attracts obligatory disqualification;
(3) on conviction of an offence attracting discretionary disqualification; and
(4) where disqualification is obligatory owing to the accumulation of penalty points for a series of offences.
(5) in addition to dealing with him in any other way, see 54–011 below.

The various systems of disqualification run parallel to each other and are not mutually exclusive (see *Jones v DPP* (2001) 165 J.P. 6).

A magistrates' court, as part of its procedures for enforcing the payment of fines and other financial penalties may, under CJA 2003, s.30, instead of issuing a warrant of commitment, or proceeding under MCA 1980, s.81 order a defaulter to be disqualified for a period not exceeding 12 months.

The provisions of C(IC)A 2003, Pt 3, govern the recognition and enforcement of disqualifications imposed on persons normally resident in the UK by courts in EC member states.

Endorsement

54–004 The particulars of all offences involving obligatory or discretionary disqualification must be endorsed on the offender's licence, unless there are special reasons for not doing so. This is irrespective of whether he is disqualified or not. RTOA 1988, s.147(3), (4), (6)

As to application for removal of an endorsement, see RTOA 1988, s.45.

Conditional and absolute discharge

54–005 Where the judge makes an order of conditional or absolute discharge in respect of an offence carrying obligatory or discretionary disqualification he may also on that occasion exercise any power conferred, and must also exercise any duty imposed, on the court by RTOA 1988, ss.34, 35, 36 or 44. RTOA 1988, s.46(1); CJA1991, Sch.11, para.38; PCC(S)A 2000, s.165, Sch.9, para.123

Mechanics of disqualification: interim disqualification

RTOA 1988, ss.29, 31; RTA 1991, s.28

54–006 In order to decide whether or not to exercise his power of disqualification, the judge may take into consideration particulars of any previous conviction or disqualification endorsed on the offender's licence.

RTOA 1988, s.26; RTA 1991, s.25; PCC(S)A 2000, s.165, Sch.9, para.119

While, in general, a disqualification will be imposed at the time sentence is pronounced, which will normally follow upon conviction:

(1) there is nothing to prevent the judge from dealing with the substantive part of the sentence on the day of conviction and postponing ancillary questions of endorsement and disqualification until the licence is produced, and any other relevant information is to hand (*R. v Annesley* (1976) 62 Cr.App.R. 113);
(2) a judge who:
  (a) defers sentence in respect of an offence carrying obligatory or discretionary disqualification; or
  (b) adjourns after convicting an offender of such an offence, before dealing with him; may order him to be disqualified until he has been dealt with for the offence.

An order under (2) ceases to have effect on the expiry of six months from the date it is made, if the offender has not been dealt with before that and, when the court comes to deal with the offender, it is precluded from disqualifying him further in respect of the same offence or any offence in respect of which an order could have been made at the time the first order was made. Where the judge proposes to disqualify, he should draw this to the attention of counsel, so that the latter may deal with the point specifically (*R. v Powell & Carvell* (1984) 6 Cr.App.R.(S.) 354).

Production of licence: suspension

RTA 1988, s.27(1), (3), (4); PCC(S)A 2000, s.165, Sch.9, para.120; CJA 2003, s.304, Sch.32, Pt 1, para.53

54–007 Before making an order the court *must require* the offender, if he is the holder of a licence, (including as community licence) to produce it, and if he has not caused it to be delivered to the court, or he does not produce it:

(1) he may be guilty of an offence; and
(2) the licence *must* be suspended until it is produced.

and the obligation imposed on him as respects the licence also applies as respects the counterpart.

1. Vehicle used for the purpose of crime

54–008 Where a person is convicted in the Crown Court or, having been convicted in the magistrates' court, is committed to the Crown Court for sentence under PCC(S)A 2000, s.3: PCC(S)A 2000, s.147

(1) for an offence punishable with imprisonment for not less than two years on indictment; or
(2) having been convicted in a magistrates' court of such an offence was committed to the Crown Court for sentence; or
(3) is convicted by or before any court of common assault, or for any other offence involving an assault, including the aiding, abetting or procuring of such an offence, or its incitement (see *R. v Rajesh Patel* (1995) 16 Cr.App.R.(S.) 756); and
(4) the judge is satisfied that a vehicle was used by that person, or by anyone else, for the purpose of committing or facilitating the commission of the offence including the taking of any steps after it was committed for the purposes of disposing of any property to which it related, or of avoiding apprehension or detection, or that the assault was committed by driving a motor vehicle,

he may disqualify that person for such period as he thinks fit.

The "offence" must, however, be that, or one of those, of which he is convicted (*R. v Parrington* (1985) 7 Cr.App.R.(S.) 18).

Important considerations

54–009 A number of points need to be noted in respect of the exercise, and the effect of exercising, this power:

(1) the power under PCC(S)A 2000, s.147 is exercisable even though the offence committed does not attract endorsement under RTOA 1988;
(2) if the driving is only incidental to the offence, the power of disqualification under s.147 should not be used (*R. v Wilmot, The Times*, January 24, 1985);
(3) the fact that the offender did not himself drive the vehicle in the course of committing the offence does not protect him from disqualification; if one of several offenders uses a vehicle for the purposes of an offence, all or any of them may be disqualified (*R. v Wilmot*, above);

(4) the power should not be exercised without first giving the defence advocate an opportunity of dealing with it (*R. v Powell & Carvell* (1984) 6 Cr.App.R.(S.) 354; *R. v Lake* (1986) 8 Cr.App.R.(S.) 69; *R. v Money* [1988] Crim.L.R. 626);

(5) the judge, in imposing a disqualification under s.147, should take account of the effect on the offender's employment prospects on his release (*R. v Wright* (1979) 1 Cr.App.R.(S.) 82, *R. v Davegun* (1985) 7 Cr.App.R.(S.) 110; *R. v Liddey* (1999) 2 Cr.App.R.(S.) 122);

(6) long periods are undesirable (*R. v Fazal* [1999] 1 Cr.App.R.(S.) 152);

(7) endorsement under s.147 does not "wipe the slate clean" of penalty points previously accumulated on the licence; nor is there any power, if the court declines to disqualify under s.147 to impose penalty points under RTOA 1988; and

(8) there is no power to order a re-test under s.147 (*R. v Rajesh Patel* (1995) 16 Cr.App.R.(S.) 756).

Obligation to produce licence

54–010 A judge ordering a disqualification under s.147 must require the offender to produce: PCC(S)A 2000, s.147(5), (7); C(IC))A 2003, s.91, Sch.5, paras 72, 74A

(1) any licence together with its counterpart (both of which expressions are defined in s.146(5));

(2) in the case where he holds a Northern Ireland licence, that licence and its counterpart, if any; and

(3) in the case of a person holding a community licence (as defined in RTA 1988, Pt III), his community licence and its counterpart.

2. Disqualification for any offence

54–011 The court before which a person is convicted of an offence committed after December 31, 1997 may: PCC(S)A 2000, s.146(1), (2), (3); CJA 2003, s.304, Sch.32, Pt 1, para.120

(1) provided the judge has been notified that he has that power;

(2) instead of, (unless the sentence is fixed by law or is one which falls to be imposed under PCC(S)A 2000, ss.110(2) or 111(2) (minimum sentences for certain repeat offences), FA 1968, s.51A(2) (minimum sentences for certain firearms offences) or CJA 2003, ss.225, 226, 227 or 228) (dangerous offenders)); or

(3) in addition to, dealing with him in any other way,

order him to be disqualified for such period as he thinks fit, for holding or obtaining a driving licence.

This power has been available since January 1, 2004 (HO Circular 59/2003).

This power is wide-ranging; it is not limited to any particular offence, nor is it necessary that the offence be connected in any way with the use of a motor vehicle (*R. v Cliff* [2005] 2 Cr.App.R.(S.) 22. see also *R. v Skitt* [2005] 2 Cr. App.R.(S.) 22).

Obligation to produce licence

54–012 A judge ordering a disqualification under s.146 must require the offender to produce: PCC(S)A 2000, s.146(4); C(IC)A 2003, s.91(1), Sch.5, paras 72, 73(a)

(1) any licence together with its counterpart (both of which expressions are defined in s.146(5));
(2) in the case where he holds a Northern Ireland licence, that licence and its counterpart, if any; and
(3) in the case of a person holding a community licence (as defined in RTA 1988, Pt III), his community licence and its counterpart.

3. Obligatory disqualification for serious RT offences

54–013 An offender *must* be disqualified, in the absence of special reasons (see below) for at least the minimum prescribed period, on conviction of any one of the following offences:

(1) manslaughter by the driver of a mechanically propelled vehicle (DD60) (indictment only—common law);
(2) causing death by dangerous driving (RTA 1988, s.1; RTA 1991, s.1 (DD70));
(3) causing death by careless driving when under the influence of drink or drugs (RTA 1988, s.3A; RTA 1991, s.3) (unfit through drink, CD40; unfit through drugs, CD50; excess alcohol, CD60; failure to provide specimen, CD70);
(4) dangerous driving (RTA 1988, s.2; RTA 1991, s.1) (DD40);
(5) driving or attempting to drive while unfit through drink or drugs (RTA 1988, s.4(1)), (through drink (DR 20), through drugs (DR 80));

(6) driving or attempting to drive with excess alcohol concentration (RTA 1988, s.5(1)(a)) (DR 10);
(7) failing without reasonable excuse to supply an evidential specimen, when driving or attempting to drive (RTA 1988, s.7(6)) (DR 30);
(8) motor racing or speed trials on the highway (RTA 1988, s.12) (MS50); and
(9) aggravated vehicle taking (TA 1968, s.12; AVTA 1992, s.3).

54–014 On conviction of any of the offences under (1) to (9) above, the offender must be disqualified for such period as the court thinks fit, for *not less than*: RTOA 1988, s.34(3), (4); RTA1991, s.26, Sch.2

(a) two years in the case of (1), (2) and (3), or 12 months in the case of (4) to (9) above; or
(b) three years, if the offender is convicted of an offence under (3), (5), (6), or (7) and was in the 10 years immediately preceding the commission of that offence convicted of a like offence;

unless for special reasons (see below) the court thinks fit to order him:

(i) *not* to be disqualified; or
(ii) to order him to be disqualified for a shorter period.

In such a case the grounds for that decision must be stated in open court (RTOA 1988, s.47(10).

On conviction of any of the offences under (1), (2) and (4) a re-test *must* be ordered and the offender remains disqualified until he has passed the appropriate driving test, which in these circumstances is an extended driving test (RTOA 1988, s.36; RTA 1991, s.32).

If on conviction of any of the offences under (1) to (9) inclusive, the court finds special reasons and does not disqualify, the licence must be endorsed with 3–11 penalty points.

Sentencing: offences under sections 1 and 3A

54–015 The maximum period of imprisonment for causing death by dangerous driving and causing death by careless driving while under the influence of drink or drugs has been is increased to 14 years' imprisonment after the coming into force of CJA 2003, s.285, February 27, 2004 (SI 2004/81). Sentencing thresholds, as set out below, will need to be adjusted accordingly.

R. v Cooksey [2003] Crim L.R. 564

54–016 CACD made the following points;

(1) it would ordinarily be obvious to an offender that his driving was dangerous, and he deserved to be punished accordingly;
(2) where death resulted this could justify a higher sentence than if it did not;
(3) the impact on the family of the victim could reasonably be taken into account;
(4) though causing death by dangerous driving was invariably a serious crime, culpability must be the dominant factor when assessing where, in the level of serious crime, the facts of the particular case came.

Aggravating features

54–017 CACD adopted the recommendations of the Sentencing Panel, that aggravating features included:

Highly culpable standard of driving at the time of the offence

(1) the consumption of alcohol or drugs (including legal medication known to cause drowsiness), ranging from a couple of drinks to a "motorised pub crawl";
(2) competitive driving against another vehicle; greatly excessive speed; showing off;
(3) disregard of warnings from passengers;
(4) a prolonged, persistent and deliberate course of bad driving;
(5) aggressive driving (such as driving too close to the vehicle in front), persistent, inappropriate attempts to overtake, cutting in after overtaking;
(6) driving whilst driver's attention is avoidably distracted, e.g. by use of mobile phone (especially when hand-held);
(7) driving when knowingly suffering from a medical condition which significantly impairs offender's driving skills;
(8) driving when knowingly deprived of adequate sleep or rest;
(9) driving a poorly maintained or dangerously loaded vehicle (especially when the driver is motivated by commercial considerations);
(10) committing the offence while on bail.

Driving habitually below careful standard

(1) other offences committed at the same time and related offences, i.e. driving without ever having had a licence; driving while disqualified; driving with no insurance, while a learner driver driving without a supervisor and so on;
(2) previous convictions for motoring offences, particularly offences which involve bad driving or the consumption of excessive alcohol before driving—in other words the man who demonstrates that he is determined to continue driving badly despite past experience;
(3) driving after having taken a vehicle without consent or in a stolen vehicle.

Outcome of offence

(1) where more than one person has been killed as a result of the offence (especially if offender knowingly put more than one person at risk, or the occurrence of multiple deaths was forseeable);
(2) severely injuring more than one victim in addition.

Irresponsible behaviour at the scene of the offence

(1) failing to stop or, even more reprehensible, trying to blame the victim for causing the collision, throwing the victim off the bonnet of the car by swerving in order to escape; and
(2) causing death in the course of dangerous driving in an attempt to avoid detection or apprehension.

Mitigating features

54–018 The offence might be mitigated by the following features:

(1) a good driving record;
(2) absence of previous convictions;
(3) a timely plea of guilty;
(4) genuine shock or remorse, which may be greater where the victim was either a close relative or friend of the offender;
(5) the offender's age (but only in cases where lack of driving experience has contributed to the commission of the offence);
(6) offender also severely injured as a result of the accident caused by his dangerous driving.

Sentencing thresholds

54–019 In *R. v Cooksey* CACD, basing its opinions on a 10 year maximum (increased to 14 years' imprisonment after the coming into force of CJA 2003, s.285, February 27, 2004 (SI 2004/81), set out four "starting points" in sentencing such offenders:

(1) no aggravating features: 12–18 months custodial sentence,
(2) intermediate culpability: two–three years,
(3) higher culpability: four–five years,
(4) most serious: six years +.

Young persons

54–020 Where an offender aged at least 14, but under 18 is convicted of an offence: PCC(S)A 2000, s.91(2), (3)

(1) of causing death by dangerous driving (RTA 1988, s.1); or
(2) of causing death by careless driving while under the influence of drink or drugs (RTA 1988, s.3A);

and the judge is of opinion that none of the other methods in which the case may be legally dealt with is suitable, he may sentence the offender to the same maximum term of 10 years as applies to an adult.

Manslaughter involving use of a motor vehicle

54–021 The maximum sentence for manslaughter is life imprisonment. The sentence for manslaughter involving the use of a motor vehicle, which involves an element of hostility, cannot be equated with other offences of causing death by driving, such as causing death by dangerous driving and causing death by careless driving, having consumed alcohol so as to be over the prescribed limit. The maximum sentence for these two offences has always corresponded and has been increased Februry 27, 2004 to 14 years.

Reduced disqualification for offender attending course

54–022 Where a person is convicted of a drink-related offence, i.e. under RTA 1988, ss.3A, 4, 5 and 7, including the "in charge" offences, and the judge makes an order disqualifying him for not less than 12 months, he may order that the period be reduced if, by a specified date, the offender satisfactorily completes a course approved by the Home Secretary specified in the order. RTOA 1988, s.34A; RTA 1991, ss.30, 31

He may only make such an order where:

(1) the offender appears to be 17 or over;
(2) he is satisfied that a place on a course is available for the offender;
(3) he explains to the offender in ordinary language the effect of the order, and the fees payable before the course begins; and
(4) the offender agrees to the order.

Note that:

(a) the reduction must be of not less than three months nor more than one-quarter of the unreduced period (thus nine months in the case of a 12-month disqualification which is the usual period for a drink-driving offence, but, of course, it may be higher according to the alcohol level);
(b) the offender disqualified for two years, as is the case under RTA 1988, s. 3A, will be eligible for a six month reduction; and
(c) the date specified as the latest date for the completion of the course must be at leas two months before the last day of the period of disqualification as reduced by the order.

4. Offences carrying discretionary disqualification

54–023 Discretionary disqualification and obligatory endorsement apply to road traffic offences which are not, like those carrying obligatory disqualification, invariably grave matters, but which may still be serious enough to justify a period of disqualification. Where the court does not exercise its power of disqualification it *must*, in the absence of special reasons, endorse the licence with the appropriate number of penalty points.

These offences are (as amended by CJA 2003, ss.281, 282 and 286 when these sections come into force):

No.	Code	Offence	Statute	Max. pen.	Pts
(10)	CDIO CD2O CD3	Careless and inconsiderate driving	RTA 1988, s.3; RTA 1991, s.2	Level 4	3–9
(11)	SPIO SF20 SF30	Speeding	RTRA 1984, s.89(1)	Level 3 or fixed penalty only	3–6 3
(12)	DR5O DR9O	In charge, while unfit through drink or drugs	RTA 1988, s.4(2)	51 weeks and/or level 4	10
(13)	DR4O	In charge, with excess alcohol	RTA 1988, s.5(l)(b)	51 weeks and/or Level 4	10
(14)	DR7O	Refusing roadside test	RTA 1988, s.6(4)	Level 3	4
(15)	DR3O DR6O	Failure to provide specimen, otherwise than in a roadside breath test	RTA 1988, s.7(6)	51 weeks and/or level 4	10
(16)		Causing danger to road users	RTA 1988, s.22A	7 yrs and/or fine on indictment	
			RTA 1991, s.6	51 weeks or level 5 or both	
(17)	MS2O	Carrying passenger incorrectly on m/cycle	RTA 1988, s.23	Level 3	3
(18)		Failure to comply with traffic directions including:	RTA 1988, ss.35, 36	Level 3	3
	TSIO	(a) signals;			
	TS2O	(b) double white lines;			
	TS3O	(c) stop sign;			
	TS4O	(d) directions of a constable;			
	TS5O	(e) others			
(19)	MSIO	Dangerous position	RTA 1988, s.22	Level 3	3
(20)	MWIO	Contravention of temporary prohibition or restriction	RTRA 1984, s.16(l)	Level 3	3–6 or 3 if fixed penalty
		Special roads regulations (except stopping)	RTRA 1984, s.17(4)	Level 4	3–6 or 3 if committed in respect

No.	Code	Offence	Statute	Max. pen.	Pts of speed restriction, 3 in any other case
(21)	PC1O PC2O PC3O	Pedestrian crossing offences	RTRA 1984, s.25(5)	Level 3	3
(22)	TS6O	School crossing patrol offence	RTRA 1984, s.28(3)	Level 5 (goods vehicles or vehicles adapted to carry more than 8 passengers); level 4 in any other case	3
(23)	CU2O	Dangerous condition	RTA 1988, s.40A		3
(24)	CUIO CU3O CU4O	Breach of requirement as to brakes, steering, tyres	RTA 1988, s.41A	Level 5 or level 4 as above	3
(25)	CU5O CU6O	Breach of requirement as to weight, goods and passengers	RTA 1988, s.41B	Level 5 or level 4 as above	
(26)	CU2O	Breach of other construction and use requirements	RTA 1988, s.42	Level 4 or level 3 as above	3
(27)	ACIO	Failing to stop and give particulars	RTA 1988, s.170(4)	51 weeks and/or level 5	5–10
(28)	AC2O	Failing to give particulars	RTA 1988, s.l70(4)	51 weeks and/or level 5	5–10
(29)	LCIO	Driving otherwise than in accordance with a licence	RTA 1988, s.87(1); RTA 1991, s.3 1	Level 3	3–6
(30)	INlO	No insurance	RTA 1988, s.143	Level 5	6–8
(31)	LC3O	Driving after making false declaration as to physical fitness	RTA 1988, s.92(10);RTA 199l, s.18	Level 4	3–6
(32)	LC4O	Driving after failing to notify S of S of disability	RTA 1988, s.94(3A); RTA 1991, s. l8	Level 3	3–6
(33)	LC5O	Driving after refusal of a licence under s.92(3)or revocation under s.93	RTA 1988, s.94A; RTA 1991, s.18(3)	6 mths and/or fine Level 5	3–6

RT DISQUALIFICATION AND ENDORSEMENT

No.	Code	Offence	Statute	Max. pen.	Pts	
(34)	MS4O	Driving with uncorrected defective eyesight	RTA 1988, s.96(1)	Level 3	3	
(35)	MS4O	Refusing to submit to eye test	RTA 1988, s.96(3)	Level 3	3	
(36)	MS3O	Playstreet offences	RTRA 1984, ss.29(3), 30(5)	Level 3	2	
(37)	LCIO	Driving a class rn/v (including LGV & PCV) not in accordance with driving licence for that class	RTA 1988, s.87(1); RTA 1991, s.31	Level 3 if disqualifiable. No discretionary disqualification, unless offence is committed by driving a rn/v where no driving licence for that vehicle could have been granted to offender or, if a provisional licence only to drive could have been granted, the driving would not have complied with the conditions 6 mths and/or level 5	3–6 RTOA 1988, s.34A; RTA1991, ss.30, 31	
(38)	BAIO	Driving while disqualified (now an arrestable offence)	RTA 1988, s.103(1)(b); Police Reform Act 2002	51 weeks and/or level 5		
(39)	UT1O	Taking or attempting w/o consent	TA 1968, s.12	Now 14 years on indictment 51 weeks and/or	–	
(40)	UT2O	Stealing or attempting to steal a rn/v		Level 5 (summary) on indictment	–	HO 1990
				7 yrs and/or fine 51 weeks and/or	–	
(41)	UT3O	Going equipped for theft, etc	TA 1968, s.25	level 5 (summary)	–	

No.	Code	Offence	Statute	Max. pen.	Pts	
				On indictment 3 yrs and/or fine Level 3		RTA 1988, s.35(1A), (5A); RTA 1991, Sch.4, para.95
(42)*		Failure of person keeping vehicle and others to give information as to driver's identity. where committed otherwise than by virtue of subs.(5) or (11)	RTA 1988, s.172; RTA 1991, s.21		3	
(43)		Aiding and abetting, etc an obligatorily disqualifiable offence	RTOA 1988, s.28(1)(b)		10	
(44)	CU5O	Load likely to cause danger because of its insecurity or position		No disqualification where offender proves that he did not know, and had no reasonable cause to suspect, that the use of vehicle involved a danger of injury to any person	3	RTOA 1988, s.28(4); RTA 1991, s.27 RTOA 1988, s.28(5); RTA 1991, s.27

*The use of a compulsory admission under the RTA 1988, s.172(2)(b) of having been the driver of a vehicle at the time of the commission of a road traffic offence does not infringe an accused's privilege against self-incrimination or his right to a fair trial under the European Convention, Art.6: *DPP v Wilson* [2002] R.T.R. 6, *cf. Brown v Procurator Fiscal*, *The Times*, February 1, 2000.

Repeated offences—penalty points

54–024 Under the penalty points system, an offender who commits a series of offences within a period of three years *must* be disqualified because of his repeated offending, whether or not the particular offence before the court would, in itself, justify disqualification.

RTOA 1988, s.35; RTA 1991,

It should be noted that:

(1) the system applies only to offences carrying obligatory disqualification in respect of an order made under RTOA 1988, s.34 as amended by RTA 1991, Sch.4, para.95 or to discretionary disqualification and obligatory endorsement as set out above; s.28; PCC(S) 2000, s.165, Sch.9, para.122A

(2) it applies in relation to an offence committed by aiding and abetting, etc. the commission of an offence such as is described in (1) above as if the offence involved discretionary disqualification;

(3) **if the court disqualifies the offender for his offence, *no penalty points* fall to be endorsed on his licence**; if he is not disqualified they are, unless there are special reasons for not doing so; where a driver is disqualified under RTOA 1988, s.34 and, has to be dealt with on the same occasion for another road traffic offence carrying an obligatory endorsement, the endorsement under s.44 should be limited to the particulars of the conviction and should not include particulars of the offence or the penalty points attributable to the offence *Martin v DPP* [2000] Crim.L.R. 320;

(4) if the offender is convicted, whether on the same occasion or not, of two or more offences committed on the same occasion and involving obligatory endorsement, **the total number of penalty points to be attributed to them is the number that would be attributed on a conviction for one of them (the most serious)**. Thus if the convictions are on separate occasions, the number to be attributed on later occasions is thereby restricted; but

(5) if (4) would ordinarily apply to two or more offences, the judge may still, if he thinks fit, decide that it will not apply to the offences, but must state his reasons for so doing in open court and enter those reasons in the register;

(6) once an offender is disqualified, the "slate is wiped clean" of all penalty points accumulated up to the time of disqualification (see *R.v Brentwood JJ. Ex p Richardson* (1992) 95 Cr.App.R. 187). HO 1990

The references in the text in bold type emphasise matters found by CACD to be ignored or not sufficiently appreciated in the Crown Court (see, in particular, *R. v Kent* (1983) 77 Cr.App.R. 120).

Repeated offences; disqualification

54–025 Disqualification under the penalty points system arises where the offender has, as a result of an offence committed within the three-year period, accumulated a total of 12 or more penalty points, including those to be endorsed on the instant occasion: RTOA 1988, s.35(4)

(1) if, taking the current offence into account, but disregarding any offence for which he is disqualified under RTOA 1988, s.34, the number of penalty points over the three year period comes to 12 points or more, the disqualification is obligatory unless there are "mitigating circumstances";
(2) the qualifying date for both the earlier and the current offences is the *date of the offence*, not the date of conviction;
(3) where the offender is convicted on *the same occasion* of more than one offence involving obligatory or discretionary disqualification, **not more than one "totting up" disqualification may be imposed, and it must be allocated to a single offence**;
(4) the *minimum period* for which such a person is to be disqualified varies according to whether he has been previously disqualified during the three years preceding the commission of the latest offence in respect of which penalty points are being taken into account. If:
    (a) there are no such disqualifications, the minimum period is *six months*;
    (b) if there is one—*12 months*; and
    (c) if there are two or more, the minimum period is *two years*.

Disqualifications by the Crown Court under PCC(S)A 2000, s.147, or interim disqualifications by a magistrates' court pending committal to the Crown Court (RTOA 1988, s.26), are not included (PCC(S)A 2000, s.147). RTOA 1988, s.36; RTA 1991, s.32

Mitigating circumstances

54–026 The judge may disqualify such an offender under the totting up provisions for a period below the minimum required under the system, or may decide not to disqualify at all, where he is satisfied that there are, **and states, the grounds** for mitigating the normal consequences of conviction, but may *not* do so where the offence is one carrying obligatory disqualification (see also *R. v Thomas* [1983] 3 All E.R. 756).

"Mitigating circumstances" are not to be equated with "special reasons" (see below). The former will, in the ordinary way, be largely circumstances pertaining to the offender, and concerned not with the gravity of the offence, but with the repetition of offences within a comparatively short period.

The statute expressly excludes from consideration any circumstances:

(1) that are alleged to make the offence(s) not serious; or
(2) that show hardship, short of "exceptional hardship"; or
(3) which have been taken into consideration already on another occasion within the three years immediately preceding the conviction.

The test of "exceptional hardship" is not the same as that for "special reasons". The judge does not need to hear sworn evidence, although obviously it will usually be desirable to do so (*Owen v Jones* [1988] R.T.R. 102). Where an offender seeks to contend that mitigating grounds which he is putting forward are other and different from those put forward to some other court within the three year period, it is for him to prove that they are different, by reference to that court's record or by calling evidence (*R. v Sandbach JJ. Ex p. Pescud* (1983) 5 Cr.App.R.(S.) 177).

Where no mitigating circumstances exist the offender must be disqualified

54–027 The references in the text in bold type emphasise matters found by CACD to be ignored or not sufficiently appreciated in the Crown Court (see, in particular, *R. v Kent* (1983) 77 Cr.App.R. 120).

Driving test order

54–028 Where:

(1) an offender:
  (a) is disqualified on conviction of manslaughter, or of an offence under RTA 1988, ss.1 or 2; or
  (b) is disqualified under s.3A (death by careless driving whilst under the influence of drink or drugs) where the offence is committed on or after January 31, 2002; or
  (c) is disqualified under RTA 1988, ss.34 or 35; or
  (d) is convicted of such other offence involving obligatory disqualification as the Home Secretary may prescribe,

the judge must (whether or not he has previously passed a test (*R. v Miller* (1994) 15 Cr.App.R.(S.) 505)) order him to be disqualified until he passes the "appropriate driving test".

(2) in the case of persons convicted of any other offence involving obligatory *endorsement* the court *may* make

such an order (whether or not he has previously passed any test).

RTOA 1988, s.22

An "appropriate driving test" means:

(a) an extended driving test where a person is convicted of an offence involving obligatory disqualification, or is disqualified under RTOA 1988, s.35; or
(b) under RTA 1999, s.36(3)(b), if the offence is committed on or after January 31, 2002, SI 2001/4051.

The judge is bound, in deciding whether to make an order, to have regard to the safety of other road users.

Such a disqualification does not expire until proof of the passing of the test is delivered to the Home Secretary.

RTOA 1988, ss.22, 40(2)(a), (b)

The superior courts have emphasised on a number of occasions (the most recent of which are *R. v Peat* (1984) 6 Cr.App.R.(S.) 311 and *R. v Lazzari* (1984) 6 Cr.App.R.(S.) 83), that such an order is *not* intended as a punishment, but to protect the public against incompetent drivers (including those not having regard for other road users (*R. v Bannister* [1991] R.T.R. 1)).

Unless obligatory, the power should be exercised only where there is reason to doubt the offender's competence to drive, whether through age, infirmity or the circumstances of the offence.

When sentencing for aggravated vehicle taking it is inappropriate to order a passenger to take an extended driving test at the end of a period of disqualification (see *R. v Bradshaw*, *The Times*, December 31, 1994).

Discretionary disqualification and totting up

54–029 Where an offender commits a motoring offence which attracts discretionary disqualification when he may also be liable for obligatory disqualification under the totting up provisions, the judge should use his discretion to consider:

RTOA 1988, s.42(1)

(1) whether the offence itself should attract discretionary disqualification, in the light of the offender's whole record, for the repetition is an aspect of the offence, as are the facts of the case before him;
(2) whether he should have a longer disqualification than the Act provides, then the judge may, instead of disqualifying him on the offence, add the appropriate points to his licence, thus leading to a totting up disqualification under s.34: *Jones v DPP*, *The Times*, October 20, 2000.

Notification of disability

54–030 Where, in any proceedings for an offence committed in respect of a motor vehicle, it appears to the judge that the accused may be suffering from any relevant disability, or prospective disability, within the meaning of RTA 1988, Pt III, he must notify the Home Secretary.

If there is evidence that an offender is liable to recurring bouts of an illness, such as hypomania, but is otherwise competent to drive, this is the course to take rather than to make a driving test order (*Hughes v Challes* (1983) 5 Cr.App.R.(S.) 374). PD 2004, IV.33.100

Proceedings after disqualification; suspension; removal

RTOA 1988, s.42(5)

54–031 The giving of notice of appeal does not operate to suspend the order of disqualification. If the order is to be suspended, it must be done by judicial act.

If an offender gives notice of appeal, or of his intention to apply for judicial review:

(1) the judge may, if he thinks fit, suspend any disqualification pending appeal;
(2) any disqualification, whether obligatory or discretionary, may be suspended:
  (a) by the Crown Court, where the offender appeals to it against conviction or sentence;
  (b) by CACD where the offender appeals or applies for leave to appeal against conviction or sentence;
  (c) by the High Court, where the offender applies to the magistrates to state a case under MCA 1980, s.87; or
  (d) by the High Court, where the offender applies, or applies for leave to apply, for a quashing order in respect of the proceedings before the magistrates' court.

Removal; procedure

54–032 A person disqualified by order of the court may apply to the court which made the order to remove it, provided that:

RTOA 1988, s.47(1)

(1) two years have elapsed, if the disqualification was for less than four years; or
(2) half the period has elapsed, if the disqualification was for not less than four and not more than 10 years; or
(3) five years have elapsed in any other case.

The judge, as he thinks fit, having regard to the character of the applicant and his subsequent conduct, the nature of the offence and any other circumstances:

(a) may, by order, remove the disqualification from such date as he may specify; or
(b) may refuse the application; but
(c) must *not* add to it any conditions or additional requirements (*R. v Bentham* (1981) 3 Cr.App.R.(S.) 229).

Application should be made to the location of the Crown Court where the order of disqualification was made.

There is no power in removing a disqualification, to remove a driving test order.

If the application is granted, the applicant may be ordered to pay the whole or any part of the costs. Where the application is refused, a further three months must elapse before another is entertained.

These provisions do not differentiate between discretionary and obligatory disqualification, and there is nothing in law to prevent the court removing an obligatory disqualification although, if it thinks fit, the court may regard it as one which it is somewhat less ready to remove than a discretionary disqualification (*Damer v Davison* [1976] R.T.R. 45).

Special reasons

54–033 Before the court can justify, for special reasons, not disqualifying for an offence where it is otherwise obligatory, or disqualifying for a period shorter than the statutory minimum, or for not ordering endorsement, four conditions must be fulfilled.

These are that the facts advanced:

(1) must amount to mitigating or extenuating circumstances;
(2) must *not* amount to a defence to the charge;
(3) must be directly connected with the commission of the offence; and
(4) must be matters which can properly be taken into account when imposing punishment (*R. v Wickens* (1958) 42 Cr.App.R. 236; *Myles v DPP* [2004] 2 All E.R. 902).

The judge **must state openly** any grounds for finding that special reasons exist for mitigating the statutory penalty.

Note that:

(a) the mere fact that the circumstances disclose a special reason does not, of itself, mean that the offender is entitled, as a matter of course, to escape disqualification;

there is a serious burden on a court to decide, in its discretion, whether to refrain from disqualifying (*Taylor v Rajan* (1974) Q.B. 424) and that discretion should be exercised only in clear and compelling circumstances (*Vaughan v Dunn* [1984] R.T.R. 376; *DPP v Bristow* [1998] R.T.R. 100).

(b) even where the above conditions are fulfilled, there may be some over-riding factor which precludes the court from regarding as "special reasons" some circumstance which at first appeared to fall within the scope of the four preconditions (*Delaroy-Hall v Tadman* (1969) 133 J.P. 127).

In an excess alcohol case where the court found special reasons, and where it was not suggested that the actual driving undertaken or even attempted could have posed any appreciable risk of danger to anyone it would be hard to justify a period of disqualification in excess of the mandatory 12 months (*R. v St Albans Crown Court Ex p. O'Donovan* [2000] 1 Cr.App.R.(S.) 344, DC).

The court is concerned not with the special reason that caused the offender to take his car onto the road, but with the special reason for not disqualifying or for imposing a lesser disqualification.

Special to the offence

54–034 The need for the facts to be directly connected with the commission of the offence, means that the facts put forward as a special reason must be "special", in contrast with those that are general, and special to the *offence* rather than to the offender. It is because of this that special reasons are not to be found in the following circumstances (for example), that:

(1) the offender is a professional driver (*Whittal v Kirby* (1947) 111 J.P. 1), or has been driving for many years without complaint (*Lines v Hersom* (1951) 115 J.P. 494), or is a careful person who would never have risked driving had he realised his condition (*Newnham v Trigg* [1970] R.T.R. 107);

(2) the offender is disabled and had no other means of getting home (*Mullarkey v Prescott* [1970] R.T.R. 296), or relies on his vehicle for transport (*R. v Jackson, R. v Hart* (1969) 133 J.P. 358), or that disqualification will cause him serious hardship and/or hardship to his family (*Rennison v Knowler* (1947) 111 J.P. 171; *Taylor v Austin* (1969) 133 J.P. 182; *Reynolds v Roche* [1972] R.T.R. 282; *East v Bladen* [1987] R.T.R. 291);

(3) the offender is a doctor, and the medical services in his area will deteriorate by reason of his being unable to drive (*Holroyd v Berry* [1973] R.T.R. 145), or a soldier on active service who must be in a position to drive (*Gordon v Smith* [1971] R.T.R. 52), or that the offender is a detective engaged in "undercover" activities which involve visiting public houses (*Vaughan v Dunn* [1984] R.T.R. 376);

(4) the offender has an idiosyncratic medical condition or diabetes (*R. v Wickins* (1958) 42 Cr.App.R. 236; *R. v Jackson, R. v Hart* (1969) 133 J.P. 358; *Jarvis v DPP, The Independent*, November 13, 2000);

(5) the offender has to drive because of his domestic situation (*Reynolds v Roche* [1972] R.T.R. 282).

Even less is it any sort of special reason that the court considers the penalty of disqualification too severe (*Williamson v Wilson* [1947] 1 All E.R. 306) or unfair (*Boliston v Gibbons* [1985] R.T.R. 176). The fact that the offence is a trivial one is not a special reason for not *endorsing*, but the court is always entitled to take account of the minor nature of the offence, and the fact that any breach was unintentional (*Hawkins v Roots, Hawkins v Smith* [1976] R.T.R. 49). An incorrect statement by a police officer to the effect that failing to provide a specimen of blood or urine would not necessarily result in disqualification which misled the defendant into refusing to supply such a specimen, can amount to a special reason (*Bobin v DPP* [1999] R.T.R. 375).

Excess alcohol offences

54–035 The vast majority of cases in which offenders seek to put forward special reasons, are those relating to excess alcohol. In deciding whether special reasons exist and whether to exercise discretion the court should consider what would a sober, reasonable and responsible friend of the defendant advise: drive or not? Discretion should be exercised in favour of the driver only if there was a real possibility rather than a mere off-chance that the friend would advise the driver to drive (*DPP v Bristow, The Times*, [1998] R.T.R. 100). The views of the superior courts over a number of years, when analysed, are that in relation to such offences:

(1) in a case under RTA 1988, ss.4, 5 and 7(6), it must be borne in mind that a person who deliberately drives, knowing that he has consumed a considerable quantity of alcohol, presents a potential danger to the public, which no private crisis can lightly excuse;

(2) in a case under s.5, the amount of excess, however small, is not capable of amounting to a special reason—the Act lays down the prescribed statutory limit (*Delaroy Hall v Tadman* (1969) 133 J.P. 127);

(3) the effect of lack of food, or the effect of drink on an empty stomach, is not capable of amounting to a special reason, whether under s.4 or s.5 (*Archer v Woodward* [1959] Crim. L.R. 461; *Knight v Baxter* [1971] R.T.R. 270), *Kinsella v DPP* [2002] EWHC 545 (Admin));

(4) the fact that an offender, unknown to him, was suffering from a disease which produced a greater degree of unfitness than would be present in a normal person, might amount to a special reason under s.4 (*R. v Wickins* (1958) 42 Cr.App.R. 236, but see *DPP v Jowle*, *The Times*, December 13, 1997), as might the fact that he had inhaled industrial fumes at work (*Brewer v MPC* (1969) 133 J.P. 185), but such factors are irrelevant on a conviction under s.5 (*Goldsmith v Laver* [1970] R.T.R. 162), see also *CPS v Jowle* 163 J.P. 85 (mouthwash containing 26.9 per cent alcohol) cf. *R. v Cambridge MC* [1992] R.T.R. 382; a motorist has a duty to enquire what he is drinking (*Robinson v DPP* [2004] Crim.L.R. 670).

(5) the court should rarely, if ever, exercise its discretion in favour of an offender where the alcohol content exceeded 100 mg per 100 ml of blood (*Taylor v. Rajan* [1974] R.T.R. 304; *Vaughan v Dunn* [1984] R.T.R. 376);

(6) the fact that the offender offered a specimen of urine when blood was required of him cannot be taken into account as a special reason (*Grix v Chief Constable of Kent* [1987] R.T.R. 193); and

(7) it is difficult to conceive of a special reason in relation to a contravention of s.7(6) (*R. v Jackson* [1970] 1 Q.B. 647, but see *DPP v Kinnersley* [1993] R.T.R. 105 (genuine fear of contracting AIDS by blowing into machine).

Sudden emergencies

54–036 A sudden emergency may amount to a special reason in cases under ss.4 and 5, as where an unexpected situation arises in which a person who has been drinking but not intending to drive, is impelled to do so by a sudden medical necessity, or in answering an emergency call (*Aichroth v Cottee* (1954) 118 J.P. 499; *Brown v Dyerson* (1969) 132 J.P. 495; *R. v Lundt-Smith* (1964) 128 J.P. 534; *R. v O'Toole* (1971) 55 Cr.App.R. 206).

A burglary at club premises where the driver was a keyholder has been held to be an emergency sufficient to justify a finding of special reasons (*DPP v Cox* [1996] R.T.R. 123, DC).

A threat by a woman to accuse a man of rape unless he drove to a cash point in order to give her money and then drove her home, amounted to special reasons (*DPP v Enston* [1996] R.T.R. 324). See also *DPP v Upchurch* [1994] R.T.R. 366, *DPP v Knight* [1994] R.T.R. 374, *DPP v Whittle* [1996] R.T.R. 154.

In dealing with such cases, the superior courts have said that the whole of the circumstances should be considered, including the nature and degree of the crisis or emergency which caused the offender to take his car onto the road, and:

(1) whether the emergency was sufficiently acute to justify the offender taking out his car;
(2) whether there were alternative means of transport available, or alternative means of dealing with the crisis;
(3) the manner of the offender's driving, the commission of traffic offences may be a consideration telling against exercise of the court's discretion; and
(4) whether the offender otherwise acted responsibly and reasonably.

These matters need to be considered objectively (*Taylor v Rajan* [1974] QB 424; *DPP v Bristow* [1998] R.T.R. 100), and it is not for the court to put itself into the offender's position in assessing "reasonableness". A driver complaining of dizziness and blurred vision did not constitute a medical emergency sufficient to justify a finding of special reasons where the passenger, her husband, who was affected by drink, decided to take over the driving (*DPP v Whittle* [1996] R.T.R. 154, DC). There is a difference in a situation presented to a driver on the outward journey and that on the homeward journey after the emergency has been dealt with (*DPP v Waller* [1989] R.T.R. 112).

It is unlikely that merely travelling to a near relative because of some emotional need will ever be able to amount to a special reason (*Thompson v Diamond* [1985] R.T.R. 316).

"Laced drinks" case

54–037 It is often put forward in excess alcohol cases that the offender's drink had been "laced" by a third party, in order to found a special reason on the ground that the drink which the offender consumed was stronger or more potent than he had anticipated. It is not enough to show that the drink was stronger than he thought.

To be capable of amounting to a special reason:

(1) there must be an element of intervention or misleading by a third party, whereby the offender was induced to take stronger drink than he would normally have done by someone who misled him, or gave him false information;
(2) it must be shown (*Pugsley v Hunter* [1973] R.T.R. 284; *Smith v Geraghty* [1986] R.T.R. 222) and the burden is on the offender to show, that the quantity of alcohol in his blood in excess of the prescribed limit:
   (a) is attributable to additional drink; and
   (b) was put into his glass without his knowledge. This will inevitably involve scientific evidence.

The judge must decide;

(i) whether the facts are capable of amounting to a special reason; and
(ii) additionally, whether the offender should have realised, when he came to drive, that he was not fit to do so by reason of the alcohol present in his body (*Pridige v Grant* [1985] R.T.R. 196; *DPP v Barker* [1990] R.T.R. 1; *Donahue v DPP* [1993] R.T.R. 156).

See also *DPP v Connor* [1992] R.T.R. 66. It is undesirable for the court to let itself be drawn into detailed scientific calculations, even where these are put before it by expert witnesses (*Smith v Geraghty* [1986] R.T.R. 222).

Factors to be considered

54–038 It was suggested in *Chatters v Burke* [1986] R.T.R. 396 that there were seven factors to be considered and taken into account when deciding whether there were special reasons for mitigating the normal consequences of a conviction, namely:

(1) how far was the vehicle driven?
(2) in what manner was it driven?
(3) the state of the vehicle;
(4) whether it was the offender's intention to go further;
(5) the conditions of road and traffic prevailing;
(6) the reason for the car being driven; and
(7) most importantly of all, whether there was a danger of the offender's coming into contact with pedestrians or other road users.

The mere fact that the offence occurred late at night, at a time and place where there were not many people about, or that the offender was merely re-parking, is not of itself capable of amounting to a special reason for not disqualifying. It might, however, amount to a special reason to show that the offender drove only a few yards in circumstances where his manoeuvres were unlikely to bring him into contact with other road users (*Mullarkey v Prescott* [1970] R.T.R. 296; *Coombs v Kehoe* [1972] 1 W.L.R. 797; and *cf. Haime v Walklett* (1983) 5 Cr.App.R.(S.) 165) but *cf DPP v Humphries* [2000] R.T.R. 52, where the offender's intention was to drive some distance had he not been apprehended; see also *DPP v Conroy* [2004] 1 Cr.App.R.(S.) 37.

Proof of special reasons

54–039 The burden of proving circumstances amounting to a special reason lies upon the offender; the standard is that of a "balance of probabilities". The court should take into account, any:

(1) relevant admissible evidence, given on oath;
(2) any admissions made in accordance with CJA 1967, s.10;
(3) any "expert reports" tendered and admissible by virtue of CJA 1988, s.30; and
(4) any submissions made by the Crown and/or defence counsel, but

evidence from the offender as to what he has heard since the incident, does not qualify (*James v Morgan* [1988] R.T.R. 85).

5. New drivers

54–040 The Road Traffic (New Drivers) Act 1995 provides for the revocation of the driving licences of new drivers who accumulate six or more penalty points within a probationary period of two years after the driver first qualified. A driver whose licence is thus revoked must pass a further test to regain his entitlement to drive.

55 SEARCH AND ACCESS WARRANTS ETC

55–001 A judge of the Crown Court may grant a production order or a search warrant under PACE 1984, and a number of orders under PCA 2002. He may grant access to bankers books under BBEA 1879, and may issue Letters of Request under CJA 1988. As to proceedings under C(IC)A 2003, ss.13–15, for the taking of evidence for overseas proceedings, see 55–033 below.

A. The Police and Criminal Evidence Act 1984

55–002 Jurisdiction is conferred upon a Circuit judge, but not upon the Crown Court (thus a Recorder has no such jurisdiction (*R. v CCC Ex p. Francis & Francis* [1988] 3 W.L.R. 989)), to entertain an application by an investigating officer to gain access to special procedure and excluded material (it makes no provision for access to legally privileged material, as to which see *R. v ILCC Ex p. Baines & Baines* (1988) 87 Cr.App.R. 111 and *R. v CCC Ex p. Francis & Francis* [1988] 3 W.L.R. 989, HL). See also *Hallinan Blackburn Gittings & Nott (A Firm) v Middlesex Guildhall CC, The Times*, November 29, 2004. He may, if he thinks fit, hear the application in chambers (*R. v CCC Ex p. DPP The Times*, April 1, 1988).

An application under PACE 1984 (as opposed to one under PCA 2002 (see 55–011 below) is appropriate where production of the material is sought for criminal investigation purposes, to determine whether an offence has been committed, and, if so, to provide evidence of it (*R. v Southwark CC* [1996] 4 All E.R. 961).

1. Production order

55–003 If, on an application made by a constable or a designated member of SOCA, a judge is satisfied that one or other of the sets of access conditions set out below is fulfilled, he may make an order that the person who appears to be in possession of the material to which the application relates:

(1) produce it to a constable or a member of SOCA for him to take away; or
(2) give him access to it,

not later than the end of the period of seven days from the making of the order, or such longer period as he may specify. Special rules apply under para.5, as amended by CJPA 2001, Sch.2, para.14, in relation to material stored in any electronic form.

A person who fails to comply with an order may be dealt with by a judge as if he had committed a contempt of the Crown Court, and enactments relating to contempt of that court have effect in relation to the matter.

Inter partes application

55–004 The preferred method of proceeding should always be by way of an *inter partes* order under para.4, after notice of application served under para.8 (*R. v Maidstone CC Ex p. Waitt* [1988] Crim.L.R. 384).

The application:

(1) must be accompanied by a document or documents containing a description of the material for which discovery is sought (*R. v CCC Ex p. Adegbesan* (1987) 84 Cr.App.R. 219), though there may be occasions on which oral information is sufficient (*R. v Manchester CC Ex p. Taylor* (1988) 87 Cr.App.R. 358);
(2) must state the general nature of the offence under investigation, though it is not necessary to state the precise section of any enactment (*R. v Manchester CC Ex p. Taylor* (above));
(3) may be served on the person concerned by leaving it at his proper address, or by posting it to him in a registered letter or by recorded delivery;
(4) may be served on one of the partners of a firm, or on the secretary, clerk, etc. of a corporation;
(5) must state the address of the premises where the material is alleged to be (*R. v CCC Ex p. Carr*, *The Independent*, March 5, May 13, 1987); and
(6) when served, prohibits the concealment, destruction, alteration or disposal of the material until the application has been dismissed or abandoned, or an order has been complied with.

Whatever material is given to the judge must be served upon the party against whom the order is sought; statements which have no substance, and which are to the prejudice of the party against whom the order is sought, ought to be ruled out by the judge (*R. v ILCC Ex p. Baines & Baines* (1988) 87 Cr.App.R. 111).

The Act does not require the suspect to be given notice when the evidence sought is in the hands of a third party (*R. v Leicester CC Ex p. DPP* [1987] 3 All E.R. 654).

The "access conditions"

55–005 Before granting an order, the judge must himself be satisfied that one or other of the access conditions contained in paras 2 and 3 of the Schedule are made out; it is not enough that the applicant believes them to be satisfied (*R. v CCC, etc.* [2002] Crim.L.R. 65). Although the strict rules of evidence do not apply to a hearing there must be evidence that the relevant set of access conditions has been fulfilled. The Act sets out two sets of "access conditions." PACE 1984, s.11

55–006 **"The first set of access conditions"** is fulfilled if:

(1) there are reasonable grounds for believing:
  (a) that a serious arrestable offence (as defined in Sch.5 to the Act) has been committed;
  (b) that there is material which consists of special procedure material as defined under s.14 or includes special procedure material and does not also include excluded material on premises specified in the application;
  (c) that the material is likely to be of substantial value (whether by itself or together with other material) to the investigation in connection with which the application is made; and
  (d) that the material is likely to be relevant evidence;

(2) other methods of obtaining the material:
  (a) have been tried without success; or
  (b) have not been tried because it appeared that they were bound to fail; and

(3) it is in the public interest, having regard:
  (a) to the benefit likely to accrue to the investigation if the material is obtained; and
  (b) to the circumstances under which the person in possession of the material holds it,

  that it should be produced or that access should be given to it.

55–007 **"The second set of access conditions"** is fulfilled if:

(1) there are reasonable grounds for believing that there is material which consists of or includes excluded material or special procedure material on premises specified in the application;

(2) but for s.9(2) of the Act a search of the premises for that material could have been authorised by the issue of a warrant to a constable under an enactment; and
(3) the issue of such a warrant would have been appropriate. PACE 1984, s.9, Sch.1, paras 12–15

Definitions

55–008 The following expressions are defined in the Act:
"Excluded material" as:

(1) personal records which a person has acquired or created in the course of any trade, business, profession or other occupation or for the purposes of any paid or unpaid office and which he holds in confidence; and
(2) human tissue or tissue fluid which has been taken for the purpose of diagnosis or medical treatment and which a person holds in confidence; and
(3) journalistic material which a person holds in confidence and which consists of:
  (a) documents, or
  (b) records other than documents.

A person holds material other than journalistic material in confidence for these purposes if he holds it subject:

(a) to an express or implied understanding to hold it in confidence; or
(b) to a restriction on disclosure or an obligation of secrecy contained in any enactment, including an enactment contained in an Act passed after PACE 1984.

A person holds journalistic material in confidence for those purposes if:

(i) he holds it subject to such an undertaking, restriction or obligation; and
(ii) it has been continuously held (by one or more persons) subject to such an undertaking, restriction or obligation since it was first acquired or created for the purposes of journalism.

Where the first set of access conditions is made out, the judge may make a production order even where it might infringe the privilege against self-incrimination (*R. v CCC Ex p. Bright, etc.* [2001] 2 All E.R. 244). Though in exercising his discretion, he should consider the implications of self-incrimination.

2. Search warrant

55–009 There will be cases where a production access order is likely to be obstructed, where only a search warrant will be appropriate, but an application under para.12 must not become a matter of common form, and where such a search is authorised the High Court has said that the reason for authorising it ought to be made clear (*R. v Maidstone CC, Ex p. Waitt* (above); *R. v Leeds CC, Ex p. Switalski* [1991] Crim.L.R. 559). Nevertheless, if, on application made by a constable or a designated member of SOCA, a circuit judge is satisfied that:

(1) either set of the access conditions set out above is fulfilled (see 55–006, 55–007 above); and
(2) that:
  (a) it is not practicable to communicate with any person entitled to grant entry to the premises to which the application relates;
  (b) it is practicable to communicate with such person, but not with any person entitled to grant access to the material;
  (c) the material contains information subject to a restriction or obligation of confidentiality (defined in s.11(2)(b) of the Act) and which is likely to be disclosed in breach of it if a warrant is not issued; or
  (d) that service of a notice of application for an access order might seriously prejudice the investigation,

he may issue a warrant authorising entry to and search of the premises under that warrant; anything for which a search has been authorised may be seized and retained.

Approach to application

55–010 An application is made *ex parte*. The authorities show that since the issue of a warrant is a very serious interference with the liberty of the subject:

(1) it should be issued only after the "most mature careful consideration of all the facts of the case" (*Williams v Summerfield* [1972] 2 Q.B. 512);
(2) the responsibility for ensuring that the procedure is not abused lies with the judge, who should be scrupulous in discharging that responsibility (*R. v Maidstone CC Ex p. Waitt* [1988] C.L.R. 384);
(3) in a case of complexity, it should not go through "on the nod", but the judge ought to give his reasons for granting the warrant, showing that he has taken the appropriate

matters into account (*R. v Southwark CC Ex p. Sorsky Defries* [1996] C.O.D. 117).

B. Proceeds of Crime Act 2002

55–011 Under PCA 2002, a judge entitled to exercise Crown Court jurisdiction may be called upon, in relation to confiscation, investigation and money laundering cases, to make orders as follows: R.62.3

(1) a production order (ss.345 to 351) requiring a person to produce any relevant material which is in his possession or under his control;
(2) a search and seizure warrant (ss.352 to 356) where a "production order" is not complied with or the requirements for the issue of a production order" are not available;
(3) a disclosure order (ss.357 to 362) requiring persons to give the DARA any relevant information; PCA 2002, s.345(4)
(4) a customer information order (ss.363 to 369) requiring a financial institution to provide information relating to the affairs of a customer;
(5) an account monitoring order (ss.370 to 375) requiring a financial institution to provide details of transactions on a particular account over a specified period of time;
(6) Letters of Request (s.376) requesting assistance relating to evidence arising outside the UK.

As to the Code of Practice issued by the Home Secretary under PCA 2002, s.377, see The Proceeds of Crime Act 2002 (Investigations in England, Wales and Northern Ireland: Code of Practice) Order 2003, SI 2003/334. PCA 2002, ss.345(1), 351(1)

In relation to applications for the purpose of a civil recovery investigation, jurisdiction is reserved to a judge of the High Court.

It was said under the previous legislation that applications under these provisions are to be contrasted with those under PACE 1984, s.9 since they are essentially appropriate where the dominant purpose of the application is to determine, in respect of a criminal offence, whether, and, if so to what extent, a person has benefited from it, or the whereabouts of any proceeds (*R. v Guildford CC* [1996] 4 All E.R. 961). PCA 2002, ss.345(2), (3)

Proof of identity and accreditation

55–012 In relation to order under PCA 2002, where:

(1) an appropriate officer (within the meaning of s.378, 55–020, below) makes an application for:

(a) a production order (s.345);
(b) a customer imformation order (s.363);
(c) an account monitoring order (s.370); PCA 2002, s.345(5)

for the purposes of a confiscation investigation or a money laundering investigation; or

(2) the DARA makes an application for a disclosure order (s.357) for the purposes of a confiscation investigation,

the appropriate officer or the Director must (subject to s.449 which provides for members of the staff of the Agency to use pseudonyms) as the case may be, must provide the judge with proof of his identity and, if he is a financial investigator, his accreditation under PCA 2002, s.3. PCA 2002, s.346

1. Production order

55–013 A production order is an order either requiring:

(1) the person the application for the order specifies as appearing to be in possession or control of material to produce it to an appropriate officer for him to take away, or
(2) the person to give an appropriate officer access to the material, within the period stated in the order.

A judge exercising the jurisdiction of the Crown Court may, on an application made to him by an appropriate officer, make a production order if he is satisfied that each of the requirements for the making of the order (set out at 55–014 below) is fulfilled.

An application for a production order (or an order to grant entry) may be made *ex parte* in chambers.

A specimen application and a draft production order are included in the Code of Practice, issued under s.337, see SI 2003/334.

The application must state that a specified person is subject to a confiscation, investigation or a money laundering investigation, and must also state that: PCA 2002, s.347

(a) the order is sought for the purposes of the investigation;
(b) the order is sought in relation to material, or material of a description, specified in the application; and
(c) a person specified in the application appears to be in possession or control of the material.

As to proof of the identity and accreditation of the applicant, see 55–012 above.

PCA 2002, ss.348(1)–(4)

The period stated in the order will be a period of seven days beginning with the day on which it is made, unless it appears to the judge by whom it is made that a longer or shorter period would be appropriate in the particular circumstances.

Requirements for making an order

55–014 Before making an order the judge must be satisfied that there are reasonable grounds for:

PCA 2002, ss.348(5)–(7)

(1) suspecting that:
  (a) in the case of a confiscation investigation, the person the application for the order specifies as being subject to the investigation has benefited from his criminal conduct;
  (b) in the case of a money laundering investigation, the person the application for the order specifies as being subject to the investigation has committed a money laundering offence; and
(2) believing that the person the application specifies as appearing to be in possession or control of the material so specified is in possession or control of it;
(3) believing that the material is likely to be of substantial value (whether or not by itself) to the investigation for the purposes of which the order is sought;
(4) believing that it is in the public interest for the material to be produced or for access to it to be given, having regard to:
  (a) the benefit likely to accrue to the investigation if the material is obtained;
  (b) the circumstances under which the person the application specifies as appearing to be in possession or control of the material holds it.

PCA 2002, ss.351(3)–(5)

Order granting entry

55–015 Where the judge makes a production order requiring a person to give an appropriate officer access to material on any premises, he may, on an application made to him by an appropriate officer and specifying the premises, make an order to grant entry in relation to the premises.

Such an order requires any person who appears to an appropriate officer to be entitled to grant entry to the premises to allow him to enter the premises to obtain access to the material.

Privileged material

55–016 A production order: PCA 2002, s.352(1), (2), (6)

(1) does not require a person to produce, or give access to, privileged material, i.e. material which the person would be entitled to refuse to produce on grounds of legal professional privilege in proceedings in the High Court;
(2) does not require a person to produce, or give access to, excluded material;
(3) has effect in spite of any restriction on the disclosure of information (however imposed).

Retention of material

PCA 2002, ss.252(2), (3)

55–017 An appropriate officer (see 55–020, below) may take copies of any material which is produced, or to which access is given, in compliance with the order and material produced in compliance with the order may be retained for so long as it is necessary to retain it (as opposed to copies of it) in connection with the investigation for the purposes of which the order was made, but if an appropriate officer has reasonable grounds for believing that: PCA 2002, s.252(5)

(1) the material may need to be produced for the purposes of any legal proceedings, and
(2) it might otherwise be unavailable for those purposes, it may be retained until the proceedings are concluded.

Special cases

55–018 Special provisions apply under s.349 to computer information, and under s.350 to government departments. PCA 2002, s.378

Discharge and variation

55–019 An application to discharge or vary a production order or an order to grant entry may be made to a judge of the Crown Court by: PCA 2002, ss.353(1), (2)

(1) the person who applied for the order;
(2) any person affected by the order and

the judge may discharge or vary the order.

If an accredited financial investigator, a constable or a customs officer applies for an order an application to discharge or vary the order need not be by the same accredited financial investigator, constable or customs officer.

Search and Access Warrants Etc

2. Search and seizure warrants

55–020 A judge may, on an application made to him by an appropriate officer (below) issue a search and seizure warrant if he is satisfied that either of the requirements for the issuing of the warrant is fulfilled, these are that a production order made in relation to material has not been complied with and there are reasonable grounds for believing that the material is on the premises specified in the application for the warrant, or that s.353 is satisfied in relation to the warrant. PCA 2002, ss.353(3), (4)

An application for such a warrant must state that a person specified in the application is subject to a confiscation investigation or a money laundering investigation.

The application must also state that the warrant is sought;

(1) for the purposes of the investigation;
(2) in relation to the premises specified in the application;
(3) in relation to material specified in the application, or that there are reasonable grounds for believing that there is material falling within ss.353(6), (7) or (8) on the premises.

A search and seizure warrant is a warrant authorising an appropriate person to enter and search the premises specified in the application for the warrant, and to seize and retain any material found there which is likely to be of substantial value (whether or not by itself) to the investigation for the purposes of which the application is made. PCA 2002, ss.353(5), (9)

A specimen application and a draft form of search and seizure warrant are included in the Code of Practice issued under s.377, see SI 2003/334.

"An appropriate officer" is, for the purposes of a confiscation investigation or a money laundering investigation, the Director, an accredited financial agent, a constable or an officer of Revenue and Customs.

Requirements where production order not available

55–021 A search and seizure warrant may be issued where there are reasonable grounds for suspecting that:

(1) in the case of a confiscation investigation, the person specified in the application for the warrant has benefited from his criminal conduct; or
(2) in the case of a money laundering investigation, the person specified in the application for the warrant has committed a money laundering offence; and PCA 2002, s.353(6)

(3) either the first or the second set of conditions is complied with.

55–022 **The first set of conditions** is that there are reasonable grounds for believing that:

(a) any material on the premises specified in the application for the warrant is likely to be of substantial value (whether or not by itself) to the investigation for the purposes of which the warrant is sought, PCA 2002, s.353(8)
(b) it is in the public interest for the material to be obtained, having regard to the benefit likely to accrue to the investigation if the material is obtained, and
(c) it would not be appropriate to make a production order for any one or more of the following:
  (i) that it is not practicable to communicate with any person against whom the production order could be made;
  (ii) that it is not practicable to communicate with any person who would be required to comply with an order to grant entry to the premises;
  (iii) that the investigation might be seriously prejudiced unless an appropriate person is able to secure immediate access to the material. PCA 2002, s.357

55–023 **The second set of conditions** is that:

(1) there are reasonable grounds for believing that there is material on the premises specified in the application for the warrant and that the material falls within subss.(6), (7) or (8),
(2) there are reasonable grounds for believing that it is in the public interest for the material to be obtained, having regard to the benefit likely to accrue to the investigation if the material is obtained, and
(3) any one or more of the requirements in subs.(9) is met, i.e.:
  (a) that it is not practicable to communicate with any person entitled to grant entry to the premises;
  (b) that entry to the premises will not be granted unless a warrant is produced;
  (c) that the investigation might be seriously prejudiced unless an appropriate person arriving at the premises is able to secure immediate entry to them.

In the case of a confiscation investigation, material falls within this provision if it cannot be identified at the time of the application but it relates to the person specified in the application, and the question whether he has benefited from his criminal conduct or any question as to the extent or whereabouts of his benefit from his criminal conduct, and is likely to be of substantial value (whether or not by itself) to the investigation for the purposes of which the warrant is sought. PCA 2002, s.358

In the case of a money laundering investigation, material falls within this provision if it cannot be identified at the time of the application but it relates to the person specified in the application or the question whether he has committed a money laundering offence, and is likely to be of substantial value (whether or not by itself) to the investigation for the purposes of which the warrant is sought.

An "appropriate person" is, if the warrant is sought for the purposes of a confiscation investigation or a money laundering investigation, a constable or a customs officer.

3. Disclosure orders

General

55–024 A judge may, on the application of the Director, make a disclosure order if he is satisfied that each of the requirements for the making of the order is fulfilled, save that no application for a disclosure order may be made in relation to a money laundering investigation.

The application must state that:

(1) a person specified is subject to a confiscation investigation which is being carried out by the Director and the order is sought for the purposes of the investigation, or PCA 2002, s.362
(2) property specified is subject to a civil recovery investigation and the order is sought for the purposes of the investigation.

A disclosure order is an order authorising the Director to give to any person he considers has relevant information notice in writing requiring him, with respect to any matter relevant to the investigation for the purposes of which the order is sought, to:

(a) answer questions, either at a time specified in the notice or at once, at a place so specified; PCA 2002, s.363
(b) provide information specified in the notice, by a time and in a manner so specified;
(c) produce documents, or documents of a description, specified in the notice, either at or by a time so specified or at once, and in a manner so specified.

As to proof of the identity and accreditation of the applicant, see 55–012 above.

Requirements for making order

55–025 For the making of a disclosure order there must be reasonable grounds for suspecting that in the case of a:

(1) confiscation investigation, the person specified in the application for the order has benefited from his criminal conduct;
(2) civil recovery investigation, the property specified in the application for the order is recoverable property or associated property.

There must be reasonable grounds for believing that information which may be provided in compliance with a requirement imposed under the order is likely to be of substantial value (whether or not, by itself) to the investigation for the purposes of which the order is sought.

There must be reasonable grounds for believing that it is in the public interest for the information to be provided, having regard to the benefit likely to accrue to the investigation if the information is obtained.

The order takers effect in spite of any restrictions on the disclosure of information, however imposed (s.351(6)); as to matters of legal privilege and excluded material, see ss.361(1)–(5). Restrictions are imposed on the use of such statements, by s.360.

Procedure

55–026 An application for a disclosure order may be made *ex parte* to a judge in chambers; Rules of Court may make provision as to the practice and procedure to be followed in connection with the proceedings. PCA 2002, s.358

An application to discharge or vary an order may be made to a judge by the Director or by any person affected by it.

4. Customer information order

Nature of order; application

55–027 A judge may, on the application of an appropriate officer (above, 55–020) make a customer information order if he is satisfied that each of the requirements for the making of the order is fulfilled.

Such an order is an order that a financial institution covered by the application for the order must, on being required to do so by notice in writing given by an appropriate officer, provide any such customer information (as defined in PCA 2002, s.364) as it has relating to the person specified in the application. A financial institution which is required to provide information under a customer information order must provide the information to an appropriate officer in such manner, and at or by such time, as an appropriate officer requires.

An application for a customer information order:

(1) *must* state that:
  (a) a person specified in the application is subject to a confiscation investigation or a money laundering investigation; or
  (b) property specified in the application is subject to a civil recovery investigation and a person specified in the application appears to hold the property;
  (c) the order is sought for the purposes of the investigation; PCA 2002, s.370
  (d) the order is sought against the financial institution or financial institutions specified in the application.

(2) *may* specify:
  (a) all financial institutions,
  (b) a particular description, or particular descriptions, of financial institutions, or
  (c) a particular financial institution or particular financial institutions.

A specimen application, a draft customer information order and a specimen notice in writing, are included in the Code of Practice issued under s.377. See SI 2003/334.

Requirements for making order

55–028 For the making of a disclosure order there must be reasonable grounds for suspecting that in the case of a:

(1) confiscation investigation, the person specified in the application for the order has benefited from his criminal conduct;
(2) a civil recovery investigation, the property specified in the application for the order is recoverable property or associated property.

There must be reasonable grounds for believing that information which may be provided in compliance with a requirement imposed under the order is likely to be of substantial value (whether or not, by itself) to the investigation for the purposes of which the order is sought.

There must be reasonable grounds for believing that it is in the public interest for the information to be provided, having regard to the benefit likely to accrue to the investigation if the information is obtained.

The order takes effect in spite of any restrictions on the disclosure of information, however imposed (s.368).

Restrictions are imposed on the use of such statements, by s.367.

As to applications to vary or discharge, see s.369, and r.62.2(1) (2).

As to proof of the identity and accreditation of the applicant, see 55–012, above.

5. Account monitoring order

55–029 A judge may, on an application made to him by an appropriate officer (55–020, above) make an account monitoring order if he is satisfied that each of the requirements set out below is fulfilled. PCA 2002, s.371

An account monitoring order is an order that the financial institution specified in the application for the order must, for the period stated in the order, provide account information of the description specified in the order to an appropriate officer in the manner, and at or by the time or times, stated in the order. The period stated in an account monitoring order must not exceed the period of 90 days beginning with the day on which the order is made.

The application for an order must state that:

(1) a person specified in the application is subject to a confiscation investigation or a money laundering investigation; or
(2) property specified in the application is subject to a civil recovery investigation and a person specified in the application appears to hold the property; and
(3) that the order is sought for the purposes of the investigation, or is sought against the financial institution specified in the application in relation to account information of the description specified.

A specimen application and a draft account monitoring order are included in the Code of Practice issued under s.377, see SI 2003/334.

"Account information" is information relating to an account or accounts held at the financial institution specified in the application by the person specified (whether solely or jointly with another).

The application may specify information relating to: BBEA 1879, s.7

(a) all accounts held by the person specified in the application for the order at the financial institution so specified;
(b) a particular description, or particular descriptions, of accounts so held; or
(c) a particular account, or particular accounts, so held.

A copy of any order made will be given by the Crown Court officer to the financial institution specified in the application (R.62.1(1)).

Requirements for making the order

55–030 In the case of:

(1) a confiscation investigation, there must be reasonable grounds for suspecting that the person specified in the application for the order has benefited from his criminal conduct;
(2) a civil recovery investigation, there must be reasonable grounds for suspecting that the property specified in the application for the order is recoverable property or associated property, and that the person specified in the application holds all or some of the property;
(3) a money laundering investigation, there must be reasonable grounds for suspecting that the person specified in the application for the order has committed a money laundering offence. C(IC)A 2003, s.7

There must be reasonable grounds for believing that information which may be provided in compliance with a requirement imposed under the order is likely to be of substantial value (whether or not by itself) to the investigation for the purposes of which the order is sought.

There must be reasonable grounds for believing that it is in the public interest for the information to be provided, having regard to the benefit likely to accrue to the investigation if the information is obtained.

As to proof of the identity and accreditation of the applicant, see 55–012, above. CCR r.32

The order takes effect in spite of any restrictions on the disclosure of information, however imposed (s.374). As to applications to vary or discharge, see s.375 and rr.62.1(2), (3).

C. Bankers' Books Evidence Act 1879

55–031 A judge may, on the application of any party to legal proceedings, order that such a party be at liberty to inspect and take copies of any entry in a banker's book for any of the purposes of such proceedings. That order may be made with or without summoning the bank or other party, and must be served on the bank three clear days before the order is to be obeyed, unless the judge otherwise orders.

Note that:

(1) before making the order the judge should satisfy himself that the application is not solely a "fishing expedition" to find material on which to hang a charge, but should consider whether the prosecution, who normally make such an application, have in their possession other evidence against the accused (*Williams v Summerfield* (1972) 56 Cr.App.R. 597);

(2) the order ought to be limited to a certain specific period, and ought not to be oppressive (*Ex p. Simpson* (1980) 70 Cr.App.R. 291); and C(IC)A 2003, ss.113–15, Sch.1

(3) the mere fact that the accused has given notice of intention to plead guilty is not a reason for refusing an order (*Owen v Sambrook* [1981] Crim.L.R. 329).

D. Letters of request

55–032 Where, on an application made to him, it appears to a judge that:

(1) an offence has been committed or that there are reasonable grounds for suspecting that an offence has been committed; and

(2) proceedings in respect of the offence have been or that the offence is being investigated,

he may request assistance in obtaining outside the UK any evidence specified in his request for use in the proceedings or investigation.

Applying for letters of request

55–033 Notice under s.3(1) is given to the Crown Court officer. It must:

(1) be made in writing, save that the court may in exceptional circumstances dispense with the need for notice;

(2) state the particulars of the offence which it is alleged has been committed or the grounds upon which it is suspected that an offence has been committed;
(3) state whether proceedings in respect of the offence have been instituted or the offence is being investigated; and
(4) include particulars of the assistance requested in the form of a draft letter of request.

The application is heard *ex parte*, and in addition and without prejudice to any other powers of the court to hear proceedings *in camera*, the court may, when hearing the application, if it thinks it necessary in the interests of justice, direct that the public be excluded from the court.

No such form of application is contained in CPR 2005.

E. Evidence for use overseas

55–034 Where a request, under the Crime (International Co-operation) Act 2003, for assistance in obtaining evidence in England and Wales is received, and the Secretary of State nominates the Crown Court to receive any evidence to which the request relates which appears appropriate to that court for the purpose of giving effect to the request or part, the following provisions apply, and:

(1) the judge has the like powers for securing the attendance of a witness as he has for the purposes of other proceedings before the court (see 12 BENCH AND WITNESS WARRANT);
(2) the court may take evidence on oath;
(3) rule 32.4 makes provision in respect of the persons entitled to appear or take part in the proceedings and for excluding the public from the proceedings; and r.32.5–9 make provision for other miscellaneous matters, such as record, interpretation, TV and telephone links;
(4) in relation to the privilege of witnesses,
    (a) a person cannot be compelled to give any evidence which he could not be compelled to give:
        (i) in criminal proceedings in England and Wales, or
        (ii) in criminal proceedings in the country from which the request for the evidence has come, provided his claim to be exempt from giving the

evidence is conceded by the court or authority which made the request; if it is not, he may be required to give the evidence to which the claim relates, but the evidence may not be forwarded to the court or authority which requested it, if a court in the country in question, on the matter being referred to it, upholds the claim.

(b) a person cannot be compelled to give any evidence if his doing so would be prejudicial to the security of the UK (a certificate signed by or on behalf of the Secretary of State is conclusive);

(c) a person cannot be compelled to give any evidence in his capacity as an officer or servant of the Crown.

(5) The evidence received by the court must be given to the court or authority that made the request or to the Secretary of State for forwarding to the court or authority that made the request; so far as may be necessary in order to comply with the request, where the evidence consists of:

(a) a document, the original or a copy must be provided,

(b) any other article, the article itself, or a description, photograph or other representation of it, must be provided.

(6) BBEA 1879 (above) applies to the proceedings as it applies to other proceedings before the court;

(7) No order for costs may be made.

"Evidence" is not confined to direct evidence for use at trial, and may extend to information which might lead to the discovery of evidence (*R. v Home Secretary Ex p. Finniuest SpA* [1997] 1 Cr.App.R. 257) (a decision under the 1990 Act). As to references to the DFFO, see *R. (Evans) v DSFO* [2003] W.L.R. 299 as to the application of "section 2 notices" (under CJA 1988, s.2).

56 SEX OFFENDER ORDERS

General

56–001 SOA 2003, repeals:

(1) SOA 1997, Pt 1, as amended by CJCSA 2000, relating to the registration of sex offenders, and abolishes restraining orders under s.5A;
(2) CDA 1998, amended by PRA 2002, and abolishes sex offender orders under that Act;

but retains the "disqualification from working with children order" under CJCSA 2000, Pt 2, see below.

The majority of these provisions, however, are re-enacted in a different form.

Of the four new orders introduced by SOA 2003: SOA 2003, s.104(1)–(3)

(a) only the sex offenders prevention order (SOPO) may be made by a judge on the conviction of an offender;
(b) notification orders, foreign travel orders under ss.114–122, and risk of sexual harm orders (RSHOs) fall to be made by magistrates' courts on the application of chief officers of police.

A. Certification

56–002 For the purposes of the notification requirements on SOA 2003, Pt 2, a certificate is required in the case of any person: SOA 2003, s.113(3)

(1) convicted of an offence listed in Sch.3 (listed in APPENDIX A, SECTION 5), or
(2) found not guilty of such an offence by reason of insanity, or
(3) found to be under a disability and to have done the act charged against him, in respect of such an offence.

The judge should certify those facts in open court, either at the time of sentence or subsequently that:

(a) on that date he was convicted, found not guilty as in (2) above, or found to be under a disability in the circumstances stated in (3) above,

(b) that the offence in question is an offence listed in Sch.3, and
(c) that he is so certifying (*R. v G (Sex Offender): Registration*), *The Times*, January 26, 2000),

so that the certificate may be used as evidence in later proceedings (see also *R. v Rawlinson, The Times*, October 14, 1999).

The imposition of a conditional or absolute discharge is not a "conviction" for these purposes and does not activate the procedure under s.92 (*R. v Longworth, The Times*, February 1, 2006, HL).

B. Sexual offences prevention order (SOPO)

General

56–003 A SOPO replaces both the sex offender order and the retraining order under the previous legislation.

Where the judge:

(1) deals with an offender, in respect of an offence listed in SOA 2003, Schs 3 or 5 (see APPENDIX A, SECTIONS 5 and 6); or
(2) deals with an accused in respect of a finding that he is:
   (a) not guilty of an offence listed in Sch.3 or 5 by reason of insanity, or
   (b) under a disability and has done the act charged against him in respect of such an offence; and
(3) is satisfied that it is *necessary* to make such an order, for the purpose of protecting the public, or any particular members of the public from serious sexual harm from the offender

he may make a SOPO prohibiting the offender from doing those things prescribed in the order. The judge must not make an order unless he considers it "necessary". The fact that it is "appropriate" is not sufficient (*R. v Halloren* [2004] 2 Cr.App.R.(S.) 57. The protection required is against "serious sexual harm". The focus of s.104 is thje risk of future offences; the judge must, therefore, conduct a risk assessment and consider the likelihood of the offender committing further Sch.3 offences (*R. v D* [2006] Crim.L.R.364).

The order has effect for a specified fixed period (of not less than five years) or until further notice (s.107(1)(2)). The prohibitions are those necessary for the purpose of protecting the public or any particular member of the public from serious sexual harm from him, that is from serious physical or psychological harm caused by his committing one or more offences listed in Sch.3.

Breach of the order is an offence carrying five years on indictment (s.113(2)); the Act expressly excludes the making of a conditional discharge (s.113(3)).

The effect of such an order on the notification provisions of SOA 2003, is set out at s.107(2), (4). Where a sexual offences prevention order is made in relation to a person already subject to such an order (whether made by that court or another), the earlier order ceases to have effect.

Orders in relation to siblings

56–004 Where the judge is considering making a sexual offences prevention order to protect from abuse within the family, particularly a sibling of the abused person, there is, and it might be desirable, to draft the order in terms that provide a link with the court's family jurisdiction.

CJCSA 2000, ss.28, 29; SOA 2003, Sch.8, para.44(5)

Under SOA 2003, s.104(1) the judge "may" make an SOPO (there is a discretion) if he is satisfied that it is "necessary" to do so to protect any member of the public from serious sexual harm from the defendant. The conduct against which protection is necessary is defined in s.106(3). When regard is had to the wording in the context of s.104 as a whole it is clear that it is the risk of future offending. Where the victim has a sibling living in the same family, the judge must conduct a risk assessment and consider:

(1) the likelihood of the offender committing a further Sch.3 offence; and
(2) the sibling being caused serious physical or psychological harm as a result, even if the offence was not directed against him.

Where the judge considers that there is a risk that the offender will in future commit one or more Sch.3 offences which, unless the sibling is protected by a SOPO, will cause him to suffer serious psychological harm it is necessary to make such an order. Under s.108 the persons who may apply for the SOPO to be varied do not include a sibling or anyone acting on his behalf. There may be occasions when a SOPO is made to protect a child of the offender where the family court's jurisdiction should be reflected in the order because of the additional flexibility that it provides. The judge has jurisdiction to make a SOPO in the following terms: "[the offender] shall not, without the order of a judge exercising jurisdiction under the *Children Act 1989*, communicate or seek to communicate, whether directly or indirectly with [the sibling] whilst he remains under the age of 16 years". In that way the child's interest in a possibly changing situation can better be met than through the blunt instrument of the SOPO alone.

R. v D (Sexual Offences Prevention Order) The Times, January 3, 2006).

Variation, renewal and discharge

56–005 Variation, renewal and discharge of such an order, under SOA 2003, s.108 is dealt with under 14 BREACH, AMENDMENT AND DISCHARGE.

CJCSA 2000, s.29A; CJA 2003, s.299, Sch.30, para.2

C. Disqualification from working with children orders

Mandatory order

56–006 Where a person is:

(1) (a) *convicted* of an offence against a child as defined in Sch.4, (as to which see APPENDIX A, SECTION 5) committed when he was aged 18 or over, and is a "qualifying" sentence imposed in respect of that offence; or

(b) *charged* with such an offence, committed when he was aged 18 or over, and a relevant order is made by the judge in respect of the act or omission charged against him as the offence,

the judge *must* order him to be disqualified from working with children, but must not so order if he is satisfied, having regard to all the circumstances, that (the offender establishes on a balance of probabilities (*R. v Clayton* [2004] 1 Cr.App.R.(S.) 29) that it is unlikely that he will commit any further offence against a child.

CJCSA 2000, s.29A; CJA 2003, s.299, Sch.30, para.2

If he does not make an order, the judge must give his reasons for not doing so and cause them to be included in the record of the proceedings.

(2) (a) is convicted of an offence against a child (as defined in Sch.4) committed at a time when he was under the age of 18 and a "qualifying" sentence is imposed in respect of it; or

(b) is *charged* with such an offence committed when he was under the of 18 and a relevant order is made by the judge in respect of the act or omission charged against him as the offence,

the judge must, if he is satisfied, having regard to all the circumstances that it is likely (the test is "probability, not the criminal standard of proof" (*R. v G* [2002] Cr.App.R.(S.) 1) that that person will commit a further offence against a child, order that he be disqualified from working with children.

Where he makes such an order, the judge must state his reasons for so doing and cause these reasons to be included in the record of the proceedings.

Discretionary order

CJCSA 2000, s.30; CJA 2003, s.299, Sch.30, paras 3, 4

56–007 Where:

(1) a person is convicted of an offence against a child (whether or not committed when he was aged 18 or over),
(2) that person is sentenced by the Crown Court (or CACD), and
(3) no "qualifying" sentence is imposed in respect of the conviction,

if the judge is satisfied, having regard to all the circumstances, that it is likely that the individual will commit a further offence against a child, he may order him to be disqualified from working with children, and if he makes an order under this section, he must state his reasons for doing so and cause those reasons to be included in the record of the proceedings. CJCSA 2000, s.30(4)

Subsequent application for order under ss.28 or 29

56–008 Where:

(1) s.28 above applies but the court has neither made an order under it , nor complied with s.28(6), or
(2) s.29 above applies and the court has not made an order under it, and it appears to the prosecutor that the court has not considered the making of an order under that section,

the prosecutor may, at any time, apply to that court for an order under s.28 or 29.

Subject to subs.(3), on such an application:

CJCSA 2000, s.31; CJA 2003, s.299, Sch.30, para.4

(a) in a case falling (1) above, the judge:
    (i) must make an order unless he is satisfied as mentioned in s.28(5), and
    (ii) if he does not make an order under that section, he must comply with s.28(6);
(b) in a case falling within (2) above, the judge:
    (i) must make an order under s.29 if he is satisfied as mentioned in s.29(4), and
    (ii) if he does so, he must comply with s.29(5).

Section 29A(2) does not enable or require an order under ss.28 or 29 to be made where the judge is satisfied that he had considered the making of an order under the section at the time when he imposed the qualifying sentence or made the relevant order (CJCSA 2000, s.29A(3)).

Definitions

56–009 A "qualifying sentence" in the sections means:

(a) a sentence of imprisonment (including a suspended sentence) for a term of 12 months or more; SOA 2003, s.92
(b) a sentence of detention in a young offender institution for a term of 12 months or more;
(c) a sentence of detention during Her Majesty's Pleasure;
(d) a sentence of detention for a period of 12 months or more under PCC(S)A 2000, s.91;
(e) a sentence of detention under CJA 2003, ss.226 or 228;
(f) a detention and training order for a term of 12 months or more imposed by court-martial or by C-MAC;
(g) a hospital order under MHA 1983; or
(h) a guardianship order under MHA 1983.

For the purpose of determining whether the individual was or was not under the age of 18 at the time the offence in question was committed, his age will be taken to be that which the court determined it to be.

A "relevant order" in the section means a guardianship order under MHA 1983.

Effect of order

56–010 A person subject to such an order commits an offence if he knowingly applies for, offers to do, accepts or does any work in a "regulated position" as defined in CJCSA 2000, s.36 (*ibid.* ss.35, 36).

Appeals

56–011 A person may appeal against an order, in the case of an order under:

(1) (a) and (b) in para.56–005, as if the order was a sentence passed upon him for the offence of which he has been convicted; or
(2) (a) and (b) in para.56–005, as if he had been convicted of an offence on indictment, and the order was a sentence passed on him for the offence;

(3) s.29A, as if the order were a sentence passed on him for the offence of which he has been convicted.

A person subject to an order has rights under the Act to apply to the Tribunal established under the Protection of Children Act 1999, for the order to be discontinued.

D. Sexual Offences Act 2003: certification

56–012 For the purposes of the notification requirements set out in SOA 2003, Pt 2, a certificate is required in the case of a person:

(1) convicted of an offence listed in s.3, or
(2) found not guilty of such an offence by reason of insanity, or
(3) found to be under a disability and to have done the act charged against him, in respect of such an offence.

The judge should state in open court, that:

(a) on that date he was convicted, found not guilty as in (2) above, or found to be under a disability in the circumstances stated in (3) above,
(b) that the offence in question is an offence listed in Sch.3 (at APPENDIX A, SECTION 5), and
(c) that he is so certifying (*R. v G (Sex Offender): Registration): The Times*, January 26, 2000)

and should certify those facts, whether at the time or subsequently, so that the certificate may be used as evidence in later proceedings (see also *R. v Rawlinson, The Times*, October 14, 1999). (SOA 2003, s.92).

57 SPECIAL MEASURES DIRECTIONS

Eligible witnesses

57–001 A witness is eligible for a special measures direction if, when the judge makes a special measures determination, that witness: YJCEA 1999, ss.16(1)–(5)

(1) is under 17, or
(2) the judge considers that the quality of evidence by the witness is likely to be diminished because the witness:
    (a) suffers from mental disorder within the meaning of the MHA 1983, or
    (b) otherwise has a significant impairment of intelligence and social functioning, or
    (c) has a physical disability or is suffering from a physical disorder.

In determining eligibility for a special measures direction, any views expressed by a witness aged 17 or over must be considered by the court.

The "quality" of a witness's evidence means quality in terms of completeness, coherence and accuracy.

57–002 Witnesses are also eligible if the judge is satisfied that the quality of evidence given by the witness is likely to be diminished by reason of fear or distress on the part of the witness. In determining whether a witness is so eligible he must take into account, in particular: YJCEA 1999, s.17(1), (2), (3)

(a) the nature and alleged circumstances of the offence;
(b) the age of the witness;
(c) his/her social and cultural background and ethnic origins;
(d) his/her domestic and employment circumstances;
(e) his/her religious beliefs or political opinions;
(f) any behaviour towards the witness on the part of:
    (i) the accused,
    (ii) members of the family or associates of the accused,
    (iii) any other person likely to be an accused or witness in the proceedings,

to the extent that these matters appear to him to be relevant. In determining that question, he must consider any views expressed by the witness.

The complainant in respect of a sexual offence is, without further qualification, eligible for special measures unless he has informed the judge of a wish not to be so eligible. YJCEA 1999, s.17(4)

The subject of witness preparation is dealt with at 57–034.

Special measures available

57–003 The measures set out below may be adopted only where the Home Secretary has notified the court that relevant arrangements may be made available in the area in which it appears that the proceedings will take place. YJCEA 1999, s.18(2)

The following measures are "special measures". YJCEA 1999, ss.23–30

(1) screening witnesses from the accused;
(2) evidence by live link;
(3) permitting evidence to be given in private;
(4) removal of gowns and wigs;
(5) video recorded evidence in chief;
(6) video recorded cross-examination or re-examination (not in force at time of going to print);
(7) examination of witness through an intermediary;
(8) aids to communication (any appropriate device to assist in overcoming communication problems due to a witness's disability, disorder or impairment).

Witnesses under 17 or who suffer from disabilities or disorders may be eligible for all these measures. Those suffering fear or distress about testifying may be considered only for those measures numbered (1) to (6) above.

The regime for child witnesses in need of special protection, where the primary rule is for video recorded evidence-in-chief, otherwise evidence by live link, may be disapplied only in limited circumstances. It is difficult to think of reasons which might make a live link or the admission of a recording unjust which are not related to:

(a) the quality of the equipment on the day;
(b) the content and quality of the video recording; or
(c) the unavailability of the witness for cross-examination.

The judge should start with the presumption that there is nothing intrinsically unfair in children giving their evidence in this way (*R. (D) v Camberwell Green YC* [2005] 1 W.L.R. 393 HL).

As to protective arrangements such as witness anonymity, voice modulation, screening and other special measures see generally *R. v Davis and Another, The Times*, June 1, 2006 where both the European jurisprudence and the domestic cases are reviewed. The overarching principle is that the trial must be fair.

Status of directions

57–004 A special measures direction is binding until the proceedings are determined or abandoned in relation to each accused. A direction may be discharged or varied in the interests of justice:

(1) on application by a party to the proceedings if there has been a material change of circumstances, or
(2) by the judge of his own motion.

The judge must state in open court his reasons for all decisions relating to special measures directions. YJCEA 1999, ss.20(1), (2)

Child witnesses

57–005 A witness under 17 is a "child witness", whether eligible for special measures directions under other provisions of the YJCEA 1999 or not, and is in need of "special protection" if the offence or any of the offences to which the proceedings relate is: YJCEA 1999, s.21

(1) a sexual offence (see s.35(3)(a) of the Act); or
(2) an offence of kidnapping, assault, etc. (see ss.35(3)(b), (c) and (d) of the Act).

The primary rule in the case of a child witness is that the court must give a special measures direction in relation to the witness which complies with the following requirements: YJCEA 1999, s.21(3)

(a) it must provide for any relevant recording to be admitted (video recorded evidence in chief);
(b) it must provide for any evidence given by the witness in the proceedings which is not given by means of a video recording (whether in chief or otherwise) to be given by means of a live link.

A special measures direction may not provide for a video recording or part of a recording to be admitted if the court is of the opinion that in all the circumstances in the interests of justice it should not be admitted. YJCEA 1999, s.27(2)

The test of admissibility should primarily depend on the answer to the question "whether a jury could be sure the child had given a creditable and accurate account on the video tape, notwithstanding any breaches of the guidelines? If 'Yes', it was a matter for the jury. If 'No' the interview would be inadmissible" (*R. v Hanton* (unreported EWCA Crim 2009). in *R. v K*

(Evidence, Child video interview), *The Times*, April 10, 2006, CACD observed that that test needed to be more widely promulgated, rather than that in *G v DPP* (1997) 2 Cr.App.R. 78), which stressed the importance of whether passages possibly influenced by others were corroborated by independent evidence, and not to extract from that case the reference to corroborating material being of central importance.

A special measures direction given in respect of a child witness eligible only because he or she was under 17 at the date of determination, and which relates to the admission of a video recording, ceases to have effect when the witness attains the age of 17 unless the witness was under 17 when the video recording was made.

There is no power to make a direction in relation to the evidence of a child witness who is the accused. (The absence of such a direction is not incompatible with ECHR, Art. 6 nor can it be said that such an accused cannot have a fair trial even when the prosecution witnesses have the benefit of a special measure: *R. v Waltham Forest YC,* QBD (Admin Court) April 3, 2004.)

Procedure

57–006 Procedure for applying for a special measures direction is governed by R.29. A form of application, etc, is set out in PD 2004, Annex D.

The applicant must send his application, providing the relevant information to the Crown Court officer, with a copy to every other party to the proceedings, and the application must be received in the Crown Court within 28 days of: R.29.1(1)–(4)

(1) the accused's committal; or
(2) consent to preferment of a voluntary bill; or
(3) the service of a notice of transfer under CJA 1991, s.53; or
(4) where a person is sent for trial under CDA 1998, s.51, the service of copies of the documents containing the evidence on which the charge(s) are based; or
(5) the service of notice of appeal from the decision of a youth court or a magistrates' court.

A party to whom an application is sent may oppose the application for a special measures direction in respect of any, or any particular, measure available in relation to the witness, whether or not the question whether the witness is eligible for assistance by virtue of s.16 or 17 of the 1999 Act is in issue. He must, within 14 days of the date the application was served on him, notify the applicant and the court officer, as the case may be, in writing of his opposition and give reasons for it. These provisions do not R.29.1(5)–(7)

apply in respect of an application for a special measures direction enabling a child witness in need of special protection to give evidence by means of a live link if the opposition is that the special measures direction is not likely to maximise the quality of the witness's evidence.

Any written notification must state whether the party: R.29.1(8)

(1) disputes that the witness is eligible for assistance by virtue of s.16 or 17 of the Act,
(2) disputes that any of the special measures available would be likely to improve the quality of evidence given by the witness or that such measures (or a combination of them) would be likely to maximise the quality of that evidence, and
(3) opposes the granting of a special measures direction; and

where the application relates to the admission of a video recording, a party who receives a recording must provide the information required by r.29.7(7) (see 57–014, below).

Where a party to the proceedings notifies the court in accordance with para.(6) of his opposition to the application, a judge of the Crown Court must direct a hearing of the application. R.29.1(9), (10)

Where a hearing of the application is to take place the Crown Court officer will notify each party to the proceedings of the time and place of the hearing, and a party so notified may be present at the hearing and be heard.

Within three days of the decision of the court in relation to the application the court officer will notify all the parties of the decision, and if the application was made for a direction enabling a video recording of an interview of a witness to be admitted as evidence in chief of that witness, the notification must state whether the whole or specified parts only of the video recording or recordings disclosed are to be admitted in evidence. R.29.1(13)

Extension of time

57–007 An application to extend the 28 day time limit for special measures applications may be made whether or not the time limit has expired. The application must be accompanied by a statement setting out the reasons why the applicant is or was unable to make the application within that period and a copy of the application and the statement must be sent to every other party to the proceedings. The application will be determined by a judge of the Crown Court without a hearing unless he otherwise directs. The court officer must notify all the parties of the court's decision. R.29.2

Late applications

57–008 Notwithstanding the requirements of r.29 an application may be made for a special measures direction orally at the trial; or, a judge may of his own motion raise the issue whether a special measures direction should be given. R.29.3

Where an application is made in this manner:

(1) the applicant must state the reasons for the late application; and the judge will need to be satisfied that the applicant was unable to make the application in accordance with r.29.1; and

(2) the judge must, before making a special measures direction:
  (a) whether to allow other parties to the proceedings to make representations on the question;
  (b) the time allowed for making such representations (if any); and
  (c) whether the question should be determined following a hearing at which the parties to the proceedings may be heard, though

(1) and (2) above do not apply in respect of an application made orally at the trial for a special measures direction:

  (i) enabling a child witness in need of special protection to give evidence by means of a live link; or
  (ii) enabling a video recording of such a child to be admitted as evidence in chief of the witness,

if the opposition is that the special measures direction will not maximise the quality of the witness's evidence.

Discharge or variation of a special measures direction

57–009 An application to discharge or vary a special measures direction under YJCEA 1999, s.20(2) must be in writing and each material change of circumstances which the applicant alleges has occurred since the direction was made must be set out. The application must be sent to the Crown Court officer as soon as reasonably practicable after the change of circumstances occur, and the applicant must also send copies of the application to each party to the proceedings at the same time as the application is sent to the court officer. R.29.4

A party to whom an application is sent may oppose the application on the ground that it discloses no material change of circumstances.

Rule 29.1(6) to (13) apply to applications to discharge or vary a special measures direction as it applies to an application for a direction.

Renewal application following a material change of circumstances

57–010 Where an application for a special measures direction has been refused the application may only be renewed ("renewal application") where there has been a material change of circumstances since the court refused the application, and the applicant must: R.29.5

(1) identify in the renewal application each material change of circumstances which is alleged to have occurred; and
(2) send the renewal application to the court officer as soon as reasonably practicable after the change occurs;
(3) send copies of the renewal application to each of the parties to the proceedings at the same time as the application is sent to the court officer.

Any party to whom the renewal application is sent may oppose the application on the ground that it discloses no material change of circumstances.

Rule 29.1(6) to (13), 29.6 and 29.7 apply to a renewal application as they apply to the application which was refused.

Directions to jury

57–011 Where on a trial on indictment with a jury, evidence has been given in accordance with a special measures direction, the judge must give the jury such warning, if any, as he considers necessary to ensure that the fact of giving a direction in relation to a witness does not prejudice the accused. YJCEA 1999, ss.32, 39; CJA 2003, s.331, Sch.36, Pt 4, paras 75, 76

A similar position obtains to ensure that the accused is not prejudiced by:

(1) inferences that might be drawn from the fact that the accused has been prevented from cross-examining the witness in person; or
(2) where the witness was cross-examined by a legal representative appointed under YJCEA 1999, s.38(4), the fact that such cross-examination was not carried out by the accused's own legal representative.

See also *R. v B(K)* [2002] 10 Archbold News 1.

Applications relating to live TV links

57–012 Where the application for a special measures direction is made for a witness to give evidence by means of a live link: R.29.6

(1) a party who seeks to oppose an application for a child witness to give evidence by means of a live link must state why in his view the giving of a special measures direction would not be likely to maximise the quality of the witness's evidence, but
(2) this does not apply in relation to a child witness in need of "special protection".

If the special measures directions combine provisions for a witness to give evidence by means of a live link with provision for the examination of the witness to be conducted through an intermediary, the witness must be accompanied at the live link only by:

(a) the intermediary; and
(b) such other persons as may be acceptable to the judge. See generally 46 LIVE LINKS.

Support for witnesses giving evidence by TV link

57–013 Where a special measures direction is made pursuant to R.29.1, enabling a vulnerable intimidated or child witness to give evidence by means of a live television link, the judge will make a direction as to the identity of the witness supporter. Where practicable that direction will be made before the trial commences. In giving the direction, the judge will balance all relevant interests (see para.1.11 of the guidance *Achieving Best Evidence in Criminal Proceedings: Guidance for Vulnerable or Intimidated Witnesses*, but see *R. v D & S* 166 J.P. 792). PD 2004, III.29.1, 2

The witness supporter should be:

(1) completely independent of the witness and his or her family; and
(2) have no knowledge of or personal involvement in the case; and also
(3) be suitably trained so as to understand the obligations of, and comply with, the National Standards relating to witness supporters.

Provided these criteria are met, the witness supporter need not be an usher or a court official.

Thus, e.g., the functions of the witness supporter may be performed by a representative of the Witness Service.

The judge should remind that person of his role and duty, and in particular that:

(a) he must be *present* in the remote witness room with his charge throughout the time that the witness is required to be there;

(b) it is his duty to ensure that no *other person* enters the room or makes any attempt to interrupt, intervene or intimidate the witness during that time;
(c) he must *not himself interrupt* or intervene during the giving of evidence or cross examination via the link with the court unless it is to report to the court that some attempt at interruption, intervention or intimidation is taking place (in which case) this must be done *immediately* he suspects anything untoward;
(d) he must *refrain* from prompting the witness in any way, offering the witness any explanation, interpretations or guidance;
(e) he must *also refrain* from making comments or signals to the witness *except* to direct the witness' attention to the questioner if the witness appears not to be concentrating;
(f) he must hand any *exhibit* to the witness without comment;
(g) in the event of an *interruption in transmission* from the court room or a failure of the equipment, he must remain with the witness; he must on no account speak to the witness about the case or the witness' evidence during any interruption in proceedings;
(h) this warning also applies to any interruptions due to the witness becoming *distressed* or unable to continue giving evidence;
(i) on termination of the witness's evidence and examination, he must ensure that a child witness or vulnerable witness is safely delivered into the care of a responsible person;
(j) he ensures before the start of the proceedings via the link that the equipment is fully operational and that the witness can clearly see and hear the transmission.

The judge must also ensure that the "accompanying person" understands his instructions and that he agrees to abide by the instructions given to him by the judge. Finally the judge should ask him if he wants to ask any questions concerning his duties.

The oath is then administered in the following words:

> *"I swear by almighty God to adhere to the instructions given by the learned Judge and to observe them fully."*

Where the witness supporter is someone other than the court usher, the usher should continue to be available both to assist the witness and the witness supporter, and to ensure that the judge's requirements are properly complied with in the CCTV room. PD 2004, III.29.3

As to compatability with ECHR, Art. 6, see *R. (D) v Camberwell YC, etc.* [2003] 167 J.P. 210.

Video recording of testimony from witnesses

57–014 Where an application is made for a special measures direction enabling a video recording of an interview of a witness to be admitted as evidence in chief of the witness, the following provisons also apply: R.29.7

(1) The application must be accompanied by the video recording which it is proposed to tender in evidence and must include:
  (a) the name of the accused and the offence to be charged;
  (b) the name and date of birth of the witness in respect of whom the application is made;
  (c) the date on which the video recording was made;
  (d) a statement as to whether, and if so at what point in the recording, an oath was administered to, or a solemn declaration made by, the witness;
  (e) a statement that, in the opinion of the applicant, either:
    (i) the witness is available for cross-examination; or
    (ii) the witness is not available for cross-examination and the parties have agreed that there is no need for the witness to be so available;
  (f) a statement of the circumstances in which the video recording was made which complies with para.(4) below; and
  (g) the date on which the video recording was disclosed to the other party or parties.

(2) where it is proposed to tender part only of a video recording of an interview with the witness the application must specify that part and be accompanied by a video recording of the entire interview, including those parts which it is not proposed to tender in evidence, and by a statement of the circumstances in which the recording of the entire interview was made which complies with para.(3) below;

(3) the statement of the circumstances in which the recording was made, referred to in para.(1)(f) and (2) above, must include the following information, except insofar as it is contained in the recording itself:
  (a) the times at which the recording commenced and finished, including details of interruptions;
  (b) the location at which the recording was made and the usual function of the premises;

(c) in relation to each person present at any point during, or immediately before, the recording:
  (i) their name, age and occupation;
  (ii) the time for which each person was present; and
  (iii) the relationship, if any, of each person to the witness and to the accused;

(d) in relation to the equipment used for the recording
  (i) a description of the equipment;
  (ii) the number of cameras used;
  (iii) whether the cameras were fixed or mobile;
  (iv) the number and location of the microphones;
  (v) the video format used; and
  (vi) whether it offered single or multiple recording facilities and, if so, which were used; and
  (vii) the location of the master tape if the video recording is a copy, and details of when and by whom the copy was made.

If the special measures directions enables a video recording of an interview of a witness to be admitted as evidence in chief of the witness with provision for the examination of the witness to be conducted through an intermediary, the information to be provided for the above must be the same as that for other persons present at the recording but with the addition of details of the declaration made by the intermediary under r.29.9.

If the special measures directions enabling a video recording of an interview of a witness to be admitted as evidence in chief of the witness with provision for the witness, in accordance with YJCEA 1999, s.30, to be provided with a device as an aid to communication during the video recording of the interview the information to be included must include also details of any such device used for the purposes of recording.

Party receiving recording

57–015 A party who receives a recording under para.(1) above must (r.29.7(7)), within 14 days of its receipt, notify the applicant and the appropriate officer, in writing: R.29.7(7)–(9)

(1) whether he objects to the admission under s.27 of any part of the video recording or recordings disclosed, giving his reasons why it would not be in the interests of justice for the recording or any part of it to be admitted;

(2) whether he would agree to the admission of part of the video recording or recordings and, if so, which part or parts; and

(3) whether he wishes to be represented at any hearing of the application.

A party who seeks to oppose an application for a special measures direction enabling a video recording of an interview of a child witness to be admitted as evidence in chief of the witness must state why in his view the giving of a special measures direction would not be likely to maximise the quality of the witness's evidence, though this provision does not apply if the witness is a child witness in need of special protection.

Accused seeking to tender video recording

57–016 Any video recording which the accused proposes to tender in evidence need not be sent to the prosecution until the close of the prosecution case at the trial, and the judge may determine an application by the accused to tender in evidence a video recording even though the recording has not been served upon the prosecution. R.29.7(10), (11)

Where a recording which is the subject of a special measures direction is sent to the prosecution after the direction has been made, the prosecutor may apply to the judge, orally for the direction to be varied or discharged, stating: R.29.7(12)–(16)

(1) why he objects to the admission under s.27 of any part of the recording or recordings disclosed, giving his reasons why it would not be in the interests of justice for the recording or any part of it to be admitted; and
(2) whether he would agree to the admission of part of the recording or recordings and, if so, which part or parts.

The judge will before determining the application:

(a) direct a hearing of the application; and
(b) allow all the parties to the proceedings to be present and be heard on the application,

and the appropriate officer will notify all parties to the proceedings of the decision as soon as may be reasonable after the decision is given.

Any decision varying a special measures direction must state whether the whole or specified parts of the video recording or recordings subject to the application are to be admitted in evidence. R.29.7(17)

Practice Direction 2004

57–017 Where:

(1) the judge, on application by a party to the proceedings or of his own motion, grants leave to admit a video recording PD 2004, IV.40.2

in evidence under YJCEA 1999, s.27(1) he may direct that any part of the recording be excluded (s.27(2) and (3));

(2) the judge gives such a direction, the party who made the application to admit it must:
   (a) edit the recording in accordance with the judge's directions; and
   (b) send a copy of the edited recording to the Crown Court officer and to every other party to the proceedings.

(3) a recording is to be adduced during proceedings before the Crown Court, it should be produced and proved by the interviewer, or any other person who was present at the interview with the witness at which the recording was made. The applicant should ensure that such a person will be available for this purpose, unless the parties have agreed to accept his written statement in lieu of attendance. PD 2004, 1V.40.3

Once a trial has begun if, by reason of faulty or inadequate preparation or for some other cause, these procedures have not been properly complied with and an application is made to edit the recording, thereby making necessary an adjournment for the work to be carried out, the judge may make, at his discretion, an appropriate award of costs. PD 2004, IV.40.4

Expert evidence

57–018 Any party to the proceedings who proposes to adduce expert evidence (whether of fact or opinion) in connection with an application or renewal application for, or for varying or discharging, a special measures direction must, not less than 14 days before the date set for the trial to begin: R.29.8

(1) furnish the other party or parties to those proceedings with a statement in writing of any finding or opinion which he proposes to adduce by way of such evidence; and

(2) where a request is made to him in that behalf by any other party to those proceedings, provide that party also with a copy of (or if it appears to the party proposing to adduce the evidence to be more practicable, a reasonable opportunity to examine) the record of any observation, test, calculation or other procedure on which such finding or opinion is based and any document or other thing or substance in respect of which any such procedure has been carried out.

Examination of witness through intermediary

57–019 A special measures direction may provide for any examination of the witness (however and wherever conducted) to be conducted through an interpreter or other person approved by the judge (i.e. "an intermediary"). YJCEA1999, s.29, r.29.9

His intermediary's function is to communicate:

(1) to the witness, questions put to the witness, and
(2) to any person asking such questions, the answers given by the witness in reply to them, and
(3) to explain such questions or answers so far as necessary to enable them to be understood by the witness or person in question.

Any such examination of the witness must take place in the presence of such persons as rules of court or the judge's direction may provide, but in circumstances in which:

(a) the judge and legal representatives acting in the proceedings are able to see and hear the examination of the witness and to communicate with the intermediary, and
(b) (except in the case of a video recorded examination) the jury (if there is one) are able to see and hear the examination of the witness.

Where two or more legal representatives are acting for a party to the proceedings, (2) above is to be regarded as satisfied in relation to those representatives if at all material times it is satisfied in relation to at least one of them.

The intermediary must not act in a particular case except after making a declaration, in the following terms:

> *"I solemnly, sincerely and truly declare that I will well and faithfully communicate questions and answers and make true explanation of all matters and things as shall be required of me according to the best of my skill and understanding."*

The provisions do not apply to an interview of the witness which is recorded by means of a video recording with a view to its admission as evidence in chief of the witness; but a special measures direction may provide for such a recording to be admitted under s.27 if the interview was conducted through an intermediary and:

(i) that person made the appropriate declaration before the interview began, and
(ii) the judge's approval for the purposes of this section is given before the direction is given.

Section 30 applies in relation to assistance for persons suffering from disability.

Reporting direction: adult witnesses

57–020 The judge may on the application of any party to the proceedings, make a reporting direction in respect of any witness in the proceedings, other than the accused, who has attained the age of 18, where he determines that: YJCEA 1999, s.46(1)–(5), (8), (12)

(1) the witness is eligible for protection, and
(2) giving a reporting direction in relation to him is likely to improve:
   (a) the quality of his evidence; or
   (b) the level of co-operation given by him to any party to the proceedings in connection with that party's preparation of its case.

"Quality" refers to the quality of the evidence in completeness, coherence and accuracy and for this purpose "coherence" refers to the witness's ability, in giving evidence, to give answers which address the questions put to him and can be understood both individually and collectively.

References to a party's preparation of the case, include, in the case of the prosecutor, the carrying out of investigations into any offence at any time charged in the proceedings.

For the purposes of this provision a witness is "eligible for protection" if the judge is satisfied that:

(i) the quality of evidence given by the witness, or
(ii) the level of co-operation given by the witness to any party to the proceedings in connection with that party's preparation of its case,

is likely to be diminished by reason of fear or distress on the part of the witness in connection with being identified by members of the public as a witness in the proceedings.

In determining whether a witness is eligible for protection the judge must take into account, in particular:

- the nature and alleged circumstances of the offence to which the proceedings relate;
- the age of the witness;
- such of the following matters as appear to the court to be relevant, namely:
  - — the social and cultural background and ethnic origins of the witness,
  - — the domestic and employment circumstances of the witness, and

— any religious beliefs or political opinions of the witness;

- any behaviour towards the witness on the part of:
  — the accused, members of the family or associates of the accused, or
  — any other person who is likely to be an accused or a witness in the proceedings, and,

in determining that question the judge, must in addition, consider any views expressed by the witness.

In determining whether to give a reporting direction the judge must consider whether it would be in the interests of justice to do so, and the public interest in avoiding the imposition of a substantial and unreasonable restriction on the reporting of the proceedings.

Effect of reporting direction

57–021 A reporting direction of this nature is a direction that no matter relating to the witness may during the witness's lifetime be included in any publication if it is likely to lead members of the public to identify him as being a witness in the proceedings. YJCEA 1999, s.46(7)

The matters in relation to which the restrictions imposed by a reporting direction apply if their inclusion in any publication is likely to have that result include in particular:

(1) the witness's name,
(2) the witness's address,
(3) the identity of any educational establishment attended by him,
(4) the identity of any place of work, and
(5) any still or moving picture of him.

Exception, revocation

57–022 The judge, or an appellate court, may by an excepting direction, dispense to any extent specified in the excepting direction, with the restrictions imposed by a reporting direction if: YJCEA 1999, ss.46(9)–(11)

(1) he is satisfied that it is necessary in the interests of justice to do so; or
(2) he is satisfied that:
   (a) the effect of those restrictions is to impose a substantial and unreasonable restriction on the reporting of the proceedings, and
   (b) it is in the public interest to remove or relax that restriction,

but no excepting direction may be given under (2) by reason only of the fact that the proceedings have been determined in any way or have been abandoned.

A reporting direction may be revoked by the judge (or by an appellate court). An excepting direction may be given at the time the reporting direction is given or subsequently; and may be varied or revoked by the judge (or by an appellate court).

Procedure

Reporting direction

57–023 An application for a reporting direction in relation to a witness is made in the form set out at PD 2004, Annex D, or orally under r.16.3. If in writing it must be sent to the court officer and copies must be sent at the same time to every other party to the proceedings. R.16.1

If the application is in writing any party to the proceedings wishing to oppose that application must notify the applicant and the court officer in writing of his opposition, giving for it, within five business days of the date the application was served on him (unless an extension of time is granted under R.16.6 below), stating whether he disputes that:

(1) the witness is eligible for protection under s.46; or R. 16.2
(2) the granting of protection would be likely to improve the quality of the evidence given by the witness or the level of co-operation given by the witness to any party to the proceedings in connection with that party's preparation of its case.

Urgent action

57–024 A judge may give a reporting direction under s.46 of the Act in relation to a witness in those proceedings, notwithstanding that the five business days specified in r.16.2(3) have not expired if: Rr.16.3(2), (3)

(1) an application is made to him it for the purpose; and
(2) he is satisfied that, due to exceptional circumstances, it is appropriate to do so.

Any party to the proceedings may make such an application whether or not an application has already been made under 16.1, and the application may be made orally or in writing. If it is made orally, the judge may hear and take into account any representations made to him by a person who in his view has a legitimate interest in the application (r.16.3(4)). The application must specify the exceptional circumstances on which the applicant relies (r.16.3(5)).

Excepting direction

57–025 An application for an excepting direction under s.46(9) (dispensing with restrictions imposed by a reporting direction) may be made by: R.16.4(1), (2)

(1) any party to the proceedings; or
(2) any person who, although not a party to the proceedings, is directly affected by a reporting direction given in relation to a witness in the proceedings,

stating why:

(a) the effect of a reporting direction places a substantial and unreasonable restriction on the reporting of the proceedings; and
(b) it is in the public interest to remove or relax those restrictions.

The application may be made in writing in the form set out in the Practice Direction at any time after the commencement of the proceedings in the court or orally at a hearing of an application for a reporting direction. The written application must be sent to the Crown Court officer and copies must be sent at the same time to every party to the proceedings. Rr.16.4(3), (4)

Any person served with a copy of an application for an excepting direction who wishes to oppose it, must notify the applicant and the court officer in writing of his opposition and give reasons for it, within five business days of the date the application was served on him (unless an extension of time is granted under r.16.6)). R.16.4(5), (6)

Variation or revocation

57–026 An application to: Rr.16.5(1)–(4)

(1) revoke a reporting direction; or
(2) vary or revoke an excepting direction,

may be made to a judge at any time after the commencement of the proceedings in the court, by:

(a) a party to the proceedings in which the direction was issued, or
(b) a person who, although not a party to those proceedings, is in the judge's opinion directly affected by the direction.

It must be made in writing and the applicant must send the application to the officer of the court in which the proceedings commenced, and at the same time copies of the application must be sent to every party or, as the case may be, every party to the proceedings, setting out in his application the reasons why he seeks to have the direction varied or, as the case may be, revoked.

A person served with a copy of an application who wishes to oppose it, must notify the applicant and the appropriate officer in writing within five business days of the date the application was served on him (unless an extension of time is granted under R.16.6 below), of his opposition and give reasons for it. R.16.5(5), (6)

Application for an extension of time

57–027 An application may be made in writing to extend the period of time for notification under r.16.2(3), 16.4(6) or 16.5(6) before that period has expired. It must be accompanied by a statement setting out the reasons why the applicant is unable to give notification within the period, and must be sent to the Crown Court officer and a copy of the application must be sent at the same time to the applicant.

Decisions of the court

57–028 The judge may: R.16.7

(1) determine any application made under r.16.1 and 16.3–16.6 without a hearing; or
(2) direct a hearing of any application.

The judge may hear and take into account representations made to him by any person who in his view has a legitimate interest in the application.

The court officer will notify all the parties of the judge's decision as soon as reasonably practicable. If a hearing of an application is to take place, the appropriate officer will notify each party to the proceedings of the time and place of the hearing.

Transfer of magistrates' courts proceedings to the Crown Court

57–029 Where proceedings are sent or transferred from a magistrates' court to the Crown Court, in which reporting directions or excepting directions have been ordered, the magistrates' court officer is under a duty to forward copies of all relevant directions to the Crown Court officer at the place to which those proceedings are sent or transferred. R.16.8

Restrictions on cross-examination of witness

57–030 Where an accused is prevented from cross-examining a witness in person by virtue of YJCEA 1999, ss.34, 35 or 36: R.31.1

(1) the judge must explain to the accused as early in the proceedings as is reasonably practicable that he is prevented from cross-examining a witness in person; and should arrange for a legal representative to act for him for the purpose of cross-examining the witness;
(2) the accused must then notify the court officer in writing within seven days of the judge giving his explanation, or within such other period as the judge may in any particular case allow, of the action, if any, that he has taken;
(3) where the judge gives his explanation to the accused either within seven days of the day set for the commencement of any hearing at which a witness in respect of whom a prohibition under ss.34, 35 or 36 applies may be cross-examined or after such a hearing has commenced, the period of seven days will be reduced in accordance with any directions issued by the judge;
(4) where the accused has arranged for a legal representative to act for him, the notification must include details of the name and address of the representative, and the Crown Court officer will notify all other parties to the proceedings of the name and address of the person, if any, appointed to act for the accused;
(5) where at the end of the period of seven days or such other period as the judge has allowed, the court has received no notification from the accused, it may grant the accused an extension of time, for such period as is considered appropriate in the circumstances of the case, whether on its own motion or on the application of the accused. Before granting of an extension, the judge may hold a hearing, at which all parties to the proceedings may attended and be heard.

Any decision as to the grant of an extension of time will be notified to the parties by the Crown Court officer.

Appointment of legal representative

57–031 Where the court decides in accordance with YJCEA 1999, s.38(4) to appoint a qualified legal representative, the Crown Court officer will notify all parties to the proceedings of the name and address of the representative. Such an appointment, except to the extent as the judge may in a particular case determine, terminates at the conclusion of the cross-examination of the relevant witness or witnesses. R.31.2

The accused may arrange for the legal representative appointed by the court to be appointed to act for him for the purpose of cross-examining any witness in respect of whom a prohibition applies.

Where such an appointment is made:

(1) both the accused and the legal representative appointed must notify the court of the appointment; and

(2) the legal representative must, from the time of his appointment, act for the accused as though the arrangement had been made under s.38(2)(a) of the 1999 Act and will cease to be the representative of the court under s.38(4);

(3) where the court receives notification of the appointment either from the legal representative or from the accused but not from both, it will investigate whether the appointment has been made, and if it concludes that the appointment has not been made, the representative will continue as if appointed by the court.

An accused may, notwithstanding an appointment by the court under s.38(4) of the 1999 Act, arrange for a legal representative to act for him for the purpose of cross-examining any witness in respect of whom a prohibition under s.34, 35 or 36 of the 1999 Act applies. Where the accused arranges for, or informs the court of his intention to arrange for, a legal representative to act for him, he must notify the court, within such period as the court may allow, of the name and address of any person appointed to act for him.

The required notifications will be made to the parties by the court officer. R.31.3

Prosecutor's application

57–032 An application by the prosecutor for the court to give a direction under YJCEA 1999, s.36 in relation to any witness must: r.31.4(1)–(4)

(1) be sent to the Crown Court officer and at the same time a copy must be sent by the applicant to every other party to the proceedings;

(2) must state why, in the prosecutor's opinion;

   (a) the evidence given by the witness is likely to be diminished if cross-examination is undertaken by the accused in person;

   (b) the evidence would be improved if a direction were given under s.36(2); and

(c) it would not be contrary to the interests of justice to give such a direction.

On receipt of the application the Crown Court officer will refer it if the trial has started, to the trial judge; or if the trial has not started when the application is received to the judge who has been designated to conduct the trial, or if no judge has been designated for that purpose, to such judge who may be designated for the purposes of hearing that application.

Where a copy of the application is received by a party to the proceedings more than 14 days before the date set for the trial to begin, that party may make observations in writing on the application to the Crown Court officer, but any such observations must be made within 14 days of the receipt of the application and be copied to the other parties to the proceedings.

Party seeking to oppose order

57–033 A party to whom such an application is sent who wishes to oppose the application must give his reasons for doing so to the Crown Court officer and the other parties to the proceedings. Those reasons must be notified: r.31.4(5)–(12)

(1) within 14 days of the date the application was served on him, if that date is more than 14 days before the date set for the trial to begin;
(2) if the trial has begun, in accordance with any directions issued by the trial judge; or
(3) if neither para.(1) or (2) applies, before the date set for the trial to begin.

Where the application is made before the date set for the trial to begin and it:

(a) is not contested by any party to the proceedings, the court may determine the application without a hearing;
(b) is contested by a party to the proceedings, the court must direct a hearing of the application.

Where the application is made after the trial has begun, the application may be made orally giving reasons why the application was not made before the trial commenced; and providing the court with the information set out in 57–031 above, and the trial judge may give such directions as he considers appropriate to deal with the application.

Where a hearing is to take place, the court officer will notify each party to the proceedings of the time and place of the hearing, and a party notified in accordance may be present at the hearing and be heard.

The court officer will, as soon as possible after the determination of the application, give notice of the decision and the reasons for it to all the parties to the proceedings.

Witness preparation

General

57–034 There is a dramatic difference between:

(1) witness training or coaching, and
(2) witness familiarisation.

The training or coaching of witnesses in criminal proceedings, whether for the prosecution or the defence, is not permitted. Such a rule:

(a) minimises the risk inherent in witness training, that a witness may tailor his evidence in the light of what someone else said, and, equally
(b) avoids any unfounded perception that he may have done so.

That is so even where the training takes place one-to-one with someone completely remote from the facts of the case; the witness may come, even unconsciously, to appreciate which aspects of his evidence are perhaps not quite consistent with what others are saying, or indeed not quite what is required of him.

But this principle does not extend to preclude pre-trial arrangements to familiarise witnesses with:

(i) the layout of the court,
(ii) the likely sequence of events when the witness is giving evidence, and
(iii) a balanced appraisal of the different responsibilities of the various participants.

Such arrangements are to be welcomed. Nor does the principle prohibit the training of expert and similar witnesses in, for example, the technique of giving comprehensive evidence of a specialist kind to a jury, or the developing of the ability to resist the inevitable pressure of going further in evidence than matters covered by the witness's specific expertise (*R. v Momodou* [2005] Crim.L.R. 588).

Guidance from CACD

57–035 CACD (in *R. v Momodou* above) stated that if arrangements are made for familiarisation with outside agencies rather than the witness service then the following guidance should be followed:

(1) in relation to prosecution witnesses, the CPS should be informed in advance of any proposal for familiarisation; if appropriate after obtaining police input, they should be invited to comment in advance on the proposals;
(2) if relevant information comes to the police, the police should inform the CPS; the proposals for the intended familiarisation programme should be reduced into writing, rather than left to informal conversations; if, having examined them, the CPS suggest that the programme may be breaching the permitted limits, it should be amended; if the defence engage in the process, it would be wise for counsel's advice to be sought, again in advance, and again with written information about the nature and extent of the training;
(3) in any event, it is a matter of professional duty on counsel and solicitors to ensure that the judge is informed of any familiarisation process organised by the defence using outside agencies, and it will follow that the prosecution will be made aware of what has happened;
(4) the familiarisation process should normally be supervised or conducted by a criminal justice process, and preferably by an organisation accredited for the purpose by the Bar Council and Law Society;
(5) none of those involved should have any personal knowledge of the matters in issue;
(6) records should be maintained of all those present and the identity of those responsible for the familiarisation process, whenever it takes place; the programme should be retained, together with all the written material (or appropriate copies) used during the familiarisation sessions; none of the material should bear any similarity whatsoever to the issues in the proceedings to be attended by the witnesses, and nothing in it should play on or trigger the witness's recollection of events;
(7) if discussion of the instant criminal proceedings begins, as it almost inevitably will, it must be stopped, and advice given about precisely why it is impermissible, with a warning against the danger of evidence contamination and the risk that the course of justice may be perverted; a note should be made if and when any such warning is given;
(8) all documents used in the process should be retained, and if relevant to prosecution witnesses, handed to the CPS

> as a matter of course, and in relation to defence witnesses, produced to the court; none should be destroyed; it should be a matter of professional obligation for lawyers involved in these processes, or indeed the trial itself, to see that the guidance is followed.

On December 20, 2004 the Attorney-General issued a report in which he signalled his decision to permit prosecutors to speak to prosecution witnesses. In the light of the judgment in *Momodou* the Professional Standards Committee of the Bar Council has set up a working group to examine, as a matter of urgency the implications for barristers involved in training witnesses.

58 SPENT CONVICTIONS

58–001 Where a person has been convicted of an offence and certain conditions are satisfied, he is, after the applicable rehabilitation period has expired, treated for the purposes of the Rehabilitation of Offenders Act 1974 as a "rehabilitated person" in respect of that conviction, and the conviction is treated as "spent".

Effect of rehabilitation

58–002 The effect of ROA 1974, s.4(1) is that a person who has become a rehabilitated person for the purpose of the Act in respect of a conviction (known as a "spent" conviction) must be treated for all purposes in law as a person who has not committed, been charged with, prosecuted for, convicted of or sentenced for the offence or offences which were the subject of that conviction. PD 2004, I.6.2

Section 4(1) does not apply, however, to evidence given in criminal proceedings (see s.7(2)(a)). Convictions are often disclosed in such criminal proceedings. When the Bill was before the House of Commons on June 28, 1974 the hope was expressed that the Lord Chief Justice would issue a practice direction for the guidance of the Crown Court with a view to reducing disclosure of spent convictions to a minimum and securing uniformity of approach. PD 2004, I.6.2

The direction is set out in the following paragraphs. PD 2004, I 16.3–7

(1) During the trial of a criminal charge, reference to previous convictions (and therefore to spent convictions) can arise in a number of ways. The most common is when the character of the accused or a witness is sought to be attacked by reference to his criminal record, but there are, of course, cases where previous convictions are relevant and admissible as, for instance, to prove system.

(2) It is not possible to give general directions which will govern all these different situations, but it is recommended that both court and advocates should give effect to the general intention of Parliament by never referring to a spent conviction when such reference can reasonably be avoided.

(3) After a verdict of guilty the judge must be provided with a statement of the offender's record for the purposes of sentence. The record supplied should contain all previous convictions, but those which are spent should, so far as practicable, be marked as such.

(4) No one should refer in open court to a spent conviction without the authority of the judge, who should not give it unless the interests of justice require.

(5) When announcing sentence the court should make no reference to a spent conviction unless it is necessary to do so for the purpose of explaining the sentence to be passed.

Excluded convictions which are "spent"

58–003 Sentences of imprisonment for life, imprisonment, youth custody or corrective training for a period exceeding 30 months, sentences of preventive detention, detention during HM pleasure or for life, or for a term exceeding 30 months passed under CYPA 1933, s.53, custody for life and a sentence of imprisonment for public protection under CJA 2003, s.225, a sentence of detention for public protection under CJA 2003, s.226, or an extended sentence under CJA 2003, s.227 or 228 are excluded from rehabilitation.

58–004 Table

Where the sentence imposed on conviction is:	The rehabilitation period begins on conviction and lasts for:	ROA 1974
Imprisonment, detention in a young offender institution, youth custody, corrective training, 6–30 months	10 years*	
Imprisonment, detention in a young offender institution, youth custody, not exceeding 6 months	7 years*	s.5(2) Table A
Fine, or any other order not specified in Table B	5 years*	
Borstal training	7 years	
Detention CYPA 1933, s.53, PCC(S)A 2000, s.91, for a term of 6–30 months	5 years	

Detention CYPA 1933, s.53, PCC(S)A 2000, s.91, for not more than 6 months	3 years	s.5(2) Table B
Detention in a detention center	3 years	
Community punishment order, or community punishment and rehabilitation in case of: (a) offender aged 18 or over at date of conviction; (b) offender under 18 at date of conviction	5 years 2½ years from conviction, or a period beginning with the date of conviction and ending when the order ceases to have effect (whichever is the longer)	CJPOA 1994, Sch.9, para.11; CJA 2003, s.304, Sch.32, para.18
Community rehabilitation (sentenced before Feb 3, 1995) community rehabilitation order (sentenced on or after Feb 3, 1995), community order under CJA 2003, s.177	Date order ceases or 1 year, whichever is the longer, 5 years for an adult, 2½ for a juvenile	
Detention and training order, PCC(S)A 2000, s.100	In the case of an offender: (a) 15 or over at date of conviction, 5 years if it was, 3½ years if it was not, for period exceeding 6 months; (b) under 15, a period beginning with date of conviction and ending 1 year after date on which order ceases to have effect	s.5(6A)
Secure training order, CJPOA 1994, s.1, conditional discharge, bind over, care order CYPA 1933, s.57, supervision order under PCC(S)A 2000, s.63(1), supervision order CYPA 1933 or CYPA 1963	Duration of order + 1 year	s.5(4), (5)
Committal to remand home CYPA 1933, s.54, committal to approved school CYPA 1933, s.57, attendance at an attendance centre	Duration of order + 1 year	s.5(6)

Hospital order with or without restriction order	5 years or duration of the order + 2 years (whichever is the longer)	s.5(7)
Disqualification, disability, prohibition or other penalty	Duration of the order	s.5(8)
Absolute discharge	6 months	s.5(3)

* Subject to a reduction by half for an offender under 18.

59 TICs

General

59–001 There is a convention, although it has no statutory authority, that where the judge, when passing sentence upon an offender for an offence:

(1) is informed that there are outstanding charges against the offender; and
(2) the offender admits each of them and asks for them to be taken into consideration,

he may formally take them into consideration, and pass a longer sentence than he would if he were dealing only with the counts on the indictment (*R. v Batchelor* (1952) 36 Cr.App.R. 64), provided that the maximum term for these offences is not exceeded.

As with other aspects of sentencing, the way in which the judge deals with such offences will depend on context. They may add nothing, or nothing very much, to the sentence he would otherwise have imposed, they may aggravate the sentence and lead to a substantial increase, particularly where the offences show a pattern of criminal activity which suggests careful planning, or if the offences were committed on bail after an earlier arrest.

When assessing their significance, the judge is likely to attach weight to the demonstrable fact that the offender has assisted the police. Such cooperative behaviour may provide its own early indication of guilt and will usually mean that no further proceedings need to be started (*R. v Miles, The Times*, April 10, 2006).

Not ranking as a conviction

59–002 Taking offences into consideration does not, technically, amount to a conviction of those offences, nor does the procedure found a subsequent plea of *autrefois convict*. It is perfectly feasible "as a matter of theoretical jurisprudence" to charge an offender with offences which have been taken into consideration. By convention it is not done, and where, perhaps in error, it is done, the judge dealing with the offences on the second occasion should see to it without any doubt whatever that no *additional* punishment is imposed on the offender on account of those offences.

Ancillary orders

59–003 Where an offence is formally taken into consideration in this manner, ancillary orders such as:

(1) a compensation order (PCC(S)A 2000, s.130); and
(2) a restitution order (PCC(S)A 2000, s.148),

may be made in respect of them. An offence involving mandatory disqualification from driving under RT legislation should not be taken into consideration (*R. v Simons* (1953) 37 Cr.App.R. 120).

Offences which may be taken into consideration

59–004 In general, offences taken into consideration should be offences similar to that or those for which the judge is passing sentence on the indictment. The judge should not take into consideration offences:

(1) without the consent of the Crown, the public interest may require an investigation of, and a trial on that offence (*R. v McLean* [1912] 6 Cr. App.R. 26);
(2) which he would have no jurisdiction to try (*R. v Simons* (above));
(3) which, though triable in the Crown Court, involve RT disqualification (*R. v Simons* (above)), unless the offender is liable to such an order under offences of which he has been convicted (*R. v Collins* [1947] KB 560; *R. v Jones* (1971) 55 Cr.App.R. 32);
(4) breaches of conditional discharge or a community order (*R. v Webb* (1953) 37 Cr.App.R. 82);
(5) offences committed outside the jurisdiction of the criminal courts of England and Wales, e.g. offences of a purely military disciplinary nature (*R. v Anderson* (1958) 42 Cr.App.R. 91) or offences committed in Scotland (see *Hilson v Easson* 1914 S.C(J) 99.

Where offences committed by a member of the armed forces are civil offences under service legislation, there is nothing to prevent their being taken into consideration (*R. v Anderson* (above)).

Community orders

59–005 The breach of a community order, should not be taken into consideration in this way (*R. v Webb*, above), but should be dealt with in the way prescribed for dealing with the breach of such orders (see 21 COMMUNITY SENTENCES).

Procedure

59–006 This procedure involves an offender, convicted of one or more offences, being punished for other offences for which he has never been arraigned, tried or convicted and to which he has never pleaded guilty. It is essential, therefore, if justice is to be done, that the judge is satisfied in respect of each offence that the offender admits it and wishes it to be taken into consideration. This is achieved by the police preparing a list of such offences, serving it, with the consent of his counsel, upon the offender and obtaining his signature to it, striking through such offences as are not admitted.

Thus:

(1) the offender (not his counsel) should be asked in open court, whether he has received the list, and if so, whether:
   (a) he admits each of the offences (not struck out); and
   (b) whether he wishes each of them to be taken into consideration;
(2) on a commital for sentence, the fact that the magistrates indicate that they have taken certain offences into consideration, does not relieve the trial judge from ensuring that the defendant still wants them taken into consideration;
(3) if there is a lengthy schedule of offences, it is not normally necessary to take him through the document page by page; but
(4) if there is any doubt as to which offences the offender admits and wishes to have taken into consideration, the issue must be resolved in open court;
(5) if the judge is not satisfied that the offender has had time to consider the list in detail, it may be necessary to adjourn (*R. v Marquis* (1951) 35 Cr.App.R. 33; *DPP v Anderson* [1978] AC 964; *R. v Nelson* (1967) 51 Cr.App.R. 98; *R. v Davies* (1981) 72 Cr.App.R. 262).

As to compensation orders made in relation to offences taken into consideration, see 23 COMPENSATION.

60 TRAVEL RESTRICTION ORDERS

General

60–001 Where an offender is convicted on **or after April 1, 2002**, and sentenced to a term of four years' imprisonment or more for a drug trafficking offence (if the offender has been convicted of more than one drug offence at any one time, only if one of those offences attracts a term of four years' imprisonment or more, but not otherwise), the judge, when sentencing him must consider whether it would be more appropriate for such sentence to include a travel restriction order. CJPA 2001, s.33(1), (2), (3); SI 2002/344

If he considers that:

(1) it is appropriate to make such an order in all the circumstances (including any other convictions of the offender for drug trafficking offences in respect of which he is also passing sentence), he should make such an order in relation him; or
(2) it is not appropriate, he must state his reasons for not making an order.

Such an order will prohibit the offender from leaving the UK at any time in the period which:

(a) begins with his release from custody; and
(b) continues after that time for such period of not less than two years as may be specified in the order.

The order cannot be made retrospectively or, in the case of offences added by statutory order under s.34(1)(c), in respect of an offence committed on or after the date of the coming into force of the relevant order.

There is no statutory maximum; the general presumption is that the travel ban should escalate based on the level of the sentence. It is for the judge to weigh the respective lengths of the term of imprisonment and the travel restriction order in any given case.

The provisions of the order do not prevent deportation, extradition or other statutory removal action, see 60–008, below.

Approach to order

60–002 In approaching the making of an order, the judge needs to bear in mind that:

(1) the section confers a discretion in broad terms;

(2) that discretion must be exercised for the purpose granted, i.e. the reduction of risk of re-offending after release, and must be proportionate;
(3) whilst the power to make such an order is not confined to important cases, the judge has a duty to consider the making of such an order, and if he makes an order must give his reasons for so doing including the reasons for the chosen length;
(4) the mere fact that the offender has been convicted of an offence of importation does not give rise to an inference that he will do it again on release; but
(5) if, on an assessment of all the circumstances, a risk does arise such as to require an order, proportionality is required as to length.

Freedom to travel is a significant aspect of modern life. In restricting a person's freedom in that respect there is a need for balance; the length of any order should be restricted to that which is necessary to protect the public. The drug trade being truly international, the Act does not contemplate an order being made in relation to certain parts of the world only. (*R. v Mee* [2004] Crim.L.R. 487.)

Direction to deliver up passport

60–003 The order may contain a direction to the offender to deliver up, or cause to be delivered up to the court, any UK passport held by him. Where such a direction is given, the court will send any passport delivered to the Secretary of State (in practice to the nearest Passport Office), who (without prejudice to any other power or duty of his to retain the passport) may retain it for so long as the prohibition imposed by the order applies to the offender, and is not for the time being suspended, and will not return the passport after the prohibition has ceased to apply, or when it is suspended, except when the passport has not expired and an application for its return is made to him by the offender. CJPA 2001, s.33(5)

Definitions

60–004 "Drug trafficking offence" has the same meaning as under the DTA 1994, s.1(3) except that it includes any such offence under the MDA 1971 as may be designated by an order made by the Home Secretary under s.34(l)(c). CJPA 2001, s.34(1), (2)

"UK passport" means a UK passport within the meaning of IA 1971. This includes a current or expired UK passport. The passports of foreign nationals and the non-British passports of those with dual nationality, whatever their domicile, remain the CJPA 2001, s.33(8) property of the issuing government. The court should record details of non-British passports.

"Release from custody" refers to an offender's first release from custody after the imposition of the travel restriction order, which is neither: CJPA 2001, s.33(7)

(1) a release on bail; nor
(2) a temporary release for a fixed period.

Revocation and suspension

60–005 An offender who has had a travel restriction order made against him may apply to the court which made the order, for the order to be either revoked or suspended subject to the following: CJPA 2001, s.35

(1) on an application for revocation made by that person at any time which is:
  (a) after the end of the minimum period; and
  (b) not within three months after the making of any previous application for the revocation of the prohibition, revoke the prohibition imposed by the order with effect from such date as the court may determine; or
(2) on an application made by that person at any time after the making of the order, suspend the prohibition imposed by the order for such period as the court may determine.

The judge must not:

  (a) revoke the prohibition unless it considers it appropriate to do so in all the circumstances of the case and having regard, in particular, to:
    (i) that person's character;
    (ii) his conduct since the making of the order; and
    (iii) the offences of which he was convicted on the occasion on which the order was made.
  (b) suspend a prohibition for any period unless he is satisfied that there are exceptional circumstances in that person's case that justify the suspension of the prohibition on compassionate grounds for that period.

When determing an application to suspend the judge must have regard to the same three requirements for revocation, mentioned above under (i), (ii) and (iii) and to any other circumstances of the case that he considers relevant.

Effect of suspension

60–006 Where the prohibition is suspended, the person who is the subject of the suspension must:

(1) be in the UK when the period of suspension ends; and
(2) if the order contains a direction under s.33(4) above, surrender, before the end of that period any passport returned or issued to him in respect of that suspension by the Secretary of State.

A passport that is required to be surrendered under (2) above, must be surrendered to the Secretary of State in such manner, or by being to such address, as he may direct at the time when he returns or issues it. CJPA 2001, s.35(5)

Where the prohibition imposed on any person by a travel restriction order is suspended for any period under this section, the end of the period of the prohibition imposed by the order is treated (except for the purposes of subs.(7) below) as postponed (or, if there has been one or more previous suspensions further postponed), by the length of the period of suspension. CJPA 2001, s.35(6)

"The minimum period" means CJPA 2001, s.35(7)

(a) in the case of a travel restriction order imposing a prohibition for a period of four years or less, the period of two years beginning at the time when the period of prohibition began;
(b) in the case of a travel restriction order imposing a prohibition of more than four but less than 10 years, the period of four years beginning at that time; and
(c) in any other case, the period of five years beginning at that time.

Contravention of order

60–007 A person commits an offence who: CJPA 2001, s.36

(1) leaves the UK at a time when he is prohibited from doing so by a travel restriction order; and
(2) is not in the UK at the end of the period during which a prohibition imposed on him by such an order has been suspended.

For each of these offences, the offender is liable, on summary conviction, to up to six months' imprisonment or to a fine not exceeding the statutory maximum, or both and, on indictment to up to five years' imprisonment, and unlimited fine, or both.

A person who fails to comply with a direction contained in a travel restriction order to deliver up, or cause to be delivered up, a passport to a court, commits an offence and is liable on summary conviction to up to six months' imprisonment or to a fine not exceeding level 5 (£5,000) on the standard scale, or to both.

Removal powers

60–008 Special savings and provisions in relation to travel restriction orders are made in respect of the Home Secretary's prescribed removal powers. CJPA 2001, s.37

61 TRIAL WITHOUT A JURY

61–001 CJA 2003, Pt 7, makes provision for trial on indictment without a jury:

(1) in certain fraud cases of a serious or complex nature; and
(2) where there is a real and present danger of jury tampering.

The provisions for fraud cases (61–002) are not yet in force; the provisions in relation to jury tampering (61–003 below) were brought into force on **July 24, 2006** (SI 2006/1835).

The effect of an order under CJA 2003, ss.43, 44, or 46(5) is that the trial to which the order relates is *conducted* without a jury; the effect of an order under s.46(3) is that the trial to which the order relates is *continued* without a jury. Where a trial is conducted or continued without a jury, the court has all the powers, authorities and jurisdiction which it would have had if the trial had been conducted or continued with a jury (including power to determine any question and to make any finding which would be required to be determined or made by a jury). CJA 2003, s.48(1), (2), (3)

Note that:

(a) except where the context otherwise requires, any reference in an enactment to a jury, the verdict of a jury or the finding of a jury is to be read, in relation to a trial conducted or continued without a jury, as a reference to the court, the verdict of the court or the finding of the court; CJA 2003, s.48(4)
(b) where a trial is conducted or continued without a jury and the court convicts an accused, the judge must give a judgment which states the reasons for the conviction at, or as soon as reasonably practicable after, the time of the conviction. CJA 2003, s.48(5)(1)

Fraud cases (not yet in force)

61–002 Where one or more accused are to be tried on indictment at the Crown Court for one or more offences, and notice has been given under CJA 1987, s.4 (notices in serious fraud cases) in respect of that offence or those offences, the prosecutor may apply to a judge for the trial to be conducted without a jury. CJA 2003, s.43(1), (2), (3), (4), (5)

On such an application the judge may order the case to be tried without a jury where he is satisfied that:

(1) the complexity of the trial, or the length of the trial (or both) is likely to make the trial so burdensome to the members of the jury hearing it,

(2) that the interests of justice require that serious consideration should be given to the question of whether the trial should be conducted without a jury,

otherwise he must refuse the application.

An order requires the approval of the Lord Chief Justice or a judge nominated by him.

In deciding whether to make an order, the judge must consider whether there are any steps which might reasonably be taken to reduce the complexity or length of the trial. Particularly relevant will be the provisions made for the preparatory hearing procedure (see 16 CASE MANAGEMENT). The judge is not, however, to regard as reasonable any measures which would significantly disadvantage the prosecution (as by severing an indictment or excluding relevant and important evidence). CJA 2003, s.43(6), (7)

Danger of jury tampering

61–003 Where one or more accused are to be tried on indictment for one or more offences, the prosecution may apply to a judge of the Crown Court for the trial to be conducted without a jury where there is said to be a real and present danger of the jury being tampered with. CJA 2003, ss.44(1)–(5)

The judge must make an order that the trial is to be conducted without a jury where he is satisfied that:

(1) there is a real and present danger that jury tampering would take place; and
(2) notwithstanding any steps (including the provision of police protection) which might reasonably be taken to prevent jury tampering, the likelihood that it would take place would be so substantial as to make it necessary in the interests of justice for the trial to be conducted without a jury,

otherwise he must refuse the application.

As to *continuing* a trial without a jury after the sitting jury has been discharged, see CJA 2003, s.46 below.

The Act gives examples of cases where there may be evidence of a "real and present danger" that jury tampering would take place, namely a case where: CJA 2003, s.44(6)

(a) the trial is a retrial and the jury in the previous trial was discharged because jury tampering had taken place;
(b) jury tampering has taken place in previous criminal proceedings involving the accused or any of the accused;
(c) there has been intimidation, or attempted intimidation of any person who is likely to be a witness at the trial.

Procedure for applications under ss.43, 44

61–004 An application under s.43 or 44 must be determined at a preparatory hearing (see 16 CASE MANAGEMENT) the parties to such preparatory hearing being given an opportunity to make representations with respect to the application. CJA 2003, s.45(1)–(3)

CJA 1987, s.7(1) (which sets out the purposes of preparatory hearings) is modified for this purpose in that for paras (a) to (c) there are substituted:

(a) identifying issues which are likely to be material to determinations and findings which are likely to be required during the trial,
(b) if there is to be a jury, assisting their comprehension of those issues and expediting the proceedings before them,
(c) determining an application to which CJA 2003, s.45 applies.

Trials under way: discharge of jury because of tampering

61–005 Where a trial on indictment is under way, and the judge is minded to discharge the jury because jury tampering appears to have taken place, he must, before taking any steps to discharge the jury: CJA 2003, ss.46(1)–(7)

(1) notify the parties that he is minded to discharge the jury,
(2) inform the parties of the grounds on which he is so minded, and
(3) allow the parties an opportunity to make representations, and

where, after considering any such representations, he discharges the jury, he may make an order that the trial is to continue without a jury if, but only if, he is satisfied:

(a) that jury tampering has taken place, and
(b) that to continue the trial without a jury would be fair to the accused, but

must if he considers that it is necessary in the interests of justice for the trial to be terminated, terminate it, and where he does so, he may make an order that any new trial which is to take place be conducted without a jury if he is satisfied in respect of the new trial that both of the conditions set out in s.44 are likely to be fulfilled.

This provision is without prejudice to any other power that the judge may have on terminating the trial, nor does anything in it affect the application of s.43 or 44, above, in relation to any new trial which takes place following the termination of the trial.

Appeal

61–006 Part 7 provides a right of appeal to CACD by the accused or the prosecutor from an order under s.46(3) or (5) but only with the leave of the judge or CACD, and the order from which the appeal lies is not to take effect before the expiration of the period for bringing the appeal, or, if such an appeal is brought, before it is finally disposed of. CJA 2003, s.47

Effect of order

61–007 Where an order is made:

CJA 2003, ss.48(1)–(3)

(1) under ss.43, 44 or 46(5) the trial to which the order relates is then conducted without a jury, and
(2) under s.46(3) the trial is continued without a jury.

In either the trial will proceed in the usual way, the judge having all the powers, authority and jurisdiction which the court would have had if the trial had been with a jury (including power to determine any question and to make any finding which would be required to be determined or made by a jury).

Except where the context otherwise requires, any reference in an enactment to a jury, the verdict of a jury or the finding of a jury, is to be read, in relation to a trial conducted or continued without a jury, as a reference to the court, the verdict of the court or the finding of the court. CJA 2003, ss.48(4), (6); DVA 2004, s.58(1), Sch.10, para.60

Where a trial is conducted or continued without a jury and the judge convicts an accused, he must give a judgment which states the reasons for the conviction at, or as soon as reasonably practicable after, the time of the conviction. CJA 2003, s.42(5)

The reference in CAA 1968, s.18(2) (notice of appeal or of application for leave to appeal to be given within 28 days from date of conviction, etc.) to the date of the conviction is to read as a reference to the date of that judgment.

Trial of part of indictment without a jury (not yet in force)

61–008 Under DVA 2004, ss.17–20 when they come into force the Crown may apply to a judge of the Crown Court for a trial to take place on the basis that the trial of some, but not all, of the counts included in the indictment be conducted without a jury where:

(1) the number of counts in the indictment is such that a trial by jury involving all of them would be impracticable;

(2) each count or group of counts which would be tried by jury if such an order was made, can be regarded as a sample of counts which could accordingly be tried without a jury; and
(3) it is in the interests of justice to do so.

A "sample count" is to be regarded as a sample of other counts where:

(a) the accused in respect of each count is the same;
(b) the evidence in respect of each count is admissible at the trial of the sample count; and
(c) the judge considers that the sample count is a sample of the other counts.

Procedure

61–009 An application is determined at a preparatory hearing under CJA 1987, or CPIA 1996 (see 16 CASE MANAGEMENT), at which both parties are given an opportunity to be heard. An interlocutory appeal lies to CACD by either party.

Effect of order

61–010 The effect of an order under DVA 2004, s.17 is that where an accused is found guilty by a jury of a count which is a "sample" of other counts to be tried in those proceedings, those other counts may be tried without a jury in those proceedings (DVA 2004, s.19).

62 TURNBULL GUIDELINES

General

62–001 *R. v Turnbull* (1976) 63 Cr.App.R. 242, laid down certain guidelines to be followed in summing up cases of disputed identity. A general warning on these lines is required in all identification cases, whether the witness identifies a person whom he purports to recognise or a stranger, and even if the sole, or main, issue raised by the defence is credibility rather than mistaken identity (*Beresford v The Queen* [1993] Crim.L.R. 944, PC).

As to rape cases see *R. v Chance* [1988] Q.B. 932.

For an example of the attitude of CACD where the judge fails to give a direction and fails to identify the weaknesses in the identification evidence, see *R. v Nash* [2005] Crim.L.R. 232).

Contents of summing up

62–002 Whenever the case against an accused depends wholly or substantially on the correctness of one or more identifications of the accused which the defence allege to be mistaken, the trial judge should:

(1) warn the jury of the special need for caution before convicting on the correctness of the identification evidence;
(2) instruct the jury as to the reasons for the need for such a warning; and
(3) make some reference to the possibility that a mistaken witness could be a convincing witness, and that a number of such witnesses could all be mistaken.

Provided this is done in clear terms, the trial judge need not use any particular form of words.

Again, the trial judge should direct the jury to examine closely the circumstances in which the identification by each witness came to be made. Thus, for example:

(a) how long did the witness have the accused under observation?
(b) at what distance?
(c) in what light?
(d) was the observation impeded in any way, as by passing traffic or press of people?

(e) had the witness ever seen the accused before?—if so, how often?—if only occasionally, had he any special reason for remembering him?

(f) how long elapsed between the original observation and subsequent identfication to the police? and

(g) was there any material discrepancy between the description of the accused given to the police by the witness when first seen, and his actual appearance?

and, finally, the judge should remind the jury of any specific weaknesses which appear in the quality of identification evidence.

Quality of the evidence

62–003 The matters set out above go to the quality of the identification evidence. If the quality is good and remains so at the close of the accused's case, the danger of mistaken identification is lessened; the poorer the quality of that evidence the greater the danger.

Where:

(1) the quality of the identification evidence is good, as where identification is made, e.g. after a long period of observation or in satisfactory conditions, by a relative, neighbour, close friend or workmate, the jury can safely be left to assess the value of the evidence, provided an adequate warning is given about the special need for caution, and this is so even though there is no other supporting evidence;

(2) the quality of the identification evidence is poor, as where, for example, it depends solely upon a fleeting glance, or on a longer observation made in difficult conditions, the trial judge should withdraw the case from the jury and direct an acquittal unless there is other evidence which goes to the correctness of the identification.

Such supporting evidence may be corroboration in the legal sense, but it need not be such if its effect is to make the jury sure that there has been no mistaken identification.

The judge should:

(a) identify to the jury the evidence which he adjudges capable of supporting the evidence of identification; and

(b) point out to them, if there is evidence which they might think was supporting that it does not have that quality.

Where accused does not give evidence

62–004 A jury may think that support for the identification evidence is to be found in the fact that the accused has not given evidence before them. Clearly the absence of the accused from the witness box does not provide evidence of anything, and the trial judge should tell the jury so. He is also entitled to tell them that, when assessing the quality of the identification evidence, they may take into consideration the fact that it is uncontradicted by any evidence coming from the accused.

Where jury reject alibi

62–005 Care should be taken by the trial judge in directing the jury about support for identification evidence to be derived from the fact that they reject an alibi.

They should be warned that:

(1) a false alibi may be put forward for a variety of reasons; an accused, for example, who has only his own truthful evidence to rely on, may stupidly fabricate an alibi and produce lying witnesses to support it, out of fear that his own evidence will not suffice;
(2) alibi witnesses often make genuine mistakes about dates and occasions, just like any other witness; and
(3) proof that the accused has told lies about his whereabouts at the material time does not prove by itself that he was where he was alleged by the identifying witness to be.

It is only where the jury is satisfied that the sole reason for fabrication is to deceive them, and that there is no other explanation for the alibi being put forward, that such fabrication can provide support for identification evidence.

Attitude of court of appeal

62–006 CACD has said that failure to follow the above guidelines is likely to result in a conviction being quashed, particularly where, on the evidence, the verdict is either unsafe or unsatisfactory. On matters of credibility, however, the court has said it will interfere only where:

(1) the jury was misdirected as to how to assess the evidence; or
(2) if there was no direction when there ought to have been one; or
(3) though such circumstances must be rare, where, on the whole of the evidence, the jury must clearly have returned a perverse verdict.

63 UNFITNESS TO PLEAD/INSANITY

General

63–001 Where, on the trial of any person, the question arises, at the instance of the defence or otherwise, whether the accused is under a disability such that, apart from the 1964 Act (as amended by the 1991 Act), would constitute a bar to his being tried, then, though ordinarily such a question falls to be determined as soon as it arises: CP(I)A 1964, ss.4(1)–(4); CJ(IUP)A 1991, s.2

(1) if, having regard to the nature of the supposed disability, the judge is of the opinion that it is inexpedient to do so, he may postpone consideration of the question of fitness to be tried, until any time up to the opening of the case for the defence; and
(2) if, before the question of fitness to be tried falls to be determined, the jury return a verdict of acquittal on all or each of the counts on which the accused is being tried, that question shall not be determined.

Proceedings under ss.4 and 4A do not offend against the provisions of ECHR Art. 6; they are not "criminal proceedings". See *R. v Kerr, Kerr and H* [2002] 1 W.L.R. 824 and the cases considered there.

Determination by judge

63–002 Where the question of fitness to be tried is raised on arraignment, it is to be determined by the judge without a jury. CP(I)A 1964, s.4(5); CP(IUP)A 1991, s.2; DVA 2004, s.22(1), (2); SI 2005/579

The judge may not make such a determination except on the written or oral evidence of two registered medical practitioners, at least one of whom is duly approved (see also *R. v Ramzi Borkan* [2004] EWCA Crim 1642). There is no need for oral evidence (*cf.* MHA 1983, s.41(2)) (*Narey v C & E Commissioners* [2005] EWCA 784 (Admin)). CP(I)A 1964, s.4(6); DVA 2004, s.22(4)

Finding that the accused did the act, etc.

63–003 Where the judge determines that the accused is under a disability, the trial will not proceed or proceed further but a jury will then determine:

(1) on the evidence, if any, already given at the trial; or

Unfitness to Plead/Insanity

(2) on such evidence as may be adduced or further adduced by the Crown, or by a person appointed by the court to put the case for the accused,

whether it is satisfied, as respects each of the counts on which he was to be, or was being, tried, that he did the act or made the omission charged against him as the offence.

If, as respects that count or any of the counts, the jury:

(a) are so satisfied, they must make a finding that he did the act or made the omission charged against him;
(b) are not so satisfied, they must return a verdict of acquittal, as if on that count the trial had proceeded to a conclusion.

Where the question of disability is determined after arraignment it is to be determined by the jury by whom the accused is being tried. CP(I)A 1964, s.4(A(1)(5); CP(IUP)A 1991, s.2; DVA 2004, ss.22(1), (4), (5)

In the exceptional case, where despite the original finding of disability, at a later hearing the accused is found to be fit to be tried, the procedure under ss.4A and 5 are inapplicable The proper course is for the judge to hold a second s.4 hearing, and if the accused is found fit to plead to order his arraignment (*Fluturim Hasani v Blackfriars CC* [2005] EWHC 3016).

Disposal

63–004 Where a special verdict is returned that the accused is not guilty by reason of insanity, or findings have been made that the accused is under a disability and that he did the act or made the omission charged against him the judge's powers of sentencing in relation to a case where the accused was arraigned **on or after March 31, 2005** are limited to making: CP(I)A 1964, s.5; CP(IUP)A 1991, s.3; DVA 2004, s.24(1)

(1) a hospital order (with or without a restriction order);
(2) a supervision order within the meaning of CP(I)A 1964, Sch.1A, Pt 1 as added by DVA 2004, s.24, Sch.2; or
(3) an order for absolute discharge.

DVA 2004 abolishes admission orders. Two important changes introduced by DVA 2004 are that the Home Secretary no longer has a role in deciding whether or not the accused is admitted to hospital, and the judge is no longer able to order the accused's admission to a psychiatric hospital without hearing any medical evidence.

Where an accused is acquitted of all counts of the indictment, save a summary offence attached to it by virtue of CJA

1988, s.40, the judge is restricted to magistrates' powers; there is no finding of guilt, as such, and the accused is not therefore an offender (*R. v Southwark CC Ex p Koncar* [1998] 1 Cr.App.R. 321).

Supervision order; CP(I)A 1964, Sch.1A

63–005 The supervision order introduced by DVA 2004 where arraignment was **on or after March 31, 2005** is an order which requires the person in respect of whom it is made ("the supervised person") to be under the supervision of a social worker or an officer of a local probation board ("the supervising officer") for a period specified in the order of not more than two years. It may require the supervised person to submit, during the whole of that period or such part of it as may be specified in the order, to treatment by or under the direction of a registered medical practitioner (CP(I)A 1964, para.1(1)).

CP(I)A 1964, s.5A, Sch.1A, para.1(1)

The judge must not make a supervision order unless he is satisfied that:

(1) having regard to all the circumstances of the case, the making of such an order is the most suitable means of dealing with the accused or appellant; and
(2) the supervising officer intended to be specified in the order is willing to undertake the supervision; and
(3) arrangements have been made for the treatment intended to be specified in the order.

The order must either:

(a) specify the local social services authority area in which the supervised person resides or will reside, and require him to be under the supervision of a social worker of the local social services authority for that area; or
(b) specify the local justice area in which that person resides or will reside, and require him to be under the supervision of an officer of a local probation board appointed for or assigned to that area.

Before making such an order, the judge must explain to the supervised person in ordinary language the effect of the order (including any requirements proposed to be included in it) and that a magistrates' court has power to review the order on the application either of the supervised person or of the supervising officer (*ibid.*, paras 2, 3(1)–(3)).

The offender has a duty to keep in touch with the supervising officer in accordance with instructions given to him and to notify him, of any change of address (*ibid.*, para.3(5)).

Administrative provisions

63–006 After making an order, the Crown Court officer will give copies of the order to an officer of a local probation board assigned to the court, and also to the supervised person; and to the supervising officer. CP(I)A 1964, Sch.1A, para.3(4)

The officer will also send to the designated officer for the local justice area in which the supervised person resides or will reside a copy of the order; and such documents and information relating to the case as it considers likely to be of assistance to a court acting for that area in the exercise of its functions in relation to the order.

Requirement as to medical treatment

63–007 An order may, if the judge is satisfied as mentioned below, include a requirement that the supervised person submit, during the whole of the period specified in the order or during such part of that period as may be so specified, to treatment by or under the direction of a registered medical practitioner with a view to the improvement of his mental condition. CP(I)A 1964, Sch.1A, paras 4(1)–(4)

The judge must however be satisfied on the written or oral evidence of two or more registered medical practitioners, at least one of whom is duly registered, that the mental condition of the supervised person:

(1) is such as requires and may be susceptible to treatment; but
(2) is not such as to warrant the making of a hospital order within the meaning of the MHA 1983.

The treatment required by the order must be one of the following kinds of treatment, specified in the order, that is to say:

(a) treatment as a non-resident patient at such institution or place as may be specified in the order; and
(b) treatment by or under the direction of such registered medical practitioner as may be so specified;

but the nature of the treatment must not be specified in the order except as mentioned in para.(a) or (b) above.

Treatment by a medical practitioner

63–008 Where the judge is satisfied on the written or oral evidence of two or more registered medical practitioners that: CP(I)A 1964, Sch.1A, para.5

because of his medical condition, other than his mental condition, the supervised person is likely to pose a risk to himself or others, and the condition may be susceptible to treatment:

(1) the order may (whether or not it includes a requirement under para.4) include a requirement that the supervised person submit, during the whole of the period specified in the order or during such part of that period as may be so specified, to treatment by or under the direction of a registered medical practitioner with a view to the improvement of the condition;
(2) the treatment required by any such order must be such one of the following as may be specified in the order:
   (a) treatment as a non-resident patient at such institution or place as may be specified in the order; and
   (b) treatment by or under the direction of such registered medical practitioner, but

the treatment must not be specified in the order except as mentioned in para.(a) or (b) above.

Where the medical practitioner by whom or under whose direction the supervised person is being treated in pursuance of a requirement is of the opinion that part of the treatment can be better or more conveniently be given in or at an institution or place which is not specified in the order, and is one in or at which the treatment of the supervised person will be given by or under the direction of a registered medical practitioner, he may, with the consent of the supervised person, make arrangements for him to be treated accordingly. Such arrangements may provide for the supervised person to receive part of his treatment as a resident patient in an institution or place of any description.

Where any such arrangements are made for the treatment of a supervised person the medical practitioner by whom the arrangements are made must give notice in writing to the supervising officer, specifying the institution or place in or at which the treatment is to be carried out; and the treatment provided for by the arrangements will be deemed to be treatment to which he is required to submit in pursuance of the supervision order. CP(I)A 1964, Sch.1A, para.5

While the supervised person is under treatment as a resident patient in pursuance of arrangements under para.6 above, the supervising officer will carry out the supervision to such extent only as may be necessary for the purpose of the revocation or amendment of the order. CP(I)A 1964, Sch.1A, para.7

Requirements as to residence

63–009 A supervision order may include requirements as to the residence of the supervised person, but before making such an order containing any such requirement, the judge must consider the home surroundings of the supervised person. CP(I)A 1964, Sch.1A, para.8

Appeal against order

63–010 In a case where arraignment took place **on or after March 31, 2005**, a person in whose case a judge of the Crown Court makes: CAA 1968, s.16A; DVA 2004, s.25

(1) a hospital order or interim hospital order by virtue of CP(I)A 1964, ss.5 or 5A or
(2) a supervision order under s.5,

may appeal to CACD against the order, but only:

(a) with the leave of CACD; or
(b) if the judge of the court of trial grants a certificate that the case is fit for appeal.

If, on such an appeal, CACD considers that the appellant should be dealt with differently from the way in which the court below dealt with him it may quash any order which is the subject of the appeal; and may make such order, whether by substitution for the original order or by variation of or addition to it, as it thinks appropriate for the case and as the court below had power to make.

Note that in relation to cases where arraignment was **on or after March 31, 2005**:

(i) the fact that an appeal is pending against an interim hospital order under MHA 1983 does not affect the power of the Crown Court to renew or terminate the order or deal with the appellant on its termination;
(ii) where CACD makes an interim hospital order by virtue of these provisions, the power of renewing or terminating it and of dealing with the appellant on its termination is exercisable by the Crown Court and not by CACD, and the Crown Court is treated for the purposes of *ibid.*, s.38(7) (absconding offenders) as the court that made the order;
(iii) the fact that an appeal is pending against a supervision order under CP(I)A 1964, s.5 does

not affect the power of the Crown Court to revoke the order.

Where CACD makes a supervision order the power of revoking or amending it is exercised as if the order had been made by the Crown Court. CAA 1968, s.16B; DVA 2004, s.25

Relevance of ECHR, Art.6

63–011 Proceedings under s.4 determine whether the accused is fit to plead; it is not a criminal charge. In proceedings under s.4A, if an accused is found to have committed the act, the verdict is not one of guilty, but a finding that he did the act or made the omission charged against him. The finding of the jury that an accused has committed the act lacks a finding as to intent and is not, therefore, a finding of guilty of the offence. The criminal charge provisions of ECHR, Art.6 do not apply to proceedings which cannot result in a conviction. Proceedings under ss.4 and 4A comply with the requirements of Art.6.

The submission that a person who is unfit to plead cannot have the fair trial required by Art.6 because he cannot sufficiently understand the proceedings or give proper instructions and may be unable to give evidence, is to confuse the rights assured by Art.6 with the enjoyment of those rights. Persons under mental disabilities, whose condition does not prevent their being fit to plead to a criminal charge, may well be under a disadvantage in legal proceedings, whether civil or criminal. A judge should do his best to minimise that disadvantage, but might be unable to remove it totally. A trial in civil or criminal proceedings where the disadvantage has been minimised could be "fair": *R. v M; R. v Kerr; R. v H.* [2002] Crim. L.R. 57, considering *T. v United Kingdom, v v United Kingdom* [2000] Crim.L.R. 187; *Brown v Stott* [2001] 2 W.L.R. 817; *R. v Antoine* [1999] 2 Cr.App.R. 225.

64 VIEW BY JURY

General

64–001 A view or inspection of real evidence may take place in the course of a trial. Where that view takes the form of a view of the *locus in quo*, it may be of two kinds:

(1) *informal*, for there is nothing to prevent an individual juror, the judge or counsel from informally viewing premises or a location for the purposes of familiarising himself with the place or surroundings concerned; or
(2) *formal*, at which witnesses give demonstrations, distances are measured off and, in effect, evidence is given.

In relation to the first kind of view, no rules can apply since such an informal inspection is no part of the trial. The judge may not, however, send one or more jurors to view the scene and report back to the others: *R. v Gurney* [1976] Crim.L.R. 567.

Formal view with jury

64–002 The trial judge, in his discretion, may permit the jury to view the *locus* at any stage of the trial up to retirement of the jury (*R. v Whalley* (1847) 2 C & K 376). In relation to a formal view, it is essential to bear in mind that it is part of the evidence given at the trial and certain basic principles apply. There is almost no relevant authority in England and Wales as to the procedure to be adopted at a formal view, and many of those held bristle with impropriety.

JA 1974, s.14, provides for rules to be made, though none have been. It is submitted that the practice adopted in the courts of many former British colonial territories, where views were frequent, is of assistance here.

Thus, since a formal view is part of the evidence:

(1) judge, jury, prosecuting counsel, the accused and defence counsel, proceed to the *locus* together with any relevant witnesses, accompanied by the clerk and a shorthand writer or logger;
(2) at the scene the witnesses point out such places or things as are relevant, and distances are measured, stepped off or otherwise arrived at;
(3) the court then re-assembles and those persons who took a material part in the view testify formally as to the part they played at the scene; and

(4) any opposing party then has the opportunity to cross-examine.

(See also the Privy Council cases of *Karamat v The Queen* [1956] A.C. 256, *Tameshwar v The Queen* (1957) 121 J.P. 477 PC, and *Goold v Evans & Co.* [1951] 2 T.L.R. 1189.)

The absence of the judge, who has a duty to prevent improper communications being made to the jurors (*R. v Martin and Webb* (1872) L.R. 1 C.C.R. 378), is a fatal flaw (*R. v Hunter* [1985] 2 All E.R. 173) even where no witnesses are present. The presence of the accused is as necessary at the view as in the courtroom. He may be able to point out matters of which his counsel is unaware or about which others attending the view are mistaken (*R. v Ely JJ. Ex p Burgess* [1992] Crim.L.R. 888).

No view after jury retire

64–003 Since a formal view is part of the evidence in the case, it follows that, as is the case where it is sought to introduce any new evidence, it must not infringe the general rule preventing the introduction of such once the jury has retired (see *R. v Davis* (1976) 62 Cr.App.R. 194, 210; *R. v Lawrence* (1968) 52 Cr.App.R. 163; *cf. R. v Nixon* (1968) 52 Cr.App.R. 218).

APPENDIX A

SECTION 1

QUALIFYING OFFENCES FOR PURPOSES OF CJA 2003, SECTION 62 (Evidentiary Rulings) (CJA 2003, SCHEDULE 4)

PART 1

LIST OF OFFENCES

Offences Against the Person

Murder
1 Murder.

Attempted murder
2 An offence under section 1 of the Criminal Attempts Act 1981 of attempting to commit murder.

Soliciting murder
3 An offence under the Offences against the Person Act 1861, s.4.

Manslaughter
4 Manslaughter.

Wounding or causing grievous bodily harm with intent
5 An offence under the Offences against the Person Act 1861, s.18.

Kidnapping
6 Kidnapping.

Sexual Offences

Rape
7 An offence under the Sexual Offences Act 1956, s.1 or the Sexual Offences Act 2003, s.1.

Attempted rape
8 An offence under the Criminal Attempts Act 1981, s.1, of attempting to commit an offence under the Sexual Offences Act 1956 s.1, or the Sexual Offences Act 2003, s.1.

Intercourse with a girl under thirteen

9 An offence under the Sexual Offences Act 1956, s.5.

Incest by a man with a girl under thirteen

10 An offence under the Sexual Offences Act 1956, s.10 alleged to have been committed with a girl under thirteen.

Assault by penetration

11 An offence under the Sexual Offences Act 2003, s.2.

Causing a person to engage in sexual activity without consent

12 An offence under the Sexual Offences Act 2003, s.4 where it is alleged that the activity caused involved penetration within subss.(4)(a) to (d) of that section.

Rape of a child under thirteen

13 An offence under the Sexual Offences Act 2003, s.5.

Attempted rape of a child under thirteen

14 An offence under the Criminal Attempts Act 1981 s.1 of attempting to commit an offence under the Sexual Offences Act 2003, s.5.

Assault of a child under thirteen by penetration

15 An offence under the Sexual Offences Act 2003, s.6.

Causing a child under thirteen to engage in sexual activity

16 An offence under the Sexual Offences Act 2003 s.8 where it is alleged that an activity involving penetration within subss. (2)(a) to (d) of that section was caused.

Sexual activity with a person with a mental disorder impeding choice

17 An offence under the Sexual Offences Act 2003, s.30 of where it is alleged that the touching involved penetration within subss.(3)(a) to (d) of that section.

Causing or inciting a person with a mental disorder impeding choice to engage in sexual activity

18 An offence under the Sexual Offences Act 2003, s.31 where it is alleged that an activity involving penetration within subss.(3)(a) to (d) of that section was caused.

Drugs Offences

Unlawful importation of Class A drug

19 An offence under the Customs and Excise Management Act 1979, s.52 alleged to have been committed in respect of a Class A drug (as defined by the Misuse of Drugs Act 1971, s.2).

Unlawful exportation of Class A drug

20 An offence under the Customs and Excise Management Act 1979, s.68(2) alleged to have been committed in respect of a Class A drug (as defined by the Misuse of Drugs Act 1971, s.2).

Fraudulent evasion in respect of Class A drug

21 An offence under the Customs and Excise Management Act 1979, s.170(1) or (2) alleged to have been committed in respect of a Class A drug (as defined by the Misuse of Drugs Act 1971, s.2).

Producing or being concerned in production of Class A drug

22 An offence under the Misuse of Drugs Act 1971, s.4(2) alleged to have been committed in relation to a Class A drug (as defined by s.2 of that Act).

Supplying or offering to supply Class A drug

23 An offence under the Misuse of Drugs Act 1971, s.4(3) of alleged to have been committed in relation to a Class A drug (as defined by s.2 of that Act).

Theft Offences

Robbery

24 An offence under the Theft Act 1968, s.8(1) where it is alleged that, at some time during the commission of the offence, the offender had in his possession a firearm or imitation firearm (as defined by s.57 of the Firearms Act 1968 (c. 27)).

Criminal Damage Offences

Arson endangering life

25 An offence under the Criminal Damage Act 1971, s.1(2) alleged to have been committed by destroying or damaging property by fire.

Causing explosion likely to endanger life or property

26 An offence under the Explosive Substances Act 1883, s.2.

Intent or conspiracy to cause explosion likely to endanger life or property

27 An offence under the Explosive Substances Act 1883, s.3(1)(a)f.

War Crimes and Terrorism

Genocide, crimes against humanity and war crimes

28 An offence under the International Criminal Court Act 2001, s.51 or s.52.

Grave breaches of the Geneva Conventions

29 An offence under the Geneva Conventions Act 1957, s.1.

Directing terrorist organisation

30 An offence under the Terrorism Act 2000, s.56.

Hostage-taking

31 An offence under the Taking of Hostages Act 1982, s.1.

Hijacking and Other Offences Relating to Aviation, Maritime and Rail Security

Hijacking of aircraft

32 An offence under the Aviation Security Act 1982, s.1.

Destroying, damaging or endangering the safety of an aircraft

33 An offence under the Aviation Security Act 1982, s.2.

Hijacking of ships

34 An offence under the Aviation and Maritime Security Act 1990, s.9.

Seizing or exercising control of fixed platforms

35 An offence under the Aviation and Maritime Security Act 1990, s.10.

Destroying ships or fixed platforms or endangering their safety

36 An offence under the Aviation and Maritime Security Act 1990, s.11.

Hijacking of Channel Tunnel trains

37 An offence under the Channel Tunnel (Security) Order 1994 (SI 1994/570), Art.4.

Seizing or exercising control of the Channel Tunnel system

38 An offence under the Channel Tunnel (Security) Order 1994, (SI 1994/570), Art.5.

Conspiracy

Conspiracy

39 An offence under the Criminal Law Act 1977, s.1 of conspiracy to commit an offence listed in this Pt of this Schedule.

PART 2

SUPPLEMENTARY

40 A reference in Pt 1 of this Schedule to an offence includes a reference to an offence of aiding, abetting, counselling or procuring the commission of the offence.

41 A reference in Pt 1 of this Schedule to an enactment includes a reference to the enactment as enacted and as amended from time to time.

SECTION 2

SPECIFIED OFFENCES
CJA 2003, Chapter 5, Pt 12
(CJA 2003, s.224, Sch.15)

SPECIFIED OFFENCES FOR PURPOSES OF CHAPTER 5 OF PART 12

PART 1

SPECIFIED VIOLENT OFFENCES

1 Manslaughter.
2 Kidnapping.
3 False imprisonment.
4 OAPA 1861, s.4 (soliciting murder).
5 OAPA 1861, s.16 (threats to kill).
6 OAPA 1861, s.18 (wounding with intent to cause grievous bodily harm).
7 OAPA 1861, s.20 (malicious wounding).
8 OAPA 1861, s.21 (attempting to choke, suffocate or strangle in order to commit or assist in committing an indictable offence).
9 OAPA 1861, s.22 (using chloroform, etc. to commit or assist in the committing of any indictable offence).
10 OAPA 1861, s.23 (maliciously administering poison, etc. so as to endanger life or inflict grievous bodily harm).
11 OAPA 1861, s.27 (abandoning children).
12 OAPA 1861, s.28 (causing bodily injury by explosives).
13 OAPA 1861, s.29 (using explosives, etc. with intent to do grievous bodily harm).
14 OAPA 1861, s.30 (placing explosives with intent to do bodily injury).

15 OAPA 1861, s.31 (setting spring guns, etc. with intent to do grievous bodily harm).
16 OAPA 1861, s.32 (endangering the safety of railway passengers).
17 OAPA 1861, s.35 (injuring persons by furious driving).
18 OAPA 1861, s.37 (assaulting officer preserving wreck).
19 OAPA 1861, s.38 (assault with intent to resist arrest).
20 OAPA 1861, s.47 (assault occasioning actual bodily harm).
21 ESA 1883, s.2 (causing explosion likely to endanger life or property).
22 ESA 1883, s.3 (attempt to cause explosion, or making or keeping explosive with intent to endanger life or property).
23 Infant Life (Preservation) Act 1929, s.1 (child destruction).
24 CYPA 1933, s.1 (cruelty to children).
25 Infanticide Act 1938, s.1 (infanticide).
26 FA 1968, s.16 (possession of firearm with intent to endanger life).
27 FA 1968, s.16A (possession of firearm with intent to cause fear of violence).
28 FA 1968, s.17(1) (use of firearm to resist arrest).
29 FA 1968, s.17(2) (possession of firearm at time of committing or being arrested for offence specified in Sch.1 to that Act).
30 FA 1968, s.18 (carrying a firearm with criminal intent).
31 TA 1968, s.8 (robbery or assault with intent to rob).
32 TA 1968, s.9 (burglary, with intent to—
   (a) inflict grievous bodily harm on a person, or
   (b) do unlawful damage to a building or anything in it).
33 TA 1968, s.10 (aggravated burglary).
34 TA 1968, s.12A (aggravated vehicle-taking involving an accident which caused the death of any person).
35 CDA 1971, s.1 (arson).
36 CDA 1971, s.1(2) (destroying or damaging property other than an offence of arson).
37 Taking of Hostages Act 1982, s.1 (hostage-taking).
38 Aviation Security Act 1982, s.1 (hijacking).
39 Aviation Security Act 1982, s.2 (destroying, damaging or endangering safety of aircraft).
40 Aviation Security Act 1982, s.3 (other acts endangering or likely to endanger safety of aircraft).
41 Aviation Security Act 1982, s.4 (offences in relation to certain dangerous articles).
42 MHA 1983, s.127 (ill-treatment of patients).

43 Prohibition of Female Circumcision Act 1985, s.1 (prohibition of female circumcision).
44 PorA 1985, s.1 (riot).
45 PorA 1985, s.2 (violent disorder).
46 PorA 1985, s.3 (affray).
47 CJA 1988, s.134 (torture).
48 RTA 1988, s.1(causing death by dangerous driving).
49 RTA 1988, s.3A (causing death by careless driving when under influence of drink or drugs).
50 Aviation and Maritime Security Act 1990, s.1 (endangering safety at aerodromes).
51 Aviation and Maritime Security Act 1990, s.9 (hijacking of ships).
52 Aviation and Maritime Security Act 1990, s.10 (seizing or exercising control of fixed platforms).
53 Aviation and Maritime Security Act 1990, s.11 (destroying fixed platforms or endangering their safety).
54 Aviation and Maritime Security Act 1990, s.12 (other acts endangering or likely to endanger safe navigation).
55 Aviation and Maritime Security Act 1990, s.13 (offences involving threats).
56 An offence under Part II of the Channel Tunnel (Security) Order 1994 (SI 1994/570) (offences relating to Channel Tunnel trains and the tunnel system).
57 PHA 1997, s.4 (putting people in fear of violence).
58 CDA 1998, s.29 (racially aggravated assaults).
59 CDA 1998, s.31(a) or (b) of that Act (racially aggravated offences under PorA 1986, ss.4 or 4A).
60 International Criminal Court Act 2001, ss.51 or 52 (genocide, crimes against humanity, war crimes and related offences, other than one involving murder).
61 Female Genital Mutilation Act 2003, s.1 (female genital mutilation).
62 Female Genital Mutilation Act 2003, s.2 (assisting a girl to mutilate her own genitals).
63 Female Genital Mutilation Act 2003, s.3 (assisting a non UK person to mutilate overseas a girl's genitals).
63A Domestic Violence, Crime and Victims Act 2004, s.5 (causing or allowing the death of a child).
64 An offence of—
   (a) aiding, abetting, counselling, procuring or inciting the commission of an offence specified in this Part of this Schedule.
   (b) conspiring to commit an offence so specified Schedule, or

(c) attempting to commit an offence so specified Schedule.

65 An attempt to commit murder or a conspiracy to commit murder.

PART 2

SPECIFIED SEXUAL OFFENCES

66 SOA 1956, s.1 (rape).
67 SOA 1956, s.2 (procurement of woman by threats).
68 SOA 1956, s.3 (procurement of woman by false pretences).
69 SOA 1956, s.4 (administering drugs to obtain or facilitate intercourse).
70 SOA 1956, s.5 (intercourse with girl under 13).
71 SOA 1956, s.6 (intercourse with girl under 16).
72 SOA 1956, s.7 (intercourse with a defective).
73 SOA 1956, s.9 (procurement of a defective).
74 SOA 1956, s.10 (incest by a man).
75 SOA 1956, s.11 (incest by a woman).
76 SOA 1956, s.14 (indecent assault on a woman).
77 SOA 1956, s.15 (indecent assault on a man).
78 SOA 1956, s.16 (assault with intent to commit buggery).
79 SOA 1956, s.17 (abduction of woman by force or for the sake of her property).
80 SOA 1956, s.19 (abduction of unmarried girl under 18 from parent or guardian).
81 SOA 1956, s.20 (abduction of unmarried girl under 16 from parent or guardian).
82 SOA 1956, s.21 (abduction of defective from parent or guardian).
83 SOA 1956, s.22 (causing prostitution of women).
84 SOA 1956, s.23 (procuration of girl under 21).
85 SOA 1956, s.24 (detention of woman in brothel).
86 SOA 1956, s.25 (permitting girl under 13 to use premises for intercourse).
87 SOA 1956, s.26 (permitting girl under 16 to use premises for intercourse).
88 SOA 1956, s.27 (permitting defective to use premises for intercourse).
89 SOA 1956, s.28 (causing or encouraging the prostitution of, intercourse with or indecent assault on girl under 16).
90 SOA 1956, s.29 (causing or encouraging prostitution of defective).
91 SOA 1956, s.32 (soliciting by men).
92 SOA 1956, s.33 (keeping a brothel).

93 MHA 1959, s.128 (sexual intercourse with patients).
94 Indecency with Children Act 1960, s.1 (indecent conduct towards young child).
95 SOA 1967, s.4 (procuring others to commit homosexual acts).
96 SOA 1967, s.5 (living on earnings of male prostitution).
97 TA 1968, s.9 (burglary with intent to commit rape).
98 CLA 1977, s.54 (inciting girl under 16 to have incestuous sexual intercourse).
99 Protection of Children Act 1978, s.1 (indecent photographs of children).
100 C&EMA, s.170 (penalty for fraudulent evasion of duty, etc.) in relation to goods prohibited to be imported under s.42 of the Customs Consolidation Act 1876 (c. 36) (indecent or obscene articles).
101 CJA 1988, s.160 (possession of indecent photograph of a child).
102 SOA 2003, s.1 (rape).
103 SOA 2003, s.2 (assault by penetration).
104 SOA 2003, s.3 (sexual assault).
105 SOA 2003, s.4 (causing a person to engage in sexual activity without consent).
106 SOA 2003, s.5 (rape of a child under 13).
107 SOA 2003, s.6 (assault of a child under 13 by penetration).
108 SOA 2003, s.7 (sexual assault of a child under 13).
109 SOA 2003. s.8 (causing or inciting a child under 13 to engage in sexual activity).
110 SOA 2003, s.9 (sexual activity with a child).
111 SOA 2003, s.10 (causing or inciting a child to engage in sexual activity).
112 SOA 2003, s.11 (engaging in sexual activity in the presence of a child).
113 SOA 2003, s.12 (causing a child to watch a sexual act).
114 SOA 2003, s.13 (child sex offences committed by children or young persons).
115 SOA 2003, s.14 (arranging or facilitating commission of a child sex offence).
116 SOA 2003, s.15 (meeting a child following sexual grooming, etc.).
117 SOA 2003, s.16 (abuse of position of trust: sexual activity with a child).
118 SOA 2003, s.17 (abuse of position of trust: causing or inciting a child to engage in sexual activity).
119 SOA 2003, s.18 (abuse of position of trust: sexual activity in the presence of a child).

120 SOA 2003, s.19 (abuse of position of trust: causing a child to watch a sexual act).
121 SOA 2003, s.25 (sexual activity with a child family member).
122 SOA 2003, s.26 (inciting a child family member to engage in sexual activity).
123 SOA 2003, s.30 (sexual activity with a person with a mental disorder impeding choice).
124 SOA 2003, s.31 (causing or inciting a person with a mental disorder impeding choice to engage in sexual activity).
125 SOA 2003, s.32 (engaging in sexual activity in the presence of a person with a mental disorder impeding choice).
126 SOA 2003, s.33 (causing a person with a mental disorder impeding choice to watch a sexual act).
127 SOA 2003, s.34 (inducement, threat or deception to procure sexual activity with a person with a mental disorder).
128 SOA 2003, s.35 (causing a person with a mental disorder to engage in or agree to engage in sexual activity by inducement, threat or deception).
129 SOA 2003, s.36 (engaging in sexual activity in the presence, procured by inducement, threat or deception, of a person with a mental disorder).
130 SOA 2003, s.37 (causing a person with a mental disorder to watch a sexual act by inducement, threat or deception).
131 SOA 2003, s.38 (care workers: sexual activity with a person with a mental disorder).
132 SOA 2003, s.39 (care workers: causing or inciting sexual activity).
133 SOA 2003, s.40 (care workers: sexual activity in the presence of a person with a mental disorder).
134 SOA 2003, s.41 (care workers: causing a person with a mental disorder to watch a sexual act).
135 SOA 2003, s.47 (paying for sexual services of a child).
136 SOA 2003, s.48 (causing or inciting child prostitution or pornography).
137 SOA 2003, s.49 (controlling a child prostitute or a child involved in pornography).
138 SOA 2003, s.50 (arranging or facilitating child prostitution or pornography).
139 SOA 2003, s.52 (causing or inciting prostitution for gain).
140 SOA 2003, s.53 (controlling prostitution for gain).
141 SOA 2003, s.57 (trafficking into the UK for sexual exploitation).
142 SOA 2003, s.58 (trafficking within the UK for sexual exploitation).

143 SOA 2003, s.59 (trafficking out of the UK for sexual exploitation).
144 SOA 2003, s.61 (administering a substance with intent).
145 SOA 2003, s.62 (committing an offence with intent to commit a sexual offence).
146 *SOA 2003, s.63 (trespass with intent to commit a sexual offence).
147 SOA 2003, s.64 (sex with an adult relative: penetration).
148 SOA 2003, s.65 (sex with an adult relative: consenting to penetration).
149 SOA 2003, s.66 (exposure).
150 SOA 2003, s.67 (voyeurism).
151 SOA 2003, s.69 (intercourse with an animal).
152 SOA 2003, s.70 (sexual penetration of a corpse).
153 An offence of—
  (a) aiding, abetting, counselling, procuring or inciting the commission of an offence specified in this Part of the Schedule,
  (b) conspiring to commit an offence so specified, or
  (c) attempting to commit an offence so specified.

NB Child abduction is *not* a sexual offence for these purposes (*R. v Bailey* [2005] Crim. L.R. 312).

SECTION 3

[PCA 2002, s.75, Sch.2]

LIFESTYLE OFFENCES: ENGLAND AND WALES

Drug trafficking

1 (1) An offence under any of the following provisions of MDA 1971:
  (a) s.4(2) or (3) (unlawful production or supply of controlled drugs);
  (b) s.5(3) (possession of controlled drug with intent to supply);
  (c) s.8 (permitting certain activities relating to controlled drugs);
  (d) s.20 (assisting in or inducing the commission outside the UK of an offence punishable under a corresponding law).

(2) An offence under any of the following provisions of CEMA 1979 if it is committed in connection with a

prohibition or restriction on importation or exportation which has effect by virtue of MDA 1971, s.3:
(a) s.50(2) or (3) (improper importation of goods);
(b) s.68(2) (exploration of prohibited or restricted goods);
(c) s.170 (fraudulent evasion).

(3) An offence under either of the following provisions of CJ(IC) A 1990:
(a) s.12 (manufacture or supply of a substance for the time being specified in Sch.2 to that Act);
(b) s.19 (using a ship for illicit traffic in controlled drugs).

Money laundering

2 An offence under either of the following provisions of this Act—
(a) s.327 (concealing, etc. criminal property);
(b) s.328 (assisting another to retain criminal property).

Directing terrorism

3 An offence under TerrA 2000, s.56 (directing the activities of a terrorist organisation).

People trafficking

4 (1) An offence under IA 1971, s.25(1) (assisting illegal entry, etc.).
(2) An offence under SOA 2003, ss.57, 59 (trafficking for sexual exploitation).

Arms trafficking

5 (1) An offence under either of the following provisions of CEMA 1979 if it is committed in connection with a firearm or ammunition;
(a) s.68(2) (exportation of prohibited goods);
(b) s.170 (fraudulent evasion).
(2) An offence under FA 1968, s.3(1) (dealing in firearms or ammunition by way of trade or business).
(3) In this paragraph "firearm" and "ammunition" have the same meanings as in FA 1968, s.57.

Counterfeiting

6 An offence under any of the following provisions of the Forgery and Counterfeiting Act 1981:
(a) s.14 (making counterfeit notes or coins);
(b) s.15 (passing, etc. counterfeit notes or coins);
(c) s.16 (having counterfeit notes or coins);

(d) s.17 (making or possessing materials or equipment for counterfeiting).

Intellectual property

7 (1) An offence under any of the following provisions of the Copyright, Designs and Patents Act 1988:
(a) s.107(1) (making or dealing in an article which infringes copyright);
(b) s.107(2) (making or possessing an article designed or adapted for making a copy of a copyright work);
(c) s.198(1) (making or dealing in an illicit recording);
(d) s.297A (making or dealing in unauthorised decoders).
(2) An offence under the Trade Marks Act 1994, s.92(1), (2) or (3) (unauthorised use etc of trade mark).

Pimps and brothels

8 (1) An offence under SOA 1956, ss.33 or 34;
(2) An offence under any of the following provisions of SOA 2003,
(a) s.14 (arranging of facilitating commission of a child sex offence);
(b) s.48 (causing or inciting child prostitution or pornography);
(c) s.49 (controlling a child prostitute or a child involved in pornography);
(d) s.50 (arranging of facilitating child prostitution or pornography);
(e) s.52 (causing or inciting prostitution for gain);
(f) s.53 (controlling prostitution for gain).

Blackmail

9 An offence under TA 1968, s.21 (blackmail).

Inchoate offences

10(1) An offence of attempting, conspiring or inciting the commission of an offence specified in this Schedule.
(2) An offence of aiding, abetting, counselling or procuring the commission of such an offence.

SECTION 4

OFFENCES QUALIFYING FOR RETRIAL UNDER CJA 2003, PT 10 [CJA 2000, s.62, Sch.4]

QUALIFYING OFFENCES FOR PURPOSES OF PT 10

PART 1

LIST OF OFFENCES

Offences Against the Person

Murder
1 Murder.

Attempted murder
2 An offence under CAA 1981, s.1 of attempting to commit murder.

Soliciting Murder
3 An offence under OAPA 1861, s.4.

Manslaughter
4 Manslaughter.

Wounding or causing grievous bodily harm with intent
5 An offence under OAPA 1861, s.18.

Kidnapping
6 Kidnapping.

Sexual Offences

Rape
7 An offence SOA 1956, s.1.

Attempted rape
8 An offence under CAA 1981, s.1 of attempting to commit an offence under SOA 1956, s.1.

Intercourse with a girl under thirteen
9 An offence under SOA 1956, s.5.

Incest by a man with a girl under thirteen
10 An offence under SOA 1956, s.10 alleged to have been committed with a girl under thirteen.

Drugs Offences

Unlawful importation of Class A drug

11 An offence under CEMA 1979, s.50(2) alleged to have been committed in respect of a Class A drug (as defined by MDA 1971, s.2.

Unlawful exportation of Class A drug

12 An offence under CEMA 1979, s.68(2) alleged to have been committed in respect of a Class A drug (as defined by MDA 1971, s.2).

Producing or being concerned in production of Class A drug

13 An offence under MDA 1971, s.4(2) alleged to have been committed in relation to a Class A drug (as defined by MDA 1971, s.2).

Supplying or offering to supply Class A drug

14 An offence under MDA 1971, s.4(3) alleged to have been committed in relation to a Class A drug (as defined by MDA 1971, s.2).

Theft Offences

Robbery

15 An offence under TA 1968, s.8(1) where it is alleged that, at some time during the commission of the offence, the defendant had in his possession a firearm or imitation firearm (as defined by FA 1968, s.57).

Criminal Damage Offences

Arson endangering life

16 An offence under CDA 1971, s.1(2) alleged to have been committed by destroying or damaging property by fire.

Causing explosion likely to endanger life or property

17 An offence under ESA 1883, s.2.

Intent or conspiracy to cause explosion likely to endanger life or property

18 An offence under ESA 1883, s.3(1)(a).

War Crimes and Terrorism

Genocide, crimes against humanity and war crimes

19 An offence under the International Criminal Court Act 2001 ss.51 or 52 (c. 17).

Grave breaches of the Geneva Conventions
20 An offence under the Geneva Conventions Act 1957, s.1.

Directing terrorist organisation
21 An offence under TerrA 2000, s.56.

Hostage-taking
22 An offence under the Taking of Hostages Act 1982, s.1.

Hijacking and Other Offences Relating to Aviation, Maritime and Rail Security

Hijacking of aircraft
23 An offence under the Aviation Security Act 1982, s.1.

Destroying, damaging or endangering the safety of an aircraft
24 An offence under the Aviation Security Act 1982, s.2.

Hijacking of ships
25 An offence under the Aviation and Maritime Security Act 1990, s.9.

Seizing or exercising control of fixed platforms
26 An offence under the Aviation and Maritime Security Act 1990, s.10.

Destroying ships or fixed platforms or endangering their safety
27 An offence under the Aviation and Maritime Security Act 1990, s.11.

Hijacking of Channel Tunnel trains
28 An offence under the Channel Tunnel (Security) Order 1994 (SI 1994/570), Art.4.

Seizing or exercising control of the Channel Tunnel system

29 An offence under the Channel Tunnel (Security) Order 1994 (SI 1994/570), Art.5.

Conspiracy

Conspiracy
30 An offence under CLA 1977, s.1 of conspiracy to commit an offence listed in this Schedule.

PART 2

SUPPLEMENTARY

31 A reference in this Schedule to an offence includes a reference to an offence of aiding, abetting, counselling or procuring the commission of the offence.

32 A reference in this Schedule to an enactment includes a reference to the enactment as enacted and as amended from time to time.

SECTION 5

SEXUAL OFFENCES FOR THE PURPOSES OF SOA 2003, s.80 [SOA 2003, Sch. 3]

England and Wales

1 An offence under SOA 1956, s.1 (rape).

2 An offence under s.5 of that Act (intercourse with girl under 13).

3 An offence under s.6 of that Act (intercourse with girl under 16), if the offender was 20 or over.

4 An offence under s.10 of that Act (incest by a man), if the victim or (as the case may be) other party was under 18.

5 An offence under s.12 of that Act (buggery) if—
- (a) the offender was 20 or over, and
- (b) the victim or (as the case may be) other party was under 18.

6 An offence under s.13 of that Act (indecency between men) if—
- (a) the offender was 20 or over, and
- (b) the victim or (as the case may be) other party was under 18.

7 An offence under s.14 of that Act (indecent assault on a woman) if—
- (a) the victim or (as the case may be) other party was under 18, or
- (b) the offender, in respect of the offence or finding, is or has been—(i) sentenced to imprisonment for a term of at least 30 months; or (ii) admitted to a hospital subject to a restriction order.

8 An offence under s.15 of that Act (indecent assault on a man) if—
- (a) the victim or (as the case may be) other party was under 18, or
- (b) the offender, in respect of the offence or finding, is or has been—
  - (i) sentenced to imprisonment for a term of at least 30 months; or
  - (ii) admitted to a hospital subject to a restriction order.

9 An offence under s.16 of that Act (assault with intent to commit buggery), if the victim or (as the case may be) other party was under 18.

10 An offence under s.28 of that Act (causing or encouraging the prostitution of, intercourse with or indecent assault on girl under 16).

11 An offence under s.1 of the Indecency with Children Act 1960 (c. 33) (indecent conduct towards young child).

12 An offence under s.54 of the Criminal Law Act 1977 (c. 45) (inciting girl under 16 to have incestuous sexual intercourse).

13 An offence under s.1 of the Protection of Children Act 1978 (c. 37) (indecent photographs of children), if the indecent photographs or pseudo-photographs showed persons under 16 and—
   (a) the conviction, finding or caution was before the commencement of this Part, or
   (b) the offender—
      (i) was 18 or over, or
      (ii) is sentenced in respect of the offence to imprisonment for a term of at least 12 months.

14 An offence under s.170 of the Customs and Excise Management Act 1979 (c. 2) (penalty for fraudulent evasion of duty, etc.) in relation to goods prohibited to be imported under s.42 of the Customs Consolidation Act 1876 (c. 36) (indecent or obscene articles), if the prohibited goods included indecent photographs of persons under 16 and—
   (a) the conviction, finding or caution was before the commencement of this Part, or
   (b) the offender—
      (i) was 18 or over, or
      (ii) is sentenced in respect of the offence to imprisonment for a term of at least 12 months.

15 An offence under s.160 of the Criminal Justice Act 1988 (c. 33) (possession of indecent photograph of a child), if the indecent photographs or pseudo-photographs showed persons under 16 and—
   (a) the conviction, finding or caution was before the commencement of this Part, or
   (b) the offender—
      (i) was 18 or over, or
      (ii) is sentenced in respect of the offence to imprisonment for a term of at least 12 months.

16 An offence under s.3 of the Sexual Offences (Amendment) Act 2000 (abuse of position of trust), if the offender was 20 or over.

17 17 An offence under s.1 or 2 of this Act (rape, assault by penetration).

18 An offence under s.3 of this Act (sexual assault) if—
  (a) where the offender was under 18, he is or has been sentenced, in respect of the offence, to imprisonment for a term of at least 12 months;
  (b) in any other case—
    (i) the victim was under 18, or
    (ii) the offender, in respect of the offence or finding, is or has been—
  (a) sentenced to a term of imprisonment,
  (b) detained in a hospital, or
  (c) made the subject of a community sentence of at least 12 months.

19 An offence under any of ss.4 to 6 of this Act (causing sexual activity without consent, rape of a child under 13, assault of a child under 13 by penetration).

20 An offence under s.7 of this Act (sexual assault of a child under 13) if the offender—
  (a) was 18 or over, or
  (b) is or has been sentenced in respect of the offence to imprisonment for a term of at least 12 months.

21 An offence under any of ss.8 to 12 of this Act (causing or inciting a child under 13 to engage in sexual activity, child sex offences committed by adults).

22 An offence under s.13 of this Act (child sex offences committed by children or young persons), if the offender is or has been sentenced, in respect of the offence, to imprisonment for a term of at least 12 months.

23 An offence under s.14 of this Act (arranging or facilitating the commission of a child sex offence) if the offender—
  (a) was 18 or over, or
  (b) is or has been sentenced, in respect of the offence, to imprisonment for a term of at least 12 months.

24 An offence under s.15 of this Act (meeting a child following sexual grooming, etc.).

25 An offence under any of ss.16 to 19 of this Act (abuse of a position of trust) if the offender, in respect of the offence, is or has been—
  (a) sentenced to a term of imprisonment,
  (b) detained in a hospital, or
  (c) made the subject of a community sentence of at least 12 months.

26 An offence under s.25 or 26 of this Act (familial child sex offences) if the offender—

(a) was 18 or over, or
(b) is or has been sentenced in respect of the offence to imprisonment for a term of at least 12 months.

27 An offence under any of ss.30 to 37 of this Act (offences against persons with a mental disorder impeding choice, inducements, etc. to persons with mental disorder).

28 An offence under any of ss.38 to 41 of this Act (care workers for persons with mental disorder) if—
(a) where the offender was under 18, he is or has been sentenced in respect of the offence to
(b) in any other case, the offender, in respect of the offence or finding, is or has been—
(i) sentenced to a term of imprisonment,
(ii) detained in a hospital, or
(iii) made the subject of a community sentence of at least 12 months.

29 An offence under s.47 of this Act (paying for sexual services of a child) if the victim or (as the case may be) other party was under 16, and the offender—
(a) was 18 or over, or
(b) is or has been sentenced in respect of the offence to imprisonment for a term of at least 12 months.

30 An offence under s.61 of this Act (administering a substance with intent).

31 An offence under s.62 or 63 of this Act (committing an offence or trespassing, with intent to commit a sexual offence) if—
(a) where the offender was under 18, he is or has been sentenced in respect of the offence to imprisonment for a term of at least 12 months;
(b) in any other case—
(i) the intended offence was an offence against a person under 18, or
(ii) the offender, in respect of the offence or finding, is or has been—
(a) sentenced to a term of imprisonment,
(b) detained in a hospital, or
(c) made the subject of a community sentence of at least 12 months.

32 An offence under s.64 or 65 of this Act (sex with an adult relative) if—
(a) where the offender was under 18, he is or has been sentenced in respect of the offence to imprisonment for a term of at least 12 months;

(b) in any other case, the offender, in respect of the offence or finding, is or has been—
(i) sentenced to a term of imprisonment, or
(ii) detained in a hospital.

33 An offence under s.66 of this Act (exposure) if—
(a) where the offender was under 18, he is or has been sentenced in respect of the offence to imprisonment for a term of at least 12 months;
(b) in any other case—
(i) the victim was under 18, or
(ii) the offender, in respect of the offence or finding, is or has been—
(a) sentenced to a term of imprisonment,
(b) detained in a hospital, or
(c) made the subject of a community sentence of at least 12 months.

34 An offence under s.67 of this Act (voyeurism) if—
(a) where the offender was under 18, he is or has been sentenced in respect of the offence to imprisonment for a term of at least 12 months;
(b) in any other case—
(i) the victim was under 18, or
(ii) the offender, in respect of the offence or finding, is or has been—
(a) sentenced to a term of imprisonment,
(b) detained in a hospital, or
(c) made the subject of a community sentence of at least 12 months.

35 An offence under s.69 or 70 of this Act (intercourse with an animal, sexual penetration of a corpse) if—
(a) where the offender was under 18, he is or has been sentenced in respect of the offence to imprisonment for a term of at least 12 months;
(b) in any other case, the offender, in respect of the offence or finding, is or has been—
(i) sentenced to a term of imprisonment, or
(ii) detained in a hospital.

And certain corresponding Scottish, Northern Ireland and Service offences.

SECTION 6

OTHER OFFENCES FOR THE PURPOSES OF SOA 2003, Pt 2, s.104

SCHEDULE 2

England and Wales

1 Murder.
2 Manslaughter.
3 Kidnapping.
4 False imprisonment.
5 An offence under s.4 of the Offences against the Person Act 1861 (soliciting murder).
6 An offence under s.16 of that Act (threats to kill).
7 An offence under s.18 of that Act (wounding with intent to cause grievous bodily harm).
8 An offence under s.20 of that Act (malicious wounding).
9 An offence under s.21 of that Act (attempting to choke, suffocate or strangle in order to commit or assist in committing an indictable offence).
10 An offence under s.22 of that Act (using chloroform, etc. to commit or assist in the committing of any indictable offence).
11 An offence under s.23 of that Act (maliciously administering poison, etc. so as to endanger life or inflict grievous bodily harm).
12 An offence under s.27 of that Act (abandoning children).
13 An offence under s.28 of that Act (causing bodily injury by explosives).
14 An offence under s.29 of that Act (using explosives, etc. with intent to do grievous bodily harm).
15 An offence under s.30 of that Act (placing explosives with intent to do bodily injury).
16 An offence under s.31 of that Act (setting spring guns, etc. with intent to do grievous bodily harm).
17 An offence under s.32 of that Act (endangering the safety of railway passengers).
18 An offence under s.35 of that Act (injuring persons by furious driving).
19 An offence under s.37 of that Act (assaulting officer preserving wreck).
20 An offence under s.38 of that Act (assault with intent to resist arrest).
21 An offence under s.47 of that Act (assault occasioning actual bodily harm).

22 An offence under s.2 of the Explosive Substances Act 1883 (c. 3) (causing explosion likely to endanger life or property).
23 An offence under s.3 of that Act (attempt to cause explosion, or making or keeping explosive with intent to endanger life or property).
24 An offence under s.1 of the Infant Life (Preservation) Act 1929 (c. 34) (child destruction).
25 An offence under s.1 of the Children and Young Persons Act 1933 (c. 12) (cruelty to children).
26 An offence under s.1 of the Infanticide Act 1938 (c. 36) (infanticide).
27 An offence under s.16 of the Firearms Act 1968 (c. 27) (possession of firearm with intent to endanger life).
28 An offence under s.16A of that Act (possession of firearm with intent to cause fear of violence).
29 An offence under s.17(1) of that Act (use of firearm to resist arrest).
30 An offence under s.17(2) of that Act (possession of firearm at time of committing or being arrested for offence specified in Sch.1 to that Act).
31 An offence under s.18 of that Act (carrying a firearm with criminal intent).
32 An offence under s.8 of the Theft Act 1968 (c. 60) (robbery or assault with intent to rob).
33 An offence under s.9 of that Act of burglary with intent to—
(a) inflict grievous bodily harm on a person, or
(b) do unlawful damage to a building or anything in it.
34 An offence under s.10 of that Act (aggravated burglary).
35 An offence under s.12A of that Act (aggravated vehicle-taking) involving an accident which caused the death of any person.
36 An offence of arson under s.1 of the Criminal Damage Act 1971 (c. 48).
37 An offence under s.1(2) of that Act (destroying or damaging property) other than an offence of arson.
38 An offence under s.1 of the Taking of Hostages Act 1982 (c. 28) (hostage-taking).
39 An offence under s.1 of the Aviation Security Act 1982 (c. 36) (hijacking).
40 An offence under s.2 of that Act (destroying, damaging or endangering safety of aircraft).
41 An offence under s.3 of that Act (other acts endangering or likely to endanger safety of aircraft).
42 An offence under s.4 of that Act (offences in relation to certain dangerous articles).

43 An offence under s.127 of the Mental Health Act 1983 (c. 20) (ill-treatment of patients).
44 An offence under s.1 of the Prohibition of Female Circumcision Act 1985 (prohibition of female circumcision).
45 An offence under s.1 of the Public Order Act 1986 (c. 64) (riot).
46 An offence under s.2 of that Act (violent disorder).
47 An offence under s.3 of that Act (affray).
48 An offence under s.134 of the Criminal Justice Act 1988 (c. 33) (torture).
49 An offence under s.1 of the Road Traffic Act 1988 (c. 52) (causing death by dangerous driving).
50 An offence under s.3A of that Act (causing death by careless driving when under influence of drink or drugs).
51 An offence under s.1 of the Aviation and Maritime Security Act 1990 (c. 31) (endangering safety at aerodromes).
52 An offence under s.9 of that Act (hijacking of ships).
53 An offence under s.10 of that Act (seizing or exercising control of fixed platforms).
54 An offence under s.11 of that Act (destroying fixed platforms or endangering their safety).
55 An offence under s.12 of that Act (other acts endangering or likely to endanger safe navigation).
56 An offence under s.13 of that Act (offences involving threats).
57 An offence under s.4 of the Protection from Harassment Act 1997 (c. 40) (putting people in fear of violence).
58 An offence under s.29 of the Crime and Disorder Act 1998 (c. 37) (racially or religiously aggravated assaults).
59 An offence falling within s.31(1)(a) or (b) of that Act (racially or religiously aggravated offences under s.4 or 4A of the Public Order Act 1986 (c. 64)).
60 An offence under Pt II of the Channel Tunnel (Security) Order 1994 (SI 1994/570) (offences relating to Channel Tunnel trains and the tunnel system).
61 An offence under s.51 or 52 of the International Criminal Court Act 2001 (c. 17) (genocide, crimes against humanity, war crimes and related offences), other than one involving murder.
62 An offence under s.47 of this Act, where the victim or (as the case may be) other party was 16 or over.
63 An offence under any of ss.48 to 53 or 57 to 59 of this Act.

63A An offence under s.5 of the Domestic Violence, Crime and Victims Act 2004, (causing or allowing the death of a child or vulnerable adult).

And certain Scottish, Northern Ireland and Service offences.

SECTION 7

Prescribed Categories of Offences for the purposes of CJA 2003, s.103(4)(b) (SI 2004/3346)

PART 1

THEFT CATEGORY

1 An offence under s.1 of the Theft Act 1968 (theft).
2 An offence under s.8 of that Act (robbery).
3 An offence under s.9(a) of that Act (burglary) if it was committed with intent to commit an offence of stealing anything in the building or part of a building in question.
4 An offence under s.9(b) of that Act (burglary) if the offender stole or attempted to steal anything in the building or that part of it.
5 An offence under s.10 of that Act (aggravated burglary) if the offender committed a burglary described in para.3 or 4 of this Part of the Schedule.
6 An offence under s.12 of that Act (taking motor vehicle or other conveyance without authority).
7 An offence under s.12A of that Act (aggravated vehicle-taking).
8 An offence under s.22 of that Act (handling stolen goods).
9 An offence under s.25 of that Act (going equipped for stealing).
10 An offence under s.3 of the Theft Act 1978 (making off without payment).
11 An offence of—
   (a) aiding, abetting, counselling, procuring or inciting the commission of an offence specified in this Part of this Schedule; or
   (b) attempting to commit an offence so specified.

PART 2

SEXUAL OFFENCES (PERSONS UNDER THE AGE OF 16) CATEGORY

1 An offence under s.1 of the Sexual Offences Act 1956 (rape) if it was committed in relation to a person under the age of 16.

2 An offence under s.5 of the Sexual Offences Act 1956 (intercourse with a girl under 13).

3 An offence under s.6 of that Act (intercourse with a girl under 16).

4 An offence under s.7 of that Act (intercourse with a defective) if it was committed in relation to a person under the age of 16.

5 An offence under s.10 of that Act (incest by a man) if it was committed in relation to a person under the age of 16.

6 An offence under s.11 of that Act (incest by a woman) if it was committed in relation to a person under the age of 16.

7 An offence under s.12 of that Act (buggery) if it was committed in relation to a person under the age of 16.

8 An offence under s.13 of that Act (indecency between men) if it was committed in relation to a person under the age of 16.

9 An offence under s.14 of that Act (indecent assault on a woman) if it was committed in relation to a person under the age of 16.

10 An offence under s.15 of that Act (indecent assault on a man) if it was committed in relation to a person under the age of 16.

11 An offence under s.128 of the Mental Health Act 1959 (sexual intercourse with patients) if it was committed in relation to a person under the age of 16.

12 An offence under s.1 of the Indecency with Children Act 1960 (indecent conduct towards young child).

13 An offence under s.54 of the Criminal Law Act 1977 (inciting a girl under 16 to have incestuous sexual intercourse).

14 An offence under s.3 of the Sexual Offences (Amendment) Act 2000 (abuse of a position of trust) if it was committed in relation to a person under the age of 16.

15 An offence under s.1 of the Sexual Offences Act 2003 (rape) if it was committed in relation to a person under the age of 16.

16 An offence under s.2 of that Act (assault by penetration) if it was committed in relation to a person under the age of 16.

17 An offence under s.3 of that Act (sexual assault) if it was committed in relation to a person under the age of 16.
18 An offence under s.4 of that Act (causing a person to engage in sexual activity without consent) if it was committed in relation to a person under the age of 16.
19 An offence under s.5 of the Sexual Offences Act 2003 (rape of a child under 13).
20 An offence under s.6 of that Act (assault of a child under 13 by penetration).
21 An offence under s.7 of that Act (sexual assault of a child under 13).
22 An offence under s.8 of that Act (causing or inciting a child under 13 to engage in sexual activity).
23 An offence under s.9 of that Act (sexual activity with a child).
24 An offence under s.10 of that Act (causing or inciting a child to engage in sexual activity).
25 An offence under s.14 of that Act if doing it will involve the commission of an offence under ss.9 and 10 of that Act (arranging or facilitating the commission of a child sex offence).
26 An offence under s.16 of that Act (abuse of position of trust: sexual activity with a child) if it was committed in relation to a person under the age of 16.
27 An offence under s.17 of that Act (abuse of position of trust: causing or inciting a child to engage in sexual activity) if it was committed in relation to a person under the age of 16.
28 An offence under s.25 of that Act (sexual activity with a child family member) if it was committed in relation to a person under the age of 16.
29 An offence under s.26 of that Act (inciting a child family member to engage in sexual activity) if it was committed in relation to a person under the age of 16.
30 An offence under s.30 of that Act (sexual activity with a person with a mental disorder impeding choice) if it was committed in relation to a person under the age of 16.
31 An offence under s.31 of that Act (causing or inciting a person with a mental disorder impeding choice to engage in sexual activity) if it was committed in relation to a person under the age of 16.
32 An offence under s.34 of that Act (inducement, threat, or deception to procure activity with a person with a mental disorder) if it was committed in relation to a person under the age of 16.
33 An offence under s.35 of that Act (causing a person with a mental disorder to engage in or agree to engage in sexual

activity by inducement, threat or deception) if it was committed in relation to a person under the age of 16.

34 An offence under s.38 of that Act (care workers: sexual activity with a person with a mental disorder) if it was committed in relation to a person under the age of 16.

35 An offence under s.39 of that Act (care workers: causing or inciting sexual activity) if it was committed in relation to a person under the age of 16.

36 An offence of—
- (a) aiding, abetting, counselling, procuring or inciting the commission of an offence specified in this Part of this Schedule; or
- (b) attempting to commit an offence so specified.

APPENDIX B PCMH FORMS

PLEA AND CASE MANAGEMENT HEARING IN THE CROWN COURT

Date of hearing: Judge:

P			represented by:		☐
D1		in custody/on bail	represented by:		☐
D2		in custody/on bail	represented by:		☐
D3		in custody/on bail	represented by:		☐
D4		in custody/on bail	represented by:		☐
D5		in custody/on bail	represented by:		☐

Tick right hand column if the advocate is instructed for trial

No. of case in Crown Court: URN:

	P	D1	D2	D3	D4	D5
Has the defendant been advised about credit for pleading guilty?		☐	☐	☐	☐	☐
Has the defendant been warned that if he is on bail and fails to attend, the proceedings may continue in his absence?		☐	☐	☐	☐	☐
Is the Crown Court Case Details form up-to-date?	☐	☐	☐	☐	☐	☐

Matters likely to be applicable to all trials

1) TRIAL JUDGE

Should the future management of the case be under the supervision of the trial or a nominated judge? **YES/NO**

2) RESOLVING THE CASE WITHOUT A TRIAL **Not applicable** ☐

	D1	D2	D3	D4	D5
a. **Might the case against a defendant be resolved by a plea of guilty to some counts on the indictment or to a lesser offence?**	☐	☐	☐	☐	☐

b. **If so, how?**

c. **Is the prosecution prepared to resolve the case in this way?** ☐ ☐ ☐ ☐ ☐

d. **If no, does the court take the provisional view that the case should be resolved in this way?** ☐ ☐ ☐ ☐ ☐

e. *If yes, the court orders:*

3) GUILTY PLEA **Not applicable** ☐

	D1	D2	D3	D4	D5
a. **Is there a written basis of plea?**	☐	☐	☐	☐	☐
b. **Is the basis of plea acceptable the prosecution?**	☐	☐	☐	☐	☐
a. Is the basis of plea acceptable to the court?	☐	☐	☐	☐	☐

b. If not acceptable, section 25 (Newton Hearing) will also apply.

c. *The defendant(s) will be sentenced on:*

d. *The prosecution to serve any further material relevant to sentence by:*

e. *The pre-sentence report, if required, to be received by the Crown Court and made available to the defence and the prosecution by:*

f. *The defence to serve any material which it wishes the court to consider when sentencing the defendant by:*

g. **Will "derogatory assertions" be made in mitigation?** ☐ ☐ ☐ ☐ ☐

h. *If yes, the court orders:*

i. **Are there any other matters which should be dealt with at the same time as these proceedings (other offences/TICs)?** ☐ ☐ ☐ ☐ ☐

j. **If yes, give brief details:**

k. *If there are other matters, the court orders:*

l. *Further orders (e.g. orders re medical or psychiatric reports or confiscation proceedings):*

4) NOT GUILTY—TRIAL DATE **Not applicable** ☐

a. **If the defendant is in custody and if the provisions regarding custody time limits apply, when does the custody time limit (or any extension thereof) expire?**

D1	D2	D3	D4	D5
☐	☐	☐	☐	☐

b. **Set out other reasons why the trial should take place earlier or later than it might otherwise?**

c. *If the defendant is in custody and the date of the trial is outside the custody time limit period, the court makes the following orders:*

d. **What is the estimated length of the prosecution, defence cases?**
Prosecution **Defence**

e. *The trial will take place on:* *and the length of it will be:*

5) READINESS FOR TRIAL

The parties' case progression officers to inform the Crown Court case progression officer in writing that the case is ready for trial, that it will proceed as a trial on the date in 4e and will take no more/less time than the period in 4e, by:

6) EVIDENCE—WITNESSES

a. **Have the parties completed Annex A?** **YES/NO**
b. If yes, does the court approve Annex A? YES/NO
c. *If the list of witnesses to be called orally is not agreed or approved, agreement (which is subject to the court's approval) must be reached and notified to the court by:*
d. *Absent agreement, the prosecution shall seek further directions by:*

7) EVIDENCE—DEFENDANTS' INTERVIEWS **Not applicable** ☐

	P	D1	D2	D3	D4	D5
a. **Should the interviews be edited before the trial?**	☐	☐	☐	☐	☐	☐

b. *Proposals for the editing of interviews shall be drafted by:* *and served by:*
c. *The other parties shall respond by:*
d. *The agreed interviews shall be filed with the court by:*
e. *Absent agreement, the party(ies) named in b) shall seek further directions by:*

8) DEFENCE STATEMENT

	D1	D2	D3	D4	D5
a. **Has a defence statement been served?**	☐	☐	☐	☐	☐
b. **Is there an issue as to its adequacy?**	☐	☐	☐	☐	☐
c. *The court gives a warning to:*	☐	☐	☐	☐	☐

d. *The court orders:*

9) PROSECUTION ADDITIONAL EVIDENCE **Not applicable** ☐

a. *Any additional evidence to be served by:*

b. **Which topic/issue will the additional evidence relate to?**

10) FURTHER PROSECUTION DISCLOSURE **Not applicable** ☐

a. *The prosecution to complete any further disclosure by:*

	D1	D2	D3	D4	D5
b. **Is the defence alleging that the prosecution has not complied with its obligation to disclose material?**	☐	☐	☐	☐	☐

c. *If yes, the court orders:*

APPENDIX B

11) EVIDENCE—ADMISSIONS/SCHEDULES

a. **Have the parties considered which admissions/schedules can be agreed:** **YES/NO**

b. *If yes and if the court agrees that the proposed admissions/schedules are sufficient, they shall be drafted by:*

c. *and sent to the other parties by:*

d. *The other parties shall respond by:*

e. *The agreed admission/schedules shall be filed with the court by:*

f. *Absent agreement, the named party in b) shall seek further directions by:*

g. *If the answer to question a. is no or if the court does not approve the proposed admissions/schedules, the court orders:*

Matters which may apply to any trial

12) EVIDENCE—EXHIBITS

a. **Have the parties completed and agreed Annex B?** **YES/NO**

b. *If Annex B is not agreed, agreement must be reached and notified to the court by:*

c. *In the absence of agreement, the prosecution shall seek further directions by:*

d. *If, in the view of the court, any exhibits should be presented in a particular way in order to be more easily understood by the jury, the court orders:*

e. *Further orders:*

13) EVIDENCE—VIDEO EVIDENCE **Not applicable** ☐

a. **Has the prosecution delivered to the defence the transcript of video witness evidence upon which it proposes to rely?**

D1	D2	D3	D4	D5
☐	☐	☐	☐	☐

b. *If no, the prosecution to do so by:*

c. *The defence shall submit any editing proposals by:*

d. *The prosecution shall respond by:*

e. *The agreed transcripts and edited video shall be filed with the court by:*

f. *Absent agreement, the prosecution shall seek further directions by:*

14) EVIDENCE—CCTV EVIDENCE **Not applicable** ☐

a. **Has any unedited CCTV evidence been made available in full to the other parties?**

P	D1	D2	D3	D4	D5
☐	☐	☐	☐	☐	☐

b. *If yes, copy of proposed composite/edited film/stills to be served by:*

c. *The other parties to respond by:*

d. *Absent agreement, the party seeking to rely on the evidence shall seek directions by:*

15) EVIDENCE—EXPERT EVIDENCE **Not applicable** ☐

a. **Expert evidence is likely to be called by:**

P	D1	D2	D3	D4	D5
☐	☐	☐	☐	☐	☐

b. **To prove/disprove. P:**
D1/2/3/4/5:

c. Does the court approve of the need for the identified expert evidence? ☐ ☐ ☐ ☐ ☐ ☐

d. If. no, why?

e. *In any event the evidence to be served by:*

f. **Should the expert evidence be presented in a particular way in order to be more easily understood by the jury?** ☐ ☐ ☐ ☐ ☐ ☐

g. *If yes, the court orders:*

h. **Would it be helpful if the experts consulted together and if possible agreed a written note of points of agreement or disagreement with a summary of reasons?** ☐ ☐ ☐ ☐ ☐ ☐

i. *If yes, and if the parties agree, the court orders:*

16) ELECTRONIC EQUIPMENT—COMPATIBILITY **Not applicable** ☐

	P	D1	D2	D3	D4	D5
a. **Does the trial courtroom have the appropriate equipment to allow the presentation of electronic evidence (CCTV, live link, audio recordings, DVD etc)?**	☐	☐	☐	☐	☐	☐

b. *If no, the court orders:*

17) EVIDENCE—SPECIAL MEASURES AND LIVE LINK **Not applicable** ☐

	D1	D2	D3	D4	D5
a. **Any outstanding issues about special measures or live links?**	☐	☐	☐	☐	☐

b. *If yes, the court orders.*

18) MISCELLANEOUS ORDERS RE. WITNESSES AND DEFENDANT **Not applicable** ☐

	P	D1	D2	D3	D4	D5
a. **Does any witness or defendant need an interpreter or have special needs for which arrangements should be made?**	☐	☐	☐	☐	☐	☐
b. *If yes, the court orders:*						
c. **Are any special arrangements needed for a child defendant?**	☐	☐	☐	☐	☐	☐
d. *If yes, the court orders:*						
e. **Will a defendant be unrepresented at trial?**	☐	☐	☐	☐	☐	☐
f. *If yes, the court orders:*						

19) HEARSAY/BAD CHARACTER EVIDENCE **Not applicable** ☐

	P	D1	D2	D3	D4	D5
a. **Further applications regarding hearsay evidence or bad character evidence are to be made by:**	☐	☐	☐	☐	☐	☐

b. *The court orders:*

APPENDIX B

20) PRODUCTION OF MATERIAL FROM THIRD PARTIES — **Not applicable** ☐

a. **Applications for production of material (e.g. social services, hospital, banking records) from third parties to be made by:**

P	D1	D2	D3	D4	D5
☐	☐	☐	☐	☐	☐

b. *The court orders:*

21) PRE-TRIAL RESOLUTION OF ISSUES — **Not applicable** ☐

a. **What are the legal or factual issues which should be resolved before the trial:**

b. *If the issues are not capable of being resolved at the plea and case management hearing, the necessary hearing will take place on* *and will last*

c. **Do the parties wish to call witnesses to give evidence orally to enable the court to resolve the issues?**

P	D1	D2	D3	D4	D5
☐	☐	☐	☐	☐	☐

d. *If yes, and if the court approves, the court makes the following orders:*

e. *Skeleton arguments to be submitted by:* P by: D1/2/3/4 by:

22) PUBLIC INTEREST IMMUNITY: ON NOTICE APPLICATIONS — **Not applicable** ☐

a. **What is the nature of the prosecution's application on notice for public interest immunity?**

b. *The court orders:*

23) FURTHER ORDERS CONCERNING THE CONDUCT OF THE TRIAL

a. *Prosecution case summary/opening, if necessary, to be served by:*

b. *To ensure that the trial does not take more time than the period in 4e., the court orders:*

24) ANY FURTHER MISCELLANEOUS ORDERS—INCLUDING ORDERS RE. LITIGATION SUPPORT

25) NEWTON HEARING — **Not applicable** ☐

a. *The Newton hearing will take place on:* *and the length of it will be:*

b. *The issues to be resolved are:*

c. *The prosecution to serve any further material by:* *and the defence by:*

d. *The following witnesses will be called to give evidence orally:*

e. *Further orders (including any orders re. hearsay/bad character):*

Judge's signature:

ANNEX A

Witnesses upon whom the prosecution intends to rely and who will give evidence orally

Name of witness	Page No.	Type of witness	Required by:						Order of calling
			P ☐	D1 ☐	D2 ☐	D3 ☐	D4 ☐	D5 ☐	
			P ☐	D1 ☐	D2 ☐	D3 ☐	D4 ☐	D5 ☐	
			P ☐	D1 ☐	D2 ☐	D3 ☐	D4 ☐	D5 ☐	
			P ☐	D1 ☐	D2 ☐	D3 ☐	D4 ☐	D5 ☐	
			P ☐	D1 ☐	D2 ☐	D3 ☐	D4 ☐	D5 ☐	
			P ☐	D1 ☐	D2 ☐	D3 ☐	D4 ☐	D5 ☐	
			P ☐	D1 ☐	D2 ☐	D3 ☐	D4 ☐	D5 ☐	
			P ☐	D1 ☐	D2 ☐	D3 ☐	D4 ☐	D5 ☐	
			P ☐	D1 ☐	D2 ☐	D3 ☐	D4 ☐	D5 ☐	
			P ☐	D1 ☐	D2 ☐	D3 ☐	D4 ☐	D5 ☐	
			P ☐	D1 ☐	D2 ☐	D3 ☐	D4 ☐	D5 ☐	
			P ☐	D1 ☐	D2 ☐	D3 ☐	D4 ☐	D5 ☐	
			P ☐	D1 ☐	D2 ☐	D3 ☐	D4 ☐	D5 ☐	
			P ☐	D1 ☐	D2 ☐	D3 ☐	D4 ☐	D5 ☐	
			P ☐	D1 ☐	D2 ☐	D3 ☐	D4 ☐	D5 ☐	
			P ☐	D1 ☐	D2 ☐	D3 ☐	D4 ☐	D5 ☐	
			P ☐	D1 ☐	D2 ☐	D3 ☐	D4 ☐	D5 ☐	
			P ☐	D1 ☐	D2 ☐	D3 ☐	D4 ☐	D5 ☐	
			P ☐	D1 ☐	D2 ☐	D3 ☐	D4 ☐	D5 ☐	
			P ☐	D1 ☐	D2 ☐	D3 ☐	D4 ☐	D5 ☐	

ANNEX B

Exhibits which the prosecution intends to make available to the jury at the start of the trial

Exhibit reference	Page No.	Exhibit reference	Page No.	Exhibit reference	Page No.

use continuation sheets as necessary

APPENDIX B PCMH FORMS

PLEA AND CASE MANAGEMENT FORM

NOTES FOR GUIDANCE

Notes relevant to specific sections. (The numbering is according to the numbering of the paragraphs on the form.)

1. Trial or nominated judge

If the case is due to last for more than four weeks or if there are issues of law to be considered or if the prosecution intends to make a public interest immunity application, then the future management of the case should normally be under the supervision of the trial judge or a nominated judge.

Where it is deemed appropriate for the management of the case to be under the supervision of the trial judge or a nominated judge the court should normally continue with the plea and case management hearing and then direct that the case be considered by the Resident Judge.

2. Resolving the case without a trial

(para.2e). The judge should normally grant the prosecution a very short adjournment to resolve the issue.

3. Guilty plea

If there is an issue about whether the accused is fit to plead the judge should be informed for the court to make appropriate orders.

(para.3i). Where the defence intend to make a "derogatory assertion" against a person's character in the course of mitigation advance notice of that intention enables the prosecution to decide whether to challenge the assertion and enables the sentencing judge to consider whether to make an order restricting the publication of the assertion under CPIA 1996, ss.58–61.

(para.3l). If the accused is facing charges in other courts give brief details of offence, court and court number.

4. Not guilty pleas – trial date

(para.4b). These reasons could include the health, vulnerability or availability of a witness or of the defendant or the fact that the defendant falls within the definition of a persistent young offender.

(para.4c). The judge should, if possible, deal with the extension of a custody time limit at this stage rather than adjourn any application to a subsequent date. Regulation 7 of the Prosecution of Offences (Custody Time Limits) Regulations 1987 permits the accused to waive the requirements of notice and gives the court authority to waive them.

(para.4e). It will often not be possible to fill in these answers until the balance of the form has been considered.

6. Evidence – witnesses

The parties must before the bearing agree or try to agree which witnesses are properly required to give oral evidence, on which day of the trial and in which order the witnesses will be called.

The parties must use their best endeavours to reduce the amount of oral evidence to a minimum, in particular by reducing the number of witnesses who give similar evidence, or by the deletion of challenged passages the omission of which will not materially affect the case for the party calling that witness, or by the use of admissions which make the calling of the witness in person unnecessary.

The parties will be expected to be able to justify to the judge what they have agreed.

7. Evidence – accused's interviews

In order to assist editing of the accused's interviews it will be helpful if the prosecution can supply interviews to the defence in an electronic form.

In the absence of agreement before the trial, the party responsible for the editing shall have available at the trial the interviews in electronic form so that the necessary editing can be done during the trial.

See also PD 2004, IV.43 in relation to interviews.

8. Defence statement

The defence is required by CPIA 1996, s.5 to serve a defence statement. The defence statement will have to comply with the new s.6A as inserted by CJA 2003, s.33. If the accused has not provided a defence statement, the court should be told what are the issues in his case.

(para.8b). See CPIA 1996, s.11 as substituted by CJA 2003, s.39.

(para.8c). The judge will have to consider whether to give a warning under of the CPIA 1996, s.5E as substituted by CJA 2003, s.36.

9. Prosecution additional evidence

The judge may wish to order that any evidence served after the due date may not be introduced without the court's permission. If so, insert that in the box.

10. Further prosecution disclosure

(para.10b). CPIA 1996, s.8 provides for an application to be made by the defence for an order obliging the prosecution to disclose material where the accused has reasonable cause to believe that the prosecution has not complied with its obligation to disclose.

11. Evidence – admissions/schedules

(para.11e). See CJA 1967, s.10.

12. Evidence – exhibits

Exhibits should be presented so that they can be easily understood by the jury, for example by the jury being given edited or summarised versions of documents, by the use of schedules, electronic presentation of material, or by the use of graphics.

13. Evidence – video evidence

Transcripts are costly and time consuming to obtain. It is the video which is the evidence, not the transcript. Therefore a transcript should normally only be obtained when there is to be a trial and a need for a transcript is identified.

14. Evidence – CCTV evidence

(para.14b). Consideration should be given to requiring the videos to be copied on to a DVD.

15. Evidence – expert evidence

(para.15c). If the judge does approve the need for the instruction of an expert on behalf of a publicly funded accused, he may wish to explain why, so that the Legal Services Commission can be informed accordingly. If the judge does not approve the need for the expert evidence, he may wish to note the reasons. If he does give reasons, those reasons must be notified to the Legal Services Commission if an application is being made for public funding of the expert's fees.

(para.15f). In order that expert evidence can be easily understood by the jury the court may order, for example, that the jury be given a copy of the report, or an edited or summarised version thereof; or may direct the use of schedules or graphics.

(para.15i). The words "if the parties agree" have been included because such an order, in the absence of agreement, may raise issues of costs and of privilege, which the Criminal Procedure Rule Committee has not yet addressed.

It must be borne in mind that the costs of an expert may not be met by the Legal Services Commission.

18. Miscellaneous orders re witnesses and the accused
(para.18a). In the event of an interpreter being required, set out the relevant language and, where applicable, the dialect. The court should establish in each case who is responsible for providing the interpreter.

(para.18c). If the accused is a child the parties and the judge should consider what provisions are required so that, in accordance with PD 2004, Part IV.39, the accused is not exposed to avoidable intimidation, humiliation or distress.

(para.18e). If the accused will not be represented at trial there are orders which may have to be made prohibiting him from cross-examining certain witnesses (see YJCEA 1999, Ch II).

20. Production of material from third parties
Note the Attorney General's 2005 Guidelines on disclosure of information in criminal proceedings.

21. Pre-trial resolution of issues
The parties must, before the hearing, agree or try to agree what legal issues are likely to be raised (joinder, severance, admissibility of evidence, abuse of process, issues of substantive law, etc.) and at what stage they should properly be resolved, and will be expected to be able to justify to the judge what they have agreed. Although PD 2004, IV.36.1 provides that written notice of an application to stay an indictment on the grounds of abuse of process must be given not later than 14 days before the date fixed or warned for trial, this issue should be considered at the PCMH.

22. Public immunity (PII); on notice applications
If the prosecution does not make an application for public interest immunity until later, the judge and the defence must be informed as soon thereafter as practicable.

24. Any further miscellaneous orders – including orders re litigation support
Note the Guide to the Award of Costs in Criminal Proceedings on www.jsboard.co.uk.

25. "Newton" hearing

The parties must agree or try to agree which witnesses are properly required to give oral evidence, in which order the witnesses will be called and what special arrangements need to be made to facilitate the giving of evidence. The parties must use their best endeavours to reduce the amount of oral evidence to a minimum, in particular by reducing the number of witnesses who give similar evidence, or by the deletion of challenged passages the omission of which will not materially affect the case for the party calling that witness, or by the use of admissions which makes the calling of the witness in person unnecessary. The court will decide which witnesses should be called to give oral evidence.

INDEX

[All entries are to paragraph number]

Index

INDEX

Index

Index

Index

INDEX

Index

Index

INDEX

Index

Index

Index

INDEX

Index

Index

Index

Index

Index

Index

Index

Index

Index

Index

Index

INDEX

Index

Index